THE MODERN GANG READER

Malcolm W. Klein
Cheryl L. Maxson
Jody Miller
University of Southern California

Roxbury Publishing Company

Library of Congress Cataloging-in-Publication Data

The modern gang reader/edited by Malcolm W. Klein, Cheryl L. Maxson, Jody Miller.
p. cm.
Includes bibliographical references.
ISBN 0-935732-66-7
1. Gangs—United States. 2. Juvenile delinquents—United States.
I. Klein, Malcolm W. II. Maxson, Cheryl L. III. Miller, Jody, 1966- .
HV6439.U5M64 1995
364.1'06'60973—dc20 94-43283
CIP

THE MODERN GANG READER

Publisher and Editor: Claude Teweles
Line Editing: Dawn VanDercreek, Sacha Howells, and Joyce Rappaport
Cover Design: Marnie Deacon
Cover Photo: James D. Vigil
Typography: Synergistic Data Systems

Printed on acid-free paper in the United States of America. This paper meets the standards for recycling of the Environmental Protection Agency.

ISBN: 0-935732-66-7

ROXBURY PUBLISHING COMPANY
P.O. Box 491044
Los Angeles, California 90049-9044
(213) 653-1068

Table of Contents

Group Process

SECTION III. CRIMINAL INVOLVEMENT OF GANGS

Delinquent and Criminal Patterns

Gangs and Drugs

SECTION IV. PROGRAMS AND POLICIES

Social Intervention

Law Enforcement

Policy Issues

General Introduction

The editors of this volume represent three generations of gang researchers. We have covered over three decades of gang study during which some fundamental changes in gang structure and function have occurred. We have tried to mirror these generations of concern in the selection of articles, but have deliberately emphasized the contemporary scene. Purists may regret the relative absence of the classic works of Frederic Thrasher, Albert Cohen, James F. Short, Jr., Richard Cloward and Lloyd Ohlin, and Lewis Yablonsky among others. We have included articles that refer to and summarize these works, but readers wishing a full background in gang theory should read these authors in their original works and review several texts such as Empey and Stafford's *American Delinquency* or Covey, Menard, and Franzese's *Juvenile Gangs*.

Our intention has not been to provide a substitute for a textbook on gangs. Rather, we have applied several criteria to the selection of gang readings that serve to raise what seem to be the most salient issues. Exposure to these issues was perhaps our highest priority. Within that broad intention, we have opted for acceptable quality and readability rather than always seeking scientific presentations; we have sought articles that best represent a larger category of material, articles that contribute to a *pattern* of information, and articles that present different or even opposing views on various topics. Consensus is not a hallmark of the gang literature; the student must be prepared to see as much controversy as agreement on the nature of gangs.

Is it time for this first collection of available gang materials? Clearly, it is. To prepare this volume, we started with a comprehensive bibliography of over 1,200 books, chapters, journal articles, unpublished research reports, and selections from newspapers, popular magazines, and government publications. Careful review led to the reading of 250 of these, of which we found 175 worthy of serious consideration. Of these, about 120 were deemed by the editors as appropriate, given our general criteria. We were not in full agreement on all of these, and forced ourselves to justify to one another each suggested choice. This process led to a "first pass" at final selection that included 69 items; from that point on, each decision to exclude an item was painful—was it redundant with another piece, was it too technical, did it come from an author already well represented, was it something that could just as well be discussed in the section introductions to be written by the editors?

The end result, we trust, is a comprehensive exposure to gang issues and controversies with plenty of room for discussion leaders to make use of their own preferences in item selection and emphasis. We have provided brief introductions to each article to facilitate this process. To aid this process further, each section introduction includes a list of additional readings that were seriously entertained for inclusion in the volume. These items provide the interested student with a carefully filtered source listing, not simply a bibliography.

The format of the book is quite straightforward. We start, in Section I, with articles divided into three subsections. The first is on definitions of gangs, raising important issues of distinguishing the essential nature of those groups that can be called gangs, depending on one's definition. Second, we provide examples of different kinds of groups that can be called gangs, depending on one's definition. Third, we offer articles specifically on females in gangs because of the much-repeated complaint that gang girls are overlooked in gang research.

Section II offers articles on how we come to know about gangs, and what is particularly special to them. Thus, the first subsection speaks to gang theories and research methods, while the second subsection provides examples of how the internal dynamics of gangs affects behaviors of the members.

Section III gets to the heart of what interests most people about gangs—their anti-social behavior. We have separated drug issues from other crimes by presenting these topics in separate sections. This is not because they are intrinsically different in the gang world, but rather because of the intense interest in gang connections to drug distribution that has captured the attention of the media and the public. In reality, the separation is quite a false one since most gangs involve themselves in a wide variety of delinquent and criminal activities, of which drug use and drug sales are merely constituent parts.

What one *does* about gangs is the most complex issue of all. Thus, the fourth and final section presents three sets of articles on three different emphases. The first set concerns the attempt to reorient gang members in more pro-social directions by various forms of social intervention stressing prevention and social change. The second subsection studies the use of strong law enforcement procedures to crack down on gangs and deter their criminal behavior. The third subsection offers examples of alternative social policies in dealing with the gang, raising not only technical issues but also ethical concerns.

We urge readers not to skip over the four section introductions, because we use these to set the stage for each group of readings. Further, we use the section introductions to discuss important materials not explicitly covered by the individual readings. The introduction to Section I on the Nature of Gangs includes an updated summary of gang proliferation, our report on the emergence of street gangs in many hundreds of towns and cities across the country, and a brief summary of gang ethnicities. The introduction to Section II on Understanding Gangs includes material on how the spread of the urban underclass and the diffusion of gang culture through the mass media have served to contribute to gang proliferation. The introduction to Section III on Criminal Involvement of Gangs describes the general patterns of gang behavior, both criminal and non-criminal. Also included is material on the motives for joining gangs and the advantages of gang membership. Finally, the introduction to Section IV on Programs and Policies includes a review of gangs outside the United States and thus provides some context for what is often thought of as a unique American phenomenon. It also discusses new attempts to write special anti-gang legislation.

Despite the programs and policies and laws, we are left with the sad but inescapable conclusion that despite many genuine efforts to develop gang intervention and control programs, we have not come far. We have learned far more about what to avoid than what can be done positively. Equally sadly, little of what has been learned has been incorporated into prevention and control programs.

To understand why this is so, it may be helpful to review several points in this general introduction. Although covered in various ways in the readings we have selected for the volume, the following points can be highlighted as background to what follows.

1. *Street Gangs and Others*: "Gang" is an ambiguous term, subject to many and changing usages over time. Most, though not all, of this book is concerned with modern *street* gangs, not with the mafia, prison gangs, terrorist groups, supremacist groups, motorcycle clubs, or the many thousands of other youth groups that are occasionally delinquent. Even with those exclusions, street gangs come in bewildering varieties. They can be as small as a dozen or so members, or they may number several hundred members or be unusual federations of several thousand members. They are primarily but not exclusively male (ratios of males to females are described as ranging from almost 1 to 1 to 10 to 1 or more; there are some all-female gangs, but these are few). Perhaps 85 percent of street gangs consist primarily of racial and ethnic minorities—black, Hispanic, Asian—and can be found in large urban centers and in suburbs and isolated towns and cities. Street gang members can range in age from pre-teens to adults in their 30s, with the average age between 16 and the early 20s in most gangs. They are usually territorial (both in the sense of living in relatively circumscribed areas and in the sense of having strong neighborhood loyalties). While most of the members' waking hours are spent in normal, even dull activities, street gang members more than most young people evidence an orientation toward anti-social behavior—various forms of delinquent and criminal behavior. In most cases, they are generalists rather than specialists in crime; that is, the crime patterns are versatile, ranging from the most minor forms of vandalism and petty theft to less common serious violent offenses. Yet it is the violence that has captured public attention and engendered the kinds of suppressive official responses described in several parts of Section IV.

Not all gangs are street gangs. The recent emergence of drug distribution gangs, for instance, has fueled much of the outcry against street gangs because the two gang forms have mistakenly been taken as synonymous. They are not. There has been some similar confusion of prison gangs and street gangs as well, while others have hoped to include white racist groups like the Skinheads in the same category as the more traditional street gangs. Every such attempt to overgeneralize yields not only conceptual confusion, but also control programs more likely to fail for bringing to bear on one gang form the beliefs about another. Category-specific kinds of intervention are needed.

2. *Gangs Then and Now*: There was a "classical" period of gang research that built upon the original work of Frederic Thrasher in 1930s' Chicago but flourished in the 1950s and 1960s in New York, Boston, Chicago, and Los Angeles. In those days, most street gangs studied were of the traditional or vertical type, each consisting of several age-specific subgroups and often one or two auxiliary girls' groups. They ranged in size from 50 to 200 members and in ages of eleven or twelve to the early twenties. Highly territorial and violent far more in talk than in actions, these gangs were black and Hispanic, but also white in the earlier years—Irish, German, Polish, Italian, and so on.

Located principally in lower- and working-class sections of major metropolitan areas, these youthful gangs fought among and between themselves, and committed a wide variety of delinquent offenses of a principally non-serious type. They were significant features of their inner-city communities, but with a few exceptions they were not the sources of fear and terror one is accustomed to hearing of now.

Things have changed. Instead of a few score gang-involved communities, we have probably a thousand or more. The variety of gang structures has grown, making generalizations more difficult. Many older young adults are now involved and firearms are readily available, yielding a far more apparent violent aspect to many gangs: *several thousand* people have been killed in gang incidents in Los Angeles County alone in the past five years. Ethnic patterns have changed as well, with most street gangs being of minority status, adding to mainstream society's disdain for gang members. Partly because of gang proliferation and increased violence levels, but also reflective of more conservative political times, the official approach to gangs has swung from prevention and social intervention to law enforcement control programs and "crack down" legislation. In reading the various selections in this volume, readers should note the years of original publications in order to set each piece in its proper context.

3. *Sources of Gang Knowledge*: As noted earlier, the selections in this book come from a wide assortment of sources, ranging from careful scientific investigation to speculative journalism. While several of our authors take swipes at the investigative methods of others, we alert our readers to the obvious truth that no one method can claim fairly to be best. Each has its problems, and we would argue for a pluralistic approach.

Ethnographic field research, usually concentrating on one or only a few gangs, seldom yields tested generalizations—gangs differ, communities differ, and researcher perspectives differ. Further, crime statistics of a reliable sort are seldom collected in such studies. Yet from such close-at-hand research, one tends to get at the perspective of the gang member that is simply not otherwise available. Ethnographers "know" gangs in a way that survey researchers and analysts of official crime data cannot hope to achieve.

By the same token, those who rely on youth or adult surveys—interviews or questionnaires—are subject to two highly suspect sets of reporters, the gang members and those who process them (such as the police and service providers). Their perspectives are sometimes self-serving and often unverifiable. On the other hand, surveys can yield systematic information on a wider population of gangs and can take into account the expertise of people who have worked extensively with gangs. A combination of ethnography and survey techniques is perhaps the best antidote.

Those who rely principally on official records—police, court, corrections—have other problems. The records contain a minimum of verifiable data about individual gang members, and far less about gang structures. The criminal records include only a small portion of actual offenses committed, and are disproportionately about the more serious offenses. Yet in no other way can so much gang crime data be gathered, nor data on large numbers of gangs across many communities. And, we have discovered, it is usually only the police who have an overview of gangs in their city; community residents and agency officials are knowledgeable—when they are—only about groups very close by.

It is well to be skeptical about any one source of gang knowledge, and about any one piece of gang description as being applicable to gangs generally. We urge caution, and we urge comprehensive review and respect for what can emerge from many sources. This volume reflects this viewpoint.

4. *Gang Contexts*: So far, we have said little about gang theories. They abound, but unfortunately tend not to be very comprehensive. We find no specific theory of gangs to be satisfactory, and no general theory to be adequate to many specific instances. Further, how one sees gangs is very dependent on the context one employs.

a. *Deviance*: Gangs and gang behavior are socially deviant, but so are many other things. Within the relatively disadvantaged neighborhoods that spawn gangs, one may well find drug sales and use, homelessness, alcoholism, high dropout rates at school, prostitution and gambling, high rates of non-marital cohabitation and teen-age pregnancy, high rates of public health problems, and so on. In other words, gangs don't appear in *gang* neighborhoods, but most often in *problem-prone* neighborhoods where gang involvement is one among many patterns of social deviance. For many gang writers, then, the gang is not the problem: the nature of the community and how it came to be that way is the problem. Gangs, like other social problems, are the by-products of their communities, and perhaps it is the source of community ills that is the appropriate target of intervention.

b. *Racism*: As noted above, most gangs are composed of racial and ethnic minorities. This is not a random pattern; it is no accident. Gangs emerge in minority communities, usually those overwhelmed by poverty, unemployment, and low levels of social services because the dominant society permits such communities to exist. Inadvertent or institutional racism—the racism of social neglect—is hard for many to face, and harder yet to combat. Yet the gangs we describe are a product of these forms of racism. Blame does not inhere in the gangs alone, and many gang researchers find modern gangs more blameless because they reflect an often insensitive white America.

c. *Youth*: As one reads media and other reports of gang activity, it is easy to form stereotypes of marauding bands, sophisticated automatic weapons, innocent victims, terrorized neighborhoods, and outmanned police handcuffed by restrictive judicial rulings. These are, in fact, occasional facets of the gang problem—very occasional. We lose sight of the humdrum life of most gang members, of their dislocation from much of mainstream America, and of the fact that so many spend their prime gang years as adolescents in trouble, not adult hoods ripping off society. One need not condone criminal behavior in order to appreciate that these are youth—*our* youth—whose futures in many instances are salvageable if we have the patience to apply the knowledge available to us and the persistence to continue supporting the research on gang youth that will yield better salvage tools.

d. *Social psychology*: Of several intellectual traditions that can be brought to bear on gang issues, social psychology seems a particularly pertinent one. Gangs are groups, and a great deal of work has been carried out by social psychologists on group structure and function. Consider just these well-researched concepts: group size, leadership, cohesiveness, group norms and values, conformity, peer pressure, intergroup relations, role-modeling, morale, rumor transmission, and communication patterns. Each has a well-documented knowledge base, and each can be applied to the understanding of gang processes. A number of gang researchers—fewer than might be hoped—have placed gangs in this intellectual context and have successfully analyzed a number of common gang patterns as well as some of the reasons gangs have been so resistant to attempts at social intervention and control.

e. *Organizational behavior*: In addition to their own group organization features, gangs are affected by social organizations whose study comprises another highly relevant intellectual context. Families, schools, community agencies, city and state legislation bodies, police, courts, and corrections personnel are all members of informal and formal organizations. As such, these people interact with gangs as organizational representatives both motivated by and constrained by organizational values and norms, bureaucratic procedures, special interests, political pressures, conflicting ideologies and perspectives, self-protection, and inertia.

Gangs develop, flourish, and languish in the contexts of these organizations. Some gang researchers have described the likely effect on gangs of existing and alternative organizational milieus, finding that such analyses help to refocus attention on non-gang factors that can exacerbate the gang situation. Again, the clear implication is that blame and credit do not belong to the gangs alone.

f. *Community structures*: Finally, there is a need to consider the macro-structure of the gang-involved communities. From Thrasher on, gang researchers have rather uniformly been sensitive to the level of structure and organization of communities as contributors to gang development and absorbers of gang activity. Socially well-organized neighborhoods can include gangs, but more commonly it is neighborhoods in transition (ethnic, economic, etc.) and socially disorganized neighborhoods that have most often been described as gang-prone.

Thus, a number of gang researchers have concentrated on ways that reorganizing and activating communities can reduce the level of gang tension and reintegrate gang members into mainstream activities. Here, the gang is at most a secondary target of intervention, and the level of a community's social capacity is the primary target. Context is all.

Each of these contexts—deviance, racism, youth, social psychology, organization, and community structure—provides a perspective from which to understand gangs. As such, each is deliberately included among the papers in this volume. Other perspectives can also be discerned; ethnic cultures constitute a prominent example. Keeping one's eye on the perspective from which an author seems to be working aids interpretation of the position taken, and provides the basis for healthy skepticism in judging the validity of the work in question. In other words, we urge our readers to be interpretive, not just to be recorders of the works presented here.

We end with one other cautionary note. As one considers the articles included in this volume and other gang-related writings as well, one should keep in mind that the gang problem is often *used* for other, usually political, purposes. Gangs have become social and political footballs, kicked around in the public arena to justify ideologies, organizational build-ups, legislative reforms, and budgetary enhancements. Each time one sees or hears of a new proposal to "deal with the gang problem," it seems fair to question the extent to which that proposal is designed to address the gang problem, and the extent to which it addresses the proposer's needs. Experience in the gang world fosters a mildly cynical outlook.

References

Covey, Herbert C., Menard, Scott, & Franzese, Robert J., *Juvenile Gangs*. Springfield, IL: Charles C. Thomas, 1992.

Empey, Lamar, & Stafford, Mark C., *American Delinquency: Its Meaning and Construction*, Third Edition. Belmont, CA: Wadsworth Publishing Company, 1991.

Thrasher, Frederic M., *The Gang: A Study of 1,313 Gangs in Chicago*. Chicago: University of Chicago Press, 1927.

Acknowledgements

The editors and the publisher would like to thank the following individuals for their insights and suggestions on an early proposal for this book: Scott H. Decker (University of Missouri—St. Louis), Finn-Aage Esbensen (University of Nebraska at Omaha), Jeffrey Fagan (Rutgers University), John M. Hagedorn (University of Wisconsin at Milwaukee), Lin Huff-Corzine (Kansas State University), Stephen P. Lab (Bowling Green State University), Scott Menard (University of Colorado, Boulder), and L. Thomas Winfree (New Mexico State University). In addition, we gratefully acknowledge the contributions of Judith Webb at the University of Southern California's Social Science Research Institute. ✦

Section I

On the Nature of Gangs

Introduction

Four general issues about the nature of gangs seem pivotal to appreciating other aspects of the gang situation. These are as follows: first, how do we resolve the problem of defining what is a gang; second, how do we categorize various forms of gangs; third, what gender and ethnic differences exist; and fourth, an issue that has only recently become important, what do we know about the proliferation of gangs to so many American towns and cities? Articles selected for this section deal with the definition, types, and gender issues, but we will discuss ethnicity and proliferation in this introduction as well.

In a widely cited paper, Ruth Horowitz has questioned whether a simple generic definition of gangs is possible, given so many special interests in the gang issue. She also asks whether attempting to achieve such a definition might not be harmful to our appreciation of the variety of gangs that exist. For instance, police definitions tend to be narrow, based primarily on crime patterns. Our view is influenced by the Horowitz position, but we are mindful as well that science seeks generalizations; and generalizations in turn require some agreement on terms if they are to be at all stable. If we cannot as yet define gangs in a concrete and exclusive fashion, perhaps we can nonetheless characterize them sufficiently to achieve reasonable communication about them. We need to know when we discuss gangs that we are discussing pretty much the same kinds of phenomena.

The papers on gang definition in Section I illustrate clearly the kinds of differences gang definitions make to theory, to different participants in the gang world, and to the conclusions we draw about gang behavior. For instance, if we define stoners, Satanic groups, and white supremacist groups like the Skinheads as not being gangs, then modern gangs will be defined almost exclusively as minority—a racial and ethnic issue more than an economic or youth issue. Or suppose we define gangs as groups of youth enduring over time with some social structure and common values and interests. By excluding territoriality and crime involvement, this definition would encompass many of the school and church groups to which so many of us have belonged.

A non-included paper by Walter Miller goes on to show as well how definitions and inclusion/exclusion of various group forms varies across cities according to various dimensions of the gang definitions—levels of organization, leadership, crime patterns, and so on. How many gangs are there? What is their essential nature? These answers, notes Miller, are very much functions of our definitions. Thus, between the contrasting positions of Horowitz and Miller—do not define gangs versus define them narrowly enough to separate them out from most youth groups—the papers offered here spell out in some detail just how the definitional issue does matter.

We offer just one further example, but a very pointed one. Much of the new anti-gang legislation appearing across the country follows the lead of California's Street Terrorism, Enforcement, and Prevention Act, which for prosecutorial purposes defines "criminal street gangs" in terms of *three or more* members. No scholar or researcher on gangs would *ever* talk about three-person gangs. Here we have a case of gang definitions determined not by *gang* realities, but by necessities of instigating successful criminal prosecutions. A limited practical goal seriously affects national law and court practice by way of a definitional stance.

Getting a handle on gang definitions naturally affects what categories of groups we do and do not include as gangs. Including street gangs as characterized in the general introduction to this volume certainly accounts for a large proportion of all gangs. If we include criminal orientation or involvement as one of the common gang ingredients, then the papers included under Types of Gangs in this section provide a good sense of the variety of groups included, groups often separated out either by their ethnic character or by their involvement in specific forms of criminal involvement.

Papers not included but well worth the reader's attention contrast nicely with Miller's depiction of various forms of what he broadly labels "law violating groups," only a small portion of which he considered to be gangs. Jeffrey Fagan's research suggests four types—social gangs, party gangs, serious delinquent gangs, and gang organizations. An article by James F. Quinn offers a dramatic image of female roles in motorcycle gangs, and is worth comparing to Baron's research on the street culture of "punks" in Victoria, British Columbia. A paper on the vicious Jamaican "Posses" by Laurie Gunst underscores as well the variety of special characters that some gangs can take on. And each of these papers can be contrasted with classic pieces by Howard and Barbara Myerhoff and by Larry Karacki and Jackson Toby on white, middle-class groups that took on gang-like characteristics yet were hard to classify as traditional youth gangs.

The included papers and those mentioned above (and referenced below for the reader's convenience) suggest some of the difficulties we face in distinguishing gang and nongang groups. Where do we place Skinheads? drug sales cliques? burglary rings? motorcycle clubs? low riders? There is still much we need to learn about gang structures and how these relate to behavior, about the disorganized versus organized and rational features of gangs, about how some youth groups do evolve into gangs while most others do not, about the reasons for some ethnic specificities in gang patterns, about gender differences in gang involvements, and about regional differences in gang patterns.

With respect to females in gangs, it is often stated that there is very little research on this topic. This is certainly true in comparison to males, but on an absolute basis, it is not true. We know that many male gangs have female gangs attached to them, often consisting of male members' sisters, cousins, and girlfriends, augmented by other friends of these girls. We know that there are sometimes a few girls more-or-less integrated into male gang structures, and that there are occasional independent female gangs. Female-to-male membership ratios tend to be in the one-to-three to one-to-ten range, but reports of equal numbers of males and females also exist.

As to crime patterns, female delinquency tends to mirror that of the male gang members, but at a far lower level. That is, males and females exhibit the same versatility of offending (although male violence is disproportionately higher), but the males simply do more of it. Reports of females carrying the guns for the males in their skirts, inflaming gang rivalries by spreading rumors or dating rival gang members, and serving as fully available sex objects for the gang, while verifiable in individual instances, are gross exaggerations of female gang roles and should not be accepted as typical aspects of girl gang life.

In preparing this volume, the editors reviewed scores of separate books and articles on female gangs or gang members. A full sixteen of these were found worthy of consideration for inclusion here. Limiting ourselves to four of these in no way reflects what is in fact available. Because of the persistence of the belief that no female gang research exists, we list below an expanded set of relevant pieces that can be recommended to the interested reader. Most of these, in addition, include references to yet other work that can be accessed. The items we have included for this volume are generic; that is, they speak to issues of female gang roles that transcend any particular female gang. The list below, however, includes a number of ethnographic depictions of specific and rather unique gangs.

Like gender, ethnicity is a demographic factor of direct relevance to gangs. We have not selected articles to illustrate race and ethnicity issues, for two reasons. First, these are issues that receive much attention in a number of the individual sections of this book; note in particular how the types of gangs described in Section I (Types of Gangs) illustrate ethnic differences. Second, in reviewing the literature, we found a great deal of excellent research about Hispanic gangs, but very little on Asian gangs and surprisingly little specifically about black gangs. A balanced selection would have been hard to present.

Nonetheless, throughout the selections in the book, the reader could keep an eye on the question of gang territoriality (Hispanic gangs are said to value this most, Asian gangs the least); versatility of crime patterns (whites and Asians are said to be most focused on a few categories of offenses); cross-generational patterns of gang succession (for Hispanics perhaps more); drug-selling for profit (Jamaican gangs, blacks focused more on crack; Hispanics more versatile). See how often Hispanic gangs are spoken of in terms of their cultural heritage, Asians in terms of national histories, and blacks are relatively ignored with respect to cultural heritage. Ethnicity and race *do* make a difference. Nonetheless, from the editors' experience and from a fair summary of available data, it may be concluded that gangs of different origin manifest far more similarities than differences.

Interesting reports by John Johnstone in 1981, by Vaughn Stapleton and Gerald Needle in 1983, and by Dennis Rosenbaum and Jane Grant also in 1983, foreshadowed a new realization and a new controversy about gangs. The realization was that gangs were becoming more common; the controversy was over whether this resulted from an outward spread from such gang centers as Chicago and Los Angeles, or from a development of indigenous, "home-grown" gangs across the nation.

The answer to the controversy has now emerged. Cheryl Maxson has stated the issues about gang member migration rather clearly, and the editors of this volume have now completed a national study which confirms that most of the gang emergence is through indigenous proliferation, not from a spread from a few major locations. A good example of a city-specific study is offered by Richard Zevitz and Susan Takata in the city of Kenosha, Wisconsin. Where gang member migration does occur, it is more often the result of normal family residence changes, or personal and job-location connections, rather than from deliberate attempts to build gang chapters or to establish new crime or drug sales territories.

Further research by the editors, reported in a new volume by Malcolm Klein, reveals that the bulk of new gangs are home-grown, not branches. The use of the names of Crips and Bloods (Los Angeles) or Latin Kings, Disciples, or Vice Lords (Chicago) is usually just a copy cat phenomenon, not an indication of branching out. Further, this research has documented almost 800 towns and cities with active gangs, and came up with a sample-based estimate of almost 1,100 by the time of the 1992 survey. These are enormous numbers; they include 90 cities with populations of 10,000 or less. Gangs are no longer a big, inner-city problem: they are suburban, sometimes even found in rural population centers.

Thus the matters described in Section I and elsewhere in this reader are no longer a matter for urban planners alone. They belong to all of us. Only three states—North Dakota, Vermont, and New Hampshire—seemed to be without at least one gang-involved city by the year 1992. A national problem has evolved.

At the same time, however, it must be noted that in the majority of these many towns and cities, the gang proliferation is of a relatively small character. The majority of the 800 documented gang cities report 500 or fewer gang members in five or fewer gangs—indicating the proliferation of a minor problem, though not a negligible one. In the big cities, of course, such is not the case, with Southern California by far the most gang-troubled area in the nation.

Yet even as we may take secondary comfort in the finding that the problem is not egregious in many locations, we would do well to be on guard. This most recent research also reveals that there are almost no ex-gang cities. Once the local gang problem emerges and gets established, it does not disappear (either on its own or because of countermeasures). Until things turn around in this country, we will have to adapt to street gangs and others as part of our national social fabric.

Additional Readings

General

Baron, Stephen W., The Canadian west coast punk subculture: A field study. *Canadian Journal of Sociology*, 1989, 14:3.

Fagan, Jeffrey, The social organization of drug use and drug dealing among urban gangs. *Criminology* 1989, 27:633-69.

Gunst, Laurie, Jamaican drug gangs: Drugs and violence in America. *The Nation*, November 13, 1989.

Horowitz, Ruth, Sociological perspectives on gangs: Conflicting definitions and concepts. In C. Ronald Huff (ed.), *Gangs in America*, pp. 37-54. Newbury Park, CA: Sage Publications, Inc., 1990.

Johnstone, John W. C., Youth gangs and black suburbs. *Pacific Sociological Review*, July 1981, 24(3):355-75.

Karacki, Larry, & Toby, Jackson, The uncommitted adolescent: Candidate for gang socialization. *Sociological Inquiry*, Spring 1962, 32:203-25.

Klein, Malcolm, *The American Street Gang: Its Nature, Prevalence, and Control*, Oxford University Press, 1995.

Maxson, Cheryl L., Investigating gang migration: Contextual issues for intervention. *The Gang Journal*, 1993, 1(2):1-8.

Miller, Walter B., Gangs, groups, and serious youth crime. In D. Shichor and D. H. Kelly, *Critical Issues in Juvenile Delinquency*. Lexington, MA: D.C. Heath, 1980.

Myerhoff, Howard L., & Myerhoff, Barbara G., Field observations of middle class gangs. *Social Forces*, March 1966, 42(3):328-36.

Quinn, James F., Sex roles and hedonism among members of "outlaw" motorcycle clubs. *Deviant Behavior*, 1987, 8(1):47-63.

Rosenbaum, Dennis, & Grant, Jane A., Gangs and Youth Problems in Evanston: Research Findings and Policy Options, July 1983, Center for Urban Affairs & Policy Research, Northwestern University.

Stapleton, Vaughn, & Needle, Gerald, Police Handling of Youth Gangs, American Justice Institute, September 1982.

Zevitz, Richard G. & Takata, Susan R., Metropolitan gang influence and the emergence of group delinquency in a regional community. *Journal of Criminal Justice*, 1992, 20(2):93-106.

Females

Bowker, Lee H., & Klein, Malcolm W., The etiology of female juvenile delinquency and gang membership: A test of psychological and social structural explanations. *Adolescence*, Winter 1983, 18(72):739-51.

Bowker, Lee H., Gross, Helen S., & Klein, Malcolm W., Female participation in delinquent gang activities. *Adolescence*, Fall 1980, 15(59):509-19.

Brown, Waln K., Black female gangs in Philadelphia. *International Journal of Offender Therapy and Comparative Criminology*, 1977, 21(3):221-28.

Campbell, Anne, Self definition by rejection: The case of gang girls. *Social Problems*, December 1987, 34(5):451-66.

——, *The Girls in the Gang*, Second Edition. Cambridge, MA: Basil Blackwell, 1991.

Miller, Walter B., The molls. *Society*, 1973, 11:32-5.

Quicker, John, *Homegirls: Characterizing Chicana Gangs, 1983*. San Pedro: International Universities Press, 1983.

Ethnicity

Chin, Ko-Lin, *Chinese Subculture and Criminality: Non-Traditional Crime Groups in America*. Westport, CT: Greenwood Press, 1990.

Moore, Joan W., *Down to the Barrio*. Philadelphia, PA: Temple University Press, 1991.

Sanders, William B., *Gangbangs and Drive-bys: Grounded Culture and Juvenile Gang Violence*. New York: Aldine De Gruyter, 1994.

Vigil, James Diego, *Barrio Gangs: Street Life and Identity in Southern California*. Houston: University of Texas Press, 1988.

Vigil, James Diego, & Yun, Steve Chong, Vietnamese youth gangs in Southern California. In C. Ronald Huff (ed.), *Gangs in America*. Newbury Park, CA: Sage Publications, 1990. ✦

Defining Gangs

1

Defining Gangs and Gang Behavior

Robert J. Bursik, Jr. and Harold G. Grasmick

Our understanding of the nature and extent of gang behavior, and our beliefs about the actions we should take to respond to it, are highly dependent on how "gang" is defined. In these pages from their book Neighborhoods and Crime, *Bursik and Grasmick discuss the variety of definitional approaches to the concept. These authors draw from the extensive gang literature to illustrate both process-based and delinquency-based approaches. Our lack of knowledge about the relationship between group dynamics and criminal behavior makes the definitional process particularly difficult.*

Peggy Sanday (1990) has provided a detailed description of the dynamics that led to a gang rape alleged to have been committed by members of a fairly well-organized, cohesive group of older adolescents in Philadelphia. Prior to this particular incident, the XYZs (a fictitious name) had already developed a widespread reputation in the neighborhood for problematic behavior. Women commonly reported that they had been verbally harassed by members of the gang who hung around drinking beer on benches along the primary street in the area. Since these benches were situated in front of their clubhouse, the group made it clear that this was their "turf" to do with as they pleased.

Although all the members of this gang were enrolled in school, the group allocated some degree of special status to those who performed poorly. One of the judges involved in the rape case noted that a statement that the XYZs had offered into evidence was "ungrammatical . . . replete with misspellings . . . garbled and incomprehensible" (Forer 1990:xvii). As Sanday has reported, new members of the community were commonly warned about the group, and women were urged to consider the potential dangers of attending the parties that were regularly thrown by the gang.

To many, this short description has all the hallmarks of classic, popular descriptions of a gang, that is, a group of inner-city adolescents, a concern with turf, harassment of local residents, an organizational structure, some degree of solidarity, and mutual participation in serious forms of illegal behavior. Sanday notes (p. 71) that during her two interviews with one of the people implicated in the gang rape, "[H]is dislike for what I was doing and his sense of superiority to people like me were expressed throughout. . . ." In general, we would guess that most readers would not consider this to be a group with which they would like to interact on a regular basis. However, we have left one very important piece of information out of our short summary of Sanday's study: these were all members of a prominent fraternity at a prestigious, upper-middle-class university; the neighborhood in question was a campus community in Philadelphia.

Perhaps some readers think that this is an inappropriate example of gang activity, for public images of such behavior usually do not include the activities of fairly affluent fraternity members at highly respected colleges. Yet consider the influential definition of a gang provided by Klein (1971:13): any identifiable group of youngsters who (a) are generally perceived as a distinct aggregation by others in their neighborhood, (b) recognize themselves as a denotable group (almost invariably with a group name), and (c) have been involved in a sufficient number of delinquent incidents to call forth a consistent negative response from neighborhood residents and/or law enforcement agencies. As anyone familiar with campus life is aware, all fraternities easily qualify under the first two conditions; each has a unique name, and highly visible, relatively arcane symbols (i.e., Greek letters) are used to signify membership in such groups. The third condition is the one that would disqualify many (and perhaps most) fraternities. Yet Sanday's ethnographic material clearly shows that the "XYZ" fraternity had a "dangerous" reputation on campus, and we would be surprised to find many college campuses without at least one such house. Nevertheless, despite the fact that the XYZs clearly qualified as a gang under Klein's definition and the fact that one of the judges described the similarities of this case to those involving more traditional gang members as "striking" (Forer 1990:xvi), there is no indication that Philadelphia's long-established Gang Crimes Unit had any involvement in the case.

Thus, we come to the heart of the problem: exactly how are we to define a gang? Without a generally accepted definition of the concept, it is impossible to make any kind of informed judgment concerning the nature and extent of gang behavior, much less changes that have occurred over time. Some criminologists would certainly include the XYZ case in the computation of rates of gang crimes;[1] others would object strongly to such a classification.

Likewise, what are we to make of the fact that many small, stable, rural communities have recently

Reprinted with the permission of Lexington Books, an imprint of The Free Press, a division of Simon and Schuster, from Neighborhoods and Crime: *The Dimensions of Effective Community Control* by Robert J. Bursik, Jr. and Harold G. Grasmick.

claimed to be the site of gang behavior? For example, a Knight-Ridder newspaper item (Wallace 1991) describes the case of Frederick, Oklahoma (population 5,200), where the local police chief believes that violent, drug-dealing gangs are staking out territory in the community. The primary basis for his conclusion is the existence of some "Bloods" graffiti in the area, a number of auto thefts, cases of shoplifting and intimidation, reports of drug dealing, and warning notes (this time from the Crips) that have been left on cars.

It is clear that one of the gravest mistakes that a community can make is to deny the existence of a gang-related problem until a series of serious incidents force the issue. Columbus, Ohio, for example, denied that it had any type of problem until members of the mayor's family were brutally attacked by people claiming gang affiliation (Huff 1989:530-531). Therefore, the situation in Frederick might be seen as an outcome of the expansion of gang-controlled drug markets that had been widely discussed (U.S. General Accounting Office 1989). However, while the concern of the Frederick police chief certainly is understandable, a healthy degree of skepticism is warranted concerning the large number of communities who suddenly have discovered a "gang problem" in their midst. Grasmick was recently told by a high school teacher from Oklahoma City (which does have a documented gang problem), that once particular symbols (such as certain forms of dress or graffiti) became associated with gang membership in his school, they quickly became adopted by many non-gang adolescents as a sign of personal rebellion.[2] Therefore, the incidents that were reported in Frederick (including the graffiti) may not be gang-related in any respect other than they represent the efforts of local youths to adopt symbols that are guaranteed to elicit a horrified reaction from the adults in their community.

There are other dynamics that also must be considered when evaluating the extent to which an area is characterized by gang activity. Many concerned communities have invited law enforcement personnel to speak to local leaders about whether they have a gang problem and, if so, what they should do about it. One of the central themes that usually emerges is that without proper action on the part of the community, it is likely to be overrun with gang-related problems in a relatively short period of time. Such messages are quickly picked up by the local media and spread to the general public. Hagedorn (1988:30), for example, reports that the elites and the media of Milwaukee adopted an image of gang behavior that was promoted by the Chicago Gang Crimes Unit and reinforced by "scary slide shows of murders and a display of gang weapons that would make the U.S. Army run for cover." During these presentations, Milwaukee was warned that if the city failed to act "in a hard line manner," Milwaukee's gangs would be like those in Chicago within five years or less. We find this passage to be especially interesting in that one member of Oklahoma City's Gang Crimes Unit has worked especially hard to promote the image of impending gang danger across the state. Recall that the principal of the junior high that was quoted in the beginning of this chapter reported that she was told that if her community took no action, gang problems would be rampant within five years.[3]

Finally, it must be noted that since access to some federally funded law enforcement programs is more likely if a gang problem can be demonstrated in a community, some agencies may have vested interests in the "discovery" of gang activity. It is impossible to determine the extent to which the apparent diffusion of gang behavior reflects such economic considerations. However, such dynamics have been suggested as an explanation of why police estimates of the number of gangs in Phoenix increased from 5 or 6 to over 100 in a very short period of time (Zatz 1987).

It certainly has not been our intention in this section to downplay the seriousness of some gang activities or to imply that most communities are exaggerating the problems they face. Rather, we have attempted to emphasize that without a precise and parsimonious understanding of what constitutes a gang and gang behavior, it is often difficult to separate fact from mythology. Unfortunately, several factors make it very difficult to arrive at such an understanding.

Crime and Delinquency as Group Phenomena

There are very few issues concerning which criminologists usually feel confident enough to make strong declarative statements. However, the group nature of delinquency is certainly one of those issues. One of the most influential findings of the Shaw and McKay research was that almost 90 percent of the delinquent events reflected in the juvenile court records of Cook County involved two or more participants (Shaw et al. 1929:7-8). The group orientation was strongly reinforced several years later when Edwin Sutherland (1934) began to develop his influential theory of differential association, which emphasized the small-group dynamics associated with the learning of delinquent and criminal behavior. More recent work has noted some important offense-specific differences in the rates of group offending. In addition, a large proportion of offenders do not engage in illegal behavior strictly in group situations (see the review of Reiss 1988). Nevertheless, the presumed group nature of illegal behavior is a generally uncontested part of criminological lore.

There have been several important criticisms of the group hypothesis. The differential association perspective suggests that the most important sources of information concerning the techniques, motivations, and justifications for illegal behavior are intimate personal groups (see Sutherland's propositions 3 and 4). Given the apparent group nature of crime and delinquency, the intimate nature of these groups might suggest that offenses occur primarily within aggregations with temporal histories, fairly developed sets of relationships among the members, and relatively high levels of cohesiveness and solidarity. However, Klein (1969) has argued that the existence of two or more offenders in a single incident does not in itself guarantee that the event represents the outcome of such group dynamics. He criticizes in particular the influence that the Shaw and McKay findings have had on the discipline, for they were based on official records in which it is impossible to determine the actual group dynamics that may have been involved.

Klein illustrates this problem with several hypothetical examples, including one in which a relatively large number of strangers are attending a party and they happen to purchase marijuana from one of the other attendees. If the police happen to bust the party and make multiple arrests for possession, the arrest reports would most likely note that several people were involved in the incident. However, they would not constitute a group in any sociological sense of the word. Rather, these people were simply "contiguous individuals" (Klein 1969:67) who were engaged in the same behavior in the same location. Because of such conceptual ambiguities, some researchers now utilize alternative phrases (such as "co-offending"; Reiss 1988) to refer to events in which more than one person was involved but in which the existence of group dynamics is not clear.[4]

Klein certainly is not arguing that group dynamics are unrelated to criminal and delinquency behavior. Rather, he is emphasizing the need to recognize the basic distinction between the sociological notions of aggregate and group processes. In that respect, some unknown percentage of illegal behavior may be more validly viewed as a form of collective behavior in which an aggregate of relative strangers respond to a particular stimulus; this aggregate may have a very limited prior history and may disband after that particular response. There is a large body of literature that indicates that persons are more likely to engage in illegal behavior if their closest friends are involved in such behavior (see Elliott et al. 1985). However, there also is evidence that many delinquent behaviors occur in the company of individuals to whom a person has relatively weak associational bonds. Martin Gold (1970:83-94) has likened this situation to a "pickup game" of basketball in which the roster of players depends on who happens to be on the playground at the same time. That is, those present may define an opportunity as suitable for basketball (delinquency), and once the game is concluded, many of them go their separate ways. While certain interesting dynamics are involved in the definition of the situation, they have a relatively short-term relevance to the participants. These are not typically the kinds of processes that sociologists attribute to groups. As a result, some criminologists have raised important questions concerning the extent to which group solidarity is reflected in the illegal behavior of co-offenders (see Morash 1983).

Much of the confusion that has arisen in the gang literature, as well as in the public's perception of gang behavior, is due to the often interchangeable use of the words "group" and "gang" (see the criticism of Klein and Maxson 1989). For example, while Walter Miller (1980) delineates twenty different types of "law-violating youth groups," he only considers three of these to represent gangs (see Table 1). If the general pattern of relationships among co-offenders is much more fluid than is usually assumed, perhaps the primary distinction between group and gang crime and delinquency pertains to the internal dynamics of the aggregate that may result in a criminal event. For example, Bernard Cohen (1969:66) considers delinquent groups to represent relatively small cliques that coalesce sporadically without apparent reason and spontaneously violate the law. Cohen considers such groups to be ephemeral, with no elaborate organizational structure, name, or sense of turf. Gangs, on the other hand, are highly developed aggregates with relatively large memberships. As opposed to delinquent groups, gangs have elaborate organizations, names, senses of corporate identity, and identifications with particular territories. A similar typology has been developed by Irving Spergel (1984). The viability of such distinctions will be examined in the next section.

Table 1

Types and Subtypes of Law-Violating Youth Groups

1	Turf gangs
2	Regularly associating disruptive local groups/crowds
3	Solidary disruptive local cliques
4	Casual disruptive local cliques
5	Gain-oriented gangs/extended networks
6	Looting groups/crowds
7	Established gain-oriented cliques/limited networks
7.1	Burglary rings
7.2	Robbery bands
7.3	Larceny cliques and networks
7.4	Extortion cliques
7.5	Drug-dealing cliques and networks
7.6	Fraudulent gain cliques
8	Casual gain-oriented cliques
9	Fighting gangs
10	Assaultive cliques and crowds
10.1	Assaultive affiliation cliques
10.2	Assaultive public-gathering crowds
11	Recurrently active assaultive cliques
12	Casual assaultive cliques

Reprinted from Miller (1980) by permission of the editors.

Defining Gang Delinquency

John Hagedorn (1988) has identified two primary ways in which the gang has been defined within the criminological literature. The first, and oldest, approach has emphasized the processes that give rise to such groups. Albert Cohen (1955), for example, defines gangs in terms of collective reactions to problems of social status, while Richard Cloward and Lloyd Ohlin (1960) focus on the interaction between legitimate and illegitimate opportunity structures. However, we feel that the most important processual definition for understanding the relationship between neighborhood dynamics and gang behavior is that of Frederic Thrasher (1927), who defines a gang as "an interstitial group originally formed spontaneously and then integrated through conflict. . . . The result of this collective behavior is the development of tradition, unreflective internal structure, esprit de corps, solidarity, morale, group awareness, and attachment to a local territory" (p.46).

Several aspects of Thrasher's definition are worth noting. First, "interstitial" has a dual connotation. Thrasher uses it in one sense to represent the period of life when one is neither a child nor an adult; gangs therefore are a reflection of the period of adjustment between childhood and maturity (p. 32). For this reason, Thrasher argues that such groups are relatively short-lived and that adult gangs or members are relatively rare.[5] Yet this does not mean that gangs are characterized by age homogeneity. Rather, as older members age out of the group, younger members join, leading to a set of loosely connected, age-based cliques within the gang.

Thrasher also used the term "interstitial" to refer to neighborhoods located between Chicago's central business district and "the better residential areas" (p. 6). Since these were areas characterized by neighborhood deterioration and residential turnover (p. 46), Thrasher's model is clearly a variation of the social disorganization approach that we have discussed extensively. The systemic implications of his approach are clearly evident in his discussion (p. 33) of the failure of "directing and controlling customs and institutions to function efficiently in the boy's experience." The spirit of this aspect of Thrasher's processual definition is evident in Spergel's (1984:201) more recent definition of integrated gangs as a reflection of the inability of primary and secondary community institutions to provide mechanisms of opportunity or control.

Second, Thrasher's emphasis on "spontaneous formation" reflects his argument that all childhood play groups represent potential forms of gangs (see pp. 23-26). Since such groups usually arise on the basis of interaction and familiarity, they tend to form around particular residential locations in a neighborhood where youths are likely to come into contact with one another. Thus, street corner groups represent the basic building block upon which Thrasher develops his thesis. The key determinant of the transition into a gang is contact with other groups (either other play groups or adults) who express disapproval or opposition to the playgroup. For example, Hagedorn (1988:57-60) observes that fierce rivalries developed among the many breakdancing groups that arose during the early 1980s in Milwaukee; gangs sometimes emerged as a result of the fights that often broke out after competitions. Such conflict can produce an awareness of the distinction between "us" and "them" and the development of a sense of solidarity among group members. The existence of a street corner group therefore can serve as a source of protection from other groups in the neighborhood (see Spergel 1984:202).

Finally, note that delinquent or criminal activities are not mentioned in Thrasher's definition. While he certainly recognized that such activities may be facilitated by gang membership, he emphasized the variability that existed in the 1,313 groups that he identified as gangs: some are good, some are bad. Thrasher's approach emphasizes the social dynamics that may lead to cohesion among a play group and the resulting development of a gang. The relationship of gangs to delinquency is therefore a key analytical issue.

Although such process-based definitions of the gang continue to appear in the literature, Hagedorn (1988:57) notes that most current research is no longer characterized by a focus on how gangs arise within particular community contexts and how they function within those social environments. Rather, he argues that the fundamental question has become "why gang members are delinquent." The definition of Klein (1971) presented earlier in this chapter, with its criterion that the number of delinquencies committed by the group has called forth some type of negative response, represents a commonly used example of such an approach. The implications of this shift in focus are much more important than they may first appear, for illegal behavior is considered to be a definitional aspect of gang activity, whereas for Thrasher it was an empirical question.

Even more so than was the case with processual definitions, there is an enormous variety of delinquency-based definitions which have become the basis for different policies, laws, and strategies. One of the most interesting attempts to produce a definition with a broad consensual base is that of Walter Miller (1975, 1980), who asked a national sample of youth service agency staff members to respond to the questions: "What is your conception of a gang? Exactly how would you define it?" His final definition is based on the responses of 309 respondents representing 121 youth serving agencies in 26 areas of the country (Miller 1980:120), including police officers, prosecutors, defenders, educators, city council members, state legislators, ex-prisoners, and past and present members of gangs and groups (1980:117).

Of the 1,400 definitional characteristics that were provided by his sample, Miller reports that there were six items with which at least 85 percent of the respondents agreed (1980:121): a youth gang is a self-formed association of peers, bound together by mutual interests, with identifiable leadership, well-developed lines of authority, and other organizational features, who act in concert to achieve a specific purpose or purposes, which generally include the conduct of illegal activity and control over a particular territory, facility, or type of enterprise.

Such delinquency-based definitions have been criticized for several reasons. Klein and Maxson (1989:205) call Miller's approach "discouraging" and argue that to define a concept on the basis of the results of a "vote" does not make it inherently more definitive or valid than other approaches. Yet their criticisms are not aimed solely at Miller, for they note that the definitional task is "difficult and arbitrary" and an "inherently unsatisfying task." The continued existence of a great variety of delinquency-based definitions (see Spergel 1990) suggests that consensus does not exist for any particular conceptualization (although the definition provided in Klein 1971 has been particularly influential). Ruth Horowitz (1990:43) notes that the variation in locally used definitions may be useful for understanding how the relationships among criminal justice personnel, the community, the gang, and the individual gang member are defined. Nevertheless, the lack of a standard, nationwide definition of a gang makes estimates that have been made concerning the number of youth gangs in the United States or comparisons that have been made over time or between communities relatively meaningless (Spergel 1990:180).

Some contemporary researchers have expressed a more general discomfort with all definitions that assume generalizable groups structures and processes or that equate crime with gang behavior (see Hagedorn 1988; Fagan 1989:643). Merry Morash (1983:310) argues that these approaches developed due to a growing reliance on definitions used by law enforcement and social work personnel. Since many of these agencies classify groups as gangs if violent or criminal activity is a major activity, gangs are by definition heavily involved in illegal behavior and Thrasher's question concerning the relationship between gang membership and delinquency becomes tautological (see Short 1990:160).

To illustrate the implications of such definitional assumptions, Morash created a scale of "gang likeness" based on an adaptation of Miller's definition.[6] While her analysis presents evidence that the gang-likeness variable has a significant effect on delinquency, more general peer group processes, such as the delinquent behavior of one's friends, are of much greater importance. Overall, she concludes (p. 325) that membership in a stereotyped gang is not a sufficient condition to stimulate serious delinquency. This seems to provide an important contradiction to the finding of many studies that gang members are involved in significantly higher levels of crime and drug use (see Fagan 1989). However, Klein and Maxson (1989:204) take issue with Morash's findings, noting that adolescent church or school groups could have qualified as gangs using her criteria.

Other characteristics of gangs that might be the subject of empirical investigation are also embedded into definitions such as that developed by Miller. For example, while some of the informants in Hagedorn's (1988) study reported that their gangs had fairly specialized and formalized ranks, others insisted that the structure was very informal; a few even stated that their gangs had no recognized leader (p. 92). Likewise, Joan Moore (1978:44) reports that the historical circumstances that set the context for the development of each of the age-based cliques *(klikas)* in Los Angeles Chicano gangs has resulted in significant differences among groupings in the same gang, each of which may have its own organizational structure (see also Keiser 1969:15).

We find the arguments of Hagedorn and Morash very persuasive, for those characteristics that are assumed by researchers such as Miller to be defining features of gangs actually exhibit a great deal of variation among groups who have been identified as gangs. Rather than taking these characteristics for granted, it would seem to be much more theoretically fruitful to examine the processes that give rise to such group variation. Perhaps one of the reasons why the Klein (1971) definition has been extremely popular is that the three criteria are extremely flexible and are relevant to a wide range of gang types.

Nevertheless, we are uncomfortable with the delinquent behavior criterion, for it makes a possible outcome of gang activity one of the defining characteristics. Klein and Maxson (1989:204) defend their position by noting that "to think of modern street gangs independent of their criminal involvement is to ignore the very factor that makes them qualitatively different from other groups of young people."[7] Despite our own misgivings concerning the presumed equivalence of gang activity and crime, there is no question that the major criterion used by many audiences in the definition of gang is the group's participation in illegal behavior (Spergel 1990:179).

Notes

1. For example, our colleague John Cochran has referred to certain fraternities on the University of Oklahoma campus as "syndicates of rate" which has made him a very popular figure in the Letters to the Editor department of the school newspaper.
2. Interestingly, at least in that high school, this meant that the dominant gang continually revised its preferred style of dress to maintain a symbolic separation between it and the general school population.
3. If the Soviet Union had had five-year plans as effective as those attributed by many authorities to street gangs, it might have survived.
4. The careful reader will note that this problem is very similar to the compositional effect-group effect issue that was discussed in Chapter 2 in respect to neighborhoods. [Editors' note: See Chapter 2 of Bursik and Grasmick, *Neighborhoods and Crime: The Dimensions of Effective Community Control*. New York: Lexington Books, 1993.)
5. A very similar argument concerning the role of gangs in adolescent development has been presented by Bloch and Neiderhoffer (1958).
6. Items included in the final scale reflected whether or not the group meets outside the home, if youths are typically members for four or more years, if the group usually meets in the same place, if the group comes from just one part of the neighborhood, if the group has a name, if the group contains older and younger kids, if the respondent meets with the group at least four days a week, and if the respondent takes part in several activities with the group.
7. Spergel (1990) notes that many gang researchers who once believed that gang behavior was not especially serious or lethal (such as Miller and Klein) now have come to the position that such groups are responsible for a large number of homicides and are active participants in widespread narcotics trafficking (see, for example, Miller 1975; Klein and Maxson 1985, 1989).

References

Bloch, Herbert A., and Arthur Niederhoffer (1958). *The Gang: A Study in Adolescent Behavior*. New York: Philosophical Library.

Bookin, Hedy, and Ruth Horowitz (1983). "The End of the Youth Gang: Fad or Fact?" *Criminology* 21:585-602.

Chambliss, William J. (1973). "The Saints and the Roughnecks." *Society* 11:24-31.

Cloward, Richard A., and Lloyd Ohlin (1960). *Delinquency and Opportunity*. New York: Free Press.

Cohen, Albert K. (1955). *Delinquent Boys*. Glencoe, IL: The Free Press.

Cohen, Bernard (1969). "The Delinquency of Gangs and Spontaneous Groups." Pp. 61-111 in *Delinquency: Selected Studies*, edited by Thorsten Sellin and Marvin E. Wolfgang. New York: Wiley.

Elliott, Delbert S., David Huizinga, and Suzanne S. Ageton (1985). *Explaining delinquency and Drug Use*. Beverly Hills, CA: Sage.

Fagan, Jeffrey (1989). "The Social Organization of Drug Use and Drug Dealing Among Urban Gangs." *Criminology* 27:633-669.

Forer, Lois G. (1990). "Foreword." Pp. xiii-xxv in *Fraternity Gang Rape: Sex, Brotherhood, and Privilege on Campus*, by Peggy Sanday. New York: New York University Press.

Gold, Martin (1970). *Delinquent Behavior in an American City*. Belmont, CA: Brooks-Cole.

Hagedorn, John M. (1988). *People and Folks: Gangs, Crime and the Underclass in a Rustbelt City*. Chicago: Lakeview Press.

Horowitz, Ruth (1990). "Sociological Perspectives on Gangs: Conflicting Definitions and Concepts." Pp. 37-54 in *Gangs in America*, edited by C. Ronald Huff. Newbury Park, CA: Sage.

Huff, C. Ronald (1989). "Youth Gangs and Public Policy." *Crime and Delinquency* 35:524-537.

Keiser, R. Lincoln (1969). *The Vice Lords: Warriors of the Streets*. New York: Holt, Rinehart and Winston.

Klein, Malcolm W. (1969). "On Group Context of Delinquency." *Sociology and Social Research* 54:63-71.

—— (1971). *Street Gangs and Street Workers*. Englewood Cliffs, NJ: Prentice-Hall.

Klein, Malcolm W. and Cheryl L. Maxson (1985). "'Rock' Sales in South Los Angeles." *Sociology and Social Research* 69:561-565.

—— (1989). "Street Gang Violence." Pp. 198-234 in *Violent Crime, Violent Criminals*, edited by Neil A. Weiner and Marvin E. Wolfgang. Newbury Park, CA: Sage.

Miller, Walter B. (1975). *Violence by Youth Gangs as a Crime Problem in Major American Cities*. National Institute for Juvenile Justice and Delinquency Prevention, U.S. Justice Department. Washington, DC: U.S. Government Printing Office.

—— (1980). "Gangs, Groups, and Serious Youth Crime." Pp. 115-138 in *Critical Issues in Juvenile Delinquency*, edited by David Schichor and Delos H. Kelly. Lexington, MA: D.C. Heath.

Moore, Joan W. (1978) *Homeboys*. Philadelphia: Temple University Press.

—— (1988). "Introduction: Gangs and the Underclass. A Comparative Perspective." Pp. 3-17 in *People and Folks: Gangs, Crime and the Underclass in a Rustbelt City*, by John M. Hagedorn. Chicago: Lakeview Press.

Morash, Merry (1983). "Gangs, Groups, and Delinquency." *British Journal of Criminology* 23:309-335.

Reiss, Albert J., Jr. (1988). "Co-Offending and Criminal Careers." Pp. 117-170 in *Crime and Justice: A Review of Research*. Vol. 10, edited by Michael Tonry and Norval Morris. Chicago: University of Chicago Press.

Sanday, Peggy (1990). *Fraternity Gang Rape: Sex, Brotherhood, and Privilege on Campus*. New York: New York University Press.

Shaw, Clifford R., Frederick M. Zorbaugh, Henry D. McKay, and Leonard S. Cottrell (1929). *Delinquency Areas*. Chicago: University of Chicago Press.

Shaw, Clifford R., and Henry D. McKay (1931). *Social Factors in Juvenile Delinquency. National Commission on Law Observation and Enforcement, No. 13, Report on the Causes of Crime, Volume II*. Washington, DC: U.S. Government Printing Office.

Short, James F., Jr. (1990). *Delinquency and Society*. Englewood Cliffs, NJ: Prentice-Hall.

Spergel, Irving A. (1984). "Violent Gangs in Chicago: In Search of Social Policy." *Social Service Review* 58:199-226.

—— (1990). "Youth Gangs: Continuity and Change." Pp. 171-275 in *Crime and Justice: A Review of Research*. Volume 12, edited by Michael Tonry and Norval Morris. Chicago: University of Chicago Press.

Spergel, Irving A., and G. David Curry (1990). "Strategies and Perceived Agency Effectiveness in Dealing with the Youth Gang Problem." Pp. 288-317 in *Gangs in America*, edited by C. Ronald Huff. Newbury Park, CA: Sage.

Sutherland, Edwin H. (1934). *Principles of Criminology*, Second Edition. Philadelphia: J.B. Lippincott.

Thrasher, Frederic M. (1927). *The Gang*. Chicago: University of Chicago Press.

United States General Accounting Office (1989). *Nontraditional Organized Crime*. Washington, DC: U.S. Government Printing Office.

Wallace, Linda S. (1991). "Big-City Terror Stalks Small-Town America." *Knight-Ridder Newspaper Service*, December 26.

Whyte, William F. (1981). *Street Corner Society*. Third Edition. Chicago: University of Chicago Press.

Zatz, Marjorie S. (1987). "Chicano Youth Gangs and Crime: The Creation of a Moral Panic. *Contemporary Crises* 11:129-158. ✦

2

Constructing Gangs: The Social Definition of Youth Activities

Scott Decker and Kimberly Kempf-Leonard

The social construction of definitions is highlighted in the following article. Decker and Kempf-Leonard gathered information about the impact and nature of St. Louis' gang situation from three types of informants: local policymakers, law enforcement officers, and juveniles detained by the juvenile court (many of whom were gang members). The diverse perceptions and knowledge levels articulated by the three groups reflect fundamentally different understandings among those responsible for responding to gangs (the police and the policymaking task force members) and the youth experiencing the highest risk of involvement and victimization.

A disturbing finding concerned the role of the media in providing the foundation of knowledge about gangs for the majority of policymakers, despite the low ratings for accuracy accorded to media coverage by all three groups. This research illustrates the importance of shared understandings, sound information, and better communication among all facets of affected communities. In particular, the authors recommend the inclusion of youths in attempts to understand and respond to gangs.

Abstract

Despite previous research, there remains no consensus on definitions of who is a gang member, what is a gang, and what is gang activity. This paper examines these issues based on results of a survey administered to two groups involved in responding to gangs—members of a gang task force and officers of an urban police department—and a group of juvenile detainees. Considerable differences are observed among the three groups in their appraisal of the extent and impact of gang activity, number of gangs and gang members, and gang-relatedness of five vignettes. The implications for formulating a policy response to gangs are discussed.

A number of problems in criminology have surfaced and faded from attention. Drugs, inequality, poverty, prisons, police powers, career criminals and victimless crimes are all problems that have peaked and faded as the object of criminological research. Another issue is the concern about gangs. Gangs have been the object of criminological attention since Thrasher's (1929) work first brought them to the fore. Since that initial treatment, interest in gangs has waxed and waned.

Explaining variation in interest in gangs involves dealing with the role of social definitions. Quinney (1970) emphasizes the importance of definitions in creating categories of crime. He stresses the function of definitions in establishing boundaries for behavior to which society responds. Gusfield (1981) underscores the effect of definitions in noting that social problems (such as drunk driving) become problems only after a process of social definition. Drunk driving, Gusfield observes, is but one of a variety of behaviors that result in painful behavior to some members of society. Yet not all such painful behaviors result in being defined as criminal or major public problems. The process by which some painful behaviors come to be defined as the targets of public attention is an important object of study.

The formulation of effective policy responses to gangs depends upon a reliable and valid foundation of knowledge of the "gang problem." This paper examines the perceptions of two groups intimately involved in such responses, and compares their responses to those of a group of juvenile detainees. The emphasis of this study is on definitions of the characteristics of gangs, and sources of knowledge about gangs. A survey was administered to assess the perceptions about gangs and gang involvement in a large city. The responses of a group of juveniles held in a detention center are compared to those of local juvenile police officers and a task force created to deal with gangs. The results will be used to demonstrate the diversity of sources of knowledge about gangs, differences in beliefs about gangs, and differences in attribution of gang-relatedness to several key features of delinquent activity. Definitions play a crucial role in the identification of problems and the formulation of responses. Recognition of variation in definitions helps us to understand the conceptual basis of social responses to problems. We are specifically interested in the role of policymakers in defining and identifying gang activity.

Literature Review

At the heart of this research is interest in what constitutes a gang. This issue involves three related questions: 1) what is a gang?, 2) who is a gang member?, and 3) what is gang activity? Interest in gangs has spanned a number of generations and a good deal of variation in the definitions of gang, gang membership and gang activity is reflected in the literature.

The last fifteen years have spawned several reviews of gangs and gang-related activities (Miller, 1975, 1976; Jackson, 1988; Spergel, 1990; Huff, 1990). Miller (1975, 1976) provided the first nationwide survey of youth gangs and youth groups. Although Miller failed to provide comprehensive definitions for a gang, a gang member, and gang activities, he later (1980) argues that it is critical for social science to establish such definitions. Jackson (1988) notes the variable definitions used in attempting to assess what identifies the three objects of the current study, gangs, gang membership, and gang activity. His work also underscores the significant variation in approaches to gangs seen during this century. More recently, Spergel (1990) distinguishes between gang and non-gang offenders in his extensive review of youth gangs, noting the historical existence of such groups. He identifies persistent involvement in criminal or delinquent activities (1990:178-179) as the halcyon characteristics of gang involvement.

The distinction between groups and gangs is not clearly made in much of the research. Even the widely accepted axiom that delinquency is group activity has been criticized. Klein (1969) and Zimring (1981) both suggest that more delinquency takes place outside the group context than traditional wisdom (DeFleur, 1967; Empey and Rabow, 1961; Empey, 1967) has suggested. These findings suggest more uncertainty among scholars concerning gang definitions, especially those which depend primarily on the use of a group context for identifying gangs and gang-related activity. This is illustrated by the sometimes unclear distinction between gangs and organized crime, a case in point being Jamaican posses.

Characteristic of the more inclusive definitions found in the literature is that provided by Miller (1976) who notes, "The term 'gang' refers to a collectivity of humans comprising identifiable persons and is conceptually analogous to terms such as 'group' or 'organization' " (1976:92). Johnstone (1981:355) provides a definition consistent with Miller's when he observes, "One person's gang may be another's peer group, street-corner group, crowd, clique, hanging group, club or simply youth group." Others report that the salient identifying characteristics of gangs are found in graffiti (Brown, 1978), normal peer group activities (Kleiner, Stub, and Lanahan, 1975), or group activities (Lerman, 1968). Indeed, Kleiner et al. note that from their perspective, ". . . use of the term gang is not intended to be a negative or derogatory reference as is often the case in both current lay and professional usage" (1975:393).

There have been several efforts to provide more conceptually useful definitions of gang activity. Arnold (1966) identifies five elements of gangs: 1) integration, 2) conflict 3) structure, 4) size, and 5) lack of a social agenda. This definition lacks a common element found among most definitions, involvement in criminal activity. Klein (1967) emphasizes the role of cohesion among gang members promoted by involvement in delinquent or criminal activities. Hagedorn (1988:5) identifies gangs as a "friendship group of adolescents who share common interests, with a more or less clearly defined territory, in which most of the members live. They are committed to defending one another, the territory, and the gang name in the status-setting fights that occur in school and or the streets." Hagedorn's definition underscores the importance of turf and solidarity which are of critical importance in understanding gangs. However, his definition fails to include a measure of criminal wrongdoing, and places too much emphasis on turf to have broad applicability. As Vigil and Yun (1990) have observed, turf is less important to many Vietnamese gangs. Fagan (1989) suggests that there are many differences both within and across gangs. His focus on drug use and drug distribution among gang members suggests yet another dimension to the ways in which gangs may vary.

Public concern over one specific gang activity—homicides—has increased over the last five years (Huff, 1990; Jackson, 1988). There is considerable disagreement about what constitutes a gang-related homicide. Disparate definitions used by Maxson, Gordon, and Klein (1985), Maxson and Klein (1990) (who use the definitions of the Los Angeles Police Department), and the Chicago Police Department (1988) provide evidence of this complication. Maxson and Klein (1990) demonstrate the significance of definitional preference for determining the level of gang-related violence, specifically homicides. The Chicago and Los Angeles police departments use different definitions for classifying a homicide as gang-related. The Los Angeles Police Department classifies a homicide as gang-related if a gang member is involved as a victim or offender. However, the Chicago Police Department classifies homicides as such only if a gang motive is evident. Obviously the more restrictive Chicago definition results in fewer homicides classified as gang-related.

The importance of understanding gang definitions is clear. Public perception of the seriousness and magnitude of the gang problem is based in large part on the definition of gangs being used. Perhaps more important than the public's perceptions of gangs are those of policymakers. Research has shown that many of the media's and public officials' views on gangs are distorted (Horowitz, 1990:39) and the portrayal of gangs and gang activity by the media has received extensive criticism in the literature (Hagedorn, 1988; Klein, 1974; Miller, 1975). This is significant, especially if a substantial portion of the knowledge policymakers use as a basis for action comes from media sources. In a very real sense, the response of policymakers to gangs defines them as a social problem. This perspective is supported by Downes' (1966) analysis that calls attention to the fact that adolescent misbehavior most often is episodic and takes place in groups. That is, though much delinquent activity takes place in groups, some of which are identified as gangs, these groups tend to coalesce and disperse around specific criminal or delinquent acts. Downes argues that little permanence exists for groups engaged in much of what is referred to as "gang delinquency." Morash (1983) analyzes the difference between practitioners' and theorists' definitions of youth gangs. She uses a scale of gang-related activity that focuses on solidarity, type of activity, and gang-likeness. Her findings support the assertion that agency personnel tend to "amplify" or overestimate gang activity. Morash underscores the need to bring "conceptual clarity" to the issue of gang-related crime.

The imputation of meanings and motives to the activities and social patterns of urban minority youths is a difficult issue, especially when there is such variation in perceptions, as the definitional variation reviewed above has shown. Understanding any phenomena requires that conceptual definitions be established, and since, as Bookin-Weiner and Horowitz (1983) note, concern about gangs seems not to be very strongly related to the volume of gang activity, the need to understand better how definitions are constructed regarding gangs, gang members and gang activities seems very significant indeed.

The present study pursues the objective of identifying the social construct of gangs. We hope to demonstrate the variation in definitions concerning youth gangs across three groups familiar with and concerned about this topic: a group of juveniles detained by Juvenile Court, police, and the members of the St. Louis Public School's Anti-Drug/Anti-Gang Task Force. In accord with previous findings (Bookin-Weiner and Horowitz, 1983; Morash, 1983), we hypothesize that these three groups will have diverse opinions about gangs. Huff (1989) observes that Task Forces play a significant role in the formulation of public policy on gangs. Thus, the perceptions held by Task Force members are an important object of study. One way to understand how social problems become policy issues is to examine those groups formally charged with developing policies to respond to such problems. It is useful to study their beliefs and knowledge of the problem, as well as the source or basis of those beliefs. In addition, the ability to compare the beliefs of those formally involved in formulating policy to those of individuals closer to, or more directly affected by the problem (such as urban adolescents and police officers) offers a unique insight into the process of policy formulation.

Gilbert (1986) has observed that there are several recurrent "episodic notions" about American delinquency. Gangs seem to be such a notion. The groups involved in creating and defining these episodes (such as Task Forces) are thus worthwhile objects of study. In a detailed history of juvenile justice reform, Sutton (1986:239) concluded that "juvenile justice reforms are best understood as symbolic efforts to dramatize an ideal vision of social order rather than instrumental attempts to control children's misbehavior." This paper attempts to understand the basis for the vision of gangs held by members of an Anti-Gang/Anti-Drug Task Force, because that vision will have important implications for policy decisions about gang activity. Findings from this study provide information about the perceptions of youth gangs held by three groups affected by their presence and activities: 1) police, 2) juveniles, and 3) policymakers.

Data Collection and Study Design

This study illustrates current inconsistencies in definitions and serves as a foundation for understanding more about what constitutes a gang, a gang member, and gang activity in the eyes of an important policymaking body. A survey aimed at the identification of conceptual and operational definitions of youth gangs was conducted during the spring of 1990. The data for this study were collected from three sources. First, perceptions about gangs were obtained from juveniles who were detained by the Juvenile Court in the city of St. Louis. Juvenile detainees were interviewed because they represent an important source of knowledge about gangs for two distinct reasons. As adolescents, they are closer in age to gang members and thus more likely to see and experience the effects of such activity. As detainees they are involved in delinquency and thus are more likely than other youth samples (e.g., those conducted at school) to be familiar with gang activity. Juveniles come into contact with gang members and their activities in a variety of settings including school, home and the neighborhood. Thus, they are at risk of being the victims of gang activity, as well as of recruitment into gangs. They are therefore closer to the problem. Hagedorn (1988) has observed that interviewing those closest to the problem may yield the most valuable insights because of their contact and familiarity with gang activities. The 79 juveniles detained during the first two weeks of April and July participated in this study. They were interviewed in an office secluded from the rest of the facility. Because of concerns about literacy and comprehension, the survey form was read to each subject. Interviews were conducted by graduate students familiar with juvenile justice and experienced in interviewing subjects in secure facilities. Only males were interviewed because so few females enter detention (fewer than 10 per month) prompting concerns about the confounding effect of gender on responses. These subjects were asked to self-report their own gang membership, in order to compare the perceptions of those who claim membership to the perceptions of those who claim no gang affiliation.[1] Just under half of the juveniles (32 or 41 percent) reported gang affiliation.

The second sample for this analysis comes from the St. Louis Public Schools Anti-Drug/Anti-Gang Task Force. This group of 90 individuals was formed by the St. Louis Public Schools in the spring of 1989 in response to perceived problems of gang activity in the schools. The Task Force is composed of roughly equivalent numbers of representatives from the schools, police, drug treatment community, juvenile services, local government, and professionals in city offices. Following the April 1990 meeting of the Task Force a questionnaire was mailed (with a self-addressed, stamped envelope) to each member of the Task Force. Responses were received from 40 members of the Task Force. The response rate was augmented by a second mailing in May to all who failed to respond to the first mailing. This effort succeeded in raising the sample size to 75 for members of the Task Force. The third source of data was the Juvenile

Division of the St. Louis Police Department. Because these officers had responsibility for responding to gang crime, their perceptions of this issue are important. A copy of the survey was distributed to the five police officers serving on the Task Force, as well as to every officer in the Juvenile Division who was not a member of the Task Force. Responses were received from all juvenile officers as well as from the five officers on the Task Force (who were included within the police sample).[2] The responses of these three groups were then compared.

The questionnaire was designed to determine the extent to which common definitions are shared within and among the three groups. Conceptual and operational definitions were distinguished for a variety of substantive issues about youth gangs. Specifically, we were interested in the factors which led to the identification of activities as gang-related, as well as in those elements which each group saw as most likely to affect a downturn in gang activity. Additionally, descriptive comparisons are made between detained youth who self-reported gang membership and those who did not. Where appropriate, significance tests are reported for the differences observed among the groups. When data are reported as means for each group, the F test of significance is used; when data are reported in tabular form, the chi square test of significance is used.[3] The results of this study should shed light on the views of three groups not often brought together to confront such issues: the policy-makers, those charged with implementing the policies and those affected by the policies.

Findings

The descriptive characteristics of the juvenile and adult groups are presented in Table 1. Data on gang membership are available for the 79 detainees. All of the police and detainee respondents are male, as is 65 percent of the Task Force. The majority of the Task Force (53 percent), gang members (91 percent) and non-gang detainees (94 percent), but only 36 percent of the police respondents, are black. A final category of comparison examines the victimization experiences of each group in the past year. The prevalence of victimization by violent crimes was substantially higher for gang members (41 percent) and non-gang members (30 percent) than for either police or Task Force members. The magnitude of difference was smaller for property crimes.

Table 1

Descriptive Characteristics of the Gang Expert Groups

	Gang Task Force (n = 75)	Police Officers (n = 22)	Non-Gang Detainees (n = 47)	Gang Members (n = 32)
Male	65%	100%	100%	100%
Race				
Black	53%	36%	94%	91%
White	45%	64%	6%	9%
Fight with more than 3 people			71%	97%
Victim of Crime in Past Year				
violent	1%	5%	30%	41%
property	15%	5%	7%	13%
both types	1%		2%	6%
not a victim	83%	90%	61%	41%

Many of the descriptive characteristics are available only for the youth. These measures include several relevant characteristics to understanding gang membership. Fights with a number of people may be taken as indicators of gang activity (Arnold, 1966; Hagedorn, 1988). The majority of gang members (97 percent) indicated that they had been involved in such altercations, compared to 71 percent of the non-gang youth. The groups are essentially similar on other characteristics.

We explore the issue of knowledge and sources of information regarding gangs in Table 2. The first measure asked how extensive gang activity was, with a lower score indicating that gang activity had more of an impact on everyday life. Police respondents had the highest score on this measure, while Task Force members and both juvenile groups had similar scores. These differences were significant at the .05 level. This finding suggests that police are less likely to view gang activity as affecting daily life than are juveniles and members of the Task Force. There was considerable agreement among police respondents about this issue (s=.7).

The analysis then moved to a consideration of the way in which respondents gained their knowledge of gangs. Clear differences (significant at the .05 level) among the groups were again observed. Firsthand experience was the primary source of knowledge about this activity for gang members. Non-gang youth learned about gangs from friends and neighbors. This reinforces Hagedorn's point (1988) about the necessity to learn from those closest to the problem. For members of the Task Force, however, the media was the primary way in which they learned about gangs. None of them learned about gangs firsthand, and only 9 percent learned of gang activity in their neighborhood. For police, the job provided the most common source of knowledge about gangs (59 percent). The second most common source of knowledge of gangs for the police was on a firsthand basis. Clearly, the source of knowledge about gangs differs across the groups. The role of the media in creating a foundation of knowledge for public policy is important, and is reinforced by the media's being the source of knowledge about gangs for most Task Force members.

Another interesting cleavage occurred among the groups when they were asked to indicate how accurately the media portrayed gangs. These differences were significant at the .001 level. The great majority of police respondents (82 percent) felt that the media sensationalized gangs. The modal response for the Task Force and both groups of juveniles was that the media failed to portray the seriousness of the problem accurately. This finding is interesting in view of the fact that Task Force members learn about gangs from

Table 2

Awareness about Gangs

How extensive is gang activity?*
(1=impacts every aspect of life, 7=has no effect)

	Mean #	S
Task Force	3.5	1.3
Police	4.5	1.7
Non-Gang Juveniles	3.2	1.6
Gang Members	3.1	1.7

	Gang Task Force (n = 75)	Police Officers (n = 22)	Non-gang Detainees (n = 47)	Gang Members (n = 32)
What is the primary way you know about gangs?*				
TV/Newspaper	52%	5%	15%	0%
Friends	4%	5%	24%	16%
Neighborhood	9%	0%	30%	9%
Job/School	30%	59%	15%	3%
Firsthand	0%	32%	7%	72%
Other	4%	0%	9%	0%
How accurately do the media portray gangs?***				
Sensationalized	30%	82%	26%	28%
Accurate	30%	9%	28%	25%
More Serious than Portrayed	39%	9%	46%	47%
How easy is it for youths to resist pressures to join gangs?***				
Very Difficult or Difficult	77%	73%	36%	40%
Moderately Hard or Not hard	23%	28%	64%	60%

* Significant at .05
** Significant at .01
*** Significant at .001

the media, yet only 30 percent of them believe the media accurately portray gangs. This calls into question how effective the Task Force may be in responding to gangs. This finding suggests a pattern that will be observed across all of the data: the police downplay the effects and presence of gang activity, whereas members of the Task Force and both groups of juveniles see the problem as much greater.

Our final consideration with regard to gang knowledge was to determine each group's perception of how difficult it is for youths to resist the pressures to join gangs. Again, significant differences (.001) among the groups were found. Because of distributional problems, we collapsed this variable to form a dichotomy representing whether it was either very difficult or difficult to resist the pressures to join gangs or moderately hard or not hard to resist these pressures. The modal response for gang members, the group closest to the problem, was that it was moderately hard or not hard to resist such pressures (60 percent); other youth reported similar perceptions (64 percent). For both the police and Task Force members the modal response was that it was very difficult or difficult to resist such pressures; 77 percent of Task Force members and 73 percent of the police felt this way. Indeed, there was little support among these two adult groups for the notion that gangs could be resisted. The irony in these findings is that the groups closest to the problem—juveniles—do not view pressures to join gangs as difficult to resist, whereas those charged with responding to the problem see such pressures as overwhelming.

We next compared the perceptions of each of the groups in assessing the status of the gang situation in St. Louis. These data are reported in Table 3. We first attempted to determine this by asking how many gangs there were in St. Louis. On average, gang members projected the highest number of gangs, followed by the police, other youth. The Task Force gave the lowest number. These differences, however, were not significant and there was considerable variation within each group. Results for a question assessing the number of gang members are presented next. The two youth groups estimated the greatest number of gang members. The police reported the fewest members, a fraction of the average number estimated by the juveniles. Task Force members projected twice as many gang members on average as did the police, but less than half as many as the two juvenile groups. These differences were significant at the .01 level. There was also considerable variation within each group on this item, as evidenced by the rather large standard deviations for each group. Most striking was the difference between police and gang members, the two groups most likely to learn about gangs on a firsthand basis. The estimates by the youths of the number of gang members were five times higher than those of the police, suggesting a fundamental difference between these groups.

A final procedure to assess the accuracy of gang knowledge was used. Thirteen real gang names obtained from the St. Louis Police Department Gang Intelligence Unit and confirmed by a street ethnographer currently studying gangs in St. Louis were embedded in a list containing several false names. Although the validity of the list is time and location specific, it was considered the best available way to assess accuracy of information among the subjects. Table 3 examines the mean number of gang names correctly identified by members of the four groups. The differences were significant at the .001 level. Both groups of juveniles and the police did relatively well at our recognition test, correctly identifying more than half of the names. Not surprisingly, gang members did the best, recognizing an average of 10.6 out of the 13 names. Members of the Task Force did very poorly, correctly identifying only 4.1 of the names.

Continued support for Hagedorn's (1988) imperative that we learn about problems from those closest to them is found in these results. On our "objective" measure of knowledge about gangs, both groups of juveniles did better than either the police or the Task Force, suggesting that policy makers would do well to pay attention to the perceptions of those nearest to the activities of youth, the youths themselves. Huff (1990) has identified the concept of "denial"—denying the existence of a gang problem—which officials in many cities have engaged in. This response seems to characterize the perceptions of the police throughout this study. However, the Task Force has quite a different perception of the extent of the gang problem, projecting more than twice as many gang members as did the police.

These results show that Task Force members project fewer gangs than either the police or detainees. In addition, juveniles believe that there are far more gang members than do either the police or members of the Task Force. On these measures, there is little difference between gang members and non-gang youth. Finally, the group charged with formulating and supporting gang policies—the Anti-Drug/Anti-Gang Task Force—was able to identify only a small number of the gangs operating in St. Louis.

Table 3

Incidence and Accuracy of Gang Knowledge

How many gangs are there in St. Louis? (N.S.)

	Mean #	S
Task Force	20	17
Police	26	20
Non-Gang Juveniles	25	32
Gang Members	29	30

How many gang members are there in the city of St. Louis?**

	Mean #	S
Task Force	952	1,529
Police	438	403
Non-Gang Juveniles	2,110	2,965
Gang Members	2,553	2,898

How many gangs were correctly identified?***

	Mean #	S
Task Force	4.1	3.3
Police	8.3	3.3
Non-Gang Juveniles	9.2	2.9
Gang Members	10.6	2.3

* Significant at .05
** Significant at .01
*** Significant at .001

Table 4

Identification of Gang-Related Scenarios

	Gang Task Force (n = 75)	Police Officers (n = 22)	Non-gang Detainees (n = 47)	Gang Members (n = 32)
The Projects	32%	1%	76%	59%***
The Softball	6%	0%	11%	34%*
The Park	83%	50%	76%	69%*
Older Brother	90%	50%	82%	91%***
Younger Brother	15%	5%	9%	9%N.S.

* Significant at .05
** Significant at .01
*** Significant at .001

Table 4 presents the results of each of the groups' appraisals of five vignettes.[4] (See Note 4 for the vignettes). Each of these scenarios was designed to highlight specific factors attributable to gang or non-gang involvement in criminal activity. The factors were selected based on the description of gang-related and gang activities identified in the literature.

The Projects scenario describes a situation where graffiti was painted following a fight of two groups over turf. These characteristics were identified as gang-related by Arnold (1966), Brown (1978), Hagedorn (1988), Johnstone (1981), Klein (1967), and Miller (1976). The great majority of non-gang youth (76 percent) identified this as gang-related, as did 59 percent of the gang members. However, only 32 percent of the Task Force, and virtually none of the police (1 percent) saw such behavior as gang-related. These findings, significant at the .001 level, show a pattern found throughout each of the scenarios—juveniles were most likely overall to identify scenarios as gang-related and police were least likely. In this case turf battles and graffiti were linked to gangs by juveniles who confront the consequences of both these issues more often than do their adult counterparts.

The Softball Game scenario involved a fight that erupted among the participants in a softball game that resulted in injuries (Arnold, 1966; Hagedorn, 1988; Kleiner et a]., 1975). None of the elements in this event could be construed as gang-related or gang-motivated by any of the definitions identified earlier. Despite this, 34 percent of the gang members saw it as gang-related. Only 11 percent of the other youth, and virtually none of the Task Force members or police associated it with gangs. This finding was significant at the .05 level and suggests that gang members are more expansive in their definitions of gang-related activities than are other youth, police or Task Force members and are likely to assign a gang label to a much broader range of activities.

The Park scenario identified a large number of teenagers in a park creating a nuisance to area residents, recruiting younger kids to join them in acting tough (Arnold, 1966; Hagedorn, 1988; Klein, 1967;

Kleiner et al., 1975). When the police respond, they find no drugs and make no arrests. This scenario sparked the concern of the Task Force, as 83 percent of them saw this incident as gang-related. Large numbers of juveniles (76 percent non-gang and 69 percent gang members) also saw this as gang-related. Only 50 percent of the police attributed gang activity to this scenario, one of only two vignettes to elicit a response from the police that identified a scenario as gang-related. The differences across groups were significant at the .05 level.

The Older Brother scenario was the most clearly gang-related. The perpetrator wore gang colors during the commission of a crime while engaged in "settling a score." These characteristics were associated with gangs by Arnold (1966), Hagedorn (1988), and Spergel (1990). Over 80 percent of the members of the Task Force and the youths saw this as gang-related; however, only 50 percent of the police saw this incident as gang-related, despite its strong gang quality. The differences here were significant at the .001 level. This again suggests the role of denial in the police response.

The final scenario depicted the revenge of an older brother for his younger brother's murder. This vignette identified gang activities as defined by Hagedorn (1988), Huff (1990), Jacobs (1974), Jackson (1988), Klein (1967). Although the younger brother was murdered over drugs, which many may link uncritically to gangs, few respondents saw the incident as gang-related. Indeed, this was the scenario in which the differences between the groups (differences which were not statistically significant) in the attribution of gang relatedness were smallest.

Discussion

This study has attempted to document differences in the understanding of gangs by many persons directly affected by gang activity and membership. The results show several disparities across the groups studied: police, members of a Task Force on gangs, and juvenile detainees, including some acknowledged gang members. The differences between these groups are important for understanding and responding to the problems presented by gangs.

The juveniles in our study were different from other members of our sample. From their perspective, gang activity had an extensive effect on daily life perhaps because of their greater firsthand knowledge of and intimate involvement with gang activity (40 percent acknowledged gang membership). On demographic traits, gang and non-gang members were virtually indistinguishable. However, gang members were more likely to have been involved in group fighting and to have been the victims of violent crime than were non-gang juvenile detainees. Both groups of youths found that it was not as difficult to resist gang pressures as either police or Task Force members perceived it to be. Juveniles perceive large numbers of gangs and gang members. When it came to identifying gang names, juveniles were much more likely to do so correctly than Task Force members and somewhat more likely to do so than police officers. As a group, youths were more likely than adults to identify scenarios that involved graffiti and group fights as gang-related. In general, juveniles used a more expansive definition of what constituted gang activity, attributing more behaviors and symbols to gangs than did either of the other groups.

Members of the Task Force had the least direct knowledge of gangs and gang activity. Their primary source of knowledge about gangs was the media, a source they thought did not accurately portray gangs. The Task Force was the group least likely to identify gang names correctly, and were also the group most likely to identify juvenile nuisance activities as gang-related. Of the groups studied, the Task Force was clearly the least informed and most dependent upon secondhand information in their understanding of gangs.

The police used the most restrictive, narrow definition of gang membership and gang activity of all the groups. They were least likely to see gang activity as pervasive in the lives of juveniles in the city. Police also were most likely to see gang activity as sensationalized in the media. They estimated about the same number of gangs, but fewer gang members than did the other groups, and were able fairly accurately to identify gang names. Finally, for every scenario the police were least likely to identify the situation as gang-related.

Responding to social problems, such as gangs, is not an easy proposition. Efforts to formulate effective responses are hindered by several factors. First, few agree on what is meant by the word gang. Our results indicate the dimensions of this disagreement. Second, there is little agreement about the prevalence and severity of gang activities, in large part due to the absence of a useful working definition. Finally, there is reason to be concerned about how well groups charged with responding to the problem understand gangs and about how they acquire their information. There have been few efforts to understand how the various groups involved in the "gang effort" define the problem to which they are responding. By documenting the differences between police, task force members and juveniles, we have identified the sources of their knowledge of gangs, as well as their perceptions of the level of the gang problem. We hope that this study will help to fill that void and stimulate subsequent research with additional groups whose perceptions on gangs may be insightful, including non-apprehended youths of all ages, especially females; gang members; and media professionals. Studies might control for exposure to different types of media and determine the extent of their influence on views about gangs.

Responding to Gangs

Responding to gangs, like any other social problem, depends on understanding the problem. For gangs, it can safely be concluded, that despite much research, not enough is known to formulate effective policy responses. Our research has demonstrated how fundamentally different the understanding of the problem is among those charged with responding to the problem and those at risk of victimization and involvement. The sometimes vast differences between the perceptions of these groups highlights the need for increased efforts targeted at understanding gangs. These efforts must, as Huff (1990:312) has noted, view gangs as both independent and dependent variables, created and affected by economic and social factors.

A dialogue is needed to educate those who wish to understand and better respond to gangs. This communication should include a variety of groups, primary among whom should be the juveniles most likely to be affected by reform efforts and policy recommendations. Because their knowledge is firsthand and they are most affected by gang activities, juveniles are integral to formulating solutions. In order to be effective, social policies directed at gangs will need the participation of young people. For these reasons, their involvement in understanding gangs and formulating responses is essential. The results of this study clearly highlight three findings. First, members of the Task Force have little basis to understand the nature or dimensions of gang problems. Members of the Task Force failed to identify actual gang names correctly. They also most often learned about gangs from the media, despite failing to have confidence in the accuracy of media reports. Second, the police have a very different perspective on gangs and gang activity than do juveniles, and use a more restrictive definition of gang activities. Police were least likely to attribute gang activity in each of the vignettes presented, and least likely to see gang activity as affecting daily life, perhaps because they estimated the lowest number of gang members. Our third finding reinforces the need to include youths in both attempts to understand and respond to gangs. Both gang members and other detainees estimated the highest number of gangs and gang members, and most often identified the scenarios as portrayals of gang-related activity. In order to better understand gangs, it is imperative that we involve the persons most likely to be affected by gang activities—juveniles.

Huff (1990) has noted that responses to gang activity can take several forms. Two typical responses are represented by the police and the juveniles in our study. The police, on the one hand, are engaged in what Huff would label "denial"—downplaying the effect of gang activity on daily life, underenumerating the number of gangs and gang members, and refusing to recognize aspects of juvenile crimes as gang-related. This pattern of response typifies cities with gang problems in their earliest phases. For every scenario, the police attributed the actions to gangs at far lower levels than did any other group. The other response, represented by the detainees, ascribes gang-relatedness to a large range of youthful group activity and a large number of young residents of the city. From this perspective, "wanna-bes" and other marginal youths are included as gang members. This all-inclusive definition is the polar opposite of the definition held by the police. Neither definition is likely to yield useful information for understanding or responding effectively to gangs. Nor are these conceptual approaches likely to avert the situation which has happened in many cities where public officials ignored gang problems until highly visible gang-related events occurred. And yet, the failure of criminal justice policies enacted in response to atypical or highly publicized cases is well known (Gilsinan, 1990:59-60). In responding to gangs effectively, our policies must not reflect "episodic notions" (Gilbert, 1986) or "symbolic dramatizations" (Sutton, 1986). More restrictive definitions are likely to lead to narrowly based, punitive responses that call only for targeted enforcement and enhanced penalties for gang activities. On the other hand, more expansive definitions would likely lead to social policy recommendations of a broader nature. Such recommendations would include policies targeted at a wide array of social institutions like schools, families, neighborhoods and the media.

Because there is no such legal term as gang in most jurisdictions, policy responses to gang activity are in large part dependent upon socially constructed definitions. The absence of an agreed upon working definition can lead either to minimizing the problem or to over-estimating its incidence. Since the definition of problems—both their nature and magnitude—drives policy, a clear definition of "the problem" is needed before goals can be set, responses formulated, policies implemented and outcomes evaluated. A number of policies are dependent upon such a definition. Those involved in juvenile justice treatment programs need to understand the perceived function served by gangs for some youths in order to respond effectively. The scope of gang activities needs to be known before greater intervention by the police and harsher sanctions by the courts are warranted. It also is important that definitions reflect a local character; efforts to arrive at a uniform definition are unlikely to be useful because gang activity and membership can change from one community or time to another.

Shared conceptual definitions and a basic understanding of social problems are essential first steps in responding to youthful misconduct. Policy responses capable of effecting change demand well-informed personnel and a plan. The results of this study suggest that such understanding has not yet been achieved. Indeed, there are substantial disagreements between the groups charged with responding to gang activity and those most affected by it. These disagreements remind us that policies to address gang problems are premature and must be reformulated to include the perspective of those most affected by such activities.

Notes

1. This question was framed as a yes/no dichotomy.
2. A comparison of the responses of police officers on the Task Force to those not on the Task Force revealed no significant differences between the two groups.
3. As these data are neither random nor experimental, the significance tests should be read with caution.
4. The vignettes:

The Projects: A group of young men from the Blumeyer Projects were playing basketball on a playground near their housing project. A car drove by and the riders shouted obscenities at the people playing basketball, who gave chase to the car. They later found a vehicle that resembled the car, turning it over and vandalizing it. They spray painted the words "Don't come back" on the hood of the car. No one was hurt, and this was the end of this particular incident.

Would you classify this incident as gang-related?
YES__ NO__

The Softball Game: A group of young men from the Compton Heights area were playing baseball one Saturday afternoon. All of the players were from the same neighborhood. A dispute about the game broke out between the two teams. The dispute ended up in a fight in which several people ended up at the hospital and the police made five arrests.

Would you classify this incident as gang-related?
YES__NO__

The Park: A group of 20 to 30 sixteen-year-olds regularly hung out together at a neighborhood park. Many people in the neighborhood considered them a nuisance. These youths generally acted tough and talked tough. They often tried to recruit younger kids in the neighborhood to join them. The police were contacted to do something about the situation, so they sent a group of officers to the park. No drugs or guns were found during a round-up of these individuals, and no criminal charges were filed against them.

Would you classify this incident as gang-related?
YES__ NO__

Older Brother: The older brother of a teenage girl found out that she had been called a "bitch" at school. He found out who had called her the name, and got two friends to go help him "settle the score." Before they left, they put on their "colors," their jackets identifying them as gang members. When he saw the boy who had slandered his sister on the sidewalk, he drove the car up on the sidewalk and struck the boy with the car. He then drove off.

Would you classify this incident as gang-related?
YES__ NO__

Younger Brother: William's younger brother was shot and killed while selling crack cocaine. William vowed to revenge his brother's death by killing the individual who had done this to his brother. He purchased a revolver from a friend and began hanging out in the area where his brother had been killed, gathering information about the killer. One night while walking alone in the area he found the person who had shot his brother. He killed this individual, screaming "This is for my brother" as he shot his brother's killer to death.

Would you classify this incident as gang-related?
YES__ NO__

References

Arnold, W. 1966. "The concept of gang." *The Sociological Quarterly*, 7:59-75.

Blauner, R. and D. Wellman. 1973. "Toward the decolonization of research." In J.A. Ladner (ed.), *The Death of White Sociology*. New York: Random House.

Bookin-Weiner, H. and R. Horowitz. 1983. "The end of the youth gang: Fad or fact." *Criminology*, 21(4):585-601.

Brown, W. K. 1978. "Black gangs as family extensions." *International Journal of Offender Therapy and Comparative Criminology*, 22(1):39-48.

Chambliss, W. J. 1973. "The saints and the roughnecks." *Society*, 20:24-31.

Chicago Police Department. 1988. *Collecting, Organizing and Reporting Street Gang Crime*. Chicago: Chicago Police Department.

De Fleur, L. 1967. "Delinquent gangs in cross-cultural perspective: The case of Cordoba." *Journal Of Research In Crime And Delinquency*, 4:132-141.

Downes, D. 1966. "The gang myth." *The Listener*, 75:534-537.

Empey, L.T. 1967. "Delinquency theory and recent research." *Journal of Research in Crime and Delinquency*, 4:28-42.

Empey, L.T. and E. Rabow. 1961. "The Provo experiment in delinquency rehabilitation." *American Sociological Review*, 26:679-695.

Fagan, J. 1989. "The social organization of drug use and drug dealing among urban gangs." *Criminology*, 27:633-669.

Gilbert, J. 1986. *A Cycle of Outrage: America's Reaction to the Juvenile Delinquent in the 1950s*. New York: Oxford University Press.

Gilsinan, J.F. 1990. *Criminology and Public Policy*. Englewood Cliffs, NJ: Prentice-Hall.

Gusfield, J.R. 1981. *The Culture of Public Problems: Drunk Driving and the Symbolic Order*. Chicago: University of Chicago.

Hagedorn, J. 1988. *People and Folks*. Chicago: Lake View Press.

Hardman, D. 1967. "Historical perspectives of gang research." *Journal of Research in Crime and Delinquency*, 4(1):5-26.

Horowitz, R. 1990. "Sociological perspectives on gangs: Conflicting definitions and concepts." In R. Huff (ed.), *Gangs in America: Diffusion, Diversity, and Public Policy*. Beverly Hills, CA: Sage.

Huff, R. 1990. "Denial, overreaction, and misidentification: A postscript on public policy." In R. Huff (ed.), *Gangs in America: Diffusion, Diversity, and Public Policy*. Beverly Hills, CA: Sage.

Jackson, P. G. 1988. *In Search of Gangs and Social Policy*. Prepared for the Office of Attorney General, Crime Prevention Center, California Department of Justice, Sacramento, CA.

Jacobs, J. 1974. "Street gangs behind bars." *Social Problems*, 21:395-409.

Johnstone, J. W. C. 1981. "Youth gangs and black suburbs." *Pacific Sociological Review*, 24:355-375.

Klein, M. 1967. "Groups, gangs, and cohesiveness." *Crime and Delinquency*, 4:63-75.

——. 1969. "On the group context of delinquency." *Sociology and Social Research*, 54:63-71.

Kleiner, R., H. Stub, and J. Lanahan. 1975. "Implications for research, action, and the role of the investigator." *Human Organization*, 34:391-394.

Kornblum, W. 1987. "Ganging together: Helping gangs go straight." *Social Issues and Health Review*, 2:99-104.

Maxson, C., M. Gordon, and M. Klein. 1985. "Differences in gang and nongang homicides." *Criminology*, 23:209-222.

Maxson, C. and M. Klein. 1990. "Street gang violence: Twice as great, or half as great." In R. Huff (ed.), *Gangs in America: Diffusion, Diversity, and Public Policy*. Beverly Hills,. CA: Sage.

Miller, W. 1975. *Violence by Youth Gangs and Youth Groups as a Crime Problem in Major American Cities*. National Institute for Juvenile Justice and Delinquency Prevention. Office of Juvenile Justice and Delinquency Prevention, U.S. Department of Justice: Washington, D.C.

——. 1976. "Youth gangs in the urban crisis era." In J. Short (ed.), *Delinquency, Crime and Society*. Chicago: University of Chicago:91-128.

——. 1976. *Violence by Youth Gangs and Youth Groups as a Crime Problem in Major American Cities, Summary Report*. National Institute for Juvenile Justice and Delinquency Prevention. Office of Juvenile Justice and Delinquency Prevention, U.S. Department of Justice: Washington, D.C.

——. 1980. "Gangs, groups, and serious youth crime." In D. Shicor and D. Kelly (eds.), *Critical Issues in Juvenile Delinquency*. Lexington, MA: Lexington.

Moore, J. W. 1973. "Social constraints on sociological knowledge: Academics and research concerning minorities." *Social Problems*, 21:65-77.

Morash, M. 1983. "Gangs, groups, and delinquency." *British Journal of Criminology*, 23:309-335.

Needle, J. A. and W. V. Stapleton. 1983. *Police Handling of Youth Gangs*. U.S. Department of Justice. Office of Juvenile Justice and Delinquency Prevention: Washington, D.C.

Quinney, E. R. 1970. *The Social Reality of Crime*. Boston: Little, Brown.

Short, J. and F. Strodbeck. 1965. *Group Process and Gang Delinquency*. Chicago: University of Chicago Press.

Spergel, I. 1966. *Street Gang Work: Theory and Practice*. Reading, MA: Addison-Wesley.

——. 1984. "Violent gangs in Chicago: In search of social policy." *Social Service Review*, 58:198-225.

——. 1986. "The violent gang problem in Chicago: A local community approach." *Social Service Review*, 60:94-131.

——. 1990. *Youth Gangs: Continuity and Change*. In M. Tonry and N. Morris (eds.), *Crime and Justice: A Review of Research*, volume 12. Chicago: University of Chicago.

Sutton, J. 1988. *Stubborn Children: Controlling Delinquency in the United States*. Berkeley: University of California Press.

Sutherland, E. H. 1924. *Principles of Criminology*. Philadelphia: Lippincott.

Thrasher, W. 1929. *The Gang*. Chicago: University of Chicago.

Vigil, J. D. and S. C. Yun. 1990. *Vietnamese Youth Gangs in Southern California*. In R. Huff (ed.), *Gangs in America*. Newbury Park, CA: Sage.

Zatz, M. S. 1987. "Chicano youth gangs and crime: The creation of a moral panic." *Contemporary Crises*, 11:129-158.

Zimring, F. 1981. "Kids, groups and crime: Some implications of a well-known secret." *Journal of Criminal Law and Criminology*, 72:867-885. ✦

3

Street Gang Violence: Twice as Great, or Half as Great?

Cheryl L. Maxson and Malcolm W. Klein

Law enforcement agencies adopt different definitional policies for tabulating and reporting "gang-related" crime. A major distinction is whether gang features are fundamental to the motive of the incident or whether gang members participate regardless of motive. Maxson and Klein apply the two definitional approaches to Los Angeles homicide data and find that the difference between the resulting case groups is less than what one might expect. Although far fewer numbers of gang-related crimes will be reported by departments using the motive definition, the overall character of the two types of gang cases is quite similar.

Attempts to develop generalizations across cities about the prevalence of gang violence need to take these definitional stances into account. However, characterizations about the nature of gang violence are less vulnerable to definitional variations. The implications of different definitional styles may be more or less important depending upon the purposes for which these data are utilized.

> *—Let me make the definitions and I'll win any argument.*
>
> anonymous attorney

Recent increases in street gang violence and the reported spread of major street gang activity to a broad array of American cities (Hagedorn, 1988; Klein & Maxson, 1989) require a careful assessment of our current state of knowledge about street gangs. Further, recent research in such gang-involved cities as Chicago (Spergel, 1985a) and Los Angeles suggests that changes of importance have taken place since the decades of the 1950s and 1960s, when much of our gang knowledge was gathered (Klein, 1971; Klein & Maxson, 1989; Quicker, 1981). For instance, this research suggests higher levels of violence, greater numbers and sophistication of weaponry, broader age ranges among gang members, especially on the adult end, and increasing involvement of gang members in drug distribution systems.

Theoretical interests among recent writers have stressed group processes and community contexts of gang activity (Horowitz, 1983; Moore, 1978; Spergel, 1984; Vigil, 1988). This chapter adds to these the issues of the social construction of the gang problem (see Zatz, 1985)—at least with respect to its seriousness—and the generalizability of the problem. Operationally, we are concerned with whether gang data gathered from one city are immediately comparable to those from another and, by extension, whether gang knowledge must be city specific or can be generalized across cities.

There are obvious policy issues here as well. How validly can we judge the seriousness of gang activity and thus its priority among an array of social problems? How sure can we be that statements of serious or spreading gang violence deserve the allocation of more municipal resources? This latter issue was highlighted in April of 1988, when the Los Angeles Police Department sought and received funds from the City Council to mount a series of 1,000-officer sweeps through various gang areas of the city, arresting anyone who looked like, talked like, or acted like a street gang member. The sweeps followed a new annual city high in gang-related homicides in 1987 that appeared to be accelerating even further in early 1988. We will suggest in pages to follow that this new rate would have been far lower with a different definition of *gang-related* to be found in other cities; would the lower rate have called forth such massive efforts at control and suppression?

Research Purposes

Recent descriptions of Chicago's gang-related homicides struck us as quite remarkable in two regards. First, the Chicago data (Spergel, 1983) closely resembled similar patterns we had noted among gang-related homicides in Los Angeles (Maxson, Gordon, and Klein, 1985). Second, the operational definition of gang-relatedness employed by the Chicago Police Department (the source of Spergel's data) was very substantively different—more restrictive—from the comprehensive definitions used by both the Los Angeles Police and Sheriff's departments, the sources of our data. Do such definitional disparities then yield similar patterns of gang activity and therefore no conceptual problem, or would adjustments to common operational definitions yield very different gang violence descriptions?

Our approach to these issues is to apply the basic Chicago definition of gang-related homicides (Block, 1985; Bobrowski, 1988; Spergel, 1983) to Los Angeles homicide data gathered as part of an earlier project (Maxson et al., 1985). This first analysis will simply "purify" the Los Angeles cases by including only those meeting the Chicago definition. This will indicate how much the gang homicide rate would be reduced by employing this more restrictive definition.

The second analysis will involve bivariate comparisons of gang and nongang homicides in Los Angeles using the Chicago definition, and comparing these to the bivariate analyses reported earlier (Maxson et al., 1985) for gang and nongang cohorts in Los Angeles. These involved both personal characteristics of gang members on victim and suspect sides of homicide incidents (age, ethnicity, and so on) and characteristics of the incidents themselves, such as type of location, numbers of participants, and involvement of autos. One might reasonably expect that the more restrictive definitions would yield "purer" gang cases and thus increase the descriptive differences between gang and nongang incidents. On the other hand, if the definitional disparities are not important, then classifying the eliminated gang cases as part of the nongang pool could reduce these differences (i.e., purifying by the Chicago definition might only mean discarding the less obvious but no less gang-involved incidents).

The third analysis will repeat our earlier application of discriminant analysis to the gang/nongang differences in Los Angeles (Maxson et al., 1985), but this time using the Chicago definition of gang-relatedness. As with the bivariate comparisons, the earlier obtained findings might be exaggerated or reduced, depending on the "real" effect of the purification by using the more restrictive definition. The results, especially in terms of classification success, should have important implications for generalizability of data on gangs across many cities, some of which use restrictive and some of which use comprehensive definitions of gang-relatedness.

Definitions

The situation in the Los Angeles Sheriff's Department is a bit unique, in that the working definition of gang-related events as reflected in the official statistics evolved principally from the concern and activities of one individual. This Sheriff's Department sergeant started collecting gang homicide statistics in 1974 in the most active gang area, East Los Angeles. He expanded the definition well beyond gang-on-gang to include almost all incidents in which any participant was a gang member. In such incidents, he looked for what he described as an "identifiable gang trait." Two examples illustrate the approach:

> (1) A gang member gets involved in an isolated incident with his nongang neighbor. The gang member is killed. This would *not* be labeled as gang-related. However, if the neighbor was the victim, then the designation would be questionable and the sergeant would look closely at the circumstance (e.g., "if he was backed up by his homies").
>
> (2) A gang member shoots a clerk in the process of robbing a store. This definitely would be labeled as gang-related because "if he were not a gang member, he probably wouldn't be carrying a weapon."

The specifics are spelled out in the Department's official statement, Procedural Memorandum 81-4:

> It is the responsibility of the Youth Services Bureau, Street Gang Detail and Safe Streets Detail, to monitor street gang members involved in criminal conduct. This directive establishes criteria for identifying incidents as street gang-related criminality.
>
> The following criteria shall determine if an incident is gang related:
>
> (1) When an incident occurs wherein participants, suspects or victims are identified gang members or associates.
>
> (2) When a reliable informant identifies an incident as gang activity.
>
> (3) When an informant of previously untested reliability identifies an incident as gang activity and it is corroborated by other attendant circumstances or independent information.
>
> (4) When there are strong indications that an incident is gang-related but it does not fit the above criteria, it shall be considered as gang activity.
>
> It is the policy of the Street Gang Unit to identify gang members based on the following criteria:
>
> (1) When an individual admits membership in a gang.
>
> (2) When a reliable informant identifies an individual as a gang member.
>
> (3) When an informant of previously untested reliability identifies an individual as a gang member and it is corroborated by independent information.
>
> (4) When an individual resides in or frequents a particular gang's area and affects its style of dress, use of hand signs, symbols, or tattoos, and associates with known gang members.
>
> (5) When an individual has been arrested several times in the company of identified gang members for offenses which are consistent with usual gang activity.
>
> (6) When there are strong indications that an individual has a close relationship with a gang but does not fit the above criteria, he shall be identified as a "gang associate."

The gang designation process in the Los Angeles Police Department differs somewhat. The official statistics come from the Gang Intelligence Unit, which receives copies of all homicide investigation reports and determines therefrom which will be listed as gang-related. This determination is based upon Special Order No. 21 (8.22.80), which reads as follows:

> *Gang-related Crime*—a) When homicide, attempted murder, assault with a deadly weapon, robbery, rape, kidnapping, shooting at inhabited dwellings, battery on a police officer or arson is reported and the suspect or victim is on file as an active gang or associate gang member. b) When the investigation reveals that the incident involves a gang member, although neither the victim nor the suspect is known to be an active or associate gang member, i.e., "A" shoots "B" and yells the name of a gang during the commission of the crime.

A supplemental description in Central Bureau in October of the same year (1980) provides even broader guidelines:

> Gang-relatedness may be established when:

a) Suspects yell a gang name during the crime or when leaving the scene;

b) Suspects yell "where are you from?" before the crime;

c) Witness says the suspects were gang members;

d) Victims are gang members.

Note: Gang affiliations may be determined by the victim's appearance, dress, vehicle, or known gang association.

Thus, in effect, the different LASD and LAPD processes yielded definitional approaches that are very similar. Official statistics for each agency are based upon very broad definitions of gang-relatedness, definitions which could yield a considerable amount of discretion in their application among cases, among investigators, among stations, and over time. Whether or not such discretion has led to systematic differences is of course an empirical question, one that has been discussed elsewhere (Klein, Gordon, & Maxson, 1986). Briefly, both departments appear to use their definitional approaches in a consistent fashion that contributes little variance to the distinctiveness of gang from nongang violence. The basic element is evidence of gang membership on either the suspect or the victim side. We will refer to this as the *gang member* definition.

The Chicago definition, especially with respect to identifying homicide cases as gang-related, is far less ambiguous: "A killing is considered gang-related only if it occurs in the course of an explicitly defined collective encounter between two or more gangs (a 'gang fight')." Further, the department is quite clear on the exclusions. Spergel (1956) notes, "Criminal and violent activity by gang members, individually or collectively, unrelated to intergang encounters is not considered gang-related."

Spergel (1985b) offers, in addition, two examples which make the contrasts with the earlier LASD examples very explicit:

> A gang-related incident, according to the Gang Crime Unit, represents a serious act or alleged act or threat of violence involving actual, suspected, or putative members of two gangs or even intragang factions. Thus, an attack on an individual mistakenly identified as a member of an opposing gang or intimidations and attempts to recruit individuals currently not gang members, are classified as gang crimes. But an act of robbery of a jewelry store by a recognized gang member, for example, is ordinarily not considered a gang crime in Chicago, as it might be in Los Angeles. (p. 16)

Although Block and, indirectly, Bobrowski dispute Spergel's statements of Chicago's reliance upon the elements of gang affiliations of the participants and the collective nature of the encounter, there is uniform agreement regarding the import of a gang-related motive to the designation of a gang-related incident in Chicago. A recent listing includes nine motives, prominent among these being retaliation, territoriality, recruiting, and "representing" (graffiti, wearing gang colors, shouting gang slogans, and so on). In practice, these overlap very substantially.

The rationale for the Chicago definition has been stated for that police department as follows:

> The presence of these indicators alone, however, does not serve to define the event as street gang related. During the review process, the report is carefully studied for information which would lead one to reasonably conclude that the incident grew out of a gang function. The gang membership of either party to the offense does not constitute gang relatedness unless the event contains some element which establishes the nexus between the incident and the animus of the gang.
>
> This definition has been viewed as somewhat restrictive as it tends to limit the volume of reported street gang crime. But it occupies a reasonable middle ground somewhere between those definitions which require that the incident involve group participation, and the other extreme, which requires only that some party to the event be a gang member. The "Chicago definition" admits the misconduct of individuals apart from the presence of the group, and is concerned with providing tactically significant information—not with describing the delinquencies of persons whose misbehavior also happens to include gang membership. If it is restrictive, it is so because it serves the interests of operational personnel concerned with interdicting the illegal activities of street gangs, and avoids the generation of a large body of less useful data. (Bobrowski, 1988, pp. 8-9)

For purposes of our analyses, we can select as Chicago-defined Los Angeles homicide incidents all those with known gang victim and suspect, and all those with clear gang motives for the encounter. Collectivity clearly is subsumed by these. The prior coding of the Los Angeles incidents fortuitously allows us to apply these Chicago criteria with considerable confidence. For purposes of this report, we will refer to this Chicago-style approach as the *gang motive* definition.

We would only add, at this point, that although the contrasting definitions come from Chicago and Los Angeles, they are not used only in those two cities. A recent symposium of police gang unit commanders[1] revealed gang motive definitions used by police departments in Philadelphia, Jackson (Mississippi), and Seattle, and gang member definitions in New York, Detroit, Evanston, Fort Worth, Miami, and Minneapolis. Five California cities that we studied recently revealed variations ranging from narrow, gang-on-gang (motive) definitions to broad, inclusive (member) definitions approaching those of Los Angeles.

The Data

The data on which the analyses are carried out were gathered in connection with the earlier project (Klein et al., 1986; Maxson et al., 1985). They were taken from the investigation files of the Los Angeles Police Department for the years 1979-81 and the Sheriff's Department for the years 1978-82. Gang-related incidents were the entire populations of homicides in 3 stations of the LAPD and 19 of the LASD, limited to cases with at least one name-identified suspect aged 10 to 30. All gang cases were so designated by the gang units of each department, a surprisingly reliable process as revealed in our earlier project (Klein et al., 1986). Comparable (one name-identified suspect aged 10 to 30) nongang homicide cases were selected by stratified sampling by proportion of gang cases per station to the total sample pool, but limited to 50 cases per year. The resulting numbers are 135 gang and 148 nongang homicides from LAPD, and 226 gang and 200 nongang cases from LASD.

Of additional relevance is the fact that 1980 was, until recently, the peak year of gang-related homicides in Los Angeles County. Thus these cases represent the situation immediately before and after a particularly horrendous period; 351 gang-related homicides were recorded throughout the county in 1980. We are comparing the effects of contrasting definitions during a period of unusual activity.

Analysis 1: Case Numbers

Included in the original Los Angeles data collection were the appearance of gang members on either the suspect side or the victim side of a gang homicide and a categorizing of motives noted in the investigation file. Motives included retaliation, territoriality, previous gang conflict, conflict over graffiti, and a residual "other" category. The basic elements of the Chicago definition are therefore available, yielding the appropriate reanalysis of the Los Angeles cases. Using the gang motive definition—a side is classified as gang if any one person on that side has a gang affiliation or suspected affiliation (via clothing or behavior)—we find that 44.4.% of the LAPD cases classified by the gang member definition would still be designated as gang-related, as would 57.1% of the LASD cases. The combined percentage (there were more LASD than LAPD cases) is 52.4%.[2]

Empirically, it seems that gang-on-gang and the presence of a gang motive, as both are recorded in gang incident investigation files, are highly redundant. Excluding cases that have only gang-on-gang *or* gang motive, the figures are reduced by only a few percentage points. It seems fair to conclude that the narrow definition of the Chicago variety would reduce the reported Los Angeles gang homicide rate by about half—more in one jurisdiction, less in the other.

In 1987, a new peak of 387 gang-related homicides was recorded in Los Angeles County. Partly on the basis of this, and the subsequent publicity associated with it and the increase in crack cocaine distribution, the police sweeps referred to earlier were inaugurated. One reasonably could question whether the same reaction would have occurred following a "peak" year of 203 cases; this latter is a figure exceeded in each of the last 10 years using the gang member definition.

Analysis 2: Bivariate Comparisons

In previous analyses, we compared gang and nongang homicides on three categories of variables; those describing the setting of the event, those describing the participants, and those relating to the thoroughness of the police investigations. The third of these is not germane to the current discussion; we compare here the differences revealed by bivariate comparisons of gang and nongang setting and participant variables, using the earlier data and the new data as created by the application of the gang motive definition.

The first step is to ask about the half of the member-defined cases that drop out using the motive definition. Does this "purification" process yield two sets of gang-related cases that are substantially different (i.e., are gang-related cases without gang motives substantively different from their motive-defined counterparts)? We can answer this question by comparing both sets of cases with respect to the incident characteristics and participant characteristics shown in our prior work to distinguish gang from nongang cases. Table 1 summarizes this comparison, based on probabilities of .05 or less associated with *t* tests and chi squares, as appropriate.

The principal finding to be derived from Table 1 is that, for the most part, cases defined by motive and cases defined by gang member involvement do *not* differ substantially. This is true in both jurisdictions. Of 29 variables describing homicide setting and participant characteristics, about one-third in LAPD and one-half in LASD yield differences attaining statistical significance. This is far more than one would expect by chance, but far fewer than might be expected from a serious attempt to alter the meaning of gang-relatedness, especially an attempt involving half (or double) the number of cases.

There are slight patterns discernible in Table 1. For instance, the significant differences relate more to participant than to setting variables. Second, a number of the significant differences make more sense with respect to the gang-on-gang than to the motive component of the Chicago-defined incidents—more drive-by shootings, more clear gang affiliations, younger victim ages, fewer robberies, and more murder attempts. Perhaps "motive" really serves as a proxy measure of gang-on-gang. Block's (1985) Chicago analysis indirectly suggested this, as almost every motive-defined case involved a gang assault rather than robbery or other offense setting. Because inferring a motive is considerably more judgmental than checking for gang affiliations in investigative and intelligence files, it may in the future be more expedient simply to look for gang membership on both sides in cities and studies opting for the narrower, motive-defined approach to gang relatedness.

We move on, now, to the more central comparison in this second approach to the analyses, the question of whether gang/nongang homicide differences are affected by the definition one uses. The data in Table 1 might lead one to predict either way, as there were a number of significant, definitionally determined gang case differences, yet not in a majority of the comparisons.

Once again, our procedure is to use selected characteristics of homicide cases. We know from our prior research which of these yielded differences between gang and nongang cases, using the gang member definition. Now we make the same comparisons using the gang motive definition, which, as described earlier, yields only about half as many cases.[3] The question here is, Do the gang/nongang differences take on a different look, either quantitatively (number of dis-

Table 1

Setting and Participant Characteristics of Gang "Motive" Versus Gang "Member" Cases in Two Jurisdictions

Characteristics	*LAPD (n = 137)*	*LASD (n = 231)*
Location[a]	no difference	no difference
Car[b] Involved	"motive" more drive-bys and other car involvement	"motive" more drive-bys and other car involvement
Time of day	no difference	no difference
Total number of weapons	no difference	"motive" more
Gun present	no difference	no difference
Knives present	no difference	no difference
Other weapons present	no difference	no difference
Presence of associated charges	no difference	no difference
Associated charge for attempted murder	"motive" more	"motive" more
robbery	"motive" fewer (in fact, none)	"motive" fewer
assault with a deadly weapon	"motive" more	no difference
other	no difference	no difference
Other injuries	no difference	no difference
Unknown suspect	no difference	no difference
Fear of retaliation	no difference	no difference
Prior contact[c]	"motive" more (in minimal category)	"motive" more (in minimal category)
All male victims	no difference	no difference
All male suspects	no difference	no difference
Affiliation of victim[d]	"motive" more	"motive" more
Affiliation of suspect[d]	"motive" more	"motive" more
Number of victim participants	"motive" more	no difference
Number of suspect participants	no difference	"motive" more
Total participants	"motive" more	no difference
Mean age, victims	"motive" younger	"motive" younger
Mean age, suspects	no difference	no difference
Proportion Black victims	no difference	"motive" fewer
Proportion Black suspects	no difference	"motive" fewer
Proportion Hispanic victims	no difference	"motive" more
Proportion Hispanic suspects	no difference	"motive" more

a. Street versus residence versus other.
b. None versus car involved versus "drive-by" shooting.
c. None versus minimal versus clear prior contact.
d. Gang affiliation explicitly noted.

tinguishing variables) or qualitatively (pattern of variables)? We present a summary in Table 2.

The proper way to read Table 2 is to read down and compare the two LAPD columns, and then the two LASD columns separately. Within the LAPD columns, we see that the character of the gang/nongang comparisons differs between the two definitional approaches for 9 of the 30 characteristics, and none of the 9 constitutes a reversal of direction. There is little pattern to the changes other than those related to associated charges cited in these incidents. When we review the LASD comparisons, we find that there are only 2 out of 30 changes, again with no reversals.

Thus, despite the loss of half the gang cases that accompanies the adoption of the motive definition, there is essentially no change in the described *character* of the homicide incidents. If we were to characterize gang-related homicides in comparison to nongang-related cases, the choice of motive or member definition would make little difference empirically, conceptually, or in policy relevance.

Analysis 3: Discriminant Functions

We come now to what is technically the most complex analysis, and one that can assess for us a bit more clearly what may be gained or lost by adopting one of the competing definitions of gang-relatedness. Discriminant analysis organizes all the variables—the characteristics listed in Tables 1 and 2—that relate to our homicide cases in such a way as to maximize their capacity to discriminate gang from nongang cases. The result is a *function* (a term referring to the variables plus the weights associated with each of them) that best separates the two kinds of cases. A perfect function will not emerge; some gang cases will look more like the typical nongang case, and some nongang cases will look quite "gangy." Still, we should be able to describe the variables that are the best discriminators between gang and nongang cases and we should be able to discern the relative contribution of each variable (the "weights") to that discrimination.

Finally, this process will permit us to ask how successfully—less than with perfection, but more than by chance—we can classify cases as gang or nongang. In this case, "successful" classification means the degree to which our variables, the setting and participant characteristics, predict the assignment of cases by the LAPD and LASD to the gang and nongang categories. We can then determine if this classification success is higher when these agencies use the member-definition or the motive-definition of gang-relatedness.

The process is similar to collecting a lot of data on variables thought to be relevant to males and females, where some official agency has separated people into those two sexes. The variables might be such things as height, weight, length of hair, occupation, mechanical skill, preferred sports, and hobbies. There is overlap on most of these items, and some are better discriminators than others. Thus we must find the best discriminators and weigh them accordingly (the discriminant functions). Having that function, we can then ask how well it correctly identifies males and females as determined by the official agency. The dif-

Table 2

Summary of Two Gang/Nongang Comparisons

Characteristics	*LAPD*		*LASD*	
	Member-Defined	*Motive-Defined*	*Member-Defined*	*Motive Defined*
Location	no difference[a]	no difference	gang more street	gang more street
Car involved	gang more drive-bys	gang more drive-bys	gang more drive-bys	gang more drive-bys
Time of day	no difference	no difference	no difference	no difference
Total number weapons	no difference	no difference	gang more	gang more
Guns present	gang more	gang more	gang more	gang more
Knives present	no difference	gang less	no difference	no difference
Other weapons present	no difference	no difference	gang more	gang more
Presence of associated charges	no difference	no difference	gang more	gang more
Number of associated charges	gang more	no difference	gang more	no difference
If associated charges, for:				
attempted murder	no difference	gang more	gang more	gang more
robbery	no difference	gang fewer	gang fewer	gang fewer
assault with a deadly weapon	no difference	gang more	gang more	gang more
other	no difference	no difference	gang fewer	gang fewer
Other injuries	no difference	gang more	gang more	gang more
Presence of unknown suspects	gang more	gang more	gang more	gang more
Fear of retaliation	gang more	gang more	gang more	gang more
Prior contact	gang more (in no prior & minimal categories)	gang more (in minimal category)	gang more (in no prior & minimal categories)	gang more (in no prior & minimal categories)
All male victims	no difference	gang more	gang more	gang more
All male suspects	gang more	no difference	gang more	no difference
Gang affiliation, victims	gang more	gang more	gang more	gang more
Gang affiliation, suspects	gang more	gang more	gang more	gang more
Number of victim participants	gang more	gang more	gang more	gang more
Number of suspect participants	gang more	gang more	gang more	gang more
Total number of participants	gang more	gang more	gang more	gang more
Mean age, victims	gang younger	gang younger	gang younger	gang younger
Mean age, suspects	gang younger	gang younger	gang younger	gang younger
Proportion Black victims	no difference	no difference	gang fewer	gang fewer
Proportion Black suspects	gang fewer	gang fewer	gang fewer	gang fewer
Proportion Hispanic victims	gang more	no difference	gang more	gang more
Proportion Hispanic suspects	gang more	gang more	gang more	gang more

a. "No difference" here means the difference is not statistically different at the .05 level. The values of location, car involved, prior contact, and gang affiliation are defined in the notes to Table 1.

ference in our analysis will be that the "official agency" can itself apply two different "gender" definitions (i.e., the member and motive definitions) so that our task is to compare *two* discriminant functions and two classification success rates.

Tables 3 and 4 list the variables,[4] the weights (*standardized discriminant coefficients* is the technical term), and two important statistics, variance explained (eta squared, technically) and classification success. The signs next to the weights indicate a positive or negative association with the gang category. The magnitude of the weights shows the relative power of that variable to distinguish between gang and nongang cases.

In the LAPD cases, the overall pattern is one of shared variables, although there are several unshared variables in each function. There is considerable shifting in the order of the weights between the two functions. Participant age loses some importance in the motive-defined function and associated charges gain importance.[5] There is a very slight gain in the amount of variance explained by the motive-defined function, as well as a gain in classification success, especially for the nongang cases.

Table 3

Summary of Discriminant Analyses, LAPD

Characteristics	*Member-defined Weights*[a]	*Motive-Defined Weights*
Mean age, suspects	-.736	-.442
Mean age, victims	-.342	-.324
Proportion Black suspects	-.248	-.243
Guns present	+.238	n.s.
Proportion male suspects	+.218	n.s.
Number of suspect participants	+.196	+.150
Prior contact[b]	+.189	-.219
Car present	+.188	+.371
Number of victim participants	-.063	+.181
Fear of retaliation	n.s.	+.360
Associated charges, attempted murder	n.s.	+.154
Associated charges, assault with a deadly weapon	n.s.	+.152
Variance explained (eta^2)	.42	.45
Classification success (%)		
gang	84.6	88.5
nongang	74.5	84.1
overall	79.2	85.2

a. These weights are taken from Maxson et al. (1990).
b. In the "member-defined" analysis, prior contact is a dichotomous variable for *no* prior contact. In the "motive-defined" analysis, prior contact is positively coded for a *clear* prior relationship between suspects and victims.

The LASD's functions show the same level of stability as LAPD's in variables emerging in the functions and the same change in the presence of associated charges; the age difference is less apparent, and the import of the lack of a clear prior relationship increases. Changes in variance explained and classification success are of the same order as in the LAPD data.

Table 4

Summary of Discriminant Analyses, LASD

Characteristics	*Member-defined Weights*[a]	*Motive-defined Weights*
Mean age, suspects	-.491	-.373
Proportion Hispanic suspects	+.415	+.264
Location on street	+.322	+.150
Number of suspect participants	+.307	+.255
Guns present	+.279	+.146
Mean age, victims	-.237	-.163
Proportion male suspects	+.185	n.s.
Prior contact[b]	+.164	-.539
Number of victim participants	+.156	+.065
Associated charges, any violent	+.152	n.s.
Mean age difference between suspect and victim	+.113	n.s.
Associated charges, attempted murder	n.s.	+.130
Car present	n.s.	+.179
Associated charges, robbery	n.s.	-.322
Fear of retaliation	n.s.	+.240
Variance explained (eta^2)	.49	.58
Classification success (%)		
gang	85	88.7
nongang	80	86
overall	82.6	87

a. These weights are taken from Maxson et al. (1990).
b. In the "member-defined" analysis, prior contact is a dichotomous variable for *no* prior contact. In the "motive-defined" analysis, prior contact is positively coded for a *clear* prior relationship between suspects and victims.

It seems reasonable to suggest that associated charges in both cases are variables that relate to the inference of gang motives since violence is more salient in gang than nongang events generally (Maxson et al., 1985; Tracy, 1979). Even more obviously, the greater weight (particularly in LASD) shown by the lack of a prior relationship in the motive-defined function speaks directly to our earlier suggestion of the redundancy between a motive definition and the presence of gang members on both sides of the fray ("gang-on-gang"). Our prior research has shown that gang violence is characterized by participants who don't know each other.

The better classification success for the motive-defined functions certainly was to be expected. However, the success of the member-defined functions was quite good to begin with, given the inherent ambiguities of homicide investigations and gang designations combined. Thus there was a limit to how much improvement might be expected for a "purer" definitional approach. A small gain in variance explained and classification success has come at the expense of giving up half the cases otherwise labeled as gang-related.

Discussion

This chapter is the latest in a series of papers in which we have used California gang incident data to test propositions about the uniqueness and generalizability of street gang offense patterns. The prior work has established that gang violence is substantively different in character from nongang violence. It has established, at least for jurisdictions with sophisticated gang intelligence units, that the character of reported gang violence is primarily a function of the setting and participant characteristics of the violent events, not the investigative and reporting procedures of the police. It has established that the character of "big city" gang violence is quite similar to that found in smaller cities with more recent development of street gangs.

In addition, we have noted in our prior work the vast increase in the number of cities facing gang problems, the changes and stability in the character of gang structure over several decades, and an early assessment of the limits of gang involvement in new patterns of drug distribution.

Throughout this work, however, we have been troubled by the realization that much of our work was based on the broad, member-defined designation of violent gang offenses. Other cities, we knew, varied in the definition of gang-relatedness, but the definitions were difficult to elicit and even more difficult to operationalize. Recent work in Chicago both by researchers and by operational personnel in the Chicago police department, in combination with the openness and cooperation of the police and sheriff's departments in Los Angeles, has provided an excellent opportunity to investigate limits to generalizability arising from differences in operational definitions. Importantly, these definitional differences can affect not only the pertinent enforcement operations but also the basic research operations upon which social science understanding of gangs largely is (or should be) based. Knowledge about street gang behavior has very limited value if its generalizability is unknown.

What we have learned from the present analysis includes the following:

(1) A motive-based definition of gang-related homicides yields about half as many gang homicides as does a member-based definition.

(2) The character of motive-defined and member-defined gang homicides are quite similar. The character of the former may be related more to the gang-on-gang nature of the incidents than to motive; certainly there is redundancy between the two.

(3) When contrasting gang with nongang homicide incidents, it does not matter much which definitional approach is used for purposes of describing the settings and participants of each.

(4) The motive-defined approach allows one to classify gang and nongang cases a bit more successfully on the basis of setting and participant characteristics, but not at all in proportion to the information at hand. That is, the slightly greater classification success is far less than might have been expected by a 50% "purification" of cases labeled as gang.

It seems clear, then, that estimates of the *prevalence* of gang violence can vary widely between cities using different definitions of gang violence. Within a given city, estimates of prevalence will be comparable over time only if the definitional operations remain constant. Comparisons across cities and across time must be made very cautiously. Studies of the etiology of gangs and gang violence which use such prevalence estimates must also be wary of the definitional problem.

Generalizations across cities with respect to the *character* of gang homicides, however, seem less vulnerable to the definitional problem. Coupled with our earlier finding of similarities in a few smaller California cities (which did not share the same definitional approaches), this suggests that gang homicides—and gang violence more generally—can be viewed in a generic fashion. This is what science hopes to find—general principals, along with situation-specific qualifications. Because gang research almost never is carried out in more than one place at a time, establishing grounds for some confidence in extrapolating findings to other places is certainly helpful.

For federal and local agencies trying to ameliorate a fast-developing national problem, it is also helpful to consider that the character of the problem being addressed has many common features across places and even across time. Current research funded by the federal Office of Juvenile Justice and Delinquency Prevention is attempting to establish intervention models that can be implemented in differing sites. Our data should be encouraging for such efforts.

Another way of contrasting the implications of the two definitions is to suggest that the character of gang violence is now less of a social science problem, and that the prevalence of gang violence is now more of a political problem. How much useful information is one willing to sacrifice in order to claim a lower level of violence?

Authors' Note:

We acknowledge with thanks the assistance of Meichun Liu Chiang in carrying out the bivariate and discriminant functions analyses. The data used in these analyses were collected as part of an earlier project funded by the National Institute of Justice, U.S. Department of Justice.

Notes

1. This symposium was held March 1, 1988, under the auspices of the University of Chicago and convened by Irving Spergel as part of a national study funded by the Office of Juvenile Justice and Delinquency Prevention.

2. The validity of the prior designation by the gang units is suggested by the fact that only 0.68% of LAPD nongang cases and 2% of LASD nongang cases fit the Chicago definition.
3. The member-defined data are taken from our prior report. Because *motive*-defined cases omit almost half the member-defined cases, some of the latter now become nongang cases under the motive definitions. These were assigned, by random selection, to the nongang category in proportion to the station contribution to the totals. This amounted to 24% of the member-defined cases in both jurisdictions.
4. The variables entered into the discriminant analysis were limited to those having significant bivariate relationships to the gang/nongang distinctions, those being nonredundant with others on the list, and those not showing heavily skewed distributions.
5. The apparent sign reversal in the prior contact variable is attributable to the different coding approaches adapted in the two analyses.

References

Block, C.B. (1985) *Lethal Violence in Chicago Over Seventeen Years: Homicides Known to the Police, 1965-1981*. Chicago: Illinois Criminal Justice Information Authority.

Bobrowski, L.J. (1988) *Collecting, Organizing and Reporting Street Gang Crime*. Chicago: Chicago Police Department, Special Functions Group.

Hagedorn, J.M. (1988) *People and Folks: Gangs, Crime, and the Underclass in a Rustbelt City*. Chicago: Lake View Press.

Horowitz, R. (1983) *Honor and the American Dream: Culture and Identity in a Chicago Community*. New Brunswick, N.J.: Rutgers University Press.

Klein, M.W. (1971) *Street Gangs and Street Workers*. Englewood Cliffs, N.J.: Prentice-Hall.

Klein, M.W., M.A. Gordon, and C.L. Maxson (1986) "The Impact of Police Investigation on Police-Reported Rates of Gang and Nongang Homicides." *Criminology* 24:489-512.

Klein, M.W. and C.L. Maxson (1989) "Street Gang Violence," pp. 198-234 in N.A. Weiner and M.E. Wolfgang (eds.), *Violent Crime, Violent Criminals*. Newbury Park, CA: Sage Publications, Inc.

Maxson, C.L., M.A. Gordon, and M.W. Klein (1985) "Differences Between Gang and Nongang Homicides." *Criminology* 23:209-222.

Moore, J.W. (1978) *Homeboys: Gangs, Drugs, and Prison in the Barrios of Los Angeles*. Philadelphia: Temple University Press.

Quicker, J.C. (1981) *Seven Decades of Gangs*. Sacramento: California Commission on Crime Control and Violence Prevention.

Spergel, I.A. (1983) *Violent Gangs in Chicago: Segmentation and Integration*. Chicago: University of Chicago, School of Social Service Administration.

—— (1984) "Violent Gangs in Chicago: In Search of Social Policy." *Social Service Review* 58(2):199-226.

—— (1985a) *The Violent Gang Problem in Chicago*. Chicago: University of Chicago, School of Social Service Administration.

—— (1985b) *Youth Gang Activity and the Chicago Public Schools*. Chicago: University of Chicago, School of Social Service Administration.

Tracy, P.E. (1979) *Subcultural Delinquency: A Comparison of the Incidence and Seriousness of Gang and Nongang Member Offensivity*. Unpublished manuscript, University of Pennsylvania, Center for Studies in Criminology and Criminal Law.

Vigil, J.D. (1988) *Barrio Gangs: Street Life and Identity in Southern California*. Austin: University of Texas Press.

Zatz, M. (1985) "Los Cholos: Legal Processing of Chicano Gang Members." *Social Problems* 33:11-30. ✦

Types of Gangs

4

L.A. Style: A Street Gang Manual of the Los Angeles County Sheriff's Department

Operation Safe Streets (OSS) Street Gang Detail

As we saw in the last section, our understanding of gangs is shaped by how we define gangs. In this manual written by the Los Angeles County Sheriff's Department, a variety of types of groups that can be defined as gangs is discussed. There are ethnic variations between groups, as well as variations resulting from social context. Although much is made in the media about the connections between prison and street gangs, it is important to note the authors' conclusion that prison gangs and street gangs are very different phenomena which should not be confused.

Relationship of Prison Gangs to Street Gangs

Essentially, there is little relationship in the sense that neither one is an extension of the other in any formal sense. From what evidence that has been found, it appears the street gang member is the future prospective raw material for the prison gang, and the majority of prison gang members were, at one time, members of either barrio, ghetto, or motorcycle gangs. The only other fact that is significant here is that since neighborhood ties are stronger than prison ties for most prospective prison gang members, the average ex-convict rejoins the street gang or outlaw motorcycle club he belonged to before entering prison.

Prison gang philosophy is very often diametrically opposed to that of the street gang. For example, loyalty is a primary requirement of both groups; but in the prison gangs, disagreements among members are many times settled by the murder of the offending member or members of his family. The killing of a homeboy, on the other hand, is alien to most street gangs. When the street gang makes raids on rival gangs, the intent is not always to kill, per se, but to terrorize their rivals. If the gang must kill to fulfill its aims, it will, with the killing itself secondary to the intent. In a prison gang, the killing is of primary importance, with the terror that the killing generates as an added extra.

The street gang operates on pure emotion. Their planning is usually unsophisticated and spontaneous. Frequently, there isn't any one person selected to be a victim. An attack on any member is an attack on the gang as a whole; therefore, any member of the opposing gang will do.

A street gang member is too undisciplined and unsophisticated to be recruited directly into a prison gang. Prison gangs, with rare exception, seldom recruit from the street. The prison gang will wait until the youthful offender has progressed through the juvenile justice system from probation camps, reform schools, and finally, prison.

A phenomena that both youth authorities and prison officials have begun to note recently is a rift between prison gangs and youth in that the street gang member seems to be achieving an independence from the prison gang. What appears to be going on is that, although young offenders continue to join prison gangs once behind bars, geographical loyalties and animosities continue even while incarcerated. Prison gangs discourage this type of rivalry between north and south or gang vs. street gang. This attitude, on the part of prison gangs, further alienates street gang members.

Some prisons are reporting that some street gangs have so many members at a particular institution that they are a force themselves. In fact, Black street gangs tend to maintain their identity so well that the many separate factions of the Crip gangs, for example, combine to present a solid front of Crips against all other Black gangs. Presently, the Crips are warring with the "Black Guerrilla Family" and "Mexican Mafia." New and powerful street gang organizations, such as the United Blood Nation (UBN), comprised of various factions of Blood street gangs, have become a significant force that authorities must contend with in the prisons and on the streets as well.

Hispanic Gangs

The structure of Hispanic street gangs is similar throughout the Western United States. Hispanic gangs have actually existed in Los Angeles County since the early years of this century. They are, as a group, very traditional and approach involvement in the gang as a "way of life," rather than random participation. Codes of conduct have been established from which traditions have evolved after generations of previous gang activity.

In the formative years, gangs developed certain styles of dress that affected their socialization into the surrounding and developing Mexican-American com-

---

Excerpted from an operating manual prepared by the Los Angeles County Sheriff's Department, Sherman Block, Sheriff. Prepared by the staff of Operation Safe Streets, Street Gang Detail.

munities. These distinctive modes of dress alienated the gang member and, in many cases, his descendants from the rest of his community. This alienation established certain traditions that today have become known as the "movidas," or rules, that Hispanic gangs live and die by.

The gangs basically began as local neighborhood groups that were oriented towards protection and self-preservation. By the late 1930s and early 40s, these Hispanic groups began to solidify into what we now recognize as street gangs. Gang rivalries evolved, and as gangs became larger, the rivalries grew in intensity and gang violence increased. The earliest Chicano gangs established turf boundaries and rivalries that exist even to this day. Their loyalties to turf are legendary, and much of the violence associated with the gangs can be directly related to this "turf protection" ideology.

A gang sees itself as the protector of its neighborhood from all aggressors, be it rival gangs or government agencies. To many gang members, this so-called turf becomes their world. In some cases, gang members do not attend school because many of the schools are located outside their turf, and they must pass through turfs of rival gangs, which is dangerous. Gang graffiti is also an extension of gang identification and used to identify the boundaries of their turf.

A gang member is loyal to the death for his gang. He is proud, even boastful, of his membership. If, for some reason, the gang member's family moves from his home gang's turf, he will usually not exchange loyalties with a gang in his new home. He will either fight them and return at every opportunity to his home gang's turf, or make an alliance with them that allows him to maintain his identification with his home gang in his new neighborhood.

Involvement in Chicano gangs has become a "hand-me-down" tradition, with many younger and older family members belonging to the same gang. Chicano gangs are now into the third or fourth generation. For the most part, those qualities that attracted the early gang members still exist:

- *A feeling of belonging*. Many gang members of all ethnic groups seek an identity. This is a result of low self-esteem and other factors that lead today's youth into gangs.
- *Identity*. Within the gang, you are a homeboy, set apart from society. You are noticed, recognized, and usually given a moniker to re-enforce your identity.
- *Lifestyle*. The lifestyle of a Chicano gang member is a "total" approach to life. Being a homeboy is not random; it is the most important and dominant aspect of their life. It replaces the family in importance.

The idea of gang involvement from the early "pachuco" to today's "cholo" is the crazy life. The "vato loco" is the epitome of the Chicano gang member. Their attitude is to be the craziest, most feared, respected gang member by whatever means necessary.

Female gang members, by contrast, have no inherent right in the gang, but belong only at the sufferance of their male counterparts. This sufferance is maintained, however, only insofar so the females conform to the mores of their male counterparts. Females have their place within the gang structure and adhere strictly to that place. The female members are, by and large, separate cliques of the larger male gang. There also are very few female gangs that are totally separate entities.

Drugs

The drugs used by Chicano gang members are split along age groups. The older "veterano" is involved with heroin, while the younger gang member is using PCP. With today's epidemic of crack cocaine, it is very popular due to its availability and relatively low cost. The newest gang members are more inclined to use crack cocaine, LSD and speed.

Style of Dress

Traditionally, Chicano gang members have chosen to wear clothes that are distinct and set them apart. Khaki pants and Pendleton shirts have been the favorite of Chicano gang members. The pants are usually heavily starched, and worn high above the waist and very baggy. The shirt is buttoned at the collar and unfastened otherwise. The style of dress has relaxed and no longer is the uniform required.

Language

Most Chicano gang members are second or third generation Americans that are not fluent Spanish speakers. They feel they are caught between two worlds without an identity. To further set themselves apart from the mainstream, they use a slang language that is a combination of Spanish and English called "calo."

Monikers

Monikers are generally associated with physical features or macho image and can be used by members of different cliques of the same gang. Examples are:

"Maton"—Killer	"Gordo"—Fat	"Shorty"
"Oso"—Bear	"Flaco"—Skinny	"Wino"
"Pata"—Feet	"Chato"—Nose	
"Pelon"—Bald	"Toro"—Bull	

Gang Structure

Leadership roles in Hispanic gangs are not formally recognized positions. No one is elected president, vice-president, or warlord, as they are in some Eastern gangs. Leadership positions are not usually assumed by any one individual on a permanent basis, but by any member who has demonstrated unique qualities of leadership needed by the gangs at a particular moment.

Chicano gangs function as one group with many "cliques." These cliques are smaller groups or subsets of the gang whose members are similar in age or live within certain areas of the gang's turf. Some gangs become so large that members don't necessarily know all of the other members; therefore, the infamous question "Where are you from?" developed among the gang members. This was to prevent mistaken assaults upon fellow homeboys or allied gangs.

On the whole, these street gangs lack a solid infrastructure of chain of command and cannot operate efficiently as a total unit. Therefore, by necessity, they have divided themselves into groupings called cliques, normally formed according to age. A clique will have its own name, such as "Winos," "Locos," "Tiny Locos," and the like.

The gangs themselves usually adopt names that have some geographical significance (street names, valleys, hills, and occasionally old, traditional, neighborhood or regional names). Examples would be "Maravilla" (regional), "18th" (street), "Lomas" (hills), or a combination such as "Geraghty Loma" (street and hill).

Graffiti

To many members of the public, graffiti represents thoughtless vandalism or childish pranks. To the youth gang member, however, graffiti is a clear marking of territorial boundaries and serves as a warning and challenge to rival gangs. The purpose of all youth gang graffiti is to glorify the gang.

Black Gangs

Black gang members are divided into two distinct, separate groups, "Bloods" and "Crips." There have been many different opinions of gang experts and gang members as to where these terms originated and how these gangs evolved. Some sources suggest Crip is a mispronunciation of the word "Crib," a term used by gang members on the East Coast. The word Crib is synonymous with one's home. Some sources suggest it was derived by gang members after the movie, "Tales of the Crypt." Others say a group of gang members beat a man so severely they crippled him and so the term Crip was coined.

The origin of the term Crip actually comes from a crippled gang member. Sources suggest that he suffered an injury in an automobile accident or was born a cripple. One thing is certain—he had a crippled leg and walked with a discernable limp. Other gang members emulated this unique way of walking and soon were referring to one another as Crips. Throughout the 1970s, gang members frequently used the term "Crippin," walking as if one's leg was crippled. Crippin also referred to the seeking out of rival gang members to assault.

The origin of the term Blood is just as hard to identify. Some sources suggest it originated from the color red, which is the primary identifying color of a Blood gang member. Some suggest they chose the color red because these gang members referred to themselves as Bloods. Others suggest simply that red and blue were the only two colors of handkerchiefs or bandanas sold at local stores in the late 1960s. Crip gang members picked blue, so Blood gang members chose red. Evidence suggests red was chosen or used by the Piru gang members prior to the term Blood coming about. The variety of colors that these gangs identify with will be discussed in more detail later.

Bloods and Crips originated in the cities of Compton and Watts, and the Willowbrook area of Southeast Los Angeles in the late 1960s. The youngsters who lived on and in the area of Piru Street, which is a street passing through this particular geographical area, formed a gang, and its members referred to themselves as the Compton Piru gang. As gang membership increased, the Compton Piru gang broke up into many different factions of Blood or Piru street gangs and became known as West Side Piru, Fruit Town Piru, Leuders Park Piru, Mob Piru, and Tree Top Piru, just to name a few.

In time, Blood gangs, such as the Bounty Hunters, Brims, and Denver Lanes, spread throughout Los Angeles County. Many gangs outside of this southeast part of Los Angeles will not refer to themselves as Piru, but identify themselves as Bloods. When asked if they are Pirus, they respond that they are not from Compton but are Bloods. However, the terms Piru and Blood are synonymous.

Crip gangs formed in the same manner as Blood gangs. Evidence shows that Crip gangs were actually formed slightly before Bloods. Crips in the cities of Willowbrook and Compton were known as the Compton Crips. Other Crip gangs formed in Watts and surrounding areas. As membership increased, these gangs broke up into many different factions, such as Santana Block Crips, Fudge Town Mafia, Corner Pocket Crips, Grandee Avenue Crips, Mona Park Crips, 62 East Coast Crips, and many more.

Prior to the existence of Bloods and Crips, there were other Black street gangs (Businessmen, Townsmen, Gladiators, Valiants, and Slauson Boys) in Los Angeles County that were significantly different than the Crips and Bloods of today. They lived in certain neighborhoods; however, they didn't identify these geographical areas as their territory. They were similar in nature to social groups and did not engage in gang activity against other gang neighborhoods. They were not well organized and did not identify their gang with colors, graffiti, or other present-day identifiers. In fact, the only characteristic that associated them as being a street gang is they identified themselves with a common street name and lived within particular geographical boundaries.

Many gang members portray themselves as experts in Black gangs, but their knowledge of gangs is very limited. They are usually only experts in their particular gang. They are familiar with their specific neighborhoods, but completely unaware of what is occurring on a state or national scale. The reality today is that we have Blood and Crip gangs throughout Los Angeles County and cities across the nation. The numbers of gangs and their members have increased and are still growing.

Black street gangs have no set rules or guidelines. Their basic characteristics are the same; however, different geographical areas, locally and nationally, have shown varying differences in their identifying characteristics.

Reasons and Types of Membership

There are many different reasons why people join gangs, and they are really no different than why anyone joins a social group or organization. Most of the time we join a club or group because our friends and associates are members of these organizations. The same is true when it comes to gang membership. The major difference, of course, is that a street gang is involved in criminal activity. Peer group pressure is a very potent force. The members of these gangs are almost always friends who attend school, play sports, go to parties, or go on dates together, etc. If one or more persons in a group becomes a gang member, there is a great deal of pressure and influence on their friends.

Identity is another strong reason that people become gang members. Most gang members have low self-esteem. Being a member of a gang gives them a sense of power, belonging, unity, a special name, a certain type and style of clothing, and even a special language.

Over the years, Black gangs mostly appeared and flourished in poverty and low income areas. Some gang members actually committed burglaries and robberies to obtain money to buy food. Today, Black gangs are appearing in middle and upper middle class neighborhoods as well. Some join gangs because they like the "life" of a gang member. They enjoy committing crimes and fighting against other gangs. Others become members for financial gain through robberies, burglaries, or narcotics trafficking. Still, some become members for protection against other gangs.

Gang membership has increased over the years. The gang has become more influential in the neighborhood and many families are bringing up their children as members of the gang. In some instances, this has created an atmosphere where it is acceptable to be a gang member. It is usually a combination of these reasons that draws a person into the gang. Being a gang member is not like deciding if you are going to be a Republican or Democrat, it is "a way of life." The gang is actually an extension of the family.

A term or word that has permeated the gang world and judicial system is "wannabe." We seem to use the term when describing a person who wants to be a member of a particular gang, or identifies or acts like a gang member but really isn't. This seems to be the commonly accepted definition. The fact of the matter is there is no such thing as a wannabe. If a person wants to be a gang member or is identifying or acting like one, it is because he is associating with gang members. In either case, he is a gang member. When a rival gang drives by to confront this gang, the defense of only being a wannabe will not spare him. It is only one type or level of membership in the gang, among several.

One level of membership is the gang member who directs and leads others in gang violence against the public and other gangs. He is in the main flow of the gang's criminal activity and often referred to as a "shot caller," because he has some type of leadership or direction in the gang. He is usually older and has gained the respect of other members of the gang as a result of his past criminal behavior. There can be one or more people falling within this category.

A second level of membership is the gang member who is part of the leaders, but also in the main flow of the gang's criminal activity, trying to earn respect within the gang. He is generally younger, but not always. The majority of gang members usually fall within this category.

The third level of membership is the person who hangs out with members of a gang, but is not directly involved with their criminal activity. He may or may not dress in gang attire. Many people will say this person is not a member of the gang, that he is merely a wannabe, but he is, in fact, a member. He is aware of the gang's criminal activity and associates with the gang members by hanging out at the gang's gathering places. He is often a victim of rival gang violence. If you associate with gang members, dress, talk, and act like a gang member, in reality, you are a gang member.

There are a variety of ways to become a member of a gang. The most common is through an initiation process of being "jumped in" or "courted in." This means you may have to physically fight two or more members of the gang for approximately 15–60 seconds. If you fight well, show that you are not afraid, and can defend the honor of the gang, you are accepted as a member.

Another way to get into a gang is to commit a criminal act, such as stealing a gun for the gang or committing an assault against a rival gang. By doing this, you can avoid being beaten up for initiation. Then again, if you have a relative who is a leader or influential figure in the gang, you can become a member by simply blending in and avoid going through the normal initiation process.

When a person no longer wishes to be a member of a gang, the common process is referred to as being "jumped out" or "courted out." This means he will have to fight two or more members of the gang for 15–60 seconds to be allowed to honorably leave the gang. It is not a prerequisite to fight well, only to survive. Not many gang members actually get jumped or courted out of the gang. More often than not, a gang member simply moves to another geographical area to end his membership.

The term "jumped," as used in the described process, is most commonly used among today's gang members. The term "courted" is a term used in the 1970s, which is not commonly used any more. In fact, many gang members today are totally unfamiliar with the term "courted."

Ages

Prior to 1977–78, the Black gang member was 13–17 years of age. When he reached 18–19, he was no longer in the gang, and when he went to prison for his crimes, he was no longer in the gang upon his return. Gang activity was somewhat restricted to specific communities. If a Crip moved to a community of a Blood, he merely became a Blood. The same was true when a Blood moved to the community of a Crip. It was common to become a member of the gang in his new neighborhood. Most gang members are unaware of this and those who do know will not freely admit it.

It was common for drive-by shootings to occur on bicycles or on foot. The mobility of the gang member during this period of time was limited due to their age. The gang member did not own or have access to a motor vehicle and was not old enough to obtain a drivers license.

Beginning around 1978, there was a change in the age group of Black gang members. When a gang member reached 18–21 years of age, he remained in the gang. When he returned from prison to the community, he retained his gang membership.

Because of the gang member's age at this point in time, his mobility increased dramatically. He was now old enough to own a vehicle, or have access to one, and obtain a drivers license. Because of this, it was not uncommon for gang members to travel significant distances to engage a rival gang. This new mobility allowed a gang member to move to rival gang neighborhoods and retain his old neighborhood gang membership. In this situation, the gang member spends most of his time in his old neighborhood, rather than his new home. If he has a problem with a gang in his new neighborhood, he needs only to summon his fellow gang members for any support he might need.

Today a gang member may be as old as 40 and as young as eight or nine. The emergence of narcotics and the profits that can be made in the trafficking of cocaine has had a major impact on gang membership. There have been people beginning their gang membership at the age of 25, solely for the financial gain in trafficking cocaine.

Hierarchy

In most organizations or groups, there is a defined position for their leaders, such as president, vice-president, etc. This is not the case when dealing with Black gangs. The structure is informal and much less organized. There is not a single person or group controlling the gang. The leader type person, or "shot caller" of the gang, more often than not, is the person who has the most money, most women, nicest car, and has gained the respect of the gang through some type of criminal act or behavior. This person usually has some type of leadership skills and degree of intelligence or he would not have been able to acquire these things.

Usually a Black gang is divided into several different groups, according to age. The gang members of similar age usually hang out with one another. These groups may fall within the following categories: 30–40 years of age, 20–30 years of age, 16–20 years of age, and 10–16 years of age. With these different groups, there may be several people falling within the role of this leader type person. In some gangs, the older, leader type persons have a large influence over members of the gang. This influence extends to all age ranges within the gang. They are looked upon as role models. This has been seen in the Santana Block Crip and Grape Street Watts Crip gangs.

Black gangs may have as few as 5–10 people or as many as 800–1,000. It was pointed out to an Anzac-Grape Street Crip gang member, by a gang investigator, that the number of members in his gang had drastically been reduced from 10 to 3 as a result of gang violence. He replied, "It only takes two; one to drive and one to shoot!" This attitude is indicative of how deeply rooted the gang life is.

Identifying Characteristics

Members of Black gangs identify their gang membership with certain colors of clothing. Bloods use red, while Crips use blue. These colors are reflected or represented in their headgear, earrings, shoelaces, handkerchiefs, belts, or bandanas, and sometimes in their vehicles. Usually the only blue a Blood will wear is in Levi pants. Usually a Crip will not wear anything red.

Over the years, many gangs have adopted colors, such as green, purple, black, and brown, to signify membership. In the Southeast Los Angeles area, green signifies being a member of a Blood gang, as a result of an extremely active gang known as Lime Hood Piru. This gang will wear green Boston Celtic attire and just about anything green. In other areas of Los Angeles County, green may not signify membership in a Blood gang, but may instead be associated with money and/or a Crip gang.

In recent years, the Grape Street Watts gang has made purple, in addition to blue, an identifying color for their gang. They will commonly wear Los Angeles Lakers attire. Several gangs have adopted brown, as well as blue, to signify their gang membership. Two of these gangs are Fudge Town Mafia and Spook Town Crips. The Santana Block Crips gang has come to identify themselves with black.

Many Black gang members will avoid wearing traditional colors in their neighborhoods to avoid attention by law enforcement. For this reason, Crips and Bloods will sometimes wear both blue and red, or neutral, clothing. This especially occurs when they are trafficking cocaine. Gang members who travel out of state to traffic cocaine usually wear some type of expensive sweatsuit with these colors.

In past years, Los Angeles Raiders and Kings caps and jackets have been worn by Blood, Crip, and non gang members. The present-day wearing of such attire in Black gang communities in Southeast Los Angeles is usually worn by Crip and non gang members. There are gang communities within Los Angeles County where Bloods still wear such attire, but it is fading out. In many communities, non gang members have been robbed of this Raiders and Kings apparel by Crip gang members.

Another item that has become an article of wear signifying Crip gang membership are British Knights tennis shoes. The monogram on the side of these shoes is "BK," which means Blood Killer in gang terminology. Many Crip gang members wear British Knights tennis shoes to show that they are members of a Crip gang and enemies of Blood gangs.

Black gang members will wear the name of their gang, monikers, and monikers of slain gang members on their headgear, shirts, and jackets.

One may find that when you experience gang members in other states, and even in other counties in California, their attire may vary or be drastically different than what has been described. This is often the result of local persons trying to emulate Los Angeles County based street gangs. It is also often the influence of a gang member who has moved from the Los Angeles area.

Unique problems have occurred within various schools in Los Angeles County concerning school colors and students' gang membership. During physical education classes, it is customary that the student wear trunks that reflect the colors of the school. There have been occasions where Crip gang members refused to dress for class because the trunks were red, and Blood gang members refused because the trunks were blue. At least one school adopted a mandatory uniform for all students, which is a neutral color, to circumvent this problem and neutralize gang identification. Most schools that have experienced problems with gangs have found it necessary to establish dress codes to avoid gang identification. Many schools have strict rules against wearing gang attire.

Black gang members use a variety of terms and words to express their membership, indicate whether they are a Crip or Blood, and identify what specific street gang they are a member of. Crips identify themselves and greet one another with "cuzz," which comes from the word cousin. The first letter is "C," which is the first letter "Crip." For example, a Crip will greet another Crip in this manner, "Hey cuzz, what it C like?", which basically means what's going on or what's happening. Another term used by Crips is "BK," which means "Blood Killer." This simply means you are a Crip and you kill Bloods. A Crip will usually avoid, if possible, using the letter "B" when talking and writing.

Blood gang members identify themselves and greet one another with the word Blood or Piru if they are from Compton, Watts, or the southeast portion of Los Angeles. The word Piru is synonymous with Blood, and the words are interchangeable, although many Bloods in other areas don't refer to themselves as Piru. The first Bloods actually resided on Piru Street (Compton Piru and West Side Piru) and came to be known as Pirus to rival Crip gang members.

As time passed, Pirus referred to themselves as Bloods. Another term used by Bloods is "CK," which means "Crip Killer." This simply means you are a Blood and you kill Crips. A Blood will usually avoid, if possible, using the letter "C" when talking and writing. A Blood will greet another Blood in this manner, "Hey Blood, what it B like?", which means what's going on or what's happening.

It is quite common for school-age gang members to write their monikers and slogans on homework assignments and school material. Students who are Bloods have actually handed in their homework with the letter "B" substituted for "C" throughout their paper. In addition, they placed their gang name and moniker at the top of the paper. The same is true of Crips substituting "C" for "B."

There are many terms commonly used by Bloods and Crips, alike. One of them is "OG," which means "original gangster." This refers to a person who has been a member of the gang for a long time or who has experience. However, it is not uncommon for young gang members, 12–14 years of age, to refer to themselves as "OG." This term is synonymous with the Hispanic term, "veterano."

A Black gang member will refer to his gang as a "set." The words set and gang are synonymous. One gang member may inquire of another gang member, "What set are you from?" or "Where you from?" He is actually asking what gang he is a member of. Another word used by Bloods and Crips is "hood." This word actually refers to neighborhood, or again, what gang you are from. The words hood and gang are synonymous.

Black gang members refer to their firearm as a "gat." A "G-ride" is a stolen car, with the letter "G" referring to "grand" theft auto. The term "cluckhead" is a person who smokes rock cocaine. A "cluck bucket" is a vehicle temporarily traded to a gang member for a rock of cocaine. The term "cluck" is attached to any item that is traded for rock cocaine. A gang member may refer to his gat (firearm) as a "duece-duece" (.22 caliber), "tray eight" (.38 caliber) or "gauge" (sawed-off shotgun). Gang members often refer to their drive-by shooting as a mission. When a gang member uses the term "gang bang," it refers to fighting with rival gangs.

Bloods and Crips use certain terms to insult one another. For instance, a Blood will call a Crip "crab," and a Crip will call a Blood a "slob." If a Blood asked a Crip, "Hey crab, what it B like?", this would be a direct challenge to fight. The same is true if a Crip approached a Blood and asked, "Hey slob, what it C like?". Another word used by Bloods to insult Crips is "E-Rickette."

Gang members will often mispronounce or change the letters in a rival gang's name to insult the gang. For instance, Bloods call Hoover Crips "Snoovers" and East Coast Crips "Cheese Toast." Crips will call Bounty Hunters "Booty Holes" and Swans "Slims."

An important thing to remember about gang terminology is that it may vary according to different geographical areas. It is also important to know that a Black gang member considers himself a "gangster," as opposed to a Hispanic gang member considering himself a "soldier," for his neighborhood.

Black gang members identify their gang membership through a variety of hand signs, commonly referred to as "flashing." A Crip will form a "C" with his fingers, generally by curling the thumb and index finger or by curling all of his fingers together, separated from his thumb. A Blood will curl the index, so it touches the thumb, and point the remaining three fingers so that it forms a "P," representative of the word Piru or Blood. Almost all Crip and Blood gangs use these two hand signs to designate whether they are a Crip or Blood. Many gangs contort their fingers into other symbols or letters to indicate what specific street gang they are a member of. It is not unusual for a Crip to challenge a Blood by flashing a Crip hand sign to him and vice versa.

Black gangs are very territorial and identify their geographical boundaries with graffiti to show it is that particular gang's "turf." Gang members will write their gang name, monikers, names of slain fellow gang members, names of gangs they are fighting, and gang slogans on residential walls, businesses, fences, poles, trees, sidewalks, and just about anything they can write on. In some areas of Los Angeles County, it is not uncommon for some Black gangs to have a Hispanic gang member, noted for their detailed and intricate printing, write the Black gang member's graffiti.

The final identifying factor concerning Black gangs is their tattoos. They often tattoo themselves with the name of their gang, their moniker, names of slain fellow gang members, and gang slogans. Most tattoos are on the arms and upper torso. It is not uncommon for Black gang members to have Hispanic gang members place tattoos on them. As in graffiti, Hispanic gang members are noted for their delicate and intricate tattoos.

Three letters commonly written on walls of gang neighborhoods and tattooed on bodies of gang members are "RIP." This just refers to a fallen member of the gang and means "Rest In Peace."

Black gangs actually learned how to gang bang from Hispanic gangs, as Hispanics were involved in gang conflicts long before the formation of Crip and Blood gangs. In many Black gang neighborhoods, Hispanic gang influence can be seen. Some Black gangs have recruited Hispanics as members. Some examples of this are in the Santana Block Crips, Leuders Park Piru, Lime Hood Piru, and Grape Street Watts gangs.

This influence can be seen in the clothes, graffiti, tattoos, and terminology of Black gangs. Many Black gangs dress like Hispanic gangs with hairnets, cut-off pants, and pendletons. These Black gang members will also, when writing graffiti, use the Hispanic method of listing all of the members of the gang and use "clouds" to signify the death of a fellow gang member.

Enemies

All Blood gangs fight against Crip gangs. The two factions almost never get along with one another. The only exception to this rule has occurred in recent years as a result of cocaine trafficking. It seems that, when large sums of money are involved, some Crip and Blood gang leaders have found that they can get along in the world of business.

Crip gangs fight against Crip gangs. Some Crip gangs are on friendly terms with other Crip gangs and unite together against other gangs. However, it is unusual for Blood gangs to fight against Blood gangs. Bloods are greatly outnumbered by Crips, in both number of gangs and amount of membership. Bloods have found it necessary to join closely together to defend themselves against Crips. A new trend, that has occurred in various areas of Los Angeles County since the early part of 1990, is gang violence between Black and Hispanic gangs. Most of these confrontations have been over territory, and some have been over narcotics. In the past, Black and Hispanic gangs coexisted in the same neighborhoods for years without confrontations of any kind.

Loyalty

It has been said that, in past years, loyalty within Black gangs was nonexistent. This was, and still is, true in many gangs. However, with the increase of age and membership in these gangs, gang loyalty has increased dramatically. Many members of these Black gangs have moved to other cities, counties, and states, and they have retained their gang loyalty and continued their gang lifestyles in these new communities.

Female Membership

If one was to talk with a so-called female Black gang member, it would be thought that the female plays a major role in Black gangs. The reality is that females play an extremely minor role. There are just a handful of females who actually participate in the activity of these gangs. It is rare to find a female that has actually been "jumped in" to the gang. They rarely hide suspects, narcotics, or firearms for gang members. There have been a few female Black gang members who have participated in gang violence against rival gangs, but the number is not remotely proportionate to Black male participation in the gang.

In some of the most hard-core Crip gang neighborhoods, you can find females wearing red attire. These same females will say they are members of the local Crip gang; however, evidence has shown this is not so. The same is true in some of the most hard-core Blood neighborhoods. The females will wear blue attire and identify themselves as being Blood gang members.

Narcotics

Prior to 1981, Black gangs were not involved in cocaine trafficking to any great extent. Some were involved in trafficking phencyclidine and marijuana during this period; however, they did not travel out of state to sell their narcotics, and it was basically sold within the Los Angeles County area.

Black gangs began to get involved in cocaine trafficking in the latter part of 1981. The sales were basically within the Los Angeles County area. When it was learned that tremendous profits could be made in other cities and states, Black gang members expanded their businesses to these areas. When doing so, they almost always went to a place where they had relatives or past acquaintances. The basic form of cocaine they were involved with was "rock" or "crack." They converted powder cocaine to "rock" form because they could double, and sometimes triple, their investment.

Some of the gangs that initially became involved in the trafficking of cocaine in other states were the Grape Street Watts Crips, Santana Block Crips, and West Side Piru. In time, many gangs became involved in this pattern of selling cocaine. Today, almost all Black gangs in Los Angeles County sell cocaine at some level.

Prior to 1981, the cost of a kilo of cocaine in Los Angeles County was approximately $55,000 to $65,000. By 1984, a kilo of cocaine could be purchased for approximately $12,000 to $16,000. The supply level of cocaine had increased dramatically and the price had dropped.

Just as in all illegal transactions where large sums of money and profits are involved, the gang member soon realized he had to justify his sudden wealth. Gang members began to invest their drug profits into auto repair and detailing, stereo shops, and a variety of other businesses to launder their drug money. They invested this money in businesses in Los Angeles County and in other States. Some gangs were now bordering on the edge of being classified as organized crime.

When these gangs initially began selling rock cocaine in their gang neighborhoods, the places of transaction were commonly referred to as "rock houses." The house would be the gang member's home or a rented home. Some gang members would rent several homes, or even pay a family, for this purpose. The gang member would almost always have security bars placed on the windows and doors to prevent law enforcement officers from entering the residences quickly, enabling the gang members or occupants to dispose of evidence. Large amounts of cocaine were often kept at these residences, as much as one to one and one-half kilos.

These gang members soon learned how to avoid law enforcement and developed new methods of handling and selling cocaine. The use of pagers, beepers, and cellular telephones made it more difficult to detect their activities. Gang members now hide their cocaine in several places, never keeping the supply in one spot. When they are detected by law enforcement, they lose only a small portion of their cocaine and money.

In Los Angeles County, a gang member of any age, as young as 12 or as old as 35, may be selling cocaine. Some of these people sell for another member of the gang and others for their own profit. Many gang members sell cocaine on a consignment or commission basis. This person receives a percentage, usually 50%, of what he sells.

The gang members use warning systems to alert fellow gang members of the presence of law enforcement when they sell cocaine on the street. When a gang member sees a patrol unit approaching, he will shout "One time!" or "Two times!", to indicate how many units are coming. Another term used to alert fellow gang members is "911." These persons, acting as "look-outs," are paid for their services in cocaine or money.

Gang members have adapted in other manners to avoid detection by law enforcement. They will avoid wearing gang identifying clothing and colors. Sometimes they will wear the colors of red and blue in their clothing to show that they are not gang members. Most of these gang members wear clothing that is neutral in color. This could be any color other than red or blue.

Gang members who are travelling out of state to other cities also try to hide their gang affiliation from law enforcement. They use a variety of transportation methods, including the airlines, bus systems (Greyhound Lines), Amtrak (rail), rental vehicles, Federal Express, and rental families. The general description of the gang member, who is involved in this process, is as follows:

- Attire is often an expensive sweat suit, not displaying gang colors.
- He is usually 20–25 years of age.
- He may be accompanied by a female.
- He almost always has no identification.
- Almost all of his transactions will be in cash; he will have large sums of money on his person.
- He will usually be wearing expensive jewelry.
- His hair will be closely cut or well groomed.
- Most of his business will be done out of local motel rooms.

The profits from the sales of cocaine are not distributed throughout the gang as one would believe. The profits are not for the benefit of the gang as a whole. One or more persons, who are leader type individuals, may control several trafficking networks within the same gang. These persons are often referred to as "high rollers." Each of these persons may have as many as three or four trusted persons who work alongside him in the distribution of the drug. In return for this trust and commitment, they are taken care of financially.

Asian Gangs

Asian Gangs Overview

This brief overview is intended to provide deputies, engaged in street enforcement activities, a practical understanding of the organization and characteristics of Asian gangs active in Los Angeles County. As with any criminal group, one will encounter individuals and specific situations which do not fit the general pattern of gang activities outlined herein. Field deputies should be alert to exceptions in specific situations and rely on their observations and experience in the interest of officer safety and the successful prosecution of suspects.

Asian gangs are frequently termed non-traditional when compared to street gangs of other ethnic groups. They are commonly referred to as organized criminal groups involved in street crimes. Most have financial profit as their primary goal; many have national and international ties. Membership behavior codes are well-defined and rigidly enforced. Acts of violence are not as random and are less frequent than with traditional gangs. Asian gang violence is committed primarily to achieve group goals. Secrecy and remaining anonymous to law enforcement is a constantly sought goal. Despite these aspects, much is known about Asian gangs. Asian gangs also share many characteristics of traditional gangs, such as territoriality, dress, graffiti, gang rivalries, etc., though these aspects are not always as obvious and are of less importance than with the traditional gangs.

Territory/Turf

With Asian gangs, "turf" is less rigid and fluctuates, as they think of territory in terms of its victim population (victims usually of the same ethnic group as the gang preying them). Acts of violence, due to gang rivalries, are infrequent as activity that does not obtain monetary gain is regarded as pointless.

If, as is the case, Koreans begin migrating to the valley, a Korean gang will regard the valley as within its area of operations. In Chinatown, the "Wah Ching"

(Cantonese Chinese) is the dominant group and regards Chinatown as its territory. During the early 1980s, the "Viet Chings" (Vietnamese of Chinese ethnicity) became active in Chinatown, and it was informally split into a southern section having a large number of Vietnamese businesses, and the northern area containing predominantly Cantonese Chinese businesses. The purpose of the division was to avoid conflicts that would result in warfare and consequently divert energy from the extortions and robberies that produce income. Turf for Asian gangs is best regarded in terms of locations and population clusters where the gangs' victim population resides and/or owns businesses. Turf doesn't recognize municipal boundaries.

Identification

Each Asian gang has its own unique characteristics. Although the average age is between 16 and 25, they may be found as young as 10 and as old as 40 and older. Hairstyles may be spiked or pompadour style, or the stereotype college student look. Clothing is most often the up-to-date styles (baggy look, fatigues, or college student look).

Tattoos and burn scars are often indicators of gang affiliation; however, they are not to be counted on. Older, hard-core gang members are most likely the ones to have tattoos, which are usually symbols of power (dragons, tigers, eagles, sailing ships, etc.). Although they may not mean anything to Western society, tattoos may have some significance in the intimidation of victims.

It should be remembered that, unlike attitudes in the West, tattoos are regarded as degrading for the most part by Asians. Most scars associated with Asian gang members are usually of the cigarette burn type and, depending on the specific gang, mean different things (initiation, victory in a fight, or ranking). These scars are usually found on the hands, wrists, forearms, or the lower legs depending on the specific gang.

Graffiti

Graffiti is of minor significance to most Asian street gangs. It serves no purpose in achieving their monetary motives, desire for secrecy, or maintenance of a low profile to the enforcement. The sophistication of these gangs vary from loosely organized street thugs to international criminal cartels. Their crimes cover the whole gambit of typical violent gang-related crimes to organized drug and theft rings. Generally speaking, the Asian gang crimes tend to be monetary motivated, but if challenged, they will react with violence just as any other street gang would.

Filipino Gangs

Gang activity in the Philippines prison system began in the 1940s. As members left prison, they banded together to control the black market of Manila. Gangs such as "Sige-Sige" and "OxO" were formed. Approximately 10 years later, these gangs were heavily recruiting Filipino youths in an attempt to keep control of their gains. New gangs such as "Sputniks" (Sige-Sige) and "Crossbones" (OxO), as well as "Bahala Na Gang" and "Tres Cantos," were formed. Some of these gangs exist in the United States today.

In the mid-1970s, the emergence of several new gangs was apparent in Los Angeles County. Immigration to the United States from the Phillipines had increased in the late 1970s and early 1980s, due to political unrest. The diversity of cultures and dialects in the Islands (approximately 2,000 inhabited islands, speaking 89 languages), coupled with the increased migration to the United States, caused the different cultures to mix together in the established Filipino communities here.

The youth that attended schools locally were faced with "street gangs" (as we relate the term to the occidental or Black and Hispanic gangs) for the first time, as well as cultural confrontations. Some of the youth subsequently reverted to a system known as "Barkada," which allows the youth to meet together in groups of several members for the purpose of socializing.

Unfortunately, many groups call themselves by a name as well as give each other nicknames. This was interpreted by both the occidental gangs as well as established Filipino gangs as "gang activity." The youth in the Barkada system then began their own means of protection, self-preservation, and retaliation. This was the birth of the Filipino gangs we see in California today.

Filipino gang members had excellent role models in the Black and Hispanic. They learned how to dress, talk, and disguise themselves in nicknames. They learned the business aspects of dealing in stolen cars, guns, and narcotics. Further, they learned to be "territorial" versus "turf" oriented so as not to be "preyed" upon by other gangs.

As with traditional gangs, Filipinos have family members, brothers, sisters, and cousins, as well as neighbors and friends in the gangs with them. Further, the members may belong to different gangs (both allied and rival) while living in the same household. Different age groups will form different "sets" or "cliques" amongst their own friends, and still identify with the "parent" gang.

Dress. The Filipino gang member will generally dress in the current fashion. Some "sets" have shown descriptive traits, such as wearing black, 3/4 length trench coats, while others may wear all white shirts and pants or have a "uniform" type of appearance. Generally speaking, these kids look very neat, clean and fashionable.

Vehicles. The vehicles of choice are the newer, imported Japanese cars, lowered, with nice sound systems, and windows tinted. They may have flared fenders and louvered back windows. The same is true for the mini pick-up trucks, with the addition of wide tires and polished wheels, that may or may not have shells on the back and truck club logos in the windows. However, not all Filipino gang members own cars, so they will drive virtually anything that their parents or relatives own.

Tattoos. The overt physical identifiers that we associate with gang members are most notably tattoos. Since there is no one tattoo that all gang members have, there are certain things to look for when dealing with them. An innocent "+" on the left middle finger of one person may not mean much; yet, if all of his friends have one, it could be an indicator. One gang tattoos their personal initials on the inside of their left index finger. Another has a complete logo that is usually tattooed somewhere on the right side of their body. It can be anywhere from their calf to their shoulder.

Another identifier is the cigarette burn mark. These burns can be located anywhere on the body but generally have been located somewhere on the hands (i.e., palm, back, or web). These burns appear to be a mark of courage or "machisimo." Generally, the more marks a person has, the worse or "crazier" he is. These marks have appeared more frequently in the younger male and female gang members and are generally worn by the self-proclaimed "hard-core" gang member.

Weapons. With the increase in membership of Filipino street gangs and their sophistication, there has also been an increase in the weaponry that we are seeing. The weapons being seized by law enforcement are no longer limited to "balisons" (or butterfly knives) and clubs, but are shotguns, rifles, and handguns. The handguns are both small and large caliber with the "automatics" being favored. It would appear that the gang member will use any gun that he can access. The ammunition for the rifles has been everything from light target type rounds to full jacketed military ammunition.

Due to the increasing market in weapons, theft and resale is an extremely profitable business. Further, gang members have been seen at military bases attempting to trade drugs for weapons (including hand grenades) with servicemen.

Graffiti. The graffiti of the Filipino gang member is very similar to that of the Black or Hispanic in its design as well as its usefulness to law enforcement. The gang's initials will appear on the walls in its neighborhood area, as will the names of some of its members and sometimes an alliance or rivalry. The Filipino gang member may have both the fantasy and cartoon type character name or nickname (resembling the Hispanic gang member, i.e., Sinbad or Aladdin), or he/she may have a gangster or Circa 1920s type name (resembling the Black gang member, i.e., Capone or Trigger).

Summary. These Filipino gangs evolved from proud, well educated and semi to very affluent families. Gangs not only terrorize their own neighborhoods, but will travel 50 miles to commit crimes in other Filipino communities. Los Angeles County gangs have subsets in San Francisco, San Diego, Hawaii, Seattle, and Las Vegas. With the mobility gang members have, now is the time to utilize available resources, identify gang members in your area, and get the needed community assistance.

Chinese Gangs

Chinese Gangs tend to be more like organized crime syndicates, not street gangs. The "Bamboo" (Mandarin speaking member from Taiwan) gang is well organized with approximately 40,000 members in Taiwan. United Bamboo (Chu Lien Bon) is a collective or umbrella term for approximately 20 gangs. It is active in Los Angeles County, preying primarily on Taiwanese immigrants. The leaders attempt to purchase legitimate businesses to accommodate their money laundering, employment for members, and to present a facade of respectability.

The Wah Ching gang is comprised of primarily Cantonese Chinese and are active not only in California, but Washington and Canada. The members tend to be youthful, illegal immigrants that prey upon legitimate Chinese businessmen. The gang members are noted for extortion rackets and drug trafficking. Much of the media attention on Asian gang violence has been a result of this gang's activity, as the membership is known to be particularly violent.

Indochinese Gangs

Indochinese Gangs (Vietnamese, Cambodian, Laotian, Thai, and Hmong) are active in welfare fraud, auto theft, commercial burglaries, and extortion. The membership is young and their dress is predominately "new wave."

There are as many as 200 different "bandit groups" (6-12 members doing crimes) operating in the Los Angeles/Orange County area. Vietnamese and Viet-Ching members can and will identify with that gang and yet may be in the company of a different gang in the bandit group. V-Boys will hang with V-Boys but commit crimes as an individual with Pomona Boyz and Santa Ana or Mohawk Boyz. They will seek out the most successful or experienced criminal to do crimes with.

Vietnamese gang members are opportunistic and will jump to another group for real or imagined personal slights and the promise of financial gain and peer respect. They are becoming increasingly sophisticated in extortions and have long been very adept at robbery. In recent years, Vietnamese have become hired "muscle" for the more sophisticated Chinese gangs.

Like Chinese and Korean gangs, Vietnamese prefer high quality firearms, including AR-15's and UZI submachine guns. Nearly all robberies of Vietnamese are perpetrated by Vietnamese gang members, just as most other ethnic Asian street crimes are committed by gang members of that ethnic group.

Vietnamese gang robberies are almost always done with the advance knowledge of money and/or jewelry to be found at the premises. The robberies are carefully planned, with individual assignments allocated during the robbery. They will occasionally photograph the location as part of the planning. Tape or pre-cut rope may be used to tie victims, and lookouts are often posted for approaching police units. Vietnamese robbery suspects are prepared to shoot it out with police and have done so on many occasions when the robbery is interrupted by the arrival of the police.

A new Vietnamese trend is for a small group to specialize in one or two financially productive crimes (GTA, robbery, etc.), travelling to several communities, wherever information indicates good opportunities. These groups don't assume group names and may be separate from any larger gang or comprise a cell within a larger group.

Korean Gangs

Although very little is known about Korean gangs, it is believed most of their activities are similar to that of the Chinese and Vietnamese. It is believed, however, that in the United States, there exists a nationwide organization which deals exclusively with prostitution. The organization strictly exploits young Korean and Vietnamese women. These women for the most part are tricked and lured into prostitution through false promises by a few older Korean women, who we term recruiters. These recruiters have found that by using their fierce loyalty in their culture, they can make large profits for a small investment.

Japanese Organized Crime

Until now, Yakuza, also known as Boryokudan (The Violent Ones), activity in the United States has been thought to consist mainly of obtaining contraband for shipment to Japan and maintaining and developing business investments in Hawaii and California. Commission research has revealed, however, that Yakuza members are involved with factions of La Costa Nostra in East Coast gambling operations catering to wealthy Japanese businessmen. This represents a serious escalation of Yakuza activity in the United States.

For at least 20 years, Yakuza members have invested in U.S. businesses in an attempt to hide their illegally earned capital from the scrutiny of the Japanese government. In the 1960s, Japanese Yakuza groups bought into enterprises in Hawaii, both legitimate businesses and massage parlors and pornography. More recently, Yakuza interests in the Los Angeles area have included import/export concerns, real estate, oil leases, night clubs, restaurants, gift shops and tour agencies. At least three Yakuza groups are known to be active in the Los Angeles area. Police in San Francisco, Las Vegas, and Denver have also reported Yakuza activity in their areas.

Pacific Islander Gangs

Pacific Islander gangs are made up of people from a number of different islands spread across many thousands of miles of ocean. Pacific Islanders began migration to the United States following the end of WWII and have increased since the 1950s, but it has not been until quite recently that we have started to notice the growing phenomenon of Pacific Islander street gangs. Their members include Samoans, Tongans, Fijians, Guamanians, and Hawaiians.

It was in Carson, California, that the first Samoan youths were observed joining in street gangs. Like most similar immigrant groups who were few in numbers, they tended to join with gangs whose reputation was already established. This is what happened in the case of the Samoans, who joined the Mexican and Black gangs they found around them when they arrived.

As their numbers increased and they became more confident, they began to withdraw from the Mexican and Black gangs and formed their own groups with their individual and meaningful names. A unique extract of the early gang involvement left the Samoan gangs with the learned behavior and attitudes of both Mexican and Black gang philosophy.

Like gangs around them, the Samoans began to identify themselves by writing their own graffiti on neighborhood walls, taking on nicknames so they would be more anonymous, acquiring tattoos, and developing similar initiation or "jumping-in" processes. In short, they began to affect all the elements which identify an individual as a gang member such as his style of dress, speech, attitude and behavior.

The early years of Pacific Islander or Samoan groups had no distinguished lines such as we recognize today as being Crip or Blood. They were involved in thefts of handguns, rifles and sawed-off shotguns. Because they were so universal amongst the various gangs, they found it profitable in selling these weapons to the gangs that allowed them to join. Soon, they were selling guns to their adversaries and were eventually forced to leave the very gang they had joined. Next, the Samoans joined Black gangs and, again, they were selling guns to their adversaries. By the late 1970s, the Samoans were large enough in numbers that they started their own gang and soon rivaled their own kind, family members from across town.

Pacific Islanders are unique among the members of Los Angeles gangs in that they adapt very easily to their surroundings and accept those parts of it which they like. Their skin coloration means they can be mistaken for Blacks or Mexicans, and they borrow heavily from both groups. They enjoy anonymity and the code of machismo, which are the markers of Mexican gangs; however, they also enjoy the styles of dress fashion and street jargon of Black gangs. Because of their Island backgrounds, they fall easily into the pattern of using warrior-type names. Different from Mexicans and Blacks, they speak a native tongue which is radically different from English. This ability gives them a yet another dimension.

In the early 1980s, they began to change these patterns and claim allegiance to either the Crip or Blood gangs. This change occurred at approximately the same time as a number of Samoan extended families were displaced from their original settlement in Carson, and moved to surrounding communities such as Long Beach, Lynwood, Compton and Harbor City. Samoan street gangs have emerged in various parts of California, as well as Seattle, Washington; Portland, Oregon; and Honolulu, Hawaii. The same graffiti and gang names are prevalent in these areas.

With the moves of their families, the young people began to be exposed to numerous different Black gangs with their own complex arrangements of loyalties and enemies. The experience of being in contact with these groups on a day-to-day basis, either in school, or on the street, meant that the Samoan youths had to choose their allegiance since they could no longer maintain a position of neutrality.

Within the Pacific Islander gangs, there are considerable historical reasons why they should not be united with one another. Although, to the outsider, all Pacific Islander gangs may look as if they present a single unit, this is not the case. Some of the fighting that takes place within Pacific Islander gangs is the result of ancient feuds between Samoans and Tongans, and Hawaiians and Samoans. In addition, there are recent feuds between island groups based on their religious preference, which is predominantly Mormon or Catholic.

One should understand that the Pacific Islanders have a cultural lifestyle that provides an inherent responsibility to take in all family members. Under this system, families are responsible for the wrongdoings of their children and must also provide work, monetary support, and shelter. Therefore, the Pacific Islander families who have established homes and work here in the Continental United States, as well as Hawaii, are forced to live in large households. The average household, per dwelling, is six families and can number as high as 10 families in the home.

Stoner Gangs

Recently, several non-traditional gang groups have developed that are not turf oriented, yet pose a tremendous threat to law enforcement personnel. The Stoners, as a group, set themselves apart from everyone and tend to be multi-racial (Mexican-American and White) in areas that are racially mixed. They dress in red or black clothing, preferring athletic jersey tops with heavy metal music stars displayed. The hair is worn longer with less emphasis on "looking sharp," as image isn't important.

Although Chicano gangs are considered traditional with close ties to family and a "Chicano" identity, a new element has entered the gang milieu and that is the "Stoner" gang lifestyle. They are less concerned with keeping ties with family or identifying with their Mexican birthright.

The "heavy metal" fad popularity greatly adds to the spread of their philosophy. Music has greatly influenced various groups, and with today's mass media, it has more impact on everyday life. Music has influenced several gang type lifestyles in the past. Some of the subcultures, many of whom have been associated with a gang lifestyle at one time, are:

- Pachucos—Swing music
- Nuros—Dance, reggae
- Cholos—Oldies but Goodies
- New Wave—Trendy
- Surfers—Surf music
- Punk—Trendy
- Breakers—Funk music
- Black Street Level—Rap
- Mods—Psychedelic music

History

Stoners have been in Los Angeles County for approximately the last decade. Named for the "Rolling Stones" or "getting stoned," they have variously been known as "Hessians," "Hippies," "Rockers," "Rebels," "Neo-Pagangs," and, prior to that, "Loadies." Stoners or Loadies was applied to the group by their teenage peers, as they were consistently under the influence of drugs or alcohol. Some Stoner gangs were formed in defense from other gangs or groups.

Stoners are generally junior high or high school students and tend to be better students, as a group, than their more traditional gang counterparts. They usually stay in school and participate in athletics. Many groups are allied with fellow Stoner gangs and feud with other music subculture groups.

Evidence of Stoner/Heavy Metal Influence

1. Symbolism: That which deals with the occult or Satanism
2. Writing Style: Uses the occult symbolism, heavy metal music oriented, and heavily influenced with the drug subcultures.
3. Musical Heroes: Tend to be from the heavy metal orientation. Some of the more popular groups are:

   A. Dio
   B. Iron Maiden
   C. Venom
   D. W.A.S.P.
   E. Slayer
   F. Ruthless
   G. Judas Priest
   H. Black Sabbath
   I. Motley Crew [*sic*]
   J. Ozzy Osbourne
   K. AC/DC

4. Other Heroes of the Stoner Membership are:

   A. Aleister Crowley
   B. Anton LeVey
   C. Adolph Hitler
   D. Charles Manson

Criminal Activity

Stoners tend to be involved in the drug subculture and commonly abuse such drugs as speed, LSD, rock cocaine, and PCP. They actively participate in both sales and use of these drugs. They easily flow into and out of gang areas because they are perceived as no threat.

Stoners tend to participate in animal sacrifice and ritual crimes such as graveyard or church desecrations. Suicides within the Stoner gangs are increasing and many researchers feel this is due to the heavy metal music influence.

This phenomenon creates various problems for law enforcement in that these gangs are different from traditional gangs. Stoner philosophy and motivation differs greatly from traditional street gangs, but their criminal potential and propensity for violence are at least as great. ✦

5
Chinese Gangs and Extortion

Ko-Lin Chin

Ethnic variations in gang formation result from differences in social and economic opportunities, community structures, and cultural values. In this article, Chin describes the involvement of Chinese youth gangs in the extortion of community businesses. According to the author, Chinese gangs are closely tied to the social and economic organization of their communities. Because the communities in which they evolve tend to be prosperous, and because they draw on Chinese subcultural norms, these gangs are able to take advantage of both legitimate and illegitimate opportunities for money and power that are not available to gang members of other ethnic groups.

Before 1965, with the exception of group conflicts among the tongs[1] in the late nineteenth and early twentieth centuries (Dillon, 1962; Gong & Grant, 1930), crime rates within the Chinese communities in North America were very low (Beach, 1932; MacGill, 1938). Chinese immigrants were generally law-abiding, hardworking, and peaceful. Official statistics show that the most common offenses were victimless crimes such as prostitution, opium smoking, drunkenness, and disorderly conduct (Tracy, 1980). Offenders were primarily adults who indulged in these culturally sanctioned recreational activities as a respite from work. Among Chinese adolescents, delinquency was also uncommon (Sung, 1977).

In considering the tranquility of Chinese communities in the past, however, it is important to note that before 1965 there were few Chinese teenagers in the United States, a result of the Chinese Exclusion Act passed in 1882 and the National Origins Act of 1924 (Fessler, 1983; Sung, 1979). The Immigration and Naturalization Act of 1965 was a turning point in the history of Chinese immigration because it not only made China a "preferred" nation but also established priorities for admission based largely on family relationships; those already living in the United States could initiate the immigration process for their families overseas (Kwong, 1987; Takagi & Platt, 1978).

Since 1965, the increasing number of Chinese immigrating to the United States has affected the stability of the Chinese communities in unprecedented ways. Traditional groups such as the family and district associations were ill prepared to cope with the influx. Because there were few social service agencies to help the newcomers, they were left mostly on their own to resolve housing, employment, education, and health problems (R. Chin, 1977; Huang & Pilisuk, 1977).

This breakdown in support, coupled with the growth of the Chinese population in isolated and fragmented communities, brought a corresponding increase in criminal activities among the Chinese (Bresler, 1981; Posner, 1988; President's Commission on Organized Crime, 1984; Robertson, 1977). Chinese gangs sprang up in San Francisco (Emch, 1973; Loo, 1976), Los Angeles (Los Angeles County Sheriffs Department, 1984), Boston (Roache, 1988), Toronto (Allen & Thomas, 1987), Vancouver (Robinson & Joe, 1980), and New York City (Chang, 1972; K. Chin, 1986). Although the number of active Chinese gang members is relatively small (there are no more than 2,000 Chinese gang members in the whole country), their involvement in some of the nation's worst gang-related violence (e.g., Daly, 1983) and heroin trafficking (U.S. Senate, 1986) has drawn the attention of law enforcement authorities. Recently, local and federal authorities have predicted that Chinese criminal organizations will emerge as the number one organized crime problem in the 1990s, when they become a dominant force in heroin trafficking, alien smuggling, money laundering, and other racketeering activities (U.S. Department of Justice, 1985, 1988, 1989; U.S. Department of State, 1988).

Although Chinese gangs have been active in the United States for more than 20 years, most of our knowledge about them has come from police and journalists. Other than a few scholarly studies carried out 10 or 15 years ago (Loo, 1976; Miller, 1975; Robinson & Joe, 1980), there has been no recent research on Chinese gangs. Thus it is imperative to improve our understanding of a social problem that law enforcement authorities have suggested is of paramount importance.

This chapter describes the individual and group characteristics of New York City's Chinese gangs and compares them with street gangs of other ethnic groups. Additionally, the social processes and functions of extortion—the type of illegal activity routinely and systematically committed by the Chinese gangs—also are considered.

This study was based on four types of data: ethnographic interviews, field notes, official reports and documents, and newspapers and magazines. People who were familiar with Chinese gangs or who had been victimized by gang members were interviewed, including members of the tongs and street gangs, social service providers, officials of civic associations, reporters, police officers, prosecutors, federal law enforcement officials, and victims.

Reprinted from C. Ronald Huff (ed.), *Gangs in America*, pp. 129-145,

To supplement interview data, I spent some time in the field. Most of my observations were made in gambling dens or bars where gang members hang out. I also reviewed and analyzed official reports and documents, and examined indictment materials and sentencing memoranda related to Chinese gangs. Finally, hundreds of English- and Chinese-language newspaper and magazine articles on Chinese gangs were collected and categorized by type of criminal organization, geographical area, and type of crime.

Demographic Characteristics

Sex

Like other ethnic gangs, Chinese gangs are composed predominantly of males. Although young females do hang around with members or live in the gangs' apartments, they are not initiated into the gangs. Except for carrying guns for their boyfriends, the girls are not involved in either property or violent crime.

Age

According to a police report, members' ages range from 13 to 37 (New York City Police Department, 1983). The mean age for the 192 registered gang members is 22.7. Most members are in their late teens or early 20s. Because the report included active, inactive, suspected, and imprisoned members, the sample may overrepresent seasoned members. Those who are new members may not yet be known to the police.

Country of Origin

In the 1960s and 1970s, most gang members were young immigrants from Hong Kong. A few were American- or Taiwan-born. Of the 25 Ghost Shadows indicted in 1985, for example, 24 were born in Hong Kong. Since the late 1970s, some Chinese gangs have recruited many Vietnam-born Chinese (President's Commission on Organized Crime, 1984). In the 1980s, many young immigrants from China were being recruited. Recently, some Korean youths also were inducted into the newly established Chinese gangs. So far, Chinese gangs have not recruited anyone who is of non-Asian origin. Most gang members, with the exception of a Taiwanese gang, speak the Cantonese dialect.

Structural Characteristics

Size

Each gang has on average about 20 to 50 hard-core members, a few inactive members, and some peripheral members. When conflicts among gangs are intense, they may seek reinforcements from other cities. Law enforcement authorities estimate a total of 200 to 400 active Chinese gang members in New York City, belonging to about nine gangs.

Organization

The structures of the gangs vary. The Ghost Shadows, for example, have four or five leaders at the top, the so-called *tai lou* (big brothers). Most other gangs have either one or two leaders. Under the leaders are a few "lieutenants," or associate leaders, in command of the street soldiers. At the bottom of the hierarchy are the street soldiers, who guard the streets and commit most of the extortion, robbery, and street violence. They are known as the *ma jai* (little horses).

Leaders maintain direct contact with certain tong elders and receive payment from them or from the gambling houses in the community. The leaders are the only liaisons between the tongs and the gangs. Leaders rarely are involved in street violence, although they give the orders. Whenever a leader wants somebody harassed or assaulted, he instructs the street leaders or members to carry out the assignment. The leader may provide the hit man with guns and pay him as a reward after he fulfills the "contract." Usually, the leader monitors the action from a nearby restaurant or gang apartment.

Although the associate leaders do not have much power in the administration of the gang, they control the ordinary members. Therefore, it is not surprising that street soldiers are more loyal to their immediate bosses than to the top leaders. Street leaders usually recruit the ordinary members. Although street leaders sometimes are involved in carrying out assignments, their usual role is that of "steerer"—they bring the street soldiers to their target and identify it for them. Street leaders do not initiate plans to attack specific people.

Among ordinary members, a few tough ones are known as "shooters"; they carry out most of the gang's assaults. The primary function of the soldiers is to watch the streets, guard the gambling places, and collect protection fees.

Most gangs have their own apartments, which are occupied mainly by street soldiers and are used as headquarters and for ammunition storage. The leaders do not live in them, although they drop by occasionally.

Except for the Ghost Shadows and the Flying Dragons, the gangs do not have splinter groups in other cities. The Ghost Shadows have chapters in Boston, Chicago, Baltimore, Houston, and Toronto, and police in New York City believe that the groups are nationally—or even internationally—linked.

Recruitment and Membership

Some youths join the gangs voluntarily, while others are coerced. Before the mid- 1970s, most youths were volunteers. Members treated one another as brothers, and it appeared that there was much camaraderie among them. From the mid 1970s through the early 1980s, however, many youths joined the gangs out of fear. Gangs have employed both subtle and crude methods to recruit new members. Gang members may treat a potential member to a good meal, show him their expensive cars, and provide him with the companionship of teenage girls. Impressionable adolescents may decide to join the gang to enjoy the putative benefits of membership. If potential recruits are unimpressed by what the gang offers, gang members send street soldiers to beat them up, a crude way of convincing them that their lives are more secure if they are gang members than if they are alone.

Usually, gang members recruit youths who are vulnerable—those who are not doing well in school or who have already dropped out. Young newcomers who have little or no command of English, poor academic records, and few job prospects are the most likely to find gang life attractive and exciting. Gang youths also approach adolescents who hang around video arcades, basketball courts, bars, and street corners, and those who talk and act arrogantly. Recruitment activities are carried out by both seasoned members and those who have been in the gang for only a short time.

Once a youth decides to join the gang, he goes through an initiation ceremony that is a simplified version of the Chinese secret societies' recruiting rituals. The youth takes his oaths, burns yellow paper, and drinks wine mixed with blood in front of the gang leaders and the altar or General Kwan, a heroic figure of the secret societies. The oaths taken by new recruits are, in essence, similar to the 36 oaths of the secret societies (see Bresler, 1981; K. Chin, 1990).

Dynamic Characteristics

Conformity to peer pressure is a strong characteristic of Chinese gang members. For instance, after six Ghost Shadows abducted and raped a White woman, two of the offenders initially opposed killing the victim. When the other four argued that she had to be killed, however, the two immediately consented. Nevertheless, group cohesion appears to be weak. Intragang conflicts erupt frequently, and members sometimes transfer from one gang to another. Within a Chinese gang there are usually two or more cliques, each consisting of a leader, one or more associate leaders, and several soldiers. These cliques usually distrust and dislike one another, and the tensions among them are exacerbated easily whenever illegal gains are not distributed properly. A review of the history of Chinese gangs in New York City indicates that leaders constantly are plotting to have one another killed (K. Chin, 1990). A Chinese gang leader is more likely to be killed by his associates than by a rival.

Some intragang conflicts are instigated by tong elders who are associated with a particular clique. These mentors prefer to have a divided rather than a united gang; therefore, they intervene to ensure that no particular clique gains enough power to challenge the supremacy of the tong.

Attachment to the gang is not absolute. To date, no gang member has been attacked by his peers simply because he decided to leave the gang. If a member joins a rival gang, however, he can provoke retaliation from his former associates. On the other hand, if the leaders of the two groups involved can reach agreement about the transfer of members, changing membership and allegiance can be arranged satisfactorily.

Comparison of Chinese Gangs With Other Ethnic Gangs

How different are Chinese gangs from other ethnic gangs? Some researchers report that Chinese gangs are similar to other ethnic gangs in several ways. For instance, Robinson and Joe (1980) found that the characteristics of the Chinese gangs in Vancouver were identical to those of American gangs. The gangs Robinson and Joe studied, however, were atypical in the sense that they were not related to community organizations as Chinese immigrant gangs in San Francisco and New York City are. They resembled American street-corner gangs or athletic clubs, and were similar to the American-born Chinese gangs that were active in the early 1960s, a period when Chinese gangs were not yet institutionalized by community associations.

Like Robinson and Joe, Takagi and Platt (1978) suggest that Chinese gangs—like other ethnic gangs—are involved only in petty crimes. In their view, the tongs and other adult associations, rather than the gangs, are responsible for the organized racketeering activities and violence within the Chinese communities. Takagi and Platt's findings are not supported by other data. Violence in Chinatown is, in most instances, instigated by Chinese gangs (K. Chin, 1990).

In contrast to scholars of gang delinquency, law enforcement authorities argue that Chinese gangs are unlike other ethnic street gangs. A former captain of the New York City Police Department suggests that Chinese gangs should not even be considered as "youth" gangs because of the way they are controlled and the age of the leaders:

> [Chinese gangs] are well-controlled and held accountable to the various associations in the Chinatown area. They are the soldiers of Oriental organized crime, with strong ties to cities throughout the United States. The associations have international ties in banking, real estate, and import/export businesses and are suspected of being involved in narcotics and alien smuggling. Members of the street gangs range in age from the mid-teens to early twenties. The street leaders are in their early twenties and thirties, with the highest leader being a mature middle-age or senior adult generally in charge of one of the associations (New York City Police Department, 1983, p.3).

The data collected for this study revealed that Chinese gangs have the following unique characteristics that set them apart from other ethnic gangs. First, they are closely associated with and are controlled by powerful community organization. Second, gang leaders invest their money in legitimate businesses and spend a large amount of time doing business. Third, Chinese gangs form national or international networks. Fourth, the gangs are influenced to a great extent by Chinese secret societies and the norms and values of the Triad[2] subculture. Fifth, gang members normally do not go through various stages in which they graduate from delinquent behavior to serious crime. New members often are assigned to carry out the most serious assaults. Sixth, Chinese gangs control large amounts of money, and making money is their main motive. Finally, Chinese gangs systematically victimize the businesses in their communities in ways no ordinary street gangs possibly could. In sum, their strong affiliation with powerful adult organizations, their high level of mobility, and their businesslike methods of wiping out rivals suggest that they more closely resemble adult criminal organizations than typical youth gangs that are concerned mainly with dress codes, turf, and involvement in nonutilitarian, negativistic activities (Cohen, 1955).

According to data collected for this study, Chinese gangs resemble Cloward and Ohlin's (1960) "criminal gangs." Chinese gangs develop in ethnic communities in which adult criminal groups exist and in which the adult criminals serve as mentors and role models for the gang members. They not only provide the youths with jobs but also offer them an opportunity structure in illegitimate activities. The youths can start working as street soldiers and then go on to become lieutenants, gang leaders, and (eventually) core members of the tong. Thus, a street youth can work his way up to become a respected, wealthy community leader through the structure of illegal activities provided by adult organizations, if he can survive his years as a gang member.

Nevertheless, gangs such as the Ghost Shadows and the Flying Dragons do not strictly follow the subculture pattern in Cloward and Ohlin's classification. Their long history of street violence shows that, besides securing income, the gangs fought constantly with rival gangs to establish their power to shake down the community. This use of violence to win status is consistent with Cloward and Ohlin's definition of "conflict gangs." It is hard to imagine, in any case, how criminal gangs could protect their illegal sources of income without violently subduing rival gangs to prevent them from encroaching on their territory. Although gang involvement in street violence is not condoned by the adult organizations and is not in the best interests of the gangs themselves, apparently the gangs believe that they must instill fear in rival groups as well as in the community as a whole.

What is the evidence for Cloward and Ohlin's third delinquent subculture, the retreatist? In a study of gangs in three cities, Fagan (1989) found drug use widespread among Black, Hispanic, and White gangs, regardless of the city. Moore's (1978) Los Angeles gangs and Hagedorn's (1988) Milwaukee gangs were involved heavily in drug use and dealing. Drug use among Chinese gang members, however, is rare. Moreover, although gang leaders are involved in drug trafficking, they themselves are not drug users. Tong members do not tolerate drug use in the gangs, and the gangs themselves are reluctant to recruit anyone who uses drugs. If a member begins using drugs, he is expelled from the gang.

Thus Chinese gangs have the characteristics of two of the subcultures described by Cloward and Ohlin: the criminal and the conflict subcultures. Because gang leaders are concerned primarily with the lucrative heroin trade and investment in legitimate businesses and are closely associated with certain tong leaders, they adhere more to norms and values of the criminal subculture as depicted by Cloward and Ohlin. Young members are concerned mostly with their macho image and therefore are more prone to commit violent acts and predatory crimes. These young members seem to be most congruent with Cloward and Ohlin's conflict gangs. Consequently, instead of labeling Chinese gangs as either criminal or conflict gangs, it is perhaps more important to consider the ages and ranks of the gang members and their criminal propensities.

Unlike Chinese gangs that are closely associated with the well-established adult groups, gangs formed by young Chinese immigrants from Vietnam and Taiwan have no adult group to emulate. As a result, these gangs are not as well organized as the Chinatown gangs. Without the stable income from protection and extortion operations that Chinatown gangs enjoy, and without a lucrative commercial district to claim as a territory, Vietnamese and Taiwanese gangs are forced to become involved primarily in extortion, robbery, and burglary. These gangs resemble Cloward and Ohlin's conflict gangs because they are prone to excessive use of violence, they lack supervision by adult criminal elements, and they are outside the illegitimate opportunity structure.

Protection and Extortion

The booming economy and the gambling industry in the Chinese community have provided Chinese gangs with ample criminal opportunities. Of the businesses in the community, gambling clubs are the most in need of the gangs' protection. In order to operate smoothly, the clubs must rely on gang members to protect them and their customers from the police, intruders, and the gangs themselves. To perform these jobs, a few members are dispersed in the street where the gambling club is located. Three or four members guard the entrance, while some stay inside. Members carry beepers to communicate with one another. Street leaders in the gang's nearby apartments oversee the entire operation. Nightclubs and massage parlors owned by Chinese and catering to Chinese patrons also require protection. These businesses need gang members to protect them from members of other gangs.

Gangs supplement their primary activity of guarding gambling dens and adjacent streets with another criminal activity: systematic extortion of Chinese businesses. Police estimate that at least 80% to 90% of Chinese businesses have to pay one or more gangs regularly or occasionally. Only those merchants who are close to the hierarchy of the tongs are said to be able to avoid paying the gangs.

Techniques of Extortion

According to police officers, prosecutors, and victims interviewed, the gangs primarily use two forms of extortion. One explicit technique is for gang members to demand money. Usually, gang members approach a new business during its opening ceremony and ask for *li shi* (lucky money). After the owner pays, they show up again later and identify themselves as gang members, explain how the racket works, and indicate that it is better to pay than to refuse. Occasionally, gang members tell the owners that they need money for food, or to help their "brothers" who have been arrested. There are also times when gang members will ask businessmen to "invest" in their business or give them a "loan."

In the second extortion technique, the demand for money is implicit. For example, the gang members will try to sell festival-related goods such as firecrackers or plants to business establishments for an inflated price. Sometimes, gang members may simply tell store owners that protection from the gang is provided to their businesses.

Gangs employ several common practices. First, a group of youths may enter a restaurant during the lunch or dinner hour, and each of them occupies a table. They tell the manager that they are waiting for friends. They sit for hours, and they act in rowdy fashion to intimidate customers. They may fight with each other, smash the dishes, or insist on remaining in the restaurant after closing hours. An experienced manager knows what the disruptive youths want.

Second, young men may go into a restaurant and order the finest dishes on the menu. When they leave, they write "Shadows" or "Dragons" on the back of the bill and do not pay. Third, some gang members may dine in a restaurant but refuse to pay the bill. While they argue with the manager about it, two or three fellow members walk in and pretend to be customers. They appear to be sympathetic to the manager and chastise the youths who refuse to pay. When the "show" is over, a gang member calls up the manager, demands protection money, and tells the manager that if similar incidents happen in the future, his gang will protect the restaurant. This technique is known as *hei bai lian* (black and white faces), meaning that while members play the role of the "bad guys," leaders will act as the "good guys" who ask money from the frightened victim.

The fourth method is called *tai jiau tsi* (carrying a sedan chair). Gang members will try to flatter a potential victim by calling him "Big Brother" and acting as though they are his loyal followers. If the businessman is unaware of the gang's tactic and associates himself with the gang, he may find out that it is too late for him to get rid of the label "Big Brother." As a "Big Brother," the victim has no other real benefits except to provide financial support to the gang.

The fifth approach is known as *wo di* (literally, undercover). A gang member infiltrates a business by seeking a job there. During his tenure he collects information about the owner, where he lives, when the business will accumulate the maximum amount of cash, and other matters. The gang member provides the information to his associates to draw up an extortion or robbery plan.

Most of the time, the owners negotiate about the amount of payment, but they do not bicker about whether they are going to pay. When the gang gets a victim paying, a schedule is arranged: several hundreds dollars monthly for large stores; less than a hundred dollars per week for modest businesses. The gang usually has designated collectors and keeps records of its income from extortion.

If a retail business refuses to pay, then the gang may vandalize, burglarize, rob, or set fire to the shop. The owner then usually relents and cooperates. In some instances gangs have beaten, shot at, or killed business and retail store owners. For those who do pay, the amount demanded by crime groups escalates rapidly, or another gang will show up soon with the same demand. When businesses are no longer able to meet the gangs' demands, they close down, move to another area, or report the crime to the police. Usually, most business owners try to satisfy the gangs by paying them the first few times. Only when they find out that they have to pay more than one gang or that their payments increase rapidly will they turn to law enforcement for help.

Types of Extortion

Extortion in Chinese communities may be classified into four types. The primary objective of the first and most prevalent type of extortion is monetary gain. The offenders and victim may not know each other prior to the incident, and the extortionate act may be perpetrated without the knowledge of the tong associated with the gang. Regardless or how the victim reacts to the offender's demand, he or she is unlikely to be assaulted physically by the offender in this type of extortion.

The second type is symbolic extortion, which is used as a display of power to indicate control over a territory. Monetary gain is not the major goal; gang members usually demand only free food or other small items such as cigarettes. They also may ask for heavy discounts from restaurant owners. This type of extortion occurs almost on a daily basis, and the victims are usually small store owners or peddlers who do businesses within a tightly controlled gang territory.

The third type is extortion for revenge. Offenders extort victims because of something the victims did to the gang previously, or the gang is hired by a victim's adversary to extort the victim as a form of revenge. Because monetary gain is not the motivating factor, victims are likely to be robbed, beaten up, or killed even if they do not resist the perpetrators. Extortion is used simply as a cover for vengeance.

The fourth type is instrumental extortion, which is used to intimidate the victim into backing down in certain business or personal conflicts. In this type of extortion, the victims are also vulnerable to assault and harassment. The extortionate act is, more than anything else, a message sent to the victim by his rival through the gang members. Gang members also may rob or extort money from the victims for their own sakes. Conflicts pertaining to business territories and business or gambling debts usually result in instrumental extortion activity.

Extortion and Territory

Through extortion, the gangs assert their firm control over certain territories in New York City's Chinese communities. When two or more gangs claim control of a specific area, or when the area is occupied by a weaker gang, store owners within that territory have to pay more than the gang. Currently, Canal Street and East Broadway, the rapidly expanding streets of Chinatown, have no single powerful gang that can claim exclusive sovereignty. Consequently, some of the store owners in those areas have to pay as many as five gangs simultaneously.

The same is true for the Chinese communities in Queens and Brooklyn. Although the White Tigers, The Green Dragons, and a Taiwanese gang are the three most active gangs in these newly established communities, more powerful gangs from Manhattan's Chinatown occasionally invade the area to commit extortion. When two or more gangs are active in a particular area and attempt to extort from the same victim simultaneously, street violence erupts as a result of the power struggle.

Before 1980, most extortionate activities were confined to Manhattan's Chinatown. Only occasionally would gang members venture outside Chinatown to extort money. Beginning in 1980, however, the gangs rapidly spread their extortionate activities to other parts of Manhattan, Queens, Brooklyn, Long Island, New Jersey, and Connecticut. Unlike extortionate activities within Manhattan's Chinatown, which are mostly spontaneous and cost the victims fairly small amounts of money, out-of-state extortion is well planned, and gang members tend to demand rather large amounts.

Since 1984, businessmen in Queens and Brooklyn have been extorted frequently. Unlike in Manhattan's Chinatown, gangs in these areas have no gambling establishments from which to collect protection money. As a result, the only likely source of funds is extortion or robbery of stores in the community. The lack of knowledge about the gangs by local precincts has also contributed to the rapid increase in extortion. In addition, business owners in Queens and Brooklyn are not protected by tongs or other traditional organizations as are business owners in Manhattan's Chinatown.

Conclusion

In order to understand Asian crime groups, the research and law enforcement communities need to broaden their perspectives. Concepts that are adequate for explaining Italian, Black, and Hispanic crime groups may not be adequate for examining criminal organizations of Asian origin. Because Asian people have diverse cultural heritages, we also need to identify the unique features of each Asian ethnic group.

We can isolate three unique characteristics that cause Chinese gangs to persist. First, unlike Black and Hispanic gangs (Hagedorn, 1988; Moore, 1978), Chinese gangs are not based on youth fads or illicit drug use. Instead, they are closely related to their communities' social and economic life. This relationship enables Chinese gangs to become deeply enmeshed in the legitimate and illegitimate enterprises in their communities. Opportunities for money, power, and prestige through various ventures are bestowed on Chinese gang members. No such distinctive opportunity exists for other minority gangs.

Second, unlike other ethnic gangs—which operate primarily in deteriorated, poor neighborhoods—Chinese gangs flourish in rapidly developing and economically robust Chinese communities that are tied closely to Chinese societies in Southeast Asia. Chinese gangs thus can become engaged in economically rewarding domestic and international ventures. Other ethnic gangs are hampered by both the lack of lucrative criminal opportunities in their own neighborhoods and the absence of contacts outside those neighborhoods.

Third, Chinese gang members are embedded in the legendary Triad subculture, a subculture established and maintained by members of the Chinese secret societies. By emulating Triad initiation rites and internalizing Triad norms and values, they can claim a certain legitimacy within their communities. This legitimacy enables them to instill a level of fear that no other ethnic gangs can match, because the community does not view them merely as street thugs.

Nevertheless, the nature, values, and norms of Chinese gangs could change in the future. Chinese gangs with no ties to the tongs or Triad subculture are emerging in newly established Chinese communities. We are now observing the rise of Vietnamese-Chinese and Fujianese gangs (Badey, 1988; Meskil, 1989). Both groups are not only unfamiliar with Triad norms and values, but their criminal patterns—such as street mugging and household robbery—are markedly different from those of the traditional Triad-inspired gangs.

Author's Note:

I am grateful to Colleen Cosgrove for her comments. This chapter is excerpted from *Chinese Subculture and Criminality: Non-Traditional Crime Groups in America* (Contributions in Criminology and Penology, No. 29, Greenwood Press, an imprint of Greenwood Publishing Group, Inc., Westport, CT, 1990).

Notes

1. *Tong* means "hall" or "gathering place." Tongs were first established in the United States during the mid-nineteenth century by the first wave of Chinese goldfield and railroad workers as self-help groups. Bloody conflicts among the tongs are known as "tong wars." The most powerful tongs in New York City are the Chih Kung, the On Leong, and the Hip Sing. Since the 1960s, in order to improve their image, the tongs have been renamed as associations. The heads of these associations are normally influential and well-respected community leaders.
2. *Triad* means a "triangle of heaven, earth, and man." Triad societies are secret societies formed by patriotic Chinese three centuries ago to fight against the oppressive and corrupt Ch'ing dynasty. When the Ch'ing government collapsed and the Republic of China was established in 1912, some of the societies began to be involved in criminal activities.

References

Allen, G., & Thomas, L. (1987). Orphans of war. *Toronto Globe and Mail*. 1(12), 34-57.

Badley, J.R. (1988). *Dragons and tigers*. Loomis, CA: Palmer Enterprises.

Beach, W.G. (1932). *Oriental crime in California*. Stanford, CA: Stanford University Press.

Bresler, F. (1981). *The Chinese mafia*. New York: Stein & Day.

Chang, H. (1972). Die today, die tomorrow: The rise and fall of Chinatown gangs. *Bridge Magazine*, 2, 10-15.

Chin, K. (1986). *Chinese triad societies, tongs, organized crime, and street gangs in Asia and the United States*. Unpublished doctoral dissertation, University of Pennsylvania.

—— (1990). *Chinese subculture and criminality: Non-traditional crime groups in America*. Westport, CT: Greenwood.

Chin, R. (1977). New York Chinatown today: Community in crisis. *Amerasia Journal*, 1(1), 1-32.

Cloward, R.A., & Ohlin, L.E. (1960). *Delinquency and opportunity: A theory of delinquent gangs*. New York: Free Press.

Cohen, A.K. (1955). *Delinquent boys: The culture of the gang*. Glencoe, IL: Free Press.

Daly, M. (1983, February). The war for Chinatown. *New York Magazine*, pp. 31-38.

Dillon, R.H. (1962). *The hatchet men*. New York: Coward-McCann.

Emch, T. (1973, September 9). The Chinatown murders. *San Francisco Sunday Examiner and Chronicle*.

Fagan, J. (1989). The social organization of drug use and drug dealing among urban gangs. *Criminology*, 27(4), 633-669.

Fessler, L.W. (Ed.). (1983). *Chinese in America: Stereotyped past, changing present*. New York: Vantage.

Gong, Y.E., & Grant, B. (1930). *Tong war!* New York: N.L. Brown.

Hagedorn, J.M. (1988). *People and folks: Gangs, crime and the underclass in a rustbelt city*. Chicago: Lake View.

Huang, K., & Pilisuk, M. (1977). At the threshold of the Golden Gate: Special problems of a neglected minority. *American Journal of Orthopsychiatry*, 47, 701-713.

Kwong, P. (1987). *The new Chinatown*. New York: Hill & Wang.

Loo, C.K. (1976). *The emergence of San Francisco Chinese juvenile gangs from the 1950s to the present*. Unpublished master's thesis, San Jose State University.

Los Angeles County Sheriffs Department (1984). *Asian criminal activities survey*. Los Angeles: Author.

MacGill, H.G. (1938). The Oriental delinquent in the Vancouver juvenile court. *Sociology and Social Research*, 12, 428-438.

Meskill, P. (1989, February 5). In the eye of the storm. *New York Daily News Magazine*, pp. 10-16.

Miller, W.B. (1975). *Violence by youth gangs and youth groups as a crime problem in major American cities*. Report to the National Institute for Juvenile Justice and Delinquency Prevention.

Moore, J.W. (1978). *Homeboys: Gangs, drugs, and prison in the barrios of Los Angeles*. Philadelphia: Temple University Press.

New York City Police Department, Fifth Precinct (1983). *Gang intelligence information*. New York: Author.

Posner, G. (1988). *Warlords of crime*. New York: McGraw-Hill.

President's Commission on Organized Crime (1984). *Organized crime of Asian origin: Record of hearing III—October 23-25, 1984, New York, New York*. Washington, DC: U.S. Government Printing Office.

Roache, F.M. (1988, January). Organized crime in Boston's Chinatown. *Police Chief*, pp. 48-51.

Robertson, F. (1977). *Triangle of death*. London: Routledge & Kegan Paul.

Robinson, N. & Joe, D. (1980). Gangs in Chinatown. *McGill Journal of Education*, 15, 149-162.

Sung, B.L. (1977). *Gangs in New York's Chinatown* (Monograph No. 6). New York: City College of New York, Department of Asian Studies.

—— (1979). *Transplanted Chinese children*. New York: City College of New York, Department of Asian Studies.

Takagi, P. & Platt, T. (1978). Behind the gilded ghetto. *Crime and Social Justice*, 9, 2-25.

Tracy, C.A. (1980, Winter). Race, crime and social policy. *Crime and Social Justice*, pp. 11-25.

U.S. Department of Justice (1985). *Oriental organized crime: A report of a research project conducted by the Organized Crime Section* (Federal Bureau of Investigation, Criminal Investigative Division). Washington, DC: U.S. Government Printing Office.

—— (1988). *Hong Kong 1997: Its impact on Chinese organized crime in the United States* (Foreign Service Institute). Washington, DC: U.S. Government Printing Office.

—— (1988). *Report on Asian organized crime*. (Criminal Division). Washington, DC: U.S. Government Printing Office.

—— (1989). *The INS enforcement approach to Chinese crime groups* (Immigration and Naturalization Service, Investigative Division). Washington, DC: U.S. Government Printing Office.

U.S. Senate (1986). *Emerging criminal groups* (Hearings before the Permanent Subcommittee on Investigations of the Committee on Governmental Affairs). Washington, DC: U.S. Government Printing Office. ✦

6

The Working Gang

Felix Padilla

The connection between drug dealing and street gangs is an issue of great public concern and speculation, and this subject will be explored in detail in Section III, Gangs and Drugs, below. In this article, Padilla provides an example of one gang that is organized around the drug trade. The reader should keep in mind that the author is describing only one type of gang structure. Padilla traces the development of this gang into a group organized around making money. He highlights the roles of legislation and the lack of economic opportunities, as well as cultural solidarity. However, in the end the author concludes that the youths' employment in drug sales finds them trapped as highly exploited workers who receive few of the benefits of their labor.

"I'm going to work," Rafael said. "I have to go and make me some bread." The day is April 17, 1989. I had just finished having lunch with Rafael in a local restaurant. Rafael is a member of a Puerto Rican youth gang in Chicago that I have been studying for over two years. He was responding to one of the questions I would ask him as we departed from the restaurant.

"Where can I drive you?" I asked. Of course I knew that he was headed to the usual street location where he had been dealing drugs for several years. After dropping him off, Rafael and a friend boarded a car, which appeared to have been waiting for his arrival. They drove away from the vicinity only to return thirty minutes later carrying a large amount of merchandise he would try selling on this day.

Once back in the neighborhood, he would position himself alongside other dealers to earn a day's pay. Rafael, as well as his co-workers, were employed by one of the distributors in his gang. Like other workers, they were expected to be at the job for a certain amount of time.

Rafael's work relations with the gang are a clear illustration of the business side of the organization. This is a topic which remains unveiled despite a fairly extensive scientific and journalistic literature on youth gangs. In the main, most accounts about gangs and drugs tend to consider "all" teenage drug dealing as an innate activity of the gang. However, this approach overlooks many cases of teenage drug dealing that are not affiliated with or sponsored by the gang.

Reprinted from *Gangs*, edited by Scott Cummings and Daniel J. Monti, by permission of the State University of New York Press, © 1993 by State University of New York Press.

There are some young men who simply establish drug-dealing networks or crews comprised of several members, but these are not gangs. They lack a formal organization and leadership stratum. Members are not expected to invest time in attending formal meetings. Nor do they pay any form of dues. Members of the network or crew do not consider this group a gang. In other cases, young people who are not affiliated with the gang manage to develop street-level dealing operations on their own. There also are instances of street-level dealing being carried out by gang members working on their own. I will demonstrate below that these three cases are unlikely to materialize where street-level dealing is controlled by a gang, though individuals continue to make attempts to establish these forms of individual undertakings.

The scholarly and journalistic writers do not make a distinction between the times when drug dealing represents a gang activity and a large portion of the earnings go to the organization and the times when drug dealing is an endeavor carried out by nongang members working only for themselves. The discussion that follows will focus primarily on street-level dealers who work for the gang, and who receive a salary for their labor. It also will touch on the experiences of several youngsters who are independent dealers, but who are still part of the gang's occupational structure. They purchase their merchandise from the gang's distributors, utilize the gang-controlled turf for retailing, and are required to pay weekly organizational dues.

The following questions will be considered. What are the reasons for the gang becoming a business organization? What does the gang look like as an entrepreneurial establishment? That is, what are its defining characteristics as a business enterprise? Which cultural elements are used by youngsters for cementing and reinforcing business relations among themselves? What is the gang's occupational structure? How does the gang generate income for itself?

Information for this chapter comes from a two-year study that I have been conducting of a Puerto Rican youth gang in Chicago. I have given the gang the fictitious name of the Diamonds. The neighborhood that serves as the Diamonds' turf is located five miles north west of the downtown area. For the last twenty years, the neighborhood has been racially and ethnically mixed, comprised of Latino (i.e., Puerto Ricans, Mexican Americans and Cubans) and white residents. Puerto Ricans, who comprise the largest group among Latinos, often refer to this neighborhood as *Suburbia* (pronounced "sooboorbia"). Living there is perceived as a measure of social prosperity and improvement. Census reports confirm this perception. In 1980, almost 40 percent of workers were employed in white-collar occupations. Only 18 percent had incomes below the poverty line and the unemployment rate was 9 percent.

The Diamonds Become a Business Gang

The history of the Diamonds dates back approximately twenty years, a relatively short period when compared to other Latino youth gangs in Chicago. At first, the Diamonds was a musical group. Members played their music on the street or in local night clubs. In 1970, a member of the musical group was mistaken for a gang member and was killed by a gunshot fired by a youngster from a rival gang. This incident sparked the reorganization of the group into a violent gang. For the next six years the Diamonds provoked fights with other groups. During most of this time, the membership of the Diamonds was quite small. The organization did not divide itself into different sections. Some members used drugs, but in the late 1970s a major change occurred in the thrust of the operations of the gang. It began taking on a business-like character. No longer were retaliation and violent behavior the mainstays of the organization. Money making through drug dealing came to represent the gang's chief activity. Several factors account for this change.

Controlled Substance Act

One gang member named Carmelo described one change:

> I remember this older guy from the neighborhood who wanted me to sell for him. He asked several of us to be his dealers. He was offering good money, but I was afraid. I didn't know what he was about. We knew that he was doing something, because all these people used to come to his house all the time. But he never dealt with us before, and then all of sudden he wanted us to work for him. I said no to the guy.

The event that precipitated the development of the gang into a business was the 1971 passage of the Illinois Controlled Substance Act. It carried heavy criminal penalties for adult heroin and cocaine dealers. Well aware that juveniles could always beat the penalties of the newly instituted law, adults who for the most part had controlled drug distribution and dealing up to this point, began enlisting some members from the Diamonds and other gangs to work the streets of particular neighborhoods. Some youngsters like Carmelo refused the job offers. Others agreed. It did not take them or leaders of the gang long to realize that they could profit substantially by controlling neighborhood drug dealing. In other words, these youngsters began to ask the question, why can't we develop our business?

Gang leaders began thinking about the gang as a wholesaler or investor. It would purchase the merchandise itself and hire its own members, especially the younger ones, to sell at the street level. Because the Diamonds viewed themselves as landlords of several *puntos* or blocks in the neighborhood, the only thing still missing for developing a business operation was the necessary capital with which to purchase large amounts of drugs.

They began pulling their money together. Sometimes two or three of the older members (or leaders) would "go into business." Sometimes the group was larger. At other times, leaders would request that all members make an investment of a certain amount and use this sum for purchasing the drugs with which to open the business.

High Demand for Drugs

The rise of the business side of the gang also was ignited by the increasing demand for drugs, particularly cocaine. The increasing popularity of drug use during the 1970s and the still blossoming international cocaine trade created a situation in which demand outstripped the supply. One distributor recalls the times when, as a street-level dealer, he would sell his merchandise so easily that some customers at times were left without goods. This was the time when the demand was greater than the supply.

> Author: How would you compare selling now to years ago?
>
> Carmelo: I was dealing in the streets back in 1974 or so. We did not have the organization that we have now. Now we deal through the gang. So, that was one difference.
>
> Author: What was another difference?
>
> Carmelo: I think it was the amount of reefer and coke, but mainly reefer that were out in the streets. Cocaine was expensive, but reefer, everybody wanted reefer and we were making all kinds of money.
>
> Author: How was that possible?
>
> Carmelo: Like I told you. There was a lot of stuff out there. There were times when I would get my supply in the morning and then go back in the afternoon and get some more. My supplier wanted me out there all the time because the stuff was selling real fast. There were times when I had to turn some of my customers on to somebody else, something I never wanted to do, but if I didn't have the stuff it was better that they cop from other guys. That way they would not want to stop using it. That's what kept us going. Yeah, but, man, that was good, today, well, you seen how that is.

The Nation Coalition

When the business side of gangs grew too large, it had to be better organized. That is when gang nations were built. "My understanding of what the nation means is that we are supposed to respect other groups from the same nation," replied Rafael when I asked him to explain the meaning of the concept. He added that

> gangbanging is nothing really hard to do. In my neighborhood, you have to hang out a lot. Our chief wants us there a lot so nobody else would try to take our neighborhood from us. And we have boundaries, and a little bit of the neighborhood we share with others from the same nation, but of a different affiliation. And we have our territory and if they were to come into our territory, we wouldn't start trouble by getting loud and stuff like that. We all respect each other pretty much, and it's alright.

At a more general level, Rafael was describing the moderate and congenial relations established by rival gangs in Chicago during the early 1980s. Peaceful relations were facilitated by the division of city areas into two gang nations or alliances, People and Folks. Suburbia's various gangs came under the auspices of the latter. No one is really certain of the lineage of the nation alliance, but rumors have it that the alignment was created from formerly rival gangs that were jailed together in 1981. It is also believed that jailed, former leaders of these two parent groups continue to play a significant role in dictating the policies and practices of street gangs in Chicago.

Theoretically, the nation approach was aimed at reducing significantly the degree of intergang violence that had been so common during the 1970s. As indicated by Rafael above, nation gangs were discouraged from invading each other's territories, and agitation and harassment were not to be brought upon coalition members. Indeed, the nation coalition contributed immensely to solidifying the business operation of the gang. "Respect for each other's territories" also came to mean the sharing of the drug consumer market. Each gang was permitted to operate its business from a relatively safe turf or marketplace, selling only to those customers who voluntarily frequented there. No longer was the gang involved in efforts to take over other turfs, hoping to expand its business boundaries beyond its immediate setting. The new nation approach called for the development of a particular gang's business enterprise in its own turf, improving the image and reputation of the business, and making it more attractive to consumers.

Since drug use was so widespread, the most rational business decision was to share the market. It was no longer necessary to fight over turfs. This also freed the neighborhood of gangbanging and provided a fairly safe "shopping area" for prospective customers. A neighborhood that was known for its ongoing gangbanging activities tended to scare off customers.

Members of the Diamonds are committed to mutual understanding and harmony with other gangs but have not abstained entirely from conflict and fighting. In fact, members of the Diamonds believe that the nation alliance has broken down as gangbanging among nation gangs is becoming routine. But the significant point is that when first started, the nation alliance reduced intergang violence substantially and enabled some gangs to establish their organizations as sound business enterprises.

Perceptions of Conventional Work

Youngsters' image of "traditional" jobs was perhaps the leading force that helped to transform the gang into a business venture. These young men began turning to the gang in search of employment opportunities, believing that available conventional work would not be sufficient for delivering the kinds of material goods they wished to secure. One youngster indicated,

> There are some jobs that people can still find, but who wants them? They don't pay. I want a job that can support me. I want a job that I could use my talents—speaking, communicating, selling and a definite goal that I'd be working towards as far as money is concerned.

These young people have a pessimistic appraisal of and outlook toward jobs in the regular economy. They have become increasingly convinced that those "jobs available to them" are essentially meaningless and far from representing the vehicles necessary for overcoming societal barriers to upward mobility. Although these youngsters have been socialized with the conventional cultural belief in achieving material success, they refuse to accept the conventional means to become successful. That is, they do not accept the "American achievement ideology," reflected in middle-class norms, and shown by Horowitz, Kornblum and Williams, and others to be widely supported by ethnic and racial minority parents and teenagers.[1] The ideology stresses that success in school leads to the attainment of managerial and professional jobs, which in turn pave the way for social and economic advancement. The youngsters' own school experiences and contact with the job market, as well as the futile and frustrating efforts of adults around them to achieve social advancement through menial, dead-end jobs, contradict the American achievement ideology. These young men do not believe in the power of education to serve as the "great equalizer." Nor do they perceive conventional jobs as leading to a successful, meaningful life.

These views reflect the tension between culturally defined goals and the ineffectiveness of socially legitimate means for achieving them that Robert Merton first described and subsequent gang studies confirmed.[2] They point to the absence of avenues and resources necessary for securing rewards which society purports to offer its members.

The decision by members of the Diamonds to sell drugs was informed by their assessment of available opportunities in the regular economy as well as their high level of aspirations. Drug dealing did not arise in deliberate violation of middle-class normative aspirations. The gang represents a "counter organization" geared to achieving things valued by the larger society and countering forces weighing heavily upon their lives. In effect, these youngsters transformed the gang into an income-generating business operation in an unconventional economy in order to "make it" in conventional American society.

Social and Cultural Components of the Ethnic Enterprise

Two questions need to be addressed at this point. First, what are the distinguishing characteristics of the gang that enable it to function as a business organization? Second, what social and cultural devices did the youngsters use for organizing the gang into a reliable money-making enterprise?

The gang has developed its own culture. The gang does this in the same way that the family unit teaches its young the norms, skills, values, beliefs, and traditions of the larger society—and the ways to communicate and reinforce that culture. At the heart of the gang culture is a collective ideology that serves to protect all the members. Collectivism also serves as the major determinant of the gang's efficient development as a business operation. The members' response to their shared conditions and circumstances is collective in the sense that they form a partnership.

For the young people I studied, collectivism translates into an ideology of strength. These young men share a belief that their capacity to earn a living or improve their life can only be realized through a "collective front." In the views of a youngster by the name of Coco, "we are a group, a community, a family—we have to learn to live together. If we separate, we will never have a chance. We need each other even to make sure that we have a spot for selling."

The collectivist nature of the gang can be said to be an extension of the traditional Puerto Rican family. In Puerto Rican immigrant society, as well as in other societies from which many other ethnic and racial groups originated, the family served as the cornerstone of the culture, defining and determining individual and social behavior. Ties between families were cemented by the establishment of *compadrazco* (godparent-godchild) relationships. Relatives by blood and ceremonial ties, as well as friends of the family, were linked together in an intricate network of reciprocal obligations. Individuals who suffered misfortunes were aided by relatives and friends. When they had re-established themselves, they shared their good fortunes with those who had helped them.

That the gang is rooted in the norms of family life and tradition can be observed from the various descriptions of the gang offered by the youngsters I studied.

> Tony: My grandmother took care of me for a long time. I guess this was part of the Puerto Rican tradition at one time. Your grandmother took care of you while your mother and father were away working. Sometimes grandmothers did not believe that their son or daughter were fit to be parents so they took the responsibility of raising their grandchildren. My grandmother is my life. Anybody who messes with my grandmother has to mess with me. The same thing with my aunt.
>
> Author: Which aunt are you referring to?
>
> Tony: This is my mother's sister, which is really weird because they are the same blood but treat me so differently. My aunt is the mother I never had. We are really closed. She is the person that I go to when I need someone to tell something to. She always listens to me.
>
> Author: And why does she always listen to you?
>
> Tony: My aunt is this wonderful woman, she's about 35 years old, who is really together. When I'm with her I feel like I can tell her anything that is in my mind. That's what family is all about. This is all in the blood. She cares because she is family. When you have a family, even if it's your aunt or uncle, you know you belong. You will always have someone looking out for you.
>
> Author: In the last interview, you talked a little about the family as it related to the gang. How similar is the gang family to what you're describing now?
>
> Tony: They are very similar. You see a family is like a fist [he pointed to his fist, clenching it and opening it to show that when it's opened it represents five fingers separated from one another]. I know that the five fingers of your hand are supposed to be related; however, what would you prefer having, a hand with five fingers or a closed fist? When the fist is closed the fingers are inseparable; when the fist is opened they stand at a distance from one another. I prefer the closed fist. That's exactly how our gang is—we are very closed. To be in our gang you need to have heart. To have heart means that you are truly committed to each other; that you'll do anything for another member because he is part of your family.

In addition to stemming directly from a Puerto Rican family tradition, ethnic solidarity served as another cultural element, used by the youngsters for cementing their business relations. As Puerto Ricans, they expressed feelings of a primordial tie, of blood kinship, said to unify them. This, in turn, provided the basis for trust. As one youngster put it: "The fact that I knew that what I liked was at another person's house—they would talk to me about things like, 'we're going to listen to Salsa music, we're going to have *arroz con gandures* [rice and pot pies]' and some other stuff, I would get more attractive to that than to other things."

Part of the collectivist, communitarian foundation of the gang was also shaped by a base of local consumers or people who are referred by friends. Their willingness to become faithful customers, to continuously purchase available goods, i.e., drugs and stolen merchandise, is viewed by gang members as an indication of membership. These customers become, in the opinion of one youngster, "one of us." The same young man also said: "People from the neighborhood know that they can get smoke, cane, and other things from us. It's risky going to other places. So they protect us. We are safe with them. So we think of them as part of the business."

The significance of collectivism for gang members can be also extracted from their views about the idea of individualism. These youngsters are not in agreement with the view that the successful exercise of individual effort in pursuit of economic and social mobility is applicable to them. To them, individualism means placing oneself at a precarious position. How can they exist or survive without one another? They are fully aware that they do not possess the traditional resources, such as money and high levels of formal education, that are used by members of the middle class to negotiate and advance their individual life chances. They believe that individual effort represents a step toward obliteration. As directly put by one youngster, "By ourselves, we are nobody. We can be had without no problem." Another's remarks were just as straightforward: "This is not a game that you can win by yourself. If you want to win, you do it as a team. If you want to lose, play alone."

Individual success honors those who have achieved it. Failure, and economic failure in particular, stigmatizes those who suffer it. Such failure can only make those who have "failed" the objects of criticism or scorn. It can also be taken to mean that they are inadequate or deficient. The individualization of "success" and "failure" in American society is unacceptable as far as these young men are concerned. For this reason, collectivism is perceived as capable of giving gang members a special sense of purpose and ability—the driving force with which to pursue economic and social success.

Rules of Collectivism

The gang adopted explicit rules aimed at enforcing communitarian behavior and discipline among its members, which was translated into economic activity. Individuals who decided to work on their own were fully aware of the severe penalties associated with such behavior if it led to problems with the "law." For example, members who are apprehended by the police for selling drugs or stealing on their own may not be entitled to receive the amenities accorded to others who engage in collective action. One youngster, who spent six months in jail, describes the consequences of working alone. "I was left to rot. My people didn't come for me. We were all warned about doing shit by ourselves. I was one who paid for not listening."

Additionally, sullen individual action can lead to severe physical harm, in particular the brutal punishment embellished in one of the most traditional rituals of the gang: the Vs. As explained by one youngster, Vs stand for "violations," which are beatings dispensed to individual members for violating certain rules of the gangs. They are often used in special ceremonies, like initiations or withdrawals of members. During these occasions an individual must walk through a line comprised of other members. The number in the line could range from ten to fifty. The line walk usually lasts three to five minutes and the individual must try to defend himself from the onslaughts of those making up the ranks of the line. If an assault causes the individual to fall, he must return to the beginning of the line and start again. If he gives up, he cannot be excused from the penalty, or accepted as member, or allowed to leave the gang. The most devastating of the Vs are those involving members wishing to quit the gang and those who violate gang rules. One young man described the violations performed during cases when a member leaves the gang:

> There are no rules when they give you a V out. They can use whatever they want on you, they can kick you wherever they want, they pull you on the floor, they can punch you wherever they want, you can't fight back. You just stand there and cover up what you can cover up, and hope that they don't hit one of your weak spots.

I was informed of many instances when individuals who violated certain rules were given severe beatings. The case of Frankie is one example.

> I came out all bruised up and had a broken rib, and that was about it. I just had lumps and bruises all over my face and on my back. It was a lot on my back. But it wasn't as hard really as I thought it would be, so it went pretty fast and I just hope for the best. I wanted to come out alright [*sic*], alive, at least.

It is to the advantage of individuals to function from the collective perspective of the gang rather than on their own. As gang members, drug dealers are offered a fairly safe marketplace from which to sell their products. The gang's turf, the location in the neighborhood where drug transactions tend to occur, is to be used by members only. In cases when a particular turf has developed a reputation for carrying stocks of reliable and good merchandise, as is true for the turfs of the section of the Diamonds I studied, youngsters can be assured of having an on-going clientele and a profitable business.

Another advantage of a collectivist approach to doing business is found in the symbolic messages this action tends to communicate, particularly to "outsiders." For example, the presence of a group of dealers on a street block or corner, usually taking turns to insure that everyone has an opportunity to make a sale, serves to discourage possible robbery attempts. Customers, users, and others not associated with the gang recognize the danger in trying to burglarize or stick up a group of dealers who are members of a particular gang. In addition, the gang provides individuals with a "reputation," serving as a defense against possible customer snitching. Customers and other individuals would be afraid and hesitant to reveal information about a particular dealer who is viewed as belonging to a particular gang. There is a widespread understanding that to snitch against one is tantamount to revealing information about the entire gang. This is an act youngsters in the streets recognize will provoke retribution and physical violence.

The gang, as representative of a collective unit, carries another advantage. It provides customers with a reputable source from which to purchase drugs and other items. In doing so, it contributes significantly to cementing seller-customer relations. Knowledge about the gang, its territory, its affiliated dealers and overall reputation present customers with the background information necessary for trusting that the merchandise they buy is authentic and good. Customers feel confident that they are not being sold a fraudulent product, or what street-level dealers call "junk."

Finally, the collective approach to selling drugs provides youngsters with protection against police invasion and apprehension. The youngsters I studied worked in groups or crews of at least three members. This work arrangement served as a reliable shield to keep each worker alert and informed of the different predators and threats around them. Otherwise, having to conduct an illicit business from an open and highly visible location, like a street corner, makes arrests a distinct possibility.

Occupational Character

The gang, as a business, is built around a fairly elementary occupational structure. Several leading jobs are found within this structure: drug suppliers/distributors, cocaine and marijuana dealers, and those involving several forms of stealing. This occupational structure, like in other business establishments, is developed in a hierarchical basis, representing a pyramid of power, prestige, authority, and information. One's position on the pyramid is correlated with one's access and possession of these attributes.

At the top level of the gang's occupational hierarchy stands the cocaine and marijuana suppliers or distributors. The number of suppliers/distributors is limited, for the smaller the number the larger the profit. Members of the Diamonds referred to their distributors/suppliers in terms of "leaders," "older guys," or simply "main heads." They thought of the distributors as individuals who had paid their dues by remaining with the gang for a very long period of time. In the process they would have gained knowledge about the drug distribution network and accumulated the necessary money for purchasing bulk quantities of drugs. Distributors hold a virtual monopoly over the purchase and supply of drugs sold by members of the Diamonds.

> Author: Who did you purchase your stuff from?
>
> Carlos: I usually bought it from my gang leaders.
>
> Author: So there was a distributor within your gang?
>
> Carlos: Yes, every gang has at least one distributor. There are times when a section may not have one, well these guys then buy from another distributor from the larger gang. My guess is that the older guys took trips to Florida, or meet people half-way. I heard some guys going downtown for the stash. Some of these people were into real estate, restaurants. But it's through some business and the owner of the business was handling the stuff. But this was all done by the older guys, the younger ones never got into this, they couldn't.
>
> Author: I heard you refer to the distributor as the "older guys."
>
> Carlos: Yes, it is the older ones who know what life is all about, who are making money and living a nice life. They are into communicating with one another and making money. But not the youth.

Distributors exercise great influence over street-level dealers through their control over drug sources. A single distributor may have as many as fifteen to twenty youngsters working for him on a regular or periodic basis. The money paid to each youngster, as well as the amount of drugs that he gives on consignment, depends on the type of relationship that is established. If he believes that an individual is not making him money, he will sever the relationship by refusing to supply him. Along with their monopoly over the supplies of cocaine and marijuana, the ability to hire and fire employees gives these distributors a considerable amount of influence over youngsters working at street-level dealing.

The distributor epitomizes success within the gang. He seduces newer members. He is not an illusion or fantasy. Rather, he embodies the dream which the larger society has denied Puerto Rican youngsters. And, in the mind of the youngsters, the distributor represents the one position within the business infrastructure of the gang that they want.

> I would see my prez and other heads, you know, two or three cars, and this and that, and they still got jobs, money, you see a bankroll in their pocket, and they be asking you what you want to eat. And this and that, and you be like, "I want to make this money and that money, I want to be like you." And he'll be like, "Ok, well I'll go buy an ounce of reefer, right, cause you ain't got the money to do it." And you know you can't do it.

Since successful drug distribution requires a great deal of secrecy, information about top-level distributors is limited. Contact between the distributor and street-level dealers is restricted to sporadic episodes, most likely involving occasions of drug dispersion and money collection. Distributors are rarely seen on the corners where drugs are presently sold.

Distributors belong to a fairly closed and exclusive club. The few individuals who remain with the gang long enough to achieve this level of job mobility are usually expected to create a new section of the gang in a different area of the neighborhood. They also might be appointed to oversee an existing section that was viewed by the leadership as nonproductive. One young man provides a precise account of the nature of the distributor's job:

> In my section, the big guys would never change. They were the distributors, the people everybody wanted to be like but couldn't. They had the control and were not going to give it to anyone. If you got big like them, you had work with another section. They didn't let you compete with them. Why should they? They were going to lose money. But I guess it's not a bad idea to create your section—it's only yours.

In effect, most workers within the Diamonds' job hierarchy occupied the position of street-level cocaine and marijuana dealers—the job directly beneath the distributor/supplier. In most cases dealers sell both drugs, though the preference is toward the cocaine business for its larger profits. Dealing cocaine and marijuana requires possessing available cash in order to purchase the drug from the supplier. Otherwise, youngsters work as sellers for the supplier who "fronts" them a certain amount of drugs—dealers receive a small percentage of the profits. There are other times when the supplier uses gang members to sell cocaine and marijuana by hiring them to make "drops" or "deposits" of specific amounts to individuals outside of the neighborhood. The profits from this job are usually small.

Because of the relatively small profits made by those working for distributors or dealers, the ultimate goal of street-level dealers is to become independent businessmen. That is, they want to amass the necessary amount of dollars to acquire and sell the product without having to share the profits with the distributor. As "independents," the youngsters know very well that the return for their investment and labor will always be higher.

> Author: How long did you stay in drug dealing?
>
> Gustavo: I'm still doing it to this day.
>
> Author: What was your biggest profit when you were working for the man?
>
> Gustavo: My biggest profit a week was about $100.00 to $150.00 a week. The profit I was making for the guy was sometimes $1,000 to 2,000.
>
> Author: So you were making very little.
>
> Gustavo: That's right. He was making all the money. There were Saturdays when I would be counting the

money that I was going to take him and there were times when on a Saturday he would make $2,000.

Author: Now that you're on your own, how much money do you make?

Gustavo: It varies. If I go and buy $800 worth of cocaine I can make $1,600—a one hundred percent profit. If I package the stuff myself into quarter bags I can make more. Any profit to me is good, as long as it's over $100. But you see, I don't make that kind of money because I don't have the money to buy that quantity.

Author: What has been the most you've ever made?

Gustavo: I bought $400 and took out that plus another $400. And I sold that on a Wednesday, Thursday, and Friday.

Similarly, as independents, dealers determine which drugs to sell, favoring cocaine over others even though the penalties for selling it are more severe. "The money is in cocaine," indicated a youngster as he described the difference between selling cocaine and marijuana. He also stated, "I have spent a lot [of] time working the streets, selling reefers and pills, but I know that I can double whatever I make in these jobs by selling cane."

Dealers from the Diamonds tend to sell both cocaine and marijuana to local consumers, though other buyers come from the "outside." In the majority of the cases, the outside buyers are young, middle-class whites, who have learned through different ways and sources about a particular corner or street block where cocaine can be readily purchased. The thing drug dealers like most about outside buyers is that they tend to become habitual customers, making purchases throughout the course of the week.

Author: You were telling me about some of your customers, and you mentioned how people from the neighborhood are not steady. What do you mean by that?

Carmelo: Friday is the big day. It's pay-day. That's when most of people come out to make their kill. Actually, the whole weekend is when we sell a lot to people from around here.

Author: And you would not consider that to be steady!

Carmelo: Well, I guess. But, you see my white customers come around all the time. These people have money all the time and don't care about spending it. They come around on a Monday or a Thursday, whenever.

Author: So are you saying that people from the neighborhood make larger purchases that last for the entire week?

Carmelo: Are you kidding? No, they buy a few hits, that's all.

Author: What happens to them during the week?

Carmelo: We work out different things. Sometimes I just give them the stuff and they pay me on Friday. Or, they bring something that they use to trade. For example, I had a guy give me this expensive watch one time. Another left his VCR. So there are different ways that we use.

Marijuana is the most readily sold drug among the youngsters I studied. Not surprisingly, the job of marijuana dealer is the one found most often within the occupational structure of the gang. Marijuana is usually sold to local clients for a very low price. Members of the Diamonds working in marijuana dealing indicated that the common use and popularity of the drug is correlated with customers' perception of it as being relatively mild, pleasurable, and easily manageable. One dealer provided what he believes to be the reasons why users or customers prefer marijuana over other drugs like cocaine.

> Because people have the opinion that cocaine is dangerous. And marijuana you just smoke it, it's like smoking a cigarette, you just smoke and get high and that's it. There's not a real big affect on you, you don't get addicted to it. You know, some people do, but they, it's controllable, it's not as bad as cocaine—you get hooked. . . . You know, you get rid of marijuana fast. Marijuana goes better than cocaine.

Youngsters also believe that the legal penalties for dealing marijuana are less severe than those for dealing cocaine. This suggests another explanation for their widespread involvement in marijuana sales. From the dealers' perspective, there is no sign of any significant enforcement apparatus and no cases of severe punishment for possessors of marijuana.

Finally, at the bottom of the gang's occupational hierarchy are those youngsters who make money through stealing. The large number of youngsters involved in acts of stealing are the newer members, called the "Pee Wees" or "Littles." In many cases, stealing represents a "special mission" that Pee Wees are instructed to carry out to demonstrate their loyalty and commitment to the gang. Although these efforts are geared to "proving themselves," they still manage to generate a profit. For other youngsters, stealing becomes a way of life. They work in crews of three or four, and the major item they target is cars. These youngsters become extremely proficient in stealing cars and make a substantial amount of money, though not as much as that generated from drug dealing.

Money-Raising Capacity

Similar to other business organizations, the gang's survival depends on its capacity to develop and maintain a sound financial base. Funds are needed to meet a wide range of organizational needs, such as purchasing weapons, making rent payments, bailing members out of jail, and paying for attorney's fees. The gang's finances are managed primarily through two major sources: one is the organization's own centralized fund, referred to by youngsters as the "box," and the other represents the private funds of the drug supplier/distributor(s) within the gang.

The centralized fund or "box" is established through membership contributions or dues, paid periodically (i.e., weekly, biweekly) to the gang's treasurer. As one youngsters put it: "Without the kitty [box] we would had [*sic*] disappeared a long time ago. We needed all kinds of money to get people out of jail because for a while we were doing some heavy gangbanging. We were paying about $10–15 a week." The significance of membership dues in terms of maintaining the gang is also described in detail by another young man:

> Author: How often did you pay dues in your gang?
>
> Hector: We pretty much paid twice a month. We were paying ten dollars per crack. To me that was a lot of money.
>
> Author: What would have happened if you didn't pay?
>
> Hector: But we had to pay—if we didn't the organization would stop. There were times when the president would give us time to raise the money, but we always had to pay. And I guess when you're part of the gang, you care for it. So if you care about the gang, you always find the way to get your hands on some money. It's like if you care for your girlfriend, you always find a way to make her happy. With the gang, you had to find the money to it happy.

Money for the centralized fund was also secured through other means, for membership dues could only raise a very limited amount. Included in these activities were the stealing and selling of weapons, car parts, and the like. While recalling his early days in the gang as a newcomer, one youngster described his working relationship with senior gang members to whom he was assigned:

> The older guys would always bring me and tell me to go steal or sell this or that. And that this would bring money for me, but most of the money had to be taken to the box for dues. They would tell me that the money would be used for getting me out of jail or any trouble that I might get into later.

A similar account was given by another youngster: "In our gang, we collected dues. Everybody had to pay. Several times I worked together with other guys pulling some jobs, we stole a car and stripped it. The guy in charge took most of the money for the box because we were empty. I guess we didn't mind that much."

The other mode for generating funds for the box is through contributions made periodically by the distributor/supplier. Because the supplier has a vested interest in the maintenance or survival of the gang, there are times when he uses his own funds for resolving certain gang-related matters. The supplier understands quite well that without his monetary donation, the gang might well fall apart. Similarly, he understands that without the gang, he could lose his business. Contributions made by the distributor are geared to protecting his workers, his street-level dealers. If they are apprehended by the police, he puts up the money for getting them out of jail. In the following exchange, Carlos provides a graphic picture of the role of the distributor as a provider toward the well-being of the organization and its members.

> Author: How often did the distributor use his money to get members out of jail?
>
> Carlos: Many. We had some times when they pull the money out of their own pockets and one of us would get bailed out. Or sometimes to pay a hospital bill or for someone who got really busted out.
>
> Author: And why did the distributor do this?
>
> Carlos: They would do it really out of their good-will, for the devotion they got for their own gang. And they want everybody in the hood; they figure the more of us who are out there, the better for them.
>
> Author: What were the other reasons the distributor used his money to get people out of jail?
>
> Carlos: One thing you have to understand that is they got their money back. The guy paid him double. It's like an investment because the guy would have to pay him two times what it cost to get him out of jail in the first place.
>
> Author: Did you ever see this happen within your gang?
>
> Carlos: Yes, I saw this happened several times. I even saw it where the big guy borrowed the money and charged double for getting this guy out. He needed money to pay his rent and went and got this money from some other guy and bailed this other one out.
>
> Author: You said earlier that one reason the big guys get others out of trouble situations is to demonstrate to everybody else that they are devoted to the gang and they care for the gang. Elaborate on this.
>
> Carlos: They want to show everybody in the gang that they are devoting everything they have into the gang to make it better. And to take, how can I say it, "look what I did for you," kind of thing. And they tell everybody, "that's why I'm leader and that's one reason I want all of you to look up to me."

Discussion

In this chapter I have provided a basic sketch of the leading components of the business youth gang. It is clear from the presentation that this kind of enterprise is quite complex. There were many factors contributing to the formation of the gang as a business operation. The examples provided indicate how external forces and conditions combined with internal cultural group dynamics to give rise to systematic and highly organized business relations among gang members.

In addition, although the description presented in the chapter suggests that the gang does indeed provide youngsters with an alternative to unemployment, it is also the case that this form of labor is highly exploitative. The street youth gang of Suburbia is far from representing a progressive cultural response to youth labor exploitation. On the contrary, it serves to reproduce that exploitation and oppression.

There are several reasons for this. Contrary to public belief, street level dealers make little money selling drugs or through stealing. In most cases, these youngsters represent another type of minimum-wage labor. The saturation of the market with mass amounts of drugs as well as the fast rise of so many gangs involved in drug selling have increased availability of drugs and decreased the cost. Youngsters' profit margins are quite small. One youngster explained this turn of events in a very interesting way. "I was planning to make enough to go legit. I wanted to do something with the money I was going to make. I know an older gang member who owns a car wash. I wanted something like that. But as I told you, I worked hard and yet I'm still standing on the corner." Another youngster put it this way:

> I guess when we joined the gang, we would see the prez and chief with so much gold and [we'd] think we're going to be the same. But then we have to face the hard facts. There is not much for most of us. But by then, you're too involved, you're a member, people see you and know you now. So you stay—you continue dealing, what else can you do?

In effect, street-level drug dealers are a cheap and permanent labor force used by a few suppliers or distributors within the gang to maintain and enhance their business interests and profits. Although the wages received from selling drugs may be higher than those earned "turning hamburgers at McDonald's," in the case of the street-level dealer upward mobility is highly unlikely. It is to the advantage of the supplier to maintain the subordination and dependency of their street-level dealers. Distributors/suppliers establish the wages of street-level dealers. Suppliers also maintain a large number of youngsters employed, establishing a very real competitive setting and compelling dealers to operate according to the rules established by suppliers.

Additionally, street-level dealing can be regarded as exploitative labor in that the occupation itself is "sporadic, having high peaks and droughts, and is full of uneven demands on [their] time"[3] (Manning and Redlinger, 1983:283). The large majority of the youngsters I studied indicated "working the block" or "standing on the corner" for a good part of their day, for there was not any established time for "making a deal." A transaction could occur at 6:00 A.M. or 12:00 midnight. In addition, competition from other dealers contributed directly to the amount of time youngsters invested working the streets or corners. As one former dealer put it:

> We used to work very long hours. There were other times that we would have to work long past 12 midnight because we got some of these people coming in on Fridays or Saturdays at 2 or 3 in the morning telling us that they just came out of after-hours and they needed it now and they would pay more for it. These were some desperate folks. But you had to deliver otherwise you would lose your clients.

Moreover, the extreme danger of drug dealing adds to the persisting strenuous nature of the occupation. These young people are the ones who do the dirty work of the business, which is often accompanied by physical harm or even death. For youngsters caught doing the gang's dirty work the common consequence is stigmatization by the larger society. Re-entering school is difficult. Obtaining employment in the conventional economy is almost out of the question.

Notes

1. Ruth Horowitz, *Honor and the American Dream* (N.J.: Rutgers University Press, 1983); William Kornblum and Terry Williams, *Growing Up Poor* (Lexington, Mass.: Lexington Books, 1985).
2. Robert K. Merton, *Social Theory and Social Structure* (Glencoe, Ill.: The Free Press, 1957); Richard A. Cloward and Lloyd Ohlin, *Delinquency and Opportunity* (New York: Free Press, 1960); Joan Moore et al., *Homeboys: Gangs, Drugs and Prison in the Barrios of Los Angeles* (Philadelphia: Temple University Press, 1978); Horowitz, *Honor and the American Dream*; Diego Vigil, *Barrio Gangs: Street Life and Identity in Southern California* (Austin: University of Texas Press, 1988).
3. Peter K. Manning and Lawrence J. Redlinger, "Drugs at Work," in *Research in the Sociology of Work*, eds., Ida H. Simpson and Richard L. Simpson (Greenwich, Conn: JAI Press, 1983), p. 283. ✦

7

The Differences Between Street Gangs and Neo-Nazi Skinheads

Mark S. Hamm

As a result of the ways in which social researchers typically define what constitutes street gangs, white supremacist youth groups are often not classified as "gangs." Hamm argues that this distinction is a valid and important one: while street gangs tend to organize as a result of shared culture and shared experiences of oppressive social and economic conditions, skinhead groups are organized explicitly around the ideology of racism. The overt political nature of skinhead groups and of their violence makes them more aptly defined as terrorist youth subcultures, according to Hamm.

The skinheads constitute a unique criminal subculture for several important reasons. To begin with, scholars have found that gangs are a largely immigrant, adolescent, underclass phenomenon, but they have not found racism to be an organizing principle for gang membership. In those instances where racism has been discovered by gang researchers, it has usually been cited as an excuse for juvenile delinquency. That is, gang delinquency is a function of youthful rebellion against oppressive conditions caused by racism in the larger society (Cloward and Ohlin, 1960; Erlanger, 1979; Hagedorn, 1988; Spergel, 1961; Vigil 1990).

This is not the case, though, for the neo-Nazi skinheads of North America. For them, we consistently discover that skinhead membership is an explicit function of their own strident racism.

Many scholars have also pointed out that violence, like racism, plays only a small role in gang behavior (Hagedorn, 1988; Klein, 1971; Merry, 1981; Miller, 1958; Morash, 1983; Moore, 1978; Suttles, 1968). In fact, some researchers have shown that gangs often have a positive relationship with their local communities and even serve as auxiliary police forces (Horowitz, 1987; Sanchez-Jankowski, 1991). Others have found that when gang violence does occur, it is often related to the use and/or distribution of highly addictive drugs such as heroin and crack cocaine (Fagan, 1989; Huff, 1989; Taylor, 1990), disputes over turf (Erlanger, 1979; Horowitz and Schwartz, 1974; Thrasher, 1927), ethnic and cultural differences between neighborhoods (Moore, 1978; Suttles, 1968), poverty and social disorganization (Curry and Spergel, 1988), or general economic interests (Spergel, 1984).

Once again, the evidence on the neo-Nazi skinheads stands in instructive contrast to this body of criminology. For the skinheads, violence is their signature trademark because *violence is part of subcultural style*. Instead of turf disputes, socioeconomic disadvantage, social disorganization, drugs, or economic interests, the skinheads seem to use violence for the explicit purpose of promoting political change by instilling fear in innocent people.

This was evident in Clark Martell's Romantic Violence, Robert Heick's American Front, David Mazzella's WAR Skins, and John Metzger's Aryan Youth Movement. It was ultimately the case in the killing of Mulugeta Seraw. There are virtually hundreds of other cases where American neo-Nazi skinheads have used violence for the specific purpose of instilling fear in innocent people.

Among these cases are the following:

- On December 4, 1987, a skinhead in Tampa, Florida (Dean McKee), used an eight-inch hunting knife to kill a homeless black man sleeping in his bedroll outside a local art museum (ADL, 1988c).
- On September 15, 1987, a skinhead in Van Nuys, California, used a switchblade knife to slit the throat of a Hispanic woman because she refused to turn off a cassette recording by the Miami Sound Machine (Klanwatch, 1989; field notes).
- On February 9, 1988, a skinhead in Las Vegas, Nevada, used a .38-caliber snub-nosed revolver to kill a young black female clerk at a 7-Eleven store. He then turned on an elderly black female customer in the 7-Eleven, and fired two shots into her spine. No money was taken from the cash register nor were the victims sexually molested (Klanwatch, 1989; field notes).
- On April 2, 1988, four members of the Detroit Area Skinheads (DASH) used knives to murder a twenty-year-old black woman. About the murder, the leader of DASH told police, "All I could do was feel confused and happy" (Dees, 1990).
- On March 4, 1988, four skinheads from La Verne, California, assaulted an Iranian couple, their two-week-old son, and a black man who tried to intervene. On arrest, the skinheads confessed that they thought the couple was Jewish (Dees, 1990).

- On December 10, 1988, a skinhead in Reno, Nevada, used a .45-caliber Smith & Wesson revolver to kill an unidentified black male (Klanwatch, 1989; field notes).
- On February 7, 1988, eight skinheads attacked a group of homeless advocates in Santa Barbara, California, stomping them with Doc Martens and beating them with baseball bats (Klanwatch, 1989).
- On January 7, 1988, seven members of San Diego's WAR Skins assaulted a group of Vietnamese immigrants outside a restaurant near Ocean Beach (ADL, 1988c).
- On January 1, 1988, seven skinheads in Washington, D.C.'s Dupont Circle attacked a party of homosexuals and beat them with baseball bats and steel batons. One of the victims, Rodney Johnson, received a fractured skull, broken ribs, and a broken shoulder as his skinhead attackers shouted, "Die, faggot, die!" On arrest, one of the skinheads told a *Washington Post* reporter that if Johnson had died, "I don't think I would have felt any remorse about it" (ADL, 1988c; Shapiro, 1990:6).
- On March 15, 1988, two skinheads approached two lesbian women outside a Philadelphia bar and beat them with beer bottles (ADL, 1988c).
- On April 21, 1988, three skinheads from Halifax, North Carolina, abducted an eighteen-year-old black male and tortured him with a boa constrictor. Then the skinheads slit the young man's throat with a hunting knife, killing him (Klanwatch, 1989; field notes).
- On December 3, 1988, five skinheads in Minneapolis, Minnesota, attacked a group of black kids playing basketball. One fourteen-year-old victim was seriously beaten with a wooden club wrapped in barbed wire (Dees, 1990).
- In July 1989, eight affluent teenagers belonging to a group known as BRASH (Buffalo Rochester Aryan Skinheads) were arrested and charged with beating a thirty-year-old man. Later, members of BRASH became suspects in more than two dozen attacks against gays in the Rochester, New York, area. One skinhead suspect told police during his interrogation: "Gay bashing is when we lure a gay guy into our path and jump him. Sometimes his wallet gets stolen, but mostly we just beat him up bad" (John Brown Anti-Klan Committee, 1990a:2).
- On March 15, 1988, two members of the Los Angeles Reich Skins plead guilty to assault with a deadly weapon for pointing a gun at a Hispanic teenager after breaking into his home (ADL, 1988c).
- On June 6, 1988, a fourteen-year-old skinhead stabbed a black junior high school student three times in the back on a playground in Ventura, California (ADL, 1988c).
- On February 4, 1989, a thirteen-year-old skinhead pulled a loaded .357 Smith and Wesson revolver and threatened to shoot a Glendale, California, teacher who refused to let the skinhead wear a white power T-shirt for his school yearbook picture (ADL, 1989b; field notes).
- On May 4, 1989, four skinhead members of Tampa's American Front were stopped in Taveras, Florida, after two of the skinheads had pulled automatic assault rifles on an elderly black couple (ADL, 1989b).
- On March 18, 1989, David Timoner was shot to death with a 9-mm automatic weapon wielded by a skinhead in Denver. The skinheads then set Timoner's car afire. During a police chase the following day, one of the skinheads took a hostage while brandishing a .22-caliber handgun, proclaiming to a police negotiator that he wanted "to go out in a blaze of glory" (ADL, 1989b).
- On February 3, 1990, five members of the Confederate Hammer Skins were found guilty of putting poison gas into a Dallas synagogue's air-conditioning system, and of other racially motivated hate crimes against Hispanics at a Dallas park during the summer of 1989 (Clarke, 1991; the *New York Times*, February 4, 1990). Since then, the Confederate Hammer Skins have been linked to more than forty hate crimes in the Dallas area, including attacks on blacks and gays, and anti-Semitic and anti-Moslem vandalism (John Brown Anti-Klan Committee, 1990b; Thornburgh, 1990).

Neo-Nazi skinheads have clubbed and knifed the punk music scene into submission in Detroit, San Diego, and Los Angeles (Coplon, 1989). And following the murder of Mulugeta Seraw, Portland skinheads were implicated in forty-six hate crimes including assaults with deadly weapons (ADL, 1988c; Shapiro, 1990). During 1989 alone, the Southern Poverty Law Center discovered more than 200 skinhead arrests and prosecutions throughout the United States for murder and assaults on blacks and minorities (Dees, 1990).

Finally, academic gang theorists have traditionally based their sociological models on the following proposition:

> The violent gang is a natural, lower-class interstitial institution, resulting mainly from the weaknesses of secondary institutions, such as schools, local communities and ethnic organizations, and to some extent from the weakness of primary institutions such as the family, to provide adequate mechanisms of opportunity and social control, particularly in the transition of males from youth to adulthood (Spergel, 1984:201-2).

This means that violent gangs are a natural outgrowth of urban, underclass cultures where schools are lousy, parents don't control their children, and there is no community or ethnic organization to join when life becomes just too much for young men to endure. This is the classic sociological definition of alienation. When this happens, contemporary criminology predicts that certain young men will meet each other in the neighborhood and start a violent street gang because it is a natural product of their environment.

Yet this pre-paradigmatic construct is based on research that focuses exclusively on poor, urban, African-American, Hispanic, or Asian youth. Rarely has a study focused exclusively on a white street gang (although Short and Strodtbeck [1965] and Yablonsky [1962] offer partial exceptions). And never has a study examined a white gang that is international, rather than interstitial, in nature.

There is good reason for this. White international criminal youth subcultures are a very recent phenomenon in America. Indeed, it was not until 1986 that the word *skinhead* was even introduced into the mainstream vernacular in the United States (Coplon, 1989). As a result, social science has yet to catch up with this unique development. For example, a recent analysis entitled *Gangs in America* (Huff, 1990) includes fourteen original criminological studies of U.S. street gangs written by foremost scholars in the field of gang research. Within this 345-page volume, the word *skinhead* is not mentioned once. Nevertheless, today thousands and thousands of violent neo-Nazi skinheads are scattered throughout the United States, Great Britain, Germany, France, Spain, Holland, Belgium, Portugal, Denmark, Canada, Australia, Brazil, and Egypt (ADL, 1989b; Jackson, 1991; Mücke, 1991; Seidelpielen, 1991; Ward, 1991; field notes).

These skinhead groups have emerged under various social, economic, and political conditions. Hence, they do not share a common street corner or neighborhood culture. But they do share a common ideology. According to every published account filed to date, this ideology is *neo-Nazism* supported and sustained by a specific *style* (shaved heads, Nazi regalia, Doc Martens, and racial/ethnic violence) and *music* (white power rock).

For these important reasons, then, the skinheads do not conform to the classic criminological definition of a street gang. In fact, the skinheads seem to violate this definition in a classical way. The skinheads represent something else; something with a wider agenda that is potentially more dangerous to society, and certainly more elusive to academic gang scholars. Hence, instead of viewing the skinheads as a street gang, we must define them for what they truly are. Because of their overt racism, political violence, and links to a homologous international subculture of neo-Nazism, the skinheads constitute what can best be described as a *terrorist youth subculture*.

References

ADL (Anti-Defamation League). 1989. *Skinheads Target the Schools*. New York: ADL.

——. 1988. *Young and Violent: The Growing Menace of America's Neo-Nazi Skinheads*. New York: ADL.

Clarke, Floyd I. 1991. "Hate, Violence in the United States." *FBI Law Enforcement Bulletin*, January:14-17.

Cloward, Richard A., and Lloyd E. Ohlin. 1960. *Delinquency and Opportunity*. Glencoe, IL: Free Press.

Coplon, Jeff. 1989. "The Skinhead Reich." *Utne Reader*, May/June:80-89.

Curry, G. David, and Irving A. Spergel. 1988. "Gang Homicide, Delinquency and Community." *Criminology*, 26:381-405.

Dees, Morris. 1990. Personal communication, letter.

Erlanger, Howard S. 1979. "Estrangement, Machismo and Gang Violence." *Social Science Quarterly* 60:235-48.

Fagan, Jeffrey. 1989. "The Social Organization of Drug Use and Drug Dealing Among Urban Gangs." *Criminology*, 27:633-69.

Hagedorn, John. 1988. *People and Folks: Gangs, Crime and the Underclass in a Rustbelt City*. Chicago: Lakeview Press.

Horowitz, Ruth. 1987. "Community Tolerance of Gang Violence." *Social Problems*, 34:437-50.

Horowitz, Ruth, and Gary Schwartz. 1974. "Honor, Normative Ambiguity and Gang Violence." *American Sociological Review*, 39:238-51.

Huff, C. Ronald. 1989. "Youth Gangs and Public Policy." *Crime and Delinquency*, 35:524-37.

Jackson, James O. 1991. "Unity's Shadows." *Time*, July 1:6-14.

John Brown Anti-Klan Committee. 1990a. "Rich Kid Skinheads Bash Gays," *No KKK—No Fascist USA*, Winter/Spring:2.

——. 1990b. "$3 Million in Stolen Loot Linked to Nazi Skinheads," *No KKK—No Fascist USA*, Winter/Spring:2.

Klanwatch. 1989. *Intelligence Report*. Montgomery, AL: Southern Poverty Law Center.

Klein, Malcolm W. 1971. *Street Gangs and Street Workers*. Englewood Cliffs, NJ: Prentice Hall.

Merry, Sally. 1981. *Urban Danger*. Philadelphia: Temple University Press.

Miller, Walter B. 1958. "Lower-Class Culture as a Generating Milieu of Gang Delinquency." *Journal of Social Issues*, 15:5-19.

Moore, Joan W. 1978. *Homeboys*. Philadelphia: Temple University Press.

Morash, Mary. 1983. "Gangs, Groups and Delinquency." *British Journal of Criminology*, 23:309-31.

Mücke, Thomas. 1991. "Bericht über das projeckt—Miteinander statt gegeneiandeer." *Jervantal*:38-47.

Sanchez-Jankowski, Martin. 1991. *Islands in the Street: Gangs in American Urban Society*. Berkeley: University of California Press.

Seidelpielen, Eberhardt. 1991. *Krieg im den Stadten*. Berlin: Rotbuch, 34.

Shapiro, Lena. 1990. "Tom Metzger and White Aryan Resistance Sued for Murder." *No KKK—No Fascist USA*, Winter/Spring:1-6.

Short, James, F., and Fred L. Strodtbeck. 1965. *Group Process and Gang Delinquency*. Chicago: University of Chicago Press.

Spergel, Irving A., 1984. "Violent Gangs in Chicago: In Search of Social Policy." *Social Service Review*, 58:199-225.

——. 1964. *Racketville, Slumtown, Haulberg*. Chicago: University of Chicago Press.

Suttles, Gerald D. 1968. *The Social Order of the Slum*. Chicago: University of Chicago Press.

Taylor, Carl S. 1990. *Dangerous Society*. East Lansing: Michigan State University Press.

Thornburgh, Dick. 1990. Address before the Simon Wiesenthal Center, Chicago, on March 6.

Thrasher, Frederic. 1927, 1963. *The Gang*. Chicago: University of Chicago Press.

Vigil, James Diego. 1990. "Cholos and Gangs: Culture Change and Street Youth in Los Angeles." In C. Ronald Huff, ed., *Gangs in America*. Newbury Park, CA: Sage.

Ward, Dick. 1991. "Hate Groups Increase in Wake of Change." *CJ Europe*, 1:1-4.

Yablonsky, Lewis. 1962. *The Violent Gang*. New York: Macmillan. ✦

8

Tagger Crews and Members of the Posse

Wayne S. Wooden

Tagging is one of the latest youth behaviors classified under the category "gang." Tagger crews are groups of youths whose organizing feature is graffiti, and who compete with other crews to see who can put up the most graffiti in a given time period and/or area. Wooden discusses the motivations for and dynamics of tagging, as well as the differences he sees between tagging and gang affiliation—notably the more transitory nature of tagger crews. However, there is evidence that some tagger crews are now carrying weapons, and their rivalries may be escalating into violent encounters more frequently.

'Complex Dynamics Shape Local Graffiti Phenomenon'

On a backyard wall, 17-year-old Shawn Carter and fellow taggers crackle mixing balls of Krylon spray paint cans and fill the air with hiss and vapors of red and black, turquoise blue and cream white.

"It's addictive, once you get started, it's like a real bad habit," said Danny Canas, 17, of his "tagging"—scrawling on everything he can find. "I quit because I've got to go to college."

Canas, a Cleveland High senior who plans to attend California State University, Northridge, said he has left his tagging crew CMF—Criminals Murdering Families. But he visits his friend's house where Carter's mother lets him spray "pieces"—short for masterpiece—in peace on the backyard wall.

The addiction has drawn thousands of teen-agers—who call themselves and their rivals "toys," "taggers" or "piecers"—to devote their time to "getting up" to attain "fame" by tagging poles, benches, utility boxes, signs, bridges and freeway signs in the San Fernando Valley with graffiti.

The taggers "battle" to see who can damage as much property as possible in a set period and area to achieve greater fame.[1]

'Life's an Exciting Game of "Tag" for This Valley Youth'

As the war on graffiti escalates, so does the rhetoric. It thundered inside a Riverside convention hall Wednesday when about 400 frustrated and angry parents from across the county spent the whole day strategizing against presumably frustrated and angry teen-agers. "I have a problem with the term 'taggers,'" said one sheriff's deputy. "Visual terrorism is a more accurate term."

The adults shared tips on stopping the terrorists. Impose tougher sentences. Take away their driver's licenses. Show them healthy ways to find adventure. Teach their parents how to raise them.

If 18-year-old Paul had been there, he would have been a damper. Paul is convinced that adults can't do a thing about tagging—conference or no conference.

Paul was 13 when he began tagging, but the real rush came in high school where he found plenty of competition. "I'd say: I can do better than that. Then I made a crew. Me and a friend of mine. We went bombing together. . . . You just go out with your can. The bigger the letters, the better the bomb. The best place would be an intersection where everybody's going to pass and no one's going to miss it." Then came his arrest. "I was like, bummed. I still didn't stop though." On he sprayed, right up until he was sent to juvenile hall. "Before I left, I was one of the best writers in this town."

"The whole point of being a writer is to be up the most. To be up more than everybody else." Up. As in: up on walls. Up on billboards. And not just up. Up with style. The best taggers practice on paper, over and over, doing justice to their obsession. "Half of them are in it to do the right thing—the way it's s'posed to be."

Style or no style, it's vandalism. Paul doesn't deny it. But he regards it as you might regard driving. It pollutes the air, but you do it anyway. An unfortunate but unavoidable reality of modern life. Besides, "I never write on anyone's house. Or on a church."

The payback of tagging is respect. "Respect from your crew and respect from everyone in the valley. That's what it's about. *Respect*." And good times. "You know people are looking for you, but they'll never get you. It's night. You're undercover. You're slick."

He hated juvenile hall. He hated boarding school. He hated disappointing his parents. Yet . . . "I still would like to be up." Especially when he sees the competition. "Every morning when I drive to school. I look up and say: Ooooo. That's a good hit! I could be there! I wanna go out and burn 'em up."[2]

Welcome to the hip-hop culture of the 1990s. Once mostly the work of street gangs staking out their turf, graffiti, or tagging as it has come to be known, is now considered sport by youth from every type of neighborhood. The newest youth culture on the suburban horizon is that of tagger crews and posses.

According to police officials, as of 1993 there were 422 active crews in Los Angeles County, with names such as NBT or Nothing But Trouble that claim 400 or more members. More alarming, there were about 30,000 taggers countywide.[3]

Referred to by a variety of names—including "graffiti bands," "tagger crews," "posses" (or mob or tribe), "piecers" (because they draw masterpieces or works of art), "housers," or "snappers,"—taggers have sprawled their three-letter monikers over the landscape of Southern California. And as their fad gains more fame, the markings of taggers will likely spread across the country as well.

Dressed in the standard garb of cockeyed baseball caps, flannel shirts, hoop earrings, and low-slung, often oversized trousers, the taggers—armed with spray-paint cans, which they often shoplift, or Mean Streak marking pens—are ready for play. Some taggers, according to police officials, even carry beepers to call for backup if they are challenged by rival tagger crews.

Some parents, knowing their kids are into tagging, let them tag the walls of their room, or the inside of a backyard wall. According to one press report, one mother, whose son was in the eighth grade, told her he had joined a tagging crew. She indicated that setting aside the wall meant that her son and his friends would have a safe outlet to express themselves.

> My first reaction was to be really upset. I had just heard of graffiti. I'm a cool mom, is what I am. I allow them to express themselves within boundaries. Parents don't understand what tagging represents. I didn't understand it at first. It took me a long time to understand it. It's their identity. It's who they are, it's what they are all about.[4]

The Dynamics of Tagging

Why do youngsters tag? Similar to standard explanations for the presence of traditional, inner-city ethnic gangs is the view that tagging provides these suburban youths with a form of status. It is a declaration of "here I am." Being a member of a group or crew and splashing their tags on overhead freeway signs—referred to as "mapping the heavens"—for instance, tells others "who we are" in a big way. Another view explains the presence of suburban taggers as a response to the ethnic gangs that may be spreading into their geographical areas. To more middle-class youths, tagging becomes a symbolic defiance of inner-city urban gangs—a stark means of saying, "I'm (or we're) not afraid of ethnic gangs!"

But tagger crews are not merely the newest form of youth culture. On the contrary, according to police, their behavior has moved beyond being a simple fad. Older taggers now carry guns for protection and to be "cool." This is referred to as "tag-banging." Yet, most taggers insist they are peaceful and they do not want to "tag bang," or escalate the use of weapons to attack tag rivals. Still others, according to police, have turned to committing other crimes such as burglary and auto theft.

What is tagged varies by the age of the tagger. The younger taggers, ages 10 to 15, typically mark school grounds and property. Older teenagers, besides defacing the overhead freeway signs, target walls, public transportation such as buses and trains, and other public areas such as traffic signs, bridges, and street poles. In effect, anything that can be viewed by the public is fair game to these graffiti vandals. Less geographically bound to protecting a particular neighborhood turf than are the ethnic and inner-city gangs, the taggers spread their marks far and wide on their nightly runs.

Typically, taggers declare all public buildings and edifices as their "turf" to display their art, whereas ethnic gangs limit their gang graffiti to the neighborhood boundaries of the gang. Taggers are driven by a need to gain "instant fame" as their "work of art" is viewed by everyone. They "battle" with rival tagger crews to see who can damage as much property as possible in a given area in a set period of time—typically a week—with someone preselected as judge to declare the winner.

The Lexicon of Taggers

Along with the dress and behavior has come an entire lexicon of tagger terms including, but not limited to, the following, listed in a Southern California newspaper:

- *all city*—tagging all over, not just in one area
- *homies*—fellow members of your crew
- *kicking it*—to relax with your homies
- *toy*—an novice, amateurish tagger
- *ranker*—a person who chickens out, does not defend his tag
- *slipping*—being caught by rival taggers without homies to back you up
- *kill* or *kill a wall*—to completely cover with graffiti
- *seek and destroy*—to tag everything in sight
- *to be down*—to be a dedicated tagger, accepted by your crew
- *to get up*—to spread your tag in as many places as possible
- *to be rank*—to have the privilege of deciding who is in and out of your crew
- *hero*—an adult who would turn in a tagger
- *landmark*—a prime spot where a tag will not be erased
- *to be buffed*—to have a tag cleaned off by authorities
- *to be crossed out*—to have a tag erased by a rival tagger[5]

Still more terms were found in another newspaper:

- *bomb*—to put a series of large letters on a wall usually in more than one color
- *bombing run*—when a tagging crew comes together for the express purpose of putting up as many of their tag names and the name of their crew as they can
- *def*—a really good tagger who is considered to be "cool"
- *dis*—to disrespect someone by writing over or on another tagger's work
- *fresh*—pieces of tagging styles that are considered good
- *head*—the best tagger in a crew artwise

- *jack*—to steal a tagger's supplies, usually by robbery
- *jump-in/out*—like street gangs, several members will beat a person who wants to get into the crew or who wants to leave the crew
- *mob*—putting as much graffiti on an object as possible; usually in a short period of time
- *rack*—stealing, shoplifting paint, markers, etc.
- *rolled-up*—arrested
- *slash*—to cross out another tagger's/crew's name; meant as an insult or challenge
- *spot*—a store to shoplift from, which is kept a secret from other taggers
- *take-out*—to defeat another tagger/crew in battle
- *throw-ups*—put large bubble-style letters on an object
- *wild style*—unique style of tagging that exhibits overlapping letters[6]

Police Definition of Taggers

Because of the widespread, wanton destructive nature of taggers, police have had to come up with definitions and criteria for tagger identification. Four such criteria have been developed that assist authorities in arresting and charging graffiti vandals. These criteria include:

1. when an individual admits to being a tagger;
2. when a reliable informant identifies an individual as a tagger;
3. when an informant of previously untested reliability identifies an individual as a tagger and it is corroborated by independent information; and
4. when an individual has been arrested several times in the company of identified taggers for offenses consistent with usual tagger activity.[7]

The Proliferation of Taggers

With over 600 tagger crews identified by the police in Los Angeles County alone, the tribes have developed a variety of names or monikers. AAA, for instance, stands for Against All Authority. Some of the more prolific crews include: TIK, Think I Kare; KMT, Kings Making Trouble; CMF, Criminals Murdering Families; EWF, Every Woman's Fantasy; KNP, Knock Out Posse; and INF, Insane Family.

Other tagger names colorfully depict the nature of their activity: ABC, Artist By Choice; ACK, Artistic Criminal Kings; AIA, Artists in Action; APT, Ambushing Public Transit; BCA, Best Creative Artist; BLA, Bombing Los Angeles; CFK, Crazy Fucking Kids; CMC, Creating Mass Confusion; DFA, Defiest Boys Around; DCP, Destroying City Property; and ETC, Elite Tagger Crew, to name but a few.

Taggers are not just limited to white juvenile males. Several tagger crews reflect both ethnic and gender diversity: TWM, Tagging With Mexicans; TUL, Three United Ladies; UMK, United Mexican Kings; and RSK, Rasta Social Kings.

To the critics of taggers and to the general public fed up with the mess these youngsters have caused, TWY—Totally Wasted Youth—seems to, unfortunately, aptly size up the situation.

What Brought About the Rise of Taggers?

The tagger scene appears to be behavior that started out as an innocent form of youth culture. Known initially as "party crews" or "housers," these were youths who organized underground parties and liked to invent new dance steps. A spinoff of "house parties" and the hip-hop dress of the early 1990s, they have come up with unusual sounding names for themselves. Like every type of clique, they travel in groups, make up T-shirt designs, and on weekends and after school gather for social occasions.

The popularity of becoming part of the tagger scene also seems to stem from suburban white youths' interest in gangsta rap, the currently popular music of some black urban youths. Enjoying hip-hop music and "getting down" becomes, for these white "home boys," their form of replicating inner-city, black ghetto "chic."

To one observer, tagger crews and posses are merely a new form of seeking a distinctive identity and gaining recognition.

> For kids, the hip lexicon of the day is to call your friends your posse. It's the influence of the street culture on kids who don't necessarily want anything to do with the street. You know, suburban kids who listen to rap and hip-hop music. They think they're Marky Mark and the Funky Bunch. Posses are the way kids seek recognition.[8]

But others see taggers in the 1990s as not a new youth phenomenon at all, pointing to a group of people in the early 1970s in New York City who called themselves "TAG" for "Tough Artist Group." In fact, according to one police official, tagging crews in Southern California first appeared in the early 1980s when youngsters began writing graffiti in an exaggerated balloon-type style of writing referred to as "bombing." The most famous "graffiti artist" in the late 1980s was a youth who used the moniker "Chakka."

Another explanation given for the presence of tagger crews is the response by suburban youths—at least in the Southern California area where they have first emerged on a grand scale—to the increasing diffusion of traditional inner-city ethnic gangs outward into suburbia. Rather than merely mimicking the delinquencies and vandalism of these urban youths, suburban tagger crews are forming to compete with or oppose them. In effect, the taggers have reversed the direction of gang diffusion from inner-city outward. That is, the tagger's movement patterns—and night runs—frequently are from suburban areas along the freeways back toward the inner-city, leaving their marks or pieces (calling cards) to indicate their presence and influence along the way.

In this regard, tagging is to these blue- and white-collar suburban youths what traditional graffiti is to lower-income, traditional ethnic gangs. Tagging becomes a response to gang diffusion. As stated earlier, it is a rallying cry, claiming, "We will not be overlooked. We will not be trampled on."

In some ways, tagging is more of a "passive-aggressive" act; one is not striking out against a particular person or group. Instead, one is attacking—through tagging—the symbols or mere edifices of society. Like juvenile firesetting (the focus of a previous study I conducted), a youngster who tags buildings is being less confrontational than overtly or personally attacking his or her enemy or antagonist. Defacing a street sign, moreover, is a less drastic form of "crying for help" than torching the local school.

Differences Between Taggers and Traditional Gangs

Several differences have been noted between tagger crews and traditional inner-city ethnic gangs. For one, the name of an individual tagger as well as one's crew can often change. However, like the traditional gang, one's name, nickname, or moniker—which becomes one's personal tag—may reflect one's physical appearance or personality quirk. One youngster interviewed is named "Lurk" because he lurks or hides behind bushes.

Not all taggers belong to a tagging crew. Some prefer to work alone. By contrast, gang members—or "OG's" for "Original Gangsters" as they are now more commonly called—nearly always "hang with their homies," maintaining steady group interaction.

Interview With Members of a Tagger Crew

In an extensive interview I conducted with four members of one tagger crew, the KMTs: Kids Making Trouble (not their real name), the adolescents said there was no detailed organizational structure to their group. One 15-year-old, "Jerry," explained,

> The only organization we have is when we are in a battle. A battle is when two or more crews get together and pick an area to tag. When we do it, the battle lasts one week. Whichever crew has their name up the most is the winner.

These tagger members also contend that, unlike gangs, they do not have any special type of initiation process. None of them were "jumped in" as is the case with traditional gangs. (Police, however, claim that tagger crews are starting to use jump-ins to initiate new members.) One 16-year-old, "Travis," maintained,

> The only thing that matters is if the other members like your (art) work. You just give them a sample and they will tell you if they like your style. That's what's important to get you accepted.

Unlike traditional gangs, taggers are not territorial. There are rarely any boundaries for a tagger. Whereas traditional gangs build up and maintain their group, taggers drift in and out of crews, often changing their names whenever they tire of the old one. The number of taggers within a crew fluctuates since it is so easy to get in or out of these groups.

The taggers interviewed indicated that the members of these crews come from all socioeconomic backgrounds and races. As another teenage tagger, "Kevin," explained,

> Taggers want to get along with gangs. We are afraid of gangs in our community. All we want is to be able to write on walls. So long as we do not write over the gang names, we are safe. However, if a crew does write over a name of a gang, they must arm themselves. This is when taggers become violent. Some gangs now require "payoffs" for taggers to move through their areas.

In response to a question of what type of weapons taggers might use to defend themselves, this juvenile replied,

> Taggers will disguise chisels in pens. These are not only for protection but to permanently write on windows. One of our greatest concerns is that at night, gangs will mistake us taggers for a rival gang member and shoot us.

Kevin maintained that at first they tagged because it was fun and exciting, but fame soon took over for the initial fear they experienced.

> Everyone knows who you are. They recognize your tag. My parents at first were angry and upset, particularly when the police arrested me. But after awhile they compensated for my behavior. They told the police, "Well, at least my kid's not shooting people. He's still alive."

In discussions with another teenager, "Fred," a self-proclaimed 18-year-old "former tagger," he indicated that tagging, for him, was just a fad.

> Tagging is associated with clothes and music which always changes. My friends and I quit tagging because after awhile, it became boring. Now we throw rave parties. This is much more profitable. (Taggers often overlap in membership to "dance crews," who attend rave parties.) We have mandatory searches for weapons on entering guests. No one is discriminated against. Anyone can attend these parties for a couple of bucks. The goal of these parties is to make money. The profits go toward throwing bigger and bigger parties.

The taggers interviewed for this study did not believe that what they do is a crime. They felt strongly that their tagging was art and an expression of themselves. "When confronted by the police," one tagger told me, "I felt insulted because he called my 'pieces' graffiti!"

References

1. Jaxon Van Derbeken, "Complex Dynamics Shape Local Graffiti Phenomenon," *The Daily News* (28 February 1993), p. A-1.
2. Shellee Nunley, "Life's an Exciting Game of 'Tag' for This Valley Youth," *The Desert Sun* (2 October 1993), p. A-3.
3. John M. Glionna, "Pals in the Posse: Teen Culture Has Seized the Word as a Hip Name for Groups; Not All Are Harmless," *The Los Angeles Times* (26 February 1993), p. B-3.
4. Van Derbeken, p. 14.
5. John M. Glionna, "Leaving Their Mark: Youths Risk Everything to Tag Walls, Buses and Traffic Signs with Graffiti," *The Los Angeles Times* (10 March 1993), p. B-1.
6. Van Derbeken, p. 14.
7. "Taggers" pamphlet, Los Angeles and Orange Counties LASD-Transit Services Bureau, February 9, 1993.
8. Glionna, "Pals in the Posse," p. 4. ✦

Female Gang Involvement

9

Female Participation in Gangs

Anne Campbell

Much early research on female gang involvement has been criticized for its reliance on and reinforcement of gender stereotypes. In this essay, Campbell provides a review of early accounts of female gang involvement, and presents a thorough assessment of the ways in which these works were shaped by an inaccurate picture of these girls as socially isolated and unable to form strong peer relationships. In contrast to the earlier work she critiques, Campbell provides evidence of the importance of peers and peer friendships among girls in gangs, and discusses the ways in which gang membership provides a means for some female youths to cope with the problems they face in their communities and society.

The Invisible Female Peer Group

The peer group has long been identified as one of the most powerful variables in explanations of male delinquency. By contrast, the female delinquent has been depicted as isolated and inept; a pitiful figure trying to assuage her loneliness through brief, promiscuous liaisons with boys (see Campbell, 1980; Giordano, Cernkovich, and Pugh, 1986). I begin this chapter by reviewing three myths that gave rise to this erroneous picture of social isolation (see Campbell, in press, for a fuller discussion).

Myth 1: Female delinquency is equivalent to sexual promiscuity, and symptomatic of maladjustment and social isolation. In 1968, Cowie, Cowie, and Slater wrote: "The nature of delinquent offenses among girls is completely different to the delinquent offenses committed by boys. A large part of the delinquencies of girls consist in sexually ill-regulated behavior of a type not to demand social sanctions in the case of an adult" (p. 43). The translation of female delinquency into sexual promiscuity led to a characterization of such girls as rejecting female peers in favor of brief, unsatisfactory affairs with exploitative older men (Cowie et al., 1968; Konopka, 1966; Richardson, 1969; Thomas, 1923; Vedder & Sommerville, 1975). Chesney-Lind (1974) challenged this view when she suggested that the prevalence of female status offenders was exaggerated by an overreliance on official juvenile court data. Although boys also engaged in precocious sex, it was girls who were processed systematically and stigmatized for it. Self-report studies of delinquency have confirmed this (Campbell, 1981; Canter, 1982b; Cernkovich & Giordano, 1979; Gold & Reimer, 1975; Hindelang, 1971; Weis, 1976). Self-report data provide no evidence that girls specialize in the solitary status offenses that previously were thought to characterize female delinquency. Indeed, Emler, Reicher, and Ross (1987) found "that girls are if anything even more likely than boys to commit any offenses in the company of others" (p. 99).

Myth 2: Family factors exert a more powerful influence on female than on male delinquents. Common sense suggests that girls are subject to much stricter control and supervision by the family than are boys, and this observation has been borne out by studies showing that daughters are perceived by their parents to be more vulnerable and to require more protection than boys (Block, 1978; Lynn, 1974; Maccoby & Jacklin, 1974). There are two fundamental issues here. First, are girls in fact subject to stricter parental control than boys? The answer is a resounding affirmative (Canter, 1982a; Cernkovich & Giordano, 1987; Hagan, Simpson, & Gillis, 1979; Singer & Levine, 1988). The second question is of greater concern: Do family variables explain more variance in female delinquency than in male delinquency? If the answer is yes, then we have found strong justification for the relative paucity of attention to the peer group as a factor in female delinquency. Loeber and Stouthamer-Loeber (1986) conducted a comprehensive meta-analysis of the impact of family factors on delinquency; they conclude: "In general, parental behavior was related to child conduct problems to the same degree for each sex" (p. 126). Subsequent studies, although finding gender differences in the nature of the family's impact on delinquency, report no significant differences in the size of the effect (Cernkovich & Giordano, 1987; Hill & Atkinson, 1988).

Myth 3: Girls do not form strong same-sex friendships. Early studies of female delinquency explicitly focused upon "relational strivings" and success in marriage as being the arena of self-expression, status, and competition among girls (Konopka, 1966; Morris, 1964; Rittenhouse, 1963; Sandhu & Allen, 1969). It is hardly surprising, then, that teenage girls were viewed as barely capable of warm same-sex friendships, because adolescence was seen as a marketplace competition for a mate. The data, however, tell a different story. Giordano et al. (1986) interviewed 942 teenagers about their friendships, using 13 dimensions of the quality of these relationships. Of these dimensions, 11 showed significant sex differences favoring girls. Girls were, among other things, more self-disclosing, more caring, and more trusting of and loyal to their friends. Giordano (1978) and Bowker and Klein (1983) found that female delinquency increased as a function of membership of a regular group, the amount of time spent in the group, and the frequency of peer contact. Figueira-McDonough, Barton, and Sarri (1981) reported striking similarity in the models of peer impact on delinquency for the two sexes. A high degree of involvement with peers and normative approval of deviant behavior explained similar amounts of variance in delinquency for boys and girls. Morash (1983) reported that the delinquent behavior of peers outweighed any other single factor in explaining individual delinquency for both sexes (.58 for boys, .44 for girls).

In sum, girls have equally good (arguably better) peer relations as boys and their delinquency depends as much on close association with delinquent others as it does for boys. In spite of this, it traditionally has been assumed that it is girls' relationships with boys, rather than with other girls, that produce delinquent behavior. When the delinquent girl is allowed a peer group, the only meaningful characters in it are male.

Early Accounts of Female Gang Participation

Not withstanding the ubiquitous problem of definition (Klein & Maxson, 1989; Miller, 1980), the gang has provided a natural forum for those interested in the interpersonal dynamics of group delinquency. Girls have been a part of gangs since the earliest accounts from New York in the early 1800s (Asbury, 1927). Their presence is not in dispute. The problematic issue revolves around the *form* of their participation.

In early writings girls were defined solely in terms of their interpersonal and structural relations to male gang members. They also were described through three layers of potential distortion: Their roles were described by male gang members to male researchers and interpreted by male academics. This does not in itself guarantee bias, but it introduces some troubling issues. Perhaps an example from the literature can illustrate. In 1965 a street worker reported:

> They just pull the girl off to the side and start rapping to her. . . . Jake will lay a broad right on the bench but most of them will take the girl off somewhere to one of these junked cars and lay her there. . . . They'll discuss who's fucking and who's not, how much time it takes for this one and how much time it takes for that one. (Short & Strodtbeck, 1965, p. 36)

At the first level, male members have much to gain by casting females in secondary roles as cheerleaders or camp followers. To the male gang worker, this reported secondary status may be accepted unproblematically because his avowed focus is upon male members and consequently his direct access to the world of the female gang member may be limited. Theorists who base their work on such information may be led to draw conclusions that fit coherently with theory but not necessarily with the facts. A. K. Cohen (1955), for example, argued that a girl is most likely to express the strain between long-term goals and the realistic likelihood of achieving them through an appropriately female channel—sexuality. Just as the "college boy" must relinquish short-term enjoyment for later benefits, so must the "good girl" learn to maintain her sexual attractiveness without becoming sexually accessible. In this way, she increases her market value in marriage, with its concomitant promise of upward social mobility. The "bad girl," who rejects this ethic, expresses her disdain by allowing free sexual access to males. From such a position, one might expect the girl to wear her promiscuity proudly, as a badge of rebellion. Those who have spoken with the girls themselves rather than accepting male gang members' accounts concur that this is not the case. Young women do not gain positive status from peers if they develop reputations for visible promiscuity (Brake, 1980; Horowitz, 1983; McRobbie, 1978; Smart & Smart, 1978).

The reliance on male gang informants began to change around 1970, and at the same time a rather different image of female participation also emerged. But it would be a mistake to conclude that male gang members had willfully given a distorted picture. It may be the case that the roles of girls did in fact alter gangs or, to put it another way, that the older material was true *at the time it was given*.

With such caveats in mind, it would be fair to say that gang girls, according to early writings, had the unenviable choice of two roles. Rice (1963) describes the problem in a nutshell:

> If a girl fights as well as a boy—and Youth Board workers know girls who do—boys don't like her, and in no walk of life is a girl who boys don't like an object of admiration or envy to other girls. By the same token, the one kind of status that carousing can confer is manly status, and to the extent that gang girls carouse they merely lessen the possibility that they will achieve the womanly status of being considered desirable mates. (p. 153)

Gang girls were either tomboys or sex objects. In terms of the literature, the latter seems to have proved more popular. In using the term *sex object*, I include those behaviors or roles that are distinguished by the fact that they conventionally require a sexually attractive female to perform them. This encompasses being a girlfriend to a male member, providing sexual services to gang boys, luring rival male members to preassigned locations (usually for the alleged purpose of sex or parties), acting as a spy by establishing a romantic relationship with a boy from an enemy gang, and carrying drugs or weapons for the boys (because girls are less likely to be searched by male police officers).

Thrasher's (1927) account of Chicago gangs found them to be overwhelmingly male. Those gangs that did include girls, however, he described as immoral rather than conflict gangs. Their chief activities included petting, necking, illicit sex, and mugging. They had names like the Tulips, the Lone Star Club, the Under the L gang and the Night Riders. They had clandestine signals that were used in the classroom to arrange secret meetings in vacant lots or deserted barns between a boy and a girl.

Bernard (1949) reported the growth of female gang membership in New York. Virtually all the female gangs were affiliated with male gangs, although they took on their own names, such as the Robinettes, the Chandeliers, and the Shangri-la Debs. Probation reports described initiation rituals that required prospective members to have intercourse with male gang members. Older girls were reported to have procured younger girls for the boys, with the express intention of rape. During the war years, groups of gang girls would pick up soldiers and lure them into side streets, where their male accomplices, too young to be drafted, would "roll" them. A girl might be dispatched to seduce rival gang leaders while her own gang notified the police of her whereabouts and claimed she was being raped. Characteristically, the girls' functions were to carry weapons (being immune to search by male officers), provide alibis, act as spies and lures, and provide sex for the male members. The overwhelming impression is of gang girls as sexual property.

The 1950s was the era of the street worker. Social workers attempted to reach and reform (or at least control) the behavior of teenage gangs. In 1950, the Welfare Council of New York City published a report on their attempt to work with Harlem gangs and their girls' affiliates. The girls were either sisters or friends of those in the male group. The majority were described as sexually promiscuous, and illegitimate births were "common." The girls incited and supported the boys' lawbreaking, while playing little part in it themselves. Occasionally, some of the girls drank or used narcotics and a few truanted from school. They are described by the street workers as passive, exploited people of low self-concept and ability. As one male member told a street worker:

> You take what you want from them. When they get off the beam and don't act right, slap them around so they'll know who's who. (Welfare Council of New York City, 1950, p. 16)

Girls were seen as sexual objects to be cajoled, tricked, or forced into sexual relations. No mention is made of the rapes, gang bangs, or homosexual prostitution of the boys—let alone their involvement in normal, if precocious, sex. The street workers' aim seems to have been not to encourage girls' independence from boys, but to inculcate "feminine" middle-class values about their sexuality and its worth by conducting classes in cosmetics and etiquette, organizing sewing parties, and getting together charity boxes to send to foreign countries.

In 1963, Rice reported on the Persian Queens in Brownsville, Brooklyn. The gang numbered only seven girls, whom Rice describes as "dim" and "exceptionally unattractive." The role that Rice concentrated upon most heavily was that of sexual consort for the boys: The girls were "delighted to drink with the Mohawks, sleep with the Mohawks and, if the occasion demanded, carry weapons and furnish alibis for the Mohawks." Hanson's (1964) account of another New York female gang, the Dagger Debs, was based upon accounts drawn from New York City Youth Board's files. The Dagger Debs numbered 12 members, and their structure included a president, a prime minister, and a war counselor. They had a "clubhouse" (an abandoned apartment) that was used for meetings and making out with members of their brother gang, the Daggers. Although Hanson makes passing reference to the girls' involvement in mugging and shoplifting, the major stress is on their sexuality. Hanson documents the girls' early initiation into sexual activities, their universal lack of genuine sexual enjoyment, and their ignorance of reproduction and birth control.

> They will oblige on rooftops or in cellars, on park benches or in the grass. They stand in halls and doorways or disappear briefly into dark corners. They behave like prostitutes, but most of them are not. They have such a low opinion of themselves, they don't even charge. (p. 70)

The street worker aimed to turn them into "ladies" by starting a charm clinic and teaching them how to eat in restaurants and shop in department stores.

Fishman (1988) has reanalyzed qualitative data also collected in the 1960s on the Vice Queens, a Black female affiliate of the Vice Kings of Chicago. Their principal roles were traditional—sexual objects, drinking partners, weapons carriers, and lookouts. They fought other female gangs, but took particular pride in exploiting their femininity to instigate inter- and intragang fights among the boys. By reporting "passes" made by members of rival gangs, they manipulated the Vice Kings into fighting for their honor. Their raison d'être was the male group, and they had "little function outside the mating-dating complex." They competed, often violently, for the attention of the male gang members, and status within the group was largely dependent on relationships with particular boys. Going steady with or having a baby by a high-status boy was prestigious, but there was no anticipation by either sex of long-term commitment or marriage.

The gang girl faced a no-win situation. If she had sex, she was rejected by the very boys she sought to attract. If instead she emulated male behavior, she ran the risk of being rejected as a tomboy. Nevertheless, early reports make it clear that some girls opted for this latter role. Asbury (1927) describes young women like Hell-Cat Maggie and Battle Annie, who, in 1850s New York, had reputations for their fighting ability. Thrasher (1927) notes that at the youngest age before adolescence, girls who took part in ganging engaged in the same kinds of misbehavior as the boys and were eager to outdo them. They excluded "feminine" girls from their gang exploits. With the awakening of interest in romantic relationships, however, the girls became self-conscious and left the gang. Miller's (1973) tomboys were the Molls, an all-White, Catholic gang of 11 girls aged between 13 and 16. The Molls played hooky, stole, drank, vandalized, and fought. They attempted to gain favor with their male companion group (the Hoods) by emulating and abetting the boys' criminal activities, but *not* by freely dispensing sexual favors to them. The girls made no effort to deny their dependence upon the Hoods, however, and in fact seemed quite proud to acknowledge their reliance upon them.

This historical emphasis upon the "rogue male" as the Svengali of gang girls has been challenged by more recent quantitative results. Giordano (1978) conducted interviews with teenage girls in which a self-report delinquency scale was used in addition to a number of questions about friendship patterns. Gang girls reported more delinquent acts than non-gang girls and, when asked about the degree of approval they would receive for delinquent acts from different members of their peer groups, the highest approval rating came from *other girls* rather than from boys. Bowker and Klein (1983) reported similar results with another female sample. They used six measures of the quality and intensity of female friendships, all of which showed a relationship with number of delinquent offenses, gang membership, or both. They conclude that "relations with *girlfriends are quite a bit more important* than relations with boyfriends in determining gang membership and the seriousness of delinquency among the girls in our study" (p. 745).

Contemporary Accounts: Gang Rhetoric

More contemporary qualitative work on female gangs (in which I include work from 1970 to 1989) has come from direct contact with the girls themselves, rather than once removed, from male members. These works, based upon intensive interviews or participant observation, have taken female gangs as collectives to be explained in their own right. Hispanic girls have been the principal objects of study, both Chicanas in Los Angeles (M.G. Harris, 1988; Quicker, 1983) and Chicago (Horowitz, 1983) and Puerto Ricans in New York (Campbell, 1984). There has been much less attention to Black, Asian, or White girls (but see Brown, 1977; Campbell, 1984; Hagedorn, 1987; Miller, 1973).

If we are to account for female gang membership in its own terms rather than as an interesting comparative footnote to the male gang, it is important to incorporate the community and class context in which these girls live and to identify what it means to be a woman growing up in and adapting to these conditions. This involves the examination of gang youth in relation to both the parent culture (the ethnic working-class or poverty-class community from which they spring) and the mainstream culture of which their class forms a marginal part. Gangs can be seen as representing a means by which some youths seek to resolve the problems presented by their structural position in relation to both these groups.

The words and actions of gang members seek to resolve the intractable problems of class by simultaneously rejecting and opposing some aspects of community and mainstream values while incorporating and internalizing others (Cohen, 1972; Hall & Jefferson, 1976). Their resulting identity is often apparently contradictory or incoherent (Campbell, 1987). They commit crimes while opposing criminals. They want independence while also wanting strong, dependable mates. They oppose hard drug use while simultaneously counting drug users among their members and dealing drugs on street corners. As Goodman (1960) puts it, "We cannot expect average kids to deviate with genius."

What are the problems that face poverty-class girls, the problems for which they seek answers in the gang?

(1) A future of meaningless domestic labor with little possibility of educational or occupational escape. For potential gang members, the possibility of a career is effectively nonexistent, and the possibility of a low-paying job is remote. Many come from mothers who have survived largely on welfare, supplemented by the marginal economy (Campbell, 1984; Moore, 1988). They are school dropouts with poor literacy skills (Moore, 1989a). When asked about jobs, their standard responses are in terms of hopelessly unattainable goals, such as being a rock star or professional model. They do not aspire to the kind of minimum-wage opportunities that are realistically available to them. Thus the future that awaits them is within the home.

(2) Subordination to the man in the house. In Hispanic culture the right of the male to dictate, control, and discipline his wife is accepted widely (Acosta-Belen & Christenson, 1979). As the breadwinner (and even when he is not a breadwinner), he will make decisions that circumscribe the possibilities that are open to her.

(3) Responsibility for children. As a mother, the Hispanic woman achieves considerable status within the household, but the practical constraints of raising children necessarily restrict her options, as does the required demeanor of motherhood (Fitzpatrick, 1971).

(4) The social isolation of the housewife. As her children grow up and pursue their lives, she will find herself trapped at home. At best she will have a circle of female kin and near-kin around the neighborhood; at worst she will be isolated in a project apartment.

(5) The powerlessness of underclass membership. Much has been written on the structural and cultural roots of powerlessness in poverty-level life (Wilson 1987). The marginality of these women in relation to the male economic and social world produces a triple remoteness from effective initiative. Handicapped by class, race, and gender, these women are victims of the system at an economic and social level. But they are also, more concretely, victims of crime and violence within their communities and their homes.

For these girls, the period of adolescence (which, defined as the cessation of childhood, may begin as early as age 8) is a brief interlude before they are incorporated into adult Hispanic identity and the economic, practical, and social constraints outlined above. The gang represents for its members an idealized collective solution to the bleak future that awaits. The members construct for themselves, at a rhetorical level, an image of the gang that counterpoints the suffocating future they face. In short, the members tacitly conspire to portray the gang to themselves—as well as to others—in a particularly romantic light. Irwin (1970) describes a similar process among adult criminals:

> This mutual support of each others' delusions among criminals is not simply dissembling. It is more a process of subtle distortion of reality by which they themselves are fooled. It is a process of selecting the most prestigious occurrences, amounts and acts for retelling and forgetting the less prestigious.

Miller (1974) has also noted the tendency for gangs to develop "standardized answers" to outsiders' questions and has expressed surprise at the extent to which their statements are given credence by researchers. Indeed, some writers do seem to have accepted the more romantic presentations given by girl gang members uncritically. The position I adopt is that such gang rhetoric is not designed solely to fool researchers, but also to fool the gang members using it.

Much is made of the "rebel" or "outlaw" nature of the gang. The gang is cast in direct opposition to the straight, anemic world of conformity. Unlike the rest of us, gang members are free from the mundane demands of Mertonian ritualism. Their dress, their swagger, their craziness are all brandished as evidence of their proud independence of the straight world.

> They can't feel the things we feel or the way our life-style is. The [mainstream] Man says, "How can you all be doing this or doing that?" He tries to analyze our life-style. "How do you do this?" and all this kind of shit. We don't want them to get inside us, we don't want them to. (Campbell, 1984)

Boyfriend-girlfriend relationships are elaborated similarly. The boy's possessiveness and his jealousy of potential rivals are seen as clear evidence of his passionate attachment to his partner. For this period of her life at least the girl is young and desirable, inciting passion and stormy emotions. Consequently, the beatings that she may receive at his hands when he believes that she has been unfaithful are interpreted as a direct index of his love for her. The problem lies not in his violent and often insecure disposition, but in the peculiarly extreme nature of their romance. This belief is adhered to even in the face of evidence that would tend to undermine it. For example, his infidelity is blamed upon his desirability to other women, rather than seen as evidence of his less-than-total commitment to her. In this way, the tyranny of males over females is translated into the problem of his passion for her, and the institutionalized female goal of attracting a man is not merely met but exceeded. She lives out the idealized female role that has been fed to her through magazines, soap operas, and romance novels (Brake, 1980; McRobbie, 1978).

> You have to be playing games with your old man. Sometimes you might have to be the sister, sometimes you have to be the lover. I don't want him to be with me because he married me and I'm his wife and he comes home every night to this wife. No, I want him to come home to his WIFE. "Wow, my wife." Sometimes I feel my love for him is too strong. It must be that love is always being jealous. Love does hurt. Love is always saying "I'm sorry." I hate him for loving him and I love him for hating him. (Campbell, 1984)

Gang members refer to one another as "sisters" or "homegirls" and to the gang as "family" (Brown, 1977; Campbell, 1984; Harris, 1988; Quicker, 1983). These terms conjure the sense of belonging and identification that are frequent themes in their conversation. The exaggerated sense of "we-ness" is best exemplified when the group is under threat from beyond, by rival gangs' incursions into the neighborhood or by police arrests. This intense in-group loyalty is particularly important to gang members. The home lives of gang girls are marked frequently by breakdown and dysfunction, at worst resulting in physical and sexual abuse (Campbell, 1984; Moore, 1988). The fragility of family relationships often is compounded by frequent changes of residence and early school truancy and dropout. The girls often speak of themselves as "loners" before joining the gang, barely connected to their schoolmates or to neighborhood peer groups.

> I don't trust anyone else, that's why. They're the only ones I can depend on, 'cause I know if I get into hassles, they'll help me. Like one time we went to B___. We used to go to hang around there, and some girls there were going to jump me, and all the girls I was with took off and they left me there alone. That's when I said I was only going to hang around with my homegirls. (Quicker, 1983)

The sisterhood of the gang is reinforced conversationally to compensate for the internal divisions that are not uncommon. Quarrels between the girls over boyfriends occur with regularity (Campbell, 1984; M. G. Harris, 1988; Horowitz, 1983; Quicker, 1983). If a girl is challenged on foreign turf, there is a normative prescription for her to state proudly her gang allegiance, even if this leads to an outnumbered attack and serious beating (M. G. Harris, 1988). Much is made of the bravery of girls who adhere to this norm to compensate for the times that discretion triumphs over valor. Even informing on fellow gang members to the police is not unknown. None of this, however, would be evident if one took at face value the idealized collective representation of loyalty in their social talk.

Street talk also highlights the glory days: the spontaneous parties, the pranks, the drink and drugs. More than anything else gang membership is seen as fun. Stories are told and retold of astonishing chemical intakes, of "crazy" behavior and "wild" parties. These events stand as a bulwark against the loneliness and drudgery of their future lives. They also belie the day-to-day reality of gang life. The lack of recreational opportunities, the long days unfilled by work or school, and the absence of money mean that hours and days are whiled away on street corners (Corrigan, 1976; Klein, 1971). "Doing nothing" means hanging out on the stoop; the hours of "bullshit" punctuated by trips to the store to buy one can of beer at a time. When an unexpected windfall arrives, marijuana and rum are purchased in bulk and the partying begins. The next day, life returns to normal.

Toughness and craziness are inextricably linked in the construction of a street reputation. Toughness denotes an unwillingness to back down in the face of threat (real or imagined); craziness indicates the labile, unpredictable nature of their response. The combination wards off the specter of people "fucking with us." As others have noted in connection with male gang members (Miller, 1966a) and British soccer fans (Marsh, Rosser, & Harre, 1978), much of the violence of these youths occurs in the world of talk rather than of action. The bellicose reputation in which they take pride is given considerably more weight in conversation than is the fear that lurks beneath it. They fear being a "dud"—a victim at the mercy of others. In their neighborhoods, where violence and even death are not uncommon, having a "rep" is preferable to walking scared, to being powerless. But the rep they work so hard to achieve sets them up as targets for others who are seeking to expand their own reps. There is the abiding fear that "there's always someone tougher than you."

> I always get nervous, even when I'm just arguing with somebody. I get nervous. There's times, yeah, I see a real big girl, then I get scared. I think, "Damn, I'm going to hurt her or she's going to hurt me." But once you're in a fight, you just think—you've got to fuck that girl up before she does it to you. You've got to really blow off on her. You just play it crazy. That's when they get scared of you. It's true—you feel proud when you see a girl that you fucked up. (Campbell, 1984)

Contemporary Accounts: Gang Life

Miller (1975) identified three possible relations between female gang members and male gangs: as independently functioning units, as regular members in "coed" gangs, and as female auxiliaries of male groups. Researchers overwhelmingly have found the last of these to be most common. Only Brown (1977) in Philadelphia has documented a wholly autonomous gang of girls. Although such groups may exist, they are far from typical. The female group usually comes into existence after the male gang has been established and often takes a feminized version of the male name. In Los Angeles, as with the male gangs, the girls may be subdivided further into age cohorts or *klikas* (M.G. Harris, 1988). The older girls may share with the boys the name of *chicas*, the younger girls *locas* (Quicker, 1983). Leadership is usually more diffuse than in the boys' groups. Typically the members insist there is no leader and that decisions are made democratically. Observation suggests that some girls clearly have more clout than others, but that this usually is not formalized as a leadership role. Some gangs have *"veteranas,"* or "godmothers," older women (often in their 20s or 30s) with considerable gang experience who often counsel on gang-related and personal problems.

Girls from the neighborhood (and beyond) are not pressured or coerced into joining. Potential members come not only through friendship networks but through family ties (M. G. Harris, 1988; Moore, 1988). Prospects or "wanna-bes" spend time with the gang and are screened informally as to their acceptability. Where a formal initiation ceremony exists, it usually takes the form of a prearranged fistfight between the prospect and an established member. The function of this "jumping in" is to prove publicly the new girl's ability to fight. She need not win the encounter; she must, however, demonstrate her "heart" or courage. This initiation also deters girls who might join for the wrong reasons—to "use" the gang as backup in some private dispute, to gain access to the boys, or to act as spies for a rival group.

The girls regulate their own affairs. They may collect dues, hold meetings, and initiate, discipline, or expel members. They are hostile to attempts by the male gang leader to intervene in these matters. Occasionally a male gang member may try to influence the girls to accept a boy's girlfriend into their ranks. The girls insist on putting her through the usual period of supervision and making their own decision. They are usually suspicious of such prospects, believing that the girl's motivation is weighted more heavily toward romance than toward sisterhood. They are possessive of their men and consequently resentful of outsiders who want the kudos of romance with a gang boy without the long-term commitment and dangers of gang loyalty. This hostility usually is couched, however, in terms of a security issue (the outsiders may be spies from other gangs) rather than as a matter of possessiveness (Campbell, 1984).

Disciplinary issues are usually informal. At a group meeting, the misbehavior is described and the group expresses its approbation, warning the offender to mend her ways or risk expulsion. Misbehaviors may include failing to support another homegirl in a fight, failing to identify oneself as a gang member when "hit up" by another gang, theft from other members, informing on group crimes, and associating with male members of rival groups. The most frequent source of conflict is stealing another girl's boyfriend (Campbell, 1984; M. G. Harris, 1988).

Gang girls exert strong normative control over one another's sexuality, as do working-class girls generally (Smart & Smart, 1978). They are acutely sensitive to the community's view of them as sexually "cheap" and—for Hispanic girls particularly—this is one of the most painful costs of gang membership (Horowitz, 1983). Serial monogamy is expected. The more cohesive the gang, the more likely it is that the girls will be expected to select their partners from the ranks of the male gang. Association with nonaligned community boys or even with members of other gangs (if they are at peace with them) may also be tolerated (M. G. Harris, 1988). Once a girl becomes involved with a boy she is expected to remain faithful until the relationship ends. Suspicion and jealousy are probably the most disruptive forces in the gang, and the strong enforcement of norms of fidelity helps to minimize the destructive potential.

Fights usually are directed at members of rival female gangs. (It is rare, but not unheard of, for the girls to take on male gang members. To do so confers particular kudos.) Enemies are disparaged as "hos" (whores) and "glue-sniffers." They frequently are characterized as the mere sex objects of their men, lacking the courage to fight for or defend them. Although often insisting that they do not look for trouble (trouble just finds them), they will enter rival territory to provoke a confrontation or to paint their *plaka* or gang symbol (M. G. Harris, 1988). This constitutes a very direct challenge to their enemies. Territory or turf remains a focal issue not only as a symbolic matter of gang integrity but as an economic base where the gang reserves the right to deal drugs. The girls view turf more in the former terms. Although the boys may use guns, the girls most often are involved in fist or knife fights (Campbell, 1984; M. G. Harris, 1988).

The tough image to which the girls aspire is a source of ambivalence for both sexes. For their part the girls take pride in their independent forays against (and triumphs over) other gangs. At the same time, they are gratified both by the boys' determination to protect them from more lethal encounters and their intervention when they see a homegirl being beaten in a fight (Horowitz, 1983; Quicker, 1983). The boys are equally proud of the girls' "heart," although there is often a somewhat patronizing tone to their accolades. They frequently insist that the gang is not the place for girls and may encourage their own girlfriends to stay out of gang affairs (Quicker, 1983).

Because the boys' approval is central to the girl gang's existence, the girls often publicly defer to the males. In Los Angeles, the girls' uniform includes Pendleton jackets, T-shirts, drapes, and flat shoes. In New York, denim sleeveless jackets with combat boots and handkerchiefs were popular. If the boys object to the outfits as too "butch," however, the girls will reserve the full outfit only for encounters with rival gang members (Campbell, 1984). When both sexes are present, the girls tend to remain quiet, allowing the boys to do most of the talking.

This deference is in marked contrast to the way the girls talk when the boys are not present. Then their attitude is transformed into indulgence. Men are infantilized in talk; they are cast as willful, hot-blooded children prone to outbursts of anger and passion. They do not always know what is good for them and it is women's place to steer the men invisibly in the direction that they wish them to go. Nowhere is this more evident than in the discussion of male infidelity. Men are, by nature, unable to refuse an offer of sex. Consequently, it is not the boy's fault when he strays but rather the other woman's. The confrontation is recast as between the girlfriend and her rival, rather than between the girl and the boy. Consequently, sexual betrayal is terminated by an attack on the rival, not on the boyfriend, who simply was following his nature. This view of men seems to be widespread in Hispanic culture, but it is realized in a more public and violent way through the encouragement of other gang members.

For most girls, leaving the gang occurs at the end of adolescence. For many it coincides with the birth of a child and the unwelcome realization of the constraints that this entails. Some have mothers who are willing to raise their children for them, but others, by choice or necessity, take on the full-time care of their children. Some find themselves in juvenile institutions, prisons, or drug treatment centers. An unfortunate few graduate to heroin use, and their dependence on the drug overtakes their loyalty to the gang. Others set up stable relationships with men and slip away from the life on the streets. Some researchers have described more ritualized exits, in which members are "jumped out" (M. G. Harris, 1988; Quicker, 1983). These involve severe beatings by a number of homegirls, sometimes resulting in hospitalization. Whether or not "jumping out" occurs seems to be a function of the extent of the girl's previous involvement, her motives for leaving, and the formality with which she announces her intended departure. Most girls are wise enough to diminish their involvement over time rather than precipitate group sanction by framing their leave-taking as an act of betrayal.

Conclusion

The picture constructed here of female gang membership is incomplete and provisional. Lack of research data makes the task of synthesis similar to trying to construct a jigsaw puzzle with most of the pieces missing. We barely have the pieces to begin a similar picture for Black and White female gangs, and even the above sketch may be distorted by the summing of data from Chicana and Puerto Rican girls (Moore, 1988). The economic and social plight of male gang members has encouraged considerable research; our concern should be no less for women than for men. Recent data suggests that the future awaiting gang girls is bleak indeed: 94% will go on to have children, and 84% will raise them without spouses (Hagedorn, 1987; Moore, 1988). One-third of them will be arrested, and the vast majority will be dependent on welfare. The attraction of the gang is no mystery in the context of the isolation and poverty that is awaiting them.

References

Acosta-Belen, E., & Christenson, E.H. (1979). *The Puerto Rican Woman*. New York: Praeger.

Asbury, H. (1927). *The Gangs of New York*. New York: Capricorn.

Bernard, W. (1949). *Jailbait*. New York: Greenberg.

Block, J.H. (1978). Another look at sex differentiation in the socialization behavior of mothers and fathers. In F. Wermarle & J. Sherman (Eds.), *Psychology of women: Future directions of research*. New York: Psychological Dimensions.

Bowker, L.H., & Klein, M.W. (1983). The etiology of female juvenile delinquency and gang membership: A test of psychological and social structural explanations. *Adolescence*, 18:740-751.

Brake, M. (1980). *The sociology of youth culture and youth subcultures*. London: Routledge & Kegan Paul.

Brown, W.K. (1977) Black female gangs in Philadelphia. *International Journal of Offender Therapy and Comparative Criminology*, 21, 221-228.

Campbell, A. (1980). Friendship as a factor in male and female delinquency. In H.C. Foot, A.J. Chapman, & J.R. Smith (Eds.), *Friendships and social relations in children*. New York: John Wiley.

——(1981). *Girl delinquents*. Oxford: Basil Blackwell.

——(1984). *The girls in the gang*. New York: Basil Blackwell.

—— (1987). Self-definition by rejection: The case of gang girls. *Social Problems*, 34, 451-466.

—— [in press]. On the invisibility of the female delinquent peer group. *Women and Criminal Justice*.

Canter, R.J. (1982a). Family correlates of male and female delinquency. *Criminology*, 20, 149-167.

—— (1982b). Sex difference in self-report delinquency. *Criminology*, 20, 373-393.

Cernkovich, S.A., & Giordano, P.C. (1979). A comparative analysis of male and female delinquency. *Sociological Quarterly*, 20, 131-145.

——(1987). Family relationships and delinquency. *Criminology*, 25, 295-319.

Chesney-Lind, M. (1974). Juvenile delinquency: The sexualization of female crime. *Psychology Today*, 8, 43ff.

Cohen, A.K. (1955). *Delinquent boys: The culture of the gang*. Glencoe, IL: Free Press.

Cohen, P. (1972). *Sub-cultural conflict and working class community* (Working Papers in Cultural Studies, No. 2). Birmingham, England: University of Birmingham.

Corrigan, P. (1976). Doing nothing. In S. Hall & T. Jefferson (Eds.), *Resistance through rituals*. London: Hutchinson.

Cowie, J., Cowie, B., & Slater, E. (1968). *Delinquency in Girls*. London: Heinemann.

Figueria-McDonough, J., Barton, W.H., & Sarri, R.C. (1981). Normal deviance: Gender similarities in adolescent subcultures. In M.Q. Warren (Ed.), *Comparing female and males offenders*. Beverly Hills: Sage.

Fishman, L. (1988). *The Vice Queens: An ethnographic study of black female gang behavior*. Paper presented at the annual meeting of the American Society of Criminology, Chicago.

Fitzpatrick, J. (1971). *Puerto Rican Americans: The meaning of migration to the mainland*. Englewood Cliffs, NJ: Prentice-Hall.

Giordano, P.C. (1978). Girls, guys, and gangs: The changing social context of female delinquency. *Journal of Criminal Law and Criminology*, 69, 126-132.

Giordano, P.C., Cernkovich, S.A., & Pugh, M.D. (1986). Friendships and delinquency. *American Journal of Sociology*, 91, 1170-1202.

Gold, M., & Reiner, D.J. (1975). Changing patterns of delinquency behavior among Americans 13 through 16 years old. *Crime and Delinquency Literature*, 7, 483-517.

Goodman, P. (1960). *Growing up absurd: Problems of youth in the organized society*. New York: Random House.

Hagan, J., Simpson, J., & Gillis, A.R. (1979). The sexual stratification of social control: A gender-based perspective on crime and delinquency. *British Journal of Sociology*, 30, 25-38.

Hagedorn, J.M. (1987). *Final report: Milwaukee Gang Research Project*. Milwaukee: University of Wisconsin, Milwaukee.

Hall, S., & Jefferson, T. (Eds.) (1976). *Resistance through rituals*. London: Hutchinson.

Hanson, K. (1964). *Rebels in the streets: The story of New York's girl gangs*. Englewood Cliffs, NJ: Prentice-Hall.

Harris, M. (1988). *Culture, people, nature: An introduction to general anthropology* (5th ed.). New York: Harper & Row.

—— (1988). *Cholas: Latino girls and gangs*. New York: AMS.

Hill, G.D., & Atkinson, M.P. (1988). Gender, familial control and delinquency. *Criminology*, 26, 127-149.

Hindelang, M.J. (1971). Age, sex and the versatility of delinquent involvements. *Social Problems*, 18, 522-535.

Horowitz, R. (1983). *Honor and the American dream: Culture and identity in a Chicano community*. New Brunswick, NJ: Rutgers University Press.

Irwin, J. (1970). *The felon*. Englewood Cliffs, NJ: Prentice-Hall.

Klein, M.W. (1971) *Street gangs and street workers*. Englewood Cliffs, NJ: Prentice-Hall.

Klein, M.W., & Maxson, C.L. (1989). Street gang violence. In N.A. Weiner & M.E. Wolfgang (Eds.), *Violent crime, violent criminals*. Newbury Park, CA: Sage.

Konopka, G. (1966). *The adolescent girl in conflict*. Englewood Cliffs, NJ: Prentice-Hall.

Loeber, R., & Stouthamer-Loeber, M. (1986). *Family factors as correlates and predictors of juvenile conduct problems and delinquency*. Unpublished manuscript.

Lynn, D.B. (1974). *The father: His role in child development*. Belmont, CA: Wadsworth.

Maccoby, E.E., & Jacklin, C.N. (1974). *The psychology of sex differences*. Stanford, CA: Stanford University Press.

Marsh, P., Rosser, E., & Harre, R. (1978). *The rules of disorder*. London: Routledge & Kegan Paul.

McRobbie, A. (1978). *Working class girls and the culture of femininity*. Unpublished master's thesis, University of Birmingham, England.

Miller, W.B. (1966a). Violent crimes by city gangs. *Annals of the American Academy of Political and Social Science*, 364, 96-112.

—— (1973). The molls. *Society*, 11, 32-35.

—— (1974). American youth gangs: Past and present. In A. Blumberg (Ed.), *Current perspectives on criminal behavior*. New York: Knopf.

—— (1975). *Violence by youth gangs and youth groups as a crime problem in major American cities*. Report to the National Institute for Juvenile Justice and Delinquency Prevention.

—— (1980). Gangs, groups and serious youth crime. In D. Shichor & D. Kelly (Eds.), *Critical issues in juvenile delinquency*. Lexington, MA: Lexington.

Moore, J.W. (1988). Changing Chicano gangs; Acculturation, generational change, evolution of deviance or emerging underclass? In J. H. Johnson, Jr. & M.L. Oliver (Eds.), *Proceedings of the Conference on Comparative Ethnicity*. Los Angeles: Institute for Social Science Research, UCLA.

—— (1989a). Is there a Hispanic underclass? *Social Science Quarterly*, 70(2), 265-285.

Morash, M. (1983). Gangs, groups and delinquency. *British Journal of Criminology*, 23(3), 309-331.

Morris, R. (1964). Female delinquents and relational problems. *Social Forces*, 43, 82-89.

Quicker, J.C. (1983). *Homegirls: Characterizing Chicano gangs*. San Pedro, CA: International University Press.

Rice, R. (1963). A report at large: The Persian Queens. *New Yorker*, 39, 135ff.

Richardson, H.J. (1969). *Adolescent girls in approved schools*. London: Routledge & Kegan Paul.

Rittenhouse, R. (1963). *A theory and comparison of male and female delinquency*. Unpublished doctoral dissertation, University of Michigan, Ann Arbor.

Sandhu, H.S. & Allen, D.E. (1969). Female delinquency, goal obstruction, and anomie. *Canadian Review of Sociology and Anthropology*, 6, 107-110.

Short, J.F., & Strodtbeck, F. (1965). *Group process and gang delinquency*. Chicago: University of Chicago Press.

Singer, S.L., & Levine, M. (1988). Power-control theory, gender and delinquency: A partial replication with additional evidence on the effects of peers. *Criminology*, 26, 627-647.

Smart, C., & Smart, B. (1978). *Women, sexuality and social control*. London: Routledge & Kegan Paul.

Thomas, W.I. (1923). *The unadjusted girl*. New York: Little, Brown.

Thrasher, F.M. (1927). *The gang: A study of 1,313 gangs in Chicago*. Chicago: University of Chicago Press.

Vedder, C.B., & Somerville, D.B. (1975). *The delinquent girl*. Springfield, IL: Charles C. Thomas.

Weis, J.G. (1976). Liberation and crime: The invention of the new female criminal. *Crime and Social Justice*, 6, 17-27.

Welfare Council of New York City (1950). *Working with teenage groups: A report on the Central Harlem Project*. New York: Author.

Wilson, W. J. (1987). *The truly disadvantaged: The inner city, the underclass, and public policy*. Chicago: University of Chicago Press. ✦

10

Female Gang Delinquency: A Search for 'Acceptably Deviant Behavior'

William J. Swart

Girls in gangs often walk a tightrope in balancing the expectations of their behavior that come from gang membership and the expectations of their behavior as females. In this essay, Swart argues that female gang members still face sanctions for not behaving in gender-appropriate ways, and he illustrates this point by examining gang members' attitudes about appropriate female conduct when it comes to issues of sexual activity, drug use, violence, and motherhood. His work is unique because he analyzes the data from numerous studies in order to develop and support his theory.

Abstract

This paper explores the forms of female gang delinquency through an analysis of ambiguous deviance norms operating within the gang structure. Caught within competing behavioral norms, female gang members are forced to "fine tune" their deviant behavior in order to make it "acceptable" to their unique position as females within a delinquent gang. The resulting behavior is a "typical" form of female delinquency which is deviant enough for gang membership but not so deviant as to be seen as a contradiction to female character expectations. The explanatory framework and coinciding specific forms of "acceptable deviance" are examined in light of the sexual promiscuity, drug use, aggressive or violent behavior, and motherhood of female gang members.

The historic commitment to the assumption that deviance is a typically male phenomenon has had a great impact on the theoretical and empirical framework from which the gang phenomenon has been studied. In general, Carol Smart (1976) has indicated that a "sexist ideology" operates within both contemporary and historic criminological theory; thus our understanding of female deviance has been biased by current gender stereotypes. Because of these assumptions about gender-typed behavior, little research exists on the role females (and more specifically, female deviant behaviors) play within gang networks. The research that does exist primarily focuses on the female role in relation to males, where males play the dominantly deviant role, and females act to support male deviance (i.e., transporting weapons, providing alibis, acting as spies and lures, and providing sex for male gang members) (Campbell, 1984, p. 14).

Reprinted from *Mid-American Review of Sociology*, 1991, Volume XV, 1:43-52. Reprinted by permission.

While such research is informative, it does little to aid our understanding of the dynamics motivating female gang members toward certain types of behavior. Why does female gang delinquency tend to be "male supportive" and of "lower intensity" than male gang delinquency? Does the gang structure have any impact on the female member's chosen forms of deviance? While current descriptions of "typical female gang delinquency" can be partly explored through Smart's theoretical sexist ideology and the related "self-fulfilling prophesy" in the arrest behavior of police, there seems to be still another dynamic involved—a dynamic which is operating on the level of the individual female gang member's perception and rooted in the gang structure itself.

In her paper on male and female gang members, Giordano (1978) discusses the relevance of peer networks to the role played by the female gang member. She concludes that "for both the white and black subsamples, there was a significant association between group affiliation and self-reported delinquency." Contrary to much research, she also concludes that "the pattern appears to be more complex than the notion that the boyfriend simply uses the female in an 'accomplice' or other passive role while he commits the crime" (1978, p. 132).

The purpose of this paper is to examine this "complex pattern" from which female gang delinquency occurs. By reviewing the analysis and conclusions of Campbell (1984, 1987), Giordano (1978), Horowitz (1986), Rice (1963), and Smith (1978), this paper will examine the role the gang plays as a "peer" network and what effect this network has on the type and extent of the female gang members' deviant behavior. Here, "female gang member" refers to a group of women who act as an auxiliary counterpart to a male gang. By taking this network into effect (as opposed to the examination of female gangs independent of and unaffiliated with male gangs), this paper will provide an alternative explanatory framework for understanding the behavior of female gang members.

In his work on gender stigma and social control, Schur (1984) identifies an attitude of ambivalence toward women present within modern social structures. A major part of Schur's work operates under the assumption that "female" is a devalued status in current society. Thus, in complex modern societies, "Extensive role-overlap and role conflict imply that often [female] behavior may be both 'conformist' and 'deviant' at the same time—depending on which set of expectations governs the evaluation." When females attempt to break out of "traditional" female behavior, "liberated" women are labeled deviant because they do not measure up to social expectations; however, acting in "traditional" female behavior patterns is itself deviant because "male" has become the expected social norm. In this event, female behavior is often "deviant either way;" whether acting in a traditional or liberated manner, female behavior "reflects the uniquely high degree of 'structural ambivalence' that has dominated thinking about women's roles. It reflects as well the generic stigma . . . ascribed merely on the basis of being a woman . . ." (1984, p. 52).

Inferring from the conclusions presented by the gang literature, it seems that an attitude of ambivalence toward women similar to that which Schur indicates is also evident among gang members. This is especially evident in the research Anne Campbell (1984, 1987) presents on female gang members' perception and self definition. In her work, Campbell (1984) identifies two factors that help interpret the role of girls in gangs: their class-value orientation (their desire and ability to be upwardly mobile in terms or their life-style), and the role that females take toward males. The typified roles that follow from these two factors can be summarized in the following table:

Role		Class-Value Orientation: Good Girls	Class-Value Orientation: Bad Girls
Toward	Complementary	Good Wives	Sex Objects
Men	Similar	Independent Women	Tomboys

In her discussion of these typified roles, Campbell alludes to the structural ambivalence mentioned above:

> These types of roles tend to suggest a no-win situation for gang girls. As Sex Objects, they are cheap women rejected by other girls, parents, social workers, and ironically often by the boys themselves. As Tomboys, they are resented by boys and ridiculed by family and friends who wait patiently for them to "grow out of it." Among lower-class women, the Independent Woman, as often as not, raises her children in an all-female household. In doing so, she becomes the target of government, academic, and media concern by those who accuse her of rearing a new cycle of delinquents or, if she works, of ousting the male from the labor force by taking low wages. . . . Clearly the most socially acceptable role is that of Good Wife. Yet even here the Woman is often characterized as the fun-spoiling petty bourgeoisie who takes the high-spirited male away from his gang friends to a future of shopping expeditions and diaper changing (1984, p. 9).

The "deviant either way" status of female gang members is also presented by Rice in his study of the Persian Queens.

> He [Rice] noted that there is nothing that females can do to achieve power or prestige in the gang world. If they fight, male gang members consider them to be deviant, and if they play a more seductive, traditionally feminine role, they are disregarded except for sexual purposes (Bowker and Klein, 1983, p. 740).

The ambivalent attitude and "deviant either way" phenomena operating within the gang plays a unique role in the deviancy of female gang members. On the one hand, the female gang member's behavior must be "deviant" to those outside of the gang in order to ensure her place within the gang itself. On the other hand, it must not be too deviant so as to be viewed negatively by other gang members (both male and female) whose perception is affected by the ambivalent attitude previously discussed. Struggling to find an "acceptable" type and measure of deviance, female gang members experience a state of "normative ambiguity" analogous to that discussed by Horowitz (1986) in her book *Honor and the American Dream*.

In her discussion of the culture and identity of a Chicano community, Horowitz identifies a two-dimensional view of culture where behavior is constrained through the normative ambiguity of two competing codes found within the social structure of the Chicano community itself. The Expressive Code, pertaining to the maintenance of personal and family honor, is deeply rooted in the Latin culture and constantly open to challenge. The Instrumental Code, on the other hand, stems from the Protestant work ethic and includes the pursuit of the American Dream through hard work and education. The tension between these two codes causes conflict because "behavior that is highly valued in one setting may be denigrated in another," while different settings occur within a single social space. Thus, the tension between these two codes "is revealed through various cultural dilemmas, which in turn reflect the disparities between economic and social aspirations and the realities of everyday life in the inner city" (1986, p. 26-27).

The normative ambiguity resulting from the ambivalent attitude of the gang toward women means that female gang members must "fine tune" their deviant behavior in much the same way as the subjects of Horowitz' study constrained their behavior to stay within the two conflicting codes. As part of a delinquent subculture, there are expectations of female gang members' behavior that are in normative conflict with the larger society; while at the same time gender-typed behavior that is synonymous with that in society as a whole is required. The result is that female gang members must operate within competing and often contradictory normative contexts, in order to find a level of behavior which is "acceptably deviant" to the other gang members.

The remainder of this paper will focus on the sexual promiscuity, drug use, aggressive or violent behavior, and motherhood of female gang members in an attempt to present the explanatory framework previously discussed.

Sexual Promiscuity

There can be little doubt that the common understanding of female delinquency predominantly rests in sexually promiscuous behavior. While current statistics show that young women are most likely to be arrested for minor status offenses (sexual promiscuity, running away, etc.), it appears that within the gang structure the promiscuity of female gang members comes under careful scrutiny by both male and female participants. This is not to deny that part of the female gang members' relation to the male gang members is sexual. One only needs to read a small sample of the available literature to understand that sexual activity on the part of both male and female gang members is one major source of deviance. However, an explanation of female gang delinquency relying solely on rampant sexual promiscuity simply isn't an adequate explanation.

The female gang member's relationship to males is important for several reasons, not the least of which is protection from the threats of the inner city. Many have indicated that the existence of the female gang itself relies upon its affiliation to a male counterpart. For this reason, many female gangs will actually take on gendered versions of the male gang name. Two of the female gangs directly studied by Campbell (1984), the Sandman Ladies and the Sex Girls, were correlates to already existing male gangs (the Sandman and the Sex Boys or Essex Boys), and Campbell indicates others in the beginning chapters of her book.

Thus, while the female gang's relation to a male counterpart is important to the existence of the female gang, the relationship is not simply sexual. In reality, while some sexual promiscuity is "normal" gang behavior, "whores" and "loose" girls are negatively sanctioned by both male and female gang participants. As Campbell (1987) indicates, "The social talk of delinquent girls generally shows that they not only reject sexual activity outside the context of a steady relationship but even reject friendships with 'loose' girls whose reputation might contaminate them by association" (pp. 451-52). In this case, rampant sexual activity among gang girls was sanctioned by other female members who wouldn't associate with them. "New girls in the group who, unaware of the prevailing norms, slept around with a variety of men were called to account for their behavior at meetings and instructed that serial monogamy was required" (p. 461).

Campbell indicates two reasons for this emphasis on serial monogamy. First, this emphasis is in part motivated by the girls' own interest in protecting their current relationships with their boyfriends. Fights among girl gang members are often the result of a breach in this gang standard. Interestingly enough, the second reason revolves around a struggle for male respect, which the female gang members felt would be lost if they participated in unselective sexual activity.

These dynamics cause female gang members to find themselves in an ambiguous situation between two conflicting norms (i.e. sexual purity and rampant sexual promiscuity). Sexual purity carries connotations of Campbell's "Good Girls," a connotation most likely not present among female gang participants. However, while a certain amount of sexual behavior is expected of female gang members as gang activity, extreme sexual promiscuity is deemed unacceptable. "Whores" are strictly sanctioned by female gang members and disregarded by their female peers if they fail to change their "loose" behavior. The resulting serial monogamy of female gang members, then, can be seen as the consequence of an attempt to act normatively in a uniquely ambiguous situation. Caught between the extremes of sexual purity and excessive promiscuity, monogamous relationships serve as an "acceptably deviant" outcome for female gang members.

Drug Use

Similar to sexual promiscuity, the use and abuse of illegal drugs is a typical form of gang delinquency. Consequently, both male and female gang members who participate in drug use are often seen as drug addicts and abusers in the eyes of the local community and police. However, inferring from the data, it is interesting to note that while female gang members are involved in the use of drugs, their involvement usually includes only the use of light drugs and is less likely to involve use and abuse of heavy drugs such as LSD, PCP, and heroin. In Campbell's (1987) work, the place of marijuana in the lives of gang members (both female and male) was "as uncontroversial as that of alcohol" (p. 458). However, the female members made a distinction between use and abuse, as well as hard and soft "types" of drugs.

> When they [the gang girls] talked about drug abuse, they drew a clear line between recreational use and addiction. . . . The girls took pains to distance themselves from any such involvement. Heroin users were seen as undependable, capricious, and irresponsible, and they were generally not welcome within the gang (Campbell 1987, p. 458).

Drug abusers were perceived by the women as unreliable, inconsistent, and committed only to themselves and their addiction. For this reason, drug addicts and abusers were usually not welcome within the female gang, and those in the gang who developed drug problems were encouraged to seek help in kicking their addiction. In addition, while men who were successful in illegal activities were sought after by females, the female members were leery of becoming involved in relationships with male drug abusers. "Males who had successful hustles were a prized commodity and addicted males were considered a liability since any income they might obtain was spent on heroin" (Campbell 1987, p. 457).

The specific use of drugs for only recreational purposes can be seen as another indicator of the female gang member's struggle to find a level of "acceptably deviant" behavior. While surrounded by a positive outlook on recreational drug use and an abundant supply of drugs, the female gang member was at the same time discouraged from drug abuse and leery of others who might have this problem. This served to define the two extremes of drug use, abstinence and addiction, from which the women were to discover an "acceptable" midpoint.

Aggressive Behavior/Violence

Current studies of female gang delinquency focus on the extent of violent female behavior in terms of its relation to male views of traditional female roles. Campbell (1984) indicates:

> "Fighters" and "drinkers" both fall into the "bad girl" category, although in different ways. A "bad girl" is one who cheapens herself by abusing her sexuality, but "bad" is also applied to girls who behave in breach of their complementary feminine role (1984, p. 31).

Thus, while aggressive behavior serves as a means for positive status among male gang members, it does the opposite for female gang members. Female gang members who are excessively violent are seen as "breaching" their feminine role, and are not usually welcome in the gang. "If a girl fights as well as a boy—boys don't like her, and in no walk of life is a girl whom boys don't like an object of admiration or envy to other girls" (Rice 1963, p. 135).

At the same time, however, a certain amount of aggression is expected of female gang members. Often one of the initiation rites for female gang members involves a test of their toughness and ability to fight. The "jumping in" process consists of the candidate subjecting (and defending, if possible) herself to a short-lived fight with the rest of the gang members or with one especially tough female member. If the candidate proves capable of defending herself and protecting gang turf, then she is allowed to enter the gang (Campbell 1984, p. 25).

These two opposite forces again serve to place the gang girls into an ambiguous situation. While displaying a certain amount of aggressive behavior is necessary for female gang members' acceptance into and participation with the gang, excessive violence is deemed a breech of appropriate female roles and is sanctioned. "Acceptably deviant" behavior is found somewhere in between these two extremes; ordinarily in female aggression against other females. This aggression usually takes the form of "cat fighting" over personal integrity or jealousy over relationships with males. At times the women might become involved in inter-gang conflict, but again, during these instances their violence is limited to fighting with members of the female auxiliary of another gang.

Motherhood

Motherhood seems to play a unique role in constraining the identity and behavior of the female gang member. While pregnancy and motherhood do not necessarily mean that female gang members have to break away from the gang, it does mean that they have to constrain their deviant behavior to the extent that it allows them to be seen as "good mothers." As Horowitz indicates in her study of Hispanic gangs:

> The Hispanic girl is likely to be deeply concerned about her identity as a good mother. To avoid any imputation of irresponsibility as a mother, she must make every effort to demonstrate her dedication to the welfare of her child. A good deal of gossip among gang members centered on girls who failed to take adequate care of their children. Motherhood did not require abandonment of the gang, but it did entail making satisfactory arrangements for the child. Girls who brought their children with them to the corner to hang out were considered irresponsible. The appropriate course of action was to leave the child with the grandmother for the night. After an all-night party, the girls would conscientiously return home in the early hours to get their children ready for school (Campbell 1987, p. 460).

In this way, the status of female gang members as mothers again places their behavior under the constraints of the gang network. Although motherhood does not require the female members to desert the gang, it does require that they amend their deviant behavior in order to adapt to their new status as mothers. Thus, motherhood brings yet another situation of normative ambiguity to the female gang member. If she remains in the gang, she is expected to participate in gang activities. However, with the onset of motherhood, her participation in these activities now comes under the unique scrutiny of the gang structure, and she is once again forced to struggle to find an "acceptable" level of deviant behavior.

The issue of abortion adds another problematic dimension to the situation of female gang mothers. Often males view fathering a child as an indication of their masculinity. Females, on the other hand, appreciate their independence and are often wary of being "controlled" by men through pregnancy. While abortion is a viable solution to this over dependence on males, excessive use of abortion carries connotations within the gang network of poor mothering.

> Wholehearted support [for abortion] might be construed as callous disregard for human life and place [the mothers] in jeopardy of being seen as "bad mothers." On the other hand, too many children could lead to a male-dependent life-style and suggest that they were vulnerable to being "conned" by men (Campbell 1987, p. 460).

Constrained by the perception of being either a bad mother or exploited by men, female gang mothers are forced to adjust their behavior between these two extremes. Thus, "abortion was accepted as legitimate after the first or second child but was generally condemned in a first pregnancy" (Campbell, 1987, p. 460). Here again the struggle within the ambiguity of competing norms of motherhood shows how opposing forces operating within the gang structure constrain and delimit appropriate female behavior.

Conclusion

This paper attempts to show that an ambivalent attitude, similar to that which Schur (1984) notes, is operating toward women within society as a whole and is also operating toward women within gang networks. I suggest that this ambivalent attitude plays a large role in defining what this paper refers to as "acceptable deviant behavior" for female gang participants. Campbell (1987) suggests something similar when she says that female gang members "arrive at a female gang identity by default rather than by affirmation":

> By "backing away" from one aspect of an assigned role, she may run the risk of being cast into another unac-

> ceptable role from which she must also extricate herself. For example, in rejecting women's passivity toward men, a girl may endorse her support for abortion. However, in doing so, she risks being seen as cheap or as a bad mother. . . . As long as her self presentation depends upon rejecting an interlocking set of actions or qualities, she is likely to find herself escaping from one rejected identity but risking entry into another (p. 452).

The model presented seeks to extend Campbell's understanding by saying that female gang members find themselves amidst the paradox of being "deviant either way." In an attempt to participate in behavior which is deviant to the social status quo, but not excessively deviant in relation to prescribed female gang roles, female gang members find themselves facing an ambiguous situation between competing behavioral norms. As this paper has argued, "typical" female gang delinquency may be more fully understood as it relates to female gang members' struggle from ambiguity to "acceptably deviant" patterns of behavior.

Before concluding this paper, it is important to note that in the previous examples given, the ambivalent attitude toward female gang members described was not simply a product of male gang members' dominance, but actually took into account the perception of both the males and females involved. Often normative constraints relied mainly on the perception of other females in the gang. Other studies support this. As Bowker and Klein (1983) indicate, "Relationships with girlfriends are more important in determining gang membership and seriousness of delinquency than any of the other variables discussed in this article" (p. 749). Campbell (1984) concludes the introduction to her book by saying "A girl's status depends to a larger (or perhaps simply more evident and self-admitted) extent on her female peers. They show their evaluation of her through their own rites and meetings" (p. 32).

This differs from Schur's notion of the source of the structural ambivalence parallel within society. While Schur implies that the devaluation of women propagates from and is supported by the behavior and perception of men, the literature cited indicates that female gang members are influenced more by the constraints of their female peers than by the perceptions of male gang members. Contrary to the literature, one could argue that because female gangs are most often auxiliary components to male gang, female gang members are more dependent upon their male counterparts to define gender-related norms than are females in the society at large, where independent female associations are more likely to occur. Nevertheless, what seems necessary is to approach female gang delinquency and the normative structure of the gang as it relates to both male and female peer influences, recognizing that both are important determinants of delinquent behavior. This paper has been an attempt to begin such a process.

References

Bowker, Lee H. and Malcolm W. Klein. 1983. "The Etiology of Female Juvenile Delinquency and Gang Membership: A Test of Psychological and Social Structural Explanations." *Adolescence* 18:738-51.

Campbell, Anne. 1987. "Self Definition by Rejection: The Case of Gang Girls." *Social Problems* 34:451-65.

——. 1984. *The Girls in the Gang*. New York: Basil Blackwell, Inc.

Giordano, Peggy C. 1978. "Girls, Guys and Gangs: The Changing Social Context of Female Delinquency." *The Journal of Criminal Law and Criminology* 69:126-32.

Horowitz, Ruth. 1986. *Honor and the American Dream: Culture and Identity in a Chicano Community*. New Brunswick, NJ: Rutgers University Press.

Rice, R. 1963. "A Reporter at Large: The Persian Queens." *New Yorker* October 19, 39:153.

Schur, Edwin M. 1984. *Labeling Women Deviant: Gender, Stigma, and Social Control*. New York: Random House, Inc.

Smart, Carol. 1976. *Women, Crime and Criminology: A Feminist Critique*. Boston: Routledge and Kegan Paul.

Smith, Lesley S. 1978. "Sexist Assumptions and Female Delinquency: An Empirical Investigation." In *Women, Sexuality and Social Control*, edited by Carol Smart and Barry Smart. London: Routledge and Kegan Paul. ✦

11

The Vice Queens: An Ethnographic Study of Black Female Gang Behavior

Laura T. Fishman

Following on the insights of Campbell's essay, Fishman's research is important because she has re-examined data gathered during the 1960s with an awareness of the pitfalls of past research, and fills in some of the historical gaps in our knowledge of girls in gangs. Her study reveals that violence in female gangs is not a new phenomenon, but existed among the Vice Queens and other earlier female gangs as well. Fishman notes that the structural constraints faced by inner-city girls in the contemporary era are more grim than those faced by girls in 1960s, and it is likely that more will turn to gang affiliation as a means of adaptation to circumstances of racism, poverty, and violence.

Abstract

This paper presents an ethnographic account of black female participation in the Vice Queens, an auxiliary to the Vice Kings, a male gang.

A combination of data sources were collected by the Youth Studies Program of the University of Chicago during the early 1960s. The re-analyzed data show that the Vice Queens have a high participation in conflict situations and in other norm-violating activities. Findings indicate that girls look to other Vice Queens for recognition and status. Status is conferred on the basis of a girl's participation in conflict situations, in the mating-dating complex, and in other norm-violating activities. It is concluded that these data suggest no significant changes in black female gang behavior since the emergence of the women's movement.

Background

While male youth gangs have been a popular subject for the media and the focus of social investigations in various academic disciplines, comparatively little attention has been paid to the role of females within the gang subculture. The present paper presents a systematic description of the multi-dimensional world of the Vice Queens, a black female auxiliary gang to a boys' conflict gang, during the early sixties.

According to reports over the past 20 years, girl gangs appear to have evolved from a predominantly auxiliary status—that is, functioning primarily to support male gang groups—to a position characterized by greater autonomy and independent activity. Some observers, most notably Freda Adler (1975), have pointed out that such changes in female gang behavior have arisen alongside, and perhaps in response to, the women's liberation movement. Although female gangs are still peripheral to the male gang, girl gang members have gradually become more highly integrated in male gang activities. At the same time, girl gangs have moved closer to becoming independent, violence-oriented groups.

Urban youth gang activity has traditionally been depicted as a predominantly male enterprise to which female gangs are auxiliaries and of only marginal importance. In the 1960s, girl gang members were perceived as maintaining traditional female roles, typically by participating in socio-sexual activities with the boys. Thrasher (1927), in his classical study of male gang members in Chicago, discussed two female gangs in which members, in general, conformed to the traditional female role. Short and Strodtbeck (1965)[1] echo this finding in their study of Chicago gangs during the 1960s, describing girl gang members as mainly sexual objects, used by the boys for sexual purposes.

Hanson (1964) reported that the Dagger Debs, a female gang in the Puerto Rican area of New York City, were instigators of the boys' fights with enemy male gangs. They spread false rumors and goaded the boys by threatening their masculinity in order to provoke inter-gang warfare. Miller (1973) observed that the Molls, a female gang in the Boston area, not only manipulated boys into gang fights but encouraged boys to steal cars and take them for joy rides.

Despite their role as instigators, gang girls have reportedly been excluded from the planning or carrying out of male gang activities, especially conflict situations. For example, Rice (1963) observed that a New York City female gang was seldom involved in gang boys' conflict situations. Rather, gang fights were at the behest of the male gang members who allowed the girls to accompany them to inter-gang "rumbles." On these occasions, they were likely to maintain their traditional roles as females and were relegated to fighting the enemy's girl gang members.

Bowker (1983) re-analyzed data on black female participation in male gang activity in Los Angeles County during the sixties and found girls still enmeshed in traditional female roles: i.e., girls were not the "cause" but the "cure" for male delinquent behavior. He reported that girls appeared to have a preventive effect on male delinquent activity in that, whenever they were present at the sites of boys' delinquent

Paper presented at the annual meetings of the American Society of Criminology, Chicago, November 1988. Reproduced with the author's permission.

activities, the boys were likely to terminate such activities.

By the mid-seventies, descriptions of girl gang roles and activities were less likely to be restricted to the traditionally female role. Gang girls were more often depicted as being actively involved in conflict situations which, in the past, were believed to be male-dominated, e.g., gang feuds, individual and gang fights. Quicker (1974), for example, reported that, while female gangs were still dependent upon male gangs for their existence, they had begun to function more autonomously and to take initiative in defining the content of their gangs. In his study of female Chicano gang members in Los Angeles, Quicker noted that girl members made their own decisions on internal matters, usually through a democratic process.

Brown (1977) also observed that female gang members in Philadelphia's black gang subculture were actively involved, along with the boys, in conflict situations. He concludes that "... the female is an intrinsic part of the gang's group identity who participates in gang activities and is involved in various gang functions, rather than just ancillary activities such as sexual fulfillment" (p. 226). Campbell's (1984) observations of three New York City girl gangs support this position. She found girl gangs to be involved in serious personal and property crimes. Furthermore, these girls appeared to take a forceful role in male gang conflict situations and to use "male" weapons such as guns and knives. They fought over boys, but they also fought in other arenas—e.g., in gang feuds, against personal insults and against the police.

Despite an apparent trend for gang girls to have moved away from traditional female roles since the early 1960s, not all reports are in agreement. For example, Miller (1975) found no evidence that female criminal behavior, in connection with gang activity, is more prevalent or violent than in the past. Rather, he reported in the mid-seventies that female participation was still traditional in content, with girl gangs still functioning as auxiliaries to male gangs, and serving as weapon carriers and as decoys. The status of girl gangs, he maintained, is directly dependent on that of male gangs (Miller 1975).

Several authors who have studied the black lower class community (Brooks, 1980; Fields & Water, 1985; Glasgow, 1981; Valentine, 1978) have noted that most males and females, being offered little from the community in the way of resources or controls, must develop some knowledge of hustling and fighting in order to survive. Low income blacks need to combine income from intermittent employment, welfare, and hustling[2] to maintain even a low standard of living. And within such communities, Brooks (1980) observes that the black woman must be socialized to defend herself, her family and her hard-earned property against aggression because she is not likely to receive protection from anyone, including the police. Brown (1977) suggests that the black female gang serves as a principal agent of socialization for poor black adolescent females, offering girls the opportunity to learn important survival strategies as well as the subtleties of lower class black lifestyle, in order to function effectively within the black community. As girls go about learning the rudiments of these strategies, they also learn the rules by which to compete successfully and gain status. Other investigators also point out that black adolescent girls who learn to handle premarital sexual experiences in a sophisticated manner and/or who give birth are conferred the highly valued status of adult women. (See for instance, Bell, 1971; Ladner, 1972; McCray, 1980; and Staples, 1973.)

On the streets, the status of girls has traditionally been dependent on that of their corresponding male gangs. In 1963, Rice concluded that the gang girls were doomed to lower status in the street gang society, which is completely controlled by males and oriented toward male activities. However, several years later, Brown (1977) observed that, while girls still placed a high value on male approval, relationships with other female gang members were more important in gaining memberships and status. On the basis of her studies of institutionalized girls who had been involved in girl gangs, Giordano (1978) also concludes that these girls were no different from boys in terms of designating their sex peer groups as the most important reference group for status achievement. Further, methods of gaining status appear to have changed since the sixties, in that, more recently, status is believed to be conferred on the basis of a girl's ability to fight. Campbell (1981, 1982) reported that girls most frequently listed maintaining personal integrity, safeguarding their tough reputations among their peer group and impressing other girls with their courage as their primary reasons for fighting.

It remains difficult to draw conclusions about changes in the function of girl gangs or their activities. Further, there is little data on female gang behavior prior to the 1970s. The present paper is based on data collected as part of a larger study of male delinquents by the Youth Studies Program of the University of Chicago in the early 1960s. At that time, the Vice Queens, a black female auxiliary to the Vice Kings, a notorious boys' conflict gang, resided in a predominantly black, lower-class community on the West Side of Chicago. Information gathered from field observations and interviews has been combined to provide an in-depth portrait of the Vice Queens' way of life and the structure and function of this particular girl gang in order to augment the existing literature on the female gang subculture of the early 1960s.

Method

The research reported here is best considered as an ethnographic account of gang girl behavior during the sixties. It is based on data collected as part of a larger study of male delinquent gangs in Chicago during 1960 and 1963. Sixteen "delinquent" gangs were assigned detached workers by the Program for Detached Workers of the YMCA on the basis of their generally "troublesome" character to the community, as judged by police complaints, reports of welfare agencies, and by field investigators of the detached worker staff. Later, in collaboration with the University of

Chicago research program, gangs were selected to fulfill research design requirements in a study of gangs representing major delinquent subcultures.[3]

The present paper is based on re-analysis of detached workers' interviews and field observer reports. The availability of detached workers as intimate observers of girl gang members provided an opportunity to gain more complete insights into the behavior of these girls than could be provided by any other methods. Weekly interviews with the workers assigned to the Vice Kings suggested that they not only shared intimately in the on going life of the boys' gang but also of the girls' auxiliary gang. These weekly interviews with detached workers began early in the project and continued until August, 1962.

In addition to the detached workers' reports, field observations by the research team also provided broad documentation of the girls' street corner behavior. The author served as a field observer of the Vice Queens during 1960 and 1963 observing the group in its setting and frequently participating in the gang's main activities. Entree to the Vice Queens was obtained through the detached worker who actively sponsored the author. Once the girls overcame their initial suspicion, the author was for the most part accepted as a peer in whose presence, it is assumed, the Vice Queens acted normally and unself-consciously.

Information from the field observer reports were compared with the detached workers' reports and with information on file at the YMCA. The data were cross-checked and re-examined in the interests of improving their reliability and validity. Not only have field observer reports and the information on file generally corroborated information provided by the detached workers, but they have added depth to the insights gained from the detached workers. The combined reports provide a detailed portrait of a black female gang during the early sixties.

The Vice Queens, an Auxiliary Gang

The Vice Queens lived in a predominantly black lower income community characterized by high physical deterioration, poverty, unemployment, illegitimacy, juvenile and adult crime. These girls learned, through gang participation, techniques necessary for functioning as adult women in their community. The Vice Queens were a loosely knit, though seldom harmonious, family for its more than 30 members, about 19 of whom form the "hard core" membership. Comprising of girls ranging in age from 13 to 19, the Vice Queens had their own leaders, meetings and activities and with other gang members, the girls found companionship, a means of achieving status and protection against undesirable men in the neighborhood. The main interests of the Vice Queens was the Vice Kings' achievements in athletics, fighting, and other activities that form the basis of male prestige. Consequently, the Vice Queens had little function outside of the mating-dating complex, since the conflict gang was largely a male world and the girls more often remained on the fringe of it. However, the Vice Queens also participated in their own activities which were functional in maintaining the group. Independent of the Vice Kings, the girls also participated in aggressive and violent actions, some norm-violating activities as well as their own athletic and social activities. Participation fluctuated with their activities. For example, more girls participated in activities that were attractive to the boys, e.g., dance and athletic events, than in conflict situations and other norm-violating activities. In general, however, fluctuations in participation took place in the fringe group rather than the core.

Unlike the Vice Kings, the Vice Queens had no rigid hierarchical or clearly defined leadership structure. Instead, leaders tended to be self appointed, with girls assuming the role of leader in situations where they could gain or maintain status. Other girls seldom threatened these function-oriented leadership positions.

The Vice Queens were not a highly cohesive group. Competition among them for the gang boys' attention often led to physical violence and sharp verbal acrimony that sometimes pervaded the entire group. Paradoxically, such competitiveness lent a measure of cohesiveness in that the girls maintained the Vice Kings' interest in them as an auxiliary group as well as individuals. The existence of a female auxiliary was a source of prestige among the Vice Kings.

Further, the Vice Queens were not bent on the establishment of "new rules" counter to middle class values, but rather pursued positive status goals within a black lower class cultural system. The Vice Queens thus provided an important milieu in which girls not only learned new roles designed to benefit the gang, but also learned the intricacies of street life.

Occupational and Educational Activities

Most of the Vice Queens did not pursue educational or occupational activities. When the girls did attend school, they often experienced conflicts with teachers and administrators who exemplified and expostulated a middle class way of life.

The resultant lack of rapport and the social distance between girls and school personnel combined with the girls' resistance to internalizing middle class educational objectives, effectively removed them from the formal objectives and programs of the school. School, from their accounts, was not a place where they prepared for future occupations or gained knowledge. It was rather, another site for gang activities—a place to learn of pending conflicts, to exchange information about the activities of other gangs, and a battleground for physical and verbal fights.

It is not surprising that most of the girls were school drop-outs. Of 19 Vice Queens, 13 had withdrawn from school, and the truancy rate of the others was so high that, for all practical purposes, they were students in name only. Quitting school did not appear to heighten the girls' motivations to obtain jobs, nor were jobs used as a reason for leaving school. Both school and work interfered with the more enjoyable pleasures derived from participation with their peers in street activities. Only two of the 19 Vice Queens had jobs at the conclusion of the field research. Of the other girls who had jobs before or during the three-year project, all had either quit or were laid off.

Most of the girls at one time or another, but never persistently, had shown an interest in working but seldom obtained jobs. As one detached worker put it, when explaining the girls' lack of interest in work:

> Some of the girls have stated that their old man will take care of them. The girls didn't want to work nor go to school and further their education. They felt education or not, they would be able to make it. They felt that they have what it takes: they were talking about sex and they figured that they can get a steady boyfriend who will give them five or maybe ten dollars a week and that would be enough to take care of them. In turn, they might live with him, and this is good enough.[4]

Disassociation from the time-consuming occupational and educational institutions permitted the girls more than ample leisure time to engage in gang activities.

Norm-Violating Activities

A significant amount of the Vice Queens' time was spent with the Vice Kings, "hanging out" on the streets, in vacant lots and at school yards, visiting one another and attending athletic and social events. Although most of this time was spent in nondelinquent activities, norm-violating activities were also of considerable importance.

Female delinquency often is thought to be extremely specialized and virtually synonymous with sexual delinquency. The Vice Queens, however, were quite diversified in delinquent activities. The group was usually the setting for norm-violating activities and, except for sexual delinquency, the solitary delinquent girl was rare. Almost all the girls were involved in such delinquent activities as running away from home, truancy, and occasional shoplifting. And most girls committed such misdemeanors as driving without a license, disturbing the peace, and loitering.

Additionally, however, some of the girls committed "male" crimes such as auto theft, purse snatching and grand larcenies which involved little planning or skills. As a rule, however, the girls' participation in these latter activities was sporadic, impulsive and experimental. An even less frequent criminal pattern among adolescent girls but one which was not rare among the Vice Queens, was strong-arming.

> They strong-arm like the boys and would strong-arm anyone who would come around; man or woman. They pick on anyone that would come along, usually three or four girls together. Certain of the girls would not participate. But they don't strong-arm too much.[5]

Unlike conflict and drinking behavior, these "female" crimes as well as "male" crimes are most often conducted by very small groups of two or three girls. The most important group activities, with their own set of rules, were conflict and drinking.

With respect to conflict, the Vice Queens acted primarily as agitators and instigators in inter- and intra-gang fights among boys. They frequently manipulated the boys into fighting over real or alleged insults or "passes" from male members of enemy gangs. Fighting over girls was common between the Vice Kings and other conflict-oriented gangs. A detached worker described this pattern vividly:

> In front of all the big fights that the Vice Kings have had, the girls have been involved. They have either started them or signified and lied so as to encourage the boys to go and fight. They have been lookouts and have seen Cobras and Comanches come in the area. They have had a lot to do with everything that had happened in respect to the big fights.[6]

Having brought about the fights in the first place, the girls then served as weapon carriers and "lookouts" for the boys. As weapon carriers, the girls provided an essential service and the Vice Kings were fully aware that the girls were less likely to be searched by the police than were the boys. Knives, guns, black jacks and other weapons were frequently hidden in a girl's clothing. For instance, a detached worker describes a fight which took place between the Vice Kings and two other gangs when the workers took some Vice Kings and Vice Queens to the amphitheater to see a basketball game.

> As we were going in, we met Gilmore's group, the southside Cobras. My boys recognized these boys and so right there in the place they had a fight. It didn't get as bad as some fights I have seen but it was on its way. Blows were passed. Just about the time we had the thing quieted down, then Charlie Brown and his group came in and the thing flared up all over again. When the ruckus started, I heard one of the boys in my group tell a girl, "Let me have the stuff!" Well this one girl produced a knife, a butcher knife, and I don't know what the other girls had but she never did get it out. Apparently it got caught in the lining of her coat or something, 'cause when we got back in the car, I heard him ask her, "Why didn't you give it to me?" and she said, "I couldn't get it out." But the implication is that they insisted these girls go along because they are the ones that carry the weapons for them.[7]

Girls would accompany boys to inter-gang fights and occasionally they would fight the enemy gang's female auxiliary members. More frequently, however, they participated independently of the boys in their own conflicts with members of other female auxiliary gangs. The Vice Queens' fights with other female auxiliary gangs usually erupted as a result of a quarrel between individual members. Typically, arguments involved the passing of threatening notes until one gang, sufficiently insulted and angered, demanded that a time and place be set for a fight. Locations for fights were usually secluded streets, movie theaters, or school yards, and seldom did more than 10 or 11 members from each gang participate. Seldom did the girls use any weapons. They usually fought with their fists and much like boys. A detached worker commented:

> They try to specialize in one punch knock-outs. They get their balance just like a man would get his and they have nice left jabs. They can almost throw them better than the boys throw their left jabs. The boys have a tendency to hook their jabs, which is very ineffective, while the girls throw their jabs right from the shoulder.[8]

Fighting other female auxiliary gangs appears closely linked with maintaining loyalty in the group and a sense of solidarity between members. Seldom did girls fight over personal grievances, rather to preserve the Vice Queens' reputation for toughness.

The Vice Queens fought with both males and females—in short, with anyone who disturbed them on the street, at parties, or at the movies. Fights generally arose over issues of integrity or loyalty.[9] Integrity issues usually center on girls' perceptions of some threat to or an attack on their public reputation. Issues generally emerged whenever other girl gang members join in on the fight, if present, on behalf of girls whose reputations had been attacked. Many girls were not at all reluctant to fight male opponents over personal grievances, as well as in response to the males initiating a violent confrontation. Some girls fought with male members as well as males from other gangs, adult males from the community and even policemen:

> The Vice Queens have been know to jump on policemen, they have been known to go to K town to fight, whether to fight boys or girls and they were known to handle themselves, they weren't scared of nobody. They would jump on sober adults, they were that strong.[10]

There is little doubt that fighting a male, and especially winning, carried a particular status among the girls. Within the black lower class culture, failure to respond in this manner constituted deviance from an implicit norm, e.g., "no one says that and gets away with it!"

The gang thus provided girls with opportunities to learn such traditional male skills as fighting skills and taking care of themselves on the streets. Within their community, there was relatively greater freedom but also less protection, for girls. It was thus expected that girls would learn to defend themselves against "abusive men," attacks on their integrity and police who were perceived as thugs, animals and "head whippers."

A considerable number of the girls consumed both alcohol and, to a lesser extent, marijuana. While both were integral to leisure time activities of the community, marijuana was not as regularly available, nor as inexpensive as alcohol. Drinking was a recurrent group recreational pattern for the Vice Queens, who occasionally drank gin, but more often, inexpensive beverages such as wine. Usually they drank in small groups, on the streets, in alleyways, but seldom in their homes, and they did not willingly share their limited liquor with the boys.

Some of the Vice Queens drank a little every day, usually in the evenings. The functional character of drinking is suggested by the fact that girls often have only half a glass of wine, but they will act drunk for the duration of the evening. The girls are boisterous, they often participate in sexual activities with the boys, and verbal and physical fights are common. The girls sometimes pool their money to buy liquor which is brought either by the Vice Queens who are legally of age or by neighborhood men and women.

Sexual Delinquency

Not all of the girls participated in the antisocial activities mentioned above, but all had prostituted themselves at one time or another, some more often than others. Prostitution, at no more than two or three dollars a customer, was a chief source of income for the girls, although they got money from other illegal activities and, occasionally, from parents. Customers were procured in taverns and on the street or at other locations not connected with organized houses of prostitution. The girls were aware of the prostituting activities of their peers and prostitution was accepted as standard behavior for the group. However, they seldom discussed with each other the details of their adventures in prostitution. The Vice Kings, who were cognizant of the prostitution even though the girls will not prostitute themselves when the boys were present, took no action to discourage the girls from earning money in this manner.

Their prostitution is the strongest indication of the Vice Queens' acceptance of female-oriented, illegitimate hustles. This should not be a surprising pattern given that the Vice Queens live in a community where hustling is a requisite for survival. The findings strongly suggest that the Vice Queens have begun to establish their style of hustling by devising a diverse package of illegal activities to produce economic gain. There are too many risks associated with hustling to restrict activities to one method. So rather than specialization in one hustle, they are generalists—building a flexible package of various hustling activities. Thus girls can not look to focus on only "female" crimes, as they are limited in scope and consequently must also look to "masculine" crimes in order to broaden their package.

Vice Queen-Vice King Relationships

During the early sixties, the most ego-involved area for female adjustment concerned relationships with the opposite sex, e.g., the types of men they dated and married, their status as sex objects and their ability to manipulate through sexual attractiveness.[11]

The primary role of girls' vis-a-vis the boys' gang was sexual. Vice Queens had sexual relations with members of the gang in the process of "going with" the boys and they bore the boys' illegitimate children. In general, the Vice Queens' relations with boys lacked the subtlety discretion consonant with middle class values. Rather than engaging in subtle or flirtatious behavior, the Vice Queens unabashedly placed themselves at the boys' disposal and openly encouraged them to fondle and to have sexual relations with them:

> The girls do not maintain the boys' interest all day, just at night. These boys all want to get a piece of ass when they want to go home at night and the girls are always accessible to them if they like the boys. I can't see certain boys getting a girl like Dorothy or Kay Bear. Some boys could rap all night long and these girls wouldn't drop their pants. But some boys, whom they like, could rap to them and they might hold out a little bit but they would come through with the goods. The girls would drop their pants just like that for a certain boy.[12]

The Vice Queens tend to accept the boys fondling them constantly, pulling on them and beating them up. In fact, one boy entered the worker's car, dragged one of the girls out and proceeded to beat her up. This girl was not going with the boy at the time and had never expressed any interest in the boy. After this incident, as she was rubbing her puffed up lips, she stated that he "sure was cute." A day later she was going with him. This frequently happens. The boy beats a girl up and then she becomes interested in him and so they are going with each other.[13]

The Vice Queens' interaction with the Vice Kings occurs within a relatively free courtship system—free in that it exists within the context of a community which is culturally permissive of such behavior. The girls associations with the Vice Kings do not take place under parental or other adult supervision.

The amount of actual dating was limited. The boys, on the whole, only paid attention to the Vice Queens when they wanted to have sexual relations. The girls, knowing this, had "steadies of the moment" with whom they had relations. It is considered usual practice that their "steadies of the moment" handle them, curse them and beat them, and little more is expected of the boys. Couples seldom shared activities and seldom did the boys treat the girls to other favors (e.g., hamburgers, cokes or flowers). A central meeting place of the Vice Kings and Vice Queens was an apartment where one of the girls lived. The girl's parents were rarely home and, consequently, this apartment became a place to participate in such norm-violating activities as gambling, fighting and sexual promiscuity. The observer, who visited this apartment, provided the following report:

> We arrived at this particular apartment house. The building was quite run down. The windows in the door were broken, the mail boxes were open, and the foyer was quite shabby. As we walked up the bleak stairs, I noticed the many obscenities written on the wall, as well as the names of the Vice Kings. . . . We entered the apartment. The dining room, crowded with kids, was the only room lit by candles. The rest of the apartment was completely dark. . . . The shades were torn but neatly covered the windows so that no one could see into the apartment. Sensuous giggles and murmurs came, intermittently, from the darkened bedrooms. . . . The apartment afforded the opportunity for everything and anything to happen.[14]

Although couples did "go steady" in the conventional sense, neither the Vice Kings nor Vice Queens perceived each other as future marriage partners. The Vice Kings perceived the Vice Queens as useful for premarital sexual relations, but for a steady girl friend, they preferred:

> . . . a girl that's unusual, who does not hang with the Vice Queens. Usually the girl they talk about is a girl who doesn't come out on the streets very often. The Vice Kings can go to her house anytime of the day and she will be there. They like this quiet life that the girl plays, instead of the girl who runs on the streets, drinks and will swing on them at any time.[15]

On the other hand, the Vice Queens felt that they could get a steady boy friend, not necessarily a Vice King, who would take care of them monetarily but not necessarily marry them. Consequently, the relationships between the Vice Kings and the Vice Queens were neither future nor marriage oriented.

Several of the girls who engaged frequently in prostitution later became involved in homosexual activities. An observer reports:

> It seems that the homosexual activities are continuing among the older girls and beginning to spread to the younger girls. Amy, an older girl whom I do not know, was seen riding Judy, a younger Vice Queen, on her bicycle down the street. Amy was seen kissing and petting Judy who seemed to be enjoying it. Also, the older Vice Queens were importing white lesbian girls into the area in order to increase their circle. This would be the first time the girls have participated in any activity with white girls. . . . The same girls who are involved in homosexual activities are still prostituting and still having sexual relations with the boys.[16]

It was reported that the girls sometimes continued homosexual patterns encouraged by matrons at correctional institutions where they had been confined. The reasons given by the Vice Queens for continued homosexual activity embraced a certain logic. First, they could be assured of not breaking their probation on grounds of pregnancy. Second, the girls were tired of treatment received from both Vice Kings and other neighborhood men, e.g., assaults, taking their money, and simply using them as sexual objects. Third, when they did become pregnant (11 of 19 girls interviewed had been pregnant), the Vice Kings claimed as the fathers, proved indifferent to the girls' predicament. Thus, the Vice Queens felt that relationships with other females could be more rewarding than their experience with male-female relationships had led them to expect. In fact, an ideal homosexual relationship was based upon values and goals romantically assumed to be characteristic of middle class male-female relationships, i.e., love, trust, tenderness and kindness. Homosexual relationships allowed relief from the demanding and competitive world of the Vice Kings and other men.

Status Seeking

The Vice Queens' role might be viewed as a traditionally female one, and, to a large extent, status was gained through sexual relationships. While granting sexual favors to the Vice Kings, the girls gained status among their female peers on the basis of gaining the boys' attention. However, maintaining status was a complex and delicate matter. It depended on being able to keep four or five boys "on the string" without any boy's knowing of the others, but at the same time, avoiding sexual relationships with too many boys at one time. Further, going from one sexual involvement to another in rapid succession, public acknowledgement of a lack of emotional involvement with the partner, or restricting sexual relations to only one boy could all result in loss of status. Under such circumstances, the other girls may react in the following manner:

> I think this girl rates a bit higher than the rest of the Vice Queens. Although the girls accept her, they still feel some hostility towards her. It became obvious to

> me that they were intent on having her taken through the mud this night. . . . The girls were anxious to see her brought to their level, so to speak, and have her share every boy in the group so they would be able to say she had been had. . . . She was drunk and I knew the other girls would have made it very convenient for as many boys as were available to pull a train on her.[17]

Status was seldom acquired by sexual liaisons with high-status Vice Kings (since these boys had relations with most of the other Vice Queens); however, status could be obtained by going steady with, or having a baby by, a high-status Vice King. These fathers-to-be rarely assumed responsibility for their pregnant girlfriends, but were more apt to assume an air of righteous indignation followed by indifference. Eventually, they would usually terminate the relationship. As a field observer noted:

> Linda then began to tell me that Duke was acting very funny toward her since he learned that she was expecting. She went over to him and informed him that she was pregnant. They then proceeded to argue about her becoming pregnant and about what responsibility he should assume. The argument ended in Duke hitting her. Now Linda is afraid to talk to Duke.[18]

Regardless of the attitude of the expectant father, status is conferred on the pregnant girl by the other Vice Queens and Kings. As one of the girls told the observer:

> Everyone comes up and hugs me; boys and girls. They tell me that they are so happy for me and it is great that I am going to give the group another Vice King or Vice Queen.[19]

The girls' incentives to proudly announcing their pregnancies are the gaining of attention from the other gang members, publicly achieving adult status, and hopefully strengthening the bonds between themselves and their boy friends. All of these incentives are culturally supported by the group. This finding strongly suggests that the girls are responding to a specific black lower class cultural pattern which confers the status of adulthood upon young women who become pregnant. They are no longer considered "little girls" but adults with all the privileges inherent in the adult status.

Another means by which a Vice Queen could attain status was by being assaulted by a high-status Vice King:

> . . . Pep, the President of the Vice Kings, has a girl. Well, her ego swells like a Peacock because she is Pep's girl. What she most likely doesn't know is that Pep has 8 or 9 girls. She has status, not in the girls' group for going with Pep because that's nothing. Pep will take a nap with any of them. But when Pep's old lady got her ass beat by Pep, she digs this. "Pep beat my ass, you know". . . . She'd tell me and the other girls this. . . . They then recognize that she got her ass beat by her old man . . . and she gets status.[20]

There is a strong suggestion that the violent forcing of physical intimacy is perceived as an indication of "true love." Assault by a high-status Vice King alerts the girls as well as other Vice Queens that he really must like her; going with such a man might lead to a "happy ending."

Outside of the mating-dating complex, the girls could derive additional status from their participation in norm-violating activities. For example, status was gained from the girls' abilities in conflict situations, e.g., the perfection of fighting techniques, the number of times the girls willingly fought and with whom they fought. A detached worker summed this up as follows:

> Keep the game up tight in the street, whipping other girls and boys in the street. Girls that keep going into Imperials' territory, keep whipping those guys there, going to K town, keeping their stuff going. The boys will probably get so excited, the girls will have all kinds of status. What it would do is create a chain reaction and then the boys would start feeling their oats and they would go too.[21]

But there was little status derived from excelling at school or in performing well in a job. In general, the girls' status within the group was achieved primary by sexual activity and by fighting.

Discussion

The picture of the Vice Queens that emerges suggests that they bear some resemblance to the gang girls described in the 1960s, but also that they were more autonomous and more prone to conflict and violence than girl gangs in the 1960s were generally perceived to be. It does appear that the Vice Queens were enmeshed in traditional female roles within a male-dominated delinquent subculture. Specifically, the Vice Queens' existence was traditional in the following ways. As an auxiliary to the Vice Kings, the girl gang members' major activities centered around providing the boys with sexual favors. The Vice Queens also sought out the status conferred through sexual liaisons with high-status Vice Kings. When the Vice Queens participated in boys' conflict situations, they usually acted as instigators and as weapon carriers, and occasionally fought against the enemy's female gang members. In this respect, they could be viewed more as a "cause" than as a "cure" for the boys' violent activities.

However, the present portrait of the Vice Queens also agrees with a number of observations of gang girl behavior in the seventies. The Vice Queens can be characterized as more autonomous than mere auxiliaries, but not fully independent of the Vice Kings. Independent of the boys, they made some of their own decisions on internal matters, and participated in conflict situations and other norm-violating activities. The Vice Queens were also actively involved in crimes traditionally viewed as "male" (e.g., strong-arming, car theft, etc.) and they engaged frequently in aggressive and violent behavior. Clearly, these black gang girls fought their own battles and took pride in their ability to look after themselves. They also competed with each other in such status-conferring arenas as conflict situations and the skillful employment of their sex.

Although the Vice Queens share some common elements with other urban female gangs prior to the seventies, it is not possible to generalize from this group to the situation of urban female gangs in general. The value of the data on the Vice Queens, however, is that it challenges these earlier ethnographic accounts' narrow focus upon a few gang girl roles: i.e., gang girls were mainly observed as sexual objects, as agent provocateurs and as "cat fighters." It would be tempting to speculate that this narrow focus reflected the prevailing cultural bias that (1) girls' delinquent behavior is synonymous with sexual delinquency or (2) that the male delinquent subculture serves as the nucleus around which girls orbit.[22] It is not possible to draw such conclusions in this regard. Instead, the account on the Vice Queens leads us to conclude that the material on the Vice Queens provides a more complex and multi-dimensional description of the nature of the female gang, during the early sixties, than previously assumed. The Vice Queens perhaps simply provide a more detailed, more revealing portrait.

The Vice Queens' behavior also bears some resemblance to those ethnographic accounts on the urban female gang after the emergence of the women's movement. The material on the Vice Queens challenges some recent observations (see Campbell, 1981, 1984; and Bowker, 1978) that girl gangs have evolved to a position of greater autonomy and independence as well as evolved to a closer approximation of the male delinquent subculture with its emphasis on violence and aggression. The present research fills an important information gap concerning the position from which girl gangs evolved. This material, then, can be considered as a forerunner to these more recent ethnographic studies which observed female gang behavior as behavior in its own right—or as a subject to be taken seriously. On this basis, we can further conclude that the research reported here and these more recent studies share a tradition of providing rich and detailed descriptions of the structure and function of female delinquent gangs. However, it would be difficult to speculate whether researchers' perceptions or perspectives of gang girls have changed.

Of particular interest here is that membership in the Vice Queens is associated with a high probability of involvement in aggressive and violent behavior as well as in more serious "male" crimes, supposedly a characteristic of black female gangs after the seventies (Brown, 1977; Campbell, 1984; and Giordano, 1978). Some observations offered in the current criminological literature to explain black females' illegal behavior as approximating the masculine crime model are of relevance here.

First, the literature on the black female offers "distinctive socialization" as a crucial factor that may explain the criminal and delinquent behavior of black females (Brooks, 1980; Datesman and Scarpitti, 1980; Lewis, 1981; Mulvihill et al., 1969). Unlike their white counterparts, lower class black male and females are both socialized to be independent, assertive and to take risks with the expectations that these are characteristics that they will need to function effectively within the black low income community. Given this, there is no tradition separating large areas of social life of black lower class boys and girls. As a consequence, black girls demonstrate, out of necessity, a greater flexibility in roles. Mulvihill et al. (1969:425) point out, "Where the cultural roles of women and men come to resemble each other, their crime rates also come closer together." The accounts on the Vice Queens as well as more recent accounts on black gang girls lend credence to these observations. The girls in these study populations participate in lower class street life and tend to participate in activities similar to those of gang boys. And thus these gang girls come to be active in "male" crimes because of their social position, a position that appears to permit these girls a great deal of freedom and lack of supervision. Within this context, the findings reported suggest that the Vice Queens utilize the female auxiliary gang as a means to acquire some knowledge of such adaptive strategies as hustling and fighting in order to be prepared to survive as independent adult women within their community.

Second, a number of researchers contend that the "status equality" of both black females and males is a crucial factor in determining black female participation in more serious "male" crimes (Adler, 1975; Brown, 1977; Lewis, 1981). Black lower class girls have "status equality" since they share the same subordinate position of males of their race. Both sexes equally experience the consequences of racism, poverty and structural constraints, share subordinate positions and have limited access to legitimate opportunity structures. Brown elaborates on this position which is as relevant to the situation of the Vice Queens as to black females who joined gangs in Philadelphia during the seventies. He points out that since girls are exposed to essentially the same milieu as that of boys in low income neighborhoods, and since these girls are in search of their identity within a community where opportunities are limited to the ghetto-specific lifestyle, violence and aggressive behavior become a viable means for establishing identity.

These factors, however, do not directly address the following issue: Although the Vice Queens participate in conflict situations, current research provides some evidence that since the emergence of the women's movement, black gang girls' involvement in conflict situations has increased (Adler, 1975; Bowker, 1978). Some researchers have suggested that perhaps black gang girls today are responding in a violent and aggressive manner to the economic conditions facing lower income blacks as well as the ambiguity of their future. There has been little improvement in the economic situation of the black community since 1965. As black females growing up, the Vice Queens' situation was bleak. They lived in a black lower income community characterized by high chronic unemployment and intermittent employment as well as high homicide, crime, drug addiction and alcoholism rates. Current examinations of the black lower income community shows that the problems of twenty years ago remain the problems of today only they are more impacted (see for instance, Cross, 1984; and Glasgow, 1980). The situation for teenage black girls today is even bleaker than it was for the Vice Queens during the early sixties. The findings suggest that as black girls are increasingly exposed to the worsening conditions within their low income neighborhoods where legitimate opportunities become increasingly restricted, then they will increasingly turn to black female auxiliary gangs which provide these girls with the opportunity to learn the skills to make adaptations to poverty, violence and racism. Thus black girls who join gangs today are no different than their sisters, the Vice Queens, but they have gone one step further. In response to the economic crisis within their communities, black female gangs today have become more entrenched, more violent and more oriented to "male" crime. These changes in the content of the black female gang appear not to be related to the women's liberation movement but to forced "emancipation" which stems from the economic crisis within the black community.

Author's Note

The author is grateful to James F. Short, Jr., who made this project feasible and provided counsel throughout its course.

Notes

1. The role of females in Chicago gangs described by Short and Strodtbeck (1965) is documented by Keiser (1969) and Dawley (1973) who provided extensive accounts of the Vice Kings' activities during the sixties.
2. According to Fields and Walters (1985) and Valentine (1978), hustling refers to a wide variety of conventional, sometimes extra-legal or illegal activities designed to produce economic gain.
3. The most comprehensive discussion of the design of this study is found in James F. Short, Jr., and Fred L. Strodtbeck, *Group Process and Gang Delinquency* (Chicago: University of Chicago Press, 1965), pp. 1-26.
4. Detached worker's interview, Youth Studies Program, University of Chicago, May, 1962.
5. Detached worker's interview, Youth Studies Program, University of Chicago, June 2, 1962.
6. Detached worker's interview, Youth Studies Program, University of Chicago, June 21, 1962.
7. Detached worker's interview, Youth Studies Program, University of Chicago, March 12, 1962.
8. Detached worker's interview, Youth Studies Program, University of Chicago, June 21, 1962.
9. A similar observation was made by Campbell (1981; 1982) in her study of female gangs in England.
10. Detached worker's interview, Youth Studies Program, University of Chicago, May 24, 1962.
11. See Cohen (1955), p. 146.
12. Detached worker's interview, Youth Studies Program, University of Chicago, June 21, 1962.
13. Observer's report, Youth Studies Program, University of Chicago, August 21, 1963.
14. Observer's report, Youth Studies Program, University of Chicago, February 8, 1962.
15. Detached worker's report, Youth Studies Program, University of Chicago, November 9, 1961.
16. Observer's report, Youth Studies Program, University of Chicago, August 21, 1963.
17. Detached worker's interview, Youth Studies Program, University of Chicago, July 16, 1962.
18. Observer's report, Youth Studies Program, University of Chicago, March 21, 1962.
19. *Ibid.*
20. Detached worker's interview, Youth Studies Program, University of Chicago, June 2, 1962.
21. Detached worker's interview, Youth Studies Program, University of Chicago, May 24, 1962.
22. According to feminist criminologists, the literature on female crime, prior to the seventies, has been hampered by a sexist translation insofar as it tended to reduce all female delinquent and criminal behavior to a fundamentally sexual level (see, for instance, Campbell, 1981, 1984; Klein, 1973; and Smart, 1977).

References

Ackley, E. and B. R. Fliegel (1960). "A Social Work Approach to Street Corner Girls." *Social Work*, 1960, 5:29-31.

Adler, F. (1975). *Sisters in Crime: The Rise of the New Female*. New York: McGraw-Hill.

Bell, R. R. (1971). "The Related Importance of Mother and Wife Roles Among Black Lower Class Women." R. Staples (ed.), *The Black Family: Essays and Studies*. Belmont, CA: Wadsworth Publishing Co., 248-255.

Bowker, L. H. (1978). "Gangs and Prostitutes: Two Case Studies of Female Crime." L. H. Bowker (ed.), *Women, Crime, and the Criminal Justice System*. Lexington, MA: 143-169.

Bowker, L. H., Gross, H.S., and Klein, M. W. (1980). "Female Participation in Delinquent Gang Activities." *Adolescence*, 15:509-519.

Bowker, L. H. and Klein, M. W. (1983). "The Etiology of Female Juvenile Delinquency and Gang Membership: A Test of Psychological and Social Structural Explanations." *Adolescence*, 18:739-751.

Brooks, A. B. (1980). "The Black Woman Within the Program and Service Delivery Systems for Battered Women: A Cultural Response." *Battered Women: An Effective Response*, Chapter 2, Minnesota Department of Corrections.

Brown, W. K. (1974). "An Expressive Culture Approach to Understanding Gang Delinquency." *American Journal of Corrections*, 36:44-46.

—— (1977). "Black Female Gangs in Philadelphia." *International Journal of Offender Therapy and Comparative Criminology*, 21:221-228.

—— (1978). "Black Gangs as Family Extensions." *International Journal of Offender Therapy and Comparative Criminology*, 22:39-45.

Campbell, A. (1981). *Girl Delinquents*. New York: St. Martin's Press.

—— (1982). "Female Aggression." P. Marsh and A. Campbell (eds.), *Aggression and Violence*. New York: St. Martin's Press, 137-150.

—— (1984). "Girl's Talk: The Social Representation of Aggression by Female Gang Members." *Criminal Justice and Behavior*, 11:139-156.

—— (1984). *The Girls in the Gang: A Report from New York City*. New York: Basil Blackwell, Inc.

Cohen, A. K. (1955). *Delinquent Boys: The Culture of the Gang*. Glencoe: The Free Press.

Cohen, A. K., and Short, Jr., J. F. (1958). "Research in Delinquent Subcultures." *Journal of Social Issues*, 14:20-37.

Cross, T. (1984). *The Black Power Imperative: Racial Inequality and the Politics of Nonviolence*. New York: Faulkner Books.

Datesman, S. K., Scarpitti, F. R., and Stephenson, R. M. (1975). "Female Delinquency: An Application of Self and Opportunities Theories." *Journal of Research in Crime and Delinquency*, 12:107-123.

Dawley, D. (1973). *A Nation of Lords: The Autobiography of the Vice Lords*. Garden City, NY: Anchor Books.

Fields, A. and Walters, J. M. (1985). "Hustling: Supporting a Heroin Habit." Hanson, B., Beschner, G., Walters, J. M., and Bovelle, E. (eds.), *Life with Heroin: Voices from the Inner City*. Lexington, MA: Lexington Books, 49-73.

Giordano, P. (1978). "Girls, Guys and Gangs: The Changing Social Context of Female Delinquency." *Journal of Criminal Law and Criminology*, 69:126-132.

Glasgow, D. G. (1980) *The Black Underclass: Poverty, Unemployment and Entrapment of Ghetto Youth.* New York: Vintage Books.

Hammond, B. E. and Ladner, J. (1969). "Socialization into Sexual Behavior in a Negro Slum Ghetto." C. B. Broderick and J. Bernard (eds.), *The Individual, Sex, and Society.* Baltimore: Johns Hopkins Press, 41-45.

Hanson, K. (1964). *Rebels in the Streets: The Story of New York's Girl Gangs.* Englewood Cliffs, NJ: Prentice-Hall.

Keiser, R. L. (1969). *The Vicelords: Warriors of the Streets.* New York: Holt, Reinhart and Winston.

Klein, D. (1973). "The Etiology of Female Crime: A Review of the Literature." *Issues in Criminology*, 8:3-30.

Ladner, J. (1972). *Tomorrow's Tomorrow: The Black Woman.* Garden City, NY: Doubleday.

Laub, J. H. and McDermott, M. J. (1985). "An Analysis of Serious Crime by Young Black Women." *Criminology*, 23:81-98.

Lewis, D. K. (1981) "Black Women Offenders and Criminal Justice: Some Theoretical Considerations." M. Q. Warren (ed.), *Comparing Female and Male Offenders.* Beverly Hills: Sage Publications, 89-103.

Luce, G. (1971). "Delinquent Girl Gangs." J. Sergel (ed.), *The Mental Health of the Child.* Washington, DC: U.S. Government Printing Office.

McCray, C. A. (1980). "The Black Woman and Family Roles." L. F. Roders-Rose, *The Black Woman.* Beverly Hills: Sage Publications, 67-78.

Miller, W. B. (1958). "Lower Class Culture as a Generating Milieu of Gang Delinquency." *Journal of Social Issues*, 14:5-19.

—— (1966). "Violent Crimes in City Gangs." *Annals of the American Academy of Political and Social Science*, 364:96-112.

—— (1973). "The Molls." *Society*, II:32-35.

—— (1975). *Violence by Youth Gangs as a Crime Problem in North American Cities.* Washington, DC: United States Government Printing Office.

Mulvihill, D., Tumin, J. M., and Curtis, L. (1969) *Crimes of Violence, Volume 12.* A staff report submitted to the National Commission on the Causes and Prevention of Violence. Washington, DC: Government Printing Office.

Quicker, J. C. (1974). "The Chicana Gang: A Preliminary Description," paper presented at the annual meeting of the Pacific Sociological Association, San Jose.

—— (1975). "Home-Girls and Home-Boys: A Theory of Female Gang Membership," which is a revision of "Chicana Gang Membership as a Function of Institutional Failure," paper presented at the annual meeting of The Pacific Sociological Association, Victoria.

Rice, R. (1963). "A Reporter at Large: The Persian Queens." *New Yorker*, 39:153-187.

Short, Jr., J. F. (1968). *Gang Delinquency and Delinquent Subcultures.* New York: Harper and Row.

Short, Jr., J. F. and Strodtbeck, F. L. (1965). *Group Process and Gang Delinquency.* Chicago: University of Chicago Press.

Smart, C. (1977). *Women, Crime and Criminology: A Feminist Critique.* London: Routledge and Kegan Paul.

Staples, R. (1973) *The Black Woman in America.* Chicago: Nelson-Hall Publishers.

Thompson, D. (1974). *Sociology of the Black Experience.* Westport, CT: Greenwood Press.

Thrasher, F. M. (1927). *The Gang.* Chicago: University of Chicago Press.

Valentine, B. (1978). *Hustling and Other Hard Work: Life Styles in the Ghetto.* New York: The Free Press.

Young, V. D. (1980). "Women, Race, and Crime." *Criminology*, 18:26-34. ✦

12

Gender Differences in Gang Participation, Delinquency, and Substance Use

Beth Bjerregaard and Carolyn Smith

Gang researchers have often treated female gang membership as if it were caused by an entirely different set of factors than those which lead males to join gangs. Bjerregaard and Smith provide one of the few comprehensive examinations of the etiology of male and female gang membership. Their study indicates that the same factors are relevant for explaining gang membership for both groups; such factors include peer delinquency and early sexual activity.

Bjerregaard and Smith's work is also important because they found the rates of female and male gang participation within high-risk communities to be comparable. In addition, they report that gang membership has an enhancement effect on delinquency for both males and females. This study highlights the importance of doing research that is comparative in nature.

The purpose of this paper is to respond to gaps in our knowledge about patterns of female gang participation and its causes and consequences. Data from the Rochester Youth Development Study, a panel study that overrepresents adolescents at high risk for delinquency, are used to compare gang participation and delinquent involvement of female and male adolescents. We then examine the role of theoretical variables associated with both female and male gang membership. The results lead us to conclude that, for females as well as males, involvement in gangs is associated with substantially increased levels of delinquency and substance use. There is also some similarity in the factors associated with gang membership for both sexes, although lack of school success emerges as a factor of particular salience for female adolescents. The results suggest that theory and intervention need to address the phenomenon of female gang membership as an important component of urban youth problems.

Reprinted from *Journal of Quantitative Criminology*, 1993, 4:329-55. © Plenum Publishing Corporation. Beth Bjerregaard teaches in the Department of Criminal Justice, University of North Carolina at Charlotte, and Carolyn Smith teaches at the School of Social Welfare, State University of New York at Albany. Authors' names are used in alphabetical order. Reprinted by permission.

1. Introduction

Although gang membership and gang-related behavior have been important topics in criminological research since the 1920s, much of our knowledge about gang behavior comes from research conducted during the 1950s and 1960s. Criminologists have studied why adolescents join gangs, what factors are related to gang membership, and whether and to what extent gangs promote delinquent and violent conduct.

During the 1980s and 1990s, a resurgence in gang research has reflected a renewal of concern about the nature and extent of gang-related crime and delinquency. Recent studies indicate that gangs have become more prevalent within the last decade and that cities throughout the United States, especially major urban centers, are contending with increasing numbers of gangs (Bryant, 1989; Miller, 1982; Hagedorn, 1988; New York State Division for Youth, 1990; Spergel, 1990). Gangs have begun to appear in suburbs and smaller towns previously thought to be immune to gang activity (New York State Division for Youth, 1990; Huff, 1990). Moreover, official data, self-reports, and observational studies converge to suggest that gangs account for disproportionate amounts of crime (Bobrowski, 1988; Curry and Spergel, 1992; Maxson and Klein, 1990; Tracy, 1987), violence (Hagedorn, 1988; Spergel, 1990; Fagan, 1990), and, increasingly, drug use (Fagan, 1989; Moore, 1991; Vigil, 1988).

1.1 Research Problem

These findings suggest that there is a basis for increased concern about gangs. However, a large proportion of the information collected on gang members and gang behavior, from both earlier studies and more recent ones, is based on male gangs and male gang members (Campbell, 1984, 1990). Even information on female gang members, as Campbell (1990) has noted, has often been gathered from male gang members talking to male researchers. Most of what we know about female gangs is also limited to a few cities and ethnic groups.[1] The purpose of this paper is to respond to this gap in our knowledge, empirically examine the patterns and nature of female gang membership, and compare it to the patterns and nature of male gang membership.

1.2. Gang Membership and Delinquency for Males and Females

Knowledge about female gangs is limited in part by the perception that female gangs are less common and less criminal than male gangs. Early studies only briefly mentioned the existence, and provided little documentation, of female participation (Thrasher, 1927). Studies examining official data generally have found that only a small percentage of officially labeled gang offenders is female (Thrasher, 1927; Miller, 1975; Spergel, 1986; Bobrowski, 1988). Moreover, females are rarely arrested for violent or weapon-related behavior (Campbell, 1984, 1990). Similarly, earlier research suggests that the delinquency of female gang members is less serious than that of males. Female gang members are often characterized as assuming auxiliary roles in gang activities or as assisting male gang members—most often by carrying weapons, providing alibis, or spying for male members (Cohen, 1955; Cloward and Ohlin, 1960; Short and Strodtbeck, 1965; Campbell, 1990; Spergel, 1990). These works stress not only the subordinate nature of the roles assumed by female gang members, but also the relatively minor nature and infrequency of offenses in which they engage.

However, more recent studies based on other sources of data suggest a somewhat different picture of female gang membership. Estimates based on recent observational and self-report studies suggest that the proportion of gang members who are female ranges from approximately 10 to 30% and is greater than official data indicate (Campbell, 1984; Miller, 1975; Esbensen et al., 1991; Moore, 1991). In addition, self-report research suggests that female gang membership may be increasing (Esbensen et al., 1991; Fagan, 1990; Winfree et al., 1992). Female gang members now face serious problems with drugs, sexual exploitation, violence, and the criminal justice system, according to observational research (Moore, 1991; Vigil, 1988, p. 101). Taken together, this work indicates the need for more extensive and systematic investigation into the gang participation of females.

1.3. Theoretical Perspectives on Gang Involvement

The theoretical literature explaining gang membership among females is relatively sparse. Theorists such as Cohen (1955), Bloch and Neiderhoffer (1958), Miller (1958), Yablonsky (1962), and Cloward and Ohlin (1960) viewed female gang membership as nonexistent, peripheral, or relatively unimportant and, instead, developed theories of male gang membership. These theories focused on sociological variables such as strain (Cloward and Ohlin, 1960), subcultural affiliation (Miller, 1958; Cohen, 1955), and neighborhood social control (Thrasher, 1927). Other approaches explained male gang membership through delinquent peer associations, social disorganization, and social class differences (Huff, 1990; Spergel, 1990).

From the literature addressing female gang participation, two schools of thought have emerged. The first argues that the factors explaining female gang membership are different in nature from those that explain male gang membership. Campbell, for example, in examining the earlier gang literature, refers to "two themes apparent in much of this early work: the psychological problems and inappropriate gender-role behavior of female gang members" (1987, p. 451). Neither of these themes was featured in research on male gangs.

The second school of thought argues that the factors explaining female gang involvement are not fundamentally different from those explaining male gang membership. According to this view, girls and boys are influenced by similar structural factors, especially marginal economic conditions (Campbell, 1994, 1990; Moore, 1991; Harris, 1988; Vigil, 1988). For example, Vigil (1988, p. 101) suggests that "the dialectic of multiple marginality applies to why females now are more active in gangs." Further, he suggests that the female gang member of today is comparable to the male gang member of the past in terms of issues such as their low social status, residence in disorganized areas, and exposure to street socialization. Others concur by indicating that female gang members have fewer opportunities to succeed—for example, with employment in well-paying jobs—than their low-income male counterparts (Covey et al., 1992, p. 83).

Because of the lack of integrated research on female and male gang membership, we have not established which of these two views has stronger support. One approach to examining the gender gap in criminological theory, as Smith and Paternoster (1987, p. 142) have noted, is to examine empirically whether concepts derived from traditional theories of male criminal behavior can also explain female criminal behavior. We move somewhat further and apply theoretical variables from the female gang literature to male gang membership, as well as the reverse. Based on the previous research on female and male gang involvement, we selected four domains for further investigation: social disorganization and poverty, delinquent peers, family processes, and personal maladjustment. The literature with respect to each is briefly discussed.

1.3.1. Social Disorganization and Poverty. Social disorganization in communities, defined as a breakdown in institutional controls generated by urban change (Kornhauser, 1978), is one of the oldest explanations of gang membership. Gang formation has been seen as a symptom of underlying disorganization in the community (Thrasher, 1927; Spergel, 1966) or even an effort to create order out of disorder in communities (Kornhauser, 1978). Empirical research has confirmed that measures of social disorganization are useful predictors of gang homicides (Curry and Spergel, 1988).

Lower social class as a distinctive factor in gang formation has also been stressed in traditional gang literature, though the mechanism linking social class and gang involvement is variously identified. Gang membership has been seen as a solution to the curtailed opportunities for traditional success available to lower-class boys (Cohen, 1955; Miller, 1958; Cloward and Ohlin, 1960). Low social class and disrupted neighborhoods also restrict educational opportunity, an important correlate of delinquency. Research on male gangs has concluded that gang boys are likely both to come from lower class neighborhoods and to do poorly in school (Cartwright et al., 1975; Curry and Spergel, 1992).

Some suggest that the strain arising from disrupted neighborhoods and restricted opportunities pushes females to precocious sexuality and personal maladjustment, as opposed to other forms of deviance (Cohen, 1955). However, there is no a priori reason to suggest that such factors would not lead girls to join gangs as well. Indeed, more contemporary research investigating the relationship between class and female gang participation contends that gang girls do indeed abandon traditional expectations for success due to their lack of educational achievement, employment opportunities, childrearing responsibilities, and social isolation, as well as the powerlessness of underclass membership (Campbell, 1990, p. 173). Other studies suggest that educational and economic marginality are related to female as well as male gang membership (Bowker and Klein, 1983; Moore, 1991). Thus it appears that for both sexes, the gang may be viewed as a response to problems inherent in disorganized neighborhoods with lower-class opportunity structures.

1.3.2. Delinquent Peers. Traditionally, gang theorists such as Thrasher (1927), Cohen (1955), Cloward and Ohlin (1960), and Miller (1958) have stressed the importance of the peer group for male gang membership. Explanations focus both on the existence of a peer network and on characteristics of that network. For example, both Miller and Cohen suggest that the gang provides males with a reference group through which nonconventional status can be achieved. Social learning theory suggests that peer groups call provide strong models and reinforcements for deviance (Akers, 1985). Empirically, a strong relationship has been demonstrated between peer relationships and gang deviance for males (Klein and Maxson, 1989).

Research on female delinquency and gang deviance also suggests that peers influence female gang membership (Brown, 1977; Bowker and Klein, 1983; Campbell, 1990; Figueira-McDonough et al., 1991; Giordano, 1978; Morash, 1983). For example, a study of incarcerated females found that females who identified themselves as being members of either a regular group or a gang were more likely to be delinquent than their counterparts and were receiving support and approval for these behaviors from their girlfriends (Giordano, 1978). Contemporary studies also suggest that the relationships of female adolescents to their girlfriends are strong predictors of both gang membership and delinquency (Bowker and Klein, 1983) and generally support the notion that peers are centrally involved with female gang choices (Campbell, 1984, 1990; Moore, 1991). The "sisterhood" of the gang appears to exert a powerful influence on female as well as male gang membership and behavior (Campbell, 1990, p. 175).

1.3.3. Family Processes. Two important dimensions of family processes associated with female deviance are affective relationships and parental control practices within the home (Maccoby and Martin, 1983; Henggeler, 1989; Geismar and Wood, 1986). Both have also been associated with female gang participation (Campbell, 1984; Moore, 1991). Research examining the role of family processes in explaining deviance suggests that these processes generally have a stronger influence on females than on males (Canter, 1982; Cernkovich and Giordano, 1987; Gibbons, 1976). A belief that females are more vulnerable to exploitation than males appears to engender both closer supervision of females and greater integration into the family (Brown, 1977; Thrasher, 1927). Males, in contrast, are afforded more freedom by their families and are less attached, especially in adolescence, than are females and, thus, have more opportunities for street activities and deviant behavior in general (Maccoby and Martin, 1983; Hill and Atkinson, 1988). Some empirical studies suggest, however, that family factors may be more strongly related to male deviance than has been theorized (Canter, 1982; Cernkovich and Giordano, 1987).

Family variables have not been a primary focus of gang research on males. Nevertheless, some research suggests that males' relationships in the family are important in understanding their gang involvement (Friedman et al., 1975). In addition, Vigil (1988) and Moore (1991) have documented the effect of family relationships on both female and male gang participation. Thus, dimensions of family life may be as important for male gang participation as they are for female participation.

1.3.4. Personal Maladjustment. A traditional explanation of female deviance, in general, and female gang membership, in particular, is that females who deviate are personally maladjusted. One type of maladjustment associated with female gang involvement is sexual activity. Cohen (1955), for example, noted that a distinguishing characteristic of female gang members was their inability to form conventional and nonsexualized relationships with the opposite sex. Precocious and indiscriminate sexuality has often been cited as a correlate of female delinquency and gang involvement, although male sexual behaviors such as rape, sexual assault, and prostitution have been ignored in research on male gang involvement (Campbell, 1984, 1990).

Yet another type of maladjustment associated with female delinquency is psychological problems (Cowie et al., 1968; Vedder and Somerville, 1975; Campbell, 1981; Morris, 1987). Several empirical studies have related female gang membership to low self-esteem (e.g., Rice, 1963; Bowker and Klein, 1983). Although low self-esteem consistently appears in the literature on female gang participation, there is little evidence on its relationship to male gang participation.

Nevertheless, self-esteem has been implicitly related to gang membership. Cohen (1955) and Yablonsky (1962) saw the gang as compensating for and reinforcing the status of its members, and recent research examining self-esteem suggests that gangs serve self-esteem enhancing functions for males (Goldstein, 1991). Research on Hispanic youth particularly has suggested that gangs become intimately tied to the youth's ego or self-respect (Vigil, 1988; Curry and Spergel, 1992; Moore, 1991). Thus, there are reasons to suggest that self-esteem, like sexual activity, is an issue in gang participation for both sexes.

1.4. Summary

This review suggests that similar risk factors may be associated with the gang participation of both females and males. However, because of the lack of integration of research on females and males, there is little empirical evidence directly comparing patterns of gang participation. We address this issue by examining two questions.

(1) Are females similar to or different from males in the extent of their gang participation, and are female gang members similar to or different from male gang members in their involvement in delinquency?

(2) Are the same risk factors related to both female and male gang participation?

2. Methods

The data for this study are from the Rochester Youth Development Study, an ongoing multiwave panel study examining the development of delinquent behavior and substance use in a predominantly high-risk, urban sample of youth. We began to ask about gang membership in wave 2, and thus we use data from waves 2 and 3 in this analysis. During wave 2, subjects were between 13 and 15 years old and were in the fall semester of the eighth or ninth grade. Wave 3 was conducted 6 months later, beginning in the spring semester of the same school year.

2.1. Sample

An important goal of the sampling strategy was to select students at high risk for delinquent conduct. The selection of Rochester as a study site was partly based on its high crime rate, which exceeds the national and New York State averages and that of New York City (Flanagan and Jamieson, 1988). To ensure that serious chronic offenders are included in the study, the sample is stratified to overrepresent high-risk youth. Males are oversampled (the sample is 75% male) because they are more likely to engage in serious delinquent behavior. Additionally, students from high-crime rate areas are oversampled, on the assumption that youths who live in such areas are at a higher risk of offending.[2] To identify high-crime rate areas, each census tract in Rochester was assigned a resident arrest rate reflecting the proportion of the tract's adult population arrested in 1986. Subjects were selected into the study with probabilities proportionate to the arrest rate in their area of residence. Because the true probability of a youth living in a particular census tract is known, the sample can be weighted to reproduce a random sample of the total seventh- and eighth-grade population of the Rochester public schools. All of the analyses which follow are weighted.[3]

Students in the final panel were selected from all students on the seventh and eighth-grade rolls in the Rochester public schools in the spring of 1988. Based on a target sample of 1000, the number of students to be selected from each census tract was determined from the arrest rate of the tract. Then students were stratified by sex and grade in school and selected at random within the tract.[4] The retention rate at wave 3 is 92% of the original panel, and the characteristics of the students retained are virtually identical to the base panel in both demographic characteristics and delinquent activities (Farnworth et al., 1990). The sample for this analysis consists of 969 adolescents who were interviewed in both wave 2 and wave 3 and whose parents were interviewed in wave 2. The sample consists of 262 females and 707 males and includes white (15.5%), African-American (67.6%), and Hispanic (16.9%) adolescents.

Face-to-face interviews with each adolescent and his or her caretaker (in 95% of the cases, the mother or stepmother) were conducted by trained interviewers at 6-month intervals. Interviews of adolescents were completed in settings that ensured confidentiality. If the student could not be contacted at school, he or she was interviewed in another private setting, usually at home. Parent or caretaker interviews were also conducted in the family home by trained interviewers. Hispanic parents were interviewed by a bilingual interviewer using a Spanish interview where necessary. Interviews with both caretakers and students were approximately 1 hr long.

Table 1

Means, Standard Deviations, and Alpha Coefficients for the Explanatory Variables[a]

	Females (*N* = 262)	Males (*N* = 707)	Total (*N* = 969)	α
Social disorganization	0.34 (0.96)	0.22 (0.96)	0.28 (0.96)	0.91
Poverty	0.38 (0.49)	0.28 (0.45)	0.33 (0.47)	
School expectations	0.88 (0.32)	0.87 (0.33)	0.87 (0.33)	
Peer delinquency	11.27 (3.81)	11.27 (3.97)	11.27 (3.88)	0.79
Parent attachment	32.09 (3.09)	32.31 (2.67)	32.30 (2.89)	0.86
Parent supervision	14.88 (1.38)	14.36 (1.62)	14.62 (1.53)	0.96
Sexual activity	0.34 (0.47)	0.51 (0.50)	0.42 (0.49)	
Self-esteem	27.42 (3.60)	27.81 (3.60)	27.62 (3.60)	0.79

[a] The coefficients presented are means, with standard deviations in parentheses.

2.2. Measurement of Variables

Variables used in the analysis are listed in Table 1, which provides descriptive data for females, males, and the total sample. Alpha reliabilities for scales are presented where appropriate.5 The text of the items is provided in the Appendix. Independent variables are drawn from the wave 2 interview schedules, with the exception of measures of social disorganization, which are derived from census tract data. Gang membership and delinquency variables combine waves 2 and 3 responses, as elaborated below. Since gang membership and delinquency cover a 1-year period preceding wave 3, the independent variables are obtained at the midpoint of this interval.

2.2.1. Independent Variables. The *social disorganization and structural domain* is represented by three variables: social disorganization, poverty, and school expectations. *Social disorganization* is measured at the census-tract level and is composed of the following variables: percentage on welfare, percentage below poverty level, population mobility, percentage of female-headed households, duration of unemployment, percentage of population with less than a high-school degree, and racial composition. These variables are from the 1980 census. The measure of social disorganization is a factor variable derived for each of 87 census tracts in the city, which is then added to the file of each individual residing in that tract. A higher score on the social disorganization variable indicates residence in a disorganized area. The variable mean is 0.28.

Poverty is measured by income data on the principal wage earner in the household. Income is dichotomized to represent those households that are at or above the national poverty level and those that are below it (U.S. Bureau of the Census, 1989). The poverty level is adjusted for household composition, allowing for the fact that a larger household puts greater pressure on a given level of family resources. Overall, about a third or the sample households report poverty level income.

School expectations is measured as a dichotomous variable indicating whether or not subjects believe they will graduate from high school. High-school graduation is considered a minimum requirement for adult employment and thus for conventional avenues of opportunity today.

Peer factors are important in a number of theoretical perspectives relevant to gang research. For this study, *peer delinquency* is measured by an eight-item scale. Subjects were asked how many of their friends committed a variety of delinquent acts within the last 6 months, ranging in severity from skipping classes to armed robbery. The four response choices range from "none of them" to "most of them." The range is 8-32, and the variable mean is 11.27. The alpha reliability for this scale is 0.79.

Family processes, as noted earlier, have been considered particularly significant for the gang involvement of females. We use two indicators of family process, one representing each of the two important domains identified earlier: attachment and control. Both measures come from questions in the student interview.[6] *Parent attachment* is measured by a scale adapted from Hudson's (1982) Child's Attitude Toward Mother (Father) Scale, a well-standardized and validated scale in the family assessment literature. The 11-item scale measures agreement on a 4-point scale with positive and negative aspects of parent-child relationships. A higher score on this scale indicates more positive and fewer negative feelings about the primary caretaker. The response range is 11-44, and the variable mean is 32.30. The reliability coefficient for this scale is 0.86.

Parent supervision is measured by a four-item scale indicating children's perceptions of the degree of supervision their parents exercise and the perceived importance of supervision to their parents. High scores on this scale indicate higher levels of parental supervision. The range is 4-16, and the mean is 14.62. The reliability coefficient for this scale is 0.96.

Personal maladjustment is a central feature of the personal pathology approach to deviance that is characteristic of earlier literature on female gangs and delinquency. We represent this domain with two indicators: sexual activity and self-esteem. *Sexual activity* is a prevalence measure indicating if the subject ever engaged in sexual intercourse up to the time of the wave 2 interview.[7] Since most respondents are age 13 or 14 during the interview period, the measure of sexual activity also captures precocious and high-risk sexual activity (Miller and Moore, 1990). The variable mean is 0.42 and is the only one on which there are substantial gender differences; the prevalence is 0.51 for males and 0.34 for females.

Self-esteem is a nine-item scale derived from Rosenberg's (1965) standardized scale measuring the extent of the subject's global self-esteem, with a high score indicating greater agreement with positive statements and greater disagreement with negative statements about oneself. The range of responses is 9-36. The variable mean is 27.62, and the alpha coefficient for this scale is 0.79.

2.2.2. Dependent Variables. One of the most significant problems plaguing gang research is the choice of an appropriate definition of a gang. Horowitz (1990) argues that our knowledge of gangs is still too fragmentary to allow precise definitions and suggests that confining the definition of the gang to specific criteria may foreclose important debate and theory. Support for this position comes from Winfree et al.(1992), who found that more restrictive measures of gang involvement were associated with less delinquent conduct compared to less restrictive measures (e.g., self-identification as a gang member). Other evidence indicates the diversity of modern gangs, such as variations in the use of gang symbols across racial and geographical lines (Curry and Spergel, 1992; Short, 1990). Many researchers agree that self-definition is a central aspect of gang membership and avoids some of the definitional debate as well as the issue of confounding definition with behavior (Fagan, 1990; Harris, 1988; Winfree et al., 1992; Zevitz and Takata, 1992). For these reasons, we allow respondents to define their own situation with respect to gang membership.8

Gang participation is measured by self-reported participation in a gang. Respondents are asked whether they belong to a gang or a "posse," the term commonly used in Rochester. Gang membership is a dichotomous measure indicating whether, in the 6 months prior to wave 2 or wave 3, the respondent reported being a member of a gang. Previous research often uses an annual report of membership because of evidence that young adolescents in particular move in and out of gangs rather frequently (Jansyn, 1966; Fagan, 1990; Moore, 1991). Twenty percent of all respondents report being members of gangs at some point during the 12-month period.

A number of self-reported *delinquency and substance use* items, adapted largely from the National Youth Survey (Elliott et al., 1985) and modified by the Denver Youth Survey (Huizinga et al., 1991a), are contained in the student interview. Five indexes are derived from the total set of items: serious delinquency, moderate delinquency, minor delinquency, alcohol use, and marijuana use. Delinquency data are summed across waves 2 and 3 to provide an estimate over 12 months.[9] Items composing each delinquency measure are given in the Appendix. Prevalence measures indicate whether or not one or more offenses in the particular index occurred in the 12-month period. Incidence refers to the mean number of offenses of a given type.

The *serious delinquency* index is an eight-item index which includes offenses of serious social concern such as car theft, assault with a weapon, and breaking and entering. The prevalence of serious delinquency in the sample is 22% and the mean incidence of serious offenses is 1.2. *Moderate delinquency* is an 11-item index that includes joyriding, fraud, and property destruction. The prevalence of moderate delinquency is 42% and the mean incidence is 3.8. *Minor delinquency* is an eight-item index that includes minor theft, being loud and rowdy in a public place, and lying about one's age. The prevalence of minor delinquency is 44% and its mean incidence is 5.9.

Substance use variables include alcohol use and marijuana use. *Alcohol use* is measured by a two-item index of drinking beer, wine, or hard liquor without parental permission. The prevalence of alcohol use is 35%, and the incidence of use, measured as the mean number of drinking episodes during the 12-month period, is 4.6. A single variable indicates *marijuana use*.[10] The prevalence of marijuana use in the sample is 17% and the mean incidence is 2.9.

Self-reported delinquency questions were asked separately from the measure of gang participation. This reduces the problem of confounding gang participation and delinquent behavior. As a consequence, our analysis examines the relationship between gang participation and involvement in delinquency and substance use, not the more specific issue of "gang delinquency." With the exception of gang fighting, we do not know if the delinquencies reported by gang members were committed as part of gang activity.

3. Results

3.1. Gang Participation

We begin by examining the extent of gang participation by females and males. Although much prior research suggests that gang membership is a predominantly male activity, our data are not consistent with this finding. In our sample, 20% (*n* = 203) of the respondents report being gang members and the prevalence rate for females (22%) is slightly higher than that for males (18%).[11] Demographic characteristics of female and male gang members are similar, with relatively more gang members of both sexes coming from racial and ethnic minority groups and from among slightly older adolescents.

Prior research suggests that gang membership enhances participation in delinquent activities (Freedman et al., 1975; Tracy, 1987; Thornberry et al., 1993b). If this is the case in our sample, the high levels of female participation in gangs should be reflected in high levels of delinquent activity by females. Thus, the second issue we examine is the extent to which female gang members are involved in delinquency and substance use, relative to male gang members and to females not in gangs.

3.2. Gang Membership and Delinquency

Rather than examining causal processes, we examine only the association between gang membership and involvement in delinquency and substance use. Other research based on RYDS data has investigated the issue of causal order across seven waves of data and found that, in general, delinquency increases after gang involvement (Thornberry et al., 1993b). Thus, gang membership appears to enhance delinquency.

Table 2

Relationship Between Gang Participation and Delinquency and Substance Use

	Gang (*N* = 203)	Nongang (*N* = 766)	Total (N = 969)
Prevalence of delinquency and substance use (%)			
Serious delinquency	73.5*	8.9	22.4
Moderate delinquency	71.1*	34.7	42.4
Minor delinquency	68.5*	37.1	43.7
Alcohol use	60.5*	28.5	35.2
Marijuana use	41.4*	10.5	17.1
Incidence of delinquency and substance use (mean)			
Serious delinquency	5.0*	0.2	1.2
Moderate delinquency	9.8*	2.2	3.8
Minor delinquency	15.7*	3.3	5.9
Alcohol use	11.6*	2.7	4.6
Marijuana use	8.0*	1.5	2.9

*P <0.01 for comparisons between gang members and nonmembers.

Several dimensions of delinquency and substance use for gang members and nonmembers are shown in Table 2. Prevalence is reported in the top panel. Each of the delinquency and substance use indexes shows significantly greater prevalence for gang members. For example, 68.5% of gang members have been involved in minor delinquency, in comparison to 37.1% of nonmembers. In fact, the discrepancy be-

Table 3

Relationship Between Gang Membership and Delinquency and Substance Use by Gender

	Females			Males		
	Gang (*N* = 60)	Nongang (*N* = 203)	Ratio	Gang (*N* = 133)	Nongang (*N* = 571)	Ratio
	Prevalence of delinquency and substance use (%)					
Serious delinquency	66.8**	6.6*	10.1	81.6	11.1*	7.4
Moderate delinquency	67.7	31.6*	2.1	75.5	37.7*	2.0
Minor delinquency	65.0	38.2*	1.7	72.7	36.2*	2.0
Alcohol use	51.4**	31.2*	1.6	71.9	25.9*	2.8
Marijuana use	43.7	11.6*	3.8	38.8	9.5*	4.0
	Incidence of delinquency and substance use (mean)					
Serious delinquency	3.7**	0.1*	37.3	6.5	0.3*	25.1
Moderate delinquency	6.2**	1.6*	3.9	14.2	2.9*	4.9
Minor delinquency	10.7**	3.5*	3.1	21.9	3.2*	6.9
Alcohol use	9.3	2.6	3.6	14.5	2.8*	5.2
Marijuana use	4.2**	0.9*	4.6	13.8	2.3*	5.9

*$P<0.05$ for comparisons between gang members and nonmembers within sex subgroups
**$P<0.05$ for comparisons between female and male gang members

tween gang members' delinquent involvement and the involvement of nonmembers is most pronounced for serious offenses (73.5% compared to 8.9%). The incidence of delinquency (bottom panel in Table 2) shows a similar pattern. Gang membership is associated with significantly more frequent involvement in delinquency and substance use and the differences between gang members and nonmembers, again, are larger for the most serious offenses.

The data in Table 3 comparing the delinquency of gang members and nonmembers for females and males separately allow us to examine two issues. First, do female and male gang members have different rates of delinquency and substance use? Second, is gang membership associated with greater involvement in delinquency for both females and males? We begin by discussing the prevalence of delinquency (top panel in Table 3).

The prevalence rates of delinquency are higher for male gang members than female gang members in four of the comparisons, but only two of the differences are significant (significance tests for this comparison are indicated by a superscript double-asterisk). However, female gang members report slightly (though not significantly) higher marijuana use than do male gang members. Compared to female gang members, male gang members are more likely to engage in serious delinquency and alcohol use but not in other forms of delinquency or substance use.

The second question concerns the relationship between gang membership and involvement in delinquency for females and males. Male gang members are significantly more likely than nonmembers to commit all types of delinquent offenses (significance tests for this comparison are indicated by a superscript asterisk in Table 3). These differences are most pronounced for more serious forms of delinquency. For example, 81.6% of the male gang members reported at least one serious delinquent offense, compared to 11.1% of nonmembers. Comparisons between gang and nongang females also show significant differences for all behaviors. For example, female gang members report a serious delinquency prevalence of 66.8%, compared to 6.6% for nonmembers.

As a summary measure of the positive association between delinquency and gang membership for females and males, ratios of gang member-to-nonmember delinquency are also reported. These standardize for different base rates of female and male delinquency. For example, 37.7% of the nongang males report moderate delinquency, as compared to 75.5% of the gang males, for a ratio of 2.0 to 1. The comparable rates for females are 31.6 and 67.7%, for a ratio of 2.1 to 1. The ratios for minor and moderate types of offenses and substance use are very similar for both females and males. Overall, prevalence ratios range between 2.0 (minor and moderate delinquency) and 7.4 (serious delinquency) for males and between 1.6 (alcohol use) and 10.1 (serious delinquency) for females, indicating similar ranges.

Incidence data are presented in the lower panel in Table 3. In all comparisons, male gang members report a significantly higher incidence of delinquency and substance use than female gang members (significance tests are indicated by a superscript double-asterisk). Only the difference for alcohol use fails to attain statistical significance. However, the association between incidence of delinquency and gang membership is similar irrespective of gender. For example, male gang members have engaged in an average of 14.2 acts of moderate delinquency, in comparison to 2.9 for nongang males. The comparable figures for females are 6.2 and 1.6. The ratios of the incidence of delinquency and substance use for males are slightly larger than for females for all but the most serious offenses.[12]

These findings indicate that for females and males, gang participation is associated with a greater prevalence and incidence of delinquency and substance use. Furthermore, the results suggest that for both sexes, the association between gang membership and a variety of measures of delinquent behavior is of a similar magnitude.

We next examine whether the risk factors associated with gang membership differ for females and males, as previous research has suggested.

Table 4

Results from Logistic Regression Equations Predicting Gang Participation for Females and Males[a]

	Female	Male	t value[b]
Social disorganization	0.13 0.19 (0.02)	0.25 0.14 (0.04)	0.74
Poverty	0.23 0.38 (0.04)	0.32 0.27 (0.05)	0.30
School examinations	-2.51** 0.72 (-0.20)	0.04 0.47 (0.01)	4.62**
Peer delinquency	0.13** 0.05 (0.02)	0.17** 0.03 (0.03)	0.95
Parent attachment	-0.12 0.06 (-0.02)	-0.06 0.05 (-0.01)	1.23
Parent supervision	- 0.01 0.14 (0.00)	-0.03 0.07 (0.00)	-0.19
Sexual activity	1.52** 0.38 (0.34)	0.91** 0.28 (0.17)	-1.96*
Self-esteem	0.01 0.05 (0.00)	-0.05 0.04 (-0.01)	-1.29

[a]The coefficients presented are, in order, parameter estimates, standard errors, and probabilities (in parentheses).
[b]Test for significance of difference between subsample coefficients.
* P.< 0.05
** P.< 0.01

3.3. Factors Associated with Gang Membership

Our dependent variable, gang membership, is dichotomous, so we use logistic regression to examine the correlates of gang membership separately for females and males. Table 4 reports the logistic regression coefficients, standard errors, and the percentage change in probability of joining a gang given an increase of one unit in each of the risk factors.[13] To determine whether differences between the female and the male equations are significant, *t* tests of subsample coefficients are reported.

The results indicate that our measure of social disorganization is not significantly associated with gang membership for either sex. Poverty, at the individual household level, is also not associated with gang membership for either females or males. The failure to find an association between either social disorganization or poverty and gang membership may relate to the sample selection process utilized here. That is, high-risk youth are oversampled and the range in the variables is, therefore, limited.

A somewhat unexpected finding is that the only variable that is uniquely associated with gang membership for females is school expectations. For females, having low expectations of completing school increases the probability of gang membership by 20%, in comparison to only 1% for males. The coefficients for the sexes are significantly different, indicating that the association between school expectations and gang membership is significantly different for females and males. This is consistent with the findings that opportunity factors have a particularly important impact on females' gang activities (Campbell, 1984, 1990; Bowker and Klein, 1983; Winfree et al., 1992).

Peer delinquency, a factor associated strongly with male gang membership in past research, is significantly associated with gang membership for males in our sample. However, peer delinquency is also significant for females, a finding consistent with research suggesting that peer behavior is critically important for females' delinquency and gang membership (Giordano et al., 1986; Bowker and Klein, 1983; Campbell, 1990). The association between delinquent friends and gang membership, while significant, is not large for either males or females, increasing the probability of gang membership for males by 3% and for females by 2%.[14]

Family processes have been associated strongly with female deviance and more weakly with male deviance. However, contrary to previous research, neither attachment to parents nor family supervision emerges as a significant correlate of gang membership for either sex once other factors are controlled. This finding contradicts the qualitative evidence from observational studies of female gang members (Moore, 1991; Harris, 1988). One explanation is that parental support and supervision have an earlier, indirect effect on gang membership, for example, through expectations and peer associations (Thornberry, 1987).[15]

Finally, although individual and sexual dysfunction has received more attention in the literature on female gang membership, we find substantive commonality between the sexes. Low self-esteem is unrelated to gang membership for both sexes, and early or precocious sexual activity is significantly associated with gang membership for both sexes. However, the association between sexual activity and gang membership is significantly stronger for females than males. Early engagement in sexual intercourse increases the probability of joining the gang for the average respondent by 17% for males and by 34% for females. An analysis of the temporal order of these two variables found only one case in which sexual activity followed reported gang membership, suggesting that this activity is not a product of having joined the gangs.[16]

4. Discussion and Conclusions

Overall, we find that the extent of female participation in gangs differs from the picture presented by earlier researchers. First, females look rather similar to males in rate of gang participation. More importantly, gang members of *both* sexes are significantly more likely to have participated in delinquency, including serious delinquency and substance abuse, and to have committed these acts at much higher frequencies than nonmembers. Thus gang membership appears to have an effect on delinquency and substance use across both sexes. Second, we also find substantial similarity in the risk factors associated with gang membership for both females and males. Peer activity, a factor more traditionally associated with male gang membership, is significantly associated with both female and male gang participation. Sexual activity, more usually associated with female gang membership, is a significant factor in the gang participation of both sexes. Self-esteem, family processes, poverty, and social disorganization are unrelated to gang participation for either sex. Only school expectations differs in its impact on female and male gang participation.

In linking these sets of findings, we see evidence of considerable commonality in the correlates and consequences of both female and male gang participation. For both sexes, gang membership is strongly associated with both the prevalence and the incidence of delinquency and substance use, with peer delinquency, and also with other problem behaviors such as early adolescent sexual activity. These patterns are consistent with the claims of researchers who suggest that adolescent groups, including gangs, arise in the context of normal adolescent developmental needs to manage substance use, sex, and aggression (Moore, 1991; Harris, 1988). It may be that adolescents engage with other youth in a constellation of "hyperadolescent" behaviors (Goldstein, 1991), characterized by early adoption of unsanctioned adult-like behavior (Jessor et al., 1991; Newcomb and Bentler, 1988). While the precise dynamics of these interrelated behaviors are not clear, their co-occurrence indicates that prevention efforts directed at gangs need to include broad-based and comprehensive intervention efforts which increase opportunity for prosocial identity formation.

Factors traditionally associated with female gang membership, but to a lesser extent with male gang membership, include family and personal maladjustment. While the family variables are unrelated to gang membership for both females and males, sexual activity emerges as significantly associated with gang membership for both sexes. Additionally, sexual involvement at an early age appears to be more strongly associated with risk of gang involvement for females than for males. This finding suggests an important area for intervention, since these females will be at especially high risk for AIDS and other sexually transmitted diseases, as well as premarital pregnancies (Biglan et al., 1990; Ensminger, 1990).

Nevertheless, some factors associated with male gang participation in traditional theory and research turned out to be relevant for female participation as well. Peer delinquent behavior is significantly associated with the probability of gang membership for both sexes. Its impact on females is approximately equal to that for males, and the two coefficients are not significantly different. Perception of limited opportunities—as indicated by expectations of school dropout—is the only variable that differs by sex, having a significant association only with gang membership for females. Campbell's (1984) thesis that females are turning to the gang as a consequence of the lack of perceived opportunity is supported by this finding. We note that, for females, lack of opportunity in the educational realm appears especially salient.

In this context, the etiology of female gang membership may merit special consideration. The effects of school expectations argue for identifying and addressing factors that could improve girls' chances for school success and increase expectations of graduation. Since strategies designed to mediate the effects of delinquent peer groups have proved ineffective (Gottfredson, 1987), the identification of additional factors such as low school expectations and risky sexual behavior that may be more easily targeted by intervention efforts may provide a more promising route to a satisfactory nongang identity for females.

The age range of our sample of predominantly younger adolescents may restrict the generalizability of the findings to some degree. Our subjects are probably younger than is typical of those initiated into gangs. We do not know if gang membership among our respondents represents the beginning of hard core structured gang activity, a more temporary coming-together of "wild" adolescents, or the desire to be associated with more established gang members. Further research is needed to pursue the meaning and value of the gang experience at these ages for both females and males. However, our study supports other evidence of the ever-younger involvement of adolescents in gangs (Taylor, 1990; Zevitz and Takata, 1992). Factors associated with initiation into gangs at these ages should be a focal point for research, in part because this activity is a signal for the co-occurrence of other problem behaviors.

This study has demonstrated that female gang membership, as well as male gang membership, needs to be addressed in efforts to reduce urban crime. Our findings as a whole support qualitative evidence that female gang membership is an important phenomenon even at young ages, in that it is indicative of other teen problems and associated with heightened propensity for delinquency. Further research could build on our findings by examining longer-term patterns and consequences of female gang membership, as well as the factors which promote resilience to and desistance from gang involvement among vulnerable youth.

Appendix

Scale Construction (with Factor Loadings Where Appropriate)

Social Disorganization

1. % welfare recipients. 96
2. % below poverty. 91
3. Mobility in census tract. 31
4. % female-headed households. 85
5. Length of unemployment. 62
6. Education, % below high school. 81
7. % Minorities in tract. 83

School Expectations

1. Taking everything into account do you really think you will graduate from high school?

Peer Delinquency

Since we interviewed you last time, how many of (these friends) . . .

1. Used a weapon or force to get money or things from people? .68
2. Attacked someone with a weapon or with the idea of seriously hurting them? .78
3. Hit someone with the idea of hurting them? .69
4. Stole something worth more than $100? .77
5. Stole something worth more than $5 but less than $50? .79
6. Damaged or destroyed someone else's property on purpose? .73
7. Took a car or motorcycle for a ride or drive without the owner's permission? .70
8. Skipped classes without an excuse? .57

Parent Attachment

How often would you say that . . .

1. You get along well with your _? .74
2. You feel that you can really trust your _? .72
3. Your _ does not understand you? .49
4. Your _ is too demanding? .51
5. You really enjoy your _? .80
6. You have a lot of respect for your _? .60
7. Your _ interferes with your activities? .49
8. You think your _ is terrific? .76
9. You feel very angry toward your _? .62
10. You feel violent toward your _? .61
11. You feel proud of your _? .73

Parent Supervision

1. In the course of a day, how often does _ know where you are? .94
2. How often would _ know who you are with when you are away from home? .93
3. How important is it to _ to know who your friends are? .93
4. How important is it to _ to know where you are? .96

Sexual Activity

1. Have you ever had sexual intercourse?

Self-Esteem

Do you strongly agree, agree, disagree, or strongly disagree with these statements about yourself?

1. In general, you are satisfied with yourself. .59
2. You have a number of good qualities. .65
3. You can do things as well as others. .68
4. You feel at least as good as others. .66
5. At times you are no good at all. .68
6. You have much to be proud of. .66
7. You feel useless at times. .59
8. You wish you would have more respect for yourself. .40
9. Sometimes you think of yourself as bad. .57

Serious Delinquency

Since we interviewed you last time, have you (how often have you) . . .

1. Gone into or tried to go into a building to steal or damage something?
2. Tried to steal or actually stolen money or things worth between $50 and $100?
3. Tried to steal or actually stolen money or things worth more than $100?
4. Stolen or tried to steal a car or other motor vehicle?
5. Attacked someone with a weapon or with the idea of seriously hurting or killing them?
6. Been involved in gang or posse fights?
7. Used a weapon or force to make someone give you money or things?
8. Had or tried to have sexual relations with someone against their will?

Moderate Delinquency

Since we interviewed you last time, have you (how often have you) . . .

1. Been drunk in a public place?
2. Damaged, destroyed, marked up, or tagged somebody else's property on purpose?
3. Tried to steal or actually stolen money or things worth $5-$50?
4. Taken someone else's car or motorcycle for a ride without the owner's permission?
5. Forged a check or used fake money to pay for something?
6. Used or tried to use a credit card, bank card, or automatic teller card without permission?
7. Tried to cheat someone by selling them something that was not what you said it was or that was worthless?
8. Hit someone with the idea of hurting them?
9. Thrown objects such as rocks or bottles at people?
10. Made obscene phone calls?
11. Physically hurt or threatened to hurt someone to get them to have sex with you?

Minor Delinquency

Since we interviewed you last time, have you (how often have you) . . .

1. Avoided paying for things, like a movie, taking bus rides, using a computer, or anything else?
2. Lied about your age to get into some place or to buy something? (for example, lying about your age to get into a movie or buy alcohol)
3. Run away from home?
4. Skipped classes without an excuse?
5. Hitchhiked a ride with a stranger?
6. Been loud or rowdy in a public place where someone complained and you got in trouble?
7. Begged for money or things from strangers?
8. Tried to steal or actually stolen money or things worth $5 or less?

Alcohol Use

Since we interviewed you last time, have you (how often have you) . . .

1. Drunk beer or wine without your parents' permission?
2. Drunk hard liquor without your parents' permission?

Marijuana Use

Since we interviewed you last time, have you (how often have you) . . .

1. Used marijuana, reefer, or pot?

Acknowledgements

This paper was prepared under Grant 86-JN-CX-0007 (S-3) from the Office of Juvenile Justice and Delinquency Prevention, Office of Justice Programs, U.S. Department of Justice, Grant 5 R01 DA05512-02 from the National Institute on Drug Abuse, and Grant SES-8912274 from the National Science Foundation.

Notes

1. Research on female gang members has been more comprehensive in its coverage of Hispanics (e.g., Harris, 1988; Horowitz, 1983; Moore, 1991).
2. Evidence that the sampling strategy selected youths with high rates of offending comes from rates of official delinquency for our sample. For example, to date 39% of our sample have an adult or juvenile police record.
3. Two distinct weighting formulas are utilized, because the sampling procedure involves stratification by census tract and also stratification by gender. The weighting procedure thus differs, depending on whether an analysis involves the total sample or separate male and female subsamples. Because of this, some apparent differences in sample numbers appear in the tables.
4. The sampling procedure is discussed in detail by Farnworth et al. (1990) and Thornberry et al. (1993a).
5. Confirmatory factor analysis was conducted on items comprising scales using principal-component analysis and a maximum-likelihood estimation procedure. Items used in each scale loaded, in all cases, on a single factor. Scale reliabilities are computed using Cronbach's alpha.
6. Parallel questions concerning family relationships are asked of both parents and students. Research has indicated that information from different family informants is not highly related, for a variety of reasons (Krohn et al., 1992). Since the nature of this study precludes including both sets of variables, we follow the more usual convention of using data from students' perceptions.
7. A measure of the frequency of intercourse is also available; preliminary analysis suggests high correspondence in results using both measures.
8. We experimented with restricting the analysis to gang members who could provide a name for their gang and those who belonged to a gang with over six members. Because a very small number of subjects were eliminated by these restrictions and substantive conclusions remained unchanged, these restrictions are not used here.
9. Follow-up items asking respondents to describe the most serious act which they have committed in each delinquency category are used by the research team to screen out inappropriate responses, trivial responses, or responses that law enforcement officials would probably ignore (e.g., sibling squabbles). If the most serious delinquency described is not rated as delinquent, the item is coded as 0; otherwise, the entire frequency is counted. Inter-rater reliability in this exercise ranged from 90 to 95%.
10. Although there are questions about the use of other drugs in the survey, the prevalence and incidence of drug use other than marijuana at these ages are too low for meaningful analysis.
11. Although at first glance this is surprising, a similar pattern was also observed in the Denver Youth Survey (Esbensen et al., 1991).
12. It is possible that inclusion of the gang fight item in the serious delinquency scale obscures differences between gang members and nonmembers. To investigate the impact of this item, we reran the analysis reported in Tables 2 and 3, omitting it from the scale. Although the differences decline somewhat (and both gang and nongang means and prevalence decline), significant differences remain for all comparisons except the incidence of serious delinquency for gang and nongang females (where the significance drops to 0.10). Thus, substantive findings are not affected.
13. See Peterson (1985) for a discussion of translating logistic regression coefficients into probabilities and for the meaning of the logistic regression formula.
14. The weak although significant showing of peer delinquency as a risk factor for gang involvement is somewhat surprising, in view of its importance in delinquency research generally. We see two possible explanations for this. First, Warr's research (1993) using the National Youth Survey suggests that the relationship between peer delinquency and deviance increases as juveniles age, peaking in the mid to late teens. This peak is older than the ages of our subjects. Second, longitudinal analysis on this sample (Thornberry et al., 1993b) supports the contention that those who are not initially highly delinquent as individuals tend to become more jointly delinquent as they participate in gangs together. Thus, our finding may be due to both the ages of our subjects and their brief exposure to the gang experience.
15. Other analyses from the RYDS project (see, e.g., Huizinga et al., 1991b), employing a wider range of family process variables, tend to confirm that perception of family attachment is the variable most consistently associated with nondeviant outcomes in the population studied.
16. We performed a subsidiary analysis to check on the temporal order of involvement in sexual activity and reports or gang membership. In all cases, we have data on the age of onset of sexual activity. Wave 2 is the earliest age at which we collect gang membership data; thus we used age at wave 2 as a proxy for the earliest age of gang involvement at wave 2 if subjects report gang membership in this wave. Otherwise, we use age at whatever wave gang membership is initially reported. We examine waves 2 through 7 data comparing ages of involvement in both gang membership and sexual activity. We find that the weight of evidence supports our contention that sexual activity generally precedes gang involvement for both females and males, often by as much as 1 or 2 years.

References

Akers, R. L. (1985). *Deviant Behavior: A Social Learning Approach*, Wadsworth, Belmont, CA.

Biglan, A., Metzler, C. W., Wirt, R., Ary, D., Noell, J., Ochs, L., French, C., and Hood, D. (1990). Social and behavioral factors associated with high-risk sexual behavior among adolescents. *J. Behav. Med.* 13: 245-261.

Bloch, R. A., and Neiderhoffer, A. (1958). *Gang: A Study of Adolescent Behavior*, Philosophical Library, New York.

Bobrowski, L. J. (1988). *Collecting, Organizing and Reporting Street Gang Crime*, Chicago Police Department, Special Functions Group, Chicago.

Bowker, L., and Klein, M. W. (1983). The etiology of female juvenile delinquency and gang membership: A test of psychological and social structural explanations. *Adolescence* 18: 739-751.

Brown, W. K. (1977). Black female gangs in Philadelphia. *Int. J. Offend. Ther. Comp. Criminol.* 21: 221-228.

Bryant, D. (1989). Communitywide responses crucial for dealing with youth gangs. *Juv. Just. Bull.*, Office of Juvenile Justice and Delinquency Prevention, Washington, DC.

Campbell, A. (1991). *Girl Delinquents*, Basil Blackwell, Oxford.

Campbell, A. (1984). *The Girls in the Gang: A Report from New York City*, Basil Blackwell, Oxford.

Campbell, A. (1987). Self-definition by rejection: The case of gang girls. *Soc. Prob*. 34: 451-466.

Campbell, A. (1990). Female gang members. In Huff, C. R. (ed.). *Gangs in America*, Sage, Newbury Park. CA.

Canter, R. J. (1982). Family correlates of male and female delinquency. *Criminology* 20: 149-168.

Cartwright, D., Thomson, B., and Schwartz, H. (1975). *Gang Delinquency*, Brooks/Cole, Monterey, CA.

Cernkovich. S., and Giordano, P. C. (1987). Family relationships and delinquency. *Criminology* 15: 295-321.

Cloward. R. A. and Ohlin. L. E. (1960). *Delinquency and Opportunity*, Free Press. New York.

Cohen. A. K. (1955). *Delinquent Boys*, Free Press, New York.

Covey, H., Menard, S., and Farnzese, R. (1992). *Juvenile Gangs*, Charles C Thomas, Springfield, IL.

Cowie, J., Cowie. V., and Slater, E. (1968). *Delinquency in Girls*, Humanities Press. Great Britain.

Curry, G. D., and Spergel, I. A. (1988). Gang homicide, delinquency and community. *Criminology* 26: 381-405.

Curry, G., and Spergel, I. A. (1992). Gang involvement and delinquency among Hispanic and African American adolescent males. *J. Res. Crime Delinq*. 29: 273-291.

Elliott, D., Huizinga. D., and Ageton, S. (1985). *Explaining Delinquency and Drug Use*, Sage, Beverly Hills, CA.

Ensminger, M. F. (1990). Sexual activity and problem behavior among black, urban adolescents. *Child Dev*. 61: 2032-2046.

Esbensen. F., Thornberry, T. P., and Huizinga. D. (1991). Gangs. In Huizinga, D., Loeber, R., and Thornberry. T. P. (eds.), *Urban Delinquency and Substance Abuse: Technical Report*, Prepared for the Office of Juvenile Justice and Delinquency Prevention, U.S. Department of Justice, Washington. DC, Sept.

Fagan, J. (1989) The social organization of drug use and drug dealing among urban gangs, *Criminology* 27: 633-666.

Fagan, J. (1990). Social processes of delinquency and drug use among urban gangs. In Huff, C. R. (ed.), *Gangs in America*, Sage, Newbury Park, CA.

Farnworth, M., Thornberry, T. P., Lizotte, A. J., and Krohn, M. D. (1990). *Technical Report No.1: Sampling Design and Implementation*, Rochester Youth Development Study.

Figueira-McDonough, J., Barton, W. H.. and Sarri. R C. (1991). Normal deviance: Gender similarities in adolescent subcultures. In Warren, M. Q. (ed.), *Comparing Female and Male Offenders*, Sage, Beverly Hills, CA.

Flanagan. T. J.. and Jamieson, K. M. (1988). *Sourcebook of Criminal Justice Statistics, 1987*, USGPO, U.S. Department of Justice, Bureau of Justice Statistics. Washington, DC.

Friedman, C. J., Mann, F., and Friedman, A. S. (1975). A profile of juvenile street gang members. *Adolescence* 10: 563 607.

Geismar, L. L., and Wood, K. M. (1996). *Family and Delinquency: Resocializing the Young Offender*, Human Sciences Press, New York.

Gibbons, D. (1976). *Delinquent Behavior*, Prentice Hall, Englewood Cliffs, NJ.

Giordano. P. (1979). Girls, guys and gangs: The changing social context of female delinquency. *J. Crim. Law Criminol*. 69: 126.

Giordano, P., Cernkovich, S., and Pugh, M. (1986). Friendships and delinquency. *Am. J. Sociol*. 91: 1170-1202.

Goldstein. A. (1991). *Delinquent Gangs: A Psychological Perspective*, Research Press, Champaign, IL.

Gottfredson, G. D. (1987). Peer group interventions to reduce the risk of delinquent behavior: A selective review and a new evaluation, *Criminology* 25: 671-714.

Hagedorn, J. M. (1988). *People and Folks: Gangs, Crime, and the underclass in a Rust Belt City*, Lake View Press, Chicago.

Harris, M. G. (1988). *Cholas: Latino Girls and Gangs*, Amas Press, New York.

Henggeler, S. W. (1989). *Delinquency in Adolescence, Vol. 18. Developmental Clinical Psychology and Psychiatry*, Sage, Newbury Park, CA.

Hill. G. D.. and Atkinson, M. P. (1998). Gender, familiar control and delinquency, *Criminology* 28: 601-626.

Horowitz, R. (1983) *Honor and the American Dream: Culture and Identity in a Chicano Community*, Rutgers University Press, New Brunswick. NJ.

Horowitz, R. (1990). Sociological perspectives on gangs: Conflicting definitions and concepts. In Huff, C. R. (ed.), *Gangs in America*, Sage, Newbury Park, CA.

Hudson, W. (1982). *The Clinical Measurement Package: A Field Manual*, Dorsey Press, Homewood, IL.

Huff, C. R. (ed.) (1990). *Gangs in America*, Sage, Newbury Park, CA

Huizinga, D. H., Esbensen, F. A., and Weiher, A. (1991a) Are there multiple paths to delinquency? *J. Crim. Law Criminol*. 82: 83-118.

Huizinga. D., Loeber, R., and Thornberry. T. P. (eds.) (1991b). *Urban Delinquency and Substance Use: Technical Report*. Prepared for the Office of Juvenile Justice and Delinquency Prevention. U.S. Department of Justice, Washington. DC, Sept.

Jansyn, L. R. (1966). Solidarity and delinquency in a street corner group. *Am. Sociol. Rev*. 31: 600-614.

Jessor, R., Donovan, J. E., and Costa, F. M. (1991). *Beyond Adolescence: Problem Behavior and Young Adult Development*, Cambridge University Press, New York.

Klein, M. W., and Maxson, C. L. (1989). Street gang violence. In Weiner, N., and Wolfgang, M. E. (eds.), *Violent Crime, Violent Criminals*, Sage. Newbury Park, CA.

Kornhauser, R. R. (1978). *Social Sources of Delinquency*, University of Chicago Press, Chicago.

Krohn, M. D., Stern, S. B., Thornberry. T. P., and Jang, S. J. (1992). The measurement of family process variables: The effect of adolescent and parent perceptions of family life on delinquent behavior. *J. Quant. Criminol*. 8: 287-315.

Maccoby, E. E., and Martin, J. A. (1983). Socialization in the context or the family: Parent-child interaction. In Hetherington. E. M. (ed.), *Handbook of Child Psychology: Socialization, Personality and Social Development*, Wiley, New York.

Maxson. C. L., and Klein. M. W. (1990). Street gang violence: Twice as great or half as great? In Huff, C. R. (ed.), *Gangs in America*, Sage, Newbury Park, CA.

Miller, B. C., and Moore, K. A. (1990). Adolescent sexual behavior, pregnancy, and parenting Research through the 1980s. *J. Marriage Family* 52: 1025-1044.

Miller, W. B. (1958). Lower class culture as a generating milieu of gang delinquency. *J. Soc. Issues* 14: 5-19.

Miller. W. B. (1975). *Violence by Youth Gangs and Youth Gangs as Crime Problem in Major American Cities*, USGPO, Office of Juvenile Justice and Delinquency Prevention. U.S. Department of Justice, Washington, DC.

Miller, W. B. (1982). *Crime by Youth Gangs and Youth Groups in the United States*, Office of Juvenile Justice and Delinquency Prevention, Washington. DC.

Moore, J. (1991). *Going Down to the Barrio: Homeboys and Homegirls in Change*, Temple University Press, Philadelphia, PA.

Morash, M. (1983). Gangs, groups and delinquency. *Br. J. Criminol*. 23: 309-331.

Morris, A. (1987). *Women, Crime, and Criminal Justice*, Basil Blackwell. Oxford.

New York State Division for Youth (1990). Reaffirming Prevention. Report of the Task Force on Juvenile Gangs.

Newcomb, M. D., and Bentler, P. M. (1988). *Consequences of Adolescent Drug Use: Impact on the Life of Young Adults*, Sage, Newbury Park, CA.

Peterson, T. (1985). A comment on presenting results from logit and probit models. *Am. Sociol. Rev.* 50: 130-131.

Rice, R. (1963). A report at large: The Persian queens. *The New Yorker* 39: 153-187.

Rosenberg, M. (1965). *Society and the Adolescent Self-Image*, Princeton University Press, Princeton, NJ.

Short, J. F. (1990). New wine in old bottles: Changes and continuity in American gangs. In Huff, C. R. (ed.), *Gangs in America*, Sage, Newbury Park. CA.

Short, J. F., and Strodtbeck, F. (1965). *Group Process and Gang Delinquency*, University of Chicago Press, Chicago.

Smith. D. A., and Paternoster, R. (1997). The gender gap in theories of deviance: Issues and evidence. *J. Res. Crime Delinq*. 24: 140-172.

Spergel, I. A. (1966). *Street Gang Work: Theory and Practice*, Addison-Wesley, Reading, MA.

Spergel. I. A. (1986). The violent gang in Chicago: A local community approach. *Soc. Serv. Rev.* 60: 94-131.

Spergel, I. A. (1990). Youth gangs: Continuity and change. In Tonry, M., and Morris. N. (eds.), *Crime and Justice: A Review of Research, Vol.* 12, University of Chicago Press, Chicago.

Taylor, C. (1990). *Dangerous Society*, State University Press, East Lansing, MI.

Thornberry, T. P. (1947). Toward an interactional theory of delinquency, *Criminology*, 863-991.

Thornberry, T. P., Bjerregaard. B., and Miles, W (1993a) The consequences of respondent attrition in panel studies: A simulation based of the Rochester Youth Development Study, *J. Quant. Criminol.* 9: 127-158.

Thornberry, T. P., Krohn, M. D., Lizotte, A. J. Chard-Wierschem, D. (1993b). The role of juvenile gang in facilitating delinquent behavior, *J. Res. Crime Delinq*. 30: 55-87.

Thrasher, F. (1927). *The Gang*, University of Chicago, Chicago.

Tracy, P. E. (1987). Subcultural delinquency: A comparison of the incidence and severity of gang and nongang member offenses, College of Criminal Justice, Northeastern University, Boston.

U.S. Bureau of the Census. (1989). *Poverty in the United States*, Series P-60 No. 163, Current Population Reports, Government Printing Office, Washington, DC.

Vedder. C. B., and Somerville, D. B. (1975). *The Delinquent Girl*, Charles C. Thomas, Springfield, IL.

Vigil, J. (1988). *Barrio Gangs: Street Life and Identity in Southern California*, University of Texas Press, Austin. TX.

Warr. M. (1993) Age, peers and delinquency. *Criminology* 31: 17-40.

Winfree, L. T., Fuller. K., Vigil, T., and Mays, G. L. (1992). The definition and measurement of "gang status": Policy implications for juvenile justice. *Juv. Family Court J.* 29-37.

Yablonsky, L. (1962) *The Violent Gang*, Macmillan, New York.

Zevitz, R., and Takata, S. (1992). Metropolitan gang influences and the emergence of group delinquency in a regional community. *J. Crim. Just.* 20:93-106. ✦

Section II

Understanding Gangs

Introduction

We are principally concerned in this section with gang theory, methods of research, and how these are played out in considering gang process or the dynamics of gangs. Gang theory, in its heyday from the 1930s to the mid-1960s, held a pivotal place in criminology because it was at the same time taken to be *delinquency* theory more generally. At the time, delinquency was thought to be disproportionately a lower-class phenomenon, and official police and court statistics provided support for this assumption. Since gangs were described as comprised of lower-class, or at most working-class groups, theoretical work on gangs was accepted as applicable to delinquency generally.

Most prominent among the gang theories were those of Fredric Thrasher, Albert Cohen, Lewis Yablonsky, and of Richard Cloward and Lloyd Ohlin among sociologists; Herbert Block and Arthur Niederhoffer among psychologists; and Walter Miller among cultural anthropologists. The first article in Section II (Understanding Gangs) reviews much of this material. But because the official statistics proved to be highly misleading, and because gangs have more recently appeared among less disadvantaged populations, the earlier gang theories have received decreasing attention. Cohen's thesis about angry, hedonistic youth subcultures, Cloward and Ohlin's postulates about patterned criminal subcultures, and Miller's notions of lower-class culture as a distinct breeder of gang values in our society have not held up well to empirical test. The most severe of these tests are the extensive and careful comparative studies reported by James F. Short, Jr., and Fred L. Strodtbeck, working with Chicago gangs. Other articles not included in Section II but which give a good sense of these theories are those by Cohen and Short and by Miller, listed below.

What do we ask of a good theory? The answer is, a great deal, and more in fact than most can supply. We seek logical consistency, good operationalization of principal concepts, parsimonious explanations, careful delineation of the theory's scope (whether broad or narrow), incorporation of known data, and the ability to predict future patterns of gang structure, functions, and crime. It's a tall order, but one well kept in mind as the reader ponders the articles included here as examples of current theoretical stances. In particular, the Sanchez Jankowski book listed in the additional readings calls for careful consideration because it posits a new view of gangs as planful, rational, materialistic, and politically adept. It is an image at variance from the others presented here, or attempted in the classical gang writings.

An approach now being applied more consistently to gangs—especially to their emergence in so many new locations—is found in part in John Hagedorn's article in this section, taken from his influential book *People and Folks*. His thesis is that gang emergence in many cities (in his case, Milwaukee) is a function of the spread and deepening of America's urban underclass as described by Chicago sociologist William Julius Wilson. The next article, by Pamela Irving Jackson, is very different in its research approach; it provides interesting support for the thesis with a sophisticated analysis of data from a large number of gang cities. The notion is that an increasing level of pervasive and persistent poverty in mainly minority communities has been fostered over the last fifteen years or more by a number of factors. These include:

- the removal of manufacturing plants and jobs from the city, leaving service jobs for which minority youth are often ill-prepared by schooling and family experience
- the migration of middle-class minority families from urban centers to more affluent suburbs, taking with them their successful social agencies and community organizing skills
- increased density of segregated minority populations
- loss of federally and state-supported social services (employment, job-training, educational, welfare, health, and other capacities)
- a resultant explosion in unemployed and underemployed minority youth of an expanded age range, attached to families seriously disrupted by these social and economic discontinuities

Hagedorn has argued persuasively that these factors are well-suited to the development of adolescent and young adult gang structures. Other gang writers have found ample evidence for the explanation in other cities as well. We would raise one caution, however, and offer a second, increasingly accepted corollary explanation for the growth in gangs. The caution is that the explanation concerning the urban underclass seems not to work as well with Hispanic as with black neighborhoods—Wilson's pivotal work concerned only the black underclass—and may logically be less pertinent to many smaller gang cities where the factors listed above may be less severe.

The corollary explanation can be labeled the "diffusion of gang culture." For decades, various fads and styles of gang costume and behavior had been limited in use to gang members and close associates. Recently, however, various aspects of outward gang culture—argot, clothing, tattoos, use of hand signals, and so on—have been picked up by manufacturers and the media, and diffused across the country. Baggy pants, Pendleton-style shirts, high-top shoes, ball caps worn backward or at angles, graffiti styles, words like "homey" and "hood," and other signs of affiliations have become part of the larger youth culture. In essence, commercial America has taught youthful America how to walk, talk, dress, and act "gangster-style."

It is no wonder, then, that "copycat" behavior is found among many youth, and when youth groups get into rivalries (over break dancing, school sports, favorite hangouts, etc.), they play out the gangster roles. Many descriptions in the crime literature now attest to these processes by which some "normal" youth groups develop into local gangs, fulfilling in their behavior the last component of gang culture, criminal involvement. It does not take an urban underclass to foster this movement. American youth in every corner of our society have learned the gang patterns. We have even seen a recent depiction of the process in The Hague, the capital of Holland. Rival groups have adopted the terms (such as "homey"), the dress, the hand signals, all the accoutrements of American gangs. They engage in a wide variety of delinquent behavior, and wear blue or red bandannas, calling themselves Crips and Bloods. There is no urban underclass in The Hague, but they do get MTV on their television.

It is, of course, one thing to theorize about gang patterns and quite another to carry out the research that tests those theories or provides the data for new ideas. In fact, Hedy Bookin-Weiner and Ruth Horowitz suggested in 1983 that the decline in gangs thought to exist then was largely a methodological artifact: researchers had simply stopped doing gang research. Funding for traditional forms of gang research, they noted, had all but dried up.

What may have been true then, however, is no longer the case. Gang research support abounds, and a new generation of gang researchers has emerged. In selecting articles to illustrate alternative research approaches, however, the editors found themselves largely stymied. Articles on qualitative approaches are plentiful—case studies, ethnographies, historical reviews—but articles explicitly discussing quantitative techniques seem almost nonexistent. Qualitative approaches are well illustrated by the Additional Readings selections by Hagedorn, Horowitz, and Joe. Quantitative methods in gang research are either assumed to be known, or seem to present so few problems that their users feel no need to discuss them in published form. An exception is the piece by Maxson listed in the Additional Readings. Our only methods article, another review by Robert Bursik and Harold Grasmick, suggests that this should not be the case; each approach has its problems. Nonetheless, any of the accepted methods is preferable to the kind of anecdotal "evidence" usually provided to us by public officials, politicians, and the news media.

Regardless of the methods employed, the study of group process within gangs has been a major part of the gang research tradition, as will be revealed in the selections of Section II (Group Process); two of the three selections appeared in the 1960s or 1970s. Most others which might have been selected also came from this earlier period. The Klein and Crawford article uses the well-established literature on *group* cohesiveness to delve into some special features of *gang* cohesiveness, relating this in turn to levels of gang delinquency. The article by Short and Strodtbeck then takes similar notions to discuss the behavior of specific individuals, gang leaders, in specific gang contexts.

These two articles stand in some contrast to two others listed in the additional readings. In one of these, Leon Jansyn illustrates a pattern suggesting that the level of delinquency in a gang can have an effect on its cohesiveness, a point corollary to but not opposite to the data presented by Klein and Crawford. Lewis Yablonsky's book, in contrast to the article by Short and Strodtbeck, points to gang leaders as sociopaths, as megalomaniacs who can sway a whole gang toward extreme exercises of violence. Yablonsky's portrayal of gang leaders has never found much support in other gang studies, but his description of gangs as "near-groups," being neither highly structured nor amorphous masses of youth, has been validated time and again. Gangs tend to manifest intermediate levels of cohesiveness, and can thus be seen as a cup half full or half empty—much ado about nothing, or a calamity about to happen. It is the eye of the beholder that is important.

In these articles on group process, scholars seem to be saying that whatever leads youth to join gangs, their behavior thereafter is most affected by group factors—norms, cohesiveness, leadership, the group identity that substitutes for individual accomplishment, and so on. This much seems clear: attempts to alter the gang situation that do not take account of the members' relationship to their group will be mired in the firmament of group process. Gang members are no longer *only* individuals; they are parts of a larger, complex whole.

The last group process article, by Terence Thornberry and his colleagues, provides a useful bridge to Section III concerning anti-social behavior. It is one of the very few that indicates clearly, thanks to the longitudinal and comparative design of the research, that gang membership itself creates greater criminal involvement among the members. There was every reason to believe this earlier. The articles by Walter Miller (Boston) and Gerald Robin (New York) listed below, as well as the work of Short and Strodtbeck cited earlier (Chicago), suggested the criminogenic nature of gang membership. Unpublished work by Paul Tracy in Philadelphia during the 1970s also provided supportive evidence, as did the gang/nongang comparisons of violence provided by Maxson et al. in Los Angeles in the 1980s. Chapter Three of John Hagedorn's *People and Folks* adds even more recent suggestions. But the Thornberry et al. article provides the most definitive proof that gang membership puts one at far more risk of delinquent involvement. It is a pivotal finding.

Additional Readings

Bloch, Herbert A., & Niederhoffer, Arthur, *The Gang*. Westport, CT: Greenwood Press, 1958.

Bookin-Weiner, Hedy, & Horowitz, Ruth, The end of the youth gang: Fad or fact? *Criminology*, November 1983, 21(4):585-602.

Cloward, Richard A., & Ohlin, Lloyd E., *Delinquency and Opportunity: A Theory of Delinquent Gangs*. New York: Free Press (Macmillan), 1960.

Cohen, Albert K., & Short, James F., Research in delinquent subcultures. *Journal of Social Issues*, 1958, 14(3):20-37.

Cohen, Albert K., *Delinquent Boys: The Culture of the Gang*. New York: Free Press (Macmillan), 1955.

Hagedorn, John M., Back in the field again: Gang research in the Nineties. In C. Ronald Huff (ed.), *Gangs in America*, pp. 240-62. Newbury Park, CA: Sage Publications, Inc., 1990.

—— *People and Folks: Gangs, Crime and the Underclass in a Rustbelt City*. Chicago: Lake View Press, 1988.

Horowitz, Ruth, Remaining an outsider: Membership as a threat to research rapport. *Urban Life*, January 1986, 14(4):409-30.

Jansyn, Leon, Solidarity and delinquency in a street corner group. *American Sociological Review*, 1967, 31:600-14.

Joe, Karen, Issues in accessing and studying ethnic youth gangs. *Gang Journal*, 1993, 1(2):9-23.

Maxson, Cheryl L., Collecting data from investigation files: Descriptions of three Los Angeles gang homicide projects. In C. R. Block and R. Block (eds.), *Questions and Answers in Lethal and Non-lethal Violence*. Washington, D.C.: National Institute of Justice, 1993.

Maxson, Cheryl L., Gordon, Margaret A., & Klein, Malcolm W., Differences between gang and nongang homicides. *Criminology* 1985, 23:209-22.

Miller, Walter B., American youth gangs: A reassessment. In L. Radzinowicz, & M.E. Wolfgang (eds.), *The Criminal in Society. Crime and Justice, Vol 1*, pp. 188-218. New York: Basic Books, 1977.

—— American youth gangs: Past and present. In A. Blumberg (ed.), *Current Perspectives on Criminal Behavior*. New York: Knopf, 1981.

Robin, Gerald, Gang member delinquency in Philadelphia. In M. W. Klein (ed.), *Juvenile Gangs in Conflict*. Englewood Cliffs, NJ: Prentice-Hall, 1967.

Sanchez Jankowski, Martin, *Islands in the Street: Gangs and American Urban Society*. Berkeley: University of California Press, 1991.

Short, J. F., Jr., & Strodtbeck, F. L., Why gangs fight. In J. F. Short, Jr. (ed.), *Gang Delinquency and Delinquent Subcultures*, pp. 246-56. New York: Harper & Row, 1968.

Tracy, Paul, Subcultural delinquency: A comparison of the incidence and seriousness of gang and nongang member offensivity. Paper presented at the American Society of Criminology, November 1979.

Yablonsky, Lewis, *The Violent Gang*. New York: Macmillan, 1962. ✦

Theory and Methods

13

The Effect of Neighborhood Dynamics on Gang Behavior

Robert J. Bursik, Jr. and Harold G. Grasmick

Over the many years that gangs have engaged the interest of social scientists, numerous theories have been proposed to explain their development and persistence. Bursik and Grasmick draw from these individual perspectives to present three sets of theoretical approaches which they then evaluate in light of empirical evidence on neighborhood characteristics and gang crime. The issues raised in the previous articles on gang definitions and types of gangs provide a context to review these theoretical thrusts and the evidence used to assess their validity.

The authors favor the systematic social disorganization approach, but note its failure to explain the existence of gangs in stable neighborhoods. The earlier statements by proponents of this explanatory framework did not anticipate certain emerging dynamics that characterize contemporary urban areas. The authors propose an expansion of social disorganization theory that addresses these criticisms of the earlier formulations.

Criminologists have identified two particular types of neighborhoods in which the development of gangs is most likely. It is often assumed that the most prevalent form of gang activity arises in unstable, institutionally weak lower-class neighborhoods. However, gang activity also has been commonly noted in relatively stable lower-class areas that are fairly well organized (Spergel 1984:203).

Three classes of theories have developed to account for these phenomena. While a systemic approach grounded in the theory of social disorganization has been the traditional explanation for the existence of gangs in the unstable areas, the presence of gangs in the second type of neighborhood usually has been accounted for either in terms of subcultures that support such behavior or, more recently, in terms of economic marginalization. The existence of such disparate approaches presents a very difficult logical problem for the development of a systemic theory of neighborhood crime, for the systemic model assumes that a general consensus exists concerning the negative evaluation of certain types of crime, whereas subcultural approaches assume that some neighborhoods may encourage such activity. Likewise, while economic factors have a primarily indirect effect on crime in a systemic model, they are at the heart of the marginalization thesis.

While it is possible that different explanations are required for different neighborhoods, it would be much more parsimonious if a single model was able to account for these situations. In this section we will examine the three frameworks, evaluate their relative validity in terms of recent empirical evidence, and examine the ability of a systemic approach to account for such findings.

The Traditional Systemic Social Disorganization Approach

Although Thrasher did not develop a systematic series of hypotheses on the basis of his data (see the criticism of Short 1963:xxi-xxii), all the elements of a systemic social disorganization model of neighborhood crime are reflected in his treatise. First, . . . he observed that delinquent gangs are most likely to arise in relatively poor, unstable neighborhoods. Such characteristics decrease the ability of local customs and institutions to control the leisure time activities of boys, which increases the likelihood of gang conflict (Thrasher 1927:33). While he considers the family to be the most important agency of control, he also discusses the inability of other institutions to restrain such behavior. Thus, all three forms of systemic control . . . are key elements of Thrasher's model (see pp. 33, 65): the private (the family), the parochial (local churches and schools), and the public (corruption and indifference in local politics and exclusion from high-paying occupations).

Several large-scale studies have provided at least partial support for the social disorganization gang approach. Desmond Cartwright and Kenneth Howard (1966) examined the neighborhood characteristics of the sixteen primary gangs who were studied in the Short and Strodtbeck (1965) research. Based on the observation that these communities are "oversupplied with young children of both sexes and undersupplied with mature adults" (p. 342), they argue that the controls that adults can impose on youth in such areas are relatively weak. However, while they did find that gangs were more likely in low-income areas, they did not find a relationship between residential mobility and the distribution of such groups, which is an important contradiction of Thrasher's model. To some extent, this may represent the fact that gangs are sometimes found in stable, low-income neighborhoods, an issue that we will address in the upcoming sections of this chapter. However, it is important to emphasize that there is a serious measurement problem in the study since the sixteen gangs examined by Short and Strodtbeck represented neither an exhaustive nor a representative sample of those in Chicago at that time (see Short and Strodtbeck 1965: Chapter 1). Therefore, some unknown proportion of the neighborhoods that are considered to be "nongang" by Cartwright and Howard are actually characterized by the presence of such groups.

More recently, Irving Spergel (1984:201-202; see also 1986) has argued that the social disorganization model may provide the best account for the development of violent gangs. However, he differentiates between two different sets of community dynamics (or, in Spergel's terms, "routes") that could give rise to such behavior. The integrated route leads to the development of violent gangs in areas newly settled by lower-class populations. While in the past these groups tended to be Irish, Italian, Jewish, Polish, German, or African-American, the contemporary immigrants are primarily Hispanic or Asian. While families in these areas may be intact, "secondary institutions . . . are weakly identified or structurally connected with the interests and needs of the population" (p. 202). Within this context, street corner groups provide a form of mutual protection.

Spergel's integrated route clearly involves the kind of systemic processes that we have discussed. However, gangs may also arise through a segmented route in relatively stable, well-organized areas with somewhat effective local institutions. Nevertheless, these communities are very poor, economically dependent, have high rates of family instability, and have been abandoned by white populations. Gangs provide a number of illegitimate opportunities in such areas and have "more of an economic-gain character" (p. 203). Spergel illustrates the complexity of these two sets of dynamics in an analysis of gang homicides in Chicago between 1978 and 1985.[5] He finds, for example, that with one exception, extremely poor, black neighborhoods with very high delinquency rates tend not to have especially high rates of gang homicides. That is, as the dynamics of the segmented route suggest, violent gang behavior is rare in such neighborhoods.

In a later paper, David Curry and Spergel (1988) utilize multivariate techniques to examine more fully the empirical relationship between community dynamics and violent gang behavior. Two of their many findings are especially important. First, after controlling for the effects of poverty, the percentage of Hispanics in a neighborhood is significantly related to the rate of gang homicide. Second, poverty is related to gang homicide in primarily black and white neighborhoods, but not in Hispanic communities. To some extent, these findings support Spergel's distinction between integrated and segmented routes to gang violence. Given the history of settlement in Chicago, Curry and Spergel (p. 387) consider the concentration of Hispanics in a neighborhood to be a "simple and gross" indicator of social disorganization (unfortunately, they have no direct measure of neighborhood stability or institutional effectiveness). To the degree that this is a valid indicator of disorganization, the high levels of gang homicide in Hispanic communities regardless of the level of poverty in those areas supports the systemic model. At the same time, the relationship between poverty and homicide in black and white neighborhoods suggests that chronic economic deprivation is also associated with gang violence.

The existence of gangs in stable neighborhoods (which has been noted by many researchers; see Whyte 1981) may appear to be an important contradiction of the systemic model and, in fact, has been a serious stumbling block for traditional social disorganization approaches. Part of the difficulty of the systemic model in this respect can be traced to the ongoing influence of early models of human ecology (such as Park and Burgess 1924; Burgess 1925), which assumed that immigrant groups eventually would be assimilated into the occupational structure of urban areas. Since residential upgrading would accompany economic mobility, these groups would relocate into progressively better neighborhoods with greater levels of systemic control. Mobility was assumed to lead to a great degree of contact between groups, which in turn would result in a decreasing relevance of racial or ethnic membership (Park and Burgess 1924:Chapter XI).

As a result, it was assumed that the racial and ethnic character of gangs would change over time. For example, because of their status as recent immigrant groups, the major street gangs that have been identified in the early nineteenth century in the United States tended to be primarily Irish (Haskins 1974:22). Even early Chinese immigrant communities, which have sometimes had a public image of being relatively gang free, gave rise to tongs, which often were involved in illegal activities (Haskins 1974:58). As the older immigrant groups became assimilated, they were replaced in their previous neighborhoods by newer arrivals, who then dominated neighborhood gang activity.

This idealized version of invasion and succession was modified by three important features of urban life. First, . . . some racial and ethnic groups were formally or informally prevented from engaging in the residential mobility that was assumed to accompany economic assimilation. As a result, some neighborhoods have mixtures of socioeconomic groups. For example, Brigitte Erbe (1975) has presented evidence that in Chicago during 1970, black professionals and managers lived in neighborhoods with occupational compositions comparable to those areas where unskilled white workers lived. Relatedly, because of their marginal economic position, certain extremely poor groups have very few prospects for residential mobility and may be "abandoned" in particular neighborhoods for several generations. Finally, certain ethnic groups have been characterized by a reluctance to move from the "old neighborhood" even when it was economically feasible to do so. The discussion of

Horowitz (1983:56) suggests that this may be due to a reliance on the expanded family for emotional and social support; she notes that even when people move away from the neighborhood, intensive relationships are often maintained.

These urban dynamics necessitate several modifications of Thrasher's argument. Most notably, his thesis suggests that the protective functions of street corner groups would decline in importance in neighborhoods with extensive formal and informal ties among the residents. Given the presumed residential mobility of racial and ethnic groups, gangs should be found primarily among the most recent groups of immigrants to an urban area. To some extent this is true. An increasing amount of attention has been paid to the apparent rise of Asian youth gangs (see Joe and Robinson 1980; Spergel 1990:212-213, 216; Chin 1990; Vigil and Yun 1990), and some parts of the United States are characterized by ongoing Hispanic in-migration, which has been associated with the development of gangs. However, Hispanic gangs have been a feature of the American Southwest for over fifty years, dating at least to the zoot suit riots during World War II (see Moore 1978). Likewise, many black gangs have extended histories, and Spergel (1990:213) notes the continued existence of gangs among second- and third-generation Italians, Irish, Polish, and middle Europeans. Therefore, gangs are not a transitory part of the urban experience of many racial and ethnic groups.

It is worth noting that the common public image is that gangs are a predominantly Hispanic and African-American phenomenon, especially since these groups currently constitute the largest numbers of youths arrested for gang offenses (Spergel 1990:213). To some extent, the apparent concentration of gang crime in these groups is to be expected given their respective histories of urban seclusion and economic marginality. However, although the data are now fairly dated, it is important to note the research of Leonard Savitz and his associates (1980), which indicates that 12 percent of black youths and 14 percent of white youths living in Philadelphia during the mid-1970s claimed gang affiliation. Similar distributional findings also have been reported by Mark Testa (1988; in Spergel 1990). Thus, blacks and Hispanics have no special predisposition to gang membership. Rather, they simply are overrepresented in those areas most likely to lead to gang activity.

Unfortunately, many media presentations give the impression either that gang activity is fairly rare in other groups or that the nature of such activity is relatively minor.[2] Such impressions are false on both counts. Seven of the thirty-seven gangs studied by Martin Sanchez Jankowski between 1978 and 1989 had a membership that was strictly white, and even in the cities in which gang behavior is predominantly black/Hispanic (such as Milwaukee; see Hagedorn 1988), a number of white gangs exist. In addition, white gangs account for their own share of seriously violent behavior, as shown in a study of a white gang located in an affluent Chicago suburb: two of the members were sentenced to six years in prison for bombing the cars of a police chief and a vice-principal (Muehlbauer and Dodder 1983).

Contemporary urban dynamics necessitate several important modifications of traditional systemic analyses of neighborhoods and gangs. First, the nature of neighborhood territoriality has changed significantly. If entire groups are geographically mobile (as assumed by Park and Burgess), then the ethnic-based gang associations might be expected to dissipate as members become dispersed throughout the city. However, when residential areas retain their racial/ethnic identity over an extended period of time, those who migrate away may retain an affinity for the "old neighborhood." While some former members join gangs that exist in their new areas, others may retain their affiliation and possibly attempt to recruit new members (see Moore et al. 1983). Thus, while the residential neighborhood may serve as the original basis for the emergence of the gang, the mobility of gang members may expand the geographic range of the group.

The prison experiences of some gang members is a second way in which a group's territorial influence may expand beyond the boundaries of the residential neighborhood, for broadly based networks and alliances often develop during incarceration (Moore 1978). At the same time, neighborhood allegiances are often heightened during these periods of separation (Moore 1978:106-109). In at least one documented case involving the Vice Lords of Chicago, the correctional experience itself led to the formation of the gang in the neighborhood after the release of several members from the Illinois State Training School for Boys (Keiser 1969; Dawley 1992).

The apparent increase in the involvement of gangs in the distribution and use of drugs is a third factor that has been suggested as an explanation for the expansion of gang influence beyond neighborhood boundaries since the relatively quick profits that can be made has encouraged some gangs to expand their markets outside of their traditional areas (see Klein and Maxson 1985; Fagan 1990). For example, some law enforcement agencies have estimated that the Bloods and the Crips, two gangs based in Los Angeles, control approximately 30 percent of the national market in crack cocaine (U.S. General Accounting Office 1989). We have used the word "apparent" because while the traditional gang literature tended to downplay the role of drugs in urban gangs, Moore (1978) notes that the use of drugs such as barbiturates could be commonly found in Los Angeles barrios as early as 1940. Again, owing to inconsistencies and changes over time in the definition of gang activity, it is impossible to confidently document trends in the distribution of drugs by gangs. For example, recall that a drug-related gang incident was definitionally impossible in the statistics collected by the Chicago Police Department until 1986.

However, presumably because of an increasing involvement in the distribution of drugs, some observers have noted a tendency for gangs to expand their sphere of influence not only into new neighborhoods, but also into new cities. Sometimes this is simply due to the residential movement of gang members and not a planned, organized expansion of activities (Huff 1989). At other times there appear to be efforts to recruit within nearby cities. However, even when gangs affiliate and identify with larger "supergangs" in other cities, most of these linkages are fairly weak and members emphasize their relative independence from these large groups. Overall, Hagedorn (1988:77) concludes that despite the apparent influence of gangs from Chicago, most Milwaukee gangs originally developed in the traditional manner described by Thrasher. This does not imply that large-city networks of gangs do not exist. Rather this represents another gang-related issue in which it is very difficult to separate fact from mythology.

Finally, Hagedorn (1988:Chapter 6) has developed the provocative argument that the desegregation of public schools has contributed to the decline of gangs as a neighborhood-based phenomenon. While over 80 percent of the black gang leaders indicated that most gangs originally had a neighborhood basis, members were bussed to public schools all over the city. In addition to increasing the alienation of these youths from local institutions such as neighborhood schools, gang members were thrown into educational environments that contained gang members from many different parts of the city. As a result, they were forced to recruit members from these schools "not based on neighborhood but on the need for protection" (p. 136). The implications of such programs on the neighborhood basis of gangs can be clearly observed in Milwaukee since its desegregation plan involved mandatory busing for only blacks. While Hagedorn (p. 137) notes that less than a third of black gang members felt that the residential area of a recruit was an important consideration, the neighborhood was an important consideration for Hispanic and white gangs.

In summary, although the traditional systemic social disorganization approach continues to be a viable explanation of the relationship between neighborhoods and gangs, it is incomplete in two respects. First, such models traditionally have had trouble accounting for the existence of gang activity in relatively stable, low-income neighborhoods. Second, certain urban dynamics that could not be foreseen by Thrasher have broadened the sphere of influence of some gangs beyond the boundaries of the residential neighborhood.

Gangs as the Carriers of Criminal and Delinquent Subcultures

The inability of the traditional systemic models of Thrasher and Shaw and McKay to account for the existence of stable neighborhoods with extensive histories of gang behavior led to the development of a very different orientation to the neighborhood and crime. While the literature contains several important variations of this perspective, all these theories hypothesize that such behavior reflects the existence of community subcultures that support gang activity.

Like the theory of social disorganization, the subcultural approach has a long criminological history, as illustrated in a passage first published in 1929: "Resistance on the part of the community to delinquent and criminal behavior is low and such behavior is tolerated and may even become accepted and approved. . . . Delinquent and criminal patterns arise and are transmitted socially just as any other cultural and social pattern is transmitted." The authors of this incipient statement concerning cultural transmission are none other than Clifford Shaw and his associates (1929:205-206), a fact that has caused a great deal of consternation among social disorganization theorists (see especially Kornhauser 1978). The subcultural elements receive even greater emphasis in their later work, in which it is stated that "within the same community, theft may be defined as right and proper in some groups and immoral, improper, and undesirable in others" (Shaw and McKay 1969:171). The primary role of the gang within such neighborhoods is the transmission of these values to its members and the fostering of behaviors that reflect these values.

Each of the three statements of the subcultural perspective that had especially important effects on the direction of gang research during the 1960s and early 1970s assumed that lower-class communities were characterized by a distinctive set of norms and values that fostered such behavior.[3] Walter Miller (1958) provided perhaps the purest cultural perspective in his discussion of "focal concerns," that is, "areas or issues which command widespread and persistent attention and a high degree of emotional involvement" (p. 7). Lower-class communities are assumed to have long-standing cultural traditions in which trouble, toughness, smartness, excitement, fate, and autonomy are important themes; in addition, lower-class boys are concerned with issues of belonging and status. Delinquent behavior, from this perspective, represents an attempt to achieve those standards of conduct.

The gang plays a central role in the daily life of boys who are raised within such communities. Miller argues that since male adults are absent from most lower-class households, or at best participate sporadically in household affairs, most lower-class families are directed by women. Therefore, he argues that belonging to a gang in which all the members are male provides "the first real opportunity to learn essential aspects of the male role in the context of peers facing similar problems of sex-role identification."

A very different subcultural approach to gangs is found in the work of Albert Cohen (1955) and Richard Cloward and Lloyd Ohlin (1960). Whereas Miller considers the subcultural features of lower-class communities to be an explicit set of norms and values with an ongoing integrity, Cohen and Cloward and Ohlin argue that these features arise in response to a rejection of particular features of the dominant middle-class culture. Since this rejection is assumed to be due to frustrations that arise when limitations in the opportunities provided to members of the lower class make it difficult to attain the dominant goals of the middle class, these two theories combine cultural and structural dynamics, making them "mixed" models of gang behavior (see Kornhauser 1978).

Cohen considers the dominant goal of all individuals to be that of status, which is generally defined as a positive recognition of an individual's personal and social attributes (p.27). In the American society, such attributions are made on the basis of the extent to which a person strives, "by dint of rational, ascetic, self-discipline and independent activity, to achieve in worldly affairs. . . . the presumption [is] that 'success' is itself a sign of the exercise of these moral qualities." Cohen argues that the primary societal context for the acquisition of such positive recognition among adolescents is the school.

This presents certain difficulties for working-class youths.[4] Schools are staffed by middle-class individuals who are expected to foster middle-class personalities by rewarding middle-class expectations (pp. 113-114). However, although "most working class Americans are under the spell of this particular set of norms" (p. 87), they tend to be perceived as failures by their teachers owing to "their relative lack of training in order and discipline, their lack of interest in intellectual achievement, and their lack of reinforcement by the home in conformity to the requirements of the school" (p.115). Given the devaluation of the working-class status in a middle-class institution, this can lead to the development of a deep sense of shame.

The basic process that leads to the formation of gangs in this context is a change of reference on the part of the adolescent from an inherently frustrating pursuit of middle-class goals to the pursuit of goals that appear to be attainable. For this "reaction formation" to be an adequate solution, working-class adolescents must convince themselves that the original goals are not worth pursuing (pp. 53-54). Since most working-class youths were originally socialized into middle-class norms, this reaction must be quite pronounced, leading to an intense hostility to the norms of middle-class society (p. 133). As a result, Cohen argues that the delinquent behavior of working-class boys represents a reversal of middle-class norms: it is nonutilitarian, malicious, negativistic, and is characterized by an emphasis on short-run hedonism and group autonomy (pp. 25, 30).

Gangs arise through the interaction of a number of adolescents who face similar problems of status attainment and who evolve similar modes of adaptation (p. 59). This interaction leads to the development of "group standards" that reflect this frame of reference and the emergence of a subculture (p.65). As long as the gang continues to serve the status needs of the age groups that succeed the original founders of the group, it will continue to exist, thereby becoming a subcultural delinquent tradition within the local community that passes on knowledge, beliefs, values, codes, tastes, and prejudices to new members (pp. 12-13).[5]

The relationship between frustrated goals and the formation of gangs is also the central theme in the work of Cloward and Ohlin. However, their work focuses on a much more limited source of status: the achievement of economic success. In one respect, the framework of Cloward and Ohlin was greatly influenced by the classic work of Robert Merton (1938), which assumed that innovative (i.e., deviant or criminal) techniques of attaining economic success are likely to be developed when the conventional institutional means (such as educational or occupational opportunities) are unavailable. If a person blames the lack of success on individual shortcomings, such innovations will most likely occur as solitary activities. However, if the sources of frustration are perceived as the result of social injustice, the first acts of deviance reflect tentative steps toward the development of norms that will put the person at odds with carriers of the dominant conventional culture. Cloward and Ohlin argue that at this stage the deviant needs "all of the encouragement and reassurance he can muster" to defend his position and finds this by searching for others who are in a similar position (p. 126). Thus, the neighborhood gang is born.

This focus on the societal distribution of legitimate opportunities for economic success is a relatively straightforward, although important, application of Merton's theory of deviance. The primary contribution of Cloward and Ohlin to the analysis of neighborhoods and gangs is their extension of that theory to include a consideration of the illegitimate opportunities that are available to a youth in a local community. The nature of these opportunities depends on two general features of the neighborhood. The first is the relationship that exists between "immature and sophisticated offenders" in an area (p. 153). Cloward and Ohlin suggest that the transmission of criminal traditions and the recruitment of young adolescents into illegal activities is more likely in areas where different age groups are integrated through stable and intimate associations. In addition, one must also consider the degree to which those people engaged in ongoing patterns of illegal behavior are integrated with conventional persons in a neighborhood to form a "single, stable structure which organizes and patterns the life of the community" (p. 156).

Cloward and Ohlin draw heavily from the work of Solomon Kobrin (1951) in their discussion of the implications of such integration on the development of gang behavior. Kobrin (p. 657) notes the existence of two polar types of communities. In some areas, there is a systematic and organized integration of illegal and conventional life-styles. For example the leaders of illegal enterprises may participate in such local institutions as churches, social groups, and political organizations. Thus, conventional and criminal value systems have a "reciprocal" (p. 658) relationship in which they reinforce one another; in such areas, delinquency arises within at least a "partial framework of social controls" and there are "effective limits of permissible activity" (p. 658). At the other extreme are those communities in which the adult criminal activity is unsystematic and disorganized and the conventional and criminal value systems are in opposition to one another. Therefore, delinquency tends to be unrestrained by any kind of control (p. 658).

Delinquent subcultures arise within gangs since particular forms of illegal behavior are seen as necessary for the performance of the dominant roles necessitated by the values of the neighborhood (Cloward and Ohlin 1960:7). Cloward and Ohlin (pp. 161-186) argue that the type of gang that emerges depends on the degree to which the conventional and illegitimate opportunity structures are integrated. *Criminal subcultures*, in which gang activity is oriented toward illegal means of securing income, are most likely in neighborhoods in which there are close bonds between different age levels and between criminal and conventional residents (p.171). *Conflict subcultures*, in which the effective use of violence is the primary source of status in the group, tend to arise in neighborhoods with low levels of age integration and severe limitations on both conventional and criminal opportunities (p.177). Finally, *retreatist subcultures*, in which the consumption of drugs is emphasized, are most likely among youth living in integrated areas who nevertheless have failed to succeed in either conventional or illegitimate activities, or among youth living in disorganized areas who are unable to successfully gain status through violent activities; in that respect Cloward and Ohlin (p. 179) refer to such gang members as double failures.

It is difficult to overstate the influence of these three theories on the development of criminological and gang theory; a recent book of James Short, Jr. (1990:148), for example, defines gangs in part as "carriers of subcultures." Not only have the predictions and assumptions of Miller, Cohen, Cloward, and Ohlin been subjected to numerable tests but they have also inspired several large-budget federal programs aimed at delinquency prevention. Klein (1971:31), for example, observes that the differential opportunity approach of Cloward and Ohlin "almost became a national policy" during the late 1960s and 1970s.

However, some important criticisms have been leveled at subcultural theories of gang behavior in general, and these three theories in particular, on both empirical and logical grounds. Several studies have failed to document the existence of a system of crime-related norms, values, and beliefs that is unique to the lower class. The most important series of research was that of Short and Fred Strodtbeck (1965), who designed their study of Chicago gangs in part as a specific test of these three theories. At a very basic level, they note that they could not find a single "full-blown" example of the criminal gangs discussed by Cloward and Ohlin, or more than one predominantly drug-using (i.e., retreatist) gang in all of Chicago despite "highly motivated" efforts to do so (p. 13); this failure led them to question the generalizability of such phenomena. Hagedorn (1988:99-100) has also been extremely critical of the Cloward and Ohlin typology, arguing that they failed to take into account the age-graded nature of gang behavior. For example, while he considers all the Milwaukee gangs included in his study to represent "fighting gangs" (which would be analogous to the conflict gang of Cloward and Ohlin), he notes that the fighting usually occurred when gang members were relatively young. As members mature, "their interests turned more to fundamental problems of survival." Such findings suggest that any particular gang may be characterized by a mixture of activities that are distributed among the members on the basis of age.

The failure to uncover the three types of gangs discussed by Cloward and Ohlin may be a function of the different localities in which these groups were situated, for we have noted the pronounced geographic variation in gang behavior. The more crucial test of the subcultural thesis is the identification of particular norms, values, and beliefs that may encourage and support delinquent behavior in lower-class neighborhoods. Such studies at best provide only partial support to these theories. Short and Strodtbeck (1965:47-76) conclude that while gang, lower-class, and middle-class boys differ in their tolerance of behaviors proscribed by the middle class, the endorsement of middle-class values is "uniformly high" (p. 76). Even gang members evaluated images associated with a middle-class life-style more positively than any subcultural images, especially those that are illegitimate (p. 59). Overall, although there was some evidence of distinctive lower-class attitudes, these were definitely secondary to conventional values and beliefs. A similar lack of support for the subcultural thesis is found in the work of Sandra Ball-Rokeach (1973).

Some criminologists have resisted the rejection of subcultural explanations, noting that there is a negative association between class and involvement in violent crime (Magura 1975; Wolfgang and Ferracuti 1982). Such arguments illustrate the primary logical problem of this class of theories. Marvin Wolfgang and Franco Ferracuti (1982:101) argue that since values can be identified in terms of expected behavior, "conduct is an external manifestation of sharing in (sub)cultural values." According to Short and Strodtbeck (p. 75), Miller inferred the existence of his focal concerns on the basis of such observational data. However, Ball-Rokeach (1975:836) has countered that even if a perfect association is observed to exist between social class and crime, it is incumbent on subcultural theorists to demonstrate that the primary source of that relationship is the existence of norms and values among the lower classes that encourage the commission of crime.

One important alternative explanation is that the prevalence of illegal behavior in particular neighborhoods represents the effects of situational exigencies caused by the social structure and is not a reflection of a "semiautonomous subculture" (Erlanger 1979:235). Without a demonstration of the independent effects of a distinctive group of norms and values, subcultural theories become exercises in circular reasoning; that is, people in lower-class neighborhoods commit crime because of a subculture that encourages such behavior, and the proof of the existence of that subculture is that people in those neighborhoods commit crime (see Kornhauser 1978:209). We do not in any way mean to deny the existence of subcultures in our society; given the diversity that exists in the United States, only a fool might suggest otherwise. Rather, the central question is whether the values that are characteristic of particular social groups directly require or condone illegal behavior (see Erlanger 1979:235).

Although there is some contradictory evidence in the literature,[6] we do not feel that the bulk of contemporary research presents a convincing case for the existence of a unique crime-based subculture within lower-class neighborhoods that can explain either the patterns of gang behavior or the development of an ongoing criminal tradition within stable neighborhoods. In fact some have questioned the existence of any distinctive subculture particular to the lower class. John Reed (1982:142-143) has outlined four implications of a subcultural theory of behavior that can be easily adapted for our purposes. First, many residents of lower-class communities will take gang behavior for granted because it is a type of activity that they find "natural." Second, gangs will not engage in illegal behavior in all circumstances but only in those where the culture permits or demands such behavior. Third, gang members are not marginal members of the community. Rather they have been well socialized into the culture of the neighborhood that gives rise to gangs. Finally, if gang behavior is part of a community's "cultural bedrock," it should be a common theme in local interactions.

There is some evidence that these criteria may be met in certain lower-class communities. For example, one of the informants quoted by Skogan (1990:25) states that a local gang has "the blessing and support of their parents and of their community." Yet Skogan's discussion implies that such support is not derived from a unique set of norms and values that encourage such behavior. Rather, this neighborhood was faced with the structural threat of racial invasion; the primary function of this gang was to "keep blacks out of the area." Based on her extensive review of the literature, Kornhauser (1978:210) has questioned the existence of any shared subculture that would unite such diverse elements of the lower class as poor whites, poor Southern blacks, poor ethnics, poor farmers, and poor slum dwellers in a distinctive set of social relationships other than "their indifference to or hatred of each other." We concur with her assessment.

It might be argued that classes are an inappropriate focus of subcultural theories. Rather, perhaps subcultural theories should focus on the development of criminal traditions within ethnic communities, whose residents clearly share a common heritage. Joan Moore (1978:52-53) has described how Chicano barrios are characterized by a wealth of shared cultural themes and long-standing family relationships. In this context, she argues that barrio gangs in Los Angeles are fully integrated parts of the community that provide the means of attaining culturally valued goals, such as the expression of maleness, competence, and "being in command." Similar observations have been made concerning Mexican-American gangs in other Chicano neighborhoods (Horowitz 1983; Vigil and Long 1990). It may therefore be possible that in such ethnic contexts, gangs serve as the carriers of neighborhood traditions and cultures.

Again, the question is the degree to which such ethnic subcultures encourage and support illegal activities. Wolfgang and Ferracuti (1982:160), for example, suggest that violent behavior is most likely in subcultures that emphasize masculinity, noting that "the adult male who does not defend his honor or his female companion will be socially emasculated . . . [and] . . . forced to move out of the territory, to find new friends, and make new alliances." Ball-Rokeach (1973:740-742) finds no support for the proposition that attitudes associated with "machismo" are significantly related to violent behavior. On the other hand, although residents of the Chicago neighborhood studied by Horowitz (1983:22-24) aspire to achieve the American Dream through traditional means, she also notes that these values coexist with a code of honor that emphasizes masculinity, the style of one's actions, and one's personal integrity. The failure to elicit respect from others is perceived as a "derogation of fundamental properties of self" (p. 23), and the subculture of the neighborhood demands a physical and sometimes violent response to such personal affronts.

Horowitz (1983:Chapter 2) extensively discusses the degree to which gang behavior is the outcome of a cultural system in which group members appraise and evaluate their behavior and that of others in terms of shared cognitive and moral categories. Not surprisingly, she concludes that culture determines the meaning of social relationships, thereby giving rise to the gang activity in the area (p. 21). Since she is dealing with only a single neighborhood, it is impossible to examine the relative effects of structure and culture on the formation and maintenance of gang behavior, and the question is moot for the 32nd Street area. However, Horowitz (p. 35) does document the very weak linkages between the neighborhood and Chicago institutions that could provide resources to the area: "The political actors ignore the area . . . the school board does little to improve its deteriorating schools, the local banks and food stores charge high prices for goods and services, and the city urban renewal plan designated many of its buildings for destruction and its residents for removal."

As we noted earlier, one of the reasons for the historical popularity of subcultural theories has been the apparent inability of systemic, social disorganization approaches to account for the presence of stable neighborhoods with ongoing traditions of gang behavior. We feel that this is due to the emphasis of Shaw and McKay on only the private level of systemic control, especially as reflected in family structures and dynamics. Because of this emphasis, the social disorganization model is at a loss when neighborhoods with fairly stable patterns of family relationships are shown to have relatively high levels of gang activity.

However, a consideration of the parochial and public dimensions of systemic control may account for such phenomena. Interestingly enough, this systemic solution is implicit to Albert Cohen's critique of social disorganization theory, in which he states that "the organization which exists may indeed not be adequate for the effective control of delinquency and for the solution of other social problems, but the qualities and defects of organization are not to be confused with the absence of organization" (p. 33). Likewise, William F. Whyte (1981:273) concluded that the primary problem of Cornerville was not its lack of organization, but its "failure to mesh with the structure of the society around it." Therefore, a systemic model of gang activity would argue in part that it is likely to arise in areas in which the networks of parochial and public control cannot effectively provide services to the neighborhood.[7] For example, Gerald Suttles (1972:225) suggests that gangs may result from the inadequacy of the police, courts and public schools to take responsibility "for the protection of property and lives and for moral education." These "urban service functions" of street gangs have been discussed extensively by Martin Sanchez Jankowski (1991:180-201), who documents gang activities ranging from the protection of elderly neighborhood residents to preventing the construction of an unwanted real estate development.

There is some limited evidence that the development of parochial and public networks of systemic control can significantly modify the nature of gang behavior in a neighborhood. Gary Schwartz (1987) has extensively discussed the differences in two working-class communities in Illinois. Cambridge, a suburban community, was characterized by a great deal of distrust between local institutions (which were dominated by middle-class professionals) and the blue-collar residents of the town. In addition, pronounced generational tensions existed. Within this setting, drug use and fighting were widespread and took on the "moral equivalence of sports" (p.144), especially among a group of youths who were highly antagonistic to authority, hypersensitive to insults, and fairly extensively involved in serious delinquency. These features are highly reminiscent of those implicated by Cohen's notion of reaction formation.

However, Schwartz discusses a second working-class community, the Parsons Park neighborhood of Chicago. In addition to its economic characteristics, Parsons Park is a primarily ethnic area that is being threatened by racial invasion. Therefore, it would seem to be an especially fruitful area for the development of a criminal tradition carried by local gangs. However, Schwartz's description gives no indication of any such behavior. While the adolescents in the area certainly get involved in delinquent activities, Schwartz notes that there is little serious juvenile crime. What does exist in the community, however, is a strong integration of family, church, and police relational networks and a clear sense of political power. It is not necessary to develop a subcultural theory to account for the antagonism toward authority that exists in Cambridge. Rather the comparison between it and Parsons Park suggests that the answer lies in the relative effectiveness of the private, parochial, and public bases of systemic control in each area.

A limited degree of support for the systemic explanation of criminal traditions can also be derived from certain incidents mentioned in the more standard gang literature. David Dawley (1992) and R. Lincoln Keiser (1969:9) describe a period during which the Vice Lords, one of the "supergangs" of Chicago, received external funding to develop community self-help and black consciousness programs. Almost all of Keiser's informants reported that "gang fighting had completely stopped" during this time (p. 11). Similarly, Howard Erlanger (1979) reports that there was a decrease in gang violence in the barrios of East Los Angeles between 1969 and 1972 when many gang members became involved with a locally based political movement.

These dynamics characterize a relatively small number of gangs and are most likely short-lived (see Short and Strodtbeck 1974). Nevertheless, such findings suggest that subcultural theories are not required to account for the existence of gang behavior in stable communities.

Neighborhood Gangs and the Urban Economy

One of the most common criticisms that has been made of contemporary gang research is that the dominant theories were developed during a period of American history in which a large number of low-skilled industrial jobs were available to immigrant gang members. These jobs provided the first steps toward economic mobility and assimilation. . . . The occupational opportunity structure of the United States has changed dramatically in that many urban areas have been characterized by significant decreases in the number of manufacturing jobs that are available to relatively low-skilled workers. Therefore, the structural sources of mobility that Thrasher or Shaw and McKay assumed to exist have narrowed considerably. The three classic subcultural theories that we discussed in the preceding section were also developed well before these shifts in the political economy began to exert their effects on urban areas. Therefore, some aspects of these traditional theories are grounded in assumptions concerning the nature of urban dynamics that are no longer relevant (see Hagedorn 1988).

No significant reformulations of gang theory were forthcoming until relatively recently, when a small group of researchers began to propose an alternative explanation for the apparent existence of gang traditions in urban neighborhoods. As opposed to the subcultural dynamics that were emphasized by the researchers discussed in the previous section, this new formulation focuses on the important contextual effect of the urban economy on the nature of the neighborhood dynamics. Although this issue has been addressed in a growing number of studies (see Horowitz 1982; Vigil 1983, 1988; Huff 1989; Fagan 1990; Jankowski 1991), the theoretical implications have been developed most fully by Joan Moore (1978, 1985, 1988; Moore et al. 1983), John Hagedorn (1988), and Mercer Sullivan (1989).

These approaches draw heavily from William Wilson's concept of "the underclass" (see Wilson 1980, 1987), which refers to those extremely poor populations that have been abandoned in the inner city owing to the exodus of the middle class; in later work (1988) he defines the underclass as residents of census tracts in which the poverty rate exceeds 40 percent. Although it does not necessarily have a racial or ethnic connotation, the term has typically been used to refer to low-income blacks and Hispanics who have been especially affected by the changing economic structure of urban areas. This is understandable, since the Hidden Employment Index developed by the National Urban League[8] indicates that 22.8 percent of all African-American workers were unemployed during the first quarter of 1991, compared to 12.3 percent of white workers (1991:1) . These problems are especially severe for teenagers seeking employment: the Hidden Employment Index suggests that 58.9 percent of such black teenagers are unemployed, compared to 30.4 percent of the whites (p. 5); similar patterns have been noted for Puerto Ricans and Mexican-Americans (Moore 1978; Hagedorn 1988). Given the changing political economies of urban areas, Wilson (1980:171) suggests that such disparities primarily are due to the differential occupational effects of these dynamics and the concentration of blacks in those occupations which have been hardest hit by the elimination of many manufacturing jobs.[9]

While "the underclass" is a very popular and controversial notion, it has been very hard to define precisely (see Will 1991). The most common use of the term within criminology has been in reference to men and women who are permanently excluded from participation in the primary labor market of mainstream occupations (Moore 1978:27-29). As a result, members of the underclass are forced to rely on one or more economic alternatives, such as taking low-paying temporary or part-time jobs in the secondary labor market, temporarily living off relatives or spouse equivalents, using transfer payments such as AFDC or General Assistance, joining subsidized employment programs like CETA, or becoming involved in hustling or street crime (Moore 1988:7-8).

Mercer Sullivan (1989) has provided a rich description of the implications of such economic dynamics on the development of gang dynamics in the "La Barriada" neighborhood of Brooklyn during the late 1970s and early 1980s. Her [sic] description of this area has all the classical features usually associated with underclass communities: most of the residents were supported by transfer payments, jobs that paid salaries just above what could be obtained through welfare, or jobs that were never officially "on the books." Economically motivated delinquency was a common behavior of young teenagers in the neighborhood, and such activities usually fulfilled a need for a short-term cash flow and excitement. However, as these adolescents aged, more regular sources of income were necessary, partly in an effort to support their families as well as their own life-styles.

Many of these youths were skeptical of the relevance of education to their future in the labor market and left school prior to graduation to obtain work.[10] However, given their relative lack of employment credentials, the positions that were available tended to be unstable, with undesirable working conditions and no chance for advancement. Since a significant proportion of these jobs were never officially recorded, many of these youths did not qualify for unemployment compensation when a position was suddenly terminated (Sullivan 1989:60-64). As a result, many of the local youths became involved in a systematic series of thefts and other economically motivated illegal activities that were coordinated through membership in local gangs (p. 117).

The image of gangs found in Sullivan's work goes beyond the play groups that are bound through conflict with other groups. Rather, as Jankowski (1991:22) has argued, "the gang emerges as one organizational response . . . seeking to improve the competitive advantage of its members in obtaining an increase in material resources." While Jankowski (p. 120) notes that gangs focus their economic activities primarily in goods, services, and recreation, "the biggest money-maker and the one product nearly every gang tries to market is drugs."

Sullivan (1989: 136) notes that some of the barrio youths that she [sic] studied greatly decreased their involvement in criminal activities after the age of eighteen because of the greater opportunities that existed for legitimate employment. Although this pattern is identical to that assumed to exist by Thrasher, there are several important differences. First, some youths had difficulty obtaining legitimate employment because of the criminal records they had compiled due to their gang involvement. Moore (1988:10-11) observes that these problems are especially severe when Chicano gang members have served time in prison or a juvenile correction facility because they often return to the neighborhoods unemployable and with a history of heroin use. Thus, the prison experience can accelerate the process of economic marginalization.

Second, those youths who were able to find legitimate employment sometimes supplemented their small salaries with the proceeds of criminal activity, which increased the likelihood of further involvement with the criminal justice system and eventual dismissal from the job. Finally, owing to problems of excess absenteeism, many of these legitimate jobs did not have a long duration. Such employment histories would necessitate further participation in gang activities for the sake of economic survival. As a result, contrary to the gangs discussed by Thrasher and many subsequent researchers, some residents have maintained their gang involvement well into early adulthood.[11] Hagedorn (1988:110) makes the important observation that this is also the case for the "Norton" gang studied by Whyte (1981), who resided in an Italian neighborhood during the Great Depression when economic opportunities were similarly limited.

Moore (1988:8) has argued that such economic processes can lead to the institutionalization of gang activities in underclass neighborhoods. While a significant proportion of gang members may mature out of such behavior (as also noted by Sullivan), some fraction is recruited into gangs during adolescence, and the process continues to reproduce itself.

It might appear that the underclass hypothesis represents an important competing alternative to the systemic social disorganization model. Like the subcultural theories that we have discussed, it is able to account for the presence of gangs in otherwise stable, low-income neighborhoods. However, the patterns that have been described in this literature are very similar to those found in Spergel's (1984) discussion of the "segmented" route to gang behavior, in which he emphasizes the economic nature of gang activity. Spergel (p. 203) noted that secondary institutions in such neighborhoods "have efficient links to the local population as well as to each other." However, these institutions are secondary to those "representing dominant city and local middle class interests." Moore (1978:21-26), for example, notes that the general absence of political "brokers" who can intercede between underclass Chicano communities and major institutional agencies (such as those connected with health education and welfare, criminal justice, education, and immigration) has left residents poorly equipped to deal with such institutions. Even programs that titularly have been designed to bring resources into the neighborhood can be perceived as self-serving and alien if there is not sufficient input and participation by local residents. As a result of these relatively weak linkages to the centers of power in a city, the potential ability of an economically marginal neighborhood to exercise effective public systemic control is very limited.

Some might argue that it is very difficult for any particular neighborhood to significantly affect the political economy of its metropolitan area to such a degree that meaningful occupational opportunities become available to residents desiring such employment. This is certainly true, for Suttles (1972) has noted that such large-scale efforts are not likely to be successful unless neighborhoods can develop alliances with other groups in the city with similar interests. While this is often extremely difficult for areas with weak bases of public control, it is not impossible. Horowitz (1983:43) notes that the 32nd Street neighborhood engaged in several indigenous collective efforts to affect the local job situation. Likewise, city governments have been lobbied to provide incentives (such as tax breaks) to encourage local employers to remain in an area or to encourage prospective employers to relocate to an area (as was the case in the recent negotiations of several cities with United Airline). The success of such efforts can in turn further strengthen the public basis of control in an area, increasing the likelihood of success in similar future efforts.

Therefore, we do not believe this body of research contradicts the assumptions of a systemic model in any way. Rather, it is simply a difference in emphasis: the traditional social disorganization research has emphasized the private level of systemic control, the "underclass" work has focused on the public level. A fully systemic model, with a consideration of the private, parochial, and public orders of control, can account for the processes described by each set of theories in a logically consistent manner.

Notes

1. Gang homicides are defined in terms of the criterion used by the Chicago Police Department: "a killing is considered gang-related only if it occurs in the course of an explicitly defined collective encounter between two or more gangs" (Spergel 1984:204). The data reflect the community in which the homicide occurred, not necessarily the residential area of the victim or offender.
2. For a good discussion of media stereotypes of gangs, see Jankowski (1991:Chapter 9).
3. The emphasis on the lower class in these theories reflects the assumption that delinquent behavior was relatively rare in other economic situations or was the result of non-sociological processes such as personal pathology. The impact of the self-report methodology, which provided evidence that apparently contradicted such an assumption, was not yet widespread when these theories were originally formulated.
4. Cohen tends to use the terms "working class" and "lower class" interchangeably in his discussion.
5. Although the neighborhood is noted in passing several times in this work, Cohen does not extensively discuss the local community bases of gang formation. However, given the class-based spatial segregation that characterizes many cities as well as the neighborhood-based schools that were dominant at the time of this work, the extension of his work to local communities per se is straightforward.
6. Contradictory evidence is especially apparent in research that has attempted to document the existence of a subculture of violence in the American South. See Loftin and Parker 1985.
7. Such an orientation is implicit to Spergel's (1984) argument concerning segmented routes to gang activity.
8. In addition to the number of people who have been officially defined as unemployed, this index includes involuntary part-time workers and those discouraged workers who have quit looking for employment.
9. A good sense of the characteristics of the underclass is provided by a recent survey of chronically poor blacks living in eight cities commissioned by the NAACP (1989; noted in Schaefer and Lamm 1992): women constitute 78 percent of the black underclass, the median income of the chronically poor households during the preceding five years was $4,900, a majority of those had not had a job in the past two years, and over 40 percent had either never held a job or received any employment training.
10. Hagedorn (1988:46), for example, notes that 40 percent of all black high school freshmen in the Milwaukee public schools drop out before their senior year. It should be noted that many of Sullivan's respondents indicated a desire to eventually return to school, or to at least complete a GED. However, very few of them did so in La Barriada.
11. The increasing presence of older gang members also has been noted by Horowitz (1983), Moore (1978), and Hagedorn (1988).

References

Ball-Rokeach, Sandra J. (1973). "Values and Violence: A Test of the Subculture of Violence Thesis." *American Sociological Review* 38:736-749.

—— (1975). "Issues and Non-issues in Testing a Subcultural Thesis: Reply to Magura." *American Sociological Review* 40:836-838.

Burgess, Ernest W. (1925). "The Growth of the City." Pp. 47-62 in *The City*, edited by Robert E. Park, Ernest W. Burgess, and Roderick D. McKenzie. Chicago: University of Chicago Press.

Cartwright, Desmond S., and Kenneth J. Howard (1966). "Multivariate Analysis of Gang Delinquency. I. Ecologic Influences." *Multivariate Behavioral Research* 1:321-371.

Chin, Ko-Lin (1990). "Chinese Gangs and Extortion." Pp. 129-145 in *Gangs in America*, edited by C. Ronald Huff. Newbury Park, CA: Sage.

Cloward, Richard A., and Lloyd Ohlin (1960). *Delinquency and Opportunity*. New York: Free Press.

Cohen, Albert K. (1955). *Delinquent Boys*. Glencoe, IL: The Free Press.

Curry, G. David, and Irving A. Spergel (1988). "Gang Homicide, Delinquency and Community." *Criminology* 26:381-405.

Dawley, David (1992). *A Nation of Lords*. Second Edition. Prospect Heights, IL: Waveland Press.

Erbe, Brigitte Mach (1975). "Race and Socioeconomic Segregation." *American Sociological Review* 40:801-812.

Erlanger, Howard S. (1979). "Estrangement, Machismo, and Gang Violence." *Social Science Quarterly* 60:235-249.

Fagan, Jeffrey (1990). "Social Processes of Delinquency and Drug Use Among Urban Gangs." Pp. 183-219 in *Gangs in America*, edited by C. Ronald Huff. Newbury Park, CA: Sage.

Hagedorn, John M. (1988). *People and Folks: Gangs, Crime and the Underclass in a Rustbelt City*. Chicago: Lakeview Press.

Haskins, James (1974). *Street Gangs: Yesterday and Today*. New York: Hastings House.

Horowitz, Ruth (1982). "Adult Delinquent Gangs in a Chicano Community: Masked Intimacy and Marginality." *Urban Life* 11:3-26.

—— (1983). *Honor and the American Dream*. New Brunswick, NJ: Rutgers University Press.

Huff, C. Ronald (1989). "Youth Gangs and Public Policy." *Crime and Delinquency* 35:524-537.

Jankowski, Martin Sanchez (1991). *Islands in the Street: Gangs and American Urban Society*. Berkeley: University of California Press.

Joe, Delbert, and Norman Robinson (1980). "Chinatown's Immigrant Gangs: The New Young Warrior Class." *Criminology* 18:337-345.

Keiser, R. Lincoln (1969). *The Vice Lords: Warriors of the Streets*. New York: Holt, Rinehart and Winston.

Klein, Malcolm W. (1971). *Street Gangs and Street Workers*. Englewood Cliffs, NJ: Prentice-Hall.

Klein, Malcolm W. and Cheryl L. Maxson (1985). "'Rock' Sales in South Los Angeles." *Sociology and Social Research* 69:561-565.

Kobrin, Solomon (1951). "The Conflict of Values in Delinquency Areas." *American Sociological Review* 16:653-661.

Kornhauser, Ruth R. (1978). *Social Sources of Delinquency*. Chicago: University of Chicago Press.

Loftin, Colin, and Robert N. Parker (1985). "The Effect of Poverty on Urban Homicide Rates: An Error in Variables Approach." *Criminology* 23:269-287.

Magura, Stephen (1975). "Is There a Subculture of Violence?" *American Sociological Review* 40:831-836.

Merton, Robert K. (1938). "Social Structure and Anomie." *American Sociological Review* 3:672-682.

Miller, Walter (1958). "Lower Class Culture as a Generating Milieu of Gang Delinquency." *Journal of Social Issues* 14:5-19.

Moore, Joan W. (1978) *Homeboys*. Philadelphia: Temple University Press.

—— (1985). "Isolation and Stigmatization in the Development of an Underclass: The Case of Chicano Gangs in East Los Angeles." *Social Problems* 33:1-12.

—— (1988). "Introduction: Gangs and the Underclass. A Comparative Perspective." Pp. 3-17 in *People and Folks: Gangs, Crime and the Underclass in a Rustbelt City*, by John M. Hagedorn. Chicago: Lake View Press.

Moore, Joan W., Diego Vigil, and Robert Garcia (1983). "Residence and Territoriality in Chicano Gangs." *Social Problems* 31:182-194.

Muehlbauer, Gene, and Laura Dodder (1983). *The Losers: Gang Delinquency in an American Suburb*. New York: Praeger.

NAACP Legal Defense and Educational Fund (1989). *The Unfinished Agenda on Race in America*. New York: NAACP Legal Defense and Educational Fund.

Park, Robert E., and Ernest W. Burgess (1924). *Introduction to the Science of Sociology*. Second Edition. Chicago: University of Chicago Press.

Reed, John Shelton (1982). *One South. An Ethnic Approach to Regional Culture*. Baton Rouge: Louisiana State University Press.

Savitz, Leonard D., Lawrence Rosen, and Michael Lalli (1980). "Delinquency and Gang Membership as Related to Victimization." *Victimology* 5:152-160.

Schaeffer, Richard T., and Robert P. Lamm (1992). *Sociology*. Fourth Edition. New York: McGraw-Hill.

Schwartz, Gary (1987). *Beyond Conformity or Rebellion*. Chicago: University of Chicago Press.

Shaw, Clifford R., Frederick M. Zorbaugh, Henry D. McKay, and Leonard S. Cottrell (1929). *Delinquency Areas*. Chicago: University of Chicago Press.

Shaw, Clifford R., and Henry D. McKay (1969). *Juvenile Delinquency and Urban Areas*. Second Edition. Chicago: University of Chicago Press.

Short, James F., Jr. (1963). "Introduction to the Abridged Edition." Pp. xv-liii in *The Gang*, by Frederic Thrasher. Chicago: University of Chicago Press.

—— (1990). *Delinquency and Society*. Englewood Cliffs, NJ: Prentice-Hall.

Short, James F., Jr., and Fred L. Strodtbeck (1965). *Group Process and Gang Delinquency*. Chicago: University of Chicago Press.

—— (1974). "Preface, 1974." Pp. v-xiv in *Group Process and Gang Delinquency*. Second Printing, by James F. Short, Jr. and Fred L. Strodtbeck. Chicago: University of Chicago Press.

Skogan, Wesley G. (1990). *Disorder and Decline: Crime and the Spiral of Decay in American Neighborhoods*. New York: Free Press.

Spergel, Irving A. (1984). "Violent Gangs in Chicago: In Search of Social Policy." *Social Service Review* 58:199-226.

—— (1986). "Violent Gangs in Chicago: A Local Community Approach." *Social Service Review* 60:94-131.

—— (1990). "Youth Gangs: Continuity and Change." Pp. 171-275 in *Crime and Justice: A Review of Research*. Volume 12, edited by Michael Tonry and Norval Morris. Chicago: University of Chicago Press.

Sullivan, Mercer L. (1989). *Getting Paid: Youth Crime and Work in the Inner City*. Ithaca, NY: Cornell University Press.

Suttles, Gerald D. (1972). *The Social Construction of Communities*. Chicago: University of Chicago Press.

Thrasher, Frederic M. (1927). *The Gang*. Chicago: University of Chicago Press.

United States General Accounting Office (1989). *Nontraditional Organized Crime*. Washington, DC: U.S. Government Printing Office.

Vigil, James D. (1983). "Chicano Gangs: One Response to Mexican Urban Adaptation." *Urban Anthropology* 12:45-75.

—— (1988). *Barrio Gangs: Street Life and Identity in Southern California*. Austin: University of Texas Press.

Vigil, James D., and John M. Long (1990). "Emic and Etic Perspectives on Gang Culture: The Chicano Case." Pp. 55-68 in *Gangs in America*, edited by C. Ronald Huff. Newbury Park, CA: Sage.

Vigil, James D., and Steve Chong Yun (1990). "Vietnamese Youth Gangs in Southern California." Pp. 146-162 in *Gangs in America*, edited by C. Ronald Huff. Newbury Park, CA: Sage.

Whyte, William F. (1981). *Street Corner Society*. Third Edition. Chicago: University of Chicago Press.

Will, Jeffrey A. (1991). "Crime, Neighborhood Perceptions, and the Underclass: An Empirical Tip Toe Through the Theory." A paper presented to the annual meeting of the American Society of Criminology, San Francisco.

Wilson, William J. (1980). *The Declining Significance of Race: Blacks and Changing American Institutions*. Second Edition. Chicago: University of Chicago Press.

—— (1987). *The Truly Disadvantaged*. Chicago: University of Chicago Press.

—— (1988). "The Ghetto Underclass and the Social Transformation of the Inner City." *Black Scholar* 19:10-17.

Wolfgang, Marvin E. and Franco Ferracuti (1982). *The Subculture of Violence: Toward an Integrated Theory in Criminology*. Beverly Hills: Sage. ✦

14

Barrio Gangs: Street Life and Identity in Southern California

James Diego Vigil

In this brief introduction to the book Barrio Gangs, *cultural anthropologist Vigil draws on historical, cultural and underclass theory to frame his notions about the development and persistence of Hispanic, or Cholo, gangs. Multiple marginality results from cultural accommodation to Anglo-American lifestyles, intergenerational culture clashes, and limited opportunities for social mobility in barrio communities. The barrio street gang is a social adaptation to the economic and cultural stressors confronting young men of Mexican descent. It is instructive to consider Vigil's position relative to the criticisms of subcultural theory presented by Bursik and Grasmick. Can the concept of multiple marginality be applied to the development of other ethnic gangs and female gang membership (as described in the articles presented in Section I)?*

A look behind the scenes of Chicano youth gang behavior is long overdue. It is important to know how the streets have become such a strong socializing force in the barrios of Southern California and why certain adolescents and youth there are particularly motivated to identify with the street gang. Many of the street gang habits and customs make better sense when considered in the context of street pressures and group identification processes. To survive in street culture, one must have a street identity. It will be revealed in this study that there are many intricacies and complexities to this street identity.

Chicano street gangs in Los Angeles and Southern California have been around for several decades (Bogardus 1926). Over the past forty years they have been viewed as a menace to society, wreaking crime and violence on the rest of the populace, or as a serious social problem with roots in the urban experience of low-income minority groups. Several explanations of Chicano gangs (McWilliams 1968; Griffith 1948; Tuck 1956; Heller 1966; Rosenquist and Megargee 1969; Klein 1971; Snyder 1977; J. Moore 1978; Horowitz 1983) advanced our understanding of the problem. However, the complexity of the street gang requires a careful separation of the cluster of factors that contribute to its formation and persistence. The lives of the street youths who comprise the barrio gang reflect multiple stresses and pressures, which result in a multiple marginality. This multiple marginality derives from various interwoven situations and conditions that tend to act and react upon one another. Although interrelated, the unfolding and interpretation of these ecological, economic, social, cultural, and psychological features of the street gang suggest a developmental sequence.

All of these considerations are integral to the relationship between multiple marginality and gang patterns. In particular, it will be clear that barrio children whose lives are most intensely affected by marginality in these dimensions are more at risk to become gang members. Moreover, use of the concept will permit an examination of gang violence and related behavior within the context of a cumulative, additive experience. My self-reflexive life history involvement with various facets of street and gang life and the life histories of different types of contemporary gang members provide insights and nuances and shifting levels of insider/outsider analysis to this perspective. This combination of ways of examining and describing the street gang will promote theory building and the integration of more narrowly focused explanations for gang phenomena that have emerged over the years.

Anyone who regularly works with street gangs can learn the answers to such questions as, Where they are located? Who are the members? What do they do and how do they do it? However, even after having gained such knowledge, few observers understand what the sources of this behavior are or when in a person's life does such behavior emerge. It is these and other such questions that should guide our discussion if we are to better comprehend the gang phenomenon. Partial, incomplete, and narrow assessments do injustice to the general public as well as to the communities where gangs are common. As an example of this narrow attitude, I once inquired of a city official, the director of community programs and affairs, what recreational and social programs were offered to the local barrio youth and whether he was familiar with some of the conditions that caused the formation of the gang. He gave a testy response: "We don't want to understand the problem, we just want to stop it." While desiring to "stop it" is understandable, such lack of analysis can only impede the official's desire.

Chicano gangs are made up largely of young males, from 13 to 25 years of age. The gang subcultural style is a response to the pressures of street life and serves to give certain barrio youth a source of familial support, goals and directives, and sanctions and guides. Although gang members typically constitute a small minority of the young in a barrio, they represent a street style that both conforms and contrasts with familiar youth patterns (Klein 1969). On the one hand, most of their time is spent in the usual cohort activities found in any neighborhood where adolescents and other youth congregate. They talk, joke, plan social events, and exchange stories of adventure and love. Their alcohol consumption and drug use shows some parallels with that of other American adolescents. Yet it is their other, violent, socially disruptive activities that distinguish gang members from most adolescents.

Reflecting the tendency among adolescents to develop new modes of dress and speech, Chicano gang members have adopted a distinctive street style of dress, speech, gestures, tattoos, and graffiti. This style is called *cholo*, a centuries-old term for some Latin American Indians who are partially acculturated to Hispanic-based elite cultures (Wolck 1973). The term also reflects the cultural transitional situation of Mexican Americans in the southwestern United States; it is a process strongly affected by underclass forces and street requisites. Many of the cholo customs symbolize an attachment to and identification with the gang, although many individuals copy the style without joining the gang. As we will note, there is a wide difference among members in degree of commitment to the gang, but generally it is those members with the most problematic lives and intense street experiences who become regular members. Over the decades, the gang has developed a subculture, that is, a social structure and cultural value system with its own age-graded cohorts, initiations, norms and goals, and roles. These now function to socialize and enculturate barrio youth. Though the emergence of a gang subculture initially resulted from urban maladaption among some segments of the Mexican immigrant population, it is now a continuing factor to which new Latino immigrants must adapt. To understand developments in this area we must look to the starting point, the inception of this country's urban revolution.

Gangs in Urban Immigrant Communities

Gangs have been an urban problem in the United States since the beginning of large-scale immigration to this country before the turn of the century (Thrasher 1963; [1927]). The processes and patterns of immigrant adaption, although different in important ways, stemmed from remarkably similar sources. The early groups were European immigrants especially from southeastern Europe, who came to this country to find work and a better life. Most of them settled in urban areas and established their own communities. The process of finding work, locating a place to live, and adjusting to urban life was repeated many times over for different ethnic groups, and the Mexican immigrant population is no different in this regard.

What characterized most of these groups was their poverty, their lack of skills. As a result, they were treated as a cheap source of labor. In addition they came from different cultural and (by contemporary definition) racial backgrounds that contrasted sharply with the dominant Anglo-American one. Anglo native-born Americans tended to view the ethnically different newcomers' appearance, behavior patterns, and poverty as a single entity; the immigrants thus faced discrimination from the native born. Their cultural difference acted in two ways to affect them. One stemmed from the changes they had to make in their own cultural values, beliefs, and patterns to adjust and acculturate to Anglo-American lifestyles. The other was a result of how the dominant Anglo culture received and accommodated them. Their own attitudes and behaviors and those of the predominant society operated to affect where they would live, what they would do for a living, and how, when, and even whether they would become "Americanized" (Handlin 1951). Exploitation and discrimination, in particular, dominated the early period after their arrival and extended to the lives of their children. The pressures and anxieties of urban poverty, of the struggle toward a better life, and of overcoming feelings of ethnic and racial inferiority made immigrant cultural adaptation problematic. Such an experience often resulted in gangs.

Throughout most of this century, researchers and writers have compiled evidence on urban gangs. The focus of these accounts varies as to ethnic group, time, and place and the theoretical emphasis. Nonetheless, there is widespread agreement among writers that gangs are an urban phenomenon, particularly so in the cases of ethnic minorities (Clinard 1968), and they represent a pattern found among lower-class adolescents (Cloward and Ohlin 1960). In fact, there is a complex of other factors that make the urban experience so remarkably uniform: a breakdown in social institutions, especially the family and schools (which often impede rather than accommodate adjustment); a first- and second-generational conflict within each ethnic group, which creates loyalty discord and identity confusions; and a noted predisposition among youth to gravitate toward street peers for sources of social associations and personal fulfillment.

Within a generation or two, most members of each early ethnic immigrant group improved their standard of living and stabilized themselves as wage earners and homemakers. Problems associated with urban adaptation, such as youth gangs, crime, poor housing, and unemployment, were initially severe. Eventually, these problems were worked through and became less serious as each group acculturated. Hence, after two generations of severe culture clash both within the ethnic community (intergenerational) and between it and the other communities, the issues that sometimes became a source of national concern, such as culture conflict, economic exploitation, and associated social disruptions, tend to dissipate.

The Nature and Persistence of Chicano Gangs

Although Mexican Americans in urban settings largely share with earlier, mostly eastern U.S. ethnics a similarity in how adaptation proceeds, there are also distinct differences between them. For one thing, Chicano youth gangs (unlike those of other immigrant groups) have shown a remarkable longevity. Moore, Vigil, and Garcia (1983) suggest reasons for this difference: "the gangs are long-lasting, not transitory phenomena. . . . With few exceptions, the Chicano communities of Los Angeles never have been invaded by another ethnic group, nor has another ethnic group succeeded them, nor has there been total cultural disintegration. Instead, there has been more or less continuous immigration of yet more Mexicans, with a reinforcement of some of the traditional culture" (p. 183). Mexican Americans remained more visually distinct from the majority than did the third generation descendants of European immigrants, and the continued presence of fully unacculturated Mexicans made their communities more culturally distinct.

Many families and their children experience acute poverty and limited social mobility opportunities in these barrios, and thus, over time, there developed an underclass with its own set of problems. It is from among these children that the youth most intensely involved in the gangs tends to come. As members of a persistent underclass within the Mexican American population, these youths come from households with even lower incomes than those of other barrio families and a higher incidence of stressful family situations. (This is perhaps reflective of what Auletta [1982] refers to as the 9 million, a subgroup of the 25 million below the national poverty level, who experience a grinding cycle of poverty. Recent reports seem to support the existence of this strata in urban centers [Bearak and Meyer 1985:14; NALEO 1985].) Poor school records and limited job options have combined to make them even more street oriented. As part of their survival on the streets, especially during adolescence, they adopt cultural values and customs that help shape their personal identities.

The youth gangs of Mexican Americans have arisen in the context of the broader pattern of Mexican adaptation to urban life in the United States. Mexican immigration has been the primary factor in the growth of the Mexican American population. The first large wave (1920s) brought anywhere from 1.5 million to 2 million immigrants, doubling the native Mexican American population (Samora 1971). In subsequent waves in the periods from 1940 to 1964 (4 million) and from 1969 through the 1970s (anywhere from 6 to 12 million), the population has continued to swell (Cornelius 1978). Throughout these decades of immigration, the population increasingly settled in urban areas, and today close to 90 percent of the Mexican America (native and immigrant alike) population is in urban areas (Alvírez, Bean, and Williams 1981). A recent report (Muller 1984) on foreign immigration to California since 1970 found that, of over 2 million who have legally settled there, "at least 1.3 million of them have settled in its seven southern counties" (p. 1); and this figure excludes the uncounted and undocumented (Cornelius, Chávez, and Castro 1982). Southern California, and Los Angeles particularly, is the urban area that has received most of these immigrants. Their adjustment and its social and cultural developments have taken different forms, depending on the work opportunities, places of settlement, and, generally, the standard of living attained by immigrants. Such continuous waves of immigrants ensure that there is always a large pool of second-generation Mexican Americans.

Bogardus (1926) noted that in the early years of Mexican immigration there was a "boy" gang problem and characterized it as an incipient form that could be remedied. However, in the following decades it was clear that the gang problem was becoming a serious one, with a formal structure and emerging set of norms and rules to attract and guide members (Bogardus 1943). Cultural change over the years was affected by barrio and underclass life and was particularly acute during the Depression, when even more Mexican youths experienced the intense pressures of urban poverty, especially the second generation. It is a second-generation urban American experience that, in the Chicano case, is a continually renewed phenomenon because of continued immigration. The second generation in the 1930s-1940s originated the *pachuco* lifestyle (a label created for those who wore zoot suits and spoke a mixed English-Spanish slang language that borrowed heavily from *caló*—this in turn, was a continuation of what the Gypsies had started in Spain and later was diffused, by bullfighters it seems, to Mexico [McWilliams 1968; G. C. Barker 1950]). Pachucos were a group who strove to reconcile the conflicting values and nascent pressures that urban adaptation brought; prolonged lower-class status and immobility shaped how Mexican culture was relinquished and American culture integrated into a street style. This style served as a mechanism of adaptation for many youth who needed a source of personal identification and human support, especially during the adolescent self-identification process where ego and peer groups merge to simplify age/sex identification. Pachucos were more than a "boy" gang of loosely aligned street children who participated primarily in street mischief. They had passed the incipient phase of gang formation, as pride in barrio affiliation, barrio conflicts, and some amount of drug use and abuse became a part of their lifestyle. Because most pachucos preferred to look "cool" in their zoot suits and have a good time, these damaging group activities were not as widespread or intense as those practiced in more recent decades. As the practice of negative group activities has escalated, the early generations of gang members, even most pachucos, can be viewed as a transitional form of gang.

A gang subculture eventually formed and became a pressing force in barrio life. Earlier, youths would join the boys on the street for play or mischief. Later, pachucos began to add their distinctive elements to the emerging street gang style. With the passage of time, and the perpetuation of situations, conditions, and social practices that helped to create it, the street style now works to socialize and enculturate youth to a rooted gang subculture with its own group norms and cholo role fronts. The street violence and other debilitating activities that are common features of barrio life can only be understood in terms of this subcultural socialization and its appeal to barrio youths with particular types of personal backgrounds that give rise to particular forms of self-identification processes.

In the 1980s, Chicano gangs comprise at least one-half of the four hundred gangs that exist in Los Angeles County (Decker 1983). This number, of course, is larger when the counties adjacent to Los Angeles are included. Notwithstanding the absolute number of Chicano gangs, however, only a small percentage of Chicano youth, perhaps only 4 to 10 percent of most barrios, are affiliated with gangs (Morales 1982). Of this relatively small percentage, there are subcategories (based upon degree and level of commitment) of regular, peripheral, temporary, and situational. For the most part, gang affiliation and gang-related behavior are primarily male phenomena, although many barrios also have smaller female cliques. The great majority of youths, as in other ethnic groups (cf., e.g., Whyte 1973), find other sources of identification and emulation.

The cultural style of the gang subculture arose partly as a response to street life. However, its major cultural forms are a reforging of Mexican and American patterns. This recombination, of course, borrowed heavily from the earlier pachuco syncretic formulation of creating a culture of mixed and blended elements (e.g., language). Cholos (the present term identifying the style as well as its bearers), share a cultural orientation that makes them distinct from other barrio youth. Although cholos are Americanized, either by accident or by design, they refuse or are unable to be totally assimilated (Vigil 1979, Buriel et al. 1982). In important ways they consider themselves traditionalists and retain certain Mexican customs, however attenuated, as part of their cultural repertoire. For example, they have retained the caló idiom of expression; the strong sense of group as family; the adolescent *palomilla* cohorting tradition (Rubel 1966), which includes many daring and bravado male patterns; and an antiauthority attitude, which is, perhaps, a reaction against *gabacho* (originally a term used for foreigners, such as the French in Mexico during the 1860s intervention, but now designating Anglos) racism (Vigil 1984).

The gangs that have been addressed by researchers range from those that began in the 1940s, and that have over time established more than a dozen identifiable age-graded cohorts (Moore 1978), to those of more recent vintage. An individual gang might include as many as two hundred or more, or as few as ten or twelve, members. It is mainly in the suburbs that the newer, smaller gangs are found. Older, larger gangs, on the other hand, are usually located in long-established urban and semirural barrios. Semirural barrios, and the gangs associated with them, have often been engulfed in recent years by rapidly expanding suburban growth. The deep-rooted presence of older barrio gangs has become a model and a stimulus for gang formation in other areas, as well as a major socialization factor throughout the barrio and nearby areas.

Acculturation is a major factor in a large urban region, such as the greater Los Angeles metropolitan area. Barrio and underclass life has shaped each new immigrant population in different ways, however, creating generational contrasts. As the decades pass, each generation, depending on sociocultural environment and historical conditions, becomes part of a process of cultural change and accommodation. What once began as a Mexican subculture is now transformed into different subcultures. It is in the second generation where the children of Mexican immigrants undergo acculturation shifts resembling a transitional (cholo subculture) phase. Sometimes the phase involves culture conflict, whereby both the donor culture and the host culture become problematic. This ambivalent cultural (and personal) identity makes the gang subculture attractive for a small but significant minority of barrio youth. Their lives are often regulated by the age-graded *klikas* (cliques, or cohorts within the gang). Older gang members also lend some sense of order to their often confused interpersonal interactions by providing vertical lines of organization (Klein 1971); and the gang's involvement in some forms of criminal behavior affords avenues for prestige and income to those who have limited chances of acquiring meaningful jobs (Moore 1978; Chicano Pinto Research Project 1979, 1981). Increasingly, in recent years, both immigrant youths from Mexico and third-generation Mexican Americans have become peripherally involved with street gangs. The Chicano Pinto Research Project (1979, 1981) has found small numbers of third-generation Chicanos, who are themselves offspring of gang members, involved in the core membership of some younger age cohorts.

Multiple Marginality and Street Adaptation

The Chicano youth gang began and grew in ecologically marginal areas of the city and surrounding countryside. It was fed by pressures generated by a marginal economic role. It is peopled by youths with marginal ethnic and personal identities. Each feature of gang life merits scrutiny by itself, but once this task is completed the next step is to search for the links between these features. For example, the interrelationships between socioeconomic condition (e.g., mother-centered households) or social event (e.g., sex identity strivings) must be assessed to understand why gangs are so important during adolescence. A multiple research strategy employing the concept of multiple marginality, which is especially useful with broad and in-depth self-reflexive and life history information, will enhance this understanding. This type of information reflects various times, places, thoughts, and events that must be unpeeled layer by layer, and thus a multiple construct facilitates such a discussion. It is a construct that views reality as a constellation of forces tending to act and react upon one another.

Multiple marginality encompasses the consequences of barrio life, low socioeconomic status, street socialization and enculturation, and problematic development of a self-identity. These gang features arise in a web of ecological, socioeconomic, cultural, and psychological factors. The use of such a concept in an analysis of Chicano youth gangs will help to avoid the difficulties stemming from single-cause examinations of previous gang studies; Cartwright et al. (1975:25-45) have addressed such problems in the second chapter of their review of juvenile gangs. The use of the concept multiple marginality can lead to what Geertz (1973:3) has called a "thick description." Looking at various circumstances and forces in a combinative way increases our understanding of the similarities and variations found within and across groups. It also affords an opportunity to make use of an analyst's personal experiences when merited. Having watched gangs and gang members for many years as an insider has enabled me to chart the flow of events and decision-making processes of street gangs.

An eclectic multiple marginality analysis makes it possible to integrate key elements of the several theories that have been formulated to explain gang delinquency and that emerged in the middle 1950s to early 1960s. (This is no coincidence, as the post-World War II urban explosion led to the development of problems among new minority groups, such as Puerto Ricans, blacks, and Mexican Americans, that were perhaps even more threatening than what had transpired earlier with white ethnics. These new phenomena led, in turn, to the reformation of old theories and the development of new theories.) In summary fashion, these theories are (1) male maturation process, "becoming a man" (e.g., Bloch and Niederhoffer 1958); (2) subcultural, collective solution of lower-class boys to acquire status (e.g., Cohen 1955); (3) lower-class cultural values (e.g., W. B. Miller 1958); (4) lower-class means and upper-class goals disjunctures or simplified means-goals discrepancy (e.g., Cloward and Ohlin 1960); and (5) sociopathic personalities that make "near-group" (e.g., Yablonsky 1959). There are several ways to assess these theories: they can either be reclassified as sociogenic (e.g., 3, 4) and psychogenic (e.g., 1, 2, 5) or, examined another way, as fitting within explanations that focus on strain (2, 4), cultural deviance (l-4), and (in varying degrees, all five) social control (Edgerton 1973; Dembo et al. 1984; Cartwright et al. 1975). Although the authors argue that their particular theory is most salient to the gang phenomenon, each theory accounts for only an aspect of the gang pattern. Yet, all the authors in fact rely on a number of related factors to arrive at their theoretical formulation. For example, Bloch and Niederhoffer (1958) maintain that the gang outlet for becoming a man results because society (through such phenomena as poverty, family stress, and urban disorganization) has failed them; and Cloward and Ohlin (1960), working on a variation of Merton's (1949) means/goals disjunctures, elaborate on the nature of low-income slum life to explain gang subcultural variations. This suggests that a cluster of factors needs to be examined to understand gang delinquency; Cloward and Ohlin say as much with these words: "gangs, or subcultures . . . are typically found among adolescent males in lowerclass areas of large urban centers" (p. 1; cf. Short and Strodtbeck 1965: 19).

The multiple marginality framework better allows for descriptions and interpretations of particular (and perhaps peculiar) facts of people, time, and place. Such a larger framework simultaneously provides for a broader and more in-depth portrayal of the various realities that gang members experience. The intensity and duration of the individual or group experience in gangs as such are better gauged in this broadly integrative way. There are several marginal situations and conditions that are a part of the Mexicans' overall adaptation to urban life. In such circumstances of "long duration . . . the individual can be born into it and live his whole life in it," becoming a participant in "even the development of a 'marginal culture'" (Dickie-Clark 1966:24).

Some researchers have noted that the concept of marginality should be carefully applied because it tends to diminish the important role of lower-income workers in a capitalist economy (Peattie 1974). Perlman (1976), in providing a sweeping critical summation of marginality theory, nevertheless recognizes the need for a construct that looks "to some set of circumstances outside individual control," such as one that "explains these conditions as expressions of the social structure and the historical process" and that looks at "different dimensions of marginality and seeks rather to examine the specificity of their interaction in each instance" (p. 251).

Mexican and Mexican American labor has definitely been significant in the economic development of the southwestern United States, for example, in mining, farming, railroading, and so on. These contributions, however, have not assured them of commensurate political and economic power, as they are excluded by leaders from decision-making processes. This marginality, moreover, is maintained by structural features in the environment to which they must adapt (Kapferer 1978; Lomnitz 1977; Barrera 1979).

The background to the current gang situation is also important, for multiple marginality has cumulative, diachronic sources, especially in group history. A *macro* (group history), *meso* (family history), and *micro* (life history) descending order of analysis is undertaken to show through time how ecological and economic conditions create sociocultural stresses and ambiguities, which, in turn, lead to subcultural and psychological mechanisms of adjustment. Descriptions of group and family history are well documented in the archives (Bogardus 1926, 1934) and in such studies as the longitudinal investigations of Moore and her *pinto* (ex-convict) associates (Moore 1978; Chicano Pinto Research Project 1979, 1981; Moore and Mata 1981). Moreover, my personal life experiences with numerous families who exemplify the multiple processes that lead to gang patterns provide for a unique insider/outsider interpretive perspective to inform these life histories and to show how these personalized events of places and living actions are refracted through the prism of multiple marginality. For example, I have gone through many experiences similar to those of gang youths . . . including being set upon and beaten by gang members into whose "turf" I had strayed. Such personal experiences inform my interpretation of such events.

A macroexamination of Mexican adaptation provides the backdrop for understanding Chicano youth gangs, for there are several areas that need to be traced. Clearly, a key focus is to examine how an emergent underclass life has affected many Mexicans. The underclass phenomenon entails the longitudinal effects of poverty. The youth groups that are produced in such nascent circumstances are quite different from, for example, the earlier nonviolent "street corner" groups reported by Whyte (1973). In fact, endemic racial barriers and cultural strains have combined with status to make this so (Wolfgang et al. 1972; Bogardus 1943). The historical record of cultural and social disparagement experienced by Mexicans is indicative of such developments (Moore and Pachón 1976; Acuña 1981; Vigil 1984).

Urban adaptation for immigrant Mexican families was problematic initially and continues to be so today. Low-paying jobs led to residence in older, run-down interstices of the city, such as sections of East Los Angeles (Gustafson 1940:25-40; Ginn 1947:18-19). Such circumstances created repercussions in other social, cultural, and psychological realms. Moreover, and similar to the experience of other immigrant groups (Feldstein and Costello 1974; Shaw and McKay 1942), schools and law enforcement often operated to aggravate rather than ameliorate problems in Mexican cultural adaptations (U.S. Commission on Civil Rights 1970, 1971). This segmented integration into American society and subsequent fragmenting of traditional social practices and cultural customs resulted in a new cultural orientation. In short, economic hardships undermined social control institutions: family life became stress ridden and schooling and contacts with law enforcement were problematic. The streets and older street youths became the major socialization and enculturation agents, with the gang representing a type of street social control institution by becoming in turn a partial substitute for *family* (providing emotional and social support networks), *school* (giving instructions on how to think and act), and *police* (authority and sanctions to enforce adherence to gang norms). The experience created a new social identity and thus a need for a new personal identity, and for street youth, the gang, both good and bad features, became a coping mechanism to ameliorate social pressures and develop avenues for personal fulfillment.

References

Acuña, Rudy, 1981. *Occupied America: A History of Chicanos*. 2nd ed. New York: Harper and Row.

Alvírez, David, Frank D. Bean, and Dorie Williams, 1981. "The Mexican American Family." In *Ethnic Families in America: Patterns and Variations*, Charles H. Mindel and Robert W. Hobenstein (eds.), pp. 269-292. New York: Elsevier.

Auletta, Ken, 1982. *The Underclass*. New York: Random House.

Barker, G.C., 1950. *Pachuco, an American-Spanish Argot and Its Social Function in Tucson, Arizona*. Tucson: University of Arizona Press.

Barrera, Mario, 1979. *Race and Class in the Southwest: A Theory of Racial Inequality*. Notre Dame: University of Notre Dame Press.

Bearak, Barry, and Richard E. Meyer, 1985. "No Tactic Yet Found to Win Poverty War." *Los Angeles Times*, August 1. [Five-part series, America and Its Poor]

Bloch, H.A. and A. Niederhoffer, 1958. *The Gang: A Study in Adolescent Behavior*. New York: Philosophical Library.

Bogardus, Emory S., 1926. *The City Boy and His Problems*. Los Angeles: House of Ralston, Rotary Club of Los Angeles.

—— 1934. *The Mexican in the United States*. USC Social Science Series, no. 8. Los Angeles: University of Southern California Press.

—— 1943. "Gangs of Mexican American Youth." *Sociology and Social Research* 28:55-56.

Buriel, Raymond, Silverio Calzada, and Richard Vasquez, 1982. "The Relationship of Traditional Mexican American Culture to Adjustment and Delinquency among Three Generations of Mexican American Male Adolescents," *Hispanic Journal of Behavioral Sciences* 4(1):41-55.

Cartwright, Desmond S., B. Tomson, and H. Schwartz, 1975. *Gang Delinquency*. Monterey, Calif: Brooks/Cole.

Chicano Pinto Research Project, 1979. *A Model for Chicano Drug Use and for Effective Utilization of Employment and Training Resources by Barrio Addicts and Ex-Offenders*. Los Angeles: Final report for the Department of Labor and National Institute of Drug Abuse.

—— 1981. *Barrio Impact of High Incarceration Rates*. By Joan W. Moore and John Long. Los Angeles: Final report for National Institute of Mental Health.

Clinard, Marshal B., 1968. *Sociology of Deviant Behavior*. New York: Holt, Rinehart and Winston.

Cloward, R.A., and L. B. Ohlin, 1960. *Delinquency and Opportunity: A Theory of Delinquent Gangs*. New York: Free Press.

Cohen, Albert K., 1955. *Delinquent Boys: The Culture of the Gang*. Glencoe, IL: Free Press.

Cornelius, Wayne A., Leo R. Chávez, and Jorge G. Castro, 1982. *Mexican Immigrants and Southern California: A Summary of Current Knowledge*. University of California, San Diego, Center for U.S.-Mexican Studies, Research Report Series, no. 36.

Decker, Cathleen, 1983. "Gang-Related Murders Fall by 38% in Los Angeles." *Los Angeles Times*, January 7.

Dembo, Richard, Nola Allen, and Harold J. Vetter, 1984. *A Framework for Understanding Nondelinquent and Delinquent Life Styles in the Inner City*. [N.p.]

Dickie-Clark, H.F., 1966. *The Marginal Situation*. London: Routledge, Keagan Paul.

Edgerton, Robert B., 1973. *Deviant Behavior and Cultural Theory*. Addison Wesley Module in Anthropology, no. 37. Reading, Mass: Addison-Wesley Publishing Co.

Feldstein, S., and L. Costello (eds.), 1974. *The Ordeal of Assimilation: A Documentary History of the White Working Class*. New York: Anchor Press/Doubleday.

Geertz, Clifford, 1973. *The Interpretation of Culture*. New York: Basic Books.

Ginn, M.D., 1947. "Social Implications of the Living Conditions of a Selected Number of Families Participating in the Cleland House Program." M.A. thesis, University of Southern California, Department of Sociology.

Griffith, Beatrice, 1948. *American Me*. Boston: Houghton Mifflin Company.

Gustafson, C.V., 1940. "An Ecological Analysis of the Hollenbeck Area of Los Angeles." M.A. thesis, University of Southern California: Department of Sociology.

Handlin, Oscar, 1951. *The Uprooted*. New York: Grosset and Dunlap.

Heller, Celia S., 1966. *Mexican American Youth: Forgotten Youth at the Crossroads*. New York: Random House.

Horowitz, Ruth, 1983. *Honor and the American Dream: Culture and Identity in a Chicano Community*. New Brunswick, NJ: Rutgers University Press.

Kapferer, Bruce, 1978, "Structural Marginality and the Urban Social Order." *Urban Anthropology* 7(3):287-320.

Klein, Malcolm W., 1968. "Impressions of Juvenile Gang Members." *Adolescence* 3(9):53-78.

—— 1971, *Street Gangs and Street Workers*. Englewood Cliffs, NJ: Prentice-Hall.

Lomnitz, Larissa A., 1977. *Networks and Marginality: Life in a Mexican Shantytown*. New York: Academic Press.

McWilliams, C., 1968. *North from Mexico—the Spanish-Speaking People of the United States*. New York: Greenwood Press.

Merton, Robert K., 1949. *Social Theory and Social Structure*. Glencoe, IL: Free Press.

Miller, Walter B., 1958. "Lower Class Culture as a Generating Milieu of Gang Delinquency." *Journal of Social Issues* 14(3):519.

Moore, Joan, 1978. *Homeboys: Gangs, Drugs, and Prison in the Barrios of Los Angeles*. Philadelphia: Temple University Press.

Moore, Joan, and Alberto Mata, 1981. *Women and Heroin in Chicano Communities*. Los Angeles: Chicano Pinto Research Project.

Moore, Joan W., and Harry Pachón, 1976. *Mexican Americans*. 2nd ed. Englewood Cliffs, NJ: Prentice-Hall.

Moore, Joan W., James Diego Vigil, and Robert Garcia, 1983. "Residence and Territoriality in Gangs." *Journal of Social Problems* 31(2):182-194.

Morales, Armando, 1982. "The Mexican American Gang Member: Evaluation and Treatment." In *Mental Health and Hispanic Americans*, Rosina M. Becerra, Marvin Karno, and Javier I. Escobar (eds.). New York: Grune and Stratton.

Muller, Thomas, 1984. *The Fourth Wave: California's Newest Immigrants*. Washington, DC: Urban Institute Press.

National Association of Latino Elected and Appointed Officials (NALEO), 1985. *Poverty's Invisible Victims: Hispanic Children; Number of Latino Poor Children Doubles in California in Past Decade*. Washington, DC: NALEO News Release.

Peattie, Lisa R., 1974. "The Concept of 'Marginality' as Applied to Squatter Settlements." In *Latin American Urban Research: Anthropological Perspectives on Latin American Urbanization*, vol. 4, ed. Wayne A. Cornelius and Felicity M. Trueblood (eds.). Beverly Hills: Sage Publications.

Perlman, Janet, 1976. *The Myth of Marginality*. Berkeley: University of California Press.

Rosenquist, C.M., and E.I. Megargee, 1969. *Delinquency in Three Cultures*. Austin: University of Texas Press.

Rubel, A.J., 1966. *Across the Tracks: Mexican Americans in a Texas City*. Austin: University of Texas Press.

Samora, J., 1971. *Los Mojados: The Wetback Story*. Notre Dame: University of Notre Dame Press.

Shaw, C., and R. McKay, 1942. *Juvenile Delinquency and Urban Areas*. Chicago: University of Chicago Press.

Short, James F., Jr., and Fred L. Strodtbeck, 1965. *Group Process and Gang Delinquency*. Chicago: University of Chicago Press.

Snyder, P.Z., 1977. "An Anthropological Description of Street Gangs in the Los Angeles Area." [A working note, prepared for the Department of Justice, by the Rand Corporation, Santa Monica, California.]

Thrasher, Frederic M., 1963. *The Gang*. Chicago: University of Chicago Press. [Originally published in 1927).

Tuck, R., 1956. *Not with the Fist: Mexican-Americans in a Southwest City*. New York: Harcourt, Brace.

United States Commission on Civil Rights, 1970. *Mexican Americans and the Administration of Justice in the Southwest*. Washington, DC: U.S. Government Printing Office.

—— 1971. *Report I: Ethnic Isolation of Mexican Americans in the Public Schools of the Southwest*. Washington, DC: U.S. Government Printing Office.

Vigil, James Diego, 1979. "Adaptation Strategies and Cultural Life Styles of Mexican American Adolescents." *Hispanic Journal of Behavioral Sciences* 1(4):375-392. [UCLA Spanish-Speaking Mental Health Research Center.]

—— 1984. *From Indians to Chicanos: The Dynamics of Mexican American Culture*. Prospect Heights, IL: Waveland Press. [Originally published as *From Indians to Chicanos: A Sociocultural History*. St. Louis: C.V. Mosby Co., 1980.]

Whyte, William F., 1973. *Street Corner Society*. Chicago: University of Chicago Press. [Originally published in 1943.]

Wolck, Wolfgang, 1973. "Attitudes toward Spanish and Quechua in Bilingual Peru." In *Language and Attitudes*. Roger Shuy and Ralph W. Fosold (eds.). Georgetown: Georgetown University Press.

Wolfgang, Marvin, Robert M. Figlio, and Thorsten Sellin, 1972. *Delinquency in a Birth Cohort*. Chicago: University of Chicago Press.

Yablonsky, L., 1959. "The Delinquent Gang as a Near-Group." *Social Problems* 7:108-117. ✦

15

What Happened to the Beer That Made Milwaukee Famous?

John Hagedorn with Perry Macon

The applicability of the tenets of social disorganization theory is challenged by Hagedorn in this chapter from People and Folks. *He charts demographic, social and economic changes in Milwaukee and suggests that the resulting demise of opportunities to mature out of delinquent activity explains the persistence of gangs in deindustrialized urban centers. This is an early and widely cited statement of the application of underclass theory to the gang situation.*

> Q. *What's the biggest cause of fights?*
>
> A. Ah . . . I think money.
>
> Q. *Money?*
>
> A. Not having money and a lot of them be frustrated, and you know they might have just enough money to get them some beer or something. Get drunk and get to going off. Talking about jobs. Everybody always talking about they want a job. Younger fellows you know. "When summer comes I'll get a summer job." Then half of them don't be able to get the summer job. So they got to run around and try to steal and shit.
>
> —*Tony, Four Corner Hustlers*

It is twenty years since rioting and unrest unsettled our nation's cities. The flames that burned on Milwaukee's Third Street in its northside black community have long since died down. But the condition of that street is today much worse than after the flames of 1967.

In place of Gimbels Department Store and the small businesses that hung on in the sixties, boarded-up stores serve as props for junkies and prostitutes. Gang graffiti tells all who can read street writing that this turf has been claimed by black youth called "Vicelords" and "Castlefolks." Though a few new buildings show that downtown is moving into the ghetto, they cannot hide the signs of economic depression. Even Schlitz, the beer that made Milwaukee famous, has moved, its jobs lost and its Third Street brewery remodeled to accommodate new county social service offices. Perhaps the closing of Schlitz best symbolizes Milwaukee's changes over the past twenty years: a large plant closed and converted to house an expanding welfare bureaucracy. Instead of industrial workers bringing home a paycheck, we have social workers mailing out welfare checks.

But isn't this just another retelling of an old story? Aren't the gangs of today basically the same delinquent boys who have plagued U.S. cities for the past sixty years? Or have the social and economic changes of the past decades had an effect on the nature of urban gangs?

Certainly, in examining Milwaukee gangs, we find they are situated in historical circumstances that have both similarities and differences from times past. Unlike those who would assert that gangs today are basically the same as gangs of the past (Miller 1976), we suspect these changed circumstances may play a role in some aspects of gang behavior, notably the process by which young gang members as they grow older "mature out" of the gang into the working class. And unlike those who study generic gangs without ethnicity and from no specific community (Cohen 1955), we believe class, ethnicity, and local community are all key variables in understanding contemporary gang developments. Because of the scarcity of modern research on black and Hispanic gangs, we believe new research is needed in the cities of the eighties. Thrasher's or Suttles' (1959) method of investigation, of emphasizing the variation in gangs and studying them as a part of a specific community, appeals to us.

We need not start without a framework. A good method of investigation would combine direct observation of gangs with a reexamination of factors that have been historically associated with gang development. Comparing the immigrant European experience of the past with the black and minority experience today may yield some insights into possible changes in the nature of today's gangs. While our data is drawn from only one "rust belt" city, Milwaukee, other cities can really compare their environments with the Milwaukee experience.

Those who think that "a gang is a gang is a gang" whether in 1920s Chicago or 1980s Milwaukee have the burden to prove their position.

Demographics: From Polka to Breakdance

Gangs in the 1920s for Thrasher and the 1940s for Whyte were youthful European immigrant gangs, jammed into crowded cities. This rapid influx of poor

---

Reprinted with permission from John M. Hagedorn with Perry Macon, *People and Folks: Gangs, Crime, and the Underclass in a Rustbelt City*. pp. 37-48.

youthful newcomers is one historical condition that led to those youth "milling about" and "ganging."

The large-scale European immigration which ended in the 1920s was seen by many as responsible for the earlier proliferation of youth gangs in Milwaukee (Schlossman 1977, 102) and other urban centers.[1] Frederic Thrasher, who studied 1,313 gangs in 1920s Chicago, provided this classic definition: "The gang is an interstitial group, originally formed spontaneously, then integrated through conflict" (Thrasher 1963, 46). By "interstitial," Thrasher meant gangs were located in the crowded "slums" surrounding the central business district. The ethnicity of gangs might change, but their location didn't. As immigrant groups moved up into better working class jobs and out of the worst housing, the new immigrant groups who took their places spawned new youth gangs who warred with gangs in neighboring areas.

By the 1960s, the ethnicity of gangs had changed. There were fewer European gangs and more black and Hispanic gangs. But the paradigm used by theorists remained the same: the gang experience was the transitory product of the social tensions of immigrant youth newly arrived in a hostile city.

Milwaukee offers a good example of U.S. urban demographic changes over the past sixty years. When Ronald Reagan visited Milwaukee during the 1984 election campaign, his aides insisted that the media event be an ethnic extravaganza, with lederhosen-dressed Herrs and pretty Frauleins and plenty of bratwurst and polish sausage. While some local Republicans objected that the ethnic image no longer fit Milwaukee, they were overruled by Washington campaign staff. To the minds of outsiders, Milwaukee is a hard-working ethnic town, with good Germans and Poles working their eight-hour day in local factories and coming home to Gemütlichkeit and Schlitz.

The President's aides were caught looking backward. Like so many other cities, Milwaukee's ethnic working class is rapidly moving to the suburbs, leaving the decaying central city to blacks and Hispanics. When Eisenhower defeated Stevenson in 1952, more than 96% of the 650,000 residents of the city of Milwaukee were white. By the time of Kennedy's "New Frontier," Milwaukee's population had risen to nearly three quarters of a million and blacks were still less than 10% of that total. By the Nixon years, Milwaukee's population still was over 700,000, but it had begun to fall. The black population topped 100,000 and whites were headed for the suburbs. When President Reagan munched on a bratwurst on his campaign stop in 1984, blacks made up more than one quarter of all city residents. Nearly one of every three Milwaukeeans today is a non-European minority.

And the black and Hispanic newcomers were youthful and poor. While the number of youth overall in Milwaukee County declined in the 1970s, the black and Hispanic youth population jumped by 25%. More importantly, there were nearly double the number of minority youth living under the poverty line in 1980 than in 1970. A majority of black children in Milwaukee now live in poverty. William Julius Wilson summarizes this phenomenon:

> The black migration to New York, Philadelphia, Chicago, and other Northern cities—the continual replenishment of black populations there by poor newcomers—predictably skewed the age profile of the urban black community and kept it relatively young. . . . In the nation's inner cities in 1977, the median age for whites was 30.3, for blacks 23.9 (Wilson 1984, 96).

In Milwaukee in 1985, the median white male age was 31.5, while the black male median was 20.8 and the Hispanic male 21.3. Milwaukee population projections forecast an absolute increase in the number of black and Hispanic children under 18 and high birth rates well into the next century.

Like immigrant gangs of the past, Milwaukee's 1980s minority youth gangs crowded on playgrounds, fought with one another, and generally made trouble. On one level all that had really changed for the young people who formed the gangs was ethnicity.

Economics: From White Working Class to Black Underclass

Gangs have been seen by most theorists as "working class" (Cohen) or "lower class" (Miller). The gang has been viewed as a single generation adolescent adaptation with the youthful delinquent eventually "maturing out" of his ganging behavior and getting on with his adult life of work and family.

For the "Chicago School" of Shaw, McKay, and Thrasher, gangs and delinquency were associated with areas of the city containing the foreign-born and black migrants. The relative abundance of industrial jobs provided a way out of poverty for some of the newcomers. Immigrant gang boys were able to mature out of delinquency in part due to an industrial-based economy which continually needed a large supply of low-skill labor. Whyte's 1930s "college boys," who were described as Italians with social mobility, differed from his "corner boys" only in degree. "Doc," the leader of the "Nortons" corner gang, worked his way into a job as a supervisor in a local plant (Kornhauser 1978, 126-30). Immigrant gang boys assimilated into American society at varying rates along with their ethnic group.

In the war years after the Depression, industrial jobs were relatively available for ethnic youth. In Milwaukee and other northern cities, discrimination and segregation restricted black entrance into basic industry in varying degrees until World War II, when the largest growth in black population occurred.[2] The black community was always relatively small in Milwaukee compared to many other Midwestern cities. The effects of the business cycle were more severely felt by Milwaukee blacks, who had a precarious hold on the "good jobs" provided by an industrial city (Trotter 1985, 60). Even the good times weren't always so good. For example, in 1950, despite a growing economy that saw only 2.7% white unemployment, 9.7% of the black workforce were unemployed (Washington and Oliver 1976, 77).

While the sixties and seventies saw their ups and downs, the eighties brought a deepening depression to the black community. It was no longer possible to step up on the industrial ladder of mobility briefly available for some after decades of discrimination. That industrial ladder was suddenly snatched away. Between 1980 and 1985, the Milwaukee area lost 35,900 manufacturing jobs. Projections by the State Department of Industry, Labor, and Human Relations forecasts that this downward trend will continue. Milwaukee now has over 15,000 more service jobs than manufacturing jobs.[3]

Change In Employment Structure
Manufacturing and Service Jobs City of Milwaukee 1975-1985

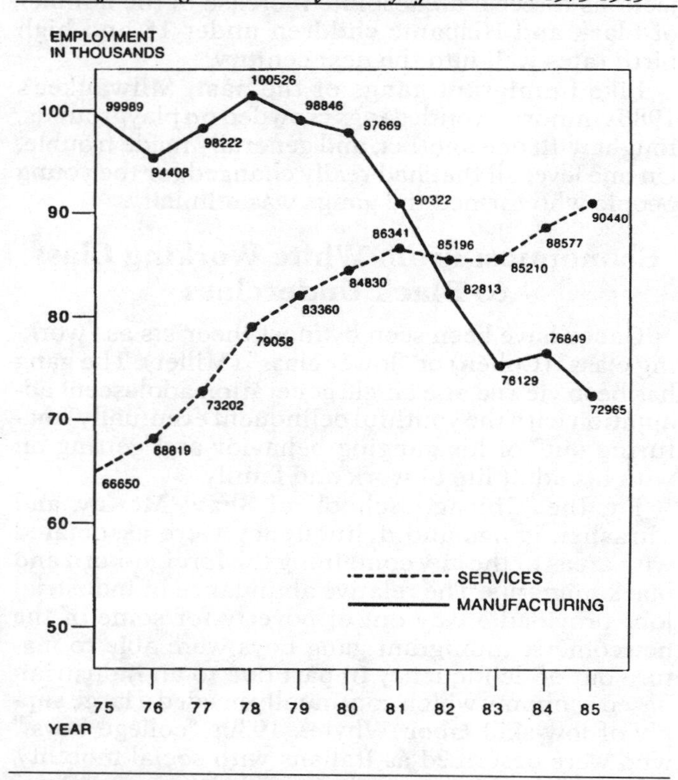

SOURCE: Wisconsin Department of Industry, Labor and Human Relations

Black workers today remain concentrated in those areas of the economy undergoing decline or paying low wages. In 1980 there were twice as many black workers in factory and low paying service jobs than blacks in managerial or professional occupations. The situation for Puerto Ricans and Mexicans was similar (Valdez 1979, 177-78; de Santiago 1980, 66). In contrast, the white ethnic working class has radically changed character. By 1980 two thirds of all white employees who lived in the city of Milwaukee were managers, in sales or other administrative support positions, or in a professional occupation. There were more white managers and supervisors alone than white industrial workers. The number of white managers has tripled since 1970. It's no surprise we could find only one white neighborhood gang in Milwaukee.[4]

The 1980s have been disastrous for the black community. A recent City of Milwaukee report found that in 1984 alone the number of households earning below $10,000 a year increased an astounding 25%. Most of these households are black or Hispanic. The 1985 Milwaukee black unemployment rate was 27.9%, second highest in the nation among larger cities. The ratio of black unemployed to white unemployed was the worst in the nation.

The significance of these developments is that a large part of the black and Hispanic communities can no longer be considered working class. Minority youth, who formed Milwaukee's 1980s gangs, will not have an industrial ladder to step on in order to "mature out" of the gang. When many black adults find employment today, the job is more likely to be part-time, temporary, and low-wage, more like their youthful jobs than the full-time, unionized stable jobs of the past.

Some sociologists and economists have understood this deindustrialization of the U.S. economy in part as the development of internal "segmented labor markets." In this segmentation, the more skilled, high-wage or primary sectors of the economy exist largely separate from the low-wage secondary sectors. Poor minority youth sell their labor almost exclusively within this secondary market in the nation's cities (Bullock 1973).

Moore (1978) points out that Los Angeles Chicano gangs exist within a labor market that consists of low-wage, usually part-time work, welfare, and the illegal economy. Within poor minority communities, a combination of the three types of subsistence is often necessary for survival. Chicano gang members in Los Angeles continue their gang life into adulthood. This closely parallels our findings in Milwaukee.

One "changed circumstance" then, from the immigrant gangs of the past to the minority gangs of the present, is the structural narrowing of the opportunity to mature out of delinquent and deviant ways of life. In the 1960s, blacks and Hispanics in large cities like Chicago and Los Angeles first felt the effects of these conditions. Gangs that formed in those cities around that time continue to exist today. In the 1980s, cities the size of Milwaukee are experiencing both economic segmentation and the reemergence of gangs. Gangs today appear to be a permanent feature of a growing urban minority underclass.[5]

Education: From Learning to Labor, to Not Learning at All

Gangs have always been associated with dropping out of school. Milwaukee's 1980s minority gangs were formed largely from youth who were on street corners rather than in a classroom. Betsy, a black sophomore bused to a southside high school far away from her all-black northside neighborhood, describes the problem best. She asked us:

"What's the difference between today (a school day in May) and last September?" She was sitting on the steps of the "Game Room," a popular local hangout overlooking a busy street. She continued: "How many buses do you see?" We could see only one yellow school bus, partially filled with black students, making the long return trip to the north side.

"In September," Betsy explained, "there are five filled buses taking kids home after school. Where are the other four buses?"

But lack of education today has a far more serious consequence for gang members than it had in the past. Historically, as Colin Greer (1972) and others have pointed out, the role of the public school was to assimilate immigrants and prepare them for work in an industrial United States. Hard work, English, and a little luck were all that was really needed to make it. The actual mobility of the German and other immigrant communities attests to the successful assimilation of these ethnic groups through public education and the long-term growth of the economy from 1920 to 1960 (Steinberg 1981).

Today, minority high school dropouts don't get jobs in factories, but work for minimum wage in fast food and other service jobs. What skills must be taught to qualify someone for such jobs? Listen to Phillip of Milwaukee's 2-4 gang explain what skills are needed to work at McDonalds:

> A. You don't have to know how to read to work at McDonalds. You just can't be color blind.
>
> Q. How's that? What do you mean?
>
> A. Color blind. You know, on the cash register. Red is for hamburger, yellow is a cheeseburger, green's a fish.

The public schools today apparently don't even need to teach reading to prepare poor youth for available work. Kenneth Polk puts the change in education in perspective.

> In decades past orderly flows existed whereby the less competent young persons would move directly into the labor market upon departure from school. . . . The availability of work provided such young persons with an alternative to school . . . one that provided both an escape from the pain of schooling and access to a job and income . . . . The fact that enough jobs existed at earlier times gave even the lower status students a sense of rationality. . . . Data from more recent years suggest an ominous change, and a new pattern whereby the lower status channels lead either to no employment, or to entrapment in the lower level of a dual labor market, a level that consists of marginal, low-paid, often part-time jobs that provide little in terms of training for the future or access to advancement. . . . This situation is creating a new class of marginal youth (Polk 1984, 467-69).[6]

Good jobs in the modern era obviously demand a much higher level of education.[7] But the new high-tech, skilled occupations are leaving poor minority youth behind. Minority students in large numbers are not only dropping out of the schools, but many of those that remain are doing terribly.

The Milwaukee Public Schools, touted as a national model of a desegregated school system, long resisted reporting on the relative performance of its black and white students. Finally, a Governor's study Commission in 1985 drew some devastating conclusions. Among them were the finding that the gap between white and black achievement, rather than narrowing as the child progressed in "desegregated" schools, continued to widen. One third of all grades received by black high school students are "F"s. Forty percent of all black high school freshmen drop out before their senior year. Any "academic progress" was confined to the college bound specialty programs. The average grade-point for black and white students in all but two college prep high schools was an astounding "D." The majority of Milwaukee Public School students, and the vast majority of its black students, were either dropping out of school or graduating with minimal skills.[8]

No black or Hispanic students went to college from Betsy's high school in 1985, but for those blacks and Hispanics who do go on to college, the outlook is also dim. The University of Wisconsin-Milwaukee, the major urban university in Milwaukee, enrolls only 20% of its freshman class from the Milwaukee Public Schools. The rest come from the nearly all-white suburbs. Only 6% of UWM's incoming freshmen are black, about the same percentage as in the total student body, but far less than the black 25.3% of Milwaukee's population.

Just as in the public schools, the problem gets worse as black students advance. Black graduate students today are less than 4% of total graduate enrollment. This reflects disturbing trends nationwide. Since 1976-77 black graduate enrollment has fallen nearly 20%, from over 65,000 to less than 53,000 in 1984-85.[9]

Black and Hispanic youth who have had a poor quality education can no longer compete for "good jobs" that could provide meaningful mobility. For a gang member, the gang experience, rather than being a transitory "rite of passage" into an adult role of family and work, continues into adult years filled with joblessness or meaningless part-time work.

From Ethnic Power to Black Powerlessness

Immigrants have always faced discrimination and unequal treatment from those with power. Gangs have always formed from powerless minorities and have often become a part of the political struggle of their ethnic group to achieve equality. Whyte's gangs were part of the political rivalry of Italians and Irish in 1940s Boston. "Doc," the leader of Whyte's "Nortons," even decided at one point to turn his widespread popularity to good use by running for office. Royko writes about the career of one prominent Chicago gang member and future mayor, Richard Daley. Daley's Hamburg Social and Athletic Club played a role in the race riots of 1919 and in Democratic ward politics. Royko describes the Irish gangs as playing an integral part in urban politics of the early 1900s (1971, 35-38).

The black experience of inequality in northern cities is a long one and was punctuated by a series of racial uprisings that shook our cities twenty years ago. The struggle for black political power in our cities has been central to the contemporary urban scene. It would seem foolish to look at the emergence of minority gangs and neglect racism and the minority experience of inequality, but almost all academic studies do just that.[10]

It would also be a mistake to think the level of racial antagonism is the same in all U.S. cities. Some cities have black mayors or police chiefs and substantial black political power, while others have changed little the past twenty years. Racism, like other attitudes, varies between people, communities, institutions, and cities. Milwaukee, compared to other cities, has a unique and persistent pattern of discrimination and racist behavior.[11]

After the disorders in 1967, a fascinating series of "race relations" surveys of elites, professionals, and black communities were taken nationwide (Rossi et al. 1974). Fifteen cities were chosen. Some, including Milwaukee, had experienced "major" disorders in 1967, some had experienced disorders earlier, and some had racial peace. The most striking fact about the surveys in Milwaukee was the agreement between random samples of local elites and members of the black community: both groups believed blacks in Milwaukee had almost no influence on decision-making in city hall. Milwaukee was near the bottom of the list among all cities surveyed on almost every measure of race relations. A 1970 follow-up study by an anti-poverty agency found that black "exclusion" from decision-making in both private enterprise and the city and county administrations was still "glaring." In 1987 there were three black aldermen, but no major city department had a black department head. Another series of surveys of Milwaukee elites in 1987 concurred with past surveys: race relations was still one of the most important unresolved problems in Milwaukee.

Milwaukee is a city that has not seemed to like change.[12] Its recently retired German mayor served seven terms, longer than any urban mayor in history. Its Irish County Executive was in office from 1976 to 1988. Its two white congressmen are seldom challenged and never defeated. Its last school superintendent served longer than any other in the country save one. Until recently, its Police Chief had a life term by state law. City Hall's political base remains the old coalition of white ethnics, big labor, and downtown business. The black and Hispanic communities have been essentially locked out of power and decision-making. And when most of a powerless community is poor, control depends upon force.

The police have always been controversial in Milwaukee. The early 1900s socialist movement aimed at control of the police in order to curtail the power of business. A socialist-populist coalition succeeded in passing a state law that gave a life term to the Milwaukee police chief to insulate him from pressure of the industrial barons and the vagaries of machine politics (Harring 1983, Conley et al. 1982).

Harold Breier was handpicked by Mayor Henry Maier to take over a corruption-riddled police department in 1964. Breier was a German cop of the old school. His popularity among whites was immense: A 1982 poll found that 74% of all whites thought he was doing an outstanding job.

But the black community had another view. In the same poll, 74% of blacks thought Breier was doing a lousy job and should resign. In 1984, no black had a rank higher than sergeant in the Milwaukee Police Department. At least ten black youths had been killed by police under suspicious circumstances while Harold Breier was Chief. Hostility to the police permeated the black community and especially its youth.

Two police killings of black youth help us better understand the extent of the black youth-police hostility. In 1958 a black youth, Daniel Bell, was killed by police. The killing was ruled "justifiable homicide." Twenty-one years later, a troubled white police officer came forward and admitted that his partner had murdered young Daniel in cold blood. While an outraged black community demanded justice, the city of Milwaukee fought to the bitter end a just settlement of the matter. In 1981 another black youth, Ernest Lacy, was killed by police as he went to a convenience store for a soda. Lacy supposedly "resembled" a rape suspect, and he died after being brutally subdued. Demonstrations of up to 10,000 for justice were ignored even after an inquest surprisingly indicted three officers for homicide. While one officer was eventually fired for his role in the killing, once again "official" Milwaukee resisted granting a "measure of justice." The killing of Ernest Lacy and the revelation of the murder of Daniel Bell took place coincidentally with the formation of black gangs. The lack of political power and the nearly universal fear of police by black youth were a component part of the Milwaukee black experience of the 1980s.

What effect has this experience of racism had on gang formation? While in the past immigrant gangs played a role within their communities' political life, Milwaukee's 1980s black gangs appear much more alienated. While thousands of their brothers and sisters marched for justice for Ernie Lacy, black gangs hung out on the playgrounds, skeptical of any "movement." The intensity of the experience of racism along with the demonstrated lack of political clout of black middle class leaders contributed to the deep sense of frustration and antagonism of black youth. Today's black gangs . . . are alienated even from their own communities.

Notes

1. Stories of Irish, Polish, and German youths "ganging" spice some histories of Milwaukee. Accounts of the "Bunker Boys" in 1861 who repeatedly escaped from reform school led to familiar citizen calls to end lenient treatment of such "hardened" youth.
2. Joe William Trotter, in an interesting account *Black Milwaukee*, looks at the black experience through a framework of black "proletarianization." The traditional framework of spatial segregation and race relations, Trotter points out, has "misrepresented two essential features of black urban life: occupational status and class structure" (Trotter 1985, 275). Trotter, whose account unfortunately ends at the conclusion of World War II, shows the central importance of industry and the wages paid the new black migrants for all classes in the black community.
3. "Wisconsin Industry Projections to 1990," DILHR Labor Market Information, Madison, 1982.
4. This data supports Wilson's provocative thesis that the economic crisis has had a differential impact on various classes within the black community. Milwaukee's black managers have increased nearly tenfold from 1970 to 1980, from less than 2% of the black workforce to about 10%. While no data is available on the 1980s, it is clear that a black professional class emerged and prospered in Milwaukee in the 1970s. See Wilson's argument in

Chapter Six of *The Declining Significance of Race*. All data listed in the text, unless otherwise noted, are from the U.S. Census Bureau, *Characteristics of the Population*, 1960, 1970, and 1980. These economic changes, of course, had been foreseen by black social scientists and others. One sociologist predicted that "the patterns of change within Milwaukee's economy are going to aggravate the economic plight of blacks and other minorities . . . blacks are going to be trapped in the more backward sectors" (Edari 1977, 31).

5. There are many other statistical indicators of the slide of much of Milwaukee's black and Hispanic communities into the underclass. AFDC cases have increased from under 5,000 in 1965 to over 35,000 cases by the mid-eighties. More than two thirds of all AFDC clients are black. General Assistance has risen from an average of about 3,000 persons in 1965 to a high of 13,500 in 1986. Eighty percent of G.A. recipients are black. Most of the increase in General Assistance and fully a third of the increase in AFDC cases have come since 1980. UWM Urban Research Center director Sammis White (1986) found that 55% of the 18 year old General Assistance enrollees were now from AFDC families. Milwaukee's highest in the nation teen pregnancy rate is a clear warning that Milwaukee's new poor underclass is beginning to reproduce itself.

   There is one other place blacks are disproportionately concentrated: in Wisconsin's prisons. While record numbers jam prisons in almost every state, Wisconsin prisons are jammed with black males. One in every one thousand white males in Wisconsin is incarcerated in a state prison; but one in every 59 black males is currently behind state prison bars, one of the highest rates in the nation. If you add to that total the number of black males incarcerated in local jails, every block in Milwaukee's black community has at least one male representative behind bars.
6. See also Colin Greer's analysis in *The Great School Legend*. As Greer put it: "The problem today is that there is an increasing shortage of even low-level employment options for those on the lower levels of the public school totem pole. As a result, the schools now produce people who are a burden upon, rather than the mainstay of, the socio-economic order" (Greer 1972, 152).
7. The Wisconsin Department of Industry, Labor, and Human Relations predicts that "Wisconsin business and industry will face a severe labor shortage in most skill areas in the last decade of the 20th Century, unless young people are trained today to meet the job needs of the 1990s" (*Wisconsin Industry Projections to 1990*, 1). Recent research in New York City concludes: "Movement toward increasingly higher levels of educational attainment has been the main direction of the American labor force. This suggests that the shift to better paying, higher quality jobs is not problem free. It has serious implications for New York City where the high school drop out rate is running at 35% . . ." (Ehrenhalt 1986).
8. The Study Commission on the Quality of Education in the Metropolitan Milwaukee Schools, October 25, 1985.
9. U.S. Department of Education quoted in the UWM Graduate School "Minority Newsletter," 1986-87. For UWM statistics, *UWM Report*, 6:16, May 6, 1986.
10. The major academic exceptions are Moore (1978) and Vigil (1983). Perkins (1987) explicitly criticizes existing gang theory for ignoring "institutional racism." The major academic gang theorists have avoided the question of racism, sometimes treating it as merely an excuse, or rationalization, as affecting only a minority of the gangs. Short claims that racist violence and the civil rights movement in 1960s Chicago had "little impact" on black gangs (1976, 133). Cohen (1955) doesn't even mention ethnicity in his classic work. Spergel (1964) carefully examines three different communities, but analyzes them in terms of "neighborhood characteristics" despite the fact each "neighborhood" analyzed was composed of several different ethnic groups. In Spergel's attempt to validate Cloward's and Ohlin's typology, ecological variables, not ethnic variables, were considered. In another work, Short and Strodtbeck explore "racial differentials" in gang behavior and find "Negro gang boys in our study are more firmly embedded in the lower regions of the lower class" (1965, 106). They conclude: "The nature of delinquency-supporting relations between adults and adolescents differs in lower class Negro and white communities . . . social control is relative, and the institutions of lower class white communities . . . are more capable of concerted effective action than is the case for Negroes" (114-15). However, while finding "community-level" differences that clearly account for differences among black and white gangs, the authors did not pursue the subject.

    On the other hand, Erlanger (1979) looks at Chicano gang violence in East Los Angeles as the result of "estrangement" of Chicano youth. He sees the violence of Chicano gangs as the result of blocked opportunities, not a "subculture of violence." Further, he finds a direct correlation between gang homicide rates and the declining political involvement of Chicano gangs in the 1970s. Suttles (1968, 216-17) found that four of the oldest black gangs in the Chicago Addams area were drawn into civil rights activity in 1964 and their gangs dissipated. However, other gangs quickly took their place.
11. Milwaukee's long socialist tradition (the city had a socialist mayor until 1960) has not exempted it from racism. Victor Berger, one of the most revered figures of Milwaukee German socialism, was an avowed racist, stating there was "no doubt that the Negroes and mulattoes constitute a lower race" (Allen 1975, 223).
12. The spring 1988 election has seated a new mayor and county executive. Change may finally be arriving.

References

Allen, Robert L., 1975. *Reluctant Reformers: Racism and Social Reform Movements in the United States*. New York: Anchor Press.

Bullock, Paul, 1973. *Aspiration vs. Opportunity: "Careers" in the Inner City*. Ann Arbor, Michigan: Institute of Labor and Industrial Relations, University of Michigan—Wayne State.

Cohen, Albert, 1955. *Delinquent Boys*. Glencoe, Illinois: The Free Press.

Conley, John, et al., 1982. "The Police in Milwaukee: Problems of Openness and Accountability." Milwaukee: Future Milwaukee.

Edari, Ronald, 1977. "The Structure of Racial Inequality in the Milwaukee Area." Milwaukee: University of Wisconsin-Milwaukee Urban Research Center.

Ehrenhalt, Samuel, 1986. "Insight and Outlook: The New York Experience as a Service Economy." Paper presented before the Nineteenth Annual Institute on Challenges of the Changing Economy of New York City, May 14, 1986.

Erlanger, Howard S., 1979. "Estrangement, Machismo and Gang Violence," *Social Science Quarterly* 60:2, 235-49.

Greer, Colin, 1972. *The Great School Legend*. New York: Basic Books.

Harring, Sidney L., 1982. "The Police Institution as a Class Question: Milwaukee Socialists and the Police, 1900-1915," *Science and Society* 46:2, 197-221.

Kornhauser, Ruth Rosner, 1978. *Social Sources of Delinquency: An Appraisal of Analytic Models*. Chicago: University of Chicago Press.

Miller, Walter, 1976. "Youth Gangs in the Urban Crisis Era," in *Delinquency, Crime, and Society*, edited by James F. Short, 91-122. Chicago: University of Chicago Press.

Moore, Joan W., 1978. With Robert Garcia, Carlos Garcia, Luis Cerda and Frank Valencia, *Homeboys*. Philadelphia: Temple University Press.

Perkins, Useni Eugene, 1987. *Explosion of Chicago's Black Street Gangs*. Chicago: Third World Press.

Polk, Kenneth, 1984. "The New Marginal Youth," *Crime and Delinquency* 30:3, 462-79.

Rossi, Peter H., Richard A. Berk, and Bettye K. Eidson, 1974. *The Roots of Urban Unrest: Public Policy, Municipal Institutions, and the Ghetto*. New York: John Wiley & Sons.

Royko, Mike, 1971. *Boss*. New York: Signet.

de Santiago, Anne Akulicz, 1980. "The Puerto Rican Community of Milwaukee: A Study of Geographic Mobility." Milwaukee: Spanish Speaking Outreach Institute, University of Wisconsin-Milwaukee.

Schlossman, Steven L., 1977. *Love and the American Delinquent*. Chicago: University of Chicago Press.

Short, James F., 1976. *Delinquency, Crime, and Society*. Chicago: University of Chicago Press.

Short, James F. and Fred L. Strodtbeck, 1965. *Group Process and Gang Delinquency*. Chicago: University of Chicago Press.

Spergel, Irving A., 1964. *Racketville Slumtown Haulberg*. Chicago: University of Chicago Press.

Steinberg, Stephen, 1981. *The Ethnic Myth*. Boston: Beacon Press.

Study Commission on the Quality of Education in the Metropolitan Milwaukee Schools, 1985. "Better Public Schools."

Suttles, Gerald D., 1959. "Territoriality, Identity, and Conduct: A Study of an Inner-City Slum with Special Reference to Street Corner Groups." Unpublished Ph.D. dissertation, Champaign: University of Illinois.

—— 1968. *The Social Order of the Slum*. Chicago: University of Chicago Press.

Thrasher, Frederic, 1963. *The Gang* (Abridged edition; orig. 1927). Chicago: University of Chicago Press.

Trotter, Joe William, 1985. *Black Milwaukee*. Chicago: University of Illinois.

United States Census Bureau, 1960, 1970, 1980. *Charactersitics of the Population*.

University of Wisconsin-Milwaukee, 1986. UWM Report 6:16, May 6, 5.

Valdez, Avelardo, 1979. "The Social and Occupational Integration among Mexican and Puerto Rican Ethnics in Urban Industrial Society." Unpublished Ph.D. dissertation, University of California at Los Angeles.

Vigil, Diego, 1983. "Chicano Gangs: One Response to Mexican Urban Adaption," *Urban Anthropology* 12:1, 45-68.

White, Sammis, 1986. *Research and Opinion*, 3:1. Milwaukee: University of Wisconsin-Milwaukee Urban Research Center.

Whyte, William Foote, 1943. *Street Corner Society*. Chicago: University of Chicago Press.

Wilson, William Julius, 1984. "The Black Underclass," *The Wilson Quarterly* 8:2, 88-99.

Wisconsin Department of Labor, Industry, and Human Relations, 1982. "Wisconsin Industry Projections to 1990." Madison: DILHR Labor Market Information ✦

16

Crime, Youth Gangs, and Urban Transition: The Social Dislocations of Postindustrial Economic Development[1]

Pamela Irving Jackson

The ability of urban underclass variables to explain the level and nature of crime and the presence of gangs in U.S. cities is the subject of this empirical article by Jackson. She finds that variables indicating demographic and economic transition have a significant impact on crime rates in the 561 cities studied. However, variables that represent competing explanatory frameworks, such as opportunities for crime and economic deprivation, also performed well in explaining crime rates. Only two of the fifteen variables tested for influence on gang presence in a smaller sample of about 50 cities proved useful. Jackson's work alerts us to the necessity of differentiating gangs from the larger spectrum of urban crime.

On the basis of a multivariate analysis of quantitative data from all U.S. cities of 25,000 or more in 1970 and 1980, this paper investigates the impact of recent economic changes and population shifts on the levels of violent and property crime. Further investigation of a subset of cities yields information on the effect of these shifts for the development of youth gangs. The findings illustrate the criminogenic consequences of transition from a manufacturing to a service economy, where changes in technological conditions undermine the comparative locational advantages of cities as industrial centers and worsen economic opportunities for the unskilled urban poor. The results suggest that higher crime rates and more youth gangs are among the unintended consequences of the nation's patterns of postindustrial development.

Policy makers and scholars recently have provided detailed testimony of the transformation of the U.S. economy from manufacturing-based to service-based (Berg 1981; Bradbury, Downs, and Small 1982; Stanback and Noyelle 1981). Current analyses have begun to explore the impact of this transformation on the urban center and the largely minority populations left behind within its boundaries. Evident in this new urban reality (cf. Peterson 1985) are the dislocations associated with economic decline, including increases in the rate of violent crime and in reliance on government provided income assistance programs (cf. Wilson 1987). Development and exacerbation of urban youth gang problems have been traced to recent declines in opportunities for unskilled labor (cf. Hagedorn and Macon 1988). Several other types of anecdotal evidence also have illustrated the problems resulting from a national economic transformation that left in its wake unskilled laborers without access to opportunities for retraining at the level required for success in the new technological environment (cf. Berry 1985; Downs 1985; Kasarda 1985).

Thus far, however, a national analysis of the effect of recent economic and social transitions on the level and nature of crime in cities and on the development of youth gangs throughout the United States has not been undertaken. Some researchers have investigated Wilson's (1987) arguments concerning class-related changes in the residential segregation of minority groups—for example, Massey and Eggers's (1990) analysis of whether middle-class minority members in 60 U.S. metropolitan areas really have removed themselves spatially from the poor. Studies also have addressed the effectiveness of varying types of city-level response to youth gang problems (cf. Spergel, Curry, Ross, and Chance 1989). Yet the impact of recent well-recognized demographic and economic transitions (cf. P. Peterson 1985) on crime and youth gangs has not been scrutinized directly in U.S. urban centers nationwide, or with appropriate attention to the influence of regional variations in these transitions.

This study fills that gap. Its central thesis is that demographic and economic transition have contributed to crime and to the presence of youth gangs in U.S. cities, even in the presence of controls for the following possibly competing explanations: opportunity factors related to the ease and profit of crime, age structure, racial and income heterogeneity, and economic deprivation. I also investigate the impact of regional variations in growth and decline on the crime rate in accordance with Wilson's prediction that such differences should be reflected in the severity of urban social dislocations.

Population, Data, and Hypotheses

The research is based on a multivariate analysis of quantitative data from all U.S. cities of 25,000 or more in 1970 and 1980. Further investigation of a subset of the cities in this analysis yields information on the

---

Reprinted from Pamela Irving Jackson, "Crime, Youth Gangs, and Urban Transition: The Social Dislocations of Postindustrial Economic Development." *Justice Quarterly* 8(3):379-397. Reprinted by permission.

impact of these shifts for the development of youth gangs. Data were obtained from the U.S. Census of Population (1970, 1980), the Uniform Crime Report (Federal Bureau of Investigation 1980), and the 1981 National Juvenile Assessment Center survey regarding youth gangs (Needle and Stapleton 1983).

I use ordinary least squares regression and logistic regression. The dependent variables of the analysis are urban crime rates and the presence of urban youth gangs. In this paper I devote primary attention to the influence of population and economic transition on the level of crime and on the presence of youth gangs. I also include the following independent variables to test the competing theoretical explanations noted above: city population size and density, climate, household activity ratio, ratio of blacks' to whites' median income, percent poor, percent unemployed, racial composition measures, and percent youth (ages 15 to 24). The operationalization of each variable is described below.

Demographic and Economic Transition

Taken together, recent work by Wilson (1987) and by Hagedorn and Macon (1988) directly advances the proposition that crime and youth gangs are among the social dislocations resulting from the U.S. transition from a manufacturing-based to a service-based economy. Wilson argues that a rise in the proportion of female-headed households, increased reliance on welfare, and a greater level of violent crime are all, in one way or another, manifestations of the social disorganization consequent to urban losses in opportunities for unskilled workers. Hagedorn, with Macon, applies this argument to his analysis of current trends in gang development in Milwaukee; he predicts that youth gangs will assume an increasing presence throughout the United States in those urban centers most affected by the demographic and economic decline inherent in the nation's postindustrial economic transition.

These propositions advanced by Wilson and Hagedorn have solid foundations in the now-classic work of Durkheim ([1893] 1965, [1895] 1965, [1897] 1951) and of Shaw and McKay (1942), in which crime and youth gangs are treated directly as consequences of the impact of demographic and economic transition on anomie and social disorganization. More current research provides further support for these links. Work by both Chamlin (1989) and Sampson and Groves (1989), for example, underscores the continued criminogenic importance of urban change. Chamlin (1989) studied the determinants of robbery and homicide in 109 large cities and demonstrated the criminogenic impact of urban structural changes that weaken social cohesion. Sampson and Groves's (1989) research on British localities provides evidence of the influence of community social disorganization on criminal victimization and offending.

Urban centers declined economically during the 1970s with the movement of manufacturing and wholesale operations, their initial reason for existence, to foreign and suburban locations, and with the national economic shift toward a service-based economy requiring technologically sophisticated training for many of the new positions it created. Kasarda's (1985) recent study of the growth of jobs with low educational requirements demonstrates that the suburbs and the exurbs have absorbed most of these positions. Herbert Jacobs (1985) examines the criminogenic implications of these changes.

In their recent book on gangs, crime, and the underclass, after reviewing the literature on gang information, Hagedorn and Macon (1988:21) note that we do not know why gangs form in some cities but not in others, or how gangs in smaller cities are similar to or different from gangs in larger cities. They point to the drastically changed economic conditions in poor, minority urban neighborhoods as having contributed to the "institutionalization of gangs as a means for young adults to cope with economic distress and social isolation" (Hagedorn and Macon 1988: 111).

Theories stressing economic and social marginality as triggers of gang formation (cf. Cloward and Ohlin 1960; Miller 1975; Moore et al. 1978, 1983) still apply, but because adulthood does not bring new opportunities for achievement, the movement up and out of the zone of transition does not occur for minority group members as it did for the European immigrants studied by the earliest researchers in this area. Hagedorn and Macon stress that "the significance of the formation of a minority urban underclass and the simultaneous emergence and entrenchment of gangs is completely overlooked" (1988: 25-26). The interstitial nature of gangs—as a bridge between youth and adulthood, occurring in the transitional zones between disorganized and stable communities—may have changed, insofar as the gang experience for many continues with joblessness and meaningless part-time work into the adult years. Work by Curry and Spergel (1988) and by Sampson and Groves (1989) underscores the effect of socioeconomic disorganization on gang activity, supporting Hagedorn and Macon's argument that recent demographic and economic changes have contributed to the development of youth gangs.

Because they reflect demographic and economic transition, economic instability and population decline are expected to be significant predictors of higher crime rates in this study, especially for crimes of violence (cf. H. Jacobs 1985: 230), and to contribute to the presence of youth gangs. The percentage change in civilian labor force opportunities in manufacturing and in wholesale and retail trades between 1970 and 1980 are included in the investigation as indicators of economic instability. Their decline represents a diminution of employment opportunities for unskilled, less educated city residents (cf. Kasarda 1985; Wilson 1987).

Percentages of city residents born in the state where they are now living (1980) and percentage of population change (1970-1980) provide indicators of long- and short-term demographic change in the city. Population decline has been viewed as indicative of "a declining city syndrome" (Clark 1985: 254; Muller 1975; G. Peterson 1976) and as a measure of "urban distress" (Clark 1985: 259; Nathon and Dommel 1977). Throughout the United States, particularly in the northeastern and north central regions, large central cities lost population during the 1970s. The declines may have reflected the loss of employment opportunities in these regions, a loss that triggered urban fiscal and social problems.

Competing Theoretical Explanations

Routine activities (cf. Cohen and Felson 1979), economic deprivation and relative deprivation (cf. Danziger and Wheeler 1975; D. Jacobs 1982; Massey and Eggers 1990; Shelley 1980), heterogeneity (cf. Blau and Blau 1982), and the age structure of a city (cf. Hindelang and McDermott 1981) may explain any observed impact of demographic and economic transition on both crime and youth gang presence. To test the influence of these competing explanations in comparison to that of the central proposition of this analysis, I bring into the analysis indicators of economic deprivation, the age structure of the population, routine activities related to the ease and profit of crime, and population heterogeneity.

Percent poor and percent unemployed in 1980 represent long- and short-term conditions of economic deprivation; the ratio of blacks' to whites' median income reflects relative deprivation. Percent black and percent Hispanic indicate population heterogeneity. In addition to these variables I include the household activity ratio—"the sum of the number of married, husband-present, female labor-force participants and the number of nonhusband-wife households, divided by the sum of the total number of households." This is Cohen and Felson's (1979: 200) indicator of the number of households likely to be without guardians because of the occupants' employment. The index provides a measure of the dispersion of activities away from the home; as a measures of the absence of guardians, I expect it to be related positively to the level of crime in cities. In addition, I expect this index to have increased along with recent urban population and economic transitions because economic instability increases the proportion of female-headed families (cf. Sampson 1987), which contribute to the number of nonhusband-wife households.

I include city population size, density, and climate in the analysis as structural indicators of the ease of crime commission in a city and because they are associated with population and economic transition, the main independent variables of this investigation. The largest, most densely settled U.S. cities are known to have experienced the greatest demographic and economic decline, especially in the northeast and north central regions, where the mean January temperature is lowest. The link between these demographic characteristics and crime is also well established. For example, I expect population size and density to influence the ease of crime commission because they heighten anonymity, reduce social cohesion, and strain law enforcement resources (cf. Boggs 1965; Harries 1975, Jackson 1984; Reppetto 1974). Climate, measured here by mean January temperature, may influence the likelihood of larceny, burglary, robbery, auto theft, and arson because milder temperatures encourage more socializing outside the home, thus increasing the vulnerability of dwellings and vehicles.

Dependent Variables

This analysis includes two dependent variables: urban crime rates and the development of urban youth gangs. I obtained information on urban crime rates from the Uniform Crime Report (Federal Bureau of Investigation 1980). Wilson's analysis of the determinants of urban social dislocations focuses on rates of violent crime in cities. In the present analysis, however, I investigate separately the determinants for each of the eight Part I index offenses because each of these direct contact predatory crimes (cf. Cohen and Felson 1979: 589) may respond to different social

Table 1

Zero-Order Correlation Matrix with Means and Standard Deviations (All cities > 25,000, N = 561) (Pearson's rs)

	1	2	3	4	5	6	7	8	9	10	11	12	13	14	15	16	$\bar{X}$	SD
Percent Black	—	.12[b]	-.17[c]	-.05	.41[c]	.40[c]	.13[b]	-.24[c]	.11[b]	.69[c]	-.27[c]	-.21[c]	.07	.10[a]	.44[c]	-.13[b]	15.5	17.1
Density		—	.28[c]	-.11[b]	.15[c]	.25[c]	-.15[c]	-.22[c]	.25[c]	.18[c]	.11[b]	-.13[b]	-.15[c]	-.03	.03	.21[c]	4324.4	3722.9
Percent Hispanic			—	-.06	-.03	-.21[c]	-.34[c]	.22[c]	.07	.21[c]	.20[c]	-.07	.24[c]	.44[c]	.06	.47[c]	8.3	13.4
Population Age 15-24				—	-.06	.28[c]	.00	.09[a]	-.05	.02	-.12[b]	.18[c]	.05	-.12[b]	-.10[a]	-.01	2.1	.5
Percent Unemployed					—	-.02	.23[c]	-.29[c]	.05	.58[c]	-.03	.08[a]	-.28[c]	-.26[c]	.23[c]	-.01	7.0	3.0
Household Activity Ratio						—	-.02	-.21[c]	.10[a]	.23[c]	-.25[c]	-.18[c]	.01	-.11[b]	.37[c]	-.07	.7	.1
Residents Born in State							—	-.38[c]	-.05	.14[c]	-.05	.08[a]	-.25[c]	-.53[c]	-.24[c]	-.37[c]	60.0	16.2
Percent Population Change								—	-.03	-.19[c]	.07	.06	.21[c]	.38[c]	-.06	.05	7.3	22.0
Population Size									—	.12[b]	-.08[a]	-.06	-.01	.01	.09[a]	.27[c]	129.1	370.2
Percent Poor										—	-.25[c]	-.11[b]	.01	.17[c]	.44[c]	.11	10.3	5.4
Blacks'/Whites' Income											—	-.04	-.05	-.12[b]	-.21[c]	.14[c]	.7	.2
Wholesale/Retail Change												—	-.25[c]	-.08[a]	-.17[c]	-.23[c]	-.1	2.25
Manufacturing Change													—	.28[c]	.11[b]	.20[c]	-2.6	4.1
January Temperature														—	.23[c]	.28[c]	36.6	13.6
Index Crime Rate															—	.07	80.1	27.8
Gang Presence[d]																—	.5	.5

[a] $p < .05$ [b] $p < .01$ [c] $p < .001$ [d] gang presence correlation based on 51 cases.

pressures. For example, the frustration produced by anomie and social disorganization may result in a link between crimes of violence and economic and social transition (cf. Bernard 1990). Although property crimes also may be influenced by transition, as deviant subcultures replace conventional normative structures eroded by change, different causal processes are at work (cf. Messner and J. Blau 1987). Hence the strength of these links may differ.

To test the effect of economic and population tradition on gangs, I use as a dependent variable data gathered in 1981 by the National Juvenile Justice Assessment Center (Needle and Stapleton 1983) on the existence of gangs in a random, representative sample of 60 U.S. cities of 100,000 or more. In each city police department, the authors interviewed gang control and youth personnel as to the existence of gangs in the city. The investigation of recognized urban gangs was based on analysis of these 60 cities which the authors selected "using population size and geographic region as major criteria for sampling" (Needle and Stapleton 1983: 1). For this subgroup of the present study's larger population of cities, I investigate the determinants of the existence of gangs recognized by the police using a dichotomous indicator of gang presence, where 0 = no police-provided evidence of gangs in the city and 1 = police-provided evidence of gangs.[2] Unfortunately the small size of this subsample precludes investigation of the regional differences that I explore in the prediction of urban crime rates.

Results

Table 1 contains associations among pairs of the urban sociopolitical characteristics included in the study. Although they are a useful starting point, these Pearson's correlation coefficients reflect only bivariate associations without controls for other possible determinants of the association. The multivariate equations in a later table are a more accurate gauge of the extent to which each independent variable influence specific crime rates and the incidence of gangs after other urban characteristics are controlled.

The bivariate associations, however, provide reason for continuation of the analysis. For example, a statistically significant relationship exists between higher crime rates and decline in the percentage of the civilian labor force employed in wholesale and retail trades (r = -.17). A bivariate relationship also exists between the percentage of residents born in the state who still live there and the total rate of index crimes; higher crime rates are found in cities with more population transition (r = -.24). This measure of long-term population transition is associated with increases in the number of manufacturing positions (r = -.25), lower levels of poverty (r = .14), and higher mean January temperatures (r = -.53).

Decline in the percentage of the civilian labor force employed in wholesale and retail positions also predicts increases in the crime rate (r = -.17), as do greater unemployment (r = .23), greater income inequality between blacks and whites (r = -.21), dispersion of activity away from the home (r = .37), and climate conducive to recreation outside the home (r = .23).

With regard to gangs, the bivariate associations suggest that they are more likely to be present in large (r = .27), densely settled (r = .21) cities with a large Hispanic population (r = .47), greater long-term population transition (r = -.37), and greater declines in the number of wholesale and retail positions (r = -.23). The multivariate equations presented below test the theoretical importance of these associations, providing evidence of the impact of economic and demographic transition on crime and gang presence when the influence of other independent variables is controlled.

Table 2 suggests that the relationship between demographic and economic transition and urban crime rates withstands controls for other, possibly competing explanatory variables. Long-term population change, as reflected in the percentage of city resi-

Table 2

Regression Equations for Index Crime Rates (1980) on Transition, Social Disorganization, Opportunity, and Other Social Characteristics of Cities (All cities > 25,000, N = 561)

	Total Crime Rate	Nonnegligent Homicide	Forcible Rape	Aggravated Assault	Robbery	Burglary	Larceny	Auto Theft	Arson
Constant	-31.310	-.060	-.654	-2.420	-6.564	-9.011	-9.546	2.738	-1.839
Mean January Temperature, Standardized Coefficient (S)	.073	.099[b]	.068	.118[a]	.018	.156[c]	.029	-.063	.118[a]
Population Size S	.029	.143[c]	.081[b]	.009	.144[c]	.010	-.001	.053	.062
Percent Change in Wholesale/Retail S	-.031	-.045	-.063[a]	.004	-.083[b]	-.050	.021	-.115[c]	-.111[b]
Ratio of Blacks' to Whites' Median Income S	-.031	-.007	-.027	.009	.053[a]	-.018	-.080[a]	.098[b]	.089[a]
Proportion Age 15-24 S	-.204[c]	-.078[b]	-.032	-.045	-.129[c]	-.212[c]	-.163[c]	-.135[c]	-.064
Percent Unemployed S	.164[c]	.142[c]	.294[c]	.102[a]	.136[c]	.124[b]	.140[b]	.071	.275[c]
Density S	-.239[c]	-.132[c]	-.233[c]	-.097[a]	.083[b]	-.109[b]	-.397[c]	.221[c]	-.042
Percent Change in Manufacturing S	.019	-.044	-.018	-.039	-.105[c]	.026	.068	.084[a]	-.018
Percent Population Change (1970-1980) S	-.057	-.043	-.040	-.037	-.104[c]	-.081[a]	-.005	.085[a]	-.018
Household Activity Ratio S	.381[c]	.068[a]	.252[c]	.110[b]	.247[c]	.298[c]	.369[c]	.165[c]	.172[c]
Percent City Residents Born in State S	-.314[c]	-.104[b]	-.271[c]	-.154[c]	-.302[c]	-.227[c]	-.256[c]	-.232[c]	-.047
Percent Hispanic S	.017	.206[c]	.130[b]	.064	.147[c]	.025	-.060	.125[b]	.070
Percent Black S	.053	.489[c]	.375[c]	.290[c]	.309[c]	.128[b]	-.116[a]	.057	-.093
Percent Poor S	.271[c]	.145[b]	.020	.244[c]	.132[b]	.268[c]	.187[b]	.210[c]	-.012
R^2	.44[c]	.60[c]	.51[c]	.38[c]	.63[c]	.47[c]	.29[c]	.42[c]	.10[c]

[a] p (one-tailed test) < .05 [b] p < .01 [c] p < .001

dents born in the state where they are now living, has a statistically significant impact on the total rate of index crimes and on each of the individual crime rates except arson. This measure of long-term population change is one of the strongest predictors of each type of crime, an indication that the lower the percentage of city residents born in the state, the greater the rate of crime. The socially disorganizing effects of such population change appear to be reflected in urban crime levels.

Percentage of city population change during the decade (1970-1980), an indicator not only of social disorganization but also of urban socioeconomic decline, has a statistically significant impact on the rates of robbery, burglary, and auto theft; population decline predicts higher crime rates. In addition, decline in labor force opportunities in manufacturing between 1970 and 1980 contributes to higher rates of robbery and auto theft; similar declines in wholesale and retail trades trigger increases in rape, robbery, auto theft, and arson rates.

The contribution of other characteristics of city structure in explaining variations in crime rates also merits attention. Unemployment, for example, short-term by its official definition, is socially disorganizing and disrupts individuals' major link with conventional society. This variable is a positive significant predictor of the total rate of index crime and of each of the individual rates of direct contact predatory crime except larceny, even after other sociodemographic characteristics of cities have been controlled. Percent poor, reflecting the extent of longer-term economic detachment in the city, also has a positive significant impact on the total crime rate, as well as on the rates of homicide, robbery, assault, burglary, larceny, and auto theft. Sampson's (1987) work suggests that this influence may result in part from the impact of economic deprivation on family structure.

Percent black and percent Hispanic, indicators of population heterogeneity, do not have a significant impact on the total rate of crime when the indicators of demographic and economic transition and the other control variables are held constant. Both, however, have a positive, statistically significant impact on the rates of three violent crimes: homicide, rape, and robbery. Percent black also has a positive impact on the rates of assault, burglary, and larceny; percent Hispanic influences the rate of auto theft.

Greater similarity of average blacks' and whites' incomes appears to contribute to the rates of robbery, auto theft, and arson in a city, even after other known crime determinants are controlled. Meriting future investigation is the question of whether this occurs because greater equality between racial groups reflects the greater criminal opportunity association with affluence or because greater interracial equality reflects widespread poverty and its associated criminogenic conditions.

City population size contributes to the rates of homicide, rape, and robbery even after demographic change, economic transition, and other predictors of the urban crime rate are controlled. The higher levels of anonymity, lower social cohesion, and weaker informal surveillance associated with large city size may undermine social restraints and provide greater opportunity for violent crime. Population density has a statistically significant negative impact on the total crime rate and on the homicide and rape rates, as well as on the rates of assault, burglary, and larceny; this finding suggests criminogenic conditions in cities with lower levels of density. Such cities were slightly more likely to be experiencing population transition in 1980 (Pearson's r for density and population change = -.22) (cf. Frey and Speare 1988).

Dispersion of activities away from the home, as measured by the household activity ratio, has a positive significant impact on the total crime rate as well as on the rate of each individual index crime. Mean January temperature, a measure of climatic conducive to interaction outside the home (cf. Cheatwood 1988), is a positive significant predictor of the rates of homicide, assault, burglary, and arson.

In summary, the multivariate equations show that urban crime rates are influenced by both long- and short-term city population change, as well as by declines in manufacturing and wholesale/retail positions, even in the face of controls for competing explanatory variables. The data support the central thesis of this paper regarding the impact of postindustrial change on crime in urban centers. Although competing explanations do not undermine this support, they shed additional light on the importance of urban characteristics that reflect the opportunity for crime. The anonymity and the household dispersion of modern life, as well as climatic conditions that encourage the pursuit of leisure and interaction outside the home, appear to be related to specific rates of urban crime.

Regional Variations

Wilson's analysis of urban deterioration in the 1970s suggests regional contextual differences that could affect the development of crime. For example, he writes that urban centers have undergone "an irreversible structural transition from centers of production and distribution of material goods to centers of administration, information exchange, and higher order provision," and notes that in northern areas in particular, city labor markets have been transformed from "centers of goods processing to centers of information processing," with consequent shifts in the educational requirements for employment (Wilson 1987: 39).

In the northeast and the midwest especially, Wilson illustrates that the jobless rate among 16- to 24-year-old black males increased sharply during the 1970s. At the same time, information processing centers have replaced jobs in manufacturing and other blue-collar industries in the north (Wilson 1987: 40). In the south and the west, he points out, the jobless rates among young black males in the central city has not risen as sharply; jobs with low educational prerequisites have not left these communities as consistently, and business migration to these areas has added others. Work by Massey and Eggers (1990: 1170) also suggests regional variations in the cumulative overall effect of these changes on urban centers, with the greatest dislocations in the northeast and the midwest.

One measure of decline in northeastern and north central cities is reflected in their 3.4 percent average population loss between 1970 and 1980. Cities in the south and the southwest, on the other hand, grew 16.4 percent on average during that decade. This growth was reflected in the fact that only 54 percent of the residents of these cities in 1980 were born in the state (44% in urban centers of the west, 62% in cities of the south). For northeastern and north central cities the figure is 68 percent, reflecting less population transition there during the decade. The average decline in manufacturing and in wholesale/retail employment was greater in northern/north central cities, 4.18 percent and .083 percent respectively, than in southern and western cities, which showed declines of only 1.3 percent and .07 percent. Even so, both population decline in the north and population growth in the south and the west manifest transition, a condition known to be criminogenic in and of itself.

Despite some differences in the extent of unemployment, youth, poverty, and minority status—all conditions conducive to the development of anomie—in 1980 the regional groupings of cities on average were not far apart on most of these control variables. Cities in the northeastern and north central regions averaged about 8 percent unemployment in 1980; the mean figure was 6 percent for southern and western cities. About 10 percent of the central city population was below the poverty level in the north, and about 11 percent in the southern/western group of cities. There was no appreciable difference in the relative size of the population aged 15 to 24, which averaged about 2 percent in each group. The proportion minority varied in expected directions. Northern cities had, on average, 14 percent black population and 4 percent from Hispanic groups. Cities in the south and west on average were 17 percent black and 12 percent Hispanic.

In 1980 the ratio of blacks' to whites' median income averaged .76 in northern cities and .68 in cities of the south and the west. Mean city population size in the north was 137,000, while it averaged about 123,000 in southern and western cities. Dispersion of activities away from the home, however, showed no major regional variation. Population density, at 5,367 persons per square mile, was considerably greater in cities of the north/north central region than in the south and the west, where cities averaged about 3,437 persons per square mile. Mean January temperature, 25 degrees in northern cities and 47 degrees in southern and western cities, indicates greater climatic conduciveness to recreation outside the home in cities of the west and the south.

In the multivariate equations for each of the regional groupings, the statistical influence of the indicators of demographic and economic transition, as well as the impact of most of the individual control variables, showed similar patterns across the regional divide. (The regional regression results are not shown in tabular form, but are available upon request.) Regional differences in the predictive ability of the model itself stand out, however. With regard to the total crime rate, for example, the model's predictive ability is more than 15 percent greater for northern cities than for southern and western cities; for homicide the difference is 18 percent; for rape, 35 percent; for robbery, 11 percent; for assault, 21 percent; for burglary, 20 percent; for arson, 12 percent. (For larceny and auto theft, there is no appreciable explanatory difference.) In every case, the explanatory difference shows that the model predicts the level of crime more accurately in northeastern and north central cities, where the greatest demographic and economic decline has occurred. In the south and the west, regions characterized by urban population growth rather than by decline, the model's predictive deficit suggests the need to look for additional determinants of crime in the nation's growth regions.

Urban Gangs

The logistic regression equation in Table 3 demonstrates the impact of demographic and economic transition on gangs after other competing explanatory variables are controlled.[3] The logit model shows that decline in the economic prospects for unskilled workers, as measured by the percentage of change in the number of wholesale and retail jobs, is a statistically significant determinant of metropolitan urban gangs. The only other significant predictor of gangs is the size of the population aged 15 to 24, the group most vulnerable to anomie and to the consequences of social disorganization.

Table 3
Logistic Regression Model of Gang Presence (N=51)

Predictor	Logistic Coefficient	Standard Error
Intercept	4.666	6.895
Mean January Temparture	.028	.029
Population Size	.001	.001
Percent Change in Wholesale/Retail	-.525[a]	.293
Ratio of Blacks' to Whites' Median Income	2.175	2.451
Proportion Age 15-24	.031[a]	.015
Percent Unemployed	-.005	.162
Density	.000	.000
Percent Change in Manufacturing	-.093	.086
Percent Population Change (1970-1980)	-.014	.015
Household Activity Ratio	-12.208	-10.852
Percent City Residents Born in State	-.011	.025
Percent Hispanic	.041	.035
Percent Black	-.020	.030
Percent Poor	-.001	.118
Total Crime Rate	.007	.015

[a] $p<.05$

These findings provide some support for Hagedorn and Macon's (1988) contention that modern urban gangs are one consequence of the inability of urban teens and young adults to achieve a firm foothold in the unskilled labor market. The anomie and the free time characteristic of youths in cities with declining economic prospects for unskilled labor may be conducive to the development and persistence of urban youth gangs and to police reports of their presence.

Conclusions and Discussion

Overall the results provide support for the central thesis of this paper. Demographic and economic transition seem to have some influence on crime and on the presence of youth gangs in U.S. cities even in the presence of controls for possibly competing explanations: opportunity factors related to the ease and profit of crime, age structure, racial and income heterogeneity, and economic and relative deprivation. Although the impact of demographic and economic change on crime rates remained stable across regions, regional differences in the model's predictive ability point to the need for further study of the impact of growth and decline on urban crime in cities.

The results of the logit model developed to explain gang presence show that decline in wholesale and retail positions was a significant predictor of gang presence, as was the size of the 15- to 24-year-old population. In the multivariate model other indicators of urban conditions, including race, ethnicity, inequality, population size, and density, did not have a statistically significant impact on urban gangs.

In investigating the influence of recent population and economic shifts in cities throughout the United States, as well as separately in regional subpopulations of cities where the nature of economic and population changes has diverged, I have focused on the criminogenic impact of population and economic transitions known to disorganize communities by reducing social cohesion and creating a mismatch between labor and jobs (cf. Kasarda 1985). The extent to which the level and the nature of urban crime have been influenced by the transitions of recent postindustrial economic development had not been investigated previously, either for cities of 25,000 or more nationally or comparatively in regions with differing patterns of urban transition. Similarly, researchers had neglected multivariate studies of the determinants of youth gangs' presence in large samples of cities.

Several other pieces of current research support and elaborate on the findings reported in this paper. They suggest that crime and youth gangs are likely consequences of the patterns of sociodemographic change recently experienced by U.S. urban centers. Work by Sampson (1987) and Sampson and Groves (1989) has investigated the influence of varying patterns of economic opportunity on the social organization and criminal involvement of specific groups and populations. With data for 150 of the largest U.S. cities, Sampson (1987: 375) demonstrated that economic deprivation and the dearth of employed black men increased the percentage of female-headed black households, and then developed a simultaneous model showing the impact of family disruption on both juvenile and adult adjusted arrest rates among blacks for robbery and homicide. The finding that family disruption influenced the juvenile offending rate even more than the adult offending rate led Sampson to suggest that "the effects of family structure are related to macrolevel patterns of social control and guardianship, especially regarding youths and their peers" (1987: 37).

In their study of 11,000 residents in 300 British localities, Sampson and Groves (1989) addressed social disorganization, a related theme, linking it to its roots in Shaw and McKay's theory and to its consequences in terms of criminal victimization and offending. They found that measures of social organization linked community structural characteristics, including socioeconomic factors, residential mobility, ethnic heterogeneity, and family disruption, to criminal victimization and offending rates based respectively on victim and self-reports. Overall the Sampson and Groves (1989) study suggests that elements which weaken a community's social cohesion thereby breed delinquency and crime.

The study described here adds to this body of research by demonstrating in U.S. cities of 25,000 or more the impact of the nation's recent postindustrial demographic and economic changes on both direct-contact predatory crime rates and reports of urban youth gangs. The influence of urban decline on urban crime rates and on gang presence survives controls for other criminogenic structural characteristics of cities, and highlights the importance of social change on the quality of life in urban centers.

The long-term consequences of crime, youth gangs, and other social dislocations resulting from the impact of these changes merit careful scrutiny. Much evidence suggests that the problems of cities have only begun. Zatz's (1985) work, for example, demonstrates the long-term criminal justice consequences for youths with gang identity and criminal involvement. In light of recent figures showing that one black male in four and one Hispanic male in 10 in the United States is under criminal justice supervision, the influence of gang involvement in channeling youths into inmate social systems cannot be ignored. It may be that without improvement in the economic prospects of urban youths, the transience of gang involvement noted by Thrasher (1927) and others will become a thing of the past. Combined with Hispanic migration to urban centers, *los cholos* and dim economic prospects may give gang involvement a permanent allure (cf. Moore 1985; Zatz 1985).

Urban decline, with its associated economic stress and social disorganization, may weaken the social cohesion and social control processes of cities, resulting in the social dislocations discussed by Wilson (1987), Hagedorn and Macon (1988), and others. As a result, higher crime rates and more youth gangs may be among the unintended consequences of the nation's postindustrial growth and development.

Notes

1. An earlier version of this paper was presented at the Twelfth World Congress of Sociology, held in Madrid, July 1990.
2. Complete data on all independent variables are available for 51 of Needle and Stapleton's cities.
3. Because the dependent variable, presence or absence of police-reported gangs in a city, is dichotomous, the logit model is appropriate in that it is designed to provide for assessment of the impact of several interval-level independent variables on a truncated dependent variable.

References

Berg, Ivar (1981) *Sociological Perspectives on Labor Markets*. New York: Academic Press.

Bernard, Thomas J. (1990) "Angry Aggression among the 'Truly Disadvantaged.'" *Criminology* 28:73-96.

Berry, Brian J.L. (1985) "Islands of Renewal in Seas of Decay." In Paul E. Peterson (ed.), *The New Urban Reality*. Washington, DC: Brookings Institute. pp. 69-98.

Blau, Judith R. and Peter M. Blau (1982) "Metropolitan Structure and Violent Crime." *American Sociological Review* 47:114-28.

Boggs, Sarah L. (1965) "Urban Crime Patterns." *American Sociological Review* 30:899-905.

Bradbury, Katherine L., Anthony Downs, and Kenneth A. Small (1982) *Urban Decline and the Future of American Cities*. Washington, DC: Brookings Institute.

Chamlin, Mitchell B. (1989) "A Macro Social Analysis of the Change in Robbery and Homicide Rates: Controlling for Static and Dynamic Effects." *Sociological Focus* 22 (4):275-86.

Cheatwood, Derrel (1988) "Is There a Season for Homicide?" *Criminology* 26(2):287-306.

Clark, Terry Nichols (1985) "Fiscal Strain: How Different Are Snow Belt and Sun Belt Cities?" In Paul E. Peterson (ed.), *The New Urban Reality*. Washington, DC: Brookings Institute, pp. 253-80.

Cloward, Richard A. and Lloyd E. Ohlin (1960) *Delinquency and Opportunity. A Theory of Delinquent Gangs*. New York: Free Press.

Cohen, Albert K. (1955) *Delinquent Boys: The Culture of the Gang*. New York: Free Press.

Cohen, Lawrence E. and Marcus Felson (1979) "Social Change and Crime Rate Trends." *American Sociological Review* 44:588-607.

Curry, G. David and Irving A. Spergel (1988) "Gang Homicide, Delinquency, and Community." *Criminology*, 26:381-405.

Danziger, S. and D. Wheeler (1975) "The Economics of Crime: Punishment of Income Redistribution." *Review of Social Economy* 33 (October):113-31.

Downs, Anthony (1985) "The Future of Industrial Cities." In Paul E. Peterson (ed.) *The New Urban Reality*. Washington, D.C. Brookings Institute, pp.281-94.

Durkheim, Emile ([1893] 1951) *The Division of Labor in Society*. New York: Free Press.

—— ([1895] 1965). *The Rules of Sociological Method*. New York: Free Press.

—— ([1897] 1951) *Suicide*. New York: Free Press.

Federal Bureau of Investigation (1980) *Uniform Crime Report*. Washington, DC: U.S. Government Printing Office.

Frey, William H. and Alden Speare, Jr. (1988) *Regional and Metropolitan Growth and Decline in the United States*. New York: Russell Sage Foundation.

Hagedorn, John M. and Perry Macon (1988) *People and Folks: Gangs, Crime and the Underclass in a Rustbelt City*. Chicago: Lake View Press.

Harries, Keith D. (1974) *The Geography of Crime and Justice*. New York: McGraw-Hill.

Hindelang, M.J. and M.J. McDermott (1981) *Juvenile Criminal Behavior: An Analysis of Rates and Victim Characteristics*. Washington, DC: U.S. Government Printing Office.

Jackson, Pamela Irving (1984) "Opportunity and Crime: A Function of City Size." *Sociology and Social Research* 2:172-92.

Jacobs, David (1982) "Inequality and Economic Crime." *Sociology and Social Research* 66:12-28.

Jacobs, Herbert (1985) "Policy Responses to Crime." In Paul E. Peterson (ed.), *The New Urban Reality*. Washington, DC: Brookings Institute, pp. 225-52.

Kasarda, John D. (1985) "Urban Change and Minority Opportunities." In Paul E. Peterson (ed.), *The New Urban Reality*. Washington, DC: Brookings Institute, pp. 33-68.

Massey, Douglas S. and Mitchell L. Eggers (1990) "The Ecology of Inequality: Minorities and the Concentration of Poverty, 1970-1980." *American Journal of Sociology* 95 (5):1153-88.

Merton, Robert K. (1968) *Social Theory and Social Structure*. New York: Free Press.

Messner, Steven F. and Judith R. Blau (1987) "Routine Leisure Activities and Rates of Crime: A Macro-Level Analysis." *Social Forces* 65:1035-51.

Miller, Walter B. (1975) *Violence by Youth Gangs and Youth Groups as a Crime Problem in Major American Cities*. Washington, DC: U.S. Department of Justice.

Moore, Joan W. (1985) "Isolation and Stigmatization in the Development of the Underclass: The Case of Chicano Gangs in East Los Angeles." *Social Problems* 33 (1):1-12.

Moore, Joan W., Diego Vigil, and Robert Garcia (1983) "Residence and Territoriality in Chicano Gangs." *Social Problems* 31 (2):182-94.

Moore, Joan W. with Robert Garcia, Carlos Garcia, Luis Cerda, and Frank Valencio (1978) *Homeboys*. Philadelphia: Temple University Press.

Muller, Thomas (1975) *Growing and Declining Urban Areas: A Fiscal Comparison*. Washington, DC: Urban Institute.

Nathan, Richard P. and Paul R. Dommel (1977) "The Cities." In Joseph A. Peckman (ed.). *Setting National Priorities: The 1978 Budget*. Washington, DC: Brookings Institute, pp. 283-316.

Needle, Jerome A. and Wm. Vaughan Stapleton (1983) *Report of the National Juvenile Justice Assessment Centers: Police Handling of Youth Gangs*. Washington, DC: U.S. Department of Justice.

Peterson, George E. (1976) "Finance." In William Gorham and Nathan Glazer (eds.), *The Urban Predicament*. Washington, DC: Urban Institute, pp. 35-118.

Peterson, Paul E. (ed.) (1985) *The New Urban Reality*. Washington, DC: Brookings Institute.

Reppetto, Thomas (1974) *Residential Crime*. Cambridge, MA: Ballinger.

Sampson, Robert J. (1987) "Urban Black Violence: The Effect of Male Joblessness and Family Disruption." *American Journal of Sociology* 93 (2):348-82.

Sampson, Robert J. and W. Byron Groves (1989) "Community Structure and Crime: Testing Social-Disorganization Theory." *American Journal of Sociology* 94 (4):774-802.

Shaw, Clifford R. and Henry D. McKay (1942) *Juvenile Delinquency and Urban Areas*. Chicago: University of Chicago Press.

Shelley, Louise (1980) *Crime and Modernization*. Carbondale: Southern Illinois University Press.

Spergel, Irving A., G. David Curry, R.A. Ross, and R. Chance (1989) "Survey of Youth Gang Problems and Programs in 45 Cities and 6 Sites." Technical report. Chicago: University of Chicago, School of Social Services Administration.

Stanback, Thomas M., Jr. and Thierry J. Noyelle (1981) *Metropolitan Labor Markets in Transition: A Study of Seven SMSAs*. Washington, DC: U.S. Department of Commerce.

Thrasher, Frederic M. (1927) *The Gang*. Chicago: University of Chicago Press.

U.S. Bureau of the Census (1970) *Characteristics of the Population*. Washington. DC: U.S. Government Printing Office.

—— (1980) *Characteristics of the Population*. Washington, DC: U.S. Government Printing Office.

Wilson, William Julius (1987) *The Truly Disadvantaged: The Inner City, the Underclass, and Public Policy*. Chicago: University of Chicago Press.

Zatz, Marjorie (1985) "Los Cholos: Legal Processing of Chicano Gang Members." *Social Problems* 33 (1):13-30. ✦

17
The Killing Fields

Ice T

In this chapter from his book, rapper Ice-T presents a unique perspective on gangs and their attraction for urban youth. This is a wide-ranging discussion about black gang culture, gang rivalries, attitudes toward violence, and the power of prison gangs. He articulates the oppositional relationships between gangs and law enforcement in Los Angeles. He challenges the efficacy of some approaches to gang intervention and offers one insider's view on how the situation might be improved. Not surprisingly, this discussion contrasts sharply with the perspectives offered in the article selections in Section IV. His comments on the gang/drug sales connection should be compared to the views found in the articles in Section III, Gangs and Drugs.

> "The most dangerous black man in America is the ghetto hustler. . . . These ghetto teenagers see the hell caught by their parents struggling to get somewhere, or they see that they have given up struggling. In the prejudiced, intolerant white man's world. . . . The ghetto hustler is internally restrained by nothing. He has no religion, no concept of morality, no civic responsibility, no fear—nothing."
>
> — Malcolm X, *The Autobiography of Malcolm X*, 1964

Gangs were born out of this chaos—the inner city. When you grow up in South Central, and you've never had anything in your life you control, you seek control. Gangs offer you ultimate control to do what you want. Just getting that for a minute is very intoxicating. Gang members are out there trying to control their own little world. It's only a little tiny place. It may not look like much to you—an alley, a street—but it's like a country to them. It's easy for outsiders to say it's just a little block, but a lot of those kids won't leave that block for years, and in some cases their entire lives. It's theirs. That becomes their whole world. Everybody wants to have power over their world.

I'm no authority on how gang warfare got started, but it's a real war. Lots of people don't see that. They just think it's stupid kids out there shooting at each other. If that's the case, then any war can be regarded as such.

Try to just imagine somebody in your family getting killed by a neighbor, maybe a teenager across the street. The police come to your door, take down the information, and don't do anything about it. Each day after that, you gotta look at these same people. Would you go over there and kill them?

I don't know. Maybe you would, maybe you wouldn't. There's a definite point where a feud begins. Once it starts, it's not easy to stop. You have a little baby my son's age growing up, and he'll put on clothes and somebody will step to him and say, "What is he doing wearing that red shirt?" A Blood—a guy from another gang—may have killed this guy's uncle. So because of this, your kid grows up in the 'hood not wearing a red T-shirt.

I've literally had friends come to my house and question what my baby boy, Ice, was wearing. "Why you putting him in this color? Why he wearing that?" I tell them, "Nigga, Ice ain't tripping with that." And they'll say, "Yeah, yeah. I'm just playing, but why don't you put him in this *blue* shirt?"

The gang scene in Los Angeles is extremely complicated and deep-rooted. The Hispanic gangs have been banging for far more years than any of the black gangs. The black gangs began to form after the Watts riots in '65, after so many brothers were thrown in jail.[1]

I first came in contact with gangs in 1974, when I started going to Crenshaw High School. I saw this one group of guys hanging out together, and I wanted to know what was going on. They were *the* unit. At this point, I unknowingly got connected in with the Crips. When you go to school, and you start hanging out with friends from one neighborhood, this immediately becomes your gang. These guys had come from Horace Mann Junior High School, and they were part of the first generation of black gangs. Across town was a gang called the Brims, which are called the Bloods now. I then started to learn all about the different groups and their idiosyncrasies.

Gang divisions are called sets. A gang member will ask you, "What set are you from?" Meaning, "Are you a Crip? Are you a Westside Crip? A Rollin' 60s Crip? Eight-Tray Gangsters? Avalon Gardens? Project Watts?"

Some of the gangs' basic characteristics are: The Crips wear blue, the Brims wear red. The Crips call you cuz. The Brims call you blood. The Crip has his left ear pierced. The Brim has his right ear pierced.

The gangbanger clothes are all based on the cheapest shit in the stores. Bandanas. Shoelaces. The Mexican kids wear pressed T-shirts; they even iron a crease in them. They wear khakis and corduroy house shoes that cost five or ten dollars. They wear Pendleton shirts that last forever. The entire dress code consists of inexpensive items, but they press them and turn

---

their dress into something that's honorable 'cause this is all they got.

Even the lowriders were a result of kids being broke. They couldn't afford to buy a new car, so they took the car they had and turned it into a flamboyant piece of art that's theirs. They took an old '60s Chevy and put some rims on it, added a custom interior and a custom paint job and made it the coolest car in the neighborhood. When they began adding hydraulic systems, lowriding even became a sport.

In black gangs, anything that's not a Crip is a Blood. This means the Blood gangs weren't all necessarily connected. You'd have the Bounty Hunters, Pirus, Denver Lanes, Villains, Swans. But they didn't get along together, and the lack of unity made them less potent than the Crip gang.

As the gangs evolved, the Crip gangs became so wild and notorious they started to prey on themselves and divide among their own sets. The Grape Street Crips in Watts would be at war with the Rollin' 60s. (The numbers, like the '60s," correspond to the street blocks. The street area where the gang activity would happen would not be too far from the west of Crenshaw Boulevard, all the way to the east as far as Long Beach Boulevard, and back into Watts. So when you hear people talk about the 20s, the "20" refers to 20th through 29th streets.)

The 30s go all the way across town, but the actual gang, the 30s, lives right around Western and the South Central police station. The 40s were the hustlers. They were the closest thing to non-gang members out of all the blocks. These were the kids who were out there gambling. They thought they were a little slicker than gang members.

Out of ten blocks, one street would be poppin' and a gang would be named after it. You had Five-Deuce (52 Hoover) Crips, Eight-Tray Crips. Before there were a Rollin' 60s and 74 Hoover—that's the hot spot of the Crip gang—they used to have a gang called 7459 Hoover Crips, which meant everything from 74th to 59th streets. And each set would have an east or a west side, like the 74 Hoover Westside or the 74 Hoover Eastside.

All these gangs have their own hand signals. A Hoover Crip would throw two fingers down and put another finger across, to look like an "H." The Crips hold up a "C." A Blood will make his fingers look like a "B." Even the hand signals are intricate. They can tell each other to fuck off from one set to another by throwing up their signals.

When a gang member gets ready for battle or goes hardcore gangbanging, they call that loc-ing. Going loc. Loc-ing up. All of a sudden the beanies will get down crazy and their pants will sag, the sunglasses are on. It's the equivalent of Native Americans going on the warpath.

I've been to parties where my homies were chillin', and even though they're in a gang, they're low-key. And a fight will break out and immediately my guys go on loc. Their hats flip up and they're ready to pop. They spread the gang energy and start vibing off each other.

Even if I didn't come out and say I was in a Crip set, a gang member reading this book will naturally know because a Blood would never use the word "loc." When it became public I was involved in a Crip gang, interviewers asked me which set I was affiliated with. I still don't think it's to anybody's advantage for me to publicly represent a set. I don't want to be responsible for somebody targeting that set for any reason. You have to remember, this is no joke on the street. People live and die over their colors.

I also run into problems when I talk to Brims about the gang truce that started in April of '92. They might not want to listen to me because I'm not in their set. Bangers would feel me out first by asking what set I was with, and each time I would tell them it's irrelevant, because now I'm trying to work for everybody.

"Oh, so you was a Blood?" they'd ask.

"Fuck a Blood," I'd snap. It's an immediate response, because a lot of my friends got killed by Bloods. A lot of my friends. The last time we were on the road, one of my buddies' brother got killed in gang violence. We had to do everything we could just to keep him from retaliating, because my buddy knew who the murderer was. His brother had called 911 right before he got shot and named the killer.

And I really felt bad for my buddy, because I used to be so emotional. I would just go on autopilot, and you couldn't talk to me. That's exactly what happens to these kids. They just go crazy. When you don't retaliate, you're just sitting around waiting, waiting on justice to be served.

The question is, will he get justice? Will these guys go to jail? Will they get served? Or will he have to issue his own form of justice?

Try to put yourself in the position of losing your sister or your brother. You'd be crazy with revenge, driving around the streets asking people, "Do you know who killed my brother?" Once you find out, your response is, "Fuck them. Just fuck them. And their whole set." That's when you got a gang situation. All of it is really, really deep, and there aren't any simple solutions.

There are three levels of gang membership: the *hardcore*, the *members*, and the *affiliates*. The *hardcore* gangster is the straight-up warrior. He's always out looking for the enemy; he's always in the attack mode. He lives the violent side of gang life and that's all he focuses on. He's equal to the army soldier who enlisted in order to go to war. "Fuck the GED. I'm here to kill some muthafuckas." He's the guy reading *Soldier of Fortune* magazine and living for the confrontation.

The *members* are in gangs primarily for the camaraderie. They'll represent their set, but they're not the guy who's sitting there nutty, just ready to go at it all the time. The members usually run the gangs because they are more levelheaded than the hardcore member. These are the guys who understand gang membership has its privileges. The Geto Boys have a song out that's titled, "Damn, It Feels Good to Be a Gangster," and the members have fun with it. They gain brotherhood and confidence that they aren't getting from anywhere else.

The *affiliates* know all the gangbangers, and they wear the colors. But they are not out there putting in the drive-bys. Usually, they just live on the same street as a set, and they abide by the rules. Sometimes, the affiliate gang members might be calling the shots because they may be a little bit more intelligent and nonviolent than the other members. I was an affiliate member, and if one of my homies from Hoover needed advice, we'd hook up and discuss tactical maneuvers. Before you know it, you're setting up a drive-by.

When you live on a certain street, you will always be held accountable for your 'hood if something goes down. In other words, a totally square kid living on 83rd Street knows his street is a Crip street and knows he can't avoid the politics of his 'hood.

I once went with my daughter to buy some sneakers. I picked out a pair for her, but she pointed to a red pair: "Let's get these." I looked at her and asked, "Red, what are you talkin' about?" But she was living near the jungle off King Boulevard and Dorsey High School and that's a Blood area.

She let me know she's not a gang member, but she's part of that environment. She told me, "I'd just rather blend in than try to fight it." If she wants to wear blue and all her girlfriends are wearing red, she's gonna create a problem, so why do that?

The first three levels of gangs really have to follow the rules completely. One of the main violations is associating with the enemy. It's like the Civil War revisited down in South Central. If you have to visit your cousin on Sunday, expect to hear about it on Monday. "Yo, cuz, I seen you with them Bloods." Kids get sweated for that all the time, because they got gang spies. If you're seen hanging on enemy turf, it's like an act of treason to your set.

The rules of gang warfare are not much different from the U.S. military. If a fight breaks out, and you run, you can get smoked for that. In the army, you could get sentenced to death. So, the kids who are more blatant with their membership—or in military-speak, gung-ho—gain the rank. In many ways, gangs are playing the same games America plays against other countries. It's a game of superiority being played out on a smaller scale. But it's essentially the same game.

The ultimate rush for any man is power. When you're in a set, you not only gain power, you gain rebellious power. You're now not answering to anybody. Once a kid can click this switch in his head and say, "I can do what I want to do. I'm here on this earth and there are laws, but I'm gonna handle it my way," his ego's boosted. He gains identity. Any time you join a fraternity, you immediately become somebody, even if it's only in your set.

In the ghetto, just the names of these gangsters have their own power. If I say I hang with Tony Bogard, everybody in the 'hood knows who he is. He's the guy who initiated the gang truce, and he's as big a gangster as anyone. Why does Bogard have juice? Because he's been shot a bunch of times, and the kids over there know he's not afraid of anyone. The buzz around town will sound like, "Oh, you know him? You know Raider from Santana block?"[2]

Who are these guys? They are not professional athletes or pop stars. But they are big shots to the ghetto kids, because they got their names from being tough. They didn't have money, so they used the one commodity they did have: strength.

Gang culture is ghetto male love being pushed to its limit. Gang members wear their colors in defiance of everything—in defiance of the cops, in defiance of other sets, even in defiance of the school system. When they wear their colors while strolling through rival turf, it's called bailing, and to anybody on the outside, they're *insane*. Why would you just walk down the street like a big target? Because in an aggressive environment, it's your way of saying, "I'm not afraid of anybody."

Gangs offer security to kids in a fucked-up environment. It's not the killing that initially draws a kid into gangs. It's the brother-like bond, because you're telling the kid, "Yo, I love you. And nothing's ever gonna happen to you, because if anything happens to you, those muthafuckas are going to be dead." You don't tell your girlfriend that. You don't tell your mother that.

They follow true on that promise. When you see these drive-bys and kids are hitting five or six people on the street, they are retaliating for the murder of one of their boys. I've seen crying men enter cars and when the doors shut, they go out and murder.

If they hit their target when they put in work, most of them will walk. They know that in Los Angeles if you go out and kill another black man, odds are you aren't going to jail. Your case isn't an LAPD priority. It's the old ghetto saying: "A nigger kills a white man. That's murder one. A white man kills a nigger. That's self-defense. A nigger kills a nigger. That's just another dead nigger."

If your case does make it to court, the witnesses they'll try to use against you to send you to jail are usually from another gang. These kids want to see any member from the other set go to jail. And once your attorney proves this, you're not going to jail. You're not gonna get popped for it. That's what is so ironic about the Rodney King trials. The witnesses for the defense were police, and that should have been a conflict right there. They are in the same gang—*Of course some of them will lie to save their buddies.*

Most of the gang killers are still out there on the street. I meet kids every day who are introduced to me as "the shooter." "This is the shooter. This is our killer." Which means this kid has killed and will kill again. This is not only what he does, it's what he's known for. Sometimes, they won't be much older than fifteen or sixteen years old.

When someone tells me, "This is the shooter," it means he got away with it a few times, and he's not afraid to do it again tomorrow. Getting away with it once is all it takes. In his mind, he's saying, "It's on."

Gangs have been able to get away with so much killing it just continues. The capability for violence in these kids is unimaginable. Last year, five of my buddies died. I don't even go to the funerals anymore. It's just so crazy. There are just so many people dying out there. Sometimes, I sit up with my friends and I think, "There will never be another time on earth where we'll all be together again." A lot of my original crew is dead. You get hard after a while. You get hard. People on the outside say, "These kids are so stone-faced; they don't show any remorse or any emotion." It's because they are so conditioned. They are conditioned, like soldiers in war, to deal with death. You just don't know what it's like unless you've been around it.

In L.A., gangbanging is done under the supervision of the police. The cops watch the gang's activity—they don't get in it, but they allow it to go down. They don't care about people hurting each other. They'll allow Al Capone to do his business, but don't hurt them. The gangs are not out to attack the police. No Mafia messes with the police, because they know the cops will come down if you hurt their own.

The gang mentality is, "This is my city, this is my 'hood, this is my world. Fuck the police. They are here to do what they got to do, and I'm here to do what I got to do." They have total disrespect for the law. Don't put them on any different level than any other gangsters—Capone or Bugsy. They had no respect for the law either. They knew the law was there, but it was simply something to get around.

They say, "We've got to go in and do our business and some of us are gonna fall, and some of us will get hit." But the gang members feel they are surviving, and they aren't really doing anything wrong. They are looking at poverty as being wrong. They figure they ain't got nothing, so fuck it.

Poverty totally instills a "Fuck it" attitude. "What am I gonna lose?" It ain't like they're coming out of nice houses in Brentwood and going out and taking a risk. They are coming out of the projects. Their homes might be as big as the average living room. My buddy Malik will tell you, "Man, I got a wife, four kids, and two pit bulls in a single apartment. So don't come tell me what to do. I'm in here just trying to live. I'm coming out here on the streets and whatever I got to do, I got to do."

Stories fly around town about cops antagonizing gang members to fight each other by going from set to set and spreading rumors about who murdered who. A lot of cops find this shit funny. If you're a real policeman, you don't want to see anybody get hurt. But you got to first put yourself in the mind-set of the cop who gets up in the morning saying, "All these fuckin' niggers, savages down here. I'm gonna go down and put some of them in jail and beat some of them up." That cop, he's causing just as much trouble as they are, because he's in there stirring them up. They'll pull you to the side of the street and tell you to get out and run. They'll tell you to fight them, and you've got to fight them.

The gangs do nothing more than act as defiant as possible toward police. A gang member will see a cop and throw his set up to him by using hand signals. They call that "giving it up" or "hitting 'em up." Like Ice Cube says on his Predator album, "See One-Time hit 'em up." He's illustrating the defiance gang members feel toward One-Time—the cops who roll through the neighborhoods. Most gang members aren't afraid of getting thrown in jail, because what do they have to lose? To most of them, jail is no different than home. They ain't gonna do nothing but kick it with the homies in jail. Everybody's there. You ain't got nothing on the street. So if you get popped, so what? If you're young, you say to yourself, "I can do two standing on my head."

Gang mentality is totally pounded into your head in prison. When you go to a prison in any section of California, you get thrown into a "car." A car is the group you hang with when you're in the joint. A ride. These are the guys you'll be rolling with in a prison riot. The first thing you'll be asked after being in prison for a while is, "What car you in?" In jail, there are Muslim cars; 415 up north; 213 in L.A.; Black Guerrilla Family; a Crip car, a Blood car. These cars are your gang and your form of protection while you're serving time.

Like in any gang situation, even if you don't side with any of them, that becomes a car—the people who ain't with anything. An inmate will ask, "You ain't with the Aryan Nation? You ain't with the Muslims?" If the answer is no, you become linked with all the other prisoners in an independent car.

If a convict goes to prison for ten years and lands in a Crips car, he's waking up every day, putting on his bandana, walking the walk. And it's no joke—when a guy who outranks you in your car comes up to you and tells you that you gotta stick some guy, you gotta do it.

There is lots of drama in jail. By the time you come home, you're really banging. When the police take you off the street and put you in jail, your criminal side is totally reemphasized. You'll see the gang tattoos. You'll see the change in their eyes.

My hope is the gang truce can reach into the prisons because the prisons are what really run the streets. In the joint, you get favors by seeing what you can do for somebody on the outside. If I were in jail with you and you wanted something done by me, or I wanted something done by you, I'd say, "Don't worry, I can reach your people and handle what you need." So, a lot of the guys who are getting killed on the streets are being reached by people in the joint. The joint contains the most hardcore gangsters.

The prisoner's mind-set is, "I'm already in jail, right? I can handle this for you. Your problem's gone." So all these shots are getting called by people in the joint, and if they decide the war is over in there, then it will be over outside, too. You can't stop on the outside without the commitment of guys in the joint. They're gonna be saying, "Yo, when I get out: Blam." It has to happen in both places simultaneously.

One of my buddies once told me, "Man, everybody wants to be special." If you can't be special by being the smartest person in school, you're gonna try to be special by being really different or really tough. The guys in Boo-Yaa Tribe wear these big braids, and they'll take a little girl's blue barrette and clip it to the end of their hair. Now, they know that looks crazy, but what they're saying is, "I'm gonna look crazy. And if you don't know better, you might say something to me about it." It gives them a distinction.

I went to the Mann's Chinese Theatre in Hollywood one time with fifty of my gangbanging buddies, right? Fifty dudes with sunglasses and baseball hats. You should have seen how the streets cleared as people got out of the way. These are kids who would never have seen that kind of power without being in a gang.

When killing becomes involved, it turns into a real dark, evil thing. If they only threw fists when a confrontation came up, there wouldn't be a problem. But somewhere along the line early on, somebody got killed, and once death came into the equation, it became a very dark, very evil, scary thing.

Whenever somebody gets power, it's inevitable it will get abused. Gangs are no different than any organization. It's not good enough to be a football team and stroll around and be nice. It's much more fun to wreck up the club.

They do what they gotta do.

In Kenneth M. Stampp's book *The Peculiar Institution*, Frederick Douglass is quoted from over 140 years ago as writing, "Everybody in the South wants the privilege of whipping somebody else." He believed that slaves, by having to submit to the power of their masters, therefore became aggressive toward each other and would whip each other even more cruelly than their masters. Frustration builds into aggressive behavior and it causes people to lash out and hurt somebody else. Anybody who suffers some kind of pain is searching to reach out. If you grow up in an aggressive environment, your threshold for pain grows higher and you're gonna do one of two things: You're gonna become extremely gentle or you're gonna become extremely violent.

I'm more or less a gentle person, but I have the ability to get extremely violent under stressful situations. I'm the person who's pleading. "Let me be nice, okay? Will you please let me be nice? I want to be nice."

Because I have a gangbanging past, people always want to test me. That's a dangerous thing, trying to push the ghetto button. People could end up dead in these situations. With gangs, you are dealing with killers, or with people who have the potential to kill. Why would you want to fuck with this guy? Why would you want to try to see if he's real? Because of his upbringing, the ghetto black man has this mechanism built in him he's trying to control. Voyeurs shouldn't push him toward the edge. Sometimes, you're dealing with people who are so frustrated, they are almost on the brink of insanity. They even got a Crip gang called the Insanes, probably because of this.

The way to deal with these guys, especially when they're attempting to break out of the gangster mindset, isn't by threatening them. In Orange County, California, politicians are threatening to crack down hard on gangs. They actually believe if they bully these kids, they will be scared out of gang membership. "Yeah, we'll scare Johnny, and he won't want to be in gangs anymore."

They don't have a clue that by the time a kid joins a gang, he's already lost all fear of what could happen to him. Nothing could be scarier than Johnny's home life and his upbringing. The killing fields have destroyed his spirit and the lives of his friends. If they were smart, they would be exploring the issues that make a kid want to join up in the first place. Why does this kid want to tag on the wall? It's so typical for the government to say, "Let's go after the kid instead of figuring out the reason he's so full of hate. Let's attack Ice T because he wrote 'Cop Killer.' We don't want to explore the reason he might have written it. That's too horrible. That's too complicated."

Because the causes are never explored, the battles will probably continue. With the injection of drugs into the gang world, you have the perfect breeding ground for organized crime.

People outside of the gang arena will always have a difficult time understanding why these kids sell drugs. They ask, "How could they hurt their own people? Why would they do that? They are hurting themselves." To understand this whole thing, I always use this scenario: Take four people, put them in a prison cell, and say to one of them, "Come to work for me. First off, none of y'all are ever getting out. You're destined to die in this prison cell. But if you poison the other three, I'll let you out. They are gonna die anyway. But you can be the one who lives. I'll allow you to kill them."

How many people in the world would be able to stay there for a hundred years and die with these people or just take a chance to get out? That's what these kids are saying. "I ain't got no way out. It's not that I want to hurt anybody, but this is my chance. I really believe the chance of escaping outweighs the harm I'm doing to other people."

When you deal dope, people are coming to you and begging you for it. You don't really see you're hurting anyone. You're quick to say:

"If I didn't give it to 'em, somebody else would."

"They want the dope. They want it. I'm fulfilling a need."

"They're feeling good."

"Well, it's their own fault, you know."

"I got to do this. For the first time, my little sister got new sneakers. My mama's car note is paid. I'm able to achieve something. I'm having things now. I ain't never had anything."

As a dealer, you become intoxicated with what it gives you, and you can't stop. People don't go into selling drugs to hurt people. If that were the case, they would take the drugs and lace them with cyanide. They are not trying to kill anyone, they are trying to get into an occupation that allows them a chance to live better than they are. Before the introduction of crack, you had units of kids that were out there fighting each other over a street, not money. Now, all of a sudden you gave them a chance to make a cash flow and these kids created their own organizations.

Dealing also helped break the gangs up into smaller units because they had the money and the opportunity to do it. Right now, crack cocaine is the number-one employer of minorities in America. It's very hard to retire from that occupation.

That's capitalism right there. Crack and cash flow has given yet another angle to the whole complex problems of gangs. Now you see the gangs spread out all over the United States, and you wonder where they come from.

They took the game on the road. The crack or dope you sell here is four times as expensive out of the state. Los Angeles right now is the number-one headquarters for cocaine in the United States. It's no longer Miami. This is the dope capital. They stopped coming in through the Miami borders, and now they're bringing it up through Mexico and Arizona, and the drugs hit in L.A. first. The gangbangers will get it, and they're already organized. Everybody's got a cousin in St. Louis or Cleveland, and they can fly out there and get their homies involved in the drug trade.

A gang member will fly out to see his relative, and since he's already got an identity to the relative, the kid out of state will listen to what he has to say. Gangsters are given respect because compared to these kids in Missouri, they've got it going on. A kid in Mississippi has never seen anything like it. He's dirt-ass poor, saying, "Hey, I wanna be in this. I like this."

The L.A. connection will tell him, "I'm from the Rollin' 60s, and I've got this product for you. If you have any problems or any drama out here, I'll have muthafuckas flown in from L.A. You see how we're kickin' up dust in Los Angeles?" And in no time, they'll turn out about ten dudes in Mississippi. They'll dress 'em up, teach them the ropes. And now Mississippi's got a gang, with real members.

Then, just like organized crime, they decide they want to take over an area out there, and they need somebody to handle it. So they fly in another kid from L.A.; he does the job and he's out of there. Straight hit. And how are you gonna bust this kid? This kid's not from Mississippi. Nobody knows anything. Nobody's ever seen him. He doesn't even know anything about who he's doing. And it's on.

The gangs grew out of control in L.A., so they were able to spread throughout the rest of the country. The problem's gotten very complex and very deep. We're looking at the breeding grounds for a black Mafia. The irony is that it's always been this way. A lot of the immigrants who came to America applied their own criminal tactics to try to get ahead.

With the onset of the gang truce, the gangs in Los Angeles are in their final bonding stages. Prior to the truce, the gangs had all bonded into small units, which I see as a death bond. If they remain separate, the war would definitely continue. By bonding together, they can step back and realize, "Yo, we've all got the same enemy. Let's stop killing each other." You would have a devastatingly, not only powerful but dangerous unit of black men in Los Angeles.

This is a situation the LAPD does not want to see happen. They do not dig this gang truce. They want to keep them separate. Once you sit down with twenty thousand guys who used to be fighting each other in groups of five or five hundred, and you set them all together, you've got some kind of new phenomena. Think about the force of these kids for a moment. If you ask, "How many people here have done a drive-by?" and two thousand hands go up, you've got some shit on your hands. You've got some hardcore soldiers. And if they decide the cops are the enemy, then the LAPD is in trouble. The cops have every reason to want these kids to remain separate; it's better for them if the kids keep killing each other.

I'm not even worried about the gangs all banding together. Once they really reevaluate their lives, they'll want to move in more mellow directions. When I was out there hustling and looking at everybody crazy, I believed that was what I always would have to do. Once I was able to change and once I had hope for a different future, I didn't have those feelings any longer. I didn't really want to hurt anybody anymore. I had no pressing reason to go out and do low. But when you're down in that hole, you feel like that's how you've got to be all day, everyday.

The whole gang attitude is something you have to be brought slowly out of. Lots of brothers can't do it. The deejay I work with, Aladdin, grew up in Compton, and even after we started working together, he used to go back to Compton every night and hang out with his homies. I used to tell him, "Yo, Aladdin, you look like a gangbanger." It was cool he was going out there to hang with his buddies, but I knew that if they committed a crime or hurt somebody, Aladdin would be nailed because he was making records. The cops could get with him. You have to remember, the brothers he's rolling with have the ability to disappear, they're unknown. That's why gang members have nicknames. The worst thing you can do is call a gangbanger by his last name. They purposely keep themselves incognito.

Aladdin knew what was going on, but he'd tell me, "I come over here and kick it with you and it's cool, but I got to go back to Compton, man. When I go back to Compton, just because I know you, everybody thinks I'm a little bit better. So I might have to stand out on the corner with my boys for an hour or so—and I might not even want to—just to prove I'm still down."

I told him he's got to start protecting himself. They might try to make him do low just out of jealousy, because they know he's got a chance to get out. His true homie will be happy for him, but these other guys might challenge him by daring him to out and commit a crime with them. They might try to test his loyalty. That's when Aladdin needed to step off and tell them he's not really down with that. He'd found his way out, and he was getting paid. If they can't understand that, then fuck 'em.

Eventually he had to get an apartment and move out. But he didn't just move, he took his real friends with him. They still come over and hang out. 'Cause even when you're in the neighborhood, you might seem like you got a lot of friends, but you really only got a couple of really true friends.

I never see the elimination of gangs. I would like to see the elimination of gang violence, though. Currently, I'm putting a lot of time and energy into Hands Across Watts, the organization in L.A. trying to see the gang truce through. Many of my friends still live in South Central or Compton, and every other phone call I get is word from the street. I'm what you call a shot caller, so I probably know more about what's going on in the 'hood than the people who live there. I'm paying for funerals and counseling kids to quit killing over colors and streets. I'm their homeboy who made it, and I'm trying to set an example that there are alternatives to violence. I have hope that peace can be instituted.

If you could just get the violence down to a standstill, you'd be left with what the rest of the world calls clubs. In a city this big, you need a group of people around you. When I was in the army, whenever we left the post the sergeants used to tell us to go in a group. "Take a gang," is what they were really saying.

The United States Army is one big gang. The cops are a gang. When they come, they come in units. So the theory of telling the kids to walk alone is bullshit. When you're in an angry environment, you need a friend. I tell women all the time to take a girlfriend if they're going out for the night. Walking alone ain't healthy when there are people out there to prey on you.

Now if you're a girl, you might just go out with your girlfriend—two might be enough. But in a rougher part of the city, you might be better off to go in threes or fours.

When you're from a rough environment like South Central, you need to ask yourself, "Are we going out looking for trouble? Or are we going out to protect each other?" The organization I created, the Rhyme Syndicate, is a business. But at the same time, it employs ex-gang members and ex-street hoods and in a way, we are a gang because people know they don't want to fuck with us. We're not looking for trouble, but we got each other's back if anyone tries to fuck with us. They are my insurance. This is nothing new. The Mafia uses the same tactics. Any organization—the FBI, the CIA—is a club and if you fuck with one member, they'll call for backup.

People have got to understand that gang warfare is not something that should be treated like some minor problem. It's gonna take a big truce. It's gonna take negotiations, and it's gonna take money. It will require a lot of effort to get it to end.

Thousands of people have died on each side of this bloody battlefield, and it's not just something that you can snap your fingers and tell people to stop. When you talk to these kids, they are like veterans from war. If you went to Beirut and asked a kid about his life, he wouldn't tell you he's at war. He'd just say, "This is how it is. You know, bombs and shit going off. I grew up with this, so this is how it is."

They are used to death. They are used to despair. On my song "Colors," I rapped:

My color's death
Though we all want peace
But this war won't end
Till all wars cease.

This gang war is just like any other war. If you think it can be easily stopped, let's go to Northern Ireland and tell them to stop. Let's go to Bosnia and tell them to quit. Don't call it anything less than what it really is. Now, once we accept that, we can begin to deal with it. As long as the media define the fighters as dumb gang members, they are undermining and not really seeing what these kids are going through.

We can say how stupid it is. We can say how ignorant it is, and I'll agree. But understand that you can say that about any war. Regard it as such.

Whenever the U.S. goes to war, there is a reason for it and there is money for it. But in reality, I can see more sense sometimes in this war out here in these streets than in some of the wars people are shipped overseas to from America. They are usually fighting something they don't even understand. They are fighting for a belief system that is American, when these kids are out fighting for somebody who hurt their family. They're on some real shit. Until you've been up and around 250-pound dudes crying while loading guns, you don't know what it's about. You don't know this is real. Why did it happen? I don't know. But the problem, the reality, is somebody's dead, and somebody wants revenge.

But that's just my opinion on the killing fields, who gives a fuck.

1. [Editor's note: This is a factual error. Black gangs were active in the late 1950s, and were the subject of a major gang intervention program as well as intensive research. See Malcolm W Klein, *Street Gangs and Street Workers*: Englewood Cliffs, NJ: Prentice-Hall, 1971.]
2. [Editor's note: Tony Bogard was shot and killed in an argument over drugs in 1994. Being involved in gang truce activities does not necessarily mean the individual has been "rehabilitated."] ✦

18
The Collection of Data for Gang Research

Robert J. Bursik, Jr. and Harold G. Grasmick

We conclude this theory section with a brief discussion of the methods used to gather information on gangs. The overview is provided by Bursik and Grasmick, in an excerpt from Neighborhoods and Crime. *The authors describe the inherent limitations of each major method and warn that the gang literature must be approached with an eye on these limitations. The editors of the volume share this concern and urge its readers to consider the methodological strategies adopted by each researcher. The representativeness of the study sample, reliability of informants, and adequacy of comparison groups are crucial elements of the context of gang research and the information it produces.*

. . . Easily the longest tradition of gang research is based on some variant of ethnographic fieldwork with gang members (or the combination of such research with supplementary forms of data collection). The work of Thrasher (1927) is exemplary in this respect. Although we know very little concerning how he actually collected his data (see Short 1963:xviii), it is clear that it represented primarily a combination of personal observation and documents that were supplemented by court records and census materials. Over the course of his seven-year study, he amassed enough material to identify 1,313 Chicago gangs.

While Bookin and Horowitz (1983) noted that fieldwork techniques had a declining popularity in sociology and predicted that they would rarely be used in future research, Horowitz (1990:37) recently has retracted that statement, for they certainly represent one of the major forms of data collection used in the study of gangs.[1] Unfortunately, ethnographers no longer have the resources at their disposal to conduct such a "census" of gangs as that of Thrasher. Therefore, the modern emphasis has been on the depth of data, rather than the breadth. Generally this is not considered a problem in fieldwork, for such research is much more concerned with the identification and analysis of process and meaning than with the ability to generalize findings to some larger population. Nevertheless, it must be emphasized that the representativeness of the gangs that have been described is not clear. Many times the gangs have been chosen on the basis of their notoriety within a community (see Keiser 1969; Muehlbauer and Dodder 1983), because of chance circumstances that bring a gang to the attention of a researcher, such as the prior participation of gang members in social service projects (Short and Strodtbeck 1965; Klein 1971; Hagedorn 1988; Harris 1988), or because of their location in particular communities upon which researchers have elected to focus (Klein 1971; Moore 1978; Horowitz 1983; Campbell 1984; Sullivan 1989; Jankowski 1991).

There are special difficulties in conducting fieldwork with gangs that do not arise in many other fields of inquiry. First, and most obviously, while most researchers are highly educated, middle-class persons, many gang members are not. It takes a skilled ethnographer to overcome the initial hostility that is often inherent to interactions with gang members (see the descriptions provided by Horowitz 1983:Chapter 1; Moore 1978:Appendix A; Hagedorn 1988:32-33). In addition to this inherent suspicion, many researchers have noted that gang members are notoriously unreliable as informants (Spergel 1990:175); Klein (1971:18) feels that "the only thing worse than the young reporter's description of a gang incident is his [sic] acceptance of the gang participant's statement about it." This problem was forcibly driven home to the first author of this book during a conversation with a friend who formerly had been a central member of one of Chicago's most notorious fighting gangs. He described with great pleasure how during times of boredom, members of his group would have an informal competition to see who could convincingly tell the most outrageous story to a social worker who had been assigned to work with the group. Therefore, the collection of valid data through fieldwork with gangs is only possible after an extended period of contact during which trust is established.

There is also a more subtle problem in the reliability of data drawn from fieldwork with gangs. An important concern in all ethnographic studies is the degree to which the presence of the researcher has a significant effect on the nature of the dynamics that are observed. For example, some of the most important studies of gang dynamics (such as that of Short and Strodtbeck 1965) have relied to a significant degree on the observations of "detached workers," that is, social service personnel who have been assigned to work with gangs in their natural settings. As Klein (1971:151) notes, those procedures that are often used to maximize contact with gangs (such as group counseling sessions or attendance at club meetings) may in fact increase group cohesiveness, which may lead to an increase in gang delinquency. In addition, the assignment of a group worker may increase the local reputation of a gang, which in turn may attract new members. Thus, the presence of a fieldworker can result in a set of group dynamics and activities that would not have occurred otherwise.

Despite these problems, ethnographic work has provided some of the most important insights that criminologists have about gangs, and much of the richest data has been obtained under situations that may have seemed doomed to failure (see Horowitz 1983). However, as we have noted, there are problems in the generalizability of such data. A second approach to gang research has attempted to overcome this limitation by incorporating surveys into the study design. While this often has been done in conjunction with ongoing fieldwork (such as Short and Strodtbeck 1965; Joe and Robinson 1980), this is not necessarily the case (Giordano 1978; Bowker et al. 1980; Morash 1983; Fagan 1989; Curry and Spergel 1991).

Many of the same problems concerning trust and hostility that characterize fieldwork studies also are present in survey-based study designs. However, two other issues make gang survey research especially problematic. The first is the sampling frame itself, that is, the population of gang members from which the respondents should be selected. Obviously, there is no "official" listing of all gang members in an area, but even if one existed, the ongoing flux in gang membership would make a list obsolete almost immediately (Short and Strodtbeck 1965:10). The police in many communities have compiled lists of suspected gang members, but these tend to be very inaccurate. Klein (1971:19) tells the story of how he examined the files kept by the police concerning the members of a particular gang. Whereas he had the names of over 100 members, the police had less than 20 and much of their information concerning addresses and offense histories was extremely dated. One solution is to administer surveys to those people who have been identified as gang members through fieldwork (see Short and Strodtbeck). Another is to interview people known to be gang members, ask them for the names of other people who should be interviewed, and continue to build the sample of respondents through such a "snowball" approach (see Fagan 1989).

While such techniques can potentially collect a great deal of useful information concerning the characteristics and behavior of gang members, it is often desirable to compare the distributions of these variables to those found among youths not involved in gang activity.[2] However, the selection of an appropriate comparison group is very difficult. The sample survey data examined in the 1989 paper of Jeffrey Fagan (1989), for example, included only the responses of gang members, and he was only able to draw comparisons with nongang youths by comparing his findings with other published research. While Short and Strodtbeck (1965) did include nongang youths in their sample, all these respondents were affiliated in some manner with youth-serving agencies (p. 5). Therefore, the degree to which these youths are representative of nongang youths in general is not clear.

Several attempts have been made to identify gang membership and make the relevant comparisons on the basis of more broadly administered surveys (Morash 1983; Rand 1987; Spergel and Curry 1988; Curry and Spergel 1991). The validity of the information that has been collected on the basis of such study designs depends on two crucial considerations. First, how likely is it that youths involved in gangs will be represented in the sample? Some researchers have tried to maximize this possibility by drawing all or part of their sample from those youths residing in correctional facilities (Bowker et al. 1980; Morash 1983). Such approaches would tend to overrepresent those youths with extensive or especially violent offense histories. Other sampling designs are likely to underrepresent active gang members. Spergel and Curry (1988) and Curry and Spergel (1991), for example, surveyed all male students in the sixth through eighth grades at four schools in Chicago. Likewise, Fagan (1990) supplemented the gang data noted earlier with information collected from a sample of high school students residing in the same three neighborhoods and a snowball sample of dropouts. However, school-based samples are especially prone to errors in studies of delinquency since the most active delinquents may be those youths who are most likely to be truant during the time of administration. In general, it is extremely difficult to draw a representative sample of gang members.

The second consideration reflects the identification of respondents as gang members. Some surveys have simply asked the respondents if they belong to a gang (Rand 1987; Johnstone 1981). While John Johnstone presents some evidence (p. 362) to suggest that the adolescents in his sample interpreted the term "gang" consistently, he does note problems with such an assumption. Other researchers assume the existence of a continuum along which a youth group is more or less like a particular operational definition of a gang (Morash 1983; Spergel and Curry 1988; Curry and Spergel 1991). We have already noted Klein and Maxson's (1989) criticism of the scale developed by Morash for its apparent inability to differentiate among dramatically different types of youth groups. The Spergel and Curry scale is a much narrower approach to the measurement of gangs and includes such items as the flashing of gang signs, the wearing of colors, and attacking (or being attacked) in a gang-related incident. One of their most important findings is that the indicators of gang involvement scaled differently for Hispanics and African-Americans, which highlights our argument that the search for a broadly relevant uniform definition of gangs may be relatively fruitless. In addition, contrary to the findings of Morash, they present evidence of a strong relationship between gang involvement and serious delinquency.

Overall, the use of surveys is no guarantee that the results of a study are any more reliable than those produced through more traditional fieldwork approaches. Rather, results are especially sensitive to the nature of the sampling design, the selection and wording of the indicators of gang membership, and the relevance of those indicators to the populations under consideration.

The final technique that has been used to collect data on gangs is based on information that has been collected by law enforcement agencies. While sometimes this information is used to supplement that derived through fieldwork or survey designs, much of the current knowledge concerning gangs is the result of studies that have been based primarily on such data (Miller 1975; Spergel 1984, 1986; Curry and Spergel 1988; Klein and Maxson 1989; Maxson et al. 1985). Bernard Cohen (1969) has argued that the Philadelphia Gang Crimes Unit uses sociologically sophisticated definitions of gang and nongang activities in its classification of criminal events. However the official classification of an offender as a gang member generally is not systematic and may not be based on reliable criteria (Klein and Maxson 1989:206).

In addition to the problem of identifying gang membership based on the information included in official records, there is an equally difficult problem in the classification of illegal events as gang-related. For example, suppose a member of a gang is arrested for the armed robbery of a convenience store. On the basis of the description of the event provided in the arrest report, it may be impossible to determine whether it was committed due to gang membership. Unfortunately, there are no national standards for the identification of a crime as gang-related. For example, the Los Angeles Police and Sheriff's Departments designate a homicide as gang-related "if either the assailant or the victim is a gang member or, failing clear identification, elements of the event, such as motive, garb, characteristic gang behavior, or attribution by witnesses, indicate the likelihood of gang involvement" (Klein and Maxson 1989:206-207). However, the Chicago Police Department uses a much more restrictive definition that is based on the evidence of "gang function or motivation" (Curry and Spergel 1988:384). Maxson and Klein (1990) note that a reclassification of the Los Angeles data on the basis of the Chicago criterion leads to a significant reduction in the estimated rate of gang homicide and question whether the massive efforts of gang control and suppression that have characterized Los Angeles would have developed if this alternative definition had been used to gauge the extent of the problem.

The existence of such definitional inconsistencies makes it very difficult to make any kind of reliable comparisons between jurisdictions concerning the level of gang activity. However, definitions may also be characterized by inconsistencies even within the same jurisdiction. For example, Curry and Spergel (1988:385) note that prior to 1986, arson, theft, burglary, and vice offenses (including those that were drug-related) were not included in the gang crime reporting system. Such changes make it nearly impossible to examine the trends in many forms of gang behavior in Chicago over time, including the changing nature of drug use and distribution that has received so much attention in other parts of the country.

Overall, the inherent limitations of the dominant forms of data collection on gangs are very serious. Therefore, in many respects, we simply cannot be as confident of our knowledge concerning gangs as we are in other areas of criminology. However, despite these problems of measurement, certain patterns have emerged in a sufficient number of studies and locations to provide at least a minimal degree of confidence in those empirical regularities. This is especially the case in gang research that has emphasized the neighborhood dynamics related to such behavior.

Notes

1. We use the term "fieldwork" in a very broad sense to refer to qualitative study designs that involve some degree of interaction between the researcher and the gang member. They can range from intensive observation conducted by the researcher over extended periods (as in Horowitz 1983, Campbell 1984, Sullivan 1989, Jankowski 1991), through the reports provided by social service workers who deal with particular gang on a regular basis (as in Short and Strodtbeck 1965, Klein 1971, or Moore 1985), to sets of intensive, unstructured interviews with respondents identified as gang members (as in Vigil 1988 or Hagedorn 1988). Many studies have combined two or more of these techniques into a single research design.
2. In fact, the availability of such information is absolutely essential to the development of processual approaches to gangs.

References

Bookin, Hedy, and Ruth Horowitz (1983). "The End of the Youth Gang: Fad or Fact?" Criminology 21:585-602.

Bowker, Lee H., Helen Shimata Gross, and Malcolm W. Klein (1980). "Female Participation in Delinquent Gang Activities." *Adolescence* 59:509-519.

Campbell, Ann (1984). *The Girls in the Gang*. Oxford: Basil Blackwell.

Cohen, Bernard (1969). "The Delinquency of Gangs and Spontaneous Groups." Pp. 61-111 in *Delinquency: Selected Studies*, edited by Thorsten Sellin and Marvin E. Wolfgang. New York: Wiley.

Curry, G. David, and Irving A. Spergel (1988). "Gang Homicide, Delinquency and Community." *Criminology* 26:381-405.

—— (1991). *Youth Gang Involvement and Delinquency: A Report to the National Youth Gang Intervention and Suppression Research and Development Project*. Office of Juvenile Justice and Delinquency Prevention, Washington, D.C.

Fagan, Jeffrey (1989). "The Social Organization of Drug Use and Drug Dealing Among Urban Gangs." *Criminology* 27:633-669.

—— (1990). "Social Processes of Delinquency and Drug Use Among Urban Gangs." Pp. 183-219 in *Gangs in America*, edited by C. Ronald Huff. Newbury Park, CA: Sage.

Giordano, Peggy C. (1978). "Girls, Guys, and Gangs: The Changing Social Context of Female Delinquency." *Journal of Criminal Law and Criminology* 69:126-132.

Hagedorn, John M. (1988). *People and Folks: Gangs, Crime and the Underclass in a Rustbelt City*. Chicago: Lake View Press.

Harris, Mary G. (1988). *Las Cholas: Latino Girls and Gangs*. New York: AMS Press.

Horowitz, Ruth,(1983). *Honor and the American Dream*. New Brunswick, NJ: Rutgers University Press.

—— (1990). "Sociological Perspectives on Gangs: Conflicting Definitions and Concepts." Pp. 37-54 in *Gangs in America*, edited by C. Ronald Huff. Newbury Park, CA: Sage.

Jankowski, Martin Sanchez (1991). *Islands in the Street: Gangs and American Urban Society*. Berkeley: University of California Press.

Joe, Delbert, and Norman Robinson (1980). "Chinatown's Immigrant Gangs: The New Young Warrior Class." *Criminology* 18:337-345.

Johnstone, John W. C. (1981). "Youth Gangs and Black Suburbs." *Pacific Sociological Review* 24:355-375.

Keiser, R. Lincoln (1969). *The Vice Lords: Warriors of the Streets*. New York: Holt, Rinehart and Winston.

Klein, Malcolm W. (1971). *Street Gangs and Street Workers*. Englewood Cliffs, NJ: Prentice-Hall.

Klein, Malcolm W., and Cheryl L. Maxson (1989). "Street Gang Violence." Pp. 198-234 in *Violent Crime, Violent Criminals*, edited by Neil A Weiner and Marvin E. Wolfgang. Newbury Park, CA: Sage.

Maxson, Cheryl L., Margaret A. Gordon, and Malcolm W. Klein (1985). "Differences Between Gang and Nongang Homicides." *Criminology* 23:209-222.

Maxson, Cheryl L., and Malcolm W. Klein (1990). "Street Gang Violence: Twice as Great or Half as Great?" Pp. 71-100 in *Gangs in America*, edited by C. Ronald Huff. Newbury Park, CA: Sage.

Miller, Walter B. (1975). *Violence by Youth Gangs as a Crime Problem in Major American Cities*. National Institute of Juvenile Justice and Delinquency Prevention. U.S. Justice Department. Washington, DC: U.S. Government Printing Office.

Moore, Joan W. (1978). *Homeboys*. Philadelphia: Temple University Press.

—— (1985). "Isolation and Stigmatization in the Development of an Underclass: The Case of Chicano Gangs in East Los Angeles." *Social Problems* 33:1-12.

Morash, Merry (1983). "Gangs, Groups, and Delinquency." *British Journal of Criminology* 23:309-335.

Muehlbauer, Gene, and Laura Dodder (1983). *The Losers: Gang Delinquency in an American Suburb*. New York: Praeger.

Rand, Alicia (1987). "Transitional Life Events and Desistance from Delinquency and Crime." Pp. 134-162 in *From Boy to Man, from Delinquency to Crime*, by Marvin E. Wolfgang, Terence P. Thornberry, and Robert M. Figlio. Chicago: University of Chicago Press.

Short, James F., Jr. (1963). "Introduction to the Abridged Edition." Pp. xv-liii in *The Gang*, by Frederic Thrasher. Chicago: University of Chicago Press.

Short, James F., Jr., and Fred L. Strodtbeck (1965). *Group Process and Gang Delinquency*. Chicago: University of Chicago Press.

Spergel, Irving A. (1984). "Violent Gangs in Chicago: In Search of Social Policy." *Social Service Review* 58:199-226.

—— (1986). "Violent Gangs in Chicago: A Local Community Approach." *Social Service Review* 60:94-131.

—— (1990). "Youth Gangs: Continuity and Change." Pp. 171-275 in *Crime and Justice: A Review of Research*. Volume 12, edited by Michael Tonry and Norval Morris. Chicago: University of Chicago Press.

Spergel, Irving A., and G. David Curry (1988). "Socialization to Gangs: Preliminary Baseline Report." School of Social Service Administration, University of Chicago.

Sullivan, Mercer L. (1989). *Getting Paid: Youth Crime and Work in the Inner City*. Ithaca, NY: Cornell University Press.

Thrasher, Frederic M. (1927). *The Gang*. Chicago: University of Chicago Press.

Vigil, James D. (1988). *Barrio Gangs: Street Life and Identity in Southern California*. Austin: University of Texas Press. ✦

Group Process

19

Groups, Gangs, and Cohesiveness

Malcolm W. Klein and Lois Y. Crawford

In order to remain intact, social groups need sources of cohesion such as common goals and shared norms. Klein and Crawford highlight the specific features of cohesiveness within gangs that make these groups unique from other social groupings. In particular, they suggest that gang cohesiveness is strengthened by the negative sanctions members receive from external sources. In addition, the authors note that delinquency is not just a product of gang membership, but also serves as a source of group cohesion for its members.

This paper is concerned with selected qualitative differences between juvenile gangs and other groups which have been the more traditional subject of empirical research. Two factors in particular are emphasized: gang cohesiveness and gang-related delinquent behavior. We take the position that the sources of gang cohesiveness are primarily external *to the group, in contrast to the findings on most groups previously studied. Gang delinquency, in addition to being the partial consequence of gang interaction, serves as an additional reinforcer of gang cohesiveness. After a brief review of the literature, we draw the conclusions that available concepts and approaches to the measurement of group cohesiveness are somewhat insufficient for application to gang research. With the use of data drawn from a study of 576 male Negro gang members in Los Angeles we illustrate several alternate measurement procedures. We view these procedures as a first step toward a sorely needed investigation of the relationship between gang cohesiveness and gang delinquency.*

"If a group lacks a task, purpose, or mission as a result of not being integrated into a demanding external system—as may in fact be the case for street-corner gangs—then it would fail to generate a major part of the rewards and sentiments which its members might expect to gain from it."[1]

This statement by Gordon, quoted by Short and Strodtbeck, derives from experience and data in the context of the Chicago juvenile gang world. It also is the nub of the position we have taken on the basis of independently collected data and experience with Los Angeles gangs. This paper is concerned with selected *qualitative differences* between juvenile gangs and other groups which have been the more traditional subject of empirical research. Our emphasis will be upon group cohesiveness and the differential nature and function of this concept when the distinctions between gangs and other groups are taken into account.

The Sherifs[2] have adopted the position, in very strong terms, that separating gang phenomena from the generic peer group context does violence to one's perspective on gangs. We agree with the *intent* of the Sherifs' argument, believing that the understanding of gang dynamics must come in the conceptual context of general group concepts and findings. We hope to demonstrate, however, that the rather extreme position taken by the Sherifs commits one to the opposite error of emasculating the juvenile gang of just those characteristics which make it stand out as a social problem.

Social Groups

Laboratory groups, T-groups, fraternities, and the other group targets of most empirical research are frequently studied in terms of the interpersonal attraction of the members and derive their cohesiveness (whether natural or experimentally induced) from such factors as common goals, explicitness of goals, shared norms and values, and stability of membership. They further tend to be characterized by behaviors and goals which are acceptable to society. Our understanding of group process and cohesiveness is colored by these facts.

It is a major thesis of this report that the existing literature on cohesiveness is less directly applicable to gangs because of qualitative factors which distinguish gangs from most other groups previously studied. As Lott and Lott observe in their review of empirical studies in the literature, while most researchers have subscribed to the position that group cohesiveness is the result of a number of independent forces, most investigations have focused on inter-member attraction. Thus, they "assume that interpersonal attraction, liking, or positive attitudes among group members is central to the cohesiveness of small groups."[3]

Juvenile Gangs

It is our contention that gang cohesiveness is based not only on these normal group processes but, to an even greater extent, on the interaction of these processes with negatively sanctioned behavior and attitudes. In the gang setting, cohesiveness and delinquent behavior are mutual interactors and reinforcers.[4] Indeed, the current literature on gangs bifurcates into these two major emphases or concerns with group variables.

One group of writers lays stress on group structure and cohesiveness per se. Thrasher,[5] for example, rec-

---

Reprinted from *Journal of Research in Crime and Delinquency*, 30(1), pp. 75-85.

ognized great variation in the size and structure of the gangs under his purview. He distinguished between "diffuse" and "solidified" gangs. A group's position along the continuum between these two categories was determined by the amount of conflict with neighboring groups. In the same vein, Yablonsky has emphasized that gang cohesiveness varies as a function of conflict, or, more accurately, of shared sociopathic withdrawal from perceived environmental threat.[6]

The other major emphasis in the current literature has to do more specifically with the modal behavior patterns of gangs. As examples, one can cite Cloward and Ohlin's[7] conception of criminal, conflict, and retreatist groups; Spergel's[8] analysis of the relationship between neighborhood characteristics and conflict, racket, theft, and drug subcultures; and the Short and Strodtbeck[9] report of five behavior factors characterizing the activities of gang members.

Thus, variations in gang cohesiveness and in gang-related behavior patterns are well established. It would appear, in addition, that group cohesiveness and group product are interdependent. The importance of this interdependence to the practitioner has been underscored by Bernstein.[10] It seems especially important at this point to investigate systematically the relationships between these two sets of variables. This paper presents preliminary analyses of the gang cohesiveness problem.

Sources of Cohesiveness

As noted above, most groups may be said to derive their cohesion primarily from "internal" sources—with respect to both origination and perpetuation of the group. In identifying these sources of cohesion as "internal" we recognize a certain semantic looseness, but our meaning may become clear when major sources of gang cohesiveness are examined.

It is our contention that internal sources operate with far less impact among gangs than among most groups and that, in contrast to other groups, gang cohesiveness derives from and is perpetuated by sources primarily external to the group. This contention is not new; most of the writers referred to above would be in sympathy with it. Cohen's[11] "reaction formation" analysis and Yinger's[12] discussion of "contraculture" are in the same tradition. We believe in addition, however, that elimination of external sources of cohesiveness of gangs, in most cases, would be followed by dissolution of a relatively large proportion of gang membership. That is, only rarely does a gang develop a sufficient number of internally-oriented systems to perpetuate itself in the absence of external pressures. This position is the result of two concomitant observations: (a) that internal sources of gang cohesion are weak and (b) that strong external pressures are present. These two characteristics of delinquent groups provide an explanation for what Gerrard[13] has described as "the intense but fragile quality of gang cohesion."

To be more specific about the weak aspects of internal sources of cohesiveness, certain characteristics can be listed.

1. Group qua *group goals* are usually minimal. The most commonly expressed group goal is the protection of members against rival gangs. Clearly this falls under what we have termed an *external* source of cohesion. Gangs assigned a detached worker sometimes learn to verbalize goals such as self-betterment, improving their group image, and "holding their cool." However, such goals are far more easily verbalized than internalized and their general acceptance, when it does take place, is more often associated with gang dissolution than with solidification.

2. Membership stability in gangs is relatively low. We have observed large groups in which the combined subgroup memberships have totaled more than two hundred over a two- to three-year period, yet at any given point of time there may be only thirty or forty active members. In other words, turnover is high; many members affiliate with the group for brief periods of from a few days to a few months, while others move out of the neighborhood or are incarcerated for periods sometimes exceeding a year. The bonds of member relationships are rendered even more transitory by the existence of intra-gang suspicions. Under these circumstances, it is hard to *conceive* of, much less observe, a continuing cohesive group. Even within gangs which have existed over several generations, the mobility factors mentioned above operate to reduce the stability of active membership, in spite of the fact that allegiance to a given group may persist for many years.

3. Group norms among gang members have received much attention in the literature, but few have been found which are distinguishable in kind from those of the social class from which gang members generally are drawn. Group *qua* group norms are relatively nonexistent in the gang world except as myths which are exploded upon test. For instance, it is often said that gang members are loyal, will not inform ("fink") on each other, and will come to each other's aid in time of threat, attack, or retaliation, yet most gang researchers report numerous occasions in which such behavior fails to materialize, or does so only among selected members. The one norm that does seem to be shared is that of acceptance of a wide variety of illegal acts. Again, however, this may be more class or subculture related than specifically gang related.

4. Role differentiation is difficult to observe in gangs. There are often official positions, such as president, vice-president, or war counselor, but the influence of the position incumbents is nebulous at best. Functional leadership related to different categories of activity is often present, but this leadership is unstable and tends to shift from one person to another during various phases of group development. A most illuminating experience in this regard is to question several members of a group about the respective roles which they expect others to assume during various anticipated future activities. Uniformity of expectation is *not* the standard finding of such an endeavor. The major agreement is on status, not role. In fact, the boys can seldom differentiate beyond the status dimension.

5. *Group names*—Gladiators, Vice Lords, Egyptian Kings—are assumed by many to indicate a common "we-feeling" among gang members. In fact, however, these names often change within a group and derive their greatest effect during conflict periods when cohesion is increased by external threat. Many gang names derive from street or neighborhood labels—Ochenta, Parks, White Fence—suggesting again an external rather than internal base for identification.

Thus, minimal group goals, membership instability, a paucity of unique group norms, little group role differentiation, and a lack of lasting identity with group names all militate against the formation of delinquent gangs based on internal sources of cohesion.

An exception is to be found among gangs with a long history, for gang tradition does seem to be a major internal source of cohesiveness. These traditions in Los Angeles extend over thirty or forty years. A boy growing up in the Clover, Hazard, or White Fence areas of East Los Angeles knows at an early age that gang membership is a highly salient opportunity. This perception is continually reinforced on the street, in school, and even in his home. In this sense, a boy living in such a neighborhood is initiated into the gang culture before he has an opportunity to make an independent decision.

In contrast to relatively weak internal sources, strong external sources of cohesion are everywhere apparent. Any informed layman can discourse on the perils of poverty, low educational performance, job skills, disrupted family relations, "social disability,"[14] and so on. It needs to be added only that these facts of urban life lead to withdrawal symptoms, as documented by Cohen and Hodges.[15] When a number of boys in a neighborhood withdraw from similar sets of environmental frustrations and interact with one another enough to recognize, and perhaps generate, common attitudes, the seeds of the group are sown. Added to threats of rival groups are the many ways in which society reinforces this tendency—police behavior, teacher reactions, lack of acceptance by adults on playgrounds and in local business establishments, etc. Adolescent behavior and adult and rival group reactions thus reinforce each other, and the range of alternatives open to these youngsters is decidedly restricted. The result is delinquent group cohesiveness, however tenuous.

The Delinquent Product

Thus far little reference has been made to the deviant behavior associated with the gang. The *delinquent product* of gang interaction is the second factor which distinguishes the juvenile gang from groups that have provided the bulk of social science knowledge of group behavior.

Society does not disapprove of gangs because they are groups, or because their membership is adolescent, or because they are urban, or because of their normal, urban, adolescent group behavior. Gangs share all of these attributes with many nondelinquent youth groups. In addition, many other youth groups originate as expressions of opposition to adult expectations concerning their behavior. However, while all the activities of these spontaneous adolescent groups may not be condoned by society, such groups are not likely to engage in behavior which will result in social rejection. Society disapproves of juvenile gangs specifically because of that small portion of member behavior labeled as delinquent. It is this delinquent product of the group that causes the reaction. Society knows this, its agents know it, and so do the boys.[16]

We have tried to indicate that gangs are distinguishable from most groups on the basis of (a) a disproportionate measure of external sources of cohesion and (b) a socially disapproved group "product." Gangs are not the only such groups in existence. Consider for example other extremist groups—motorcycle clubs, beatniks, the Black Muslims, the KKK, and some inmate cultures. In most of these cases, however, there are specifiable common goals for which the groups are originated. This and sometimes other internal sources of cohesion distinguish them from the gang. The closest parallels to the juvenile gang may in fact be inmate cultures and San Francisco's now defunct North Beach beatnik colony.[17]

Traditional Approaches to Cohesiveness

In relating gang cohesiveness to gang-connected delinquency, one must choose among available conceptions and measures of cohesiveness or create new ones. A review of the literature strongly suggests that one should create new measures of cohesiveness to fit this particular problem.

Cohesiveness, like patient care in medical sociology or morale in industrial psychology, proves on examination to be a complex concept. It has been used as independent variable,[18] dependent variable,[19] intervening variable,[20] and hypothetical construct.[21] It has been used as an experimental gimmick, induced so that relationships between other variables might be illuminated.[22]

Cohesiveness, nominally, has referred to mutual liking or acceptance,[23] attraction to group,[24] degree of shared norms or values,[25] and resistance to disruptive forces.[26] Operationally, it has been measured by coordination of efforts,[27] summated attractiveness scores,[28] reaction to threat,[29] choice of group over other alternatives,[30] ratio of in-group to out-group choices or contacts,[31] and so on.

So many dimensions of cohesiveness run through the literature that cohesiveness can hardly be considered a definitive concept. Resolution of this problem is perhaps best solved with reference to one's particular interests based on relevant theoretical concerns.

We have said that the delinquent product of the gang makes it a special case. Further, it is generally acknowledged that gang membership increases delinquency involvement. The question is, how much and why? The "why," we suggest, is in part a function of cohesiveness; the "how much" is ultimately an empirical question.

Why should high cohesiveness lead to high delinquency in the gang? It is not just the external sources of cohesiveness that bring this about; these have to do with gang formation before reinforcement. Most gang theorists presently concur that, if offenses are affected by gang membership, it is because the antecedent deviant values, the requisite skills, and the opportunities for misbehavior are learned and reinforced through association with other members. Status forces are also operative. We would add only that these processes can occur and persist because the external sources of cohesion continually throw gang members together, forcing the kinds of interaction which are preliminary to increased gang-related offenses. These interactions become secondary sources of cohesion in conjunction with offense behavior, each reinforcing the other as the members mingle and verbalize the deviance which labels them as different.

Some of the jargon, the "tough" talk, and the recounting of delinquent exploits engaged in by gang members probably serve the function of reinforcing the weak affiliative bonds within the group. Several writers have analyzed both individual and group offenses at critical points in gang development—points of low status and low cohesiveness—to indicate how these offenses revitalize failing group patterns.[32]

Thus a measure of cohesiveness which might relate most directly to gang delinquency must involve *member interaction*. It should not rely on members' verbal responses to an investigator, however, since those willing to respond are not likely to constitute a representative sample of the membership. Interviewing and questionnaire responses are of limited value for the task at hand.

Group *qua* group measures are also inappropriate for they reflect only *indirectly* a presumed summation of member interaction. This eliminates retaliations against rival groups as a measure, an infrequent occurrence in any case.

Index measures which are based on the attractiveness of gang participation as the numerator and alternatives as the denominator are suspect because the researcher cannot adequately assess these alternatives. We have attempted one such analysis, using average distance from member homes to evening meeting sites as representing a summation of barriers overcome to join in group activities. This measure yields findings which are highly gang-specific, rather than generalizable. In some groups, it is related to attendance figures, in others it is not. The variance seems more a function of core than of fringe members in the analysis of between-gang differences, and variance is far greater between gang clusters than within subgroups of the same cluster.[33] All in all, we see little advantage in continuing to use this approach.

A Suggested Approach

Another approach seems more promising. This method is not dependent upon member responses, presents fewer sampling problems, and is a direct measure of member interaction, our primary criterion. It requires the presence of an observer—in our case, a "detached worker."

For the past four years, the authors and their colleagues have been conducting studies of gang intervention practices employed by detached workers with Negro juvenile gangs in Los Angeles. As part of this project, we have received daily "Contact Reports" from the gang workers assigned to *four large Negro gang clusters* (involving sixteen separate gang groups). These Contact Reports give an account of all individuals seen by the workers in the course of each day. The report lists the names of the persons seen and indicates the site, duration, and mode of contact initiation in each case, as well as the content of the conversation between the worker and the person contacted. There is also an indication of the grouping of persons involved in each interaction situation. Thus, for any given gang member, it can be determined not only how often he has been seen by the worker during a specified time period, but also with which other members he is seen most frequently.

Approximately six hundred male and two hundred female gang members have been identified through these Contact Reports in combination with other data-collecting procedures. Most of these members have interacted with the detached workers numerous times.

Table 1 summarizes the intragroup companionship patterns for one gang over a six-month period and indicates how often each member contacted each of the other members in the presence of the worker. For example, member #l was seen most often with members #13, 15, and 22, and he was never seen in the company of fifteen of the thirty-two members contacted by the worker during this time period.

Using data such as those presented in the model in Table 1, we explored the ability of various combinations of the data to differentiate one group from another. The indices explored are summarized below, using the data in Table 1 for illustrative purposes. The first five indices are measures of subgroup or clique cohesiveness.

1. Number of Cliques. Any approach to analysis based on a factor analytic model can be used to reveal subgroupings among the members. For instance, if one applies the first steps of McQuitty's Elementary Linkage Analysis[34] to Table 1, two cliques emerge. The first involves members #1, 4, 6, 9, 13, 15, 17, 22, and 26 and the second involves members #5, 24, 25, 27, and 31. The relationships within each group are shown in Figure 1, following McQuitty's procedure.

In this illustration, we have *arbitrarily* limited potential clique members to those who have at least ten contacts with one other member. The arbitrariness introduced has no theoretical or statistical justification,

Figure 1

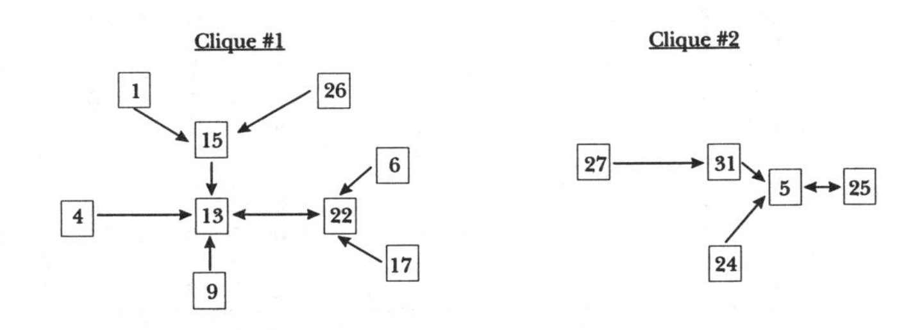

but this presents no problem so long as the index is used for *comparative* purposes, i.e., for comparing one group to another or comparing different time periods involving the same group.

One other cautionary note is required here. This analysis employs only those members contacted during the time period selected. In other situations, it might be preferable to include in the contact matrix all known gang members, whether contacted or not. This choice applies equally to the other indices cited below.

2. *Percentage of Members in Cliques*. This index consists of the number of clique members divided by the total membership (however defined—see previous paragraph). In the case of Table 1, the index yields a figure of .44 (14/32).

3. *Percentage of Clique Members with 50 per cent or More of Their Contacts within Their Own Cliques*. The 50 per cent figure is obviously an arbitrary choice. This provides a measure of clique cohesiveness rather than of overall gang cohesiveness, although the two obviously will be positively related. In our illustration, all fourteen clique members fall above the 50 per cent figure, ranging from 58 per cent for number 31 to 100 per cent for number 24.

4. *Average Within-clique Over All-contacts Ratio*. In this index, one determines, for each clique member, the ratio of his contacts within his clique to the sum of his contacts, then sums over all clique members and divides by the number of clique members. The index figure in our illustration is 77 per cent.

5. *Percentage of Clique Membership with Core Status*. Most gang workers make a gross distinction between two classes of gang membership: core and fringe. Using the worker's designation as the operational definition of core and fringe status, this index states the ratio of core to fringe members within identifiable cliques.

The first five possible indices of gang cohesiveness all deal with clique membership. The potential importance of such indices is that the clique members clearly constitute friendship groups within a larger and somewhat amorphous collection of individuals. From a practical viewpoint, the practitioner concerned with decreasing the cohesive bonds of a juvenile gang must understand the nature and intensity of these bonds where they are the strongest, that is, within natural friendship groups. A suitable index of the relative extent and intensity of clique relationships is the first order of business.

The remaining indices refer to the entire matrix of contacts representing an attempt to measure total gang cohesiveness rather than the tightness of selected subgroups.

6. *Number of Contacts Per Cell*. Referring again to Table 1, it can be seen that a total of 808 mutual contacts was made (1,616 contact notations in the two symmetric halves of the matrix). There are 32x31/2 or 496 possible combinations of individuals who might have made mutual contacts. This index divides the first figure by the second to arrive at an overall measure of the relative frequency of gang interaction (in the illustration, this figure is 1.63).

7. *Percentage of Empty Cells*. It is one of the interesting facets of our obtained matrices that a number of gang members are never seen together, with the

Table 1

	1	2	3	4	5	6	7	8	9	10	11	12	13	14	15	16	17	18	19	20	21	22	23	24	25	26	27	28	29	30	31	32	
1		2	0	12	1	5	0	0	4	0	0	0	17	0	18	1	2	0	5	0	4	17	5	0	1	9	0	0	5	0	0	0	108
2	2		0	3	0	2	0	0	2	0	0	2	4	2	2	0	2	0	2	0	6	4	2	0	0	2	0	0	2	0	0	0	39
3	0	0		0	0	0	0	0	0	0	0	0	0	0	0	0	0	0	0	1	0	0	0	0	0	0	0	0	0	0	0	0	1
4	12	3	0		1	9	3	0	11	1	0	0	18	0	11	1	7	0	4	0	2	16	6	0	1	7	1	0	0	0	0	0	114
5	1	0	0	1		0	1	0	0	0	0	0	3	0	1	5	0	0	0	0	0	1	0	14	21	1	1	0	5	0	10	1	66
6	5	2	0	9	0		0	0	6	2	0	0	7	0	7	0	4	0	4	0	2	11	6	0	0	5	0	0	4	0	0	0	74
7	0	0	0	3	1	0		0	0	0	0	0	0	0	0	0	3	0	0	0	0	0	0	0	0	0	0	0	0	0	3	0	10
8	0	0	0	0	0	0	0		1	0	0	0	2	0	2	0	0	0	0	0	0	1	0	0	0	0	0	0	1	0	0	0	7
9	4	2	0	11	0	6	0	1		1	0	0	18	0	14	0	3	0	6	0	2	15	5	0	0	9	0	0	5	0	0	0	102
10	0	0	0	1	0	2	0	0	1		0	0	2	0	0	0	1	0	1	0	0	0	0	0	0	0	0	0	0	0	0	0	8
11	0	0	0	0	0	0	0	0	0	0		0	1	0	1	0	0	0	0	0	0	1	0	0	0	0	0	0	0	0	0	0	3
12	0	2	0	0	0	0	0	0	0	0	0		3	2	0	0	0	0	0	0	2	2	0	0	0	0	0	0	0	0	0	0	11
13	17	4	0	18	3	7	0	2	18	2	1	3		2	37	1	5	0	5	0	6	40	6	0	1	11	1	0	5	0	4	3	202
14	0	2	0	0	0	0	0	0	0	0	0	2	2		0	0	0	0	0	0	2	2	0	0	0	0	0	0	0	0	0	0	10
15	18	2	0	11	1	7	0	2	14	0	1	0	37	0		1	3	0	5	0	4	34	5	0	0	12	1	0	4	0	0	0	162
16	1	0	0	1	5	0	0	0	0	0	0	0	1	0	1		0	0	0	1	0	1	0	0	2	1	0	0	0	0	3	6	23
17	2	2	0	7	0	4	3	0	3	1	0	0	5	0	3	0		0	3	0	2	10	2	0	0	3	0	0	2	0	5	0	57
18	0	0	0	0	0	0	0	0	0	0	0	0	0	0	0	0	0		1	0	0	0	0	0	0	0	0	0	0	0	0	0	1
19	5	2	0	4	0	4	0	0	6	1	0	0	5	0	5	0	3	1		0	2	6	4	0	0	5	0	0	4	0	0	0	57
20	0	0	1	0	0	0	0	0	0	0	0	0	0	0	0	1	0	0	0		0	0	0	0	0	0	0	0	0	0	1	0	3
21	4	6	0	2	0	2	0	0	2	0	0	2	6	2	4	0	2	0	2	0		4	2	0	0	2	0	0	2	0	0	0	44
22	17	4	0	16	1	11	0	1	15	0	1	2	40	2	34	1	10	0	6	0	4		6	0	1	11	1	0	5	0	0	0	189
23	5	2	0	6	0	6	0	0	5	0	0	0	6	0	5	0	2	0	4	0	2	6		0	0	5	0	0	4	0	0	0	58
24	0	0	0	0	14	0	0	0	0	0	0	0	0	0	0	0	0	0	0	0	0	0	0		2	0	0	0	0	0	0	0	16
25	1	0	0	1	21	0	0	0	0	0	0	0	1	0	0	2	0	0	0	0	0	1	0	2		1	0	0	0	0	3	0	33
26	9	2	0	7	1	5	0	0	9	0	0	0	11	0	12	1	3	0	5	0	2	11	5	0	1		0	0	4	0	0	0	88
27	0	0	0	1	1	0	0	0	0	0	0	0	1	0	1	0	0	0	0	0	0	1	0	0	0	0		1	0	0	13	0	19
28	0	0	0	0	0	0	0	0	0	0	0	0	0	0	0	0	0	0	0	0	0	0	0	0	0	0	1		0	0	0	0	1
29	5	2	0	0	5	4	0	1	5	0	0	0	5	0	4	0	2	0	4	0	2	5	4	0	0	4	0	0		0	0	0	52
30	0	0	0	0	0	0	0	0	0	0	0	0	0	0	0	0	0	0	0	0	0	0	0	0	0	0	0	0	0		1	0	1
31	0	0	0	0	10	0	3	0	0	0	0	0	4	0	0	3	5	0	0	1	0	0	0	0	3	0	13	0	0	1		2	45
32	0	0	0	0	1	0	0	0	0	0	0	0	3	0	0	6	0	0	0	0	0	0	0	0	0	0	0	0	0	0	2		12
																																	1616

result that many of the matrix cells are empty. Much of this lack of contact is due to age differentials among the members. Ages range from twelve to the early twenties and, as with all adolescents, friendship patterns are strongly related to the age dimension. Younger boys are seldom seen in the company of older boys within the gang. Another contributing factor is the inclusion of many fringe members, boys who have fewer contacts "across the board." This index provides a measure of these factors as they and others affect behavioral interactions. In the illustration, 68 per cent of the matrix cells are empty, indicating no observed contact between the individuals concerned.

8. *Percentage of Single-contact Cells out of All Contact Cells*. Given the relatively high index figures resulting from index #7 (percentage of empty cells), we thought that we should obtain a similar measure among those boys who *were* in contact with each other. This index is derived by dividing the number of cells with only one entry by all cells containing one or more entries. In Table 1, the result is 78/322 or 24 percent.

9. *Percentage of Empty and Single Cells*. This is a combination of the numerators of the 7th and 8th indices, using the total number of cells as the denominator. For our example, the index percentage is 75 per cent.

Results

No doubt other combinations may occur to the reader, but the foregoing are sufficient to illustrate the general approach. We have been unashamedly exploratory in the absence of consistent theoretical guidelines in the literature on group cohesiveness. We had hoped that some of the above indices, along with meeting attendance and average residential "spread," as mentioned earlier, might be differentially related to the current status of the four gang clusters involved in our Los Angeles study. From many sources we know that gang Clusters A and B have continued the gang pattern far longer than have Clusters C and D. Further, we know from structural premises that cohesiveness declines with age beyond a certain point. In comparing the indices of cohesiveness taken from the workers' Contact Reports, we have found the following (see Table 2).

Table 2

Cohesiveness Measures in Four Gang Clusters

	Higher Delinquency Clusters		Lower Delinquency Clusters	
	A	B	C	D
a. Clique members/all members	.42	.43	.16	.15
b. Mutual contacts /n(n - 1)	.81	.72	.20	.32
c. Single contacts/all contact	.54	.35	.73	.77
d. In-clique contacts/all clique contacts	.82	.73	.47	.40

1. The number of identifiable sub cliques within a cluster seems unrelated to overall cluster patterns, but the proportion of boys identifiable as clique members *is* related. These proportions in Clusters A, B, C, and D are .42, .43, .16, and .15 respectively. Remember, throughout these items, that Clusters C and D are the ones with lower delinquency involvement.

2. The index based on the number of mutual contacts between members divided by the number of boys contacted, squared (actually n x n —1), clearly differentiates between clusters. In the same order as above, the index figures are .81, .72, .20, and .32.

3. Similarly, the number of single mutual contact situations (two boys see each other just once during a standard period of time) over the number of all mutual contact situations yields indices of .54 for Cluster A., .35 for B, .73 for C, and .77 for D.

4. Among clique members, the proportion of in-clique contacts to all clique member contacts is related in a fashion similar to the above. For Clusters A, B, C, and D, the figures are .82, .73, .47, and .40.

5. The remaining indices failed to differentiate between the four groups.

That the indices listed refer to more than differences between clusters is revealed by a pilot analysis carried out on Cluster A. The older and younger members were compared on two indices over three consecutive six-month periods, with the results shown in Table 3.

Table 3

Cohesiveness Index Changes Among Older and Younger Members of Cluster A

Index	Age Group	July-Dec. '63	Jan.-June '64	July-Dec. '64
# Contacts/n(n-1)	Older	.25	.25	.16
	Younger	.21	.25	.29
# Non-single contacts/Total contacts	Older	.65	.54	.51
	Younger	.60	.57	.70

Preliminary data indicate that the increase in cohesiveness among the younger boys and the decrease among the older boys parallels similar trends in recorded offense rates. In any case, it is clear from both tables that we are employing indices of some sensitivity. It remains to be shown just how directly they are related to gang offense patterns, but our hopes are high.

The development of these indices of cohesiveness is an effort to assess this group variable as it is found in delinquent gangs. Our concurrent development of offense measures endeavors to ascertain the seriousness of the delinquent product.[35] The interaction patterns of these measures of gang cohesiveness and juvenile offenses, we believe, represent a sorely needed investigation in our understanding of group delinquency phenomena. If our investigation adds to the placement of these phenomena within the larger context of group process and outcome relationships, we shall be doubly rewarded.[36]

Notes

1. Robert A. Gordon, "Social Level, Social Disability, and Gang Interaction," unpublished paper quoted in James F. Short, Jr. and Fred L. Strodtbeck, *Group Process and Gang Delinquency* (Chicago, (University of Chicago Press, 1965), pp. 272-73.
2. Muzafer and Carolyn Sherif, *Reference Groups* (New York: Harper and Row, 1964), pp. 48-49.
3. Albert J. and Bernice E. Lott, "Group Cohesiveness as Interpersonal Attraction: A review of relationships with antecedent and consequent variables," *Psychological Bulletin*, October 1965, pp. 259-309.
4. This point—the interaction of normal group processes with delinquency involvement and the consequent impact on group structure—is overlooked by the Sherifs in their argument, although they quote Polsky on just this issue; see Sherif and Sherif, op. cit. supra note 2, p. 129.
5. Frederic M. Thrasher, *The Gang: A Study of 1,313 Gangs in Chicago*, abridged and with a new introduction by James F. Short, Jr. (Chicago: University of Chicago Press, 1963), particularly chs. 4 and 14.
6. Lewis Yablonsky, *The Violent Gang* (New York: MacMillan, 1962), particularly ch. 13. Yablonsky's seemingly overstated interest in violence, paranoia, and sociopathic characteristics should not blind one to his legitimate contribution to the placement of gangs in the group-structure tradition.
7. Richard A. Cloward and Lloyd E. Ohlin, *Delinquency and Opportunity: A Theory of Delinquent Gangs* (Glencoe: The Free Press, 1960).
8. Irving Spergel, *Racketville, Slumtown, Haulburg: An Exploratory Study of Delinquent Subcultures* (Chicago: University of Chicago Press, 1964).
9. Short and Strodtbeck, *op. cit. supra* note 1, ch. 4.
10. Saul Bernstein, Youth on the Streets: Work with Alienated Youth Groups (New York: Association Press, 1964), pp. 98-100.
11. Albert K. Cohen, *Delinquent Boys* (Glencoe: The Free Press, 1955).
12. J. Milton Yinger, "Contraculture and Subculture," *American Sociological Review*, October 1960, pp. 625-35.
13. Nathan L. Gerrard, "The Core Member of the Gang," *British Journal of Criminology*, April 1964, pp. 361-71.
14. Short and Strodtbeck. *op. cit. supra* note 1, ch. 10.
15. Albert K. Cohen and Harold M. Hodges, "Lower-Blue-Collar-Class Characteristics," *Social Problems*, Spring 1963, pp. 303-34.
16. Parenthetically, it is often the failure to separate specific delinquent acts from the offender which makes for the inefficiency of many of our delinquency prevention programs. Perhaps due to stimulus generalization, it is the whole boy and the whole group which is condemned, rather than their delinquent product alone.
17. Francis J. Rigney and L. Douglas Smith, *The Real Bohemia: A Sociological and Psychological Study of the "Beats"* (New York: Basic Books, 1961).
18. J. Downing, "Cohesiveness, Perception, and Values," *Human Relations*, May 1958, pp. 157-66; A. Pepitone and G. Reichling, "Group Cohesiveness and the Expression of Hostility," *Human Relations*, August 1955, pp. 327-37; S. Schacter, N. Ellertson, Dorothy McBride, and Doris Gregory, "An Experimental Study of Cohesiveness and Productivity," *Human Relations*, August 1951, pp. 229-38.
19. B. N. Phillips and L. A. D'Amico, "Effects of Cooperation and Competition on the Cohesiveness of Small Face-to-Face Groups," *Journal of Educational Psychology*, February 1956, pp. 65-70; H. P. Shelley, "Focused Leadership and Cohesiveness in Small Groups," Sociometry, June 1960, pp. 209-16; J. W. Thibaut, "An Experimental Study of the Cohesiveness of Underprivileged Groups,"Human Relations, August 1950, pp. 251-78.
20. R. S. Albert, "Comments on the Scientific Function of the Concept of Cohesiveness," *American Journal of Sociology*, November 1953, pp. 231-34.
21. A. J. Lott and Bernice E. Lott, "Group Cohesiveness, Communication Level and Conformity," *Journal of Abnormal and Social Psychology*, March 1961, pp. 408-12.
22. L. Berkowitz, "Group Standards, Cohesiveness, and Productivity," *Human Relations*, November 1954, pp. 509-19.
23. B. N. Phillips and L. A. D'Amico, *op. cit. supra* note 19; Bernice Eisman, "Some Operational Measures of Cohesiveness and Their Interrelations," *Human Relations*, May 1959, pp. 183-89; Warren O. Hagstrom and Hanan C. Selvin, "Two Dimensions of Cohesiveness in Small Groups," *Sociometry*, March 1965, p. 1, 30-43.
24. Leon Festinger, "Group Attraction and Membership," *Group Dynamics, Research and Theory*, Dorwin Cartwright and Alvin Zander, eds. (Evanston, Ill.: Row, Peterson Company, 1953), pp. 92-101; Annie Van Bergen and J. Koskebakker, "Group Cohesiveness in Laboratory Experiments," *Acta Psychologica* (2), 1959, pp. 81-98; Hagstrom and Selvin, *op. cit. supra* note 23; Eisman, op. cit. supra note 23.
25. Eisman, *op. cit. supra* note 23; Hagstrom and Selvin, op. cit. supra note 23.
26. Neal Gross and William E. Martin, "On Group Cohesiveness," *American Journal Sociology*, May 1952, pp. 546-54.
27. Cartwright and Zander, *op. cit. supra* note 24, p. 76.
28. Lott and Lott, *op. cit. supra* note 21.
29. A. Pepitone and R. Kleiner, "The Effects of Threat and Frustration on Group Cohesiveness," *Journal of Abnormal and Social Psychology*, March 1957, pp. 192-99.
30. Sherif and Sherif, *op. cit. supra* note 2, p. 242.
31. Gross and Martin, *op. cit. supra* note 26; Sherif and Sherif, op. cit. supra note 2; Leon Festinger, Stanley Schacter, and Kurt Back, *Social Pressures in Informal Groups* (New York: Harper, 1950); P. R. Hofstaetter, "A Note on Group Cohesiveness," *American Journal of Sociology*, September 1952, pp. 198-200.
32. Short and Strodtbeck, *op. cit. supra* note 1, especially chs. 8 and 9; also see Leon Jansyn, *Solidarity and Delinquency in a Street Corner Group*, unpublished Master's thesis, University of Chicago, 1960.
33. A gang "cluster" refers to a pattern of inter-gang affiliations commonly observed among traditional gangs in Los Angeles. Typically, a cluster consists of three or four age-graded male subgroups plus a girls' group. Each subgroup maintains its own self identity, yet clearly affiliates with the overall cluster and its "generic" name. See Malcolm W. Klein, "Internal Structures and Age Distributions in Four Delinquent Negro Gangs," paper presented at the annual meetings of the California State Psychological Association, Los Angeles, 1964 (Youth Studies Center, University of Southern California, mimeo).
34. Louis L. McQuitty, "Elementary Linkage Analysis for Isolating Orthogonal and Oblique Types and Typal Relevancies," *Educational and Psychological Measurement*, Summer 1957, pp. 207-29.

35. Richard I. Martin and Malcolm W. Klein, "A Comparative Analysis of Four Measures of Delinquency Seriousness," paper presented at the annual meeting of the Pacific Sociological Association, Salt Lake City, April 1965 (Youth Studies Center, University of Southern California, mimeo).
36. This paper will appear in *Gang Delinquency and Delinquent Subcultures*, James F. Short, Jr., ed. (New York: Harper and Row, 1967). An earlier version of this paper was presented at the annual meeting of the Pacific Sociological Association in Vancouver, B. C., April 1966. It reports one aspect of a larger project funded by the Ford Foundation and carried out in collaboration with the Los Angeles County Probation Department. The authors are grateful to LaMar Empey, Solomon Kobrin, Barbara Myerhoff, and George Newland for their constructive criticisms of an earlier draft.✦

20

The Response of Gang Leaders to Status Threats: An Observation on Group Process and Delinquent Behavior[1]

Fred L. Strodtbeck and James F. Short, Jr.

As Klein and Crawford's article reveals, out-group aggression builds cohesion within the gang. Building on this insight, Short and Strodtbeck examine the ways in which gang leaders initiate fights with outside groups such as other gangs in order to reduce threats to their status within the gang. Because fighting skills and delinquency are among the few available means for gang youth to gain status among their peers, out-group aggression heightens group solidarity and provides gang leaders with the means to maintain their status in the group.

Abstract

For the explanation of aggressive episodes, group process is seen as an important adjunct both to subcultural and individualistic theories of gang delinquency. Gang leaders are observed to precipitate acts of aggression that are directed outside their group when their status is threatened. This is believed to arise because the leaders' control of internal resources is limited. It also requires the support of aggressive norms within the group for such behavior is not appropriate in a group with "retreatist" norms. The interpretation is based upon instances drawn from observations of a dozen Chicago gangs over a three-year period.

This paper describes a particular type of delinquent episode which arises when a gang leader acts to reduce threats to his status by instigating out-group aggression. Our view is that leaders resort to this action because of the limited resources they have for internal control of their group—particularly when their status is attacked.

Unlike other syndrome explanations, such as that of Bloch and Flynn[2] who related delinquency to particular types of parent-child relations, or the various theories that are concerned with the emergence of delinquent subcultures,[3] this paper attempts to provide a clearer understanding of the precipitation of episodes within "delinquent gangs." The focus is on the ongoing relations of group members rather than on the boys' family backgrounds or the position of lower-class adolescents within the social structure. The argument is not that family background and social class position are unimportant but, rather, that these factors cannot explain the emergence of particular instances of aggressive delinquency from the on-going, largely nondelinquent, behavior of gang boys.

We decided to develop this paper with liberal use of illustrative instances in order to correct the impression that would exist if William Foote Whyte's superb description of Doc and the Nortons in *Street Corner Society*[4] were permitted to carry the full burden of our need for knowledge about subinstitutionalized elementary social behavior of corner groups.[5] It is almost necessary to protest that Whyte's corner boys were not delinquents, they were older, and they were much more stable as a group than are adolescent delinquent gangs. When one turns to the narrative materials of the delinquency literature, it comes as a surprise to find how little illumination of group process they provide. For any but the most broadly formulated hypotheses concerning the nature of group life among the boys studied, we find these materials inadequate. By contrast, the strength of *Street Corner Society* lies exactly in the fact that the descriptions are given in such a way that the group process is explicit.

One notable instance of experimental research specifically related to delinquency is the investigation of Lippitt, Polansky, Redl, and Rosen in which deliberately frustrated camp boys followed in delinquent activity an impulsive boy who was ordinarily given low rank in the group.[6] These authors did not intend to suggest, however, that the mechanism revealed by this ingenious experiment is the typical process for delinquent groups in their natural setting. Similarly, Polsky and Kohn's description of the process by which "delinquency in its collective form" emerges "out of the interaction of a group of youngsters" within a juvenile correctional institution[7] is not meant to serve as the model for collective delinquency outside of a "total institutional" context.[8]

The closest parallel to our concern with group factors in delinquency outside the context of a camp or treatment institution is Jansyn's study of the social system of a gang with whom he worked as a "detached worker."[9] He found that, for this group of boys, delinquent behavior, on both an individual and a group basis, served to increase the solidarity of the group, and that group leadership and membership varied according to specific group goals being implemented. Fur-

Reprinted by permission from Fred L. Strodtbeck and James F. Short, Jr., "The response of gang leaders to status threats," *American Journal of Sociology*, 1983, 68:571-578.

ther, the boys' perceptions of who was and who was not a member of the group, how large the group was, the importance and even the existence of a conception of "turf" or "territory" were responsive to the situation in which the group found itself.

The shifting character of the group structure that Jansyn describes for the white gang he worked with is present in the white gangs contacted in the present project, and in the Negro gangs as well. Central to our present argument is the proposition that flux in membership and amorphous group boundaries reduces the latitude the leader has in dealing with status threats. But, as the case material illustrates, the disposition of the threatened leader to use out-group aggression to deal with the threat involves further premises about group norms and the required fluctuation in role behavior by the leader. Eight cases, followed by brief interpretative sections, will be presented.

Detached Worker Case Reports

For a three-year period of the research some eight to ten detached workers[10] assigned by the YMCA to highly delinquent gangs were interviewed on a weekly basis. These interviews were reviewed by the research staff and representative selections have been made. In proceeding with the selection, we reasoned somewhat as one would in the review of cases in law. The principle is illustrated as it emerges in different form over the range of specific fact situations that might be encountered with street-corner groups.

Case 1. Duke is the leader of the King Rattlers, a conflict-oriented group of approximately fifty Negro boys, aged fifteen to nineteen who live on the periphery of a commercial area in the inner city. Duke is a good fighter, having risen to his leadership status in the group by being quick and effective with his fists while, at the same time, playing it very cool. Duke does not get caught. The detached worker reaffirmed Duke's status by working through him and was quickly successful in suppressing intergang fighting. Duke's leadership style capitalizes on his coolness and on his ability to both negotiate in intergang councils and to control his boys.

Despite his coolness, Duke did become implicated in a shooting incident that involved other members of the Rattlers and was sent to jail. The boys eventually "beat the rap," but they were held in detention for two and one-half months. While Duke and the others were absent from "the scene," new officers were "elected" by the worker and the group. It was understood that when Duke returned he would be president again. Upon Duke's return, despite the celebrations attending it, no formal recognition was made of his leadership. It was shortly after this that the detached worker with the Rattlers made the following observations in a weekly interview:

> A: . . . Duke is acting very unusual. It's not the same Duke.
>
> Q: What's happened?
>
> A: I don't know. I feel maybe it's because he's been in jail and he's trying to release a lot of energy. Maybe after a while, he'll settle down. As of yet he hasn't settled down. He is one of the real instigators in fightin'. They say, "You know, Duke is acting like us now." The boys even notice the difference in him. It isn't just me.
>
> Q: Do they appreciate this or don't they like this?
>
> A: They appreciate it because now they have no more problems. All of them like to fight. If Duke chips in, that's better yet. But they notice the change in him. I keep tellin' Duke, "Be careful, boy, you'll be right back in jail."

The worker then described Duke's behavior at a basketball game which had been scheduled with the Jr. Lords.

> A: Duke was calling them "mother fucker," and "The Lords ain't shit." Duke walked up to them—Duke doin' all the talkin'—instigator. Bill next to him and Harry listening. Everybody was listening but Duke, and I was having a problem trying to get Duke down there so he could get himself dressed and leave. Duke walked up and said, "[Y]ou ain't shit. The Jr. Lords ain't shit. Are you a Jr.?" The boys said, "No." And he said, "A fuckin' old Lord, I'm King Rattler." Duke walked all through all of them, "You ain't shit," trying to get a fight. "Come on, Duke," I said, trying to push him down the stairs. But each time he'd get away and go over there, "You Lords ain't shit . . . we're Rattlers. We're Eastside Rattlers."
>
> Q: Was he drunk?
>
> A: No, he's sober but he's changed. Big change. Bill was watchin' him and goin' along. I told Harry to grab him and told Henry to get Duke and take him. I had to grab him—he wouldn't listen. The rest of the Rattlers wanted to fight too. So I had to take Duke downstairs, and while they were getting their clothes on we had a problem with hats. They wanted the new hats of the other team which they could see on the rack. Duke owns a brown hat, but he had worn a gray one over there. By mistake, I gave him a brown hat which belonged to the Lords. When I saw what had happened, I tried to get it back but no one knew where it was.

The prognosis one would make from the hat and fighting incidents would be one of a growing gap between the detached worker and Duke. Such a gap did not, in fact, materialize. Just a week later, the worker took Duke to a large department store where he secured a job as messenger-boy. Duke's behavior was exemplary. His "strange behavior" did not recur, and he resumed a steadying, essentially non-aggressive and non-delinquent influence on the group.

It is to be noted in the detached worker's report quoted above that the boys approved of Duke's aggressiveness, were willing to fight, and, against the express desires of the detached worker, were willing to help Duke conceal the stolen hat. After this brief period of catering to the most broadly held norms of aggressive behavior, Duke resumed the "cool" image that had distinguished him from the group he led. The Duke incident occurred despite the conscious intention of the detached worker to support Duke's leadership.

It is our interpretation that the tough, highly aggressive, behavior was adopted by Duke to clarify the uncertain leadership situation that had arisen as a result of his detention. In the next case, the status threat arises from a detached worker's failure to understand the previously existing leadership structure.

Case 2. A worker who had been successful in reaching, and in reducing the delinquency of a leadership clique known as the "Big Five," suddenly found that a group of his boys were following another boy in predatory and assaultive delinquency. It developed that this new leader had been in jail during the several months that the worker had been with the group. The worker was only dimly aware of the boy's existence and not at all aware of his former leadership position. Upon release from jail, this boy gathered "lower-echelon" boys about himself and led them in a variety of aggressive delinquencies. This situation was well under way before it was understood by the worker but, when he did turn his attention to the errant group, he brought the aggressive behavior of the subgroup under relative control by "capturing" their leader.

Case 3. A contrasting case involves the return from Army duty of a leader of the Midget Lords, a segment of a large conflict oriented gang complex known as the "Nation of Lords." It resulted in what we call "The Great Train Robbery."

Johnnie was by far the strongest leader of the Lords. When a new worker was assigned to the group, Johnnie was in the service. The worker was told about Johnnie, however, and upon the latter's return to the group late in the summer of 1960, he was introduced to the worker. The worker was not able to "capture" Johnnie immediately and, in fact, found that he was somewhat uncomfortable with Johnnie and the clique of boys who were most directly involved with him. The worker continued, therefore, to spend the majority of his time with the less delinquent boys who were not Johnnie's immediate followers.

One evening Johnnie and his clique asked the worker to take them "out South" to a party. Figuring that this would at least remove a troublesome element from the area, the worker agreed to the request. Rather than staying with the boys, however, the worker returned to the area where he contacted other members of the Midgets.

On their own return trip, Johnnie and his boys made a spur-of-the-moment decision to hold up the car on the elevated train on which they were traveling. They beat one man and took cash from passengers.

If this dramatic demonstration of the toughness and daring had been successful, it would have reaffirmed Johnnie's leadership role in his clique, solidified the subgroup, and, in all probability, have drawn the worker into closer work with Johnnie's clique. The interpretation of this incident in terms of status implications is by no means unequivocal but, since the robbery cannot be understood as the actions of boys rationally oriented toward crime as a way of life, the need for an alternative interpretation is clear.

Case 4. The protagonist, Lawrence, was an influential member of a group for which there was no single and most powerful leader. To maintain his position of influence, Lawrence was required to play a central role in many of the varied activities of the group. The incident in question turned around a "quarter party," which Lawrence was "putting down," primarily out of his embarrassment over having no money. Several of the other chiefs were employed at this time, but Lawrence was not. He deprecated the party and urged the Chiefs to join him in "turning it out," that is, in breaking it up.[11] When the other Chiefs refused to go along with the suggestion despite his urging, Lawrence did not pursue the issue further. Instead, he borrowed money from the worker because, we believe, his position in the group made asking for money from another group member untenable.

During the course of the evening, Big Daddy, another member of the Chiefs, started after a member of the Cobras with a hammer. The detached worker grabbed Lawrence and, in recognition of his status and ability to control the other boys, said, "Look. I don't want no crap. What about you?" Lawrence replied, "Don't worry, ain't gonna be no crap," and proceeded to help the worker bring about order.

If we view Lawrence's threat to turn the party out as a way of "saving face" when his financial dilemma further complicated the status ambiguity attendant upon the entry of a new worker into the group, then the recognition of status ambiguity by the loan and the request from the worker for help may be regarded as having prevented the delinquency.

The next two cases are parallel. They both involve a detached worker's problem in dealing with a highly aggressive boy who had an established role of instigating delinquent episodes.

Case 5. In the first case, the boy, Commando, was known for his daring and for being in the middle of whatever was happening. When the Lords came together as a fighting group, under pressure from a rival gang who were "wolf-packing" in the area, Commando became one of the boys who was most difficult to control. He instigated trouble in a way that captured attention, and he set a style of violence by sometimes carrying a shotgun.

The worker decided to "put down" Commando in front of the rest of the group by telling him that he really was not tough or brave. He concluded by saying, "You ain't nothin'." Commando reacted by being even more reckless in his actions, particularly when members of the rival group were on the scene. He continued to demonstrate to the group that he was not chicken and that he *was* somebody until the worker ceased his public ridicule.

When the worker shifted to a nurturant relation and impressed Commando privately with his responsibility, as a leader, for curbing conflict, the boy became less aggressive and aided the worker. The worker still feels, however, that in a conflict situation, without a worker present, Commando would find it difficult not to "sell wolf tickets" (i.e., challenge) to rival gang members and instigate conflict. Commando appears not to be motivated to convert status won by aggression to a more stabilized rank in the group.

Case 6. A comparable case involved Bill, a tough and influential member of the Pizza Grill Boys. These boys lived in an area where organized crime was firmly entrenched. The boys stole automobiles, auto parts, and many other articles, hot-rodded their cars, and drank excessively. They were not a fighting gang. The worker with these boys had been an intercollegiate boxing champion and had engaged in a brief professional career as a boxer. He taught Bill and others in the group a great deal about boxing. Bill proceeded to employ these skills in beating up on boys in the area. The worker strongly and publicly reprimanded Bill for doing this, indicating that this behavior was stupid and cowardly rather than brave, tough, and skilled. Bill's subsequent action was to drink excessively and then proceed to get into fights that demonstrated how tough he was.

After winning a fight, Bill did not have the skills to convert the advantage to generalized rank. Cases 5 and 6 both involve inflexibility in role shift after aggression thus suggesting that flexibility is required if a boy is to cope successfully with leadership demands of groups such as these.

The next case is interesting from two perspectives. First, it indicates that the outcome of competitive sports activities, even when supervised, may release a need for status equilibration that results in overt aggression. Second, it provides a commentary on what the participants understand concerning their own motivation.

Case 7. Gary, one of the three top "influentials" among the King Rattlers, was captain of one of the two pool teams from this gang. The other Rattler team won their division play while Gary's team placed second in their division. In the championship playoffs, Gary's team was eliminated in the first round of play, while the other group, which had advanced to the semifinals, wound up in fourth place. Feelings ran high at the playoffs, and individual and team winners received a great deal of praise.

Gary and his team watched first the finals, then the presentation of the individual trophies to the other team from their gang. The trophies, which were proudly displayed upon the return to the Rattler area, re-emphasized Gary's failure in this formal leadership role. The timing was particularly bad because Gary had emerged as one of two major influentials among the Rattlers since the employment and marriage of Duke, the former leader, who was at this time spending less time with the group. But Gary himself had recently obtained a job and had not spent much time on the streets. Gary had been paid on the day of the tournament and, at the tournament, he had the substantial sum of between $50 and $80 in his pocket. For this reason, the gang, which placed a high value on strong-arming, was not clear whether Gary would continue to lead them in this activity.

Although we should like to have more detailed information, we know only that, after the tournament sessions were over, Gary and two members of his team strong-armed a man. The team members held the man and Gary hit him; the take was $18. Gary's subsequent comment to the worker was, "Shit, I wasted my time." This was as far as he could go to explain why he had strong-armed with money in his pocket. He told the worker simply, "... saw him walking down the street and just got him—for no reason, just got him."

The salient elements in Gary's case are these: (a) he was adept at strong-arming, (b) strong-arming was status-conferring in the group, and (c) Gary played a crucial role in the incident in question. While these facts are not sufficient to establish the relationship, they are all consistent with the interpretation that Gary's action was specifically related to his need for status reaffirmation following the perceived loss in connection with the pool tournament.

Case 8. On a note of caution, we shall close with an observation concerning a drug-using group of white boys who resisted taking up an invitation to aggressive behavior under highly provocative circumstances. The group was oriented primarily around the use of drugs in pill form, though the boys smoked marijuana heavily, drank excessively, and, when they could afford it (and it was available), used heroin. According to the worker, these boys "looked upon fighting as being 'square'."

The incident to be reported concerns the summer, 1961, "wade-ins" by Negroes and whites at "white" beaches on Chicago's South Side in protest against the segregation of beach facilities. When the possibility of the "wade-ins" became known to a large white gang from the same area as the drug-users, they immediately took up a battle cry and proceeded to plan the co-ordination of groups in opposition to the "wade-ins." Excitement ran high and they admonished the drug-using group to lend support to the cause. The worker reported that the drug using group "expressed considerable racial hostility" and "talked about getting into the coming battle," but when the "wade-ins" occurred they chose to separate themselves from the milling hostile crowd that gathered on the beach. Instead, they proceeded to get "high" on pills. While six of them did go to the beach, they chose to sit beneath a tree—at the far end of the beach, away from the "wade-in"—and play cards. In the words of the worker, "they could hardly have been less concerned with who was going to occupy the beach."

These boys, in contrast to previous cases cited, had been urged to fight, with clear insinuations that anyone who did not was "chicken," yet they chose to turn away. Their reaction to this threat was withdrawal from the larger group and participation in activity expressive of the norms which distinguished them from the conflict oriented boys, namely, drug use. This instance does not involve any separate threat to the leader of this group, for all members seemed to agree easily on the course of action. However, this response, in this situation, suggests that, in groups in which the leader's prestige is bound up in competence at enjoying esoteric "kicks," it may well be doubted that status threat would result in aggressive behavior.

From the practical standpoint of understanding of gang functioning, this reservation may not be important for it is the observation of our group and other workers that individual boys who adopt strong retreatist adaptations (such as drug use) do not continue as prominent members of large gangs. They drift off into small cliques, and in many cases appear to behave as an isolated individual who moves (without developing strong interpersonal ties) into loci of heightened collective emphasis on retreatist norms. From the theoretical standpoint, this instance suggests a possible dependence between group norms and modes of status reaffirmation and, at the same time, reminds us that there was a high evaluation of aggression in the functioning of the groups from which the other examples were collected. By an extension of this thinking, if one doubts that aggression would confer higher status in retreatist groups, it is also plausible to doubt that aggression would confer higher status in middle-class adolescent groups—though for different reasons.

Targets and Functions of Aggression

Miller and his associates suggest in "Aggression in a Boys' Street-Corner Group" that verbal aggression "was an essential element of behavioral mechanisms which operated to delineate standards of personal worth, to facilitate effective collective functioning, to maintain relations of reciprocity and equality, to define attitudes toward those outside the group and their values, to indicate the *limits* of acceptable behavior and to provide effective sanctions against deviation from group-supported standards."[12] For our groups, also, the level of intragroup aggression in such forms as "body-punching" and "signifying" is high but intragroup dominance-seeking aggressive behavior by gang members, including acknowledged leaders, is not supported by group norms and is rarely resorted to by gang leaders.

Leaders we have observed are cautious not to exercise their leadership arbitrarily, and often overtly disavow that they lead the gangs. The percentage of total activities that are formally organized is low, and leaders are, in general, very careful to obtain clearance from other high-status group members before staking their prestige on a given course of action. We do not, in many cases, know how the original hierarchy of status was established, but clearly it is not maintained by aggressive dominance-seeking by leaders.[13] Except when other boys in the gang directly challenge their status, leaders of even the toughest fighting gangs do not engage in dominating, aggressive interpersonal relationships within the gang. Among conflict gangs, the leaders are known to have the capacity to function aggressively against other members when necessary to maintain their dominance, but the overwhelming preponderance of their actions are co-ordinating and nurturant.

Discussion

In Cases 5 and 6, the principals, Commando and Bill, made their bids for attention through aggressive behavior but, when the tension was past, they were not able to shift roles. Neither maintained a following. The observation that a good suitor may not make a good husband, or a good campaigner a good president, is applicable in other contexts. It is our thought that similar shifts in system requirements occur with great frequency on the corner. The leaders who persist over long periods, like Duke (Case 1), do have aggressive skills as well as the ability to use them selectively.

The quickened tempo of the testing of relationships on corners, in contrast with, for example, work groups, arises in part because leaders do not control important amounts of property, because there are few privileges or immunities they can bestow, and because there are no external institutional pressures that constrain members to accept the discipline of the gang. Gang membership is very fluid,[14] particularly among fringe members. The leader cannot crassly dominate a person who is dissatisfied with the allocation of rewards within the group because of the effectiveness of the threat of splintering away. The result is that the successful gang leader is surprisingly conciliatory in his corner relations.

The recourse to aggressive behavior toward an out-group object is viewed as being a part of the sensitivity to role requirements. Out-group aggression does not undercut the gratification that membership confers and does not expose the relationship to the threat of splintering. The foray provides excitement, a heightened need for leadership, and a non-disruptive way for the leader to exercise his aggressive skills.

We do not mean to imply that all attempts at status re-equilibration through out-group aggression are successful. Sometimes they are not, and when they are not, the consequences can be grave. Kobrin and Finestone describe a case in which a boy withdrew from the gang and began to smoke marijuana,[15] and another case, known to us by correspondence, resulted in suicide. Most failures are unquestionably less dramatic than these, but a social cost is surely involved.

This formulation has specific explanatory implications that may be illustrated by comparisons with Cloward and Ohlin's comment on the reduction of intergang fighting that comes about when detached workers become associated with gangs:

> The reduction in conflict may reflect the skill of the social workers, but another explanation may be that *the advent of the street gang worker symbolized the end of social rejection and the beginning of social accommodation*. To the extent that violence represents an effort to win deference, one would logically expect it to diminish once that end has been achieved.[16]

Instead of viewing the presence of the worker solely as symbolic of the interest of the larger society, we would also stress that his presence stabilizes what we have come to call "the leadership structure." And, in so doing, we believe it makes less frequent the need for status-maintaining aggressiveness by leaders. We believe that the gang also recognizes its obligation to the worker as a *quid pro quo* for services performed by the worker and for the additional status within the gang world that accrues to a gang by virtue of their having a worker.[17] Both of these points relate to status-maintaining mechanisms within more immediate systems—the gang itself and the gangs of the area—rather than to the "end of rejection" at the hands of a somewhat amorphous middle-class society.

In conclusion, it is to be emphasized that we do not suppose the usual elementary approval and disapproval mechanisms are absent in the gang situation; it is more that we believe gang leaders to be particularly vulnerable when they try to use negative sanctions to maintain their rank. While we view the hypothesis as plausible, we believe it highly desirable to test it by purposive, experimental intervention in the functioning of on-going groups (e.g., by having a detached worker deliberately frustrate a leader). Because of the serious consequences that might follow from the resulting aggressions, we have not made such attempts with the groups presently under observation.

Notes

1. This is a revision of a paper read at the annual meeting of the American Sociological Association, August 1961. This investigation was a part of the Youth Studies Research Program supported by Research Grant M-3301 from the Behavioral Science Study Section, National Institutes of Health, Public Health Service, and directed by James F. Short, Jr., at the University of Chicago.
2. Herbert A. Bloch and Frank T. Flynn, *Delinquency: The Juvenile Offender in America Today* (New York: Random House, 1956), pp. 151-75.
3. See Albert K. Cohen, *Delinquent Boys: The Culture of the Gang* (Glencoe, Ill.: Free Press, 1955); Albert K. Cohen and James F. Short, Jr., "Research in Delinquent Subcultures," *Journal of Social Issues*, XXIV (1958), 20-37; and Richard A. Cloward and Lloyd E. Ohlin, *Delinquency and Opportunity: A Theory of Delinquent Gangs* (Glencoe, Il.: Free Press, 1960).
4. *Street Corner Society* (Chicago: University of Chicago Press, 1943); 2nd ed., 1955).
5. See George Homans, *The Human Group* (New York: Harcourt, Brace & Co., 1950); and George Homans, *Social Behavior: Its Elementary Forms* (New York: Harcourt, Brace & Co., 1961).
6. Ronald Lippitt, Norman Polansky, Fritz Redl, and Sidney Rosen, "The Dynamics of Power: A Field Study of Social Influence in Groups of Children," in *Readings in Social Psychology*, ed. Eleanor Maccoby, Theodore M. Newcomb, and Eugene S. Hartley (New York: Henry Holt & Co., 1958).
7. See Howard Polsky, "Changing Delinquent Subcultures: A Social Psychological Approach," reprinted from *Social Work* (October, 1959), pp. 1-15; and Howard Polsky and Martin Kohn, "Participant Observation in a Delinquent Subculture," *American Journal of Orthopsychiatry*, XXIX (October, 1959), 73-51.
8. Erving Goffman, "On the Characteristics of Total Institutions: The Inmate World," and "Staff-inmate Relations." In *The Prison: Studies in Institutional Organization and Change*, ed. Donald R. Cressey (New York: Holt, Rinehart & Winston, 1961), chaps. i and ii, pp. 15-106.
9. Leon Jansyn, "Solidarity and Delinquency in a Street Corner Group: A Study of the Relationship Between Changes in Specified Aspects of Group Structure and Variations in the Frequency of Delinquent Activity" (unpublished Master's thesis, University of Chicago, 1960).
10. "Detached work" is a form of service currently being practiced by a number of agencies to reach groups of youth who are ordinarily inaccessible through more conventional channels, such as schools and churches, whose families do not send them to the agencies, and who do not themselves voluntarily come to the agencies. Such workers may be either male or female, depending usually on the sex of the client group, and typically they are young adults. In the YMCA project from which the following cases are drawn, workers are males, aged 25-30. Negro gangs have Negro workers, and white gangs have white workers. Our special thanks go to the staff of the Program for Detached Workers of the YMCA of Metropolitan Chicago for their excellent co-operation and stimulating ideas that have contributed much to the research.
11. Whyte reports Doc's similar plight, though Doc did not suggest a delinquent way out of his dilemma (see Whyte, *op. cit.*).
12. Walter B. Miller, Hildred S. Geertz, and Henry S. G. Cutter, "Aggression in a Boys' Street-Corner Group," *Psychiatry*, XXIV (November, 1961), 283-98.
13. Mandel recently discussed the severe sociometric costs of interpersonally aggressive dominance-seeking among the boarding-school boys he studied. See Rudolf Mandel, *Die Aggressivität bei Schulern: Beobachtung und Analyse des Aggressiven Verhaltens einer Knapengruppe im Pubertätsalter* (Bern and Stuttgart: Verlag Hans Huber, 1959); also Miller *et al.*, *ibid.*
14. Our gangs are definitely not the very fluid near-group phenomena which Yablonsky describes, although we can imagine our boys answering as his respondents did after they were picked up (see Lewis Yablonsky, "The Delinquent Gang as a Near-Group," Social Problems, VII [Fall, 1959], 108-17; and Harold W. Pfautz, "Near-Group Theory and Collective Behavior," *Social Problems*, IX [Fall, 1961], 167-74).
15. Solomon Kobrin and Harold Finestone, "Towards a Framework for the Analysis of Juvenile Delinquency" (paper read at the annual meeting of the American Sociological Association, 1958). (Dittoed.)
16. Cloward and Ohlin, *op. cit.*, p. 176. Their italics.
17. James F. Short, Jr., "Street Corner Groups and Patterns of Delinquency: A Progress Report from National Institute of Mental Health Research Grant M-3301" (March 1, 1961). (Mimeographed.) ✦

21

The Role of Juvenile Gangs in Facilitating Delinquent Behavior

Terence B. Thornberry, Marvin D. Krohn, Alan J. Lizotte, and Deborah Chard-Wierschem

The behavior of youths who are members of street gangs is invariably shaped by group norms, values, and dynamics. Thornberry and his colleagues provide one of the few comprehensive examinations of the relationship between gang membership and delinquent involvement. Because their study is longitudinal and comparative in nature, they were able to follow youths' crime patterns prior to, during, and after gang involvement. This work is important because it provides the strongest evidence to date that gang membership itself increases youths' involvement in crime and delinquency.

Abstract

This study examines alternative explanations for why gang members are more likely to have higher rates of serious and violent crime than nongang members. Specifically, three models are posited: (a) a selection or "kind of person" model; (b) a social facilitation or "kind of group" model; and (c) an enhancement model that combines aspects of the selection and social facilitation models. Each model has different implications for the rate of delinquency and drug use of gang members before, during, and after membership in a gang. Data from the Rochester Youth Development Study, a panel study that overrepresents adolescents at high risk for serious delinquent behavior and drug use, are used to compare these models. Findings indicate that gang members, as compared to nongang members, did not have higher rates of delinquent behavior or drug use before entering the gang, but once they became members, their rates increased substantially. Moreover, when gang members left the gang their rates of delinquency typically were reduced. These results are interpreted as being supportive of the social facilitation model.

Criminological research has clearly demonstrated that gang members are more likely than nongang members to commit offenses, especially serious and violent offenses, and to do so with high frequency (see Spergel, 1990, for a thorough review of this literature). This relationship is remarkably robust, being reported in virtually all American studies of gang behavior regardless of when, where, or how the data were collected.

Reprinted from the *Journal of Research in Crime and Delinquency*, 30(1): pp. 55-87.

The link between gang membership and delinquency appears indisputable, but there is little information about the causal mechanisms that bring it about. That is, although we know that gang members are involved in more delinquency and drug use than nongang members, we know surprisingly little about whether gangs *attract* adolescents who are already highly delinquent or whether they *create* highly delinquent adolescents as part of the gang process. The present article addresses this issue by examining the delinquent careers of gang members before, during, and after their involvement with gangs and by comparing their delinquent behavior to that of nongang members.

Gang Membership and Delinquency

Perhaps the oldest and most common method of collecting data about the behavior of gang members is through direct observation. Beginning with the work of Thrasher (1927) in Chicago, observational studies have consistently shown that gang members have high rates of delinquency and, in more recent studies, drug use. This is also evident in the older work of Spergel (1964), Miller (1966), and Klein (1971), and the spate of more recent observational studies by such authors as Moore (1978), Hagedorn (1988), Vigil (1988), and Taylor (1990). Studies that rely on official data to compare gang and nongang members also report a strong relationship between gang membership and criminal involvement. See, for example, the research of Cohen (1969), Klein, Gordon, and Maxson (1986) and Maxson and Klein (1990). Finally, studies that use survey research techniques find that gang members report higher rates of criminal involvement than nongang members. See, for example, the research by Short and Strodtbeck (1965), Tracy (1979), Fagan, Piper, and Moore (1986) and Fagan (1989, 1990).

Although there is tremendous consistency in these findings, they should not be taken to mean that gangs are a homogeneous blob with no variation in their behaviors or characteristics. There is in fact considerable diversity in contemporary American gangs, as ably demonstrated in Huff's (1990) recent anthology on gang research. Some gangs are more violent than others, some are more instrumental than others, some are more involved in drug use than others, and so on. Although this variation across gangs exists, it does not detract from the virtually universal finding that gang members are much more heavily involved in delinquency and drug use than nongang members.

This finding is hardly surprising because gangs are groups that are organized to some extent around delinquent conduct. Cohen, for example, defines them as collectivities that engage in deviant, disruptive, antisocial, or criminal behavior (1990, pp. 9-10). Although there is no universally accepted definition of a juvenile gang (Horowitz 1990), and even some disagreement about whether involvement in criminality should be a formal part of the definition (compare Klein and Maxson [1989] with Short [1990]), gangs clearly connote groups that have some deviant or criminal orientation. Spergel (1990) states that "the principal criterion currently used to define a 'gang' may be the group's participation in illegal activity" (1990, p. 179). Thus the relationship between gang membership and high rates of involvement in delinquency and drug use is not at all surprising. Indeed, if it were not found it would raise serious questions about the validity of one or both measures.

Casual Mechanisms

Prior research in criminology, therefore, has demonstrated a strong link between gang membership and delinquency. It has not, however, identified the causal mechanisms that bring it about; in fact, there is very little empirical information available to account for or explain the relationship between gang membership and delinquency. As Fagan (1990) has noted: "it is uncertain whether the differences reflect the positive correlation between group crime and violence, features of the gang itself, or the state of social controls in the inner cities where gangs are most evident" (p. 186). By extending Fagan's argument, three somewhat competing models that could account for the relationship between gang membership and delinquency can be identified.

The first is a *selection* or a "kind of person" model. It posits that gangs recruit their members from adolescents who are already delinquent, or at least who have a high propensity for delinquency. These individuals are likely to engage in delinquency and drug use regardless of their membership in gangs. Thus gangs do not cause their members to be delinquent; they recruit or attract people who are already delinquent.[1] This view is consistent with a social control perspective (Hirschi 1969) and especially Gottfredson and Hirschi's (1990) propensity theory of crime. The gang attracts adolescents who lack self-control and, therefore, may already be involved in delinquency.

If the selection or "kind of person" model is accurate we would expect to observe two relationships. First, gang members would have higher rates of delinquency than nongang members, and second, this would hold across time—before, during, and after their membership in the gang. That is, if gang members are truly different kinds of people—those with high propensities toward deviance—they are likely to act out those propensities regardless of their gang membership status at any particular time. Indeed, in a pure version of the selection model the gang becomes epiphenomenal:

> Given the large numbers of adolescents with relatively low self-control living in close proximity, and given the relatively low level of supervision exercised over them, it is inevitable that from time to time they will congregate in the streets of U.S. cities. Given these facts, it is also inevitable that the "gang" will occasionally engage in delinquent and criminal activities, ranging from shoplifting cigarettes and intimidating the elderly to using heavy drugs and participating in drive-by shootings directed at no one in particular. (Gottfredson and Hirschi 1990, p. 209)

The gang itself, however, appears to have no causal impact on these behaviors.

The selection model is also consistent with the view that "the gang is an aggregate of individuals with 'shared incapacities' " (Spergel 1990, p. 230). Such a perspective is seen in the work of Yablonsky (1962), Gerrard (1964), and others, especially those approaching gang research from a psychiatric or clinical perspective (see Spergel 1990, pp. 229-31).

The second model is a *social facilitation* or a "kind of group" model. In its pure form it posits that gang members are intrinsically no different from nongang members in terms of delinquency or drug use. They do not have a stronger propensity toward these behaviors and, left to their own devices, they are no more likely to engage in delinquency or drug use than are nongang members. If they do join a gang, however, the normative structure and group processes of the gang are likely to bring about high rates of delinquency and drug use. Gang membership is thus viewed as a major cause of deviant behavior.

If the social facilitation model is accurate it implies that gang members will differ from nongang members in terms of delinquency and drug use only when they are active members of a gang. Before and after they are gang members they should not differ substantially from nongang members because they are, after all, not different "kinds of people." When they are members of a gang, however, they should have higher rates of delinquency and drug use because of the influence of gang processes on their behavior. In their classic study of gangs in Chicago, Short and Strodtbeck (1965) describe a number of group processes that bring about high rates of delinquency for active gang members. For example, when the status of gang leaders is threatened they often resort to out-group aggression "because of the limited resources they have for internal control of the group" (1965, p. 185). More generally, threats to the status of gangs and gang members are likely to lead to delinquent behavior, especially violent behavior, as a way of regaining status:

> Specifically, it is our hypothesis that much of what has previously been described as short-run hedonism may, under closer scrutiny, be revealed to be a rational balancing from the actor's perspective, of the near certainty of *immediate* loss of status in the group against the remote possibility of punishment by the larger society *if* the most serious outcome eventuates. (Strodtbeck 1965, p. 250; emphasis in original)

Other gang researchers have also pointed to group processes that are likely to increase the involvement of delinquency by active gang members. Miller, Geertz, and Cutter (1961), report that aggression is important for creating and maintaining group cohesion and Jansyn (1966) reports that delinquency is often a response to threats to the gang's solidarity.

In brief, a variety of gang studies suggest that group processes revolving around such dimensions as status, solidarity, and cohesion are likely to increase the level of delinquency for gang members. Because these are properties of the group, however, they ought to have no impact on facilitating delinquent behavior either before or after the person is a gang member.

The third model for accounting for the strong relationship between gang membership and delinquency combines the other two into a mixed model, what might be called an *enhancement* model. Here, gangs recruit their members from adolescents who are already delinquent. However, because the gang provides an atmosphere that encourages delinquency and, in some cases, makes delinquency easier, the enactment of the member's delinquent propensities becomes more likely. In other words, both processes—selection and facilitation—are at work.

If the enhancement model is accurate we would expect gang members to have generally higher rates of delinquency and drug use than nongang members, and this difference would be particularly noticeable when they are active gang members. The enhancement model is consistent with the empirical findings of Sarnecki's (1990) study of Swedish delinquent networks. Members of the more active delinquent gangs he studied were recruited from networks that were characterized by common delinquency.

In sum, there are three plausible models that could account for the established relationship between gang membership and delinquency, but there is surprisingly little empirical information about the relative validity of these competing models. To separate them empirically, two types of hypotheses need to be tested. The first concerns group differences because the models make different hypotheses about whether gang members will differ from nongang members in terms of delinquency and drug use; the second concerns temporal differences because the models make different hypotheses about when—before, during, or after periods of active gang membership—delinquency and drug use will be highest. To our knowledge these hypotheses have not been tested in the gang research literature.

This seems to be due primarily to the design of prior gang studies. They tend to study either gang members exclusively, as in participant observation studies, or to compare active gang members to nongang members. Both strategies focus so much attention on active gang members they lose sight of the fact that gang members have delinquent careers before and after they are gang members. Because of that, prior studies cannot test the temporal hypotheses and therefore cannot validate which of these three models is most consistent with the data. As Spergel (1990) has noted: "researchers have tended to employ nonrepresentative or age-truncated samples and limited data-gathering technologies. . . . Longitudinal studies that examine the stability and character of [gang] structures and processes over time have not been conducted" (p. 177).

Thus prior research leaves us with the observation that gang members are more delinquent than nongang members but little explanation of why. To examine the underlying dynamic of this relationship requires longitudinal data on a general sample, containing gang members and nongang members, followed long enough to observe their behavior before, during, and after their period of active gang membership. The remainder of this article tests these hypotheses on a data set with these characteristics.

Methods

The data are drawn from the Rochester Youth Development Study (RYDS), a multiwave panel study designed to examine the causes and correlates of serious delinquent behavior and drug use. Adolescents and the adult primarily responsible for their care are interviewed at 6-month intervals. In addition, data are collected from the Rochester schools, police, and other agencies that have contact with youth. The current analysis is based on information collected in adolescent interviews at Waves 2 through 7. At Wave 2 the students were in the fall semester of their 8th or 9th grade and at Wave 7 they were in the spring semester of their 10th or 11th grade.

Sample

To obtain a sufficient number of youth who are at high risk for committing serious delinquent behavior and to be gang members, the following sampling strategy is used. First, public school students of Rochester, New York were selected as the target population. Rochester has a diverse population and a crime rate that is considerably above the national and New York State averages, and even exceeds that of New York City (Flanagan and Jamieson 1988). Second, the sample was stratified on two dimensions. Males are overrepresented (75% to 25%) because they are more likely than females to be chronic offenders and to engage in serious delinquency (Blumstein, Cohen, Roth, and Visher 1986). Second, students from high-crime areas of the city were oversampled on the assumption that they would be at greater risk for offending. To indicate the criminality of areas, each census tract in Rochester was assigned a resident arrest rate reflecting the proportion of the tract's total population arrested by the Rochester police in 1986.

Of the 4,013 students in the seventh and eighth grades in the Spring of 1988, 3,372 (84%) were eligible for the sample. To generate a final panel of 1,000 students, all eligible students were assigned to their census tract of residence and 1,334 were selected based on an estimated nonparticipation rate of 25% (Elliott, Ageton, Huizinga, Knowles, and Canter 1983; Capaldi and Patterson 1987). All students in the census tracts with the highest resident arrest rates (approximately the top one third) were asked to participate, whereas students in the remaining census tracts were selected at a rate proportionate to the tract's contribution to the overall resident arrest rate. Once the number of students to be selected from each tract was determined, the student population was stratified by sex and grade in school and students were selected from those strata at random. A final panel of 987 students and their families was selected for the study.[2]

Because the true probability of each adolescent being selected is known, the sample can be weighted to represent all seventh and eighth graders in the Rochester Public Schools. The sample is weighted in the analysis to follow.

Current analysis is based on interview data from Wave 2 through Wave 7, because items on gang membership were not asked in Wave 1. It is also limited to males because the number of female gang members, especially in the last two waves, is too small for the type of analysis conducted here. Males constituted 74.1% of the initial panel and 74.0% of those interviewed at Wave 7. Of the males in the total panel, 90.5% were reinterviewed at Wave 7.

Table 1

Characteristics of Sample Members at Wave 1 and at Wave 7 (in percentages)

	Wave 1(n = 708)	*Wave 7(n = 651)*
Race/ethnicity		
African-American	63.7	62.5
Hispanic	17.9	18.3
White	18.4	19.2
Age at Wave 1		
11-12	13.6	14.3
13	36.5	38.7
14	37.3	26.4
15	12.6	10.6
Census tracts grouped by resident arrest rates		
1 (highest rate)	30.1	29.6
2	34.2	35.0
3	19.4	19.0
4	8.9	8.2
5 (lowest rate)	7.5	8.2
Ever prevalence of self-reported delinquency at Wave 1		
General	50.6	48.8
Violence	31.1	30.1
Property	20.2	19.8
Drug use	6.8	6.6

Table 1 presents basic descriptive data about the male respondents at Waves 1 and 7. As is evident there is very little differential attrition by race/ethnicity, age, census tract of residence, or Wave 1 self-reported delinquency and drug use. For example, at Wave 1 50.6% of the boys reported involvement in general delinquency and that same statistic, based only on those still interviewed at Wave 7, is 48.8%.

Although the present analysis uses data from six waves of the study, because of relatively low base rates of gang membership at any one wave, data are combined into three annual time periods. Time 1 combines responses from Waves 2 and 3; Time 2 combines responses from Waves 4 and 5; and, Time 3 combines responses from Waves 6 and 7.

Measurement

Two variables are used in the analysis to follow: gang membership and self-reported delinquency. Both are measured from interview responses.[3]

Gang Membership

At each interview, beginning with Wave 2, respondents were asked if they belonged to a street gang or "posse," the term commonly used in Rochester. Respondents who answered in the affirmative are considered gang members in this article.[4] More specifically, if they responded yes at either the Wave 2 or 3 interview they are considered a gang member at Time 1; if they responded yes at Wave 4 or 5 they are a gang member at Time 2; and if they responded yes at Wave 6 or 7 they are a gang member at Time 3.

Moreover, because the key hypotheses in this study compare delinquency before, during, and after periods of active gang membership (see below), groups that allow for clear temporal comparisons are needed; therefore, the following groups will be used in the analysis. Respondents are grouped on the basis of those who were gang members at:

Time 1 only
Time 2 only
Time 3 only
Times 1 and 2 only
Times 2 and 3 only
Times 1, 2, and 3[5]

The modifier "only" will not be used in the text but the reader should bear in mind that this is how the groups are defined.

Delinquency and Drug Use

The dependent variable is self-reported delinquency and drug use. The items in the self-report index are derived in large part from the National Youth Survey (Elliott, Huizinga, and Ageton 1985) as modified by the Denver Youth Survey (Huizinga, Esbensen, and Weiher 1991). From the total set of items five subindexes that cover domains of delinquent activity that have been hypothesized to be related to gang behavior are used in this analysis.[6] They are: crimes against the person, six items covering relatively serious violent offenses;[7] crimes against property, 17 items covering theft; drug selling, two items covering the sale of marijuana or harder drugs; and general delinquency, a composite of the other three indexes. In addition, drug use is measured by a nine-item index which, at these ages, refers primarily to marijuana use.

All self-reported delinquency responses are screened to determine whether they fit the type of delinquency measured by the item and are "actionable" offenses. The latter criterion is intended to screen out trivial offenses (e.g., siblings' squabbles with one another in response to a question about serious assault) that law enforcement officials would, in all probability, ignore.[8] If the response meets these two criteria, the total frequency for each offense is counted to construct each summated delinquency index.

Although the analysis is based on annual time periods, the self-reported delinquency measures presented in the Tables refer to the frequency of involvement in delinquency per half-year. For the vast majority of subjects these frequencies were generated by taking the average of the responses on the two interviews; for example, at Time 1 the reported frequency is the average of the responses provided at Waves 2 and 3. This, rather than simply summing the two frequencies, was done so that the few subjects interviewed at only one of the two waves at each time period could be included in the analysis.[9] For them the response they provided at the single wave is used, based on the reasonable assumption that there are not huge changes in behavior in adjacent 6-month intervals.

Table 2

Sample Matrix for Describing the Relationship of When Delinquency Occurs to Periods of Active Gang Membership

	Time 1	*Time 2*	*Time 3*
Nongang members	Before	Before	Before
Transient gang members			
Time 1 only	During	After	After
Time 2 only	Before	During	After
Time 3 only	Before	Before	During
Stable gang members			
Times 1 and 2 only	During	During	After
Times 1 and 3 only	Before	During	During
Times 1, 2, and 3	During	During	During

Hypotheses

Two types of hypotheses are tested in this article. The first are cross-time comparisons, comparing the delinquency and drug use of gang members when they are active gang members and when they are not. The second are cross-group comparisons, comparing the delinquency and drug use of gang members and nongang members. To test these hypotheses the data are arrayed as in Table 2, which indicates whether the delinquency rate in each cell covers the time period before, during, or after active membership. For example, for "Time 2 only" gang members, delinquency committed at Time 1 is before their active gang membership, at Time 2 it is during their gang membership and at Time 3 it is after their gang membership. Because the nongang members could join a gang in the future their delinquency is labeled "before" in Table 2.

Row comparisons test the temporal hypotheses of differences in behavior before, during, and after gang membership. *Column comparisons* test the cross-group hypotheses of whether gang members are more delinquent than nongang members.

With these comparisons in mind, the substantive hypotheses that relate to each of the three models can be presented. They are

1. The *selection* or kind of person model hypothesizes that:
   a. Gang members will have equal rates of delinquency and drug use at all three time periods, regardless of whether they are an active gang member (a row comparison); *and*
   b. Gang members will have higher rates of delinquency and drug use than nongang members at all three time periods (a column comparison).
2. The *social facilitation* or kind of group model hypothesizes that:
   c. Gang members will have significantly higher rates of delinquency and drug use when they are in a gang as compared to when they are not in a gang (a row comparison); *and*
   d. Gang members will have higher rates of delinquency and drug use than nongang members only when they are active gang members. At the other periods the groups will not differ (a column comparison).
3. The *enhancement* or mixed model would be supported if hypotheses B and C are supported. That is, gang members should have generally higher rates of delinquency and drug use than nongang members, but especially high rates when they are active gang members.[10]

Types of Gang Members

To this point each of the three models has been presented as if it applied to all gang members equally well. That is, the selection model has been presented as a general explanation for the relationship between gang membership and delinquency, as have the social facilitation and enhancement models. There are, however, different types of gang members and it is possible that one model may be more appropriate for certain types of members and another model for other types.

The gang literature often distinguishes between leaders and regular members (Yablonsky 1962; Klein 1971). It also distinguishes between core and fringe members; the former being characterized as having higher levels of commitment to and participation in the gang than the latter (Klein 1971, pp. 70-76). In addition, gang members differ on the permanency of their gang involvement; some members are rather transient—joining a gang for relatively brief periods of time, and others are more stable—remaining in the gang over longer periods of time. Moreover, these dimensions appear to be interrelated, with leadership, core member status, and stable membership going together and regular members, fringe member status, and more transient membership going together.

In the analysis that follows we will see if the three models under examination here apply equally well to stable and transient members. This variable is selected because there are too few leaders in any time period—never more than nine—to allow for analysis and because there is no available measure of core/fringe membership status in this data set.

Stable members are defined as those who were members in 2 or more years, and transient members are those who were members in 1 year only (Time 1 only, Time 2 only, or Time 3 only). Fifty-five percent of the gang boys are categorized as transient members and 45% as stable members. Moreover, at each time, stable members are significantly more likely than transient members to report being a leader or one of the "top people" in the gang.

Table 3

Mean Frequency of Self-Reported Delinquency for Gang Members (*N* = 175) and Nongang Members (*N* = 488)

	Time 1	*Time 2*	*Time 3*
General delinquency			
Gang members	18.16**	15.37**	14.89**
Nongang members	4.68	3.74	5.09
Person offenses			
Gang members	11.58**	8.61**	7.82**
Nongang members	2.69	2.31	3.37
Property offenses			
Gang members	4.83**	3.17**	2.64*
Nongang members	1.44	0.85	0.83
Drug sales			
Gang members	1.75*	3.59**	4.44**
Nongang members	0.55	0.58	0.90
Drug use			
Gang members	4.58*	8.52**	7.00**
Nongang members	1.35	2.02	2.17

*$p < .01$; **$p < .001$.

Results

We begin the analysis by comparing the delinquency and drug use of boys who were *ever* members of a gang and those who were not (Table 3). These results, which ignore temporal variation, replicate prior studies of the relationship between gang membership and delinquent activity. At all three time periods the gang members have substantially higher rates of delinquency and drug use than do the nongang members.[11] For example, at Time 1 boys who were ever members of a gang have an average frequency on the general delinquency scale of 18.16, whereas adolescents who were never members of a gang have an average frequency of 4.68. This type of disparity is seen across all three time periods and all five measures of delinquency and drug use. In general, the rates for gang members are about four to five times as high as those for nongang members.

These results indicate that the boys of the Rochester Youth Development Study are much like those in other studies of street gangs; gang members are much more delinquent than nongang members. (These findings also provide support for the validity of our measure of gang membership.) Attention now turns to the issue of whether this disparity is best accounted for by a model that says gangs recruit adolescents who are already delinquent or a model that says the gang process creates delinquents.

General Delinquency

Table 4 presents the data needed to test the substantive hypotheses for general delinquency. We begin by discussing the data for the more transient members—presented in the top panel of Table 4. Results for the more stable gang members are discussed in the following section.

Transient Gang Members. The temporal hypotheses, which are row comparisons, are discussed first. (Significance levels for these comparisons are labeled a, b, and c.) As a point of departure, we note that there is no clear temporal trend for the nongang members across the three time periods; the mean frequency of general delinquency changes from 4.68 at Time 1, to 3.74 at Time 2, to 5.09 at Time 3.[12] More patterned temporal changes are noted for the gang members, however. This can be seen in a cursory way by examining the entries along the main diagonal that indicate the level of delinquency for gang members for the time period when they were active members. All of these frequencies are the highest in their respective rows.

Those respondents who were gang members during Time 1 and not in Times 2 or 3—the first row of the top panel of Table 4—report significantly higher rates of general delinquency during Time 1, when they were in a gang, than during Times 2 or 3, when they were not. At Time 1 their rate is 18.85 and that drops to 7.71 at Time 2, when they have left the gang, and drops further to 6.79 at Time 3. This pattern is consistent with the social facilitation hypothesis—gang members are more delinquent when they are in a gang than when they are not.

Results for those boys who were gang members during Time 2 (the second row of the panel), are not quite as consistent with the social facilitation hypothesis. As expected, their delinquency rate increases significantly from Time 1 (4.90) to Time 2 (12.05) but it drops only slightly at Time 3, to 11.04. For Time 3 gang members (the third row of the panel) the results are again consistent with a social facilitation model. Their rates before joining the gang are low (Time 1 = 1.97; Time 2 = 5.96) but increase substantially when they join the gang during Time 3, to 14.78.

Overall, the temporal comparisons for general delinquency are consistent with the expectations of the social facilitation or kind of group explanations. Gang members are not uniformly delinquent; when they are in a gang their frequency of general delinquency is high, when they are not in a gang, it is substantially lower.

Table 4

Relationship Between Active Gang Membership and Frequency of General Delinquency

		Time 1	*Time 2*	*Time 3*	*n*
Nongang members		4.68	3.74	5.09	488
Transient gang members					
Time 1 only	a = .010				
	b = .003	18.85	7.71	6.79	53
	c = n.s.				
Time 2 only	a = .025				
	b = .088	4.90	12.05	11.04	19
	c = n.s.				
Time 3 only	a = .086				
	b = .044	1.97	5.96	14.78	15
	c = .095				
	d =	.002	.047	n.s.	
	e =	n.s.	.030	n.s.	
	f =	n.s.	n.s.	.088	
Stable gang members					
Times 1 and 2 only	a = n.s.				
	b = .026	29.69	37.04	13.26	24
	c = .004				
Times 2 and 3 only	a = n.s.				
	b = .076	5.02	8.05	16.69	13
	c = n. s.				
Times 1, 2, and 3	a = n.s.				
	b = n.s.	28.96	20.60	29.40	34
	c = .061				
	g =	.002	.001	.080	
	h =	n.s.	n.s.	.074	
	i =	.005	.001	.000	

NOTE:
Row comparison
a = difference between Time 1 and 2.
b = difference between Time 1 and 3.
c = difference between Time 2 and 3.
Column comparison
d = difference between Time l only and nongang members.
e = difference between Time 2 only and nongang members.
f = difference between Time 3 only and nongang members.
g = difference between Time l and 2 only and nongang members.
h = difference between Time 2 and 3 only and nongang members.
i = difference between Time 1, 2, and 3 and nongang members.
n.s. = not significant.

The second type of hypothesis concerns group comparisons—between gang and nongang members—at each time period. These are column comparisons and significance levels are labeled d, e, and f.

The comparisons do not support the selection argument that gang members always have higher rates of delinquency than nongang members. When gang members are active in the gang they have higher rates of delinquency than do the nongang members. This can be seen by comparing the diagonal entries with the respective column entry for the nongang members. All the diagonal frequencies are significantly higher than the frequencies for the nongang members. That is, 18.85 is significantly higher than 4.68 at Time 1, 12.05 is higher than 3.74 at Time 2, and 14.78 is higher than 5.09 at Time 3.

But the off-diagonal elements are even more informative. Only one of the six comparisons is significant, suggesting that transient gang members, *when they are not active members of a gang*, are not uniformly more delinquent than nongang members. This is most clearly seen in the upper right hand and lower left hand cells of the top panel, the points at which there is the greatest distance from the time the respondent was an active gang member. At Time 1, those who were gang members only during Time 3, actually have lower rates of general delinquency than nongang members (1.97 vs. 4.68); at Time 3, those who were only gang members during Time 1, do not differ significantly from nongang members (6.79 vs. 5.09).

The pattern of these results is simply not consistent with a selection model. Based on the cross-group comparisons, gang members do not seem to be different "kinds of people" than nongang members. This is especially so as the time between active gang membership and the observation period increases. Further, the temporal pattern of delinquency is consistent with the social facilitation model. They suggest that active gang membership makes a difference in behavior. The highest frequencies of general delinquency for the transient gang boys are observed during the time period of their active membership.

Stable Gang Members. The bottom panel of Table 4 presents the same types of relationships for the more stable gang members—those boys who joined a gang and remained a member across at least two consecutive years. Discussion begins with the cross-group comparisons.

When the stable gang members are active in the gang they report substantially higher rates of general delinquency than do the nongang members (or the transient gang members for that matter). Significance levels for *t* tests comparing the stable gang members with the nongang members are labeled g, h, and i. Seven of the nine comparisons are significant and the differences in the size of the means are usually substantial. For example, the Times 1 and 2 gang members report frequencies of 29.69 and 37.04 at Times 1 and 2 respectively, compared to frequencies of 4.68 and 3.74 for the nongang members.

When the stable gang members are not active in a gang, however, the picture changes somewhat. Unfortunately there are only two cells in which this is the case; the upper right hand cell—Time 3 delinquency for Times 1 and 2 gang members, and the first cell in row 2—Time 1 delinquency for Times 2 and 3 gang members. Only the first of these comparisons is significant (p<.08). Thus the evidence that the stable gang members are more delinquent than nongang members even when they are not active gang members is mixed. Nevertheless, the overall magnitude of the means reported in the lower panel of Table 4 suggests that stable gang members have generally higher rates of delinquency than nongang members and transient gang members.

Even though stable gang members have generally high rates of delinquency, the temporal comparisons still indicate that gang membership greatly facilitates their involvement in delinquency. For those boys who were gang members during Time 1 and Time 2 (the first row), their rates are significantly higher at Times 1 and 2 than at Time 3 (29.69 and 37.04 vs. 13.26). Those who were gang members at Times 2 and 3 have their lowest rate of delinquency at Time 1 (5.02), before they were gang members; the rate increases to 8.05 at Time 2 and 16.69 at Time 3. Finally, those boys who were gang members at all three times have consistently high rates of general delinquency (28.96, 20.60, and 29.40 from Time 1 to Time 3) and these rates are not significantly different from one another. In addition to this major pattern, it also seems that stable gang members who joined the gang at an earlier time (Time 1) are somewhat more delinquent than those who joined the gang at a later time. This may reflect criminogenic influences of the early onset of problem behaviors.

Summary. Results for the transient members—those who were gang members for only one year and presumably less committed to the gang—are most consistent with the social facilitation model. Involvement in delinquency is particularly high when the boy is an active gang member but these boys are not consistently more delinquent than nongang members when they are not active in the gang. Results for the stable gang members—those who remain as members for at least 2 years and who are presumably more committed to the gang—are slightly more consistent with the enhancement model. In general, these boys exhibit the highest rates of general delinquency. But even for them, delinquent involvement is greatest during their years of active gang membership. None of these results are consistent with a pure selection model. . . .

Discussion

There is little dispute that gang members are more likely to commit more offenses, especially serious and violent offenses, than are nongang members. Prior research has largely ignored the question of why such differences in behavior exist, however. This important gap in our knowledge is, to a large extent, a result of the limitations created by prior research strategies. Both direct observation and analysis of official statistics and cross-sectional survey data have generated a wealth of knowledge about gangs, but they share an important limitation. These methods focus on the behavior of active gang members and typically fail to examine the delinquent careers of gang members before and after they are members of the gang. However, examining these careers is a crucial step in the process of determining why gang members exhibit such high rates of delinquent behavior.

The present study, using data from a panel study of adolescents, attempts to fill this lacuna. In doing so, it identifies and investigates the viability of three alternative explanations for the relationship between gang membership and delinquent behavior. The selection model asserts that gang members are recruited from adolescents who are already delinquent or who have a high propensity for delinquency. The social facilitation model suggests that gang members are intrinsically no different than nongang members. Rather, group processes of the gang and the normative support it provides for delinquent behavior generate a context in which such behavior flourishes. Finally, the enhancement model combines these two explanations, asserting that the gang recruits members from adolescents who are already delinquent but then facilitates the enactment of such behavior.

If gang members are selected on the basis of their propensity for delinquency, then their rates of delinquent behavior before, during, and after gang membership should be relatively high, and they should differ significantly from nongang members. On the other hand, if being a member of the gang facilitates delinquent behavior, then gang members should only exhibit high rates of delinquent behavior when they are active members of the gang; their rates before and after membership should be relatively low and not strikingly different from those of nongang members. If both processes are at work, the rates of delinquency should be high before and after gang membership, but active members should exhibit even higher rates.

The most general results reported here, those covering the general delinquency index, are most consistent with the social facilitation model. This is especially the case for the transient gang members—those who stayed in the gang for no more than a single year. These boys, when they are active members of the gang, exhibit high rates of delinquency; before and after active gang membership, however, their mean level of delinquent behavior is not significantly higher than those boys who never belonged to a gang. For transient gang members there is no evidence of a selection effect.

Among boys who were more stable gang members—those who remained in the gang for at least two consecutive years—the social facilitation model, and perhaps the enhancement model, most accurately describe the causal mechanism that appears to be operating. When they are active members of the gang, their rate of delinquency is substantially higher than it was either before or after gang membership and it is substantially higher than the rate for nongang members.

When data are analyzed within categories of offense types, the overall patterns observed are supportive of the social facilitation model for person crimes, drug sales, and drug use. The only offense type that does not exhibit a pattern supportive of the social facilitation model is property crime. Here, none of the models describe the behavior patterns of either transient or stable gang members when compared with nongang members. Indeed, gang membership seems to have little effect on the frequency of property crime.[13]

Perhaps the strongest support for the social facilitation model is found in the analysis of the type of behavior most often associated with gangs—crimes against the person. Transient and stable gang members have higher rates of person offenses only when they are active gang members. Of particular interest is the drop-off in the rate of person crimes once boys leave the gang. The means for crimes against the person for boys when they are active members of the gang are, by and large, at least twice as high as when they are not. Clearly, being in the gang is generative of violent behavior among these boys. This result is quite consistent with the group process perspective on gang behavior that argues that threats to status, cohesion, solidarity, and so forth are more apt to be responded to by aggressive, violent acts than by other forms of delinquency (Jansyn 1966; Miller et al. 1961; Short and Strodtbeck 1965).

Study Limitations

Although support has been found for the social facilitation model, the interpretation of these findings needs to be tempered by the recognition that the design of the study limits the degree to which they can be generalized. When they were interviewed, the boys in this study were at the younger end of the age continuum for gang members (Klein 1971, pp. 76-77). The gang experience may have a different meaning for these younger boys than for those who are active members in later adolescence. If there is a selection factor in joining a gang, it may well be more evident at older ages when boys have established more discernible behavioral patterns.

The ability to generalize from these findings is also limited by the fact that the sample comes from only one city, Rochester, New York. Although these findings are very similar to those reported by the Denver Youth Survey (Esbensen, Thornberry, and Huizinga 1991), it is not clear that they generalize to all other "gang cities." Klein (1992) identified both Rochester and Denver as cities that have an emerging gang problem, rather than ones in which gang behavior is an established practice. The meaning of being a gang member in a location where gangs are a relatively new phenomenon may be quite different than in a city that has an established tradition of gangs (see, for example, Hagedorn 1988).

Whether older respondents or a different research site would lead to different conclusions regarding the social facilitation and selection models is unknown. To the extent that the present findings can be generalized, however, they have implications for theory and research regarding gang behavior.

Theoretical Implications

The results have been discussed in the context of what we have called the selection, social facilitation, and enhancement models. However, findings that support or refute these models have broader implications for traditional theories of crime and delinquency.

The failure to find support for the argument that gang members are recruited because they already have a high propensity for delinquent behavior is damaging to advocates of social control theories. If these boys are not bonded to conventional people, institutions, or beliefs (Hirschi 1969) or if they simply lack self-control (Gottfredson and Hirschi 1990), they should exhibit higher rates of delinquent behavior regardless of their status in the gang. Although Gottfredson and Hirschi's theory recognizes that gang membership might provide the opportunity for an underlying delinquent propensity to be manifested more often and, thus, be able to account for the higher delinquency rates of active gang members, their theory has much more difficulty coming to grips with the fact that these gang members are *not* more delinquent than nongang members before or after they are active in the gang. In particular, it is difficult to account for the substantial drop-off in delinquent activity after leaving the gang if, indeed, these boys lack self-control.

While damaging to social control theories, the results are encouraging to adherents of socialization theories like differential association (Sutherland and Cressey 1978) or social learning theories (Akers 1985). Clearly, the group (gang) is having an effect on the behavior of these boys. What is not addressed with these data are the reasons for the group's effect. It could be that the gang is effective at communicating definitions and teaching techniques as Sutherland would argue. Or the causal processes might better be accounted for by referring to the reward structure of the group (Akers 1985). Or the types of group processes described by Short and Strodtbeck (1965) and others could be at play. What is evident from these results, however, is that in pursuing an explanation of why gang members have a higher rate of delinquency than nongang members, the structure and dynamics of the group context must be the central focus.

Research Implications

Virtually all prior studies of gang behavior only observe gang members during their periods of active membership. This is true of participant observation studies by definition and is generally true of studies that rely on official and self-reported delinquency measures as well. The results of the present investigation demonstrate the limitations of those designs and suggest the importance of extending observations to cover periods before and after, as well as during, gang membership. The longitudinal data used here show that gang membership is more apt to be fleeting than permanent; only 21% of the gang members were gang members at all three time periods. Gang membership, therefore, cannot be treated as a stable trait or characteristic of its members.

Because of that, it is important to understand the role of gang membership in the overall delinquent careers of these subjects rather than focusing attention exclusively on that part of the career that overlaps with active membership. Doing so should increase our understanding of the causal mechanisms that link gang membership to high rates of delinquency, especially crimes against the person. It should also increase our understanding of how gang membership influences other aspects of the overall delinquent career, for example, the length of careers and the timing of desistance from them. In general, the findings of this study suggest that future gang research should be less myopic and observe gang members through longer portions of the life course.

Future research should also examine the causal mechanisms identified in this article in much more detail than we have been able to do. Our research clearly suggests that a social facilitation, not a selection, model is important in accounting for the generally observed correlation between gang membership and delinquency. But this research does not examine how the process works. Future gang research should be designed to address these process issues directly.

In addition, research should attempt to identify systematically those factors that separate the more transient from the more permanent gang members. Although these types do not appear to differ on prior levels of delinquency they may differ on the reasons they join or the reasons they leave gangs. Also, the gang may play a different role in the overall friendship networks of these types of youth. The identification of these factors is an important theoretical issue that may also lead to the development of techniques for reducing the rate of gang membership in a community.

Clearly, the current study does not provide the answers to the theoretical and research implications that are raised by its results. By focusing on the role of gang membership in the more general career of the subjects, however, it does suggest that participation in the gang is a more important factor in generating delinquency than is the type of person who is recruited to join the gang. This finding provides an important perspective for understanding the relationship between gang membership and delinquency. It also provides a direction for future research and policy efforts.[14]

Appendix

List of Items in Self-Reported Delinquency and Drug Use Indexes

Person
- Carried weapon
- Used weapon with idea of seriously hurting someone
- Hit someone with idea of hurting them
- Threw objects at people
- Used weapon to get money or things
- Physically hurt someone to get them to have sex

Property
- Damaged property
- Set fire
- Avoided paying
- Broke into building
- Stole < $5
- Stole $5-$50
- Stole $50-$100
- Stole > $100
- Shoplifted
- Snatched purse
- Stole something from car
- Bought/sold stolen goods
- Went for a joyride
- Stole a car
- Forged a check
- Used a credit card without permission
- Cheated someone by selling them something worthless

Drug sales
- Sold marijuana
- Sold other drugs

General
- Sum of above three indexes

Drug use
- Marijuana
- Hallucinogens
- Cocaine
- Crack
- Heroin
- Angel dust
- Tranquilizers
- Barbiturates
- Amphetamines

Notes

1. It is not clear if gangs recruit certain people to join or if certain persons are attracted to the gang. In the former the gang is the active agent in selecting members; in the latter, the member is the active agent in selecting the gang. The terms "recruit" and "attract" are used interchangeably in this article to refer to this process.
2. A More detailed description of the sampling procedures of the Rochester Youth Development Study is presented in Farnworth, Thornberry, Lizotte, and Krohn 1990 and in Thornberry, Bjeregaard, and Miles forthcoming.
3. The interviews were conducted by RYDS staff members, generally in private rooms provided by the Rochester schools. Students who could not be contacted at school were interviewed at home and students who moved from Rochester were followed and interviewed. Interviews were about an hour in length.
4. We experimented with eliminating gang members who could not provide a name for their gang or who belonged to a gang with fewer than six members, to help distinguish between street gangs and friendship groups. These screening criteria eliminated few respondents, in some waves none and in no wave more than three, however. Because of that these restrictions are not used in this analysis. The substantive results are not affected by this decision.
5. The other possibility, gang members at Times 1 and 3 only, had too few members (5) to warrant analysis. Because of this, and occasional missing values, the total number of cases in the tables is sometimes slightly less than the total sample size of 651.
6. The items appear in the appendix.
7. This scale does not include gang fights.
8. To determine that the offenses reported are "actionable," respondents are asked to describe the most serious (or only) act committed in a category. Coders rate the act as being actionable or not. The interrater reliability ranged from 90% to 95%. If the most serious delinquency described is not rated as delinquent, the item is coded as a zero, otherwise, the total frequency is counted.
9. The percentage of the total of boys who remained in the panel who were not interviewed in both waves of any one time period is 5.2% for Time 1, 3.8% for Time 2, and 3% for Time 3.
10. All of these hypotheses are directional, positing that gang members have higher (or equal) rates of delinquency and drug use than nongang members and that active members have higher (or equal) rates than non-

active members. There are no hypotheses that rates are lower for gang members. Because of that, one-tailed *t* tests are used throughout the analysis. Also, because the number of subjects in the six gang member groups is rather small, and because this study is somewhat exploratory in light of the absence of prior research on this topic, significance levels up to $p < .10$ are reported.

11. All analyses were replicated using prevalence measures. The pattern of results is virtually identical to that reported below. We also replicated the analyses when the nongang members were restricted to: (a) those who lived in the same census tracts as the gang members, and (b) only nongang members who were delinquent. The former restriction recognizes that gang activity is more prevalent in inner city areas and the latter restriction adjusts for the lower overall rate of delinquency exhibited by nongang members. Neither of these adjustments, however, altered the substantive conclusions and we report only comparisons based on all nongang members.
12. Significance levels are not reported for the nongang members because there are no temporal hypotheses offered for this group and, because of the large sample size (n = 488), many differences that are substantively quite small are statistically significant.
13. [Editor's Note: The data and discussion referred to in this paragraph, consisting of eight pages in the original, have been deleted by the editors to conserve space.]
14. The authors would like to thank Hans Toch of the University at Albany, State University of New York for commenting on an earlier draft. Prepared under Grant No. 86-JN-CX-0007 (S-3) from the Office of Juvenile Justice and Delinquency Prevention, Office of Justice Programs, U.S. Department of Justice, Grant No. 5 R01 DA05512-02 from the National Institute on Drug Abuse, and Grant No. SES-8912274 from the National Science Foundation. Points of view or opinions in this document are those of the authors and do not necessarily represent the official position or policies of the funding agencies.

References

Akers, Ronald L. 1985. *Deviant Behavior: A Social Learning Approach*. 3rd ed. Belmont, CA: Wadsworth.

Blumstein, Alfred, Jacqueline Cohen, Jeffrey A. Roth, and Christy A. Visher. 1986. *Criminal Careers and "Career Criminals."* Washington, DC: National Academy Press.

Capaldi, D. and G. Patterson. 1987. "An Approach to the Problem of Recruitment and Retention Rates for Longitudinal Research." *Behavioral Assessment* 9:169-77.

Cohen, Albert K. 1990. "Foreword and Overview." Pp. 7-21 in *Gangs in America*, edited by C. Ronald Huff. Newbury Park: Sage.

Cohen, Bernard. 1969. "The Delinquency of Gangs and Spontaneous Groups." In *Delinquency: Selected Studies*, edited by Thorsten Sellin and Marvin E. Wolfgang. New York: Wiley.

Elliott, Delbert S., Suzanne S. Ageton, David H. Huizinga, B. A. Knowles, and Rachel J. Canter. 1983. *The Prevalence and Incidence of Delinquent Behavior, 1976-1980* (National Youth Survey Report No. 26). Boulder, CO: Behavioral Research Institute.

Elliott, Delbert S., David H. Huizinga, and Suzanne S. Ageton. 1985. *Explaining Delinquency and Drug Use*. Beverly Hills, CA: Sage.

Esbensen, Finn-Aage, Terence P. Thornberry, and David Huizinga. 1991. "Gangs." Chapter 14 in *Urban Delinquency and Substance Abuse*, edited by David Huizinga, Rolf Loeber, and Terence P. Thornberry. (Technical Report submitted to Office of Juvenile Justice and Delinquency Prevention).

Fagan, Jeffrey. 1989. "The Social Organization of Drug Use and Drug Dealing Among Urban Gangs." *Criminology* 27:633-69.

——. 1990. "Social Processes of Delinquency and Drug Use Among Urban Gangs." Pp. 183-219 in *Gangs in America*, edited by C. Ronald Huff. Newbury Park, CA: Sage.

Fagan, Jeffrey, Elizabeth Piper, and Melinda Moore. 1986. "Violent Delinquents and Urban Youths." *Criminology* 24:439-71.

Farnworth, Margaret, Terence P. Thornberry, Alan J. Lizotte, and Marvin D. Krohn. 1990. *Sampling Design and Implementation* (Technical Report No. 1). Rochester Youth Development Study.

Flanagan, Timothy J. and Katherine M. Jamieson, eds. 1988. *Sourcebook of Criminal Justice Statistics—1987* (U.S. Department of Justice, Bureau of Justice Statistics). Washington, DC: U.S. Government Printing Office.

Gerrard, Nathan L. 1964. "The Core Member of the Gang." *British Journal of Criminology* 4:361-71,

Gottfredson, Michael and Travis Hirschi. 1990. *A General Theory of Crime*. Stanford, CA: Stanford University Press.

Hagedorn, John. 1988. *People and Folks: Gangs, Crime and the Underclass in a Rustbelt City*. Chicago: Lake View Press.

Hirschi, Travis. 1969. *Causes of Delinquency*. Berkeley: University of California Press.

Horowitz, Ruth. 1990. "Sociological Perspectives on Gangs: Conflicting Definitions and Concepts." Pp. 37-54 in *Gangs in America*, edited by C. Ronald Huff. Newbury Park, CA: Sage.

Huff, C. Ronald, cd. 1990. *Gangs in America*. Newbury Park, CA: Sage.

Huizinga, David H., Finn-Aage Esbensen, and Anne Weiher. 1991. "Are There Multiple Paths to Delinquency?" *Journal of Criminal Law and Criminology* 82:83-118.

Jansyn, Leon R., Jr. 1966. "Solidarity and Delinquency in a Street Corner Group." *American Sociological Review* 31:600-614.

Klein, Malcolm W. 1971., *Street Gangs and Street Workers*. Englewood Cliffs, NJ: Prentice-Hall.

——. 1992. *Twenty-Five Years of Youth Gangs and Violence*. Paper presented at the meetings of the American Association for the Advancement of Science, Chicago, February.

Klein, Malcolm W., M. A. Gordon, and Cheryl L. Maxson. 1986. "The Impact of Police Investigation on Police-Reported Rates of Gang and Nongang Homicides." *Criminology* 24:489-512.

Klein, Malcolm W. and Cheryl L. Maxson. 1989. "Street Gang Violence." In *Violent Crime, Violent Criminals*, edited by N. A. Weiner and M. E. Wolfgang. Newbury Park, CA: Sage.

Maxson, Cheryl L. and Malcolm W. Klein. 1990. "Street Gang Violence: Twice as Great, or Half as Great?" Pp. 71 -100 in *Gangs in America*, edited by C. Ronald Huff. Newbury Park, CA: Sage.

Miller, W. B. 1966. "Violent Crimes by City Gangs." *Annals of the American Academy of Political and Social Science* 364:96-112.

Miller, Walter B., Mildred Geertz, and Henry S. G. Cutter. 1961. "Aggression in a Boys' Street-Corner Group." *Psychiatry* 24:283-98.

Moore, Joan W. 1978. *Homeboys*. Philadelphia, PA: Temple University Press.

Sarnecki, Jerzy. 1990. "Delinquent Networks in Sweden." *Journal of Quantitative Criminology* 6:31-50.

Short, James F. 1990. "New Wine in Old Bottles: Changes and Continuity in American Gangs." Pp. 223-39 in *Gangs in America*, edited by C. Ronald Huff. Newbury Park, CA: Sage.

Short, James F. and Fred L. Strodtbeck. 1965. *Group Process and Gang Delinquency*. Chicago: University of Chicago Press.

Spergel, Irving A. 1964. *Slumtown, Racketville, Haulburg*. Chicago: University of Chicago Press.

——. 1990. "Youth Gangs: Continuity and Change." Pp. 171-275 in *Crime and Justice: A Review of Research, Vol. 12*, edited by Michael Tonry and Norval Morris. Chicago: University of Chicago Press.

Sutherland, E. H. and D. P. Cressey. 1978. *Criminology*. 10th ed. Philadelphia, PA: Lippincott.

Taylor,Carl S. 1990. "Gang Imperialism," Pp. 103-15 in *Gangs in America*, edited by C. Ronald Huff. Newbury Park, CA: Sage.

Thornberry, Terence P., Beth Bjerregaard, and William Miles. Forthcoming. "The Consequences of Respondent Attrition in Panel Studies: A Simulation Based on the Rochester Youth Development Study." *Journal of Quantitative Criminology*.

Thrasher,Fredrick M. 1927. *The Gang: A Study of 1,313 Gangs in Chicago*. Chicago: University of Chicago Press.

Tracy, Paul E. 1979. *"Subcultural Delinquency: A Comparison of the Incidence and Seriousness of Gang and Nongang Member Offensivity.* " Unpublished manuscript, University of Pennsylvania, Center for Studies in Criminology and Criminal Law.

Vigil, J. D. 1988. *Barrio Gangs: Street Life and Identify in Southern California*. Austin: University of Texas Press.

Yablonsky, Lewis. 1962. *The Violent Gang*. New York: Macmillan. ✦

Section III

Criminal Involvement of Gangs

Introduction

We tend to concentrate, especially in these days when gang violence garners so much attention, on the anti-social behavior of gang members, and we overlook the ways they spend most of their time. Similarly, we tend to ignore the fact that gang members, in most cases, represent the minority of gang-age youth in their communities. These are points to be pondered and facts to be given their due in the context of gang activity.

In one sense, gang members are little different from their nongang peers. They sleep, they eat, they go to school (typically less often and for fewer years), they spend time with family and friends, they watch TV and engage in sex—in short, they are youth. Most of us are probably used to quite a bit of structure in our daily lives. On week days, we get up at a standard time in order to have breakfast and attend class, or go to our job. We tend to stay in the school or workplace until late afternoon, and then return home in time for dinner and the evening with classmates or family. The routine is broken by sports or entertainment, but normally in a predictable pattern.

For many, many gang members, this regular, routinized pattern of varied activities is not typical. Their days are far less structured because they are often out of school, out of work, and out of sorts with their families. Rising late, eating episodically, disinterested in organized sports or recreation, often unhappy in the home, the gang member occupies much of his or her time thinking up or looking for something to do, something to fill the time. That something, as often as not, involves his or her gang friends. Peer dependence fills the voids—and causes many of the problems. It needs to be stated, clearly, that most of the gang member's time is in fact spent doing very little of anything. Delinquent and criminal activity help fill the voids, but not much. *Talking* about such activities fills more of the time.

So who and what are these young people, so similar and yet somehow different? In the mid-sixties, Klein found core members of gangs to have more personal deficits (e.g., lower I.Q., lower impulse control, less independence, more aggressiveness) than those on the fringe of gang membership, and to be more delinquent as well. Yet they did not differ at all in sociodemographic factors such as family composition, family income, length of local residence, parental education, and so on. In the mid-seventies, Friedman, Mann and Friedman compared gang and nongang members on several score variables, yet found only three or four to be of any significance, including general aggressiveness and violence between youth and parents. More recent attempts at understanding motives for gang membership can be reviewed by the interested reader in other articles listed in the additional readings by Ko-Lin Chin and Jeffrey Fagan on Asian gangs in New York and by Calvin Toy on Asian gangs in San Francisco.

Gang members have been described as more shy than their nongang peers, less socially skilled, and less prepared for the world of work. They have fewer contacts with adults who could serve as positive role models and more with adults who can lead them astray. They are, it would seem, the most at risk of getting into trouble, and the least protected from engagement in illegal activities. And so they are, in those smaller portions of their daily lives, more open to, tempted, and excited by the chance to get into trouble.

One would never know from reading the newspaper and tuning in the six o'clock news, but the illegal acts most commonly engaged in by gang members (as by many nongang youth as well) are things like petty theft, truancy, smoking dope, writing graffiti, drinking alcohol, and just plain scaring people by seeming to take over street corners, parks, arcades, and the like. When we say gang members are into everything, that "everything" is usually of the bothersome but non-serious type.

Yet it is the street crime, the acts of violence, that catch the attention of the public and of the justice system—and rightly so. Homicide is rare but devastating. The open street drug market serves willing customers, but can seriously disrupt the street life of the local residents.

Thus we have chosen not to emphasize the generally non-serious forms of gang crime in our selected articles. Rather, with the exception of the first article describing this general pattern, we have offered articles that describe specific forms of gang crime such as homicide and drive-by shootings. In these selections, we hope to give the reader more of an in-depth sampling of specific gang crime patterns, with the understanding that these normally fit into a far wider variety of crimes. It is the variety that is the hallmark of *street* gangs in particular, more so than most others.

In the second part of this section, we have separated out for special attention the controversial issue of gang involvement in drug distribution and sales, a relatively new concern, triggered principally by the explosion in crack cocaine sales in the mid-1980s. We have done so because the gang and drug connection has been so badly overstated over the past decade. We would hope that five or ten years from now, such special attention to gangs in drugs sales would no longer be necessary.

Gang scholars have recognized for decades that drug *use* is one of the many illegal offenses engaged in by gang members. Many of the same scholars have reported as well that drug sales are either fairly uncommon, or limited primarily to dealing among friends. Drug sales and distribution have not generally been a part of gang (especially street gang) tradition. In many reported cases, in fact, these activities have been forbidden by gang leadership.

Beginning in the mid-1980s with the appearance of crack cocaine, this situation changed somewhat—emphasis on the *somewhat*. Some gang members became engaged in the occasionally lucrative crack trade, especially at the lowest or street level of dealing. In addition, some cliques from within gangs separated out to concentrate on drug dealing while in other cases gangs developed *de novo* to engage in drug sales. Finally, there were a number of instances in which gang members from one city set out deliberately to establish new drug sales markets in other cities.

The issue is not whether these patterns emerged, but how much; to what extent did gangs (a) take over crack distribution, (b) franchise it across the country, and (c) thereby create much of the gang proliferation that has taken place? To what extent has this purported connection led to a rise in gang violence? The evidence for the centrality of gangs to crack and gang proliferation is in such articles as those included here by Jerome Skolnick and Jesse Katz. The evidence against is illustrated by the articles of Cheryl Maxson, and of James Meehan and Patrick W. O'Carroll. National-level research undertaken by the editors comes down strongly on the side of the latter two papers, but it is nevertheless common to hear public officials and news reporters continue the overstatements about street gang involvement in and control of crack and other drug markets.

Other articles dealing directly with this controversy are those listed below by Joan Moore, Jeffrey Fagan, Malcolm Klein, and John Hagedorn. Also interesting and very readable are the pieces by Scott Decker and Barrik Van Winkle, Laurie Gunst, and Dan Waldorf and David Lauderback, as well as the Padilla article on a drug distribution gang already included in Section I. Each of these studies emanates from a different city, adding to the sense of the wide variety of situations in drug dealing among gang members.

Additional Readings

Social and Antisocial Behavior

Chin, Ko-Lin, & Fagan, Jeffrey, Social Order and Gang Formation in Chinatown. In Freda Adler & William Laufer (eds.), *Advances in Criminological Theory*, Vol. 6. New Brunswick, NJ: Transaction Publishers, 1994 (in press).

Friedman, C. Jack, Mann, Fredrica, & Friedman, Alfred S., A profile of juvenile street gang members. *Adolescence*, 1975, 10(40):563-607.

Hagedorn, John, M., *People and Folks: Gangs, Crime and the Underclass in a Rustbelt City*. Chicago: Lake View Press, 1988.

Klein, Malcolm W., *Street Gangs and Street Workers*. Englewood Cliffs, NJ: Prentice-Hall, 1971.

Maxson, Cheryl L., Gordon, Margaret A., & Klein, Malcolm W., Differences between gang and nongang homicides. *Criminology*, May 1985, 23(2):209-222.

Miller, Walter B., Theft behavior in city gangs. In M.W. Klein (ed.), *Juvenile Gangs in Context: Theory, Research and Action*. Englewood Cliffs, NJ: Prentice-Hall, 1967.

Robin, G., Gang membership delinquency: Its extent, sequence, and pattern. *Journal of Criminal Law, Criminology and Police Science*, 1964, 55:59-69.

Toy, Calvin, Coming out to play: Reasons to join and participate in Asian gangs. *The Gang Journal*, 1992 1(1):13-29.

Tracy, Paul, Subcultural Delinquency: A Comparison of the Incidence and Seriousness of Gang and Nongang Member Offensivity. Paper presented at American Society of Criminology, November 1979.

Drugs

Decker, Scott, & Van Winkle, Barrik, "'Slinging Dope': The Role of Gangs and Gang Members in Drug Sales." *Justice Quarterly*, forthcoming.

Erlanger, Howard S., Estrangement, machismo and gang violence. *Social Science Quarterly*, September 1979, 60(2):235-48.

Fagan, Jeffrey, Drug selling and licit income in distressed neighborhoods: The economic lives of street-level drug users and dealers. In Adele Harrell & George Peterson (eds.), *Drugs, Crime and Urban Opportunity*. Washington, D.C.: Urban Institute Press, 1992.

Gunst, Laurie, Jamaican drug gangs: Drugs and violence in America. *The Nation*, November 13, 1989, 1:529-62.

Hagedorn, John M., Neighborhoods, markets, and gang drug organization. University of Wisconsin, Milwaukee, 1993, unpublished.

Hutchison, Ray, & Kyle, Charles, Hispanic street gangs in the Chicago public schools. In Scott Cummings & Daniel J. Monti (eds.), *Gangs: The Origins and Impact of Contemporary Youth Gangs in the United States*. Albany: State University of New York Press, 1991.

Klein, Malcolm, Juvenile Crime, Drugs and Gangs: Romancing the Rocks, an address delivered to Communities Take Action: A Governor's Conference on Juvenile Crime, Drugs and Gangs, April 1, 1992 (Milwaukee, Wisconsin). University of Southern California, unpublished.

Lopez, Jose, & Mirande, Alfredo, Chicano urban youth gangs: A critical analysis of a social problem? *Latino Studies Journal*, September 1992, 3(3):15.

Moore, Joan, Gangs, drugs, and violence. *National Institute on Drug Abuse Research Monograph Series, Research Monograph 103*, pp. 160-76, 1990.

Waldorf, Daniel, & Lauderback, David, Don't be your own best customer—Drug use of street ethnic gang drug sellers. *Crime, Law and Social Change*, July 1993, 19(1):1-15. ✦

Delinquent and Criminal Patterns

22

Gang and Non-gang Youth: Differences in Explanatory Factors

Finn-Aage Esbensen, David Huizinga, and Anne W. Weiher

Personal interviews with a representative sample of youths living in high-risk Denver neighborhoods provide the data used by these authors to measure the extent to which gang members differ from two types of youth: serious street offenders and less serious or nonoffending youth. Gang members generally reported more delinquency involvement than other youth; however, their patterns of drug sales and use matched those of non-gang serious offenders. The three categories of youths were similar on several social-psychological dimensions: involvement in conventional activities, perceptions of both social isolation and limited opportunities, and self-esteem. Gang members and street offenders shared differences from nonoffenders in their attitudes toward illegal activities, negative peer commitments, and normlessness. The findings call into question certain tenets of popular theoretical approaches and suggest some redirections for gang intervention efforts.

Abstract

An apparently common assumption about juvenile gangs is that they are composed of individuals who are substantially different from other youth that are not gang members. Little empirical evidence exists to support such an assumption. This can, in part, be attributed to the fact that most knowledge about gangs has been derived from data gathered by police gang units or from observational or case studies. Very little information has been derived from surveys or interviews with a general sample of youth. In this paper, data from the Denver Youth Survey, a longitudinal study of families, are used to examine the characteristics of gang members and to explore the extent to which gang members differ from non-gang members on key theoretical variables. Findings suggest that while gang members differ from nonoffending youth on a number of social psychological variables, they do not differ from other youth involved in serious "street" level offending.

While juvenile gangs have been a part of American history for at least the past one hundred years, the study of gangs has been sporadic and usually descriptive in nature (e.g., Asbury, 1927; Campbell 1991; Cohen 1955; Hagedorn 1988; Miller 1958; Moore 1978; Puffer 1912; Short and Strodtbeck 1965; Spergel 1966; Thrasher 1927; and Vigil 1988). In spite of these descriptive accounts, however, little information exists regarding the extent to which gang members differ from non-gang members. The vast majority of research has relied upon observational methods and has provided a wealth of information about specific gangs and their members. In the recent genre, Campbell (1991), Hagedorn (1988), MacLeod (1987), Sullivan (1989), and Vigil (1988) provide excellent descriptive accounts of their particular samples.

In other instances, research has relied upon law enforcement records to examine gang offenses and to describe gang members (e.g., Maxson and Klein 1990; and Spergel 1990), while others have used survey methods to study gang behavior (e.g., Esbensen and Huizinga 1993; Fagan 1989; Thornberry, Krohn, Lizotte, and Chard-Wierschem 1993; and Winfree, Vigil, and Mays 1991). Interestingly, regardless of study design or research methodology, considerable consensus exists regarding the high rate of criminal offending—including crimes against person and property, substance use, and drug distribution and sale—among gang members.

Relatively few of the numerous gang studies, however, have used survey data, especially of a representative sample of a general population, to examine the extent to which gang members are differentially involved in delinquency and drug use, or the extent to which they differ from other youth. Some notable and relatively recent examples of such efforts include Bowker and Klein (1983), Esbensen and Huizinga (1993), Fagan (1989), Klein (1971), Morash (1983), Thornberry et al. (1993), and Winfree et al. (1991).

The research reported by Fagan (1989) relied upon interviews with a snowball sample of gang members in three different cities in the United States. Examination of the relationship between gang membership, violent behavior, and drug use/selling allowed Fagan to classify gangs according to gang structure and the dominant type of illegal activity in which the gangs were involved.

The remaining six publications cited above used interviews with more representative samples of youth. Based upon a sample of youth enrolled in school and of juveniles that had penetrated the justice system, Morash (1983:325) reported that the level of peer group organization was "not a sufficient condition to stimulate delinquency among members." That is, she found that while gang members were highly involved in delinquent activities, they were only negligibly more criminally involved than other non-gang youth that were also categorized as high rate serious offenders. More recently, Esbensen and Huizinga

Reprinted with permission from the *Journal of Contemporary Criminal Justice*, 1993, 9:94-116.

(1993) and Thornberry et al. (1993) examined the temporal relationship between gang membership and involvement in delinquent activity among a household sample of urban youth. Both sets of findings, contrary to Morash, indicated that gang members were significantly more criminally active than were non-gang members.

The Klein (1971) and the Bowker and Klein (1983) research reports are based on data obtained from male and female gang members and a comparison group of youth from similar neighborhoods. Both of these publications included analyses of theoretically relevant variables associated with gang membership. Bowker and Klein, for example, contrasted social structural effects with psychological factors and report that the "data were found to be more consistent with social structural explanations of gang membership and juvenile delinquency than explanations which depend on psychological constructs" (1983:750). Winfree et al. (1991), on the other hand, report that social learning variables were more instrumental in explaining gang membership than were their measures of social structural characteristics. Although there is some work testing theoretical relationships, there is a relative paucity of studies utilizing representative samples and/or survey methods in the study of gangs and competing theories of gang behavior have not been adequately tested. This should raise some concern regarding the reliability and validity of the current state of gang knowledge.

This is not to suggest that gang research based on observational and police data has been atheoretical. In fact, the past eighty years of gang research have generated numerous theoretical statements and have served as the basis for much criminological theory development. With regard to the past fifteen years of gang research, however, Covey, Menard, and Franzese (1992) suggest that gang theory has been virtually stagnant. In fact, they comment that "if one were to read reviews of theories of juvenile gangs written in the last decade . . . one might well be excused for thinking that theoretical developments on the topic of juvenile gangs stopped with the publication of *Group Processes and Gang Delinquency*" in 1965 (Covey et al. 1992: 175).

The cultural deviance perspective initiated by Shaw and McKay (1942) and perpetuated by Miller (1958) served as an early example of theoretical explanations of gang activity. Cloward and Ohlin (1960) and Cohen (1955) advanced the social strain perspective as an explanation for male gang delinquency. In addition to these lines of theoretical development which were largely motivated by attempts to account for gang behavior, Hirschi's social bond theory (1969), and learning theory—both Sutherland's differential association (1970) and Akers' (1985) version in which operant conditioning is included as an integral component—have been widely cited as explanation for all forms of juvenile delinquency.

During the past twenty years, criminology has witnessed a movement towards the combination or integration of dominant theoretical perspectives, on the assumption that no singular perspective can explain the variety of pathways to legal violations (see, for example, Elliott 1985; Messner, Krohn, and Liska 1989; and Thornberry 1987). In the spirit of this integration movement, our purpose in the research reported here is to provide a descriptive analysis of the extent to which gang members[1] differ from non-gang members across key theoretical concepts borrowed from social learning, social control, and social strain theory. Also, given the continuing interest in the labeling perspective (e.g., Gove 1980) and in the role of self-concept in delinquency (e.g., Kaplan 1980), measures of these theoretical constructs have also been included in the analyses. We view this as an important first step toward more thorough examination of theoretical explanations of gang behavior.

Study Description

The research reported here is part of an ongoing longitudinal study investigating the causes and correlates of delinquency and drug use in a "high risk" sample.[2] Census data were used to identify "high risk" neighborhoods in Denver, Colorado. From these neighborhoods a probability sample of households was selected and interviews were conducted with 1527 youth between the ages of 7 and 15 years and one of their parents. The data used here are self-reported measures of gang membership, delinquent activity, and attitudinal measures obtained from the youth during the third and fourth years of the panel. The primary reason for limiting the analyses to these years is that the cohorts are older and allow for a better examination of gang activity. Only the four oldest cohorts (ages 12 to 18 years in year 4) are included.

Sample and Ecological Areas

In order to insure sufficient numbers of serious or chronic juvenile offenders in the sample, "high risk" neighborhoods were identified. Based upon the results of earlier studies, we selected 35 variables from the 1980 census data representing seven conceptual areas: family structure, ethnicity, socioeconomic status, housing, mobility, marital status, and age composition. Factor analysis was used to identify distinct factors and then a cluster analysis was conducted to identify and combine similar block groups of the city. Seven distinct clusters emerged, with three clusters very loosely identified as being "socially disorganized."

The geographic areas covered by these clusters include areas identified by arrest data from the Denver Police Department as having high crime rates. Using arrest data, we identified those neighborhoods within the socially disorganized areas that were in the upper one-third of the crime distribution.[3] These socially disorganized high crime areas became the neighborhoods for inclusion in the study sample. A more detailed description of the sampling design and the social ecology analysis is provided in Esbensen and Huizinga (1990).

Selection of Respondents

The overall design of the ongoing research project is based on a prospective sequential longitudinal survey. The longitudinal survey involves a sequence of annual personal interviews with five different birth cohorts. At the point of the first annual survey, the birth cohorts were 7, 9, 11, 13, and 15 years of age.

To identify study participants, a stratified probability sample of 20,300 households was selected from the 48,000 in the targeted neighborhoods. Then a screening questionnaire was used to identify those households that contained an appropriately aged respondent (i.e., a 7, 9, 11, 13, or 15 year old person). This sampling procedure resulted in 1527 completed interviews in the first year, with youths distributed across the five cohorts (a completion rate of 85% among identified eligible youth). The sample consists of 52 percent males, 48 percent females; 33 percent Black, 45 percent Hispanic, 10 percent Anglo, and 12 percent Other (primarily Asian and American-Indian).

Annual retention rates for the first four annual in-person interviews have been high by prevailing standards, 91–93 percent, and complete data covering the third and fourth years are available for 90 percent of the original sample.[4] In this report, only data from the four oldest cohorts (n=1095) are used for the analyses due to the distinctly different developmental stages represented by the youngest cohort (aged nine and ten during the third and fourth annual data collection periods), for whom gang involvement was not a major factor.

Methods

The survey collected considerable data about gang membership. One early finding from this line of questioning was that approximately five percent of youth in the DYS indicated that they were gang members in any given year (41 in Wave 3, and 76 in Wave 4). Respondents were asked early in the interview if they were "members of a street or youth gang." All those responding affirmatively were later asked a series of questions about their gangs.[5] Examination of this follow-up information indicated that what some of these youth described as gangs could best be defined as informal youth groups or, in some instances, church groups that did not necessarily include involvement in delinquent behavior. To be considered a gang member, the youth had to indicate that the gang was involved in illegal activity. Affirmative responses to either one of two follow-up questions were used to exclude non-delinquent gangs from the analysis (perceived gang involvement in fights with other gangs and participation in illegal activities). While the exclusion of respondents who indicated their gang was not involved in these activities reduced the number of potential gang members in the third year (32 in Wave 3 and 68 in Wave 4), this process allows for a more stringent and, arguably, more accurate description of juvenile *delinquent* gang membership and activity. The 32 gang members in Wave 3 represent 2.7 percent of the general sample of youth aged 11 to 17, while the 68 Wave 4 gang members represents 6.7 percent of the youth when they were 12 to 18 years of age. From this one might conclude that even though gang membership increases with the aging of these cohorts, gang membership remains a relatively infrequent phenomenon in Denver, even in this "high-risk" sample of urban youth.

Self-report delinquency data were also collected from all respondents. These measures are improved versions of our earlier work (e.g., Huizinga and Elliott 1986) and avoid some of the problems of even earlier self-report inventories. An attempt has been made to measure when an offense or offenses occurred during the reporting year. This permits examination of episodic behavior and the effect of specific life events such as beginning junior high school. Trivial offenses such as defying parental authority were eliminated and serious offenses often excluded from earlier works (e.g., rape, robbery, and aggravated assault) were included. Additionally, follow-up questions were included as integral parts of the measures. These follow-up questions allow for determination of the seriousness and appropriateness of initial responses. If, for example, a respondent indicated that they had committed one aggravated assault during the prior year but the follow-up information revealed that it was accidental and that the person truly was not injured, the original response was changed to zero.

For analysis purposes, the delinquency and drug use measures focus on those behaviors often considered to be of greatest concern. To this end, four different levels of delinquency were developed: 1) street offending, 2) other serious offending, 3) minor offending, and 4) non-offending. Street crimes focus on serious crimes that occur on the street and are often of concern to the average citizen and policy makers, alike. Due to the perception that gang members are disproportionately involved in the sale and distribution of drugs, a specific measure of drug sales was created and used in some analyses.[6] Other serious delinquency includes behaviors that, while not in the street crime category, are nevertheless considered as serious delinquency. Minor delinquency refers primarily to status offenses and other public nuisance type behaviors. These categories of delinquent behavior generally reflect the seriousness weighting obtained by Wolfgang, Figlio, Tracy and Singer (1985). Drug use was dichotomized into alcohol use and "other drug use," including marijuana and other illicit drugs. For the analyses reported below, all youth were categorized based upon their most serious level of involvement in delinquency and drug use. Thus, if an individual reported committing a minor, a serious, and a street offense in a given year, that individual was classified as a street offender. Appendix A provides a listing of the items included in the self-reported delinquency and drug use classifications.

To allow for closer examination of the extent to which gang members differed not only from non-gang members, but from youth who also reported involvement in "street level offending," respondents were categorized into three groups: 1) self admitted gang members (n=68); 2) individuals who were not gang members but reported some involvement in street level offending (n=124); and 3) non-street offenders, i.e., youth who reported no street level offending and were not gang members (n=901), who in this report are referred to as "non-offenders."

Eighteen different theoretical measures were included in the analyses reported in this paper. The scales represent constructs from the dominant theoretical perspectives in the study of delinquency: social learning, social control, labeling, strain, and self-concept. See Appendix B for a summary of scale characteristics. The longitudinal data from this panel study allow for a temporally controlled analysis of theoretical variables relative to the dependent variables of gang membership and delinquent activity. The social-psychological measures were all obtained during the Year 3 interview (conducted in early 1990), while gang membership in 1990 and delinquent behaviors committed during calendar year 1990 were collected in Year 4.

Brief descriptions of the social-psychological scales are provided below:

1. Religiosity: four items measuring the extent to which the respondent is a religious person, the level of participation in religious activities and the amount of satisfaction derived from religious activities.
2. Commitment to Negative Peers: three questions such as "If your friends were getting you in trouble at home, how likely is it that you would still hang out with them?"
3. Commitment to Positive Peers: two questions such as "if your friends told you not to do something because it was against the law, how likely is it that you would listen to them?"
4. Attitudes to Delinquency: twelve questions asking respondents how wrong they think it is to do a variety of things such as skip school, steal, hit people, or sell drugs.
5. Attitudes to Alcohol: one question about how wrong it is to use alcohol.
6. Attitudes to Drug Use: two questions about how wrong it is to use marijuana and "hard drugs."
7. Social Isolation: three separate scales measuring social isolation within the three contextual areas of: a) family, b) peers, and c) school. Included are questions such as "I feel close to my friends" and "I feel like an outsider in my family."
8. Normlessness: three separate scales measuring normlessness in three contexts: a) family, b) peers, and c) school. Items included statements such as "It's okay to lie if it keeps your friends out of trouble" and "You can make it without having to cheat on exams or tests."
9. Limited Opportunity: two scales measuring perceived limited opportunities in a) education and b) other areas. Items included such statements as "You'll never have enough money to go to college" and "You are as well off as most people."
10. Perceived Labeling by Teachers: three distinct scales measuring the respondents' perceptions that teachers have of them with regard to being: a) good, b) bad, or c) disturbed. Respondents indicated the extent to which they thought their teachers would agree that they were: well-liked, a bad kid, or in need of help.
11. Self-Concept: a ten item scale consisting of statements such as: "I am a useful person to have around" and "Sometimes I think I am no good at all."

Results

Before describing the demographic characteristics of the gang members included in this sample, it may be beneficial to provide a description of the nature of these gangs with regard to the members' perceptions of structural and behavioral characteristics. Descriptive data provided by respondents paint a picture of what Yablonsky (1959:109) referred to as "near groups"—characterized by limited cohesion, impermanence, shifting membership, and diffuse role definition, but at the same time groups that had some level of identification as a gang as evidenced by having a gang name, the presence of colors and initiation rites. Year 4 data are representative of the descriptive information provided across the first four years of data collection: 97 percent of the members indicated their gangs had a formal name (there were 37 different gangs identified by the 68 gang members, with many being affiliates of the Bloods and Crips); 87 percent said their gang had initiation rites; 33 percent said their gang had regular meetings; only 5 percent reported having members under 10 years of age while 90 percent indicated members were 16 and older; 97 percent said their gang had symbols or colors; and 49 percent reported members have specific roles although only 28 percent said there were roles for each age group and 43 percent said there were roles for girls. With regard to shifting membership and impermanence, when asked what role they would like to have or what role they expect to have in the gang someday, over 60 percent of Year 4 gang members indicated that they would like to *not* be a member and expected *not* to be a member sometime in the future.

Gang Member Demographics

Gangs have traditionally been thought of as being a predominantly male phenomenon but some studies have documented the role of females in the juvenile gang world (e.g., Bowker and Klein 1983; Campbell 1991; Giordano 1978; Hanson 1964; Harris 1988; Morash 1983; and Quicker 1983). One result of this focus on male gang members has been considerable ignorance concerning not only the role of female gang members, but also the extent to which females are involved in gang activity. Campbell (1991) suggests that approximately 10 percent of New York City gang members were female, and that female membership might have been as high as 33 percent in one gang. Fagan (1990) also reported female gang membership to be approximately 33 percent in his survey.

The DYS data confirm that a significant proportion of all gang members are females—a fact not generally acknowledged in media presentations of gangs. In the fourth study year, for example, 20 percent of gang members were female. Thus, while there is evidence that gang members are primarily males, there is reason to believe that females are more involved in gangs than is generally acknowledged. As we have reported elsewhere, however, while female gang membership may well be greater than that presented in the popular press, female gang members are less likely to report high levels of involvement in delinquent activity (Esbensen and Huizinga 1993).

As with gender, it is often assumed that gang members are youth from ethnic/racial minority backgrounds (e.g., Fagan 1989; Spergel 1990). In a 1989 survey of law enforcement officials in 45 cities across the nation, it was found that African American and Hispanics made up 87 percent of gang membership (cited in Gurule, 1991). Due to the nature of the DYS sample, 78 percent of the sample is African American or Hispanic, it is not prudent to address the ethnic distribution of gang membership. Given the disproportionate number of minority youth in the sample, it should be expected that the majority of gang members also would be African American or Hispanic.

Gang membership does appear to be associated with age. Among the year 4 gang members, nine percent were 12 years old, 35 percent were 14 year olds, 31 percent were 16 years old, and 26 percent were 18 year olds.

Another demographic characteristic receiving attention in the delinquency and gang literature is family structure. Consistent with literature describing socially disorganized areas, the most common living arrangement for all youth in this sample was single parent homes (40% of non-offenders, 44% of street offenders, and 47% of gang members). Gang members were less likely to live in intact families—being more apt to live some "other" living arrangement such as with friends or cohabitating. Twenty-three percent of gang members lived in some such "other" living arrangement compared with nine percent of non-offenders and only half as many gang members reported living in intact families as did the non-offenders (16% versus 35%).

Theoretical Variables

Based on social bond theory, there is reason to believe that involvement in conventional activities such as school, work, and religion should be associated with lower levels of delinquency and a reduction in the probability of belonging to a gang. In Table 1, the results reveal no differences in the extent to which gang members, non-gang street offenders, and non-offenders are involved in eight different conventional activities. Approximately 40 percent of all three groups reported having a job during the school year and during summer vacation. Ninety percent reported being enrolled in school and of these, approximately one-third of each group indicated involvement in after school athletic teams. Approximately 25 percent were involved in school activities such as student government and special interest clubs. These school related activities refer only to the school year, while the measures of community and religious involvement are estimates for the entire calendar year. A smaller percentage of youth were involved in community sponsored athletics and activities (between nine and 22 percent). Non-offenders reported slightly higher rates of participation in religious activities (significant at the .10 level) than did gang members and street offenders. These data, clearly, do not lend support to a central tenet of social control theory: involvement in conventional activities was not found to be negatively associated with delinquency, nor do they distinguish gang members from other delinquent youth.

Table 1
***Involvement in Conventional Activities*[1]**

	Non-Offender[2]		Non-Gang Street-Offenders		Gang Members	
	N	%	N	%	N	%
School-Year Job						
No	550	61%	68	55%	40	59%
Yes	350	39%	56	45%	28	41%
Total	900		124		68	
Summer Job						
No	557	62%	71	57%	38	57%
Yes	343	38%	53	43%	29	43%
Total	900		124		68	
Attend School						
No	66	7%	12	10%	7	11%
Yes	835	93%	113	90%	61	91%
Total	901		124		68	
School Athletics						
No	548	66%	72	65%	39	65%
Yes	283	34%	39	35%	21	35%
Total	831		111		60	
School Activities						
No	617	74%	84	74%	40	67%
Yes	214	26%	29	26%	20	33%
Total	830		113		61	
Comm Athletics						
No	735	82%	97	78%	56	84%
Yes	166	18%	28	22%	11	16%
Total	900		124		67	
Comm Activities						
No	780	87%	110	88%	61	91%
Yes	121	14%	14	12%	6	9%
Total	900		124		67	
Religious Activities						
No	338	37%	57	46%	30	44%
Yes	564	63%	68	54%	38	56%
Total	901		124		68	

1. Due to weighting of the sample, the frequencies do not always add up to the total.
2. None of these analyses are statistically significant.

Analysis of the theoretical variables was conducted by the use of multiple T-Tests, using the separate variance estimate of t to test for statistical significance. This procedure was used due to the heteroscedasticity of variables that violates an [assumption] required for use of analysis of variance.

With respect to attitudes and self-perceptions, differences in mean scale scores indicate a number of statistically significant differences between non-gang members and both the street offenders and gang members. There were virtually no differences, however, between the gang members and the street offenders who were not gang members. With respect to commitment to negative peers, for example, non-offenders were much less likely than either of the other two groups to indicate that they would continue to associate with their friends if they were getting them in trouble at home, at school, or with the police. Commitment to positive peers revealed the opposite—gang members and street offenders were less likely to listen to friends if they told them that it was wrong to do something. Gang members and street offenders expressed virtually the same level of religiosity while the street offenders reported statistically lower levels than did non-offenders (a group mean of 11.53 for gang members compared with a group mean of 12.15 for non-offenders and 11.21 for street offenders, so differences on this measure are relatively small).

The same trend is evident throughout all of these analyses, the street offenders are quite similar to the gang offenders on the attitudinal measures while the both of these two groups are distinct from the non-offenders. Exceptions to this general finding are the social isolation, perceived limited opportunities, and self-concept measures, which revealed no differences among the three groups.

Two of the three labeling scales, however, did indicate differences between all three groups. Gang members are much more likely to perceive their teachers as labeling them as either bad or disturbed than are members of either of the other two groups. This, however, is not the case for the perception of the teachers' labeling the respondents as good.

Table 2
Mean Attitudinal Scores of Non-Offenders, Street Offenders and Gang Members

	Non-Offenders	Non-Gang Street-Offenders	Gang Members
Attitudinal Scales			
Religiosity[a]	12.15	11.21	11.53
Commitment to Negative Peers[ab]	5.39	6.46	6.95
Commitment to Positive Peers[ab]	8.28	7.78	7.36
Attitudes to Delinquency[ab]	42.93	40.24	39.64
Attitudes to Alcohol[ab]	3.39	3.01	2.85
Attitudes to Drug Use[ab]	7.42	6.88	6.76
Social Isolation-Family	10.26	10.53	10.41
Social Isolation-Peers	10.66	10.92	10.29
Social Isolation-School	10.83	10.82	10.42
Normlessness-Family[ab]	8.82	9.59	9.58
Normlessness-Peers[ab]	8.49	9.79	9.86
Normlessness-School[ab]	10.88	11.92	11.80
Limited Opp-Educ	8.49	8.89	9.04
Limited Opp-Other	18.87	19.40	18.60
Labeling-Good	15.73	15.57	15.22
Labeling-Bad[ab]	8.25	9.49	10.94
Labeling-Disturbed[bc]	9.30	9.56	10.49
Self-Esteem	41.07	40.23	41.65

a. $p<.05$ T-test for Non-Offenders and Non-Gang Street Offenders
b. $p<.05$ T-test for Non-Offenders and Gang Members
c. $p<.05$ T-test for Non-Gang Street Offenders and Gang Members

Delinquent Behavior

As reported elsewhere, involvement in illegal activities appears to be the most statistically significant and substantive difference between gang members and other youth. The analyses reported in Table 3 extend this generalization—not only are gang members more delinquent than other youth in general, they also report higher levels of delinquent activity than other youth that are involved in street level offending. The average number of offenses committed by each group of youth is reported in Table 3. While the non-offenders, by definition, were not involved in street level offending, they did indicate some degree of involvement in other forms of delinquent activities. The mean scores reported in Table 3 are group means and *not* individual offending rates or lambdas. Clearly, gang members reported substantially higher average levels of involvement in all types of delinquent behavior, be it minor offending, legal substance use, drug sales, or street (i.e., UCR Index level) offending.

Table 3
Mean Delinquency Scores of Non-Offenders, Street Offenders and Gang Members

	Non-Offenders	Non-Gang Street-Offenders	Gang Members
Behavior Type			
Street[abc]	0.00	6.74	16.07
Serious[abc]	1.49	9.71	21.85
Minor[abc]	4.93	13.67	23.76
Drug Sales[ab]	0.00	4.05	5.64
Alcohol Use[abc]	5.45	16.82	34.31
Drug Use[ab]	1.50	11.92	21.69

a. $p<.05$ T-test for Non-Offenders and Non-Gang Street Offenders
b. $p<.05$ T-test for Non-Offenders and Gang Members
c. $p<.05$ T-test for Non-Gang Street Offenders and Gang Members

Summary

To counter-balance the reliance upon observational studies and police data for knowledge about gangs and gang members, we have used data from a representative sample of urban youth to provide a descriptive account of gang members and the activities of their gangs. Analyses were conducted to determine the extent to which gang members differed from non-gang members on theoretical measures representing five different perspectives in criminology: social control; social learning; social strain; labeling; and self-concept.

The importance of general surveys is highlighted by examination of the demographic characteristics of gang members. Contrary to popular perception, females were found to be quite active in gangs (20 percent of Year 4 gang members were female). While this is higher than the prevailing stereotype, it is consistent with Fagan's (1990) and Campbell's (1991) estimates.[7]

Due to the nature of the DYS sample, it is not possible to discuss the ethnic/racial composition of gangs in Denver. There were simply too few Anglo youth in the general sample to adequately address this issue. Consistent with other research is the finding that gang membership did not appear to be common among the younger respondents; respondents in their mid teens had the highest rates of gang membership. Gang members were also more likely than their non-gang counterparts to live in "other" (i.e., non-familial) living arrangements.

Analyses presented in this paper confirm the general finding that gang members have higher rates of criminal offending than do non-gang members. Table 3 reported that youth who were neither gang members nor involved in street level offending had the lowest rates of any type of offending. The rate of offending by non-gang street offenders were at least three times the rate of the "non-offenders," while the rate for gang members was generally twice that of the street offenders. Little doubt remains that, at least with respect to law violating behavior, gang members are indeed different from non-gang youth, even those youth who have reported some level of involvement in street level offending.

Several analyses addressed the question of whether there are differences between gang members and non-gang members on key theoretical measures. No support was found for the involvement construct of social control theory. Gang members and the non-gang street level offenders were as involved in eight conventional activities as were the youth defined as non-offenders. This finding has serious ramifications not only for social control theory, but for social policy. A number of current anti-gang and anti-delinquency policies and programs are based on an assumption that getting "kids" involved in after school activities will reduce their delinquent activity, or that summer jobs will reduce gang activity. These analyses call such proposals into question.

Other analyses suggested that social psychological measures representative of five different theoretical perspectives produced statistically significant differences between non-offenders and both gang members and youth who report committing street level offenses. Virtually no differences, however, were found between the gang youth and the non-gang street offenders.

Both the gang members and the street offenders reported a greater likelihood of continuing to associate with friends even though those friends may get them into trouble. At the same time they indicated that they would be less likely to listen when friends told them not to do something that was wrong or against the law. It appears that the these delinquent youth have become more imbedded in their peer subculture than have the non-offenders. This level of commitment to peers and its apparent relationship to delinquent activity is contrary to Hirschi's (1969: 145) statement of control theory. Whereas Hirschi felt that commitment to peers would serve as an insulator against delinquency, these data suggest that youth who express a willingness to tolerate criminal activity on the part of their peers are more likely to become gang members or to participate in street level offenses than are youth who are less tolerant of other youths' transgressions.

While the social psychological measures included in these analyses can be classified as measures of five different theoretical perspectives (social learning, social control, social strain, labeling, and self-concept), we have intentionally referred to them only as social psychological measures. Although several of these measures have been widely used, a lack of consensus exists with regard to which theoretical perspective they best measure. The normlessness and isolation measures, for example, could be classified in accordance with Seeman's (1959) elaboration of alienation and the notion that alienation is an individualized form of the Durkheimian concept of anomie. Some researchers and theorists, however, have classified these measures of normlessness and social isolation as indicators of attachment in social control theory (e.g., Agnew 1991; and Elliott et al. 1985). This inconsistency of classification underscores the need for both more rigorous conceptualization in criminological theorizing and operationalization of concepts in criminological research. Whether indicators of strain theory or bonding theory, gang members and street offenders were more likely than were the non-offenders to agree that norm violating behavior was appropriate under certain conditions.

Less ambiguity surrounds the measures of the labeling perspective. For these measures, some support was found for differences in perceived negative labeling. While all three group means indicated disagreement with the statements, the gang members reported lower levels of disagreement than did the other youth. That is, the gang youth believed that their teachers viewed them less favorably than did the other youth.

In summary, compared to gang members and street offenders, non-offenders can be described as reporting: 1) lower levels of commitment to delinquent peers; 2) higher commitment to positive peers; 3) lower levels of normlessness in three different contexts (family, peer group, and school); 4) less negative labeling by teachers; and 5) lower tolerance for deviance. With regard to comparisons between gang members and street offenders, the only observed difference was that gang members reported significantly more negative labeling by their teachers than did the street offenders.

An important aspect of this research is identification of street level offenders that were not gang members. This allowed for comparison of the behaviors and attitudes of gang members with youth involved in equally serious criminal activity. Given the lack of differences on key theoretical variables reported in Tables 1 and 2, there does not appear to be a substantive difference between gang members and other youth involved in street level offending. Thus, the issue raised by Fagan (1990) concerning the high rates of offending among gang members can be partially addressed. It is, in all likelihood, not simply the state of controls in the inner city that is responsible for the higher rates of offending. As Thornberry et al. (1993:82) note, to fully understand the high level of offending, emphasis will need to be placed on "the structure and dynamics of the group context."[8]

Notes

1. With regard to a definition of gangs, our purposes are best met by relying upon a succinct definition of

gangs—one that includes only those gangs that are involved in criminal activity. More than twenty years ago, Klein (1971) argued for such a definition in that it is those youth groups that commit illegal acts that are of interest to criminologists. In accordance with this criteria, our focus is exclusively on *delinquent* gangs. Other criteria such as having a gang name, colors and symbols, and being identified as a gang by others are of secondary importance but nonetheless essential to distinguishing between gangs and informal law violating groups.

2. This research is part of the Program of Research on the Causes and Correlates of Delinquency, with companion projects at the University at Albany-SUNY and the University of Pittsburgh.
3. A number of block groups defined as socially disorganized did not have high crime rates and therefore were excluded from the sample. Conversely, block groups having high crime rates but socially disorganized according to our analysis also were excluded from the high-risk sample.
4. Given that the survey was conducted in "high risk" neighborhoods with high rates of mobility, these high retention rates are a testament to the diligence and expertise of the field staff that are involved in tracking respondents in the study.
5. In Wave 4, we added a validity check by asking an additional question at the end of the gang section. The respondent was asked if they had ever been in a gang. A respondent's gang membership status was adjusted based on responses to this and other follow-up questions.
6. We are aware that drug sales are included in the street offenses measure but due to the heightened interest in the role of gangs in drug distribution we extracted these items for specific analyses. In additional analyses, we determined that the drug sales items were not "driving" the more general street offending scale.
7. Several possible reasons for the perception that females are not as involved in gangs include the following: 1) most gang research has been conducted by men focusing on male behavior; 2) reliance on official data and/or purposive samples of gangs; and 3) an actual historical change with females becoming more involved in gangs in the latter part of the twentieth century.
8. This research was supported by grants from the Office of Juvenile Justice and Delinquency Prevention, Office of Justice Programs, U.S. Department of Justice (Grant No. 86-JN-CX-0006), and the National Institute of Drug Abuse (Grant No. R01-DA-05183). Points of view or opinions expressed in this paper are those of the authors and do not necessarily represent the official position or policies of these agencies. We are indebted to Linda P. Cunningham, Meg Dyer, Amanda Elliott, Linda Kuhn, Judy Armstrong Laurie, Deantha Ashby Menon, Judy D. Perry, Sylvia Portillo, and Jennifer West, the dedicated research staff, without whom the data could never have been collected, nor the data so meticulously prepared for analysis.

References

Agnew, Robert. 1991. "The Interactive Effect of Peer Variables on Delinquency." *Criminology* 29:47-72.

Akers, Ronald, L. 1985. *Deviant Behavior: A Social Learning Approach 3rd Edition*. Belmont, CA: Wadsworth.

Asbury, H. 1927. *The Gangs of New York*. New York: Capricorn.

Bowker, Lee H. and Malcolm W. Klein. 1983. "The Etiology of Female Juvenile Delinquency and Gang Membership: A Test of Psychological and Social Structural Explanations." *Adolescence* 18:740-751.

Campbell, Anne. 1991. *The Girls in the Gang. 2nd. edition*. Cambridge, MA: Basil Blackwell.

Cloward, Richard A. and Lloyd E. Ohlin. 1960. *Delinquency and Opportunity: A Theory of Delinquent Gangs*. New York: Free Press.

Cohen, Albert. 1955. *Delinquent Boys: The Culture of the Gang*. Glencoe, IL: Free Press.

Covey, Herbert C., Scott Menard, and Robert J. Franzese. 1992. *Juvenile Gangs*. Springfield, IL: Charles C. Thomas Publisher.

Elliott, Delbert S. 1985. "The Assumption that Theories Can Be Combined with Increased Explanatory Power: Theoretical Integrations." In Robert F. Meier (ed.) *Theoretical Methods in Criminology*. Beverly Hills, CA: Sage.

Elliott, Delbert S., David Huizinga, and Suzanne S. Ageton. 1985. *Explaining Delinquency and Drug Use*. Newbury Park, CA: Sage.

Esbensen, Finn-Aage and David Huizinga. 1993 "Gangs, Drugs, and Delinquency in a Survey of Urban Youth." *Criminology* (in press).

Esbensen, Finn-Aage and David Huizinga. 1990. "Community Structure and Drug Use: From a Social Disorganization Perspective." *Justice Quarterly* 7:691-709.

Fagan, Jeffrey. 1990. "Social Processes of Delinquency and Drug Use Among Urban Gangs." pp. 183-219 in C. Ronald Huff (ed.) *Gangs in America*. Newbury Park, CA: Sage.

Fagan, Jeffrey. 1989. "The Social Organization of Drug Use and Drug Dealing Among Urban Gangs." *Criminology* 27:633-669.

Giordano, Peggy C. 1978. "Girls, Guys, and Gangs: The Changing Social Context of Female Delinquency." *Journal of Criminal Law and Criminology* 69:126-132.

Gove, Walter R., 1980. *The Labelling of Deviance*. Beverly Hills, CA: Sage.

Gurule, Jimmy. 1991. "The OJP Initiative on Gangs: Drugs and Violence in America." *NIJ Reports* 224:4-5.

Hagedorn, John M. 1988. *People and Folks: Gangs, Crime and the Underclass in a Rustbelt City*. Chicago, IL: Lakeview Press.

Hanson, K. 1964. *Rebels in the Street: The Story of New York's Girl Gangs*. Englewood Cliffs, NJ: Prentice-Hall.

Harris, Mary G. 1988. *Cholas: Latino Girls and Gangs*. New York:AMS.

Hirschi, Travis. 1969. *Causes of Delinquency*. Berkeley, CA: University of California Press.

Huizinga, David and Delbert S. Elliott. 1986. "Reassessing the Reliability and Validity of Self-Report Delinquency Measures." *Journal of Quantitative Criminology* 2:293-327.

Kaplan, Howard B. 1980. *Deviant Behavior in Defense of Self*. New York, NY: Academic Press.

Klein, Malcolm W. 1971. *Street Gangs and Street Workers*. Englewood Cliffs, NJ: Prentice-Hall.

Klein, Malcolm W. 1984. "Offense Specialization and Versatility Among Juveniles." *British Journal of Criminology* 24:185-194.

MacLeod, Jay. 1987. *Ain't No Makin' It: Leveled Aspirations in a Low-Income Neighborhood*. Boulder, CO: Westview Press.

Maxson, Cheryl L. and Malcolm Klein. 1990. "Street Gang Violence: Twice as Great or Half as Great?" pp. 71-100 in C. Ronald Huff (ed.) *Gangs in America*. Newbury Park, CA:Sage.

Messner, Steven F., Marvin D. Krohn, and Allen E. Liska. 1989. *Theoretical Integration in the Study of Deviance and Crime*. Albany, NY: State University of New York Press.

Miller, Walter B. 1990. "Why the United States Has Failed to Solve its Youth Gang Problem." pp. 263-287 in C. Ronald Huff (ed.) *Gangs in America*. Newbury Park, CA: Sage.

Miller, Walter B. 1958. "Lower Class Culture as a Generating Milieu for Gang Delinquency." *Journal of Social Issues* 14:5-19.

Moore, Joan W. 1978. *Homeboys: Gangs, Drugs, and Prison in the Barrios of Los Angeles*. Philadelphia, PA: Temple University Press.

Morash, Merry. 1983. "Gangs, Groups, and Delinquency." *British Journal of Criminology* 23:309-331.

Puffer, J. Adams. 1912. *The Boy and His Gang*. Boston: Houghton Mifflin.

Quicker, John C. 1983. *Homegirls: Characterizing Chicano Gangs*. San Pedro, CA: International University Press.

Seeman, Melvin. 1959. "On the Meaning of Alienation." *American Sociological Review* 24:783-791.

Short, James F. and Fred L. Strodtbeck. 1965. *Group Processes and Gang Delinquency*. Chicago: University of Chicago Press.

Spergel, Irving A. 1990. "Youth Gangs: Continuity and Change." pp. 171-275 in Norval Morris and Michael Tonry (eds.) *Crime and Justice: An Annual Review of Research*. Chicago: University of Chicago Press.

Spergel, Irving A. 1966. *Street Gang Work: Theory and Practice*. Reading, MA: Addison-Wesley.

Sullivan, Mercer L. 1989. *Getting Paid: Youth Crime and Work in the Inner City*. Ithica, NY: Cornell University Press.

Sutherland, Edwin H. and Donald R. Cressey. 1970. *Criminology*. New York, NY: J.B. Lippincott.

Thornberry, Terence P. 1987. "Toward and Interactional Theory of Delinquency." *Criminology* 25:863-891.

Thornberry, Terence P., Marvin D. Krohn, Alan J. Lizotte, and Deborah Chard-Wierschem. 1993. "The Role of Juvenile Gangs in Facilitating Delinquent Behavior." *Journal of Research in Crime and Delinquency* 30:55-87.

Thrasher, Frederick M. 1927. *The Gang: A Study of One Thousand Three Hundred Thirteen Gangs in Chicago*. Chicago: University of Chicago Press.

Vigil, James D. 1988. *Barrio Gangs: Street Life and Identity in Southern California*. Austin, TX: University of Texas Press.

Winfree, L. Thomas, Teresa Vigil, and G. Larry Mays. 1991. "Social Learning Theory and Youth Gangs: A Comparison of High School Students and Adjudicated Delinquents." Paper presented at the Annual Meeting of the American Society of Criminology, San Francisco.

Wolfgang, Marvin, Robert M. Figlio, Paul E. Tracy, and Simon I. Singer. 1985. *The National Survey of Crime Severity*. Washington, DC: U.S. Government Printing Office.

Yablonsky, Lewis. 1959. "The Delinquent Gang as a Near Group." *Social Problems* 7:108-117.

Appendix A: Self-Report and Drug Use Scales

Street Delinquency

1. Stolen or tried to steal money or things worth more than $50 but less than $100.
2. Stolen or tried to steal money or things worth more than $100.
3. Stolen or tried to steal a motor vehicle.
4. Gone into or tried to go into a building to steal something.
5. Attacked someone with a weapon or with the idea of seriously hurting or killing someone.
6. Used a weapon, force, or strongarm methods to get money or things from people.
7. Physically hurt or threatened to hurt someone to get them to have sex with you.
8. Been involved in gang fights.
9. Snatched someone's purse or wallet or picked someone's pocket.
10. Stolen something from a car.
11. Sold marijuana.
12. Sold hard drugs.
13. Knowingly bought, sold, or held stolen goods or tried to do any of these things.

Other Serious Delinquency

1. Stolen or tried to steal money or things worth more than $5 but less than $50.
2. Stolen or tried to steal money or things worth more than $5.
3. Gone joyriding.
4. Hit someone with the idea of hurting them.
5. Thrown object such as rocks or bottles at people.
6. Had or tried to sexual relations with someone against their will.
7. Carried a hidden weapon.
8. Purposely damaged or destroyed property that did not belong to you.
9. Purposely set fire to a house, building, car, or other property or tried to do so.
10. Used checks illegally or used a slug or fake money to pay for something.
11. Used or tried to use credit or bank cards without the owner's permission.

Minor Delinquency

1. Avoided paying for things such as movies, bus or subway rides, food, or computer services.
2. Lied about your age to get into some place or to buy something.
3. Run away from home.
4. Skipped classes without an excuse.
5. Hitchhiked where it was illegal to do so.
6. Been loud, rowdy, or unruly in a public place.
7. Begged for money or things from strangers.
8. Been drunk in a public place.
9. Been paid for having sexual relations with someone.

Alcohol Use

1. Drunk beer.
2. Drunk wine.
3. Drunk hard liquor.

Other Drug Use

1. Used marijuana or hashish.
2. Used tranquilizers such as valium, librium, thorazine, miltown, equanil, meprobamate.
3. Used barbiturates, downers, reds, yellows, blues.
4. Used amphetamines, uppers, ups, speed, pep pills, or bennies.
5. Used hallucinogens, LSD, acid, peyote, mescaline, psilocybin.
6. Used cocaine or coke other than crack.
7. Used crack.
8. Used heroin.
9. Used angel dust or PCP.

Appendix B: Social Psychological Scale Characteristics

1. Religiosity: 4 item scale
Mean=12.01 SD=3.88 Range 4 - 20 alpha=.75
2. Commitment to Negative Peers: 3 item scale
Mean= 5.65 SD=2.72 Range 3 - 15 alpha=.81
3. Commitment to Positive Peers: 2 item scale
Mean= 8.14 SD=2.02 Range 2 - 10 alpha=.72
4. Attitudes to Delinquency: 12 item scale
Mean=42.38 SD=5.26 Range 12 - 48 alpha=.90
5. Attitudes to Alcohol Use: 1 item
Mean=3.31 SD=0.83 Range 1 - 4
6. Attitudes to Illegal Drug Use
Mean=7.32 SD=1.00 Range 2 - 8 alpha=.61
7. Social Isolation - Family: 5 item scale
Mean=10.30 SD=3.02 Range 4 - 20 alpha=.80
8. Social Isolation - Peers: 5 item scale
Mean=10.71 SD=2.71 Range 5 - 25 alpha=.71
9. Social Isolation - School: 5 item scale
Mean=10.81 SD=2.88 Range 5 - 25 alpha=.70
10. Normlessness - Family: 4 item scale
Mean=8.98 SD=2.38 Range 4 - 20 alpha=.57
11. Normlessness - Peers: 4 item scale
Mean=8.75 SD=2.44 Range 4 - 20 alpha=.66
12. Normlessness - School: 5 item scale
Mean=11.19 SD=2.79 Range 5 - 25 alpha=.57
13. Limited Opportunities - Education: 4 item scale

Mean=8.66 SD=2.38 Range 4 - 20 alpha=.66
14. Limited Opportunities - Other: 8 item scale
Mean=19.00 SD=3.91 Range 8 - 40 alpha=.68
15. Teacher Labeling - Good: 4 item scale
Mean=15.63 SD=2.13 Range 4 - 20 alpha=.64
16. Teacher Labeling - Bad: 5 item scale
Mean=8.63 SD=2.53 Range 5 - 25 alpha=.79
17. Teacher Labeling - Disturbed: 4 item scale
Mean=9.46 SD=2.47 Range 4 - 20 alpha=.64
18. Self-Esteem: 10 item scale
Mean=40.91 SD=5.39 Range 10 - 50 alpha=.78 ✦

23

Street Gang Crime in Chicago

Carolyn Rebecca Block and Richard Block

In this report prepared for the U.S. Department of Justice, the Blocks draw from extensive data on gang crime in Chicago. The definition of gang crime is limited to actions specifically linked to gang function. The complexity of the relationship between crime and gang involvement is revealed in the ebb and flow of gang homicide over a 25-year period, in the differential patterns of lethal and nonlethal violence, and in the variations in level and type of crime among the 40 major street gangs active in this city. The Blocks have pioneered the use of computer mapping to enhance intervention efforts. By identifying concentrations of gang crime in certain neighborhoods, "hotspots" can be pinpointed to focus law enforcement and prevention resources.

Street gang activity—legal and illegal, violent and nonviolent, lethal and nonlethal—occurs disproportionately among neighborhoods and population groups. Types of incidents tend to cluster and increase in bursts in specific neighborhoods and among specific gangs.

Neighborhoods often differ sharply in the predominant type of street gang-motivated incidents they experience. For example, one city neighborhood may be unaffected by street gang activity, while another close by may be a marketplace for a street gang's drug operation, and yet a third may be plagued by frequent and lethal turf battles.

In addition, the chief criminal activities of one street gang often differ from those of another. For example, one outbreak of lethal street gang violence may be characterized by escalating retribution and revenge, while another may be associated with expansion of a drug business into new territory. Consequently, street gangs and the crimes in which they engage cannot be viewed as monolithic in nature.

This Research in Brief describes these and other patterns of street gang-related violence in a major U.S. city—Chicago. All available information, including Chicago police records of illegal street gang-motivated activity—from vandalism to drug offenses to violent offenses (both lethal and nonlethal)—was examined across time, neighborhood, and street gang affiliation. Individual, gang-level, and neighborhood-level characteristics were also analyzed to determine the relationships among these three factors. The results of the analysis give one of the most complete pictures of street gang crime available today.

Revised and reprinted from *Research in Brief*, December 1993. National Institute of Justice, Office of Justice Programs, U.S. Department of Justice.

Issues and Findings

Discussed in the Brief

A study supported by the National Institute of Justice of street gang-motivated violence in one major U.S. city—Chicago. Analysis of police homicide records over 26 years and gang-motivated incident records over 3 years revealed the street gang affiliation of every offender and the location of each offense, which gives a detailed picture of gang activity and the relationships of individual, gang, and neighborhood characteristics.

Key Issues

Gangs—and gang-related violence and drug trafficking—are growing problems across the country. Street gangs and the crimes in which they engage cannot be viewed as monolithic: One neighborhood may be unaffected, while nearby, another is the marketplace for a gang's drug operation or the center of lethal turf battles. Bursts of gang-related violence appear among specific gangs and suddenly stop.

Key Findings

For a 3-year period, 1987-1990, the study results included the following:

- Gang-related, high-crime neighborhoods can be classified into three types: turf hot spots, where gangs fight over territory control; drug hot spots, where gang-motivated drug offenses concentrate; and turf and drug hot spots, where gang-motivated crimes relate to both.
- Gang involvement in violence and homicide is more often turf-related than drug-related. Only 8 of 288 gang-motivated homicides were related to drugs.
- The city's four largest street gangs were identified with most of the street gang crime. Representing 51 percent of all street gang members, they accounted for 69 percent of recorded criminal incidents.
- The rate of street gang-motivated crime in the 2 most dangerous areas was 76 times that of the 2 safest.
- A gun was the lethal weapon used in almost all gang-motivated homicides. Use of high-caliber, automatic, or semiautomatic weapons dramatically increased.

These and other findings of the research have policy implications for formulating intervention strategies:

- Programs to reduce nonlethal street gang violence must be targeted to the specific street gang problems in each neighborhood.
- Effective intervention strategies must be built on continuously updated information.

Target Audience

Law enforcement officials, community leaders, policymakers, and researchers.

Study Methodology

Researchers examined Chicago gang homicide data over a 26-year period, from 1965 through 1990, and detailed information on other gang-related crime from 1987 to 1990. Two methods of analysis were used to determine the extent to which neighborhoods differed in the type and concentration of street gang activity and to examine the neighborhood characteristics that were associated with high levels of lethal and nonlethal street gang activity.[1] The information analyzed was primarily from Chicago Police Department (CPD) records, which were organized into three sets of data on Chicago homicides, street gang-motivated offenses, and street gang territories. Neighborhood characteristics and population data for rate calculation were obtained from the U.S. Bureau of the Census. This information was gathered by tract and aggregated into the 77 Chicago community areas (exhibit 1).[2]

Researchers geocoded the address of each homicide and street gang-motivated incident. Boundaries of the community areas were mapped, geocoded offenses were aggregated by community area, and offenses were analyzed in relation to population and other community characteristics. Finally, the densest concentrations (hot spot areas) of individual addresses of street gang-related incidents were identified regardless of arbitrary boundaries and related to gang turfs, gang activity, and community characteristics.

Exhibit 1

Non-Lethal & Lethal Street Gang Motivated Crimes: 1987–1990

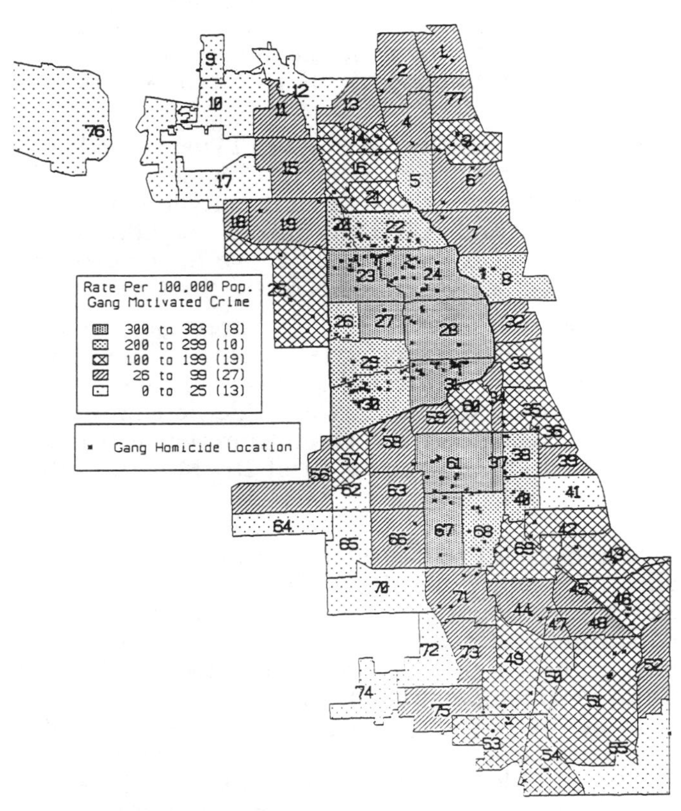

SOURCE: Chicago Police Department

Data on Homicides

One of the largest and most detailed data sets on violence ever collected in the United States, the Chicago homicide data set contains information on every homicide in police records from 1965 to 1990.[3] More than 200 variables were collected for the 19,323 homicides in this data set. The crime analysis unit of the Chicago Police Department has maintained a summary—Murder Analysis Report (MAR)—of each homicide over the 26-year period. On the basis of these reports, 1,311 homicides were classified as street gang-motivated.

Data on Street-Gang–Motivated Offenses

This data set included information on 17,085 criminal offenses that occurred from 1987 to 1990 that were classified by the police as street gang-related. These offenses were categorized as follows:

- 288 homicides.
- 8,828 nonlethal violent offenses (aggravated and simple assault and battery).
- 5,888 drug offenses (violations related to possession or sale of hard or soft drugs).
- 2,081 other offenses (includes more than 100 specific crimes ranging from liquor law violations to intimidation, mob action, vandalism, robbery, and weapons law violations).[4]

Data on Street-Gang Territory Boundaries

This data set included the location of street gang territory boundaries in early 1991. These boundaries were based on maps drawn by street gang officers in Chicago's 26 districts, who identified the territories of 45 street gangs—both major and minor—and noted areas that were in dispute between one or more street gangs.[5]

Defining Gang Affiliation

These three data sets included several possible aspects of street gang affiliation for each incident—for example, the street gang affiliation of the offender or offenders, the affiliation of the victim or victims (if any), and the location of the incident within the boundaries of a gang's turf. In this study researchers classified street gang-motivated criminal incidents according to the affiliation of the offender(s).

Street Gangs in the City

More than 40 major street gangs are active in the city of Chicago.[6] Researchers in this study concentrated on the four largest and most criminally active street gangs, each of which was responsible for at least 1,000 police-recorded criminal incidents from 1987 to 1990:

- *Black Gangster Disciples Nation (BGDN)*. Descended from the Woodlawn Disciples, BGDN is strongest on Chicago's South Side. The gang is known for its turf wars with the Blackstone

Rangers in the late 1960s and early 1970s and the Black Disciples in 1991.[7]

- *Latin Disciples*. A racially and ethnically mixed street gang allied with BGDN, the Latin Disciples operate mainly in the integrated Northwest Side neighborhoods of Humboldt Park and Logan Square.[8]
- *Latin Kings*. The oldest (over 25 years) and largest Latino street gang in Chicago, the Latin Kings operate throughout the city in Latino and racially and ethnically mixed neighborhoods. The gang is particularly active in the growing Mexican neighborhoods on the Southwest Side.
- *Vice Lords*. One of the oldest street gangs in Chicago, the Vice Lords date from the 1950s. The gang operates throughout the city, but is strongest in the very poor West Side neighborhoods that have never recovered from the destruction that followed the death of Dr. Martin Luther King in 1968.[9]

Members of BGDN and the Vice Lords are almost all black men, while the Latin Disciples and Latin Kings are predominantly Latino men. Rough police department estimates indicate that the 19,000 members of these four gangs constitute about half of all Chicago street gang members.

In the mid-1980s BGDN and the Latin Disciples formed the folk alliance. Soon after the Latin Kings and Vice Lords formed the People alliance. Both "super alliances" of street gangs appeared following an increase of street gang-related homicide.

The contrasting size and longevity of Chicago black and Latino street gangs is in part a reflection of the city's population dynamics. In general, the black population of Chicago has declined[10] and some black neighborhoods have been abandoned, while the Latino population has grown and the population of Latino neighborhoods has climbed. For example, over the past 25 years, the population of East Garfield Park (area 27) has fallen by 60 percent and many commercial and residential buildings have been lost, while the population of South Lawndale (area 30) has expanded by 31 percent and changed from a Czech to a Mexican neighborhood (now called Little Village).

With the growth of the Latino population and the expansion of Latino neighborhoods, many small street gangs have emerged. Given their limited territories, these small neighborhood street gangs battle each other frequently and often have to defend their turf against the more established Latino street gangs.

Criminal Activities of Street Gangs

From 1987 to 1990, the four largest street gangs were also the most criminally active. They accounted for 69 percent of all street gang-motivated crimes and 56 percent of all street gang-motivated homicides in which the street gang affiliation of the offender was known. Of the 17,085 street gang-motivated offenses recorded during this period, BGDN was responsible for 4,843 offenses; the Vice Lords for 3,116; the Latin Kings for 2,868; and the Latin Disciples for 1,011.

However, taken as a whole, street gangs other than the top four were responsible for more police-recorded offenses (5,207 from 1987 to 1990) than any one of the top four. Many of these smaller street gangs were relatively new, predominantly Latino, and fighting among themselves over limited turfs.

Drug Offenses

The four major street gangs varied sharply in the degree to which drug crimes dominated their illegal activity (exhibit 2). For example, of the 2,868 incidents committed by the Latin Kings from 1987 through 1990, only 19 percent were drug offenses, compared to 56 percent of the 3,116 incidents attributed to the Vice Lords. More incidents of cocaine possession (the most common drug offense) were attributed to the Vice Lords or to the Black Gangster Disciples Nation than to all other street gangs combined. The Vice Lords were also active in heroin possession offenses, with twice as many incidents attributed to them than to all other street gangs combined.

The reintroduction of heroin to Chicago by the Vice Lords and Black Gangster Disciples Nation was particularly disturbing to police and community workers. From 1987 to 1990, the number of incidents of possession of white heroin rapidly escalated from 11 to 165, while possession of brown heroin declined from 77 to 64, probably reflecting the reentry of Asian heroin into the Chicago market. Meanwhile, the number of inci-

Definition of a Street Gang

The Chicago Police Department defines "street gang" as an association of individuals who exhibit the following characteristics in varying degrees:

- A gang name and recognizable symbols.
- A geographic territory.
- A regular meeting pattern.
- An organized, continuous course of criminality.

An incident is defined as street gang-related if the evidence indicates that the action grew out of a street gang function. Gang membership is not enough to determine gang-relatedness. To determine if an incident is street gang-related, police investigators analyze each case for application of the following criteria:

- Representing—Offenses growing out of a signification of gang identity or alliance (such as hand signs, language, and clothing).
- Recruitment—Offenses relating to recruiting members for a street gang, which include intimidating a victim or witness.
- Extortion—Efforts to compel membership or to exact tribute for the gang.
- Turf violation—Offenses committed to disrespect another gang's territory.
- Prestige—Offenses committed either to glorify the street gang or to gain rank within the gang.
- Personal conflict—Conflicts involving leadership or punitive action within the rank and file of a gang.
- Vice—Activities generally involving the street-level distribution of narcotics by street gang members.
- Retaliation—Acts of revenge for offenses against the gang by rival gang members.[11]

Exhibit 2

Street Gang Incidents: 1987–1990 Four Largest & Other Gangs

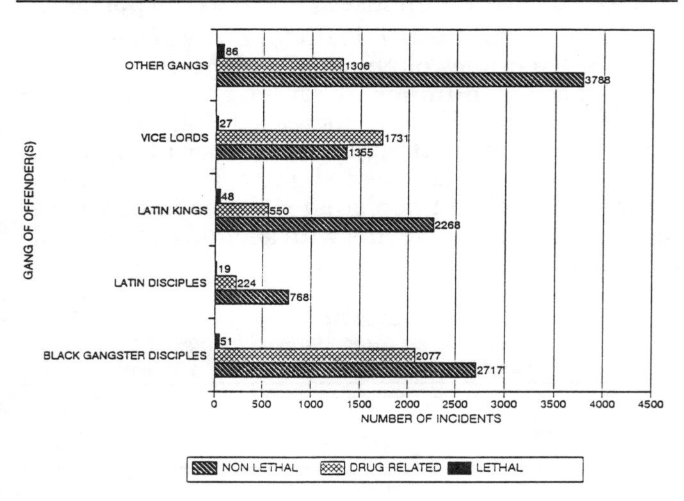

dents of hard drug possession involving the Latin Kings, Latin Disciples, and other street gangs remained low.

Only 8 of the 288 street gang-motivated homicides between 1987 and 1990 were drug related.[12] Five of these, all of which occurred in 1989 or 1990, were related to the business of drugs. As researchers in Los Angeles also found, the connection between street gangs, drugs, and homicide was weak and could not explain the rapid increase in homicide in the late 1980s.[13]

Competition, Violence, and Other Confrontations Over Turf

Most of the nonlethal, nondrug offenses attributed to street gangs were violent confrontations (assault and battery) or damage to property (graffiti); see exhibit 3. Other Index crimes such as robbery and burglary were relatively rare, and only six sexual assaults were determined to be street gang-motivated from 1987 to 1990.[14]

Exhibit 3

Non-Lethal Street Gang Crimes Four Largest & Other Gangs

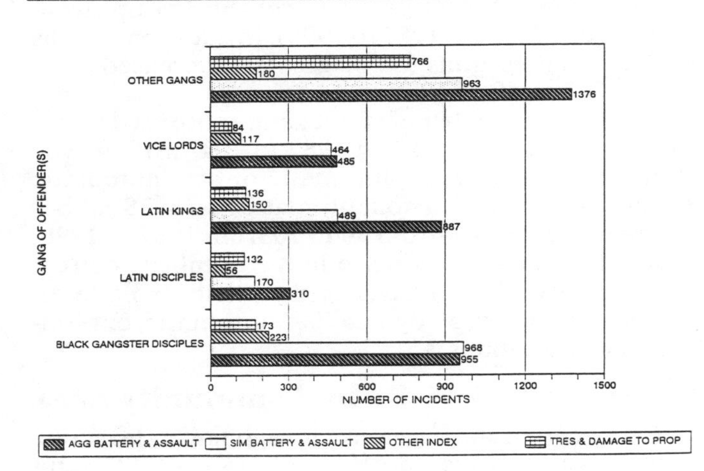

Violent incidents involving the Vice Lords or BGDN were evenly divided between simple battery and assault (no weapon) and aggravated battery and assault. Offenses attributed to the Latin Disciples, Latin Kings, or smaller street gangs (which were also mostly Latino) were more likely to be aggravated than simple assault or battery.

The Vice Lords' West Side turf (see exhibit 4) was remarkably free of graffiti. The gang was so much in command that they did not need many physical markers to identify their turf. In contrast, the constricted turfs of the smaller street gangs were well marked with graffiti and other identifiers. Driving south on Pulaski Road from Vice Lords' turf in North Lawndale (area 29) toward Two Sixers', Deuces', and Latin Vikings' territories in South Lawndale (area 30), researchers observed a remarkable transformation in neighborhoods. In North Lawndale stood many abandoned factories and apartments and empty lots, but not much graffiti. In thriving South Lawndale (Little Village), buildings were covered with multiple layers of insignia. Competing for scarce territory, the street gangs in Little Village had to identify and violently defend their domains.

Both the amount of graffiti and number of violent turf defense incidents appear related to competition. West Side gangs knew which neighborhoods were under the Vice Lords' control and infrequently challenged that control. In contrast, battles between rival street gangs were a regular occurrence in the expanding Mexican neighborhoods on the Southwest Side. Thus, symbolic "face maintenance," graffiti contests, and violent territorial defense actions were relatively frequent in street gangs more threatened by competition.

Exhibit 4

Street Gang Motivated Homicide, Other Violence & Drug Crimes: 1987–1990

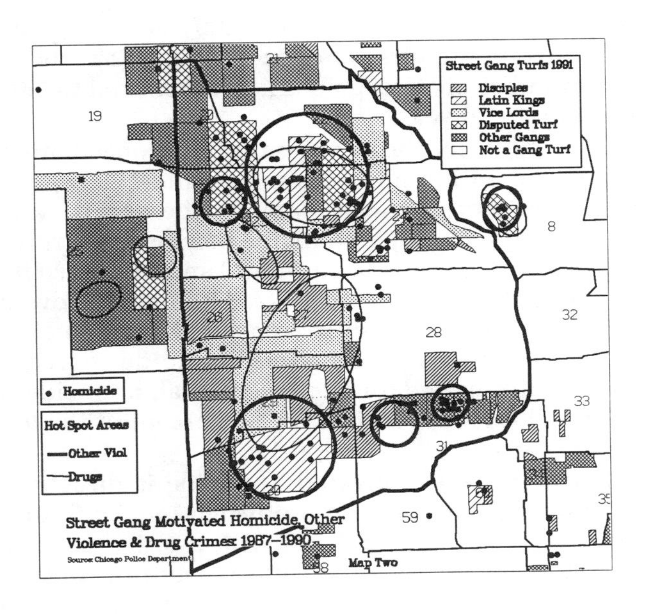

Trends in Homicides

In contrast to domestic or acquaintance killings, street gang homicides occurred in bursts (exhibit 5).[15]

Exhibit 5
Street Gang Motivated Homicides, 1965–1990
(Number & rate per 100,000)

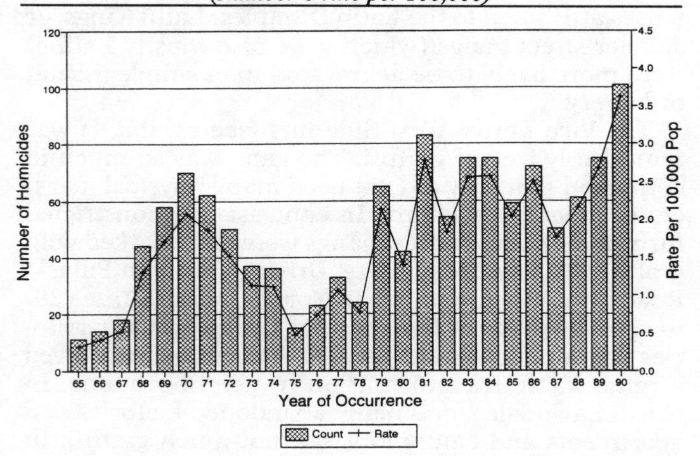

Years with only a few homicides were punctuated by years with many. In 1965 only 11 street gang-motivated homicides occurred (2.8 percent of all homicides); but in 1970, 70 occurred (8.7 percent of the total). The risk of being murdered in a street gang confrontation was more than five times higher in 1970 than in 1965. This early surge in homicide reflected BGDN wars on Chicago's South Side.

By 1975 the number of street gang-motivated homicides was again as low as the mid-1960s, even though 1974 and 1975 were record years for other types of homicide. This brief respite was followed by eruptions of lethal street gang violence in 1979 and again in 1981, when there were 65 and 83 deaths, respectively. However, the formation in the mid-1980s of the two gang super alliances, People and Folk, may have brought relative stability in street gang-motivated violence for a few years. Only 50 street gang-motivated homicides were recorded in 1987, and the total number of Chicago homicides reached the lowest point in 20 years.

Unfortunately, the rivalries that developed both between and within alliances in the mid-1980s generated even more violence later in the decade when street gang-motivated homicide increased sharply to 101 in 1990 (then an all-time high) and surpassed that to 121 in 1991 and 133 in 1992. Although the overall level of homicide also increased rapidly in those years, street gang-motivated homicide increased faster. It accounted for 12 percent of all homicides in 1990 and was responsible for 33 percent of the total increase from 1987 through 1990.

If street gang-motivated homicide is directly related to other street gang-motivated incidents and if the proportion of incidents with a lethal outcome does not change, then the pattern over time of lethal incidents should parallel the pattern of nonlethal incidents. Although the data show some similarity in the short-term pattern of street gang-motivated lethal versus nonlethal incidents, the overall trend is very different (see exhibit 6).[16]

- In 1987 1 street gang-motivated homicide occurred for every 44 street gang-motivated personal violence offenses known to the police.
- In 1990 there was 1 death for every 20 police-recorded crimes of personal violence.

Indeed, the number of street gang-motivated deaths in a typical month increased sharply over the 3-year period, even though the number of nonlethal violent incidents declined slightly. These divergent trends in lethal and nonlethal violence indicate that the proportion of incidents with a lethal outcome has increased.

Exhibit 6
Trends in Street Gang-Motivated Violence
Lethal and Nonlethal (3 Month Moving Average)

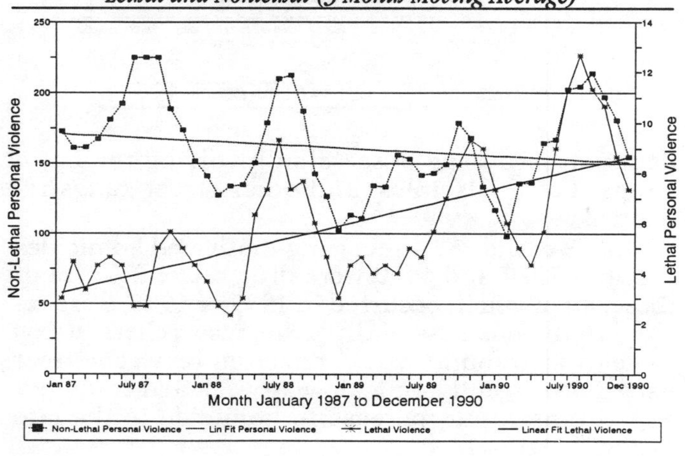

The Role of Guns

One explanation for the increasing lethality of street gang-motivated violent incidents could be an increase in gang use of guns. From 1987 to 1990, the proportion of nonlethal street gang-motivated violent offenses that were committed with a gun increased slightly from 27.3 percent to 31.5 percent. In contrast, a gun was the lethal weapon in almost all street gang-motivated homicides—96 percent in 1987 and 94 percent in 1990.

Furthermore, the proportion of murder weapons that were automatics or semiautomatics increased from 22 percent to 31 percent over the 3 years (from 11 to 31 deaths from 1987 to 1990). In addition, deaths by large-caliber guns (38 or greater) increased from 13 in 1987 to 39 in 1990.

Overall the number of street gang-motivated homicides increased from 51 in 1987 to 101 in 1990. The number killed with an automatic or semiautomatic (any caliber) or with a nonautomatic gun of 38 caliber or greater increased from 24 to 70 from 1987 to 1990. Virtually the entire increase in the number of street gang-motivated homicides seems attributable to an increase in the use of high-caliber, automatic, or semiautomatic weapons.

Street Gang Activity by Community Area

Every community area in Chicago had at least one street gang-motivated offense between 1987 and 1990. However, the two most dangerous communities, East Garfield Park (area 27) and Humboldt Park (area 23), had a mean annual rate of street gang-motivated crimes (381.5) that was 76 times the mean annual rate (5.0) in the two least dangerous neighborhoods, Mt. Greenwood (area 74) and Edison Park (area 9); see exhibit 1. The community areas with the highest levels of street gang-motivated crime were on the West Side (areas 23, 24, 27, 28, and 31); in the south central neighborhoods of New City (area 61) and Fuller Park (area 37); and in West Englewood (area 67), the scene of a burst of street gang violence in 1990 and 1991.

Homicides

Street gang-motivated homicides were also concentrated in two corridors on the Northwest and Southwest Sides. Of Chicago's 77 community areas, 17 had no street gang-motivated homicide from 1965 to 1990. Many had only one. None of the 13 community areas with the lowest rates of street gang-motivated crime had a street gang-motivated homicide between 1987 and 1990. At the other extreme, the Lower West Side (area 31) averaged more than 6 street gang-motivated homicides per 100,000 people per year over that same time period.

The risk of becoming a homicide victim or offender was far higher for young Latino men than for other Latinos or for non-Latino whites, and equal to that for young black men. The risk of homicide for other Latinos was not exceptionally high,[17] but the risk of homicide for non-Latino blacks was higher than for non-Latino whites, regardless of age or gender, and higher than for all Latinos except young men.

These individual differences were reflected in community differences as well.

Community Differences

Black neighborhoods with high rates of street gang homicide also had high rates of other forms of homicide. But this was not necessarily true in other communities. For example, the mostly mixed and Latino neighborhoods on the Northwest and Southwest Sides had many street gang-motivated killings, but relatively few killings for other reasons.[18] As a result, the rate of street gang-motivated homicide and the rate of other forms of homicide from 1987 though 1990 were only weakly correlated (.287) across community areas.

Compared to the relationship over time (exhibit 6), the relationship between lethal and nonlethal violence across geographic areas appeared to be higher, but the strength of the relationship depended on the type of violence. Five of the six community areas with the highest rates of street gang-motivated nonlethal personal violence (assault and battery) also ranked among the six with the highest rates of street gang-motivated homicide. In contrast, only one of the six community areas that had the highest rate of street gang-motivated drug crime in the years 1987 to 1990 also ranked among the top six in street gang-motivated homicide rates. Only one community area, Humboldt Park (area 23), ranked among the top six in all three rates—street gang-motivated lethal violence, nonlethal personal violence, and drug offenses. Overall the correlation across the 77 community areas between rates of street gang-motivated drug crime and homicide was moderate (.401), while the correlation was much stronger (.728) between street gang-motivated homicide and rates of street gang-motivated assault and battery.

Hot Spot Areas of Street Gang Activity

Fifty-one percent of the city's street gang-motivated homicides and 35 percent of nonlethal street gang-motivated offenses occurred in 10 community areas on the West Side. Three kinds of neighborhood situations can be seen in this West Side map (exhibit 4).[19]

- Neighborhoods with a turf hot spot area (heavy concentration of nonlethal personal violent activity to defend turf).
- Neighborhoods with a drug hot spot area (heavy concentration of street gang-motivated drug offenses).
- Neighborhoods plagued by both a turf and drug hot spot area.

Residents in these neighborhoods tend to view street gang activity very differently. For example, a resident living in a drug hot spot area is likely to consider the neighborhood street gang problem to be primarily a drug problem. A resident living in a turf hot spot area may consider the neighborhood street gang problem to revolve around violent defense of turf. And a resident of a community in which a drug and a turf hot spot area intersect experiences the worst of both.

In specific neighborhood areas, the link between incidents of street gang-motivated nonlethal and lethal personal violence was far stronger than that between drug crimes and lethal violence. For example, street gang-motivated homicides tended to occur within or close to the boundaries of turf hot spot areas, and only rarely in drug hot spot areas except when a drug hot spot area intersected a turf hot spot area.[20] Of the 169 street gang-motivated homicides in the 10 community areas shown in exhibit 4, 94 occurred in hot spot areas, as follows: 37 in neighborhoods where a drug hot spot area and a turf hot spot area intersected (28 in Humboldt Park, 4 in Little Village, and 5 in Cabrini Green), 48 in turf hot spot areas only, and 9 in drug hot spot areas only. The turf hot spot area in Little Village (in the southwest corner) experienced more than 7 homicides per square mile, while the Pilsen hot spot area (southeast corner) experienced 48, and the turf hot spot area around Humboldt Park, which intersected with a drug hot spot area, was the site of 16 homicides per square mile over the 3-year period.

Highlights of Major Findings

This study painted a more complete picture of the reality of street gang crime than is usually the case in studies of gangs. By analyzing police records of lethal and nonlethal street gang-motivated crimes, examining temporal and spatial patterns of those crimes, and describing the criminal activities of Chicago's four largest street gangs, researchers sought to uncover typical patterns of street gang life.

The patterns of street gang activity can be summarized as follows:

- Chicago's largest street gangs can be identified with most of the city's street gang crime. These four street gangs (representing about 10 percent of all street gangs and 51 percent of the estimated number of all street gang members) accounted for 69 percent of police-recorded street gang-motivated criminal incidents and 55 percent of all street gang-motivated homicides from 1987 to 1990.
- Street gangs varied in the types of activities in which they were engaged. Some specialized in incidents of expressive violence while others focused on instrumental violence (see "Expressive Versus Instrumental Violence"). For example, the Vice Lords and BGDN were much more involved in acts of instrumental violence (such as possession or sale of drugs), while the Latin Disciples, Latin Kings, and smaller gangs specialized in acts of expressive violence (such as turf defense). Most of the criminal activity in smaller street gangs centered on representation turf defense. The most lethal street gang hot spot areas are along disputed boundaries between small street gangs.
- Types of street gang crime clustered in specific neighborhoods. Street gangs specializing in instrumental violence were strongest in disrupted and declining neighborhoods. Street gangs specializing in expressive violence were strongest and most violent in relatively prosperous neighborhoods with expanding populations.
- The rate of street gang-motivated crime in the 2 most dangerous Chicago communities was 76 times that of the 2 safest. However, every community area in Chicago had at least one street gang-motivated criminal incident between 1987 and 1990.
- Most of the lethal gang-related crimes occurred in neighborhoods where street gang activity centered on turf battles, not in neighborhoods where street gang activity focused on drug offenses. Of 288 street gang-motivated homicides from 1987 to 1990, only 8 also involved drug use or a drug-related motive.
- A gun was the lethal weapon in almost all Chicago street gang-motivated homicides from 1987 to 1990. Incidents involving a high-caliber, automatic, or semiautomatic weapon accounted for most of the increase in homicides over this period.
- Many community areas with high levels of lethal and nonlethal street gang-motivated personal violence and homicide had relatively low levels of other forms of homicide. Although hot spot areas of street gang-motivated drug offenses were usually low in street gang homicide, some were high in other kinds of homicide.

Policy Implications

As this report shows, street gang violence has been a continuing problem in Chicago since the late 1960s. The years 1990, 1991, and 1992 broke records for street gang violence, and the number of incidents continued to grow in 1993.

Expressive Versus Instrumental Violence

A growing body of literature indicates that violence is not one type of event but many.[21] Almost all acts of lethal violence begin as another type of confrontation—for example, as an argument between spouses, a fight or brawl between acquaintances, a robbery, an act of sexual violence, or a street gang confrontation—that escalates to death. To understand lethal violence, the reasons why some—and only some—of these violent events become lethal must first be understood. The answer differs for those fatal and nonfatal "sibling" offenses such as assault homicide and assault compared to robbery homicide and robbery, which occupy different points on the expressive-versus-instrumental continuum.

In general, the dynamics of a violent situation are governed by the degree to which *expressive* versus *instrumental* motives predominate as the assailant's primary and immediate goal. In an expressive violent confrontation, the primary goal is violence or injury itself, and other motives are secondary. In contrast, the primary purpose of an act of instrumental violence is not to hurt, injure, or kill, but to acquire money or property. In addition, situational factors—such as possession of a weapon—that might affect the likelihood of a fatal outcome operate differently in expressive and instrumental confrontations.

Street gang-motivated violence often contains many expressive aspects—such as impulsive and emotional defense of one's identity as a gang member, defense and glorification of the reputation of the gang and gang members, and expansion of the membership and territory of the gang. Though some of these turf activities may involve acquisition, the primary motive is expressive. On the other hand, other types of street gang violence, such as formation and maintenance of a lucrative drug business and other entrepreneurial activities, are fundamentally instrumental. In this study researchers found that some gangs specialized in expressive violence, while others specialized in instrumental violence.

Intervention programs whose aim is to reduce nonlethal street gang violence will probably also reduce lethal violence. To be effective, however, these intervention programs must be built on a foundation of current information about the types of street gangs and street gang activity in each specific neighborhood.

As shown by this research, street gang-motivated crime is not random. In Chicago it occurred in specific neighborhoods and was concentrated in limited time periods. Some street gangs spent much of their time defending or expanding their turf while others were actively involved in the business of illegal drugs. Programs to reduce street gang-motivated violence must recognize these differences. For example, a program to reduce gang involvement in drugs in a community in which gang members are most concerned with defense of turf has little chance of success.

Furthermore, because the predominant type of street gang activity in a neighborhood may change from year to year or month to month, and because the level of street gang-motivated violence tends to occur in spurts, effective intervention strategies must be built on continuously updated information.

Another focus of control over gang violence should be on weapons. The death weapon in almost all gang-motivated homicides in Chicago was a gun, and much of the increase in gang-motivated homicides from 1987 to 1990 was an increase in killings with large-caliber, automatic, or semiautomatic weapons. Therefore, reducing the availability of these most dangerous weapons may also reduce the risk of death in street gang-plagued communities.

Street gang membership, street gang-related violence, and other illegal street gang activity must be understood in light of both long-term or chronic social patterns, and current or acute conditions. Street gang patterns and trends reflect not only chronic problems, such as racial and class discrimination and adjustment of immigrants, but also acute, often rapidly changing problems stemming from the existing economic situation, weapon availability, drug markets, and the spatial arrangement of street gang territories across a city.

Obviously, the chronic problem of street gang violence cannot be solved with a quick fix; the ultimate solution rests on a coordinated criminal justice response, changes in educational opportunities, racial and ethnic attitudes, and job structure. On the other hand, while waiting for these long-term strategies to take effect, lives can be saved and serious injury prevented by targeting the causes of short-term or acute escalations in violence levels.[22]

Notes

1. Two types of spatial analysis were used: correlational community area analysis and identification of hot spot areas of dense street gang activity concentrations. Hot spot areas were identified using the hot spot ellipse capability of the STAC (Spatial and Temporal Analysis of Crime) package, which was developed by the Illinois Criminal Justice Information Authority. STAC used an iterative search that identified the densest clusters of events on the map, calculated a standard deviational ellipse fitting each cluster, and mapped the events and the ellipses. STAC delineated, regardless of artificial boundaries, the areas of the map that contained the densest clusters of events. It was thus a data based-driven, objective tool for identifying nonarbitrary summary areas from the actual scatter of events on the map. For further information about STAC, see C. R. Block, "Hot Spots and Isocrimes in Law Enforcement Decisionmaking," paper presented at the Conference on Police and Community Responses to Drugs: Frontline Strategies in the Drug War, University of Illinois at Chicago, December 1990.
2. Community areas are aggregations of census tracts, usually including several neighborhoods but sometimes only one, identified by an official name and number. Since the Chicago School sociologists first identified them in the 1930s, a plethora of data has been collected and analyzed by community area. For more detail, see exhibit 1 and Chicago Factbook Consortium, *Local Community Fact Book: Chicago Metropolitan Area* (Chicago: University of Illinois Department of Sociology, 1980).
3. Data from 1965 through 1981 are currently available in the National Archive of Criminal Justice Data of the Inter-University Consortium for Political and Social Research, and a completely updated data set from 1965 through 1990 is being prepared for the archive. The ultimate source of all information for all years was the Murder Analysis Report (MAR), a two-page summary of each homicide maintained since 1965 by the Crime Analysis Unit of the Chicago Police Department. Since its inception in 1965, MAR has consistently flagged cases in which there was positive evidence that the homicide was motivated by street gang activity.
4. Although a single incident may have involved multiple offenders or multiple victims, data were analyzed at the incident level. If more than one offense occurred in an incident, the incident was classified according to the most serious violation. All data are from 1987 to 1990, except for homicides; the homicide data include murders that occurred from 1965 to 1990.
5. It is quite possible that the territories defined by police officers differ from the territories that would be defined by street gang members, agency workers, community members, or even by police officers assigned to another division such as narcotics. Also, because street gangs disappear, merge, or change names over time, it would have been preferable to have a turf map that was contemporaneous with the street gang incident data. However, the turfs are probably a fairly accurate representation of the later part of the study period.
6. Chicago Police Department, Gang Crime Section, "Street Gangs (internal report), 1992.
7. In the 1960s and 1970s, the Woodlawn Disciples battled the Blackstone Rangers (later called the Black P Stone Nation and then changed to El Rukins), which resulted in an upsurge in homicides. In 1991, renamed BGDN, the gang fought the normally allied Black Disciples gang for control of Englewood.
8. Much of the discussion on gang structure, history, and current activities depends upon two police department sources: L.J. Bobrowski, "Collecting, Organizing, and Reporting Street Gang Crime," paper presented at the annual meeting of the American Society of Criminology, Chicago, 1988; and Chicago Police Department, "Street Gangs," 1992.
9. R.J. Sampson and W.J. Wilson, "Toward a Theory of Race, Crime, and Urban Inequality," paper presented at the annual meeting of the American Society of Criminology, San Francisco, 1991.
10. C. R. Block, "Lethal Violence in the Chicago Latino Community," in *Homicide: The Victim-Offender Connection*, ed. A.V Wilson (Cincinnati: Anderson Pub. Co., 1993), 267-342.
11. For further information, see Bobrowski, "Collecting, Organizing and Reporting Street Gang Crime," and Chicago Police Department, "Street Gangs," 1992.
12. A homicide was defined as drug-related if drugs were a motivation for the crime or if the victim or offender was under the influence of drugs during the incident. Drug-motivated homicides included those involving the business or sale of drugs, those that resulted from a crime committed to get drugs or money for drugs, those that resulted from an argument or confrontation about drugs, and "other" (such as an infant starving to death because both parents were high). This definition follows that of P.J. Goldstein, "The Drugs/Violence Nexus: A Tripartite Conceptual Framework," *Journal of Drug Issues* 14 (1985): 493-506. Note that drug-related information was not available for nonlethal incidents.
13. M. W. Klein, C. L. Maxson, and L. C. Cunningham, "'Crack,' Street Gangs, and Violence," *Criminology* 29(4) (1991): 701-717.
14. Non-Index offenses, such as intimidation, mob action, and weapons and liquor law violations, are not shown in exhibit 3.
15. Yearly totals in exhibit 5, which refer to the year of occurrence of the homicide (year of the incident) may differ from police totals, which refer to the year in which the police "booked" the offense.
16. The data here are 3-month moving averages.
17. C. R. Block, "Lethal Violence in the Chicago Latino Community," 1993.

18. R. Block and C. R. Block, "Homicide Syndromes and Vulnerability: Violence in Chicago's Community Areas Over 25 Years," in *Studies on Crime and Crime Prevention*, v. 1. (Oslo/Stockholm: Scandinavian University Press, 1992), 61-87.
19. Because of space considerations, the actual locations of the drug or nonlethal violent incidents that formed the basis for these hot spot areas are not depicted in exhibit 4. The location of street gang-motivated homicides, which were not included in the calculation of the hot spot area ellipses shown on the map, are depicted by black dots.
20. Note that only nonlethal offenses, not homicides, were included in the calculation of hot spot areas depicted in exhibit 4.
21. For more information on this issue, see R. Block and C. R. Block, "Homicide Syndromes and Vulnerability," 1992.
22. The authors acknowledge also the assistance of the Chicago Police Department in preparing this study, especially Commander Robert Dart of the Gang Crime Section, Commander James Maurer of Area Four Violent Crimes, Gang Crimes Specialist Lawrence J. Bobrowski of the Bureau of Operational Services, and Detective Al Kettman (retired) of the Crime Analysis Unit. Findings and conclusions of the research reported here are those of the authors and do not necessarily reflect the official position or policies of the U.S. Department of Justice.

References

Block, Carolyn Rebecca. "Hot Spots and Isocrimes in Law Enforcement Decisionmaking." Paper presented at the Conference on Police and Community Responses to Drugs: Frontline Strategies in the Drug War. University of Illinois at Chicago, December 1990.

——. "Lethal Violence in the Chicago Latino Community." In *Homicide: The Victim-Offender Connection*, ed. Anna V. Wilson. Cincinnati: Anderson Pub. Co., 1993, pp. 267-342.

Block, Carolyn Rebecca, and Richard Block. "Beyond Wolfgang: An Agenda for Homicide Research in the 1990s." *Journal of Criminal Justice* 14 (1992): 31-70.

Block, Richard, and Carolyn Rebecca Block. "Homicide Syndromes and Vulnerability: Violence in Chicago's Community Areas Over 25 Years." *Studies on Crime and Crime Prevention*, v. 1. Oslo/ Stockholm: Scandinavian University Press. 1992, pp. 61-87.

Bobrowski, Lawrence J. "Collecting, Organizing, and Reporting Street Gang Crime." Paper presented at the annual meeting of the American Society of Criminology, Chicago, 1988.

Chicago Factbook Consortium. *Local Community Fact Book: Chicago Metropolitan Area, 1980*. Chicago: University of Illinois Department of Sociology, 1980.

Chicago Police Department, Gang Crime Section. "Street Gangs." Internal report, 1992.

Curry, G. David. and Irving Spergel. "Gang Homicide, Delinquency, and Community." *Criminology* 26(3) (1988): 381-405.

Goldstein, Paul J. "The Drugs/Violence Nexus: A Tripartite Conceptual Framework." *Journal of Drug Issues* 14 (1985): 493-506.

Klein, Malcolm W., Cheryl L. Maxson, and Lea C. Cunningham. "'Crack,' Street Gangs, and Violence." *Criminology* 29(4) (1991): 701-717.

Sampson, Robert J., and William Julius Wilson. "Toward a Theory of Race, Crime, and Urban Inequality." Paper presented at the annual meeting of the American Society of Criminology, San Francisco, 1991.

Spergel, Irving A. "Youth Gangs: Continuity and Change." In *Crime and Justice: A Review of Research*, vol. 12, eds. Michael Tonry and Norval Morris. Chicago: University of Chicago Press, 1990, pp. 171-275.

Wacquant, Loic, and William Julius Wilson. "Poverty, Joblessness, and the Social Transformation of the Inner City." In *Welfare Policies for the 1990s*, eds. Phoebe H. Cottingham and David T. Ellwood. Cambridge, Mass.: Harvard University Press, 1989, pp. 70-102. ✦

24
Drive-bys

William Sanders

In this chapter from Gangbangs and Drive-bys, *Sanders describes several features of what has become the quintessential form of gang violence, the drive-by shooting. The author approaches these events as strategic interactions, reinforced by the grounded values and norms of gang culture and yielding considerable benefits to identity and status. Although Sanders relies on law enforcement sources, supplemented with interviews with San Diego gang informants, his framework of analysis contrasts markedly with other researchers' use of police data. His focus on situational interactions reinforces the importance of group dynamics in understanding gang behavior.*

Introduction

This chapter closely examines one of the key violent situations associated with gang life: drive-by shootings. I have attempted to explore this phenomenon from several different angles in order to provide a fully developed understanding of it. First, it is examined in terms of a historical background to see how drive-bys replaced other types of gang violence as a favored tactic. Then, using Erving Goffman's concept of *strategic interaction*, we evaluate drive-bys as a strategy. Further using Goffman's notions of character and identity developed in situations, we see how a gang identity can be found in the context of a drive-by. Finally, we look at the different types of situations where drive-bys develop and how they develop.

The Drive-by Shooting in the Context of Gang Warfare

A drive-by shooting occurs when members of one gang drive a vehicle into a rival gang's area and shoot at someone. As used here, the drive-by is a hit and run tactic and does not include situations where members of one gang, who happen to have guns, arrive at a location in a car, and then later on encounter rival gang members and use their guns. However, drive-bys *do* include situations where gang members drive to a location, find a target, jump out of the car, chase the victim down, and then flee in the car after the shooting. The idea of a drive-by is that it is a hit-and-run maneuver, and whether or not someone temporarily leaves their car is not considered analytically important. The following examples provide a sense of the range of types of drive-by shootings:

> The victims, some members of Da Boys, were at home. Some Be Down Boys drove up, got out of the car and shot at the victims, their car, and dog. After firing several shots, they got back in their car and drove away.

> Members of Eastside Piru were hanging out in front of a liquor store when a car drove by. Some Crips in the car said, "What's up, Blood?" The Pirus ignored them and walked away. After a Piru member refused to come over to their car, the Crips began firing, hitting the victim three times. Then the Crips drove away.

> A member of the Neighborhood Crips was sitting on a wall when he heard a car drive up. He turned to look at the car and then turned back. At this point he was shot in the head. The victim ran into a friend's house, noting only that the shooter was wearing red. [Red is the color of the Crips' rivals, the Bloods/Pirus.]

> Some VELs were standing in front of their house when two 70s on a motorcycle drove by and shot a pistol at the house and car, hitting the car.

> Some Varrio Market Street boys were standing outside when four VELs drove up and yelled, "Encanto, Encanto!" and asked, "Where are you from?" When the victims replied "Varrio Market!" the VELs started shooting.

Sometime after World War II, gangs introduced the term *japping* to refer to hit and run attacks (Klein, 1971: 24). The term came from certain unorthodox strategies used in the war by Japanese soldiers, especially shooting from hidden positions behind Allied lines. It was an unconventional mobile warfare discovered by the gangs. Walter Miller (1975: 36-38) used the term *foray* to characterize these mobile tactics. This type of gang warfare is in contrast to the melee or rumble, where gangs would meet at appointed places and times to do battle in large groups.

In the traditional East Coast cities with high density populations, narrow streets, and congested traffic, a foray was often conducted on foot or bicycle. The neighborhoods are relatively close, and gang members were able to make a quick attack, and get back to the safety of their own area before the other gang could mobilize for a counterstrike. It would even be possible to make a hit-and-run attack using public transportation, such as the subway.

On the West Coast, particularly in Southern California, the neighborhoods are further apart, more spread out, more likely to be on the ground level, and have lower density. There is an excellent road system and relatively little public transportation. The automobile is the primary mode of transportation, and using the freeway system, an attacker can quickly return to his home base miles away from the site of the shooting. It was in this type of situation that the drive-by shooting developed.

In San Diego, there was an increasing use of the drive-by shooting from the early 1980s to the end of the decade. Table 1 shows the jump in drive-by shootings as a percentage of gang attacks from the early 1980s to the later part of the decade. As can be seen, the drive-by almost doubled in proportion to non-drive-by assaults from the beginning to the end of the decade.

Table 1

Percentage of all gang assaults that are drive-by shootings

Year	Drive-bys
1981	23 .7
1988	40.8

Strategic Interaction and Drive-by Shootings

Analytically, we can understand drive-by shootings as a rational reaction to the conditions of gang warfare. Erving Goffman (1969:100-101) describes *strategic interaction* as those situations where people come together under conditions of mutual fatefulness. The *players* in these situations attempt to dope out what the other is going to do, and make the best possible *move* to maximize their chances of surviving the encounter. Since the level of violence used has escalated in the situations of gang warfare, they are literally life-and-death ones.

As situations come to be more and more those of life and death, the notion of chivalry takes on a different tone. In encounters with knives and clubs, one could well spare the life of (or limit the wounds upon) an opponent. It was not only a chivalrous move, it was one that may be repaid later, and as such, was a strategic move. A victor who did not finish off an opponent with a fatal blow or shot could receive as much honor for chivalry as he could for ending the opponent's life. The value was in the honor, not just the victory.

In gang warfare, as it became clear that face-to-face encounters with manufactured guns should be short in duration, the automobile was seen as a resource to make such meetings as brief as possible. Only in situations of pure recklessness would an assembled group stand before opponents who were displaying firearms.

When manufactured firearms began to be used by gangs on a large scale in the 1970s, the old style rumble was replaced without ceremony by the *foray* (Miller, 1975). In the wide open spaces of Southern California, the drive-by became the adopted style of the foray.

In the context of gang warfare the drive-by shooting is the military equivalent of getting hit by an unseen shell. Since there is an almost constant enemy but there are not constant staged battles, a drive-by is something that can happen anywhere, any time. What's more, a drive-by is hidden in the normal appearances of its surroundings (Goffman, 1971:238-82). A car driving down San Diego streets is a normal occurrence, and like all such mundane events is seen but unnoticed. When bullets or shotgun pellets suddenly begin spewing from a car, it is too late. Since about 80 percent of all drive-by shootings were in the evening or at night (between 6 p.m. and 6 a.m.), noting a vehicle belonging to a rival gang is even more problematic. The following case provides an instance where the most mundane of situations can be transformed into a deadly one:

> The victim, a Syndo Mob member, was working inside his car on the back window. He saw a white van back down the alley. When the van's passenger side door came in front of his car, a Piru pointed an Uzi machine gun at him and fired eighteen rounds, hitting his car several times but missing him.

Given the swift and deadly nature of drive-by shootings, gang members live in a very real situation of sudden death. Considering the stances to unpredictable danger, Goffman suggests postures that can be "deer-like, ever ready to be startled, . . . cow-like, slow to be mobilized, or lion-like, unconcerned about predators and wary chiefly when stalking prey" (1971:242-43). One might expect the general stance to be either deerlike, especially when separated from fellow gang members, or lionlike, demonstrating heart to the gang. However, a good deal of the postures of the targets appeared to be cowlike. This could be due to the frequent use of alcohol and drugs by gang members. Since partying was a major pastime for gang members, and parties consisted of drinking, illicit drug use, dancing, and sex, it would be trying indeed to maintain full alert on such occasions. Intoxicated gang members make easy targets. The following illustrates a relaxed interlude being transformed into a situation of high alarm:

> A member of the Neighborhood Crips and his girlfriend were sitting on what was described as an "electrical box" [possibly a phone company switching box]. He heard several shots fired and pulled his girlfriend towards him when he realized she had been shot.

. . . The term *kicking back* was used by gang members to convey a desired stance of relaxing or having fun. Not only was this a general term favored by youth in the area, gang members used it to describe everything from parties to hanging out at their favorite haunts. Jankowski (1991:81) found the identical term and sentiment used among Chicano gangs.

Returning to the relaxed stance that seemed to be a dominant posture of the targets of the drive-by shootings, we can understand their lack of alertness in terms of kicked-back situations. Goffman (1961:37) explains fun in terms of *spontaneous involvement*. To be spontaneously involved is to disattend to all but the unfolding moment. If one must concern oneself with external matters that take attention away from being engrossed in kicking back, then one cannot enjoy the fun of the gathering. At parties, a sure bore is one who brings up unpleasant chores at the office, unfinished homework, a dying relative, or anything else that takes away from being caught up in the moment of the gathering. Constant reminders of the *possibility* of a drive-by and the need for alertness are also undesirable in kicked-back situations, because they put a damper on the spirit of the occasion. Furthermore, one who shows too much alertness may be accused of lacking the heart for gang life. So, for those with a nervous alertness, there is a need to manage the impression that they are indifferent to the dangers of drive-bys, and they may in fact let down their guard in the *performance* of doing so.

To the extent people can disattend to external matters in a situation, we can say they are at *ease* (Goffman, 1961:41-45). *Tension* is defined as a "sensed discrepancy between the world that spontaneously becomes real to the individual, or the one he is able to accept as the current reality, and the one in which he is obliged to dwell" (Goffman 1961:43). For the gang members, kicking back and enjoying any ease contrasts dramatically with the state of alertness necessary to survive a drive-by shooting. Since the weather in Southern California is conducive to year-round outdoor activity, gang members spend a good deal of time outside. In about 90 percent of the cases, the victims were outside when attacked in a drive-by shooting. In several cases, those who were shot outside were spillovers from an indoor party. The following is typical of a kicked back occasion that was disrupted by a drive-by:

> Some VELs were leaving a party when a car drove by with some boys who yelled "Logan, Logan" and shot them. Later, several other people who were at the party showed up at the hospital with stab and gunshot wounds.

The irony of gangs is that the very kicked-back lifestyle that is an important part of their life is disrupted by the tension of drive-by shootings, another part of gang life.

In the aftermath of drive-by shootings where someone is actually killed or severely wounded, the reaction of the gang members and others in the neighborhood is disbelief that it really happened. Even though violence is a major part of gang life in terms of topics of conversation, tattoos proclaiming violence, and carrying weapons, that actual situation of violence always produces trauma.

So the unprepared posture often taken in the face of danger appears to be more a matter of denial than it is of either bravery or ignorance. There may be a temporary alertness after a drive-by against a gang, but it seems to be short-lived. In one instance, a boy from the Shelltown gang had been murdered two weeks prior to a drive-by shooting where a second Shelltown member was gunned down. The denial cannot be maintained indefinitely, and some gangs do post sentries and/or have their gatherings in *cul de sacs* or other locations where drive-by shootings are difficult. However, the overall attitude is one that recognizes the drive-by shooting as a possibility, but gangs filter it out as an external matter. To give it too much attention takes away from the *vida loca* (the crazy life), but to be wholly unaware of it can have fatal consequences. So drive-bys are viewed as something to avoid (as a target), hoping oneself is not the victim.

Grounded Values and the Drive-by Shooting

Up to this point we have discussed drive-by shootings primarily from the point of view of the target: a contingency in the life of a gang member. Now, I would like to examine drive-by shootings from the point of view of the shooters. How can we understand what it takes to get in a car with one's homeboys and deliberately go hunting for someone to shoot? It is true that some drive-bys seem to be unplanned in that someone just happens to have a gun in a car and starts shooting, but interviews with former gang members show that drive-bys can be fairly deliberate hunting expeditions for human quarry.

One argument explaining deliberate initiated violence is to classify individuals who do such things as sociopaths, psychopaths or some similar label implying that they are violent and without scruples or conscience. Likewise, we could argue that the core gang members suffer from sociopathic maladies, as did Yablonsky (1962) and that those with these dysfunctions are attracted to the most violent element of gangs. Thus, we would conclude, boys who engage in drive-by shootings are *really* suffering from individual problems and would be violent no matter what.

There are several problems with such individualistic arguments. First of all, they tend to be tautological. To wit: if a person engages in drive-by shootings he must be sociopathic, and sociopaths are defined as those who are involved in drive-by shootings. The same problem existed in pre-classical criminological thought. The offensive act and offensive person are wrapped together into a single entity: evil (Sylvester, 1972:3). Distinctions between the evil *act* and evil *actor* become blurred. Second of all, gangs are a group phenomenon. If sociopaths are persons without regard for others, they would not be subject to or care about others in their gang. Since observers of gang life report that there is very much a concern for the options of fellow gang members, it would be difficult to argue for a sociopathic personality generating gang behavior. On their own, sociopaths or psychopaths may generate all kinds of bizarre behavior, but involvement in a drive-by shooting in cooperation with fellow gang members in a car hardly seems to fit in with the wholly antisocial nature of this personality type. Finally, those who seem to fit the sociopathic and psychopathic labels tend to be loners, and the nature of their offenses is different from patterned crime.

Gang members involved in drive-by shootings talk about their feats in the same displaced way that bomber pilots talk of hitting targets. The gang boys are proud of that fact that they had the heart to point the gun and pull the trigger at an enemy, *not necessarily that they may have killed someone*. Short and Strodtbeck (1964:25-29), in their examination behind why gangs fight, point out that gang boys need to maintain status. They get the status by performing well in gang-gang encounters. In quoting gang boys' elation after one such encounter, Short and Strodtbeck illustrate the combined pride and tension relief:

> "Baby, did you see the way I swung on that kid?" "Man, did we tell them off?" "Did you see them take off when I leveled my gun?" "You were great, baby. . . ."
>
> The tension was relieved. They had performed well and could be proud (1964:26).

Those who could not or would not perform by going along on a drive-by were judged as lacking heart. They could still be part of the gang, but like the rear echelon troops in a battle zone, they are given no hero status or meaningful medals.

The gang, as a group or organization, provides the situation of the drive-by shooting. We might say that in the same way that situations have realized resources as described by Goffman (1961:28), gangs too have realized resources. One of the resources that can be realized by gang membership is participation in a drive-by shooting. The guns, the cars, the rival, and even the accounts (Scott and Lyman, 1968:46-62) are gang-provided resources.

Of the gang-provided resources, the least important are the guns and automobiles. Virtually anyone can get cars and guns in San Diego without much trouble. However, coming up with *murderous* rivals and the *accounts* necessary for shooting at them is another matter. The rivals are generated as part of gang lore, accidental encounters, and contingency of ethnic group and location. As part of gang lore, images of rivals as cowardly, venal, dangerous, and worthy of disdain are passed on from one generation to the next. The rivalry between the Crips and Bloods/Pirus in San Diego is traced to a rivalry in Los Angeles, one that had nothing to do with anyone in San Diego. When the gangs in San Diego started using Crips and Bloods/Pirus in their names, they based their rivalry on the Los Angeles gangs' lore. Within the lore are the accounts for any enmity between the two groups. Likewise, an accidental encounter between non-rival gangs may result in a fight or a killing. Once that occurs, a vendetta may be established that will work into a full-time rivalry. Finally, a rivalry may simply crop up because of the proximity of two gangs. The 70s and VELs are the Mexican-American gangs nearest to one another, and that seems to be the basis for their rivalry. Likewise, since ethnic lines are generally uncrossed boundaries in San Diego gang life, two gangs such as the West Coast Crips (African-American) and the Calle 30 (Mexican-American) are not rivals although they are adjacent and even part of the same area.

Knowing the accounts, justifications, and meanings generated in gang life to participate in drive-by shootings is core to understanding gang violence. One of the most difficult matters to resolve in this research was how to make sense of a kid sticking a gun out the window of a car and intentionally shooting another human being. Gang members learn accounts or vocabularies of motives (Mills, 1940:904-913) in gang situations. For example, a gang boy who is attacked and beaten, shot at, or stabbed has two experiences. First, he has *empirical* evidence of a physically painful and/or frightening experience. Second, he has a *rational* experience in that he seeks a reason—a motive or account—for the experience. The rational account is not an automatic calculation of costs and benefits in the classical or neoclassical sense. The rational account is weighing the empirical experience against ways of talking about what has happened.

A middle-class youth who was subject to a near-miss in a drive-by shooting would be given the account that he was in the wrong place. He would be given advice to avoid those situations by avoiding the neighborhoods where gangs exist. Low-income non-gang youths in the community who cannot avoid such neighborhoods will be given advice to avoid certain individuals or places in the neighborhood. However, gang youths who experience being a target of a drive-by are provided with very different accounts. They hear about revenge, heart, courage, balls, honor, and perhaps even how weak the attacker is if no one is harmed. So the rational experience of the gang boy is one of dealing with the problem by means other than avoidance. Even the meekest members of the gang are glad there are other members who have the heart to drive-by and "mess up" their rivals. Instead of hearing about the futility of endless vendettas, gang boys come to *understand* that only a powerful counterstrike can thwart future drive-bys. The gangs honor is at stake, but the honor is more than saving face. If a gang is seen to have honor, it is seen as a gang that should not be trifled with. As such, it is a safer, *more rational*, gang. So instead of being merely an act of vengeance, a drive-by shooting is seen as a rational action to protect the gang. Those in the role of drive-by shooters are seen as protecting not only the gang's honor but also its life and limb.

The accounts and understanding of what a drive-by shooting means as a protective measure are grounded in the gang-generated situations. The values and norms surrounding and justifying drive-bys, either as a rational battle plan in view of the available weapons or as a defensive act to stave off drive-bys in one's own patch, find their specific meaning in the way the gangs talk about the situations of their occurrence. In turn, the *talk* is justified by the empirical reference of what happens in their neighborhoods and to them as gangs.

Action and the Drive-by Shooting

Goffman (1967:185) defines *action* as taking on fatefulness for its of sake. A drive-by shooting clearly has the makings of a fateful situation. It is risky in that those who drive by and shoot at a rival may become the target themselves, or they may be caught by the police. It is consequential since what occurs in the occasion of the drive-by will almost certainly have significant effects on the shooters' future.

Horowitz and Schwartz (1974) argue that honor in gangs is a key to understanding their violence. One can gain honor by acting bravely in a gang encounter, establishing character for oneself and possibly robbing it from an opponent. Since character contests make up a part of gang warfare, both individually and collectively, we must examine the drive-by in this light. As noted above, not all members of a gang have the mettle to sit in a car with a gun and go hunt rival members. Those who do can demonstrate they have character or heart. This is understood in Goffman's (1967:214) use of the term *character*. To wit, a gang boy has the opportunity to demonstrate he has the ability to act coolly and deliberately even though alarms may be going off inside that tell him to get out of the car and away from the danger.

At the same time there is a concrete, grounded situation in which to establish character, there is the excitement in taking chances. The adrenaline that pumps through one in the face of danger creates a heightened awareness, but its effects must be kept in check to demonstrate coolness. Once the firing begins, the pent up feelings can be released in firing the gun or listening to it go off, and there is a spontaneous involvement in the moment. Also, there is the excitement of the recognition of the fellow gang members. Their praise for heart and bravery provide another high in the aftermath of the shooting. All of the excitement is grounded in the drive-by shooting. In the telling of the drive-by, future drive-bys are preordained, for the telling provides the grounds for others to establish themselves and feel the thrill of danger.

Normative and Strategic Interaction in Drive-by Shootings

Goffman (1969:130) notes that while it is possible to conceive of strategic interaction as free of norms, it is usually very difficult in reality. We can examine drive-by shootings as purely tactical moves based on the most efficient way to do in a rival, but upon closer examination, there is a good deal else that goes on and *does not* go on to make the move a purely strategic one.

Above we noted that norms appear *not* to keep gangbangers from blasting away at dwellings with non-gang members inside, but because norms against shooting at dwellings where a rival's family members may be present are not included in the moral code of the gang does not mean that norms do not exist at all. There do seem to be norms against singling out an innocent relative of a gang member and shooting at him or her. The lack of remorse shown by gang members when asked about killing babies, small children, and women is not an attitude of condoning such killings. It is a reflection of their view of reality. They will readily defend themselves by pointing out they were not *trying* to harm innocents, but that is one of the unfortunate side effects of gang warfare—just like any other warfare. In the same way that the rules of war "protect" noncombatants from being shot at *intentionally*, women and children have never been protected from the consequences of area shelling or bombing. As long as they can demonstrate that they did not knowingly and intentionally kill non-gangs members, they can maintain a normatively correct posture.

Emergent Norms in a Drive-by

While it was possible to gather data on the events of a drive-by shooting during the immediate time of the shooting, it was not possible to gather much data on what led up to the shooting. In other words, there were few data that show how a drive-by emerges. From the data that were collected, widely different circumstances seem to be involved.

In one case, a police informant was at a party with some Logan gang members. As the party developed, gang members became more intoxicated with alcohol, drugs, or both and decided to "hit" the Sherman gang. It is not clear whether they decided to do the drive-by first and then became intoxicated to bolster their resolve, or after becoming intoxicated the idea of a drive-by seemed like a good one. In interviews with a former gang member, it seemed that he and his fellow gang members were "loaded" a good deal of the time, regardless of the situation. Thus, while drugs and/or alcohol may have been present in drive-by situations, they do not seem to explain how the kernel of the idea of a drive-by developed since the same state of intoxication was present when drive-by shootings were the furthest thing from gang members' minds.

In another shooting where data were available concerning the events that led up to the drive-by, two of the people in the shooting car were literally innocent bystanders. It involved a girl whose boyfriend's brother was a gang member. The following transcript excerpts show how the drive-by evolved:

> [F]irst, it started from my house and it was about 4 o'clock in the afternoon. Me and my boyfriend were talking inside this car and we decided to go for a ride around the block cause he wanted to drive. And around two blocks away from my house, we saw his brother. And uh, he asked us to stop the car so he can get in the car with us. So when uh, we stopped the car, he asked us to go to another block to pick up two of his friends. When we went out there, we saw two of his friends with something in their hands. We . . . picked them up. They asked me to open the trunk of the car. First, I didn't want to but then my boyfriend told me to do it. Cause, uh, well he probably thought it was something else but he didn't know if they had a gun with them. Whatever they had in their hands that was in the back of my car. So they get in the car and we left. So they asked us to go where I live at.
>
> We went down there, and they went across the street to pick up a friend. We stopped the car and [name] got out of the car and went to pick up [name]. So when [he] come out of the house, he had a gun with him. A small gun with him. And then, uh, he got into the car and he told us to drive. I didn't want to. My boyfriend didn't want to either. But then [the boy with the gun] pulled my hair, and he told me to do it. He told me "Come on girl, do it." So my boyfriend, he got out of the car and he said, "Don't be pulling her hair" and [the boy with gun] said, "Man, don' start nothing with me right now. I'm drunk, I'm loaded right now." So my boyfriend told me, "[girl's name] get in the car and then let's go." But then uh, first, uh, my boyfriend was talking so when we, he found out what they put into the trunk was two guns, a gun, he didn't want to talk no more. He wanted to stay [at the girl's house]. And then, he told me to stay too, I didn't want to. I said "Whatever my car was . . ." [the car belonged to the girl.]
>
> And he pointed the gun to him [girl's boyfriend]. I don't know if he mean it to point it to him or not but I know he pointed to him, he said, "Man, let's get out

of here." So my boyfriend said, "We better go before we get shot." So we go into the car, and we started driving around by the park, I don't know the name of the park. And when we saw two guys come. They were coming around by the park, [the boy with the gun] said, "Man, stop. Stop the car." [At this point, the girl narrating the drive-by was in the back seat of her own car with her boyfriend. Two of the boys in the front seat jumped out of the car and began shooting at the boys in the park, hitting one.]

If the girl was telling the truth and was not involved with the gang members from the outset, it appears that the situation for a drive-by was an opportunistic one. That is, it was known that someone had guns and wanted to shoot at a rival gang. When the opportunity of an available automobile came about, the gang members took over the car and went looking for targets. When they found the targets, they simply shot at them.

The transformation of the situation of one from "driving around" to a drive-by started when the guns were brought into the car and the driver and her boyfriend were forced to accompany the shooters. Since the girl and her boyfriend were unwilling participants, they were under the coercive rule of the gun and not the rules of situated norms. The two others in the car who did not participate in the shooting were "along for the ride" and made no attempt to gain the release of the girl and her boyfriend. Their lack of action and failure to indicate they did not want to be along suggests they were non-shooting drive-by participants. It was an exciting outing for them. (Indeed, it may have been an exciting outing for all of them, and after deciding who was going to take the fall for the offense, the others may have openly cooperated with the police.)

More data on the nature of the emergent norms in drive-by shootings is needed. The accounts provided by researchers like Jankowski are reflections of commonsense reasoning by the gang members in the context of their social reality. However, such accounts tell us little of how actual situations of gang violence evolve or about the situations themselves. Like we do with other data that have emerged in the study of crime, we tend to want to know more about the actors than the situations they create and in turn become caught up. However, since the actors are behaving in the way they are because of the nature of the situation, we need to know more about those situations.

Situations of Drive-by Shootings

In looking at some situations where drive-by shootings occur, we can get an inkling of the strategies and norms behind these attacks. The kinds of situations that occur prior to a drive-by shooting are often vague, but we will attempt to classify those that are the most common and provide some examples to see the characteristics of the situations and shootings.

Emergent Arguments

The type of drive-by that occurs more or less accidentally or spontaneously emerges out of arguments. Typically, some gang members in a car with a gun will say something to a person in a rival's neighborhood. Often the statement will be a gang challenge. For example, the following driving-shooting occurred when three Little Africa Pirus encountered four Eastside Pirus. Since usually Pirus fight Crips, this incident stands as an exception to the unstated alliance, but the example clearly illustrates the type of situation where cars and guns are used in emergent arguments:

Three Little Africa Pirus were at a stoplight at an intersection when a car with four Eastside Pirus pulled up next to them. One of the Little Africa Pirus said, "What's up blood?" to the boys in the other car. After some further verbal exchanges, one of the Eastside Piru members pulled out a handgun and shot several bullets into the Little Africa Pirus' car. Two of the occupants were wounded, and jumped out of the car and ran to a nearby gas station. The Eastside Pirus drove off.

It is possible that the shooter thought the boys in the Little Africa Pirus' car were Crips, since the statement, "What's up blood?" often prefaces a shooting by the Crips. (The Pirus preface their attacks of Crips with "What's up, cuz?")

Sometimes, the targets may actually initiate the violence. These are cases where the target says or does something to intentionally antagonize the shooters in the car. For example, the following cases illustrate interchanges that resulted in a shooting from a passing car:

Three East Side Pirus were in front of their house lifting weights when a car with West Coast Crips drove by and one of the occupants shouted, "Fuck the Pirus!" The Pirus left the yard and walked down the street, where the car passed them again. The second time it passed, a shotgun was pointed at them from the rear window. One of the Pirus, who apparently did not see the shotgun, threw a rock at the car. The car continued down the street, made a U-turn, and came back toward the Pirus. As it passed the third time, two shots were fired from the car, hitting one of the Pirus in the back.

A third type of emergent argument occurs when there is an immediate attack on the drivers and counter-attack by the shooters in the car. This type of emergent argument typically occurs when a car with known rival gang members appears in another gang's home territory and is recognized. The target gang mobilizes and attacks the drivers. The following incident, described by non-gang and gang witnesses, involved the West Coast Crips and Lincoln Park Pirus:

Two West Coast Crips drove into a parking lot in front of a fried chicken franchise and record store that was the home territory of the Lincoln Park Pirus. When they drove into the lot, they were recognized by the Lincoln Park Pirus, who began attacking them. A non-gang witness said, "I pulled into the lot and everybody was throwing rocks and bottles at each other. These dudes got out of this green Chevy that was parked in front of Dr. J's lot and started shooting. There were two people in the car. The driver got out of the car and fired six shots. There was one other guy in the car. Then they both jumped in the car and tried to run over some of the people that were throwing rocks at them."

A Lincoln Park Piru, who was shot and wounded in the drive-by, provided the following account of the same incident.

> I was just standing on Lowe's lot with a couple of my homeboys, and these two dudes in a six-nine Chevy pulled onto the lot. I don't know either one of them by name but I know they were from the Coast [West Coast Crips]. I had seen them around a couple of times before. There was an "18 and over" party at the record shop. A couple of my homeboys and them got into an argument and my homeboys said something like, "fuck the Coast." Then the dude that was driving pulled out a gun. It looked like he really meant to shoot me 'cause he pointed the gun right at me. I hear a couple of shots, and then I knew I was hit, but I kept on running. I got dizzy and fell down. The next thing I remember the paramedics were there.

Such encounters provide members of both gangs with enough evidence that they showed heart, demonstrated character, and were generally tried-and-true gangbangers. The shooters in the car could claim they took on a numerically superior group and wounded one. The target gang could claim they faced a gun with mere rocks and bottles. Furthermore, the situation grounded the beliefs of both gangs in empirical experience, giving them substance. It showed the necessity of fighting back, the nefarious nature of each other's opponents, and the reality of establishing character. All of these could further be attributed, *positively*, from the gang boys perspective, to gang affiliation.

Hanging Out

The situation of the last two examples of emergent argument were also examples of drive-bys occurring in situations where the target gang is hanging out. A distinction is made here between emergent arguments and hanging out as situations of drive-by shootings on the basis of one generating a situated reason for the shooting. In emergent arguments, the shooter can always point to something that the target did or said on the shooting occasion that resulted in the shooting. In the preceding example, something was said or some action was taken by the target gang before the shooting gang began firing.

The difference between a hanging-out situation and one of emergent argument is that in a hanging-out situation, the target has little time to say or do anything before the shooting starts. We can review emergent argument situations and say that were it not for the fact that the target gang *did* say or do something to antagonize the shooter, the shooting may not have occurred. In other words, we can argue that emergent argument situations are in part *situationally victim precipitated*. That means that something the target group did *in the situation* of the drive-by shooting helped justify the shooting.

By contrast, hanging-out situations, while they may be victim precipitated, are not situationally victim precipitated. For example, suppose a gang crosses out another gangs *placaso* (gang signature). The gang whose *placaso* has been defaced justifies a drive-by shooting against the offending gang. They execute the drive-by later that day, that week, or even that month. We can say that the gang who crossed out the *placaso* contributed to its being targeted for a drive-by. In that sense, the drive-by is victim precipitated. However, it is not *situationally* precipitated because the offending action occurred in an occasion separate from the drive-by. The following is an example of this type of hanging-out situation that was precipitated by a member of the target gang. The shooter had been beaten up by some Neighborhood Crips. The drive-by was in retaliation for the "jumping" (beating). The following was related by the shooting victim:

> I was talking to a couple of fellow at Gompers Park . . . when we saw this car turn the corner at Hilltop and Carolina. It started moving toward us. They were yelling "Piru" several times, and we all started running. I could hear them yelling "Piru," and I also hear one of them yell, "What are you running for, blood?" While I was running away, I saw the passenger behind the driver point what appeared to be a double barrel shotgun and fire two shots. . . . [T]he first shot hit me in the back, and I continued running toward 47th Street, through the park. We kept on running until we were somewhere near C Street and Myron helped carry me to a house where he called the police.

As can be seen from the example, there was nothing that the targets did in the situation to precipitate the shooting during the occasion of the shooting. However, it became clear in the investigation that the shooter was involved in the drive-by because of an earlier offense by Neighborhood Crips. Thus, the case is victim-precipitated but not situationally so.

Parties

In most ways there is not a lot of difference between a drive-by targeting a group hanging out and one that targets a party. Parties were selected as targets because they provided an opportunity for a gang to show it would fearlessly attack a massed rival, and party gatherings provided large targets. The shooters may also have considered parties a good target since the party-goers were likely to be intoxicated and not be able to quickly respond:

> Some Shelltown homeboys were at a birthday party for one of the boys' grandmother when some VELs drove by. One Shelltown boy was standing on the street when two VELs got out of the car and said, "Where are you from?" He replied, "Shelltown," and they responded, "Encanto, Encanto!" [VEL is an acronym for Varrio Encanto Locos—roughly translated it means, "The crazy guys from the Encanto neighborhood."] The Shelltown boy ducked down when the VELs began shooting at him before they drove off.

The details of the shooting itself are little differentiated from one where shots are fired in a hanging-out situation. In some of the drive-by shootings observed at parties, it was noted that there tended to be a larger grouping, and girls were more likely to be present. In some of the drive-bys at parties, girls in fact were wounded. Since females are not usually targeted in drive-bys, they are considered innocent bystanders, but there does not seem to be remorse or embarrassment when girls or other innocent bystanders are shot. The view is, "They shouldn't party with those guys if they don't want get shot at."

Another reason that gangs target parties is to enhance their reputation. This can occur when there is little or no past conflict between the gangs. By hitting a party, there is an immediate and wide recognition of the event since the party is likely not only to attract most of the gang members, but also others who attend the occasion as dates or guests of gang members. In one such event, the Spring Valley Locos attacked a Shelltown party. The Shelltown boy who was gunned down in the drive-by was considered a fringe member and had no record of violence himself. In interviews after the incident the partygoers all said that there was no rivalry between the two gangs. Since the gangs were separated by about twelve miles, they did not attend the same schools, and they had no common territorial boundary, it was unclear why the attack occurred. Eventually, some Shelltown boys pointed out that Spring Valley Locos wanted to enhance their reputation. The attack and killing would get around and the Spring Valley Locos would be seen as a gang of heart.

Since two weeks prior to the drive-by, a Shelltown boy had been killed in the Spring Valley Locos territory, it would seem that the Spring Valley Locos had already made their reputation as a dangerous gang. An alternative accounting would be that the Spring Valley Locos attack was to thwart a *payback* (revenge attack) by Shelltown. Jankowski (1991:164) cited fear of being attacked by a rival as a reason to strike first. The first strike is supposed to generate fear that attempts at revenge will call on more retaliation. From this research, it appears that fear is not so much a *factor* as Jankowski used the term, but rather it is a gang *account*. That is, in the vocabulary of motives for engaging in a drive-by shooting, *fear* is an acceptable account if presented correctly. None of the gang members want to appear cowardly in front of their fellow gang members, and so fear must be presented as a rationally grounded reason instead of a gut reaction. In citing Jankowski's own example, we can see the rational account more so than the fear:

> That's it man, we attack the [rival gang's name] and leveled some impressive destruction. . . . No, I don't know if they were planning to attack us or not. If they weren't thinking of it now, they would have had to think of it in the future, so it was best we got them now (Jankowski, 1991:164).

The account may have implied fear, but it also implied an empirically grounded account for making an attack based on what other gangs honor. Whether it is running from fear or leaping into a situation bringing on honor and the identity associated with it is not so important as was the fact that the reasoning is considered a valid accounting of the events by gang members. Thus, it is not context-free rationality, but rather a rationality grounded in the gang culture, which itself is reflexively grounded in the gang situations.

Business Competition

In the early 1980s, business competition did not appear to be a reason for gang violence at all in San Diego. However, by 1988, many of the gang-related drive-by shootings, especially among African-American gang members, did appear to be connected to the sale and distribution of crack cocaine.

The profits from the sale of crack cocaine were so great that the African-American gangs were all engaging in it to some extent. With wider distribution, sales and profits would increase. In an attempt to expand their business, Los Angeles gangs attempted to take over some of the San Diego areas serviced by local African-American gangs. When this occurred, the rivalry between the local Crips and Pirus was suspended while both gangs fought off the challenge from Los Angeles. However, the Los Angeles gangs were not going to be run off easily. The following attack was made by a Los Angeles gang on West Coast Crips:

> Two West Coast Crips and a non-gang member were walking along the sidewalk when a car drove by and shot at them with an automatic rifle (machine gun). The non-gang member was suspected in a shooting a few days previously.

The non-gang member with the two Crips may have been involved in drug deals, and the gang violence thus may have been a reflection of violence among drug dealers for customers. The increase in drive-by shootings in 1988 makes it clear that *something* occurred that year to make the number increase so dramatically. Since crack cocaine was introduced to the neighborhoods primarily through African-American gangs at that time, sales competition is hypothesized to be a primary cause.

Non-Person Targets

In addition to shooting at people who could be seen, targets in drive-by shootings also were physical objects that belonged to targets. Most common were automobiles and houses. In the cases of targeting automobiles, it was fairly clear whether or not someone was in the car. However, houses were sometimes occupied and sometimes not.

Shooting at a gang member's house or car can cause damage to the physical target, breaking windows, and putting holes in the stucco walls and metal car panels. In addition, such attacks threaten the victim, and the shooters can claim they have caused a loss of face for the rival gang.

The most problematic issue that arises in examining drive-by shootings at houses is the nature of norms in the context of strategic interaction. While gang members are definitely the desired target if anyone happens to be at home, there is a good chance that others in the house may be wounded or killed. Do norms exist that protect innocent family members? They do not seem to, for drive-by shootings include shooting at houses when parents and siblings of gang members are at home. A former gang member recalled when his family at dinner had to dive for the floor as a rival gang sprayed the house with bullets. He was the only gang member in the family even though he had several brothers and sisters.

Conclusion

Drive-by shootings have become synonymous with gang violence. As a strategy in the context of rival gangs armed with manufactured firearms, it is far superior to other forms of gang warfare. A gang can hit a target miles away from its home territory, and then speed away unscathed. In these situations, gang members can build an identity as having "heart" and live to tell about it. While risky in terms of counter-strikes by the rival gang and police apprehension, a drive-by can be conducted by virtually anyone who can ride in a car and shoot a gun. As such, this type of violence is the most deadly and is likely to be a continuing source of gang power.

References

Goffman, Erving. 1961. *Encounters: Two Studies in the Sociology of Interaction*. Indianapolis: Bobbs-Merrill.

——. 1967. *Interaction Ritual*. Garden City, NY: Doubleday.

——. 1969. *Strategic Interaction*. Philadelphia: University of Pennsylvania Press.

——. 1971. *Relations in Public*. New York: Harper and Row.

Horowitz, Ruth and Gary Schwartz. 1974. "Honor, Normative Ambiguity and Gang Violence." *American Sociological Review* 39 (April): 238-251.

Jankowski, Martin Sanchez. 1991. *Islands in the Street: Gangs and American Urban Society*. Berkeley: University of California Press.

Klein, Malcolm W. 1971. *Street Gangs and Street Workers*. Englewood Cliffs, NJ: Prentice-Hall.

Miller, Walter B. 1975. *Violence by Youth Gangs and Youth Groups As a Crime Problem in Major American Cities*. Washington, DC: U.S. Department of Justice.

Mills, C. Wright. 1940. "Situated Actions and Vocabularies of Motive." *American Sociological Review* 5: 904-13.

Scott, Marvin B. and Sanford Lyman. 1968. "Accounts." *American Sociological Review* (February): 46-62.

Short, James F. and Fred L. Strodtbeck. 1964. "Why Gangs Fight." *Trans-action* I (6, Sept.-Oct.): 25-29.

Sylvester, Sawyer F., Jr. 1972. *The Heritage of Modern Criminology*. Cambridge, MA: Schenkman.

Yablonsky, Lewis. 1962. *The Violent Gang*. New York: Macmillan. ✦

Gangs and Drugs

25

Gangs and Crime Old as Time; But Drugs Change Gang Culture

Jerome H. Skolnick

The nature and scope of gang involvement in drug distribution, and its relationship to violence levels, are a matter of considerable debate. Drawing from interviews with prison inmates and law enforcement officers, Skolnick distinguishes instrumental, or entrepreneurial, gangs from cultural gangs, based upon the degree to which gang organization revolves around the drug business. In this description, drug sales, facilitated by gang norms and values, are said to emerge as a pervasive aspect of California gangs. Some cultural gangs may be evolving toward the instrumental model and this would pose new challenges for law enforcement and local communities.

Although many of us may long for the safe streets of the "good old days," gang kids and street crime are scarcely a novel feature of the urban American landscape. The benchmark study of the urban gang is still Frederick Thrasher's of 1,313 Chicago gangs, first published in 1927. The disorder and violence of these gangs appalled Thrasher, who observed that the gangs were beyond the ordinary controls of police and other social agencies, beyond the pale of civil society. He saw "regions of conflict" that were "like a frontier." He described gang youth as "lawless, godless, wild."

Of these youthful gangsters, only 7.2 percent were identified as "Negro." Located in economically disadvantaged neighborhoods, the Chicago gangs of the 1920s were composed of the children of immigrants—mostly Poles, Italians, and Irish, mixed with Jews, Slavs, Germans, and Swedes. Their moral posture seems scarcely different from that of today's young gang members. "Stealing, the leading predatory activity of the adolescent gang," Thrasher wrote, "is regarded as perfectly natural and contains no more moral opprobrium for the gang boy than smoking a cigarette." Today's youthful gangsters sell illegal drugs, particularly crack cocaine, with similar moral abandon. Armed with semi-automatic military weapons, they are capable of far greater injury to themselves and others.

These past two summers, my students and I interviewed more than 100 youthful drug dealers serving time in California prisons. We interviewed more than 100 law enforcement officers as well. The dealers were tough kids, all of whom said they had participated in violent acts. In their world, a youngster proves manhood by fighting other gang members; or dispatching himself fearlessly in conflict with outsiders. We learned some very interesting things about these kids, their gangs, and their participation in the drug trade, and we gained some insights that might help us control their illicit activities.

One of the first questions we asked ourselves was how gangs and street drug distribution were related. To ask the question presupposes that there is some inherent relationship between gangs and drugs, or that in some way gangs are synonymous with drugs. Our data suggest this is not true, nor should it be assumed that just because gang members participate in the sale or use of controlled substances that gangs have some pre-established arrangement to do so. Our research indicates that the relationship between the traditional or neighborhood-based gang—which we call the "cultural gang"—and drugs is not so casual. On the contrary, the cultural gang is strongly grounded in a neighborhood identity which may extend through generations.

We designate these gangs as cultural to distinguish them from opportunistic groups of young men calling themselves gangs or mobs, but which are vertically organized primarily for the purpose of distributing drugs. This type of gang dominates the drug trade in northern California and in other parts of the United States in which gangs do not entertain such a developed ideology of neighborhood loyalty.

Such gangs are usually regarded by their members as "organizations" and are considered strictly business operations. They are organized primarily to engage in criminal activities. We call these "entrepreneurial" gangs in the sense that the fealty of membership depends on the opportunities offered by leaders, usually those who can claim a reliable connection to a source of drugs. These gangs are thus less neighborhood centered and more business focused, although recruitment usually occurs within an identifiable neighborhood or housing project.

Like any other capitalist enterprise, these drug marketing organizations are motivated by profits and the control of a particular market or markets. But unlike many capitalist enterprises, not all drug organizations strive for growth or expansion. They often perceive themselves to be local businesses. Some may merely seek to control drug sales and distribution

Reprinted from "Commentary," pp. 171-79 in *Crime and Delinquency in California, 1980-1989*. Sacramento, CA: Bureau of Criminal Statistics and Special Services, Office of the Attorney General, Department of Justice, State of California.

within territorial boundaries, such as a part of the city or a housing project.

The data we have collected suggest that mob-associated violence in northern California tends to be instrumental, that is, for the purpose of controlling a drug territory or for enforcing norms of loyalty to the organization. By contrast, Los Angeles drug dealers engage in both cultural and instrumental violence. Cultural violence is called "gang banging"—a symbolic aspect of gang loyalty and social identity. But the Los Angeles gangs seem to be changing, indeed dynamically so, as the values associated with drug marketing come to the fore and gang members migrate as markets expand.

Although we did not find a causal link between gangs and drug distribution, our research did indicate that most, if not all, cultural gang members had their first contact with drugs, either as sellers or users, as members of the gang or the "set." For the most part, they started off as users, doing drugs with other gang members, first smoking marijuana and then moving on to more potent or sophisticated drugs, such as PCP, cocaine, or heroin.

None of our respondents claimed to be a member of a gang which had neither used nor sold drugs. We were told that older gang members routinely assist younger ones to sell drugs. This is considered to be a friendly gesture, a measure of economic opportunity. An older "homeboy" in any gang may help out a younger one by consigning or "fronting" some drugs to him. Since most gang members come from economically depressed communities and backgrounds, the drug selling business is very appealing, especially in Los Angeles where the protection of the gang is also assumed. There are more youngsters, we were consistently told, who want to sell drugs than can be accommodated.

Once a youngster is accepted into a cultural gang, participation in the drug business can facilitate upward mobility. To advance your position in a gang, it is important to show that you are willing to take risks, are fearless, are willing to hurt and be hurt, and can be trusted. Drug related activities—especially intergang violence for Crips and Bloods gang members—present some of the most risky, and therefore the most rewarding of gang activities. This is nothing new. Thrasher makes a similar observation regarding the 1920s Chicago gangs: "The gang is a conflict group. It develops through strife and thrives on warfare."

Virtually every gang member we interviewed had been attacked or injured with a deadly weapon. Several had been shot more than once. Gang members prize the capacity to injure and accept injury. Violence is, in effect, a moral injunction and of instrumental value in supporting participation in a dangerous and lucrative business. Although the cultural gang is not organized for the express purpose of selling drugs, this activity is facilitated by gang norms, values, and organization.

Criminal activities—stealing hubcaps, stealing cars, burglaries—have never been uncommon in the southern California cultural gang. As Joan Moore points out in *Homeboys: Gangs, Drugs, and Prison in the Barrios of Los Angeles*, "In the poverty environment, small scale extortion was (and is) fairly common among teenagers to obtain public consumption ends." Malcolm Klein's study of an east Los Angeles gang in *Street Gangs and Street Workers* shows similar patterns of delinquency—theft, truancy, status offenses such as incorrigibility—as a minor part of gang life. Moreover, gangs have always formed some important part of the illegal economy, with the sale of drugs, particularly marijuana, heroin, and PCP, as part of an innovative response to economic deprivation and restricted economic opportunity in the larger society.

Nevertheless, in contrast to the instrumental gang, the cultural gang exists prior to and independently of the illegal activities in which it is engaged. At least on an ideological level, gang and neighborhood values dominate financial ones. Thus, a young man who describes himself as a "Rollin' 60s Crip" denies that his organization is primarily a drug dealing gang:

> Nah, it's for fun. It's part of being bad and being part of the neighborhood. Like if someone come shooting up our neighborhood, we go back and shoot up theirs.

How similar this seems to Thrasher's gang members who, he says, ". . . are impelled, in a way, to fight: so much of their activity is outside the law that fighting is the only means of avenging injuries and maintaining the code."

Members of cultural gangs refer to themselves as an extended family, as a community. Our respondents said that notions of brotherhood, sisterhood, loyalty and respect, especially for those who are more experienced or older, are important values. They are frequently described as sacred and form the backbone of gang organizational structure. Thus, the gang is considered to be a familial resource, with strongly held values of attachment and loyalty. The cultural gang is a place where individuals can turn to homeboys for financial support, physical protection, and other assistance when necessary.

Significant ethnic differences are also apparent between L.A. neighborhood gangs. Family and community ties are most apparent among Chicano gangs. Such ties are sometimes traceable through several generations. The newer black gangs, while they observe similar conventions of respect, loyalty, and brotherhood, do not have the stability and historic roots of the Chicano gangs. And although black gangs identify with neighborhoods, they do not seem to command the solidarity and traditional values of local Chicano neighborhood gangs.

Indeed, our interviews suggest that black neighborhood gangs are increasingly organized for financial reasons. Individuals are attracted to gangs, not for what gangs represent to others in the neighborhood, nor for what they represent to other gangs, but rather for the opportunity they provide for dealing drugs.

Nonetheless, cultural gang control of drug dealing seems to have intensified, partly due to the social organization of the gang, which offers trust, knowledge of others, common values, and thus helps meet the economic needs of a drug dealing organization. Drug dealing then becomes a paramount value, particularly as the gang member ages. One of our 20-year-old gangsters said, "There's still a lot of gang bangin' goin' on, but it's the younger generation. The people my age, they kickin' back now, they out selling drugs." He said it almost wistfully, as if the older gangsters were selling out by losing interest in gang values.

The concept of rivalry is significant for these cultural gangs, with violence as a symbol of personal and neighborhood respect and identity. A Crip will fight a Blood for a cause seemingly similar to that which might motivate a Serbian to fight a Croatian—perceived traditional rivalry. Imprisoned gang members we interviewed have been involved in numerous encounters. When asked why he shot someone, the gang member will say, "Because he dis'd (disrespected) me," or "They shot my homeboy."

Youngsters grow up and distinguish themselves in gang banging or "putting in work for the gang" that is, in fighting with other gangs over matters that are seen as central to identity. On the other hand, one of our interviewees offered an instrumental interpretation to gang banging. "Reputation," he said, "is the most important thing. They want the reputation as being crazy, going out and shooting, because with the reputation will come the money."

The predominantly entrepreneurial gangs in Oakland and San Francisco do not on the whole recognize or give deference to such traditional rivalries. This does not mean that they will refuse to engage in violence. On the contrary, they can be pitilessly savage. But when such violence occurs, it is instrumental—the gang seeks to maintain or expand its territory, to enrich its economic opportunities, or to protect its authority. As self-perceived organized criminals, they prefer to develop understanding of territorial boundaries, an almost rational sharing. Of course, rational sharing doesn't always happen among entrepreneurial gangs anymore than it does among traditional Mafia families. But youthful and symbolic gang banging in general is viewed with disdain.

In Northern California, entrepreneurial gang members develop reputations by performing economic services, such as acting as lookouts for police while drug dealing is in progress, or steering customers to drug dealers. Many L.A. gangs, by contrast, require each member to satisfy some membership criteria before he can be considered a homeboy or an official member. Membership criteria may include anything from getting beaten, often referred to as getting jumped, to selling drugs, to killing a rival gang member.

Violence is thus a central aspect of both cultural and entrepreneurial gang activity. But the purpose of the violence often differs between gangs. Purpose in turn affects the frequency of violence, the resources gangs are likely to have for engaging in violent activity, and ultimately, the degree to which gang violence can be controlled by law enforcement. The violence of cultural gangs has traditionally centered on retribution and the assertion of neighborhood-gang identity. Entrepreneurial gangs, by contrast, employ violence to control or expand their drug business and markets. Thus, depending upon the stability of the market, the entrepreneurial gang may be more or less violent than the cultural gang.

If a market becomes destabilized, whether by a rival entrepreneurial gang or by law enforcement, then violence is likely to erupt, as it did in Oakland after the arrest and conviction of three major drug dealers and their lieutenants. There also appears to be an inherent instability in markets where the gang's predilection is to expand; or where a valuable territory is targeted by other gangs. The entrepreneurial gang exists and thrives only insofar as it can control a market and intimidate its competitors. By contrast, the authority of the leaders of cultural gangs rest on tradition as well as power. But the cultural gang comes to look more like a drug organization as pecuniary values come to dominate. As one interviewee said, "Red and blue don't matter so much anymore. I wear a green rag. My color is green."

The organized gang offers several advantages to the drug dealer who is a member. First, the gang member can rely on his homeboys for protection if anything were to happen to him in or outside gang turf. Second, gang members enjoy easy control and access to territorial markets. They can sell drugs in their own neighborhood without intruding upon the turf of others. In return, they can exclude others from selling on their turf, a territorial monopoly backed by force. Third, trust inheres in the homeboy relationship, so gang members are expected not to betray other members to the police or rival gangs. And finally, gangs offer a rich source of shared marketing information—about who sells what for what price and who has which drugs available is easily communicated among gang members.

Individual drug dealers do not enjoy the same advantages. They must develop their own reliable connections with suppliers. They must establish their own turf and be careful not to intrude upon gang turf. They must establish their own clientele. They do, however, enjoy the advantage of not having to fulfill gang obligations, which in Los Angeles may result in serious injury or in death.

Our interviewers found that correctional facilities are a fertile ground both for developing drug business contacts during incarceration, and for affirming the identity of gang members. Prisoners say, and correctional officials confirm, that drugs are routinely marketed even in prisons, although prices are much higher.

Well-intentioned correctional officials seek to identify the putative gang affiliation of every inmate and ward as a means of avoiding conflict and bloodshed among rival gangs. In one institution, drug dealers from northern California are referred to, by both themselves and the prison officials, as 415s—the area code for the San Francisco Bay Area.

But by structuring inmate assignments along gang lines, the correctional system ironically supports the gang identity of inmates. Moreover, the identification of one's self as a person who has served time affords the inmate an alternative kind of homeboy status—the prison becomes a kind of neighborhood.

Today's California correctional institutions—overcrowded as they are with parole violators who have failed drug testing—have become, in effect, schools for advanced drug dealing connections. Drug dealers who leave prison are rarely, if ever, reformed. On the contrary, imprisonment for drug dealers, both gang and individual, may well serve functions similar to those that conferences perform for business people, scholars, and police chiefs—an opportunity for "networking."

One of our more intriguing findings was that, unlike heroin dealers, successful crack dealers don't use the product. What is more, they disdain users. One said:

> People who buy the drugs . . . we call them "cluckheads," "caneheads," "crackheads," things like that. You can't sell drugs and use dope at the same time, 'cause you won't get nowhere. You're not going to make no money. So, basically, I try to keep myself away from people who sell and use drugs, 'cause otherwise you come up short for money.

Successful dealers consider use a business impediment. In one dealer's words:

> I never use cocaine; it's not real when they say that a person that sells ends up using his drugs; that's not true, he's like an outcast . . . you get beat up, dogged out; nobody respects you anymore, it turns you scandalous; the s— will make you steal from your mama.

This suggests that, however compelling the drug, those who try it and use it are not necessarily hooked. Consistently in our interviews we found gang members who claimed they had given up any drug use that would impair their ability to function in their business or to maximize profits.

Another interesting market finding is that although a variety of dangerous drugs are sold on the street, in bars, at truck stops, and in houses, crack cocaine selling seems to be associated primarily with black youth. There seems to be little disagreement about the relative lack of involvement by Chicano youth in the crack cocaine trade in Los Angeles. To the extent they indulge in drug trafficking, Chicanos seem to prefer, for both sale and use, Phencyclidine (PCP) and marijuana.

We did not discover, nor did anyone we interviewed—police, psychiatrists, sellers, or users—offer a compelling explanation of why drug sales and use vary with ethnicity. Individuals in all groups apparently use alcohol, cigarettes, and marijuana. When we explore harder drug use, however, all of our subjects across the spectrum report that whites prefer speed and powder cocaine and some heroin; Mexicans prefer PCP and heroin, and may be beginning to use crack; and while older blacks prefer heroin, younger blacks prefer crack cocaine or PCP. Even in San Quentin, we were told by prison officials, psychiatrists, and prisoners without exception that whites used "crank" (amphetamines), blacks used crack, and Mexicans used PCP. Some prisoners, especially whites, extolled the pleasures of combinations—heroin and coke, or heroin, crank and coke.

Heroin seems, however, no longer to be a drug of choice among younger users in any ethnic group. As heroin users die off, we may well find a sharp decline in heroin use over the next decade. This is especially true in the black community, where crack cocaine appears to have replaced heroin as the initiate's drug of choice. On the other hand, heroin mixed with other drugs may make a comeback.

The contemporary drug distribution pattern suggests something about drug markets that we also know from history—which drug preference, the epidemiology of drug use—seems less related to the intrinsic properties of the drug than to the social definition of a particular substance as the drug of choice. Suppose we actually could destroy the Peruvian, Bolivian, and Columbian cocaine fields? Lurking in the background are a variety of manufactured drugs. It is likely that those trained in faster living through chemistry can design and manufacture what addicts would consider the ideal drug—one with the kick of crack and the longevity of crank.

We could find ourselves looking at a designer drug problem more potent and destructive than anything we've yet seen. Indeed, a powerful new drug, a colorless and odorless form of crystal methamphetamine with the street name of "ice" is said to be sweeping Hawaii and is threatening to invade the West Coast ports of San Francisco, Los Angeles, and Portland. It may only be a matter of time before the drug finds its way across the country to replace "crack" as the drug of choice during the 1990s. The only good news ice will bring is its economic challenge to the Medellin Cartel—but it is doubtful that the distributors of the new drug will prove more concerned for public health than the cocaine producers.

But back to crack cocaine—the drug of the moment. Dealers told us that wholesaling is generally considered to be safer than retailing even though less profitable, since law enforcement is most limited at that level. Thus, Los Angeles gangs have taken to becoming wholesale distributors throughout the western part of the United States.

This is not to suggest that wholesaling is without risk and considerable anxiety, not so much from being caught—this is a remote concern—as from being killed or injured by other drug dealers. As one of our higher level dealers said:

> About selling dope, it's money, you have a good life. But the worst thing about it is buying it. When you sitting up there in a little motel room and everybody got guns, holding guns, and counting money, you sweatin'. No windows open—nothin' can be open 'cause you got all that dope. And you're talkin' about price. Then I say, "Well, I can only give you seventeen for this right here." And he says, "F— that, on the phone you told me different." You don't want to look weak and he don't want to look weak. All that tension. If I could ever find a way where I didn't have to buy nothing, just trust somebody with all that money, I'd never buy again.

Any discussion of the business arrangements of street drug dealing requires mention of the several alarming ways drug dealers—particularly cultural gang dealers—are developing increasingly sophisticated business practices. Many of these practices comprise tricks of the trade which are most readily and easily passed between gang members and hence must be seen as yet another advantage gang dealers enjoy over independent street drug dealers.

- First, since a dealer has a drug-selling organization at this disposal, lower-downs in the organization can be and routinely are employed to handle the high risk work of handling drugs.
- Second, the gangs have learned to employ novices—particularly young women whom they exploit mercilessly—to distribute drugs around the country.
- Third, they have learned that law enforcement is well aware of color identification of gangs, and so they report that gang dealers have learned to avoid colors, switch colors, or wear neutral colors when completing drug deals.
- Fourth, they have learned that it is wise to have an effective lawyer.
- Fifth, dealers are more aware of legal risks and associated penalties. Thus, they generally dislike dealing from houses, because there is too much evidence to be found. On the other hand, those who manage crack houses are not necessarily directly involved with the drug deals being made there. One of our dealers described his strategies for avoiding arrest:

> I got a basehead's apartment. It be in his name, but I pay the rent. That be my dope house. I have a couple of dudes known for killin' people—everybody know you don't f— with them—they work in the house. Then I had other people on the roof, riding bikes and stuff, with walkie talkies, watchin' out for police. I was in the city with a beeper, if they need me or they need more dope. I had girls or somebody young deliver the dope so that if they get popped they don't do a lot of time.

In 1989 our interviews focused on gang migration, and examined two conflicting explanations for that phenomenon. One is that these well organized groups target a particular market and quite consciously move in, retaining strong links with the "mother" or "host" gang. Another is that individuals opportunistically move to another city, set up a new gang with few or no links to the old, while using the old gang's name and symbols. Neither of these explanations is entirely accurate. The right answer seems somewhere in between.

Our findings indicate that gang members are motivated to move out of Los Angeles partly because the L.A. police are said to be sophisticated about drug dealing, and thus more of a threat; but mainly because there is too much competition among L.A. sellers. They can make more money, doubling and sometimes tripling the price outside the greater Los Angeles area.

Individuals or groups of gang members usually migrate to places where they have relatives or trusted friends. There seems to be a settlement pattern in places like Seattle and Portland, relatively close to Los Angeles, but a little too far for an easy drive. L.A. gang members usually don't settle in Sacramento, but instead come up for a weekend, and sell drugs out of a motel, then return home. Nor do they seem to settle in places like Kansas City. Instead, they develop connections with relatives, and supply them with powder cocaine, which is cooked in Kansas City.

Police infiltration in such situations is difficult, but not impossible, because eventually drugs must be sold to local people. A street-smart Kansas City black female officer told me that despite executing several search warrants and making undercover buys, she wasn't aware that the sellers were L.A. gang-related until they were apprehended and their backgrounds investigated.

Our study of gangs and drug dealing would suggest then that drugs are a national as well as a local crime problem. In a sense, every drug sale is potentially a federal crime, and policy—usually federal—determines whether drug crimes will be federally or locally prosecuted.

If our goal is to toughen law enforcement, federal prosecution surely has that effect. Joint federal and local law enforcement is more likely to apprehend and convict the migrating drug dealer. The local police provide on-the-scene intelligence, and the feds offer greater financial resources, plus the advantages of federal criminal procedures. L.A. or Jamaican drug dealers who are federally prosecuted will typically not qualify for bail, will have little opportunity for plea bargaining, and will likely be sentenced severely. Thus, Kansas City is reportedly known as a black hole to Jamaican drug dealers since, once arrested, they will not see the street for a long time, perhaps 20 to 30 years.

Nevertheless, law enforcement's ability to fight the drug problem is limited. There is also a danger in the "take back the streets" tactic. If police become too tough on the street and employ harassment measures, they may succeed in deterring some dealers, but they may also inflame anti-police attitudes at a time when it is essential that police be responsive to communities.

There is also a more general law enforcement dilemma, which I call the Darwinian Trafficker dilemma. As law enforcement officials develop increasingly sophisticated strategies, the strongest operatives survive. That is why the gangs have been successful. In the face of more effective law enforcement, they have learned to organize vertically, pull together and seek wider markets, particularly in economically distressed communities.

Such communities will need to have resources, not just for exiling offenders to prison, but for creating a social and economic climate where the drug business is not the major avenue of economic opportunity. Drug enterprising will scarcely be affected unless significant alternatives exist and are seen to be available.

The inner city drug dealers we talked with can be dangerous, sometimes violent criminals. But they can also be described as rational, calculating, enterprising entrepreneurs who are anything but risk averse. Today's gangsters appear morally similar but technologically superior to the traditional gangs described by generations of gang researchers for Thrasher through such contemporary gang researchers as Malcolm Klein, Irving Spergel, and Joan Moore. In some respects, they appear more like organized criminals than youth gangs. But, as Thrasher pointed out during the Prohibition Era, "There is no hard and fast dividing line between predatory gangs of boys and criminal groups of younger and older adults."

It is worthwhile recalling that the legendary gangsters of that era were still teenagers when the constitutional amendment that instituted prohibition was passed—Meyer Lansky, for example, was 17, Bugsy Seigel 15. Our new prohibition has created the opportunity for a 21st century generation of organized entrepreneurial criminals from the underclass—this time around, primarily from black, Asian, and Hispanic backgrounds instead of Thrasher's children of East European immigrants. Our challenge as a society continues to be to turn the energy and intelligence of these illegal entrepreneurs into socially constructive channels—and to reduce significantly the demand for their attractive and dangerous product. ✦

26

Research in Brief: Street Gangs and Drug Sales in Two Suburban Cities[1]

Cheryl L. Maxson

A contrasting view of the connections between gangs and drug sales is offered in the following article. In a study of arrest reports for drug sales in two Southern California cities, Maxson finds gang members to be less prevalent than would be expected from Skolnick's work. Gang involvement did not appear to generate special impacts on the nature of these drug transactions. Taken together, the two studies demonstrate that varying data sources and research methodologies sometimes can produce different conclusions. The studies reinforce the need to examine issues like gang/drug sales/violence linkages from different perspectives.

Abstract

Gang members were arrested in 27 percent of the 1,563 cocaine sales arrest incidents occurring between 1989 and 1991 in two Los Angeles suburban cities.

Rock or crack forms of cocaine were more often present in gang cases, but most aspects of cocaine sales incidents (e.g. location, firearms presence and amount of cash) did not vary with gang involvement. Cases with gang members were more likely to include males, younger ages, and black ethnicity.

Rates of gang involvement and gang/nongang differences were very similar to those reported from Los Angeles in 1985.

The presence of gang members in arrest incidents for sales other than cocaine was far lower; less than 12 percent of the 471 cases involved identified gang members. There were no differences in the incident characteristics of the two types of cases. Other drug cases had higher rates of Hispanics arrested than cocaine sales incidents, but black suspects of younger ages were more common in gang cases.

The lower than expected rates of gang involvement in drug sales, coupled with the lack of evidence of special impacts associated with gang involvement, suggests a reconsideration of gang specialization in narcotics enforcement.

The degree to which street gang involvement in drug distribution presents special and substantial difficulties to law enforcement is a matter of some debate in police and academic circles. Most of the literature emanating from law enforcement sources suggests a strong connection, with gangs portrayed as organized entrepreneurs battling traditional drug distributors for dominance of a lucrative business. Increases in violence are often attributed to gang involvement in the drug trade.

The academic literature reflects more diversity regarding the scope and nature of the gang/drug sales connection. Some authors report well-organized drug distribution operations by gangs in California and the Midwest.[2] Other researchers have disputed this characterization of highly entrepreneurial gangs.[3] A study of gangs in three U.S. cities suggested the causal independence of gangs, drug sales and violence; some gangs were involved in drug sales and others, not—some violent, and others not.[4] Interviews with gang members in five recent studies have yielded widely varying reports of rates of drug sales involvement—the lowest figure was 30% and the highest 95%.[5] Perceptions of a close relationship between gangs, drug sales and homicides have been challenged by a number of recent studies in Chicago, Boston and Los Angeles.[6]

With the exception of the homicide studies, personal interviews, questionnaires, and/or participant observations of gang members were the primary research methods used. A distinguishing feature of the research described here is the use of law enforcement records to assess gang/drug/violence linkages in areas characterized by high incidence of both gang and drug sales activity. The emergence of "rock," or "crack," cocaine in Los Angeles in the early eighties piqued interest because almost immediately police and media reports linked gangs to crack distribution.[7] In an earlier study, law enforcement arrest, investigation, and gang records were used to investigate the magnitude and nature of gang involvement in cocaine sales arrest incidents in South Central Los Angeles between 1983 and 1985. Despite a dramatic increase in gang-involved cocaine sales from nine percent in 1983 to almost 25 percent in 1985, there was no evidence of gang domination at the street level or mid-level sales as recorded by the police.[8] The connection between street gangs, drug sales and violence appeared to have been overstated by media reports.

The incident and drug features of these cases were quite similar regardless of gang member participation. On the other hand, the participant characteristics displayed marked contrasts between the two groups of cases. These differences mirrored those emerging from prior studies of gang and nongang violent incidents in Los Angeles and elsewhere:[9] drug sales cases with gang members involved had more

Forthcoming as Research in Brief. National Institute of Justice, Office of Justice Programs, U.S. Department of Justice.

participants, of younger ages, more males and more blacks than cases without gang members. These data provided no evidence of organized gang incursions into the drug market and predictions of increased violence or firearm presence in gang cases were not supported.

By the mid-to-late eighties, crack had appeared, often reported to be tied to gangs, in most major cities across the nation. Also during this period and into the early nineties, hundreds of mid-sized and smaller cities and towns experienced gang problems for the first time.[10] Law enforcement informants in the majority of these newer, smaller gang cities reported moderate to heavy gang involvement in drug distribution.

The current study was initiated to assess the generalizability of the Los Angeles findings to smaller suburban gang cities and to investigate whether sales incidents involving drugs other than cocaine might display different patterns. The research objectives were:

1. to assess the magnitude of gang involvement in cocaine and other drug sales in two suburban cities;
2. to compare the characteristics of gang involved drug sales incidents with those without gang involvement;
3. to assess the generalizability of findings on cocaine to other drugs, and from urban to more suburban settings; and
4. to translate the implications of the research findings into the development of law enforcement strategies.

Methods

Site Selection. Pasadena and Pomona were selected as study sites for several reasons. Both are mid-sized (about 130,000 population), suburban cities; Pasadena is immediately adjacent to the city of Los Angeles whereas Pomona lies 25 miles to the east, but is still well within the metropolitan area. Both cities have long-standing gang problems and enforcement personnel reported to us very active involvement by both black and Hispanic gang members in the distribution of a variety of drugs. Finally, Pasadena and Pomona have well-developed gang units and have maintained gang membership files for several years.

How do Pasadena and Pomona compare with other U.S. gang cities? Table 1 provides data on the local gang situations in these two cities and the 37 other U.S. cities with a population ranging from one to three hundred thousand that reported the onset of gangs prior to 1981.[11] Spanning all regions of the country, the comparison group includes such cities as Hartford (CT), Jersey City (NJ), Flint (MI), Kansas City (KS), Lubbock (TX), Hayward (CA), and Las Vegas (NV).

Pasadena reports more gangs, and both cities have more gang members and more gang homicides than other gang cities of this size. Three-fourths of the comparison cities have at least 40 percent Hispanic gang members, while about one-third report a comparable percentage of black gang members. Generally, the Pasadena and Pomona figures fall into the upper-mid range compared with other gang cities, but have a greater representation of black gang members. Despite their proximity to Los Angeles, the two study sites are by no means unique; the research findings are relevant to a number of cities across the country.

Table 1

Gang Characteristics of Mid-sized Gang Cities with Onset of Gangs Prior to 1981

	Pasadena	Pomona	37 Other Gang Cities[a]
Number Gangs	32	14	24
Number Gang Members	2,200	2,000	1,243
Percent Black Gang Members	50%	48%	30%
Percent Hispanic Gang Members	40%	50%	53%
Number of Gang Homicides in 1991[b]	13	7	4.5

[a] Group means for each characteristic are reported. An alternative measure is the range represented by the middle 50 percent of cities: number gangs, 8-31; gang members, 300-1,100; percent black gang members, 3-48; percent Hispanic gang members, 40-77; gang homicids, 1-7.

[b] "During 1991, what was the number homicides in your jurisdiction that involved gang members?"

Sampling. Drug sales incidents were defined by the arrest of at least one suspect for a drug sales offense.[12] Computer-generated lists of all suspects arrested for these offenses between 1989 and 1991, along with co-arrestees charged with incident-related offenses, formed the population of drug sales cases. In general, a sales "incident" was defined as such by the assignment of a departmental identification number to that case. Incidents were categorized as cocaine-involved or not and cases including the sales of other drugs in addition to cocaine were placed in the cocaine group. The number of drug sales incidents eligible for sampling in each department is reported in Table 2.

Table 2

Drug Sales Incidents in Pasadena and Pomona

	Pasadena		Pomona	
	Cocaine	Noncocaine	Cocaine	Noncocaine
1989	343	34	325	74
1990	330	48	141	134
1991	243	47	181	134
Total	916	129	647	342

While the magnitude of any arrest figures, or in our case, arrest incidents, are always heavily influenced by police enforcement activity, the numbers displayed in Table 2 reflect substantial drug sales activity in both cities. Clearly, drug sales incidents involving cocaine are far more numerous than those without cocaine, particularly in Pasadena. Sales of other drugs in Pomona outnumber those in Pasadena.

Gang cases were defined by the arrest of at least one identified gang member in the drug sales incident. The gang membership files maintained by the gang unit in each department was the major source of gang case identifications. The gang units in both cities have maintained their gang files for several years. Criteria for entry approximate the definitional guidelines of most Southern California cities with which we are familiar: self-acknowledgment, identification by an informant proven reliable in the past, corroboration of identification by informants of an untested nature and so on. In both departments, gang member elections from patrol or detective sections are reviewed and verified by gang unit personnel in both departments. Neither unit had purged its file of inactive gang members.

In Pomona, an alphabetically ordered printout of about 1,800 entries from the automated gang file facilitated the matching process. Full name, birth date, moniker, and gang name were included. Each name on the arrestee list was checked against the gang roster. Alternative spelling variations (e.g., common misspellings, nicknames and slight phonetic variations), different name ordering (e.g., a first name that could plausibly be a last name), and any aliases provided on the arrest list were explored. Only minor variation in names or birthdates were allowed, except where there was a clear match on a very unusual name.

Pasadena gang files were not automated; membership cards were located in four different boxes or card file drawers. The two major black gang groupings in the Los Angeles area, Crips and Bloods, each had their own box with about 700 cards in the Blood file and about 300 in the Crip box. About 700 cards were located in the Hispanic gang box and these were separated into seven major gang sections. Finally, about 275 cards, mainly with older dates of entry, were contained in a box marked "miscellaneous." Except for the multiple sources investigated, the matching procedures mirrored those in Pomona.[13]

This initial check of drug arrestee names in the gang files yielded four groups of cases for sampling: gang and nongang; cocaine and noncocaine. Up to one hundred cases in each group were sampled randomly from the lists constructed for each city. Whenever a case was dropped during collection, it was replaced by a random selection from the appropriate nonsampled pool. New gang information did surface in the drug incident case file material and required transfers from nongang to gang status. A clear attribution of gang membership in the case material was considered valid even if the suspect did not appear in the gang files. Also, new arrestees not on the original arrest list and new aliases emerged during the case review and were checked against the gang rosters. Occasionally, drug information surfaced in the case file which necessitated reclassification (e.g., drug "resembled" cocaine, but tested positive for heroin). We accommodated these transfers until the sample goals of 100 cases per group had been fulfilled; fourteen eligible cases were dropped because the accurate gang or drug information emerged too late to include the case in the correct sampling pool.

Several limitations to the sources of information used in this study should be noted. Few cities would claim that their gang files accurately represent all that city's gang members. Many gang members fail to come to the attention of police while some individuals with only marginal or transitory involvement inevitably slip through the sieve of even the most rigorous gang designation procedures. Moreover, drug sales arrests reflect drug enforcement activity (e.g. departmental allocation of resources and officer discretion) as well as the level and visibility of drug sales activity. Many, perhaps most, drug transactions are not detected by police. The purpose of this study was to use law enforcement gang files and arrest records to assess empirically the views, held by law enforcement and communicated to the public through the media, of the scope and nature of gang involvement in drug sales. Different techniques, such as interviewing gang members about drug sales activity, have been used by others to investigate this issue.

Collection and Coding Procedures. Teams of students, trained and supervised by a field coordinator well versed in the ambiguities of law enforcement case file material, extracted information relevant to the incident, police activity, drug sales activity and the participants. The collection form was pretested and the case file content reviewed to ensure that the information we sought was available in both departments.

As a reliability check, a random sample of 10 percent of the collected cases was drawn for duplicate coding. The overall discrepancy rate was quite low, two percent for case level variables and one percent for participant variables. For no variables did the correspondence between the two coding passes fall below 91 percent.

Departmental Differences. Any multi-site study raises concern regarding inter-departmental differences. Variations in gang rostering procedures, the arrest logs from which we identified the samples, and the contents of case material could all introduce differences between the two cities. As noted earlier, differences in officer levels and deployment, narcotics enforcement and arrest policies, and recording practices influence the degree to which these arrests reflect the actual level of sales activity in these cities. Interviews with key informants and observations in the stations during the data collection period assessed interdepartmental differences in the manner in which gang and nongang sales activity was handled. Except for the differences in the gang file structures reported earlier, no dramatic variations between the two departments' narcotic or gang enforcement activities were noted. Both departments had street narcotic enforcement operations with teams of gang, narcotics and patrol officers conducting undercover buys and sweeps of the visible, street level dealers and well-known sales locations.

Gang and nongang cases from both drug groups were combined (328 from Pasadena and 326 from Pomona) to assess the differences between the two departments. Very few significant (p.<05) differences between the two cities emerged in this analysis. Indications of gang membership in the case files and the number of gang members per case were at similar levels. There were no location differences, but the presence of firearms was slightly higher in Pomona (14 percent vs. 5 percent). Amounts of each type of drug taken into evidence were similar, but Pomona incidents were slightly more likely to involve marijuana sales charges (36 percent vs. 28 percent) and slightly less likely to be for heroin (five percent vs. nine percent). The total number of suspects per case, and their mean ages, did not differ, but Pomona incidents had proportionally more Hispanics (.41 vs. .16) and fewer blacks (.52 vs. .78). Pomona cases yielded slightly higher proportions of male suspects (.86 vs. .82).

Most of these differences are quite small, and those reaching statistical significance are few. The data from the two stations are combined for all subsequent analyses.

Figure 1
Levels of Gang Involvement in Cocaine Sales Arrest Incidents (1989–91)

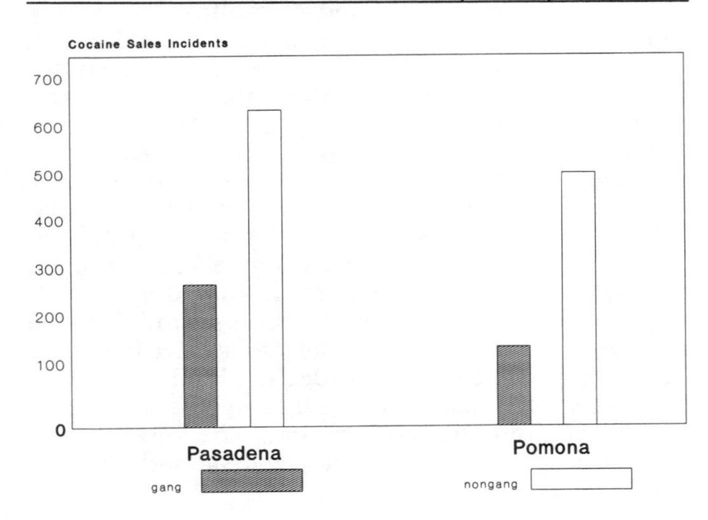

Findings

Cocaine Sales

Recalling the definition of gang cases as including at least one identified gang member arrested in a sales incident, Figure 1 displays the level of gang involvement in the 1,563 cocaine sales incidents. The proportion of cases with gang members in Pasadena is about 30 percent (279/916) and in Pomona, just over 21 percent (139/647). The combined rate is 26.7 percent, indicating that there is substantial gang involvement, yet cocaine distribution is hardly *dominated* by gangs in these two suburban cities. A "one-out-of-four" figure would represent significant gang presence in drug sales for many jurisdictions, yet is much lower than the estimates offered by our law enforcement collaborators prior to data collection. "Almost all," "upward of 90 percent" were not uncommon responses from both gang and narcotics experts in Los Angeles. Pasadena and Pomona estimates were more accurate, but still ranged from about 30-50 percent. In any case, it should be noted that these gang member arrestees may be individual entrepreneurs and involvement of the gang, minimal.

Table 3

Characteristics in Gang and Nongang Cocaine Sales Arrest Events

Incident Characteristics	Nongang N=200	Gang N=200	p[a]
Location			
Dwelling	21% (42)	16% (33)	
Vehicle/open access	70% (141)	79% (158)	NS
Other	9% (17)	5% (9)	
Violence present	6% (13)	5% (10)	NA
Firearms present	10% (21)	10% (19)	NS
Mean number of firearms (among cases with firearms)	2.00	1.16	NS
Cash taken into evidence	48% (97)	54% (109)	NS
Mean amount cash (among cases with cash)	$393	$235	NS
Rock/crack form present	75% (150)	86% (173)	p<.01
Amount of rock/crack (grams) (among cases with rock)	2.40	2.26	NS
Amount any form cocaine (grams)	6.95	3.55	p<.05
Other (than cocaine) drug sales charges present	6% (13)	4% (9)	NS
Known narcotics sales location	36% (73)	44% (87)	NS
Fortifications at location	2% (4)	1% (2)	NA
"Multiple handlers" in sales transaction	21% (42)	24% (48)	NS
Participant Characteristics[b]			
Mean number of offenders	1.68	1.86	NS
Proportion male	.76	.91	p<.001
Proportion black	.76	.92	p<.001
Proportion Hispanic	.20	.07	p<.001
Mean age	38.32	22.48	p<.001

[a] Probability based upon chi-square or T-tests comparisons of means. NS = p>.05: NA = chi square test not valid due to low cell counts.

[b] Participant characteristics calculated over all suspects charged in case. Ninety-two percent of all suspects were charged for cocaine sales offenses.

This combined rate is quite close to the figure of 25 percent reported for the Los Angeles cocaine sales cases in 1985. Thus, the scope of gang involvement in Pasadena and Pomona does not seem to exceed that in South Central Los Angeles in the mid-eighties. Yet, these levels of gang involvement would be more than sufficient to concern law enforcement if gang presence is associated with special features of drug sales.

For example, multiple drugs sold in larger amounts, or a higher likelihood of firearm presence might suggest increasing law enforcement resources to target gang cocaine sellers. The gang/nongang comparative data permit the assessment of this issue. Table 3 displays the data on gang and nongang cocaine sales incidents. The majority of sales occurred on the street or in open access settings, and rarely involved violence or even the presence of firearms[14]. The rock or crack form is more prevalent than powdered cocaine, small amounts are the norm, and the sales of multiple drug types are uncommon. The majority of the incidents did not involve multiple participants engaged in different distribution roles (labeled "multiple handlers" in Table 3).

Very few of the incident characteristics yielded statistically significant differences. Rock sales surface more often in gang cases, but the drug amounts retrieved for evidence are quite similar and just over two grams. The higher figures for cocaine amounts in any form is attributable to the inclusion of cocaine powder; amounts retrieved in nongang cases are almost double that in gang incidents.[15] More cash is taken into evidence in nongang cases, although this difference does not reach statistical significance. No differences emerge in the nature of the sales location (including knowledge by enforcement of prior sales occurring at that site), violence associated with the drug transaction or arrest, or the potential for violence represented by firearms. There is no evidence the cases with gang members are more serious than other cases.

The pattern of similarity between gang and nongang *incident* descriptions changes dramatically when we examine the *participant* characteristics reported on the lower third of Table 3. Most of the cocaine sales incidents involve male black offenders in their twenties. While the total number of offenders per case is the same in the two groups, all the demographic descriptors show marked differences. Gang involvement yields a greater likelihood of male, black suspects of younger ages when compared with cases without gang members. In general, females and Hispanics are not often engaged in cocaine sales in these two cities but they are even less likely to be involved in gang transactions.

The pattern of participant demographic differences mirrors that which emerged from other studies of gang and nongang homicide and other violent incidents.[16] Participants in gang crimes tend to be younger, male and either black or Hispanic. The lack of differences in the cocaine sales incident descriptors suggests that gang involvement has only a negligible impact on the *nature* of these drug transactions. Gang presence is not associated with increased seriousness, *by any measure*.

The earlier Los Angeles cocaine sales data yielded quite similar patterns. A comparison of the outcomes of the statistical tests for gang and nongang distinctions on an array of variables is instructive:

- Location—no difference, both studies
- Firearms—no difference, both studies
- Cash taken—no difference, Pomona and Pasadena; higher in Los Angeles gang cases
- Rock present—gang higher in both studies
- Rock amount—no difference, both studies
- Other drugs present—no difference, both studies
- Fortifications—no difference, both studies
- Multiple handlers—no difference, Pomona and Pasadena; higher in Los Angeles gang cases
- Number suspects—no difference, Pomona and Pasadena; higher in Los Angeles gang cases
- Proportion male—gang higher in both studies
- Proportion black—gang higher in both studies
- Proportion Hispanic—gang lower in both studies
- Age—gang lower in both studies

The differences observed in whether cash was taken into evidence in the Los Angeles cases did not emerge in the current study. The higher number of offenders in gang cases in the first project, and the associated greater likelihood of multiple offenders, did not distinguish gang and nongang incidents in the suburban cities. However, these are rather minor differences within the overall context of similarity between the two time periods and locations.

Moreover, the general nature of cocaine sales incidents appears remarkably stable over time and city. Characteristically, they involve street sales of relatively small amounts of the rock/crack form of cocaine. The majority of these drug sellers are male, black and in their twenties. Very few incidents of violence were recorded in either time period, but the more recent cases were less likely to involve firearms. Firearms presence was recorded in about one-fourth of the 1984-85 incidents, but displayed a *decreasing* pattern of gun presence over time. The lower rate of about one in ten incidents in Pasadena and Pomona is encouraging.

Noncocaine Drug Sales

The design of the current project permitted an examination of the magnitude and character of gang involvement in sales of drugs other than cocaine. Law enforcement informants reported that gangs are prominent in the distribution of marijuana, heroin and PCP, although less so than in cocaine. A higher presence of Hispanic gang members in the sale of these other drugs was anticipated.

The approach to identifying gang-involved sales of other drugs and the data collection procedures paralleled that adopted for cocaine cases. Figure 2 reports the level of gang involvement in the 471 noncocaine sales incidents. The overall proportion of gang involvement is 11.5 percent, much lower than in cocaine cases. There are notable differences between the two cities. The total volume of other drug sales activity is almost three times as high in Pomona (342 incidents vs. 129 incidents), but the number of cases with gang involvement is nearly identical (26 in Pomona vs. 28 in Pasadena).[17] Thus, the percentage of gang involvement is three times higher in Pasadena

(22 percent) than in Pomona (eight percent). Although nearly 500 arrest incidents reflect considerable sales activity (particularly in Pomona), the rate of gang involvement does not suggest that particular concern about gang dealers is warranted. Nevertheless, a unique impact associated with gang presence could imply special law enforcement training or operational procedures.

Figure 2
Levels of Gang Involment in Noncocain Sales Arrest Incidents (1989–91)

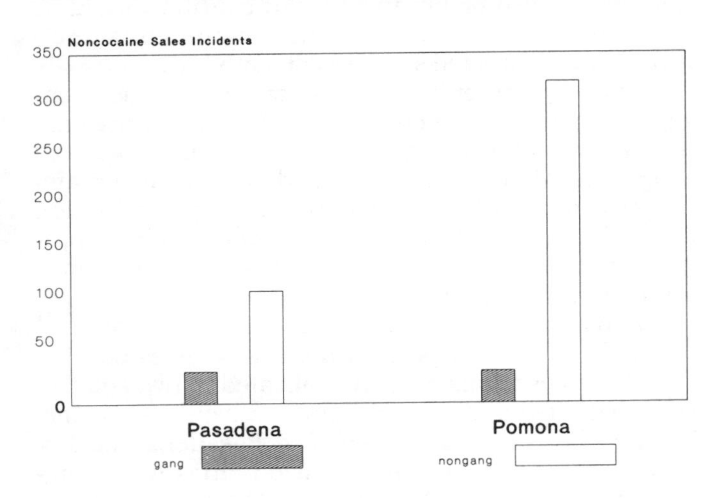

The combined total of just over 50 gang cases provided an upper limit for the gang noncocaine collection sample. Two hundred nongang cases were sampled for collection of the incident and participant descriptors from the case file materials.

Even fewer gang/nongang differences emerged in the noncocaine sales cases. There are *no* significant differences in the incident characteristics and only the proportion of black suspects and mean age distinguish the participants in gang and nongang events. The proportion of black and Hispanic offenders is more evenly distributed than in cocaine cases; in other drug sales, gang involvement is associated with a slightly higher proportion of blacks (.48) than is no gang involvement (.31). In other words, gang cases are about equally likely to involve blacks and Hispanics; nongang sales offenders are more often Hispanic. The pattern of offender ages is quite similar to that found in the cocaine incidents.

Drug Type Comparison

. . . The lack of distinction between cocaine sales cases with and without gang involvement is reflected in noncocaine incidents as well. We combined gang and nongang cases together to test for significant differences between the two drug groups and surprisingly few distinctions emerged. Cocaine events were less likely to have cash taken into evidence (52 percent of cases vs. 62 percent of the noncocaine incidents), but differences in cash amounts did not reach statistically significant levels. The average number of offenders was slightly higher in cocaine sales (1.77 vs. 1.52) as was the increased likelihood of "multiple handlers" (22 percent in cocaine and 9 percent in other drug cases). Finally, the proportion of gang offenders per incident was higher as well (.39 vs. .17).

Perhaps the most interesting distinction between the two drug groups is the ethnic pattern just noted above; Hispanics are more involved in the sale of drugs other than cocaine. However, this difference does not appear to affect the character of drug sales activity generally, nor does it seem to introduce differences dependent on whether the involved Hispanics are gang members.

The Distribution of Drug Arrestees Within Gangs

The case material was inadequate for empirical analyses of "drug gangs." Typical street gang structures are not supportive of organized drug distribution,[18] but the emergence of drug-selling cliques within typically offense-diversified street gangs is quite plausible. Ethnographic methods are more appropriate to this research question and the law enforcement records allow us to speak to this issue only tangentially.

The written narratives in the arrest investigation files did not yield descriptions of recurrent drug-selling groups within gangs, nor did they address the *organization* of drug distribution within a street gang context. In fact, gang information within the case material was limited to occasional references to membership, or to the frequent drug sales activities among certain street gangs. While some drug dealers were arrested for more than one sales incident over the three year time period, no clear gang pattern among these repeat offenders was discernible.

The gang names of the drug arrestees were tallied for both cities. In Pomona, 15 separate gang names were noted among 113 offenders.[19] Nine gangs yielded three or fewer arrests suggesting that most Pomona gangs have very limited involvement in drug sales. On the other hand, one gang generated 45 arrests and two others, about 15 each. In other words, about 70 percent of the gang-named drug offenders were affiliated with just three gangs. Two gang members from the highest volume gang were arrested together in only four *incidents*. The data available do not address the role that the gang played in these drug transactions. It is not clear whether the offenders are individual entrepreneurs, working in several small groups or are concentrated within one or two cliques; ethnographic methods would be required to investigate relationship patterns among drug sellers within this high volume gang.

This pattern of concentration emerged even more dramatically in Pasadena. Eighteen gang names were recorded for 132 gang suspects. Only two gangs generated more than a handful of arrests, but one of these yielded 91 arrests. Only nine *incidents* involved the arrests of two members of this gang together.

The gang members arrested for drug sales during this period represent a clear minority of the gang membership, even in the high volume gangs. There is no evidence of widespread involvement by the membership of either gang and thus neither gang can be characterized as a drug gang. The vast majority of gangs in both cities yielded very few arrests for drug sales during this period. On the other hand, just a few gangs are responsible for most of the gang-involved drug sales in these cities. These gangs are quite logical targets for collaboration between gang and narcotic units. However, it should be noted that the role of the gang *per se* in drug sales operations is unclear and requires more assessment.

Conclusions and Policy Recommendations

Relying upon law enforcement arrest records and gang membership files places some limits on this investigation of gang involvement in drug sales. These data describe the proportion of drug sales *resulting in an arrest* that involve *identified* gang members; other sales transactions, and gang members unrecognized as such by police, are not included. Moreover, this study does not directly address the question of what proportion of all gang members engage in drug sales. Nevertheless, several conclusions derive from these data.

Gang member presence in drug distribution in these two smaller cities can be characterized as substantial, but not overwhelming. Rates of involvement in cocaine sales are of sufficient levels to raise some concern for law enforcement, yet hardly sufficient to cause alarm. The even lower rates of gang presence in transactions of drugs other than cocaine requires little specialized attention by law enforcement.

The degree to which these levels resemble the relative rates of gang involvement in other types of offenses might be instructive. For example, in 1993, gang members were suspects or victims in about one-third of all homicides in Los Angeles county (LASD, 1994). Figures for other offenses are not available, but levels of gang involvement in burglary, vehicle theft or assault might well equal or exceed the rates found in cocaine sales incidents, particularly in areas with high gang activity.

The data did not support an assessment of whether gang members were involved in individual entrepreneurial activities or drug sales directly related to gang functions. However, the majority of gangs contributed very few arrests; in both cities, significant sales activity was associated with just one gang. There was no evidence of widespread involvement of gangs in drug distribution.

Furthermore, there is little evidence of special impacts associated with gang involvement in drug sales of any type. *Gang cases are not more serious*. Gang cocaine sales involve more young, black males in transactions more often including crack rather than the powdered form. The gender differences should allay a growing concern about increased involvement by female gang members.[20] Drug distribution is overwhelmingly a male enterprise, and particularly so in gang cases. Increased likelihood of black and younger offenders also characterize the sales of other drugs by gang members and Hispanics are more often involved in sales of drugs other than cocaine. No policy implications based on these differences would appear to be appropriate. There is little that is unique in the gang drug sale *settings*, wherein policy implications could be quite meaningful. The finding that most gangs contribute few arrests for drug sales suggests that police gang experts should focus their attention on other forms of illegal activity.

In fact, the clearest policy implication emerging from this study is a recommendation to *move away* from gang specialization in narcotics enforcement. The exception may lie in the unusual case of the extremely involved drug selling street gang. Here, intelligence building and sharing between gang and narcotics units may be beneficial. Collaboration in street operations and investigations might also be productive, but caution should be exercised regarding possible cohesion-building side effects of gang-targeted suppression activities.

Social agency practitioners, particularly those engaged in gang-targeted programs, should exercise caution in assuming strong ties between gang clients and drug sales. Many gang members do not sell drugs and few are engaged in highly lucrative drug distribution networks. The discouraging reports of job training programs in competition with vast amounts of drug money are likely exaggerations. Well-conceived gang prevention and intervention programs should be supported.[21]

Finally, the findings from the Los Angeles cocaine sales have been substantially replicated in two smaller, suburban cities and relative to drugs other than cocaine. Earlier, the resemblance between Pasadena and Pomona and several dozen mid-sized cities with long-standing gang problems was noted. About sixty percent of the 37 comparison cities reported that local black gang members are *heavily* involved in drug distribution, most frequently, crack cocaine. The figures for Hispanic gang members are somewhat lower, yet still substantial. Future research should assess these estimates with methods similar to those used in this study, particularly in cities outside the Los Angeles area. Law enforcement gang experts in these cities may be overestimating the scope of the problem, as did many in the Los Angeles area. Regardless of the magnitude of gang involvement, the current study has produced little basis for *specific* concern regarding gangs selling drugs, and suggests that narcotic enforcement operations would benefit little from street gang expertise.

Notes

1. Malcolm Klein and Lea Cunningham contributed significantly to the research design and implementation. This research would not have been possible without the cooperation and assistance from the personnel of the Pasadena Police Department and the Pomona Police Department. Permission was provided by Pomona Police Chief Lloyd Wood and Pasadena Police Chief Jerry Oliver and facilitated by numerous people within the command structures. Personnel within the records and computer divisions provided us with the required case materials and work space. Finally, the officers in both gang units responded to our many questions and helped us with the gang files. Access to records was facilitated by a court order provided by the Honorable Jaime Corral, Presiding Judge, Los Angeles Juvenile Court. The research was supported under award # 91-IJ-CX-K010 from the National Institute of Justice Office of Justice Programs, U.S. Department of Justice. Points of view in this document are those of the author and do not necessarily express the official position of the U.S. Department of Justice.

2. Skolnick, J.H., The social structure of street drug dealing. *American Journal of Police*, 9(1990):1-41; Taylor, C.S., *Dangerous Society*. East Lansing, Mich.: Michigan State University Press, 1989; and Padilla, F., *The Gang as an American Enterprise*. New Brunswick, New Jersey: Rutgers University Press, 1992.
3. Waldorf, D., and Lauderback, D., Gang drug sales in San Francisco: Organized or freelance? Alameda, Calif.: Institute for Scientific Analysis, 1993; Quicker, J.C., Galeai, Y.N., and Batani-Khalfani, A., Bootstrap or noose: Drugs in South Central Los Angeles, draft report to the Social Science Research Council, 1991, cited with permission of the authors; Decker, S., and Van Winkle, B., Slinging dope: The role of gangs and gang members in drug sales. St. Louis: University of Missouri, 1994; and Hagedorn, J. Neighborhoods, markets, and gang drug organization. *Journal of Research in Crime and Delinquency* (1994): forthcoming.
4. Fagan, J., The social organization of drug use and drug dealing among urban gangs. *Criminology*, 27 (1989):633-67.
5. Esbenson, F.A. and Huizinga, D., Gangs, drugs, and delinquency in a survey of urban youth. *Criminology*, 31(1993):565-586; Pennell, S., Evans, E., Melton, R. and Hinson, S., Down for the set: Defining and describing gangs in San Diego. Report to the Administration of Children, Youth and Families. San Diego: San Diego Association of Governments, 1994; Spergel, I.A., personal communication regarding current study of gang members in Chicago, September 1993; Decker, S. and Van Winkle, B., op. cit., 1994; Hagedorn, J., Homeboys, Dope Fiends, Legits and New Jacks. *Criminology*, 32 (1994):197-219. Note that with the exception of the Esbenson and Huizinga work, all studies employed selective samples of gang members.
6. Block, C.B., and Block, R., Street gang crime in Chicago. NIJ Research in Brief, Washington, D.C.: National Institute of Justice; Miller, W.B., memo to James Howell reporting analysis of violent crimes involving youth gangs in Boston, 1984-94, no date; Maxson, C.L., Klein, M.W., and Cunningham, L.C., Definitional variations affecting drug and homicide issues. Los Angeles: University of Southern California, 1992.
7. See Klein, M.W., & Maxson, C.L., Rock sales in south Los Angeles. *Sociology and Social Research*, 69 (1985):561-65, for our first impressions based largely on these sources.
8. Klein, M.W., Maxson, C.L., and Cunningham, L.C., Gang involvement in cocaine "rock" trafficking. Final report to the National Institute of Justice. Los Angeles, Calif.: University of Southern California, 1988; and Klein, M.W., Maxson, C.L., and Cunningham, L.C., "Crack," street gangs, and violence, *Criminology*, 29 (1991):623-50.
9. Maxson, C.L., Gordon, M., and Klein, M.W., Differences between gang and nongang homicide. *Criminology*, 23 (1985):209-222; Klein, M.W., Maxson, C.L., and Gordon, M., Police response to street gang violence: Improving the investigative process. Report to the National Institute of Justice. Los Angeles: University of Southern California, 1987; Bailey, Gary, and Unnithan, Prabha, Gang homicides in California. Paper presented to the American Society of Criminology, 1993.
10. Maxson, C.L., and Klein, M.W., The scope of street gang migration in the U.S.: An interim report to survey participants. Los Angeles: University of Southern California, 1993.
11. These data were gathered in 1992 in an NIJ-funded study on gang migration (#91-IJ-CX-K004). A survey of law enforcement in over 1,100 U.S. cities, including all cities with a population of over 100,000, yielded almost 800 with local street gangs. This comparison is limited to cities of comparable size and relatively early onset dates. The 37 cities constitute about one-third of the gang cities in this population range. Only 10 similar-sized cities reported no gang problems.
12. Thirteen sections of California Health and Safety codes pertain to illegal drug sales or possession for sale. A list of these codes is available from the author.
13. It is possible that gang members from other cities were arrested for drug sales in Pasadena or Pomona and yet did not appear in these two cities' gang files. A check of a sample of 50 arrestees from each department in the county-wide GREAT system maintained by the Los Angeles Sheriff's Department suggested that this was not a concern. Only two of the 100 arrests were in GREAT but not the station gang files. Our thanks to Sgt. Wesley McBride, LASD, for facilitating this procedure. A discussion of the inadequacies and limitations of large computerized files on gang membership can be found in the recent GAO report included in the US House of Representatives Subcommittee on Civil and Constitutional Rights of the Judiciary Committee hearings on developing a national gang data base.
14. Group means can be inflated by a few extreme cases. The frequency distributions for all continuous variables were reviewed. A small number of cases were identified, without regard to gang status, as extremes and omitted from the calculation of group means. This procedure had no impact on the outcome of tests for statistical significance. For example, one nongang case with 23 firearms, if included, would increase the mean number to three guns. The mean amount of cash taken in nongang incidents rises to $1,416 unless one case is dropped from the analysis. Two cases (one from each group) were deleted from the calculation of the mean amount of rock, generating a decrease of about one-half gram in each group. One incident involved more than 10 kilograms of powdered cocaine and four others had more than 1,000 grams. The deletion of these five cases, all nongang, dramatically lowered the group mean from 195 grams to 7 grams. The difference between these two figures serves as a reminder to be cautious about the well-publicized, dramatic bust; the lower figure is a much more accurate measure of the "average" amount of cocaine in these cases. All five large volume cases were the result of long term investigations by the narcotics units in each department.
15. The group means for drug amounts were calculated among cases with cocaine taken into evidence. Thirty-nine of 400 cases had no cocaine counted, usually because laboratory analysis of the retrieved substance tested negative for cocaine or other illegal drugs. Common bar soap was often used to imitate cocaine rocks.
16. Maxson et al., op. cit., 1985; Klein et al., op. cit., 1991; Maxson, et al., op. cit., 1992.
17. These figures would increase only slightly had the cases with multiple drug types including cocaine been placed here rather than in the cocaine group (see Table 3).
18. Klein, M.W., *The American Street Gang*. New York: Oxford University Press, forthcoming.
19. Includes drug sales of all types; multiple arrests of the same offender inflate this figure somewhat. A specific gang name was not available for about ten percent of the gang offenders. Note that the unit of analysis has shifted from incident to individuals.
20. Taylor, C.S., *Girls, Gangs, Women and Drugs*. East Lansing, Michigan: State University Press, 1993.
21. An anonymous review suggested this implication from the study findings. ✦

27

Gangs, Drugs, and Homicide in Los Angeles

Patrick J. Meehan and Patrick W. O'Carroll

Recently, public health practitioners have framed a national campaign on violence as a public health issue. In this article, two physicians from the Centers for Disease Control present their research on the relationships between gangs, drug sales, and violence. Their point of departure is homicide, and thus, their study strikes a contrast with Skolnick's gang drug sellers and Maxson's drug sales incidents. Meehan and O'Carroll utilize homicide investigation reports and coroner's data to study both the drug aspects in gang homicides and gang involvement in drug homicides. The public health orientation of these authors is reflected in the component of the research that assesses homicide victims' cocaine use and narcotic arrest history as differential risk factors in gang and nongang homicides.

Abstract

Objective: To assess the theory that youth homicides in Los Angeles, Calif, are largely attributable to gang involvement in the trafficking or use of drugs.

Design, Setting, and Participants: First, we analyzed all homicides in a police database that occurred in Los Angeles between January 1, 1986, and August 31, 1988, to examine the association between gang activity and narcotic use and trafficking. Second, we used detailed data from police files to examine the same associations for a subset of homicides in south central Los Angeles. Third, we investigated the association between gang homicide victimization and victim cocaine use for all 1987 Los Angeles homicides. Finally, we compared narcotics arrest histories for gang homicide victims with histories for other homicide victims.

Results: Gang-motivated homicides were less likely than other homicides to involve narcotics, and narcotics-motivated homicides were less likely to involve a gang member. Victims of gang-motivated homicides in 1987 were less likely than other homicide victims to have detectable levels of blood cocaine. Finally, young victims of gang-involved homicide were no more likely to have a history of narcotics arrests than other victims.

Conclusions: Our investigation does not support the theory that a substantial proportion of homicides are attributable to gang involvement in narcotics trafficking. (AJDC. 1992;146:683-687)

Between 1980 and 1988, the homicide rate in Los Angeles, Calif, was more than double the rate for the state of California (unpublished data, Los Angeles Police Department [LAPD] and the California Department of Health Services, 1989). According to the gang investigation unit of the LAPD, gang-related homicides constitute an increasingly large proportion of all homicides in Los Angeles. In 1983, 14.8% of all homicides were gang-related compared with 25.2% in 1987.

There is also objective evidence that cocaine abuse and trafficking have increased in Los Angeles. Both the number of medical encounters for problems related to cocaine abuse and cocaine seizures by law enforcement agencies have increased.[1] Furthermore, in 1987, cocaine or cocaine metabolites were detected in the blood of more than one of every five homicide victims in Los Angeles County at the time of death.[2]

Both gang activities and narcotics trafficking are inherently violent activities that are independently associated with an increased risk of homicide perpetration and victimization.[3] However, a prevalent theory in Los Angeles in the late 1980s was that a substantial proportion of the increasing incidence of homicide among the youth in that city was attributable to the increasing involvement of gang members in illicit drug trafficking, drug use, or both. According to this theory, the involvement of gangs in the narcotics trade is a particularly explosive mix, resulting in increases in violence far beyond what might be expected from the sum of the independent contributions of gang activity and narcotics trafficking. The general acceptance of this theory is reflected in both the popular media (*Los Angeles Herald Examiner*, January 14, 1989:A4; *Rolling Stone*, September 22, 1988:64-72, 114-116) and in official reports, such as the 1988 report from the California Council on Criminal Justice Task Force on Gangs and Drugs.[4] The hypothesized interaction of gangs and narcotics in causing homicide is generally thought to involve narcotics trafficking, particularly cocaine trafficking. It is also conceivable, however, that increasing *use* of narcotics by gang members could contribute to higher homicide rates, either because of direct pharmacologic effects of narcotics that promote violent behavior or because of the need of narcotics users to commit violent crimes to supply their addictions.[5]

Despite its popularity, there is little evidence to support the theory that gang involvement in the narcotics trade is responsible for a substantial proportion of homicide among youth in Los Angeles. This issue should be critically examined because it has direct relevance to the design of homicide prevention pro-

Reprinted with permission from the *American Journal of Diseases of Children*, 1992, 146:683-87.

grams. If a large proportion of homicides are attributable to this intersection of gang activity and narcotics trafficking (or use), then increased efforts to prevent gangs from selling (or using) narcotics might be the most effective short-term strategy for reducing the death toll from homicide in Los Angeles. If, on the other hand, narcotics trafficking and gang activity are more important as independent contributors to homicide than as cofactors, a prevention strategy targeted primarily at the intersection of these two inherently violent activities would be misdirected.

Unfortunately, no single data source is sufficient for a comprehensive examination of the various possible relationships between gangs, narcotics, and homicide. Police files, vital statistics, and medical examiner's data files provide relevant information, but each data source has limitations that prevent a straightforward epidemiologic investigation. As part of an investigation of homicides in Los Angeles, however, we were able to make use of several distinct but complementary data sources, each of which provided some evidence about the hypothesized association between gang activity, narcotics use or trafficking, and homicide.

Materials and Methods

The available data sources permitted us to evaluate the following four hypotheses: (1) homicides due to gang rivalry (gang-motivated homicides) are more likely than others to involve narcotics; (2) homicides resulting from conflicts related to narcotics trafficking (narcotics-motivated homicides) are more likely than others to involve gang members; (3) victims of gang-motivated homicides are more likely than others to have been using cocaine before death; and (4) victims of homicides involving a gang member (gang-involved homicides) are more likely to have a history of arrests related to narcotics (possession or distribution) than are victims of homicides that involved neither gangs nor narcotics.

Each of these hypotheses posits possible associations between narcotics trafficking or use and gang involvement in homicides in Los Angeles. Because street gang members are mostly younger than 25 years, our analysis emphasizes youth homicides.

Narcotics and Gang Involvement in Homicides

We used two separate data sources to examine the first two hypotheses. The first is a database maintained by the homicide unit of the LAPD primarily for investigative purposes, which we refer to as the *LAPD database* (Table 1).

It contains information on homicide victim demographics, crime circumstances, motives, weapons, and suspects, as well as a brief summary of the incident. Information on homicides is entered by detectives at the outset of an investigation and is updated periodically. Motive was entered by the detective as a word or short phrase ("gang," "gang fight," "domestic," "narco dispute," etc). Motive was then counted by us as "narcotics-motivated" if narcotics appeared in the description of motive, "gang-motivated" if gang appeared in the description, or "motivated by one of a variety of other factors." Apart from the primary motive, "narcotics involvement" and "gang involvement" were entered by the police as separate variables. By definition, all narcotics-motivated homicides were "narcotics-involved," and all gang-motivated homicides were "gang-involved."

Table 1

Study Questions and Data Sources

Question No.	Study Questions	Data Sources Used
1.	Are gang-motivated homicides more likely than other homicides to involve narcotics?	LAPD database,* SCLA investigative files+
2.	Are narcotics-motivated homicides more likely than other homicides to involve gangs?	LAPD database,* SCLA investigative files+
3.	Are victims in gang-motivated homicides more likely than other homicide victims to have been using cocaine?	LAPD database, linked with LA County Coroner's data**
4.	Are victims of gang-involved homicides more likely to have a narcotics-related arrest than are victims of homicides that were neither gang nor narcotics involved?	LAPD database (sample),++ LAPD arrest records

* Based on information from the Los Angeles Police Department (LAPD) database, 2,162 homicide victims between January 1986 and August 1988 were aged 10 years or older.

+ Based on south central Los Angeles (SCLA) investigative files, 114 homicide victims were aged between 10 and 19 years.

** Based on blood cocaine levels of 74% of 618 homicide victims in the LAPD database in 1987.

++ Randomly selected homicide victims in south central Los Angeles aged 15 to 24 years between January 1986 and August 1988 included 31 cases (gang-involved homicides) and 36 controls (neither gang- nor narcotics-involved homicides).

The LAPD defines a gang as "a group of persons working to an unlawful or antisocial end" (from LAPD intradepartmental correspondence). Operationally, gang membership is ascertained by detectives entering the data, based on whether the subject is listed in the computerized gang roster of the LAPD or based on characteristics of the event, including use of known hand signals used by gangs, gang-specific clothing, and witness statements.[3]

We verified the completeness of this database by manually comparing homicides in it with those in the master crime file housed in the LAPD data unit's mainframe computer. For the period of study, 97% of the homicides in the master file were also found in the LAPD investigative database. The determination of gang motive by the LAPD had previously been validated.[6] Further, an independent gang unit of the LAPD examined each 1988 homicide to ascertain whether it was gang-motivated. Of the 82 homicides determined to be gang-motivated by the unit, 64 (78%) were described as having a gang motive in the LAPD database. Of the 416 homicides not ascertained to be gang-motivated by the gang investigation unit, 385 (93%) were also described as other than gang-motivated in the LAPD database.

We determined that data had been reliably entered into the LAPD database for the period of January 1, 1986, through August 31, 1988. We therefore analyzed data on the victims of all homicides that occurred in Los Angeles during this period, excluding homicides due to legal intervention (during the interruption of a crime). We constructed a set of contingency tables to compare the frequency of gang involvement in narcotics motivated homicides with that in other homicides. We also constructed contingency tables to compare the frequency of narcotic involvement in gang-motivated homicides with that in other homicides. In our analysis, we stratified the victims into two age groups: 10 to 24 years old, and 25 years and older.

Our second data source was the investigative homicide files kept in police district offices. Of 18 police districts in the city, the police had identified four contiguous districts as having the highest concentration of youths involved in gangs and homicides involving gangs. We refer to this area as *south central Los Angeles*. District office files for each homicide contain initial investigative reports and summary follow-up reports. We limited the case subjects in this analysis to a subset of the population that we studied using the LAPD database: homicide victims aged 10 to 19 years who died in south central Los Angeles from January 1, 1987, through August 31, 1988 (Table 1). We extracted demographic data, information on the weapons used, motive, relationship of victim to offender, whether narcotics were involved, and various incident characteristics.

For this part of the analysis, we defined a gang-involved homicide as one in which either the victim or perpetrator was identified as a gang member through the evidence collected. We defined a gang-motivated homicide as one that resulted from violence between rival gang factions. We defined a narcotics-involved homicide as one in which narcotics were found at the scene of the homicide or on the body of the victim or perpetrator, or in which evidence indicated that narcotic sales or use was occurring at or near the time of the homicide. Finally, we defined a narcotics-motivated homicide as one that resulted from a violent conflict over a narcotics transaction. As with the LAPD database, we used these data to look at the levels of involvement of gangs and narcotics in narcotics-motivated and gang-motivated homicides, respectively.

Cocaine Use by Homicide Victims

To examine the third hypothesis, we supplemented data contained in the LAPD database with records from the Los Angeles County Coroner's Office for 1987. The Los Angeles County Coroner's Office analyzes blood specimens from all homicide victims in Los Angeles County for the presence of cocaine and a cocaine metabolite (benzoylecgonine) according to methods described elsewhere.[2] Detection of either compound was considered evidence of recent cocaine use. Complete data were available for homicides in 1987, and we were able to link the databases from the LAPD and the Coroner's Office for 74% of the homicides that occurred in Los Angeles in 1987 (Table 1). Homicide cases that could not be linked to data from the Coroner's Office did not differ substantially from those that could in terms of the victim's age, sex, or race, the police division in which the homicide occurred, or the perpetrator's motives. The most common reason for a failed linkage was inability to match records by the common identification number.

We examined the hypothesized association between recent cocaine use and being a victim of a gang-motivated homicide by comparing the frequency of positive cocaine levels in the blood of victims of gang-motivated homicide with those in victims of homicides not motivated by gangs.

Past Narcotics Arrests Among Homicide Victims

We tested our fourth hypothesis using a case-control study design. We defined case subjects as victims of gang-involved homicides and control subjects as victims of homicides that were neither gang- nor narcotics-involved. We evaluated the prevalence of history of narcotics arrest among cases compared with controls.

We randomly selected 36 case and 36 control victims of homicide from the LAPD database of ages 15 to 24 years who resided in one of the census tracts within south central Los Angeles and were killed between January 1, 1987, and August 31, 1988 (Table 1). Correct addresses were not available for five of the sampled gang-involved homicide victims, leaving 31 case and 36 control subjects.

We assessed the decedent's history of narcotics arrests using data from computerized county arrest records. After obtaining court permission, we searched computerized law enforcement databases using the decedent's name, address, and date of birth. Any arrest history was noted, including any history of narcotics arrests (for possession or for selling). We found that 42 of the 67 study victims had arrest records. We assumed that the absence of an arrest record was indicative of a victim having no arrests for any offense. We also assumed that the possibility that a record was not found because of an incorrect name or other clerical error was equally likely for case and control subjects.

Statistical Methods

Statistical testing was done using either the Mantel-Hantzel x^2 test or a two-tailed Fisher's exact test. Odds ratios and 95% confidence intervals (obtained from Cornfield's approximation) were calculated with Epiinfo software (Centers for Disease Control, Atlanta, Ga).

Results

Narcotics Involvement in Gang-Motivated Homicides

The LAPD database contained data on 2,162 homicides that occurred between January 1, 1986, and August 31, 1988. Overall, it was noted that 18 (5%) of 345 gang-motivated homicides involved narcotics, whereas 416 (23%) of 1817 other homicides involved narcotics (P«.01; Table 2). For both younger and older homicide victims, gang-motivated homicides were significantly less likely to have involved narcotics than were other homicides.

Table 2

Narcotics Involvement in Gang-Motivated Homicides in Los Angeles from January 1986 Through August 1988

Victims	Gang Motivated	Other Motive	
10 to 24 years old			
Narcotics involved	11	135	$P < 10^{-7}$
Narcotics not involved	259	375	
Total	**270**	**510**	**780**
25 years and older			
Narcotics involved	7	281	$P < .05$
Narcotics not involved	68	1026	
Total	**75**	**1307**	**1382**
Total 10 years and older			
Narcotics involved	18	416	$P < 10^{-7}$
Narcotics not involved	327	1401	
Total	**345**	**1817**	**2162**

Since all the narcotics-motivated homicides (conflict due to narcotics trafficking) are by definition in the "other" (comparison) homicide group when gang-motivated homicides are being examined, and since narcotics-motivated homicides are always narcotics involved, there is an intrinsic bias toward finding more narcotics involvement in the "other" homicide group than in the gang-motivated homicide group. To account for this bias, we compared the frequency of narcotics involvement in gang-motivated homicides with that for homicides that were neither gang- nor narcotics-motivated. Gang-motivated homicides were still less likely to have involved narcotics than were other homicides. This finding held for all ages combined (P<.005) and for victims aged 10 to 24 years (P<.001). For victims 25 years and older, homicides that were gang-motivated were just as likely to involve narcotics as were homicides that were neither gang- nor narcotics-motivated (difference is not significant).

We obtained similar results from our detailed examination of investigation files for homicides among adolescents that occurred in south central Los Angeles. During the 20-month period from January 1, 1987, through August 31, 1988, there were 116 homicides in south central Los Angeles involving victims aged 10 to 19 years. We reviewed the investigative files of 114 of these homicides (records for two homicides were not available) and found that none of the 40 gang-motivated homicides involved narcotics.

Gang Involvement in Narcotics-Motivated Homicides

Overall, narcotics-motivated homicides were less likely than other homicides to have involved gangs (Table 3). Of the 281 narcotics-motivated homicides in the LAPD database, 30 (11%) were also noted to have involved gangs. Of the 1881 other homicides, 442 (23%) involved gang members (P«.01). When the victims were stratified by age, this negative association between narcotics-motivated homicides and gang involvement was found only for those homicides involving victims younger than 25 years. The most common motive for homicides involving gang members was a gang conflict.

Table 3

Gang Involvement in Narcotics-Motivated Homicides in Los Angeles from January 1986 Through August 1988

Victims	Narcotics Motivated	Other Motive	
10 to 24 years old			
Gangs involved	16	324	$P < 10^{-7}$
Gangs not involved	81	359	
Total	**97**	**683**	**780**
25 years and older			
Gangs involved	14	118	$P < .3$
Gangs not involved	171	1078	
Total	**185**	**1196**	**1381***
Total 10 years and older			
Gangs involved	30	442	$P < 10^{-5}$
Gangs not involved	251	1439	
Total	**281**	**1881**	**2162**

* Information for gang involvement was not available for one case.

Since gang-motivated homicides (involving gang conflict) are always gang-involved (include a gang member as victim or perpetrator), and since gang-motivated homicides are by definition included in the comparison group in the preceding analysis, the negative association we found between narcotics-motivated homicides and gang involvement could theoretically be due to an artifactual bias. We therefore also compared gang involvement in narcotics-motivated homicides with gang involvement in homicides that were neither gang- nor narcotics-motivated. Still, narcotics-motivated homicides were less likely to have involved gangs than were homicides that were neither gang- nor narcotics-motivated for all ages combined (P<.05) and for victims 25 years or older (P=.05). For victims aged 10 to 24 years, narcotics-motivated homicides were no more or less likely to involve gangs than were homicides that were neither gang- nor narcotics-motivated (difference is not significant).

Of the 114 homicides in south central Los Angeles for which we reviewed actual investigative files, three were found to be narcotics-motivated. None of those three homicides involved gang members.

Cocaine Use by Homicide Victims

Victims of gang-motivated homicides in 1987 were significantly less likely than victims of other homicides to have cocaine or cocaine metabolites in their bloodstreams (P<.0001; Table 4). This negative association between being a victim of a gang-motivated homicide and recent cocaine use was found only for homicides involving victims between 10 and 24 years old (P<.0005). Among those 25 years and older, no such association was found.

Table 4

Detection of Cocaine or Cocaine Metabolite in the Blood of Homicide Victims in Los Angeles in 1987

Victims	Gang Motivated	Other Motive	
10 to 24 years old			
Cocaine present	4	36	*P*<.0005
Cocaine not present	78	110	
25 years and older			
Cocaine present	8	119	P=.7
Cocaine not present	14	249	
Total 10 years and older			
Cocaine present	12	155	*P<.0001*
Cocaine not present	92	359	

Past Arrest Histories of Homicide Victims

Eight (26%) of 31 victims of gang-involved homicides had a history of narcotics arrests, whereas nine (25%) of 36 control homicide victims had a history of narcotics arrests (Table 5). Thus, victims of gang-involved homicides were no more likely to have a history of narcotics arrests than were victims of homicides that were neither gang nor narcotics-involved (odds ratio, 1.0; 95% confidence interval, 0.30 to 3.6).

Table 5

Comparison of Narcotics Arrest Histories for Homicide Victims Between Ages 15 and 24 Years in South Central Los Angeles From January 1987 Through August 1988

Narcotic Arrest History	Homicides Involving Gangs	Homicides Involving Neither Gangs Nor Narcotics	Odds Ratio (95% Confidence Interval)
History of arrest	8	9	1.0 (0.3-3.6)
No history of arrest	23	27	

Comment

There is no question that a substantial proportion of homicides in urban America are attributable to gang activity and to narcotics trafficking. ln Los Angeles during the period studied, 16% of the homicides among persons aged 10 years and older were gang-motivated, and 13% were narcotics-motivated (Tables 2 and 3). Thus, three out of every 10 homicide victims died from violence between rival gang factions or from violence associated with narcotics trafficking. The results of our investigation, however, do not support the popular theory that a substantial proportion of homicides are attributable to gang involvement in narcotics trafficking. Indeed, our analysis of available data sources suggests that gang-motivated homicides do not tend to involve narcotics trafficking (or victim drug use), and narcotics-motivated homicides do not tend to involve gangs.

Past research on the relationship between gangs, narcotics trafficking, and violence is inconclusive.[7] In contrast to our findings, for example, Skolnick and colleagues[8] concluded (based on a series of interviews in California with inmates of correctional institutions and police and correctional officers) that street drug dealing in California is dominated by Black gangs organized specifically for the purpose of distributing crack cocaine (institutional gangs). Such gangs are said to be distinct from the more traditional neighborhood or cultural gangs. Klein and Maxson,[3] however, have suggested that it may be tautological to define gangs in terms of the common criminal activity that brings the members together as with institutional cocaine distributing gangs. It is quite possible that violence involving traditional youth street gangs that are loosely tied together by neighborhood allegiance is a phenomenon distinct from violence involving more highly organized institutional gangs or networks that exist for the purpose of marketing narcotics.

The hypothesis that the increasing rates of gang-related homicide result from an increasing gang involvement in narcotics trafficking presupposes that gang involvement in narcotics trafficking has actually increased. There is evidence, however, that this is not the case. A 1988 study by Klein et al.[9] did not show a relationship between the dramatic increase in crack cocaine sales in Los Angeles during 1983 to 1985 and gang involvement in cocaine distribution. Fagan[10] interviewed 151 gang members younger than 21 years from three inner-city, high-crime neighborhoods, including south central Los Angeles. He concluded that illicit drug use and violence were widespread among gangs but that serious drug use and dealing by individual gang members occurred regardless of the prevalence of drug dealing within the individual's particular gang. He also concluded that drug use and sales by gang members did not necessarily increase the frequency or severity of violent behavior.

Each of the four data sources we used in our analysis has certain limitations. We were concerned, for instance, that in an atmosphere of heightened concern about gang violence there might be a bias in the LAPD database toward coding homicides involving gang members as gang-motivated or gang-involved without noting the roles of narcotics or other factors. It is also possible that police may purposely downplay the role of narcotics in a homicide to avoid the introduction of mental impairment as a defense in court proceedings. Our own review of police investigation files for a subset of homicides (those occurring in south central Los Angeles and involving victims aged 11 to 19 years) helps validate the data obtained from the LAPD database; however, since the findings were similar, we cannot completely rule out such misclassification bias. We compared gang classification within the LAPD database with an independent classification provided by the gang investigation unit of the LAPD and found reasonably good agreement, and past research has provided evidence of the validity of gang involvement in homicides by the LAPD.[6] Thus, misclassification bias of gang status is unlikely. In the future, researchers who evaluate existing police data may benefit from using court records or other sources of information to check further for misclassification bias.

We were able to obtain whole blood cocaine levels on a large, representative sample of homicide victims for 1987. The hypothesized association between illicit drug use and participation in violence would clearly be better tested by using data on drug use by all crime participants, including perpetrators. Unfortunately, existing data sources did not permit us to analyze the drug use of perpetrators.

Our finding that little or no association existed between narcotics-related arrests and gang-motivated homicide victimization further supports our conclusion that gang conflicts that result in a homicide are often independent of narcotics use and trafficking. Two limitations to this part of the analysis should be noted, however. First, we used the victims' history of narcotics arrests as a marker for their involvement in narcotics use or trafficking, and an arrest history may be an insensitive measure of such involvement. Second, the power of our analysis to detect a difference is limited by the small number of homicides that we studied. A separate, larger-scale study would be useful for confirming or refuting our findings.

Despite these limitations, we believe that the consistency of our findings across these different data sets strongly suggests that if gang activity and narcotics trafficking (or use) do interact to increase the risk of homicide, this interaction does not account for a large proportion of homicides (i.e., the attributable risk percent is small). In light of this, we recommend that gang activity and narcotics trafficking or use be addressed as separate, important risk factors for homicide rather than as interrelated cofactors.

Author's Note:

From the Division of Injury Control, National Center for Environmental Health and Injury Control, Centers for Disease Control, Public Health Service, US Department of Health and Human Services, Atlanta, GA 30333.

Notes

1. McAllister, D, Speckart, G. Current trends and patterns of drug abuse in Los Angeles County, California 1984-1986. In: *Patterns and Trends of Drug Abuse in the United States and Europe*. Rockville, MD: National Institute on Drug Abuse, 1987;2:88-113.
2. Budd, RD. Cocaine abuse and violent death. *American Journal of Drug and Alcohol Abuse*. 1989;15:375-382.
3. Klein, MW, Maxson, CL. Street gang violence. In: Weiner, NA, Wolfgang ME, eds. *Violent Crime, Violent Criminals*. Newbury Park, Calif: Sage Publications; 1989:198-234.
4. California Council on Criminal Justice. *Task Force Report on Gangs and Drugs*. Sacramento: California Council on Criminal Justice; 1989.
5. Goldstein PJ. Drugs and violent crime. In: Weiner NA, Wolfgang ME, eds. *Pathways to Criminal Violence*. Newbury Park. Calif: Sage Publications 1989:16-48.
6. Klein MW, Gordon MA, Maxson CL. The impact of police investigations on police-reported rates of gang and nongang homicides. *Criminology*. 1986;24:489-511.
7. Clark CS. Youth gangs. *Congressional Quarterly Research*. 1991;22:755-771.
8. Skolnick JH, Correl T, Navarro E, Rabb R. The social structure of street drug dealing. In: *BCS Forum: The Social Structure of Street Drug Dealing*. Berkeley, Calif: University of California; 1989.
9. Klein MW, Maxson CL, Cunningham L. *Gang Involvement in Cocaine Rock Trafficking: Final Report to the National Institute of Justice*. Los Angeles: University of Southern California; 1988.
10. Fagan J. The social organization of drug use and drug dealing among urban gangs. *Criminology*. 1989; 27:633-665. ✦

28

An Ethic Dies With Gang Chief

Jesse Katz

We come full circle in this section with the following journalistic account of one long-term gang member's violent death. Katz' depiction of the evolution of this notorious gang resonates with Skolnick's description of the impact of drug trafficking on the social organization and violent behavior of black cultural gangs. While mindful that this account focuses on the unusual member of an atypical gang in a city often dubbed "the gang capital" of the nation, the story of "Stone" raises the issue of a "tipping point" wherein the destructiveness of some aspects of gang life might lead even the most committed participants to reconsider the lifestyle.

When the partially decomposed body of Keith Cardell Thomas turned up in a San Gabriel Valley avocado grove two months ago—handcuffed, shot in the head and stuffed into the back of a rented Ford Explorer—it sparked some rare introspection by Los Angeles' most notorious street gang.

At 30, he was among the oldest and most respected leaders of the Rollin' 60s—a group of Crips whose fierceness and reckless exploits have fueled the city's worst fears about gang violence.

But Stone, as he was known around Crenshaw Boulevard, was different from the new generation of gangsters filling the ranks of the Rollin' 60s, teenagers blinded by the lure of fast cash and gold chains.

In many ways, he was a throw-back to the Crips' origins in the 1970s, when the battles were over community control, when loyalty to the neighborhood—being "down for the 'hood"—meant self-determination, not self-destruction.

Even as he became a ruthless henchman in the gang's violent push into the rock cocaine trade, Stone clung to an old-fashioned code of honor, cautioning that cutthroat greed within its ranks was undermining the ethos of unity and devotion. Much like a weary Mafia don, he had begun making peaceful overtures to rival gangs, wearing wooden African beads and seeking inspiration in the teachings of Malcolm X and Louis Farrakhan.

Although some Rollin' 60s listened—if only out of respect—Stone's assassination drove home a point they could not ignore: The violence that he had both warned against and wreaked is careening out of control.

"We started out as brothers loving brothers," one veteran Rollin' 60s member said. "Now, the neighborhood don't really trust each other no more. . . . There used to be respect. Now, it's like everybody's against everybody."

Los Angeles County sheriff's officials, while declining to discuss details of the case, say Stone's execution has all the markings of a soured drug deal, in which he was either the victim or the perpetrator of a rip-off. Stone's body was found Feb. 1 by a caretaker in the isolated avocado grove in Duarte, where he was lying face-down inside the truck alongside his friend Daniel J. Chapman, 28, who had also been handcuffed and shot in the head.

"This is not poo-butt street stuff," said Sheriff's Homicide Lt. Frank Merriman. "You're talking major league gangs and major league dope."

That Stone's call for self-examination had struck a nerve in the Rollin' 60s was evident at his funeral, where an anguished crowd of nearly 400 packed the pews and stood in the aisles of Grace Chapel at Inglewood Park Cemetery.

The mourners formed a sea of blue—hardened young men in baggy pants and carefully creased shirts—as Stone was remembered as "a warrior," "Six-O all the way."

But unlike most gang funerals, this one was not an affirmation of the criminal life. Instead, a burly man known as Keta Roc, who has "Rollin' 60s" tattooed across his neck, took the microphone and made the kind of speech that normally only the preacher dares deliver.

The gang, he said in emotion-choked spurts, must face its culpability in Stone's death. The homeboys were so busy thinking about themselves that they had failed to protect one of their own. As the mourners shifted uncomfortably, Keta Roc said in a rising voice that they were all to blame.

"The 'hood," he said, "is liable."

The Rollin' 60s' evolution from a unified band of neighborhood enforcers to a collection of well armed, for-profit factions is being mirrored in gangs throughout Los Angeles County. While gangs have always been brutal, they resort to violence more quickly and more indiscriminately now because the stakes are about money, not just turf or pride, according to police and gang authorities.

This transformation has jarred not only the gang world, but has turned their neighborhoods into virtual war zones, where innocent bystanders are consumed by the mayhem, victims of geography.

In gang and law enforcement circles, there are no illusions that the Rollin' 60s' soul-searching, triggered by Stone's execution, will make any difference in the escalating violence that last year claimed a record 771 lives in the county.

But when even hard-core gang members say they have grown tired of the bloodshed and treachery, it underscores the bitter truth of what Crippin' has become.

"Once upon a time, the Rollin' 60s were a family," said Chilton Alphonse, a Crenshaw District gang worker. "Now, I think a lot of these youngsters are beginning to question, is it really worth it."

When Keith Thomas was born in 1961, Crips did not exist.

Their roots are usually traced to a Fremont High School student named Raymond Washington, who had been steeped in the Black Panther rhetoric of pride, protection and community control. In 1972, when a gang of followers from his neighborhood beat a teenager to death for his leather jacket, they became a legend.

Word spread about the tough-looking young men, who some said carried canes and walked with a limp—cripples, or crips, they were called for short. But their significance went beyond just a few heralded street fights. Before long, some were saying that Crip was an acronym for Community Revolution in Progress.

"There was a point at which Crips had a more favorable reputation and position in the community," said Donald Bakeer, a teacher of African-American literature at Washington High School, who has written a historical novel about the Crips. "Today, all the destruction and murder and terror seem crazy. . . . But in the late '70s, every youngster in junior high wanted to be a Crip—there was mystery and glamour, like tales of the Old West."

It was an attractive notion to the young men growing up in the western fringes of South Los Angeles, where many black families had sought refuge in the late 1960s after the tumultuous events in Watts. The Rollin' 60s, who take their name from the numbered streets between Slauson and Florence avenues, were one of the first cliques—or "sets"—of the Crips to take root in the area. They viewed their new turf as a prized possession—a symbol of manhood and existence.

Even back then, the Rollin' 60s could be vicious in their defense of the neighborhood. You seized your piece of the pie with fearlessness and audacity. Being crazier than the next guy was part of the mystique.

In those days, however, they tended to view their enemy as the society that had kept them powerless. When cheap crack cocaine began pouring into the community in the 1980s, that changed. The high-stakes battle for drug turf turned Crips against Crips, and eventually, Rollin' 60s against Rollin' 60s.

The 60s were one of the first Los Angeles gangs to cash in on the drug trade, shifting their focus from neighborhood rule to for-profit endeavors. They were also one of the first to heavily arm themselves; according to urban folklore, they hold a cache of automatic weapons stolen from a National Guard Armory.

"The 60s are one of the most violent, active gangs in the city," said Sgt. Steve La Roche of the Los Angeles Police Department's antigang CRASH unit. "They're so big that their own internal factions frequently get into it with each other."

In a confidential LAPD report prepared in 1989, detectives identified 459 hard-core members of the Rollin' 60s, who had been arrested a total of 3,527 times. Those arrests had resulted in convictions for 17 murders, four attempted murders, seven assaults with a deadly weapon, 35 robberies, five burglaries, eight auto thefts, 20 narcotics sales, three rapes and two forgeries, among other things.

The report also noted that members of the gang were suspected of 37 bank robberies in Southern California, a jewelry store holdup in Modesto, transporting cocaine to Dallas, a drive-by shooting in West Covina and barging into motel rooms in Southwest Los Angeles, and robbing the occupants at gunpoint.

Moreover, officials found no evidence of a formal leadership structure. Apart from two cliques devoted to drug trafficking, the report said, most of the gang members commit crimes for their personal gain and "hold no allegiance to any organization and do not act at the direction of a recognized leader."

In one of their most savage exploits, two Rollin' 60s members barged into the home of former NFL star Kermit Alexander's family in 1984, killing his 58-year-old mother in the kitchen and his sister and two young nephews in their beds. The attack was supposedly a murder for hire; the only hitch was, the killers had misread the address and gone into the wrong house.

Four years later, another act of reckless shooting erupted into arguably the single most significant event in Los Angeles gang history. Durrell DeWitt Collins, a 23-year old member of the Rollin' 60s, spotted a rival on a crowded Westwood street and approached him, saying: "C'mon, I got something for you."

Collins then pulled a gun and fired twice, missing his target, but striking Karen Toshima, a graphic artist from Long Beach who was strolling with a friend. The shooting was a watershed, shocking middle-class corners of the city with the realization that gang violence can occur anywhere, while minority leaders complained that killings in their communities rarely generate the same outrage.

There were also the cases of David (Let Loose) Cole, convicted of killing a 10-year-old girl after the bullets he fired pierced the walls of her Inglewood home; Anthony Wayne Fagan, sentenced to 25 years in prison for selling rock cocaine from a house across the street from Hyde Park Elementary School, and George Brett Williams, who killed two men during a scheme to buy cocaine from them with bundles of shredded telephone books disguised as cash.

Last December, 26-year-old Eugene Henley, one of the gang's de facto leaders and one of Stone's closest confidants—was arrested in a drug sting after he allegedly tried to rob an undercover sheriff's deputy of 33 pounds of cocaine. He is being held in lieu of $2 million bail.

"You can't predict what we do," said a 16-year-old gang member known as Mike Dog, as he scrawled RSC—Rollin' 60s Crips—on the metal gate of an apartment building. "If we let people run over the 60s, we wouldn't have no 'hood."

Like many of his friends, young Keith (Stone) Thomas had no father in the house—a two-bedroom, 1920s-era bungalow on Cimarron Street. His mother, a UCLA graduate and public health nurse for the county, struggled to raise two sons on her own.

Although she managed to provide the basics of a middle-class life—Keith collected pigeons and played Little League baseball—not all of their hurdles were economic. All around, they faced reminders, some blatant, others insidious, that race was still a defining factor.

"You have a generation of young black children, especially males, that feel disenfranchised, that feel used, that feel the system is out to get them," said Alphonse, director of the Community Youth Sports and Art Foundation. "So, they think, what the hell, I'm down with gangsterism. It's their way of paying society back."

When he was 13, Keith's mother took him and a cousin to a West Los Angeles bank, where a teller suspected that the two teenagers were robbers—"not because of their behavior, but because of their physical appearance," his mother wrote in an obituary printed on the back of his funeral program.

More than a dozen police officers showed up and pointed their guns at Keith and his cousin, the only two black youths in the bank. "I didn't do nothing," Keith cried, as his mother pleaded for the officers to hold their fire.

The misunderstanding was cleared up, but the incident remained "a confusing trauma in his life," his mother wrote. It was the kind of experience, he later learned, that was "shared by the very many friends and brothers he made."

"Kids in this neighborhood get labeled," his mother, Billie L. Thomas, said in an interview. "Nobody is trying to include them in mainstream America. A child here has to fight for his self-esteem, his friendships and his belonging."

As a teen-ager at Crenshaw High School, that meant Stone stood behind his fists and never shied from a challenge, even when the taunts came from an older or bigger kid. Later, when he had earned the title of O.G., an Original Gangster, he would invite 50 friends to his place, send out for $300 worth of barbecued ribs and crack open a few gallons of his favorite vice—Hennessy cognac.

It also meant there were times when he had to, as they say on the streets, take care of business. Stone—a name he adopted because of its flinty sound, as did other old-timers with monikers such as Roc and Bone—could be ferocious and merciless. One gang authority described him as a henchman akin to Luca Brasi, the beefy enforcer in "The Godfather."

Yet, as in the early days of the Mob, there were also rules to be followed. You didn't shoot little children or somebody's mother, let alone fire on a cemetery, hospital or church. A dispute might still turn murderous, but it was understood that the beef was only with that rival, not his entire gang.

"Stone was an O.G. with love for the 'hood, but he wasn't down for that stupid gang-banging, that senseless killing stuff," said one Rollin' 60s member, who asked that his name not be used. "Now, I ain't gonna say that he never did no shooting. . . . But it wasn't like these kids now, who shoot nine or 10 times, then open their eyes to see what they hit."

When he was coming of age, it was easier to live by such rules, in part, because not everyone had a gun. If they did, it was most likely to be a .22, not some imported military-style rifle that could fire 16 rounds without reloading. Drive-bys were also kept in check because few could afford a car.

But Stone, who was convicted in 1981 of burglary and being an accessory to a robbery, also subscribed to a different ethic. Gang was synonymous with neighborhood, and you protected the neighborhood by not turning every dispute into a war. Stone would even party with rivals, walking from 60th Street down to Century Boulevard—now unthinkable—in search of a beer bash, dancing or female companionship.

"The whole nature of the beast has been transformed over the last 15 years," said Jim Galipeau, a deputy probation officer who knew Stone. "There was a time when there was heart, when guys fought from the shoulders, when there was camaraderie and devotion. All there is now is screw your buddy."

That change—"a reflection of the breakdown of society in general," as Galipeau sees it—began in the avaricious 1980s, as scandals were brewing on Wall Street, in the savings and loan industry, among overcharging defense contractors and swindling televangelists.

California replaced Florida as the chief port for the Colombian cocaine cartels. Weapons were circulating widely. Easy money was close behind. The most aggressive and ambitious members of the Rollin' 60s, lacking other economic opportunities, responded to the message of the day and did whatever necessary to survive.

"These kids read the newspapers and watch the news and see what's going on in the world," said Ed Turley, a manager for Community Youth Gang Services. "The persons who are the shot-callers are very charismatic and could have been corporate raiders. The ones with entrepreneurial abilities, who maybe because of lack of resources or a positive family structure didn't get to college, took to selling drugs."

Stone, who bore no tattoos and had abandoned the saggy pants and blue rags in favor of close-cropped hair and a short goatee, was not going to turn his back on the action, despite being grounded in the old ways of the gang.

He organized drug-selling "crews" that branched out to other states, colleagues said, bought speedboats, all-terrain vehicles and a classic 1963 Chevy with hydraulic lifts and vanity plates, STONE63. When he supplied his people with guns, according to one associate, he cautioned them "not to hurt anybody that don't gotta be hurt."

He bought a gated home at the base of Windsor Hills, with a gym in the den and big-screen TV for watching Raiders games and his favorite movie, "Scarface." On weekends, drug profits fueled high-stakes games of dice and dominoes. Entertainment was supplied by Stone's coterie of exotic dancers—

four scantily clad women who appear in provocative poses on business cards bearing his home phone and pager numbers.

"Stone didn't change with the times—the times changed him," said a member of the gang. "When the dope hit the scene, some could grab it, sell it and rise up to fame. He was one of the lucky ones, the blessed ones—and it brought him up, in a sense of speaking."

Yet Stone, a father of three, did not approve of his friends using cocaine, associates said, and he did not deal in his own community.

He generously shared his wealth, buying remote-control model airplanes for poor youths and opening his home to anybody who needed a safe place to chill when the streets got too hot. One teen-ager from the neighborhood whose older brother was arrested said Stone took him under his wing and kept him out of trouble.

"For that, I'm forever grateful," the youth said.

Last April, on the night of the touted boxing match between George Foreman and Evander Holyfield, Stone invited a group of friends, including some from rival gangs, to celebrate at his place. Although there might have been a time when some of the guests would have bristled at the thought, the mood was jovial, the cognac flowed freely and the bikini dancers paraded for tips between rounds.

"Stone was a kid in transition," said Jim Brown, the former pro football star, who had recently made Stone a leader in Amer-I-Can Inc., his self-esteem course for gang members. "He tried to bring peace and reach out to other gangs without losing respect in his own neighborhood. . . . But there is not some magic dust that you just sprinkle on a gang member and get him to go to church."

That all this madness would one day claim Stone probably could have been predicted. But the shock wave that rippled through the Rollin' 60s after his death was as much a function of the way he was killed as the level of respect he commanded.

Stone, the theory goes, must have trusted his killer for that person to have gotten so close. He weighed 210 pounds, looked like he could bench-press 400 and would not go down without a fight.

When he was stopped by police on Christmas Day, 1990, for driving his 1988 Bonneville with a broken taillight, officers found a stolen .38-caliber Smith & Wesson under the front seat. "That's my gun," Stone confessed, according to a police report. "I need it for protection."

In the old days, there were many things you would die for—neighborhood, family, pride—but a bag of dope was not one of them. Back then, no one would have even been able to get close enough to betray Stone. His homeboys would have been watching.

"If he had been with some trustworthy brothers, Stone wouldn't be dead," a member of the 60s said. "If the homeboys weren't fighting each other and tripping all the time, I wouldn't have to be grieving."

At Stone's funeral, the Marvin Gaye song "What's Goin' On?" was playing in the chapel. Many of the mourners mouthed the words, shaking their heads.

A young man who called himself Bronco choked back sobs to recite a poem:

Hey, brother, where you going?
Hey, brother, where you been?
Can we reach the mountaintop?
And stop following that same old trend?

As they filed past Stone's body, a young woman turned to her friend. "The homies keep leaving us," she said. "I'm getting so sick of this."

But by the same evening, many of the toughest youths were already back on the streets, sucking down 40-ounce bottles of malt liquor, building up each other's courage. Even with the tears barely dried in their eyes, the talk was of revenge. ✦

Section IV

Programs and Policies

Introduction

How have gangs been responded to in the past? How should we respond to them in the future? The saddest message of all is simply this: little that has been done can be demonstrated to have been useful. Thus, the clues for the future have less to do with what might work, than with avoiding in the future what has not worked. For this final section of the volume, we have selected articles roughly falling into three categories: social intervention programs, law enforcement programs, and policy implications.

By social intervention programs, we mean those aimed either at changing the life situations of gang members, or at changing aspects of the community that foster or reinforce their gang status. At the individual level, this can involve social or psychological counseling, help with school or job situations, dealing with family problems or disputes, providing adult role models, or other direct attempts to help the individual. At the community level, intervention targets tend to be the social institutions that impinge on youths' lives. Parks and recreational facilities closed to gang members can be opened up; schools quick to expel can be helped to tolerate gang members and provide supervision of them; job openings can be sought and connections made; police and gang members can be brought together for conversations and shared activities; welfare aid can be sought or facilitated for needy gang families, and so on. Community agencies and residents can be organized to support anti-gang programs and to provide activities for would-be gang members. In such programs, gang members tend to be thought of more as "clients" than as offenders.

By way of contrast, law enforcement programs generally eschew interest in the social situations of gang members but see these persons as law violators and disruptors of community order. Any gang offender, of course, is subject to the usual laws and procedures of the justice system—no need to pay special attention to them. But gangs tend to bring out more concentrated law enforcement efforts, or special "suppression" programs as they have come to be known. One hears of special police gang units, harassment or selective enforcement, wholesale police sweeps of gang areas, special gang prosecution programs, and the like. Sometimes probation and parole departments develop special gang caseloads to increase surveillance on gang members and more easily return them to incarceration.

A related category of approaches could not be included in the book but is becoming of increasing importance, namely the development of special anti-gang legislation. The article referenced below by Alexander Molina describes the most typical of these approaches, Street Terrorism Enforcement and Prevention (STEP) acts, originated in California and now widely copied elsewhere. STEP acts make membership in gangs (legislatively defined as criminal gangs) a special status, subject to special enforcement procedures and increased sentences upon conviction. Some sense of this can be obtained by the included article by Kent and Smith in Section IV (Law Enforcement). Other articles referenced below by Patrick Jackson and Cary Rudman and by the Institute for Law and Justice provide reviews of the extensive anti-gang legislation now sweeping the nation. States are not simply tinkering with existing laws; they are creating a whole set of *new* laws, expanding the legal consequences of gang membership and gang behavior.

These new approaches are not only interesting as policy formulations, but they are symptomatic of the 180-degree shift in gang intervention that has occurred over the years. Their intent is almost exclusively to crack down on gangs, to suppress gang crime and deter gang membership. Little attention is paid to the prevention or amelioration of gang-producing conditions, or treatment services for young gang members, or attempts to rehabilitate older members. For instance, laws to prohibit gang member use of public parks do nothing to suggest alternative activities, leaving gang members to hang out on the street corners even more. The concern with job training and employment, educational support, family counseling, recreation, and other alternative activities, or street worker connections with gang members—the essence of 1950s and 1960s interventions—are not the concern of this new legislative thrust. Nor is the earlier belief in the value of community organization to be found.

As the prevention versus enforcement confrontation becomes more intense and uncompromising, policy issues become more clear because communities must make policy choices. Some have begun to use a public health metaphor, even defining gang violence as a public health issue: if violence is epidemic, it can be treated much as a spreading disease; "primary" (prevention), "secondary" (intervention), and "tertiary" (rehabilitation) approaches to spreading disease are applied to spreading violence.

But this is not a metaphor that provides an obvious place for law enforcement or prosecution or corrections as these ordinarily define themselves. Therefore, they develop "equal and opposite" policy options—special gang suppression efforts and stiffer laws. The articles in Section IV (Policy Issues) have been selected to highlight these opposing options and the political and philosophical stances that underlie them. The intransigence of the viewpoints is worth noting.

The three categories of articles in the following pages offer the reader wide exposure to the social versus law enforcement approaches to gang problems. The contrasts come close to constituting conflicting philosophical and political stands, in which the stance—or ideology—is more important than the actual interventions. Most often missing, therefore, are empirical evaluations of interventions, because the issues are so often unrelated to the advantages of one approach over another to gangs or their communities. Program success comes to mean not program effect, but program implementation or credit for doing something. For example, in Philadelphia in the mid-1970s, a social intervention program with surveillance overtones claimed *success*, based on reductions in gang homicides, even before the program got started. In Chicago and Los Angeles in the 1960s, social intervention programs claimed success on the basis of the *level of effort* they put out, only to learn later that they had failed to reduce, or had actually increased, the rates of gang crime. And in Los Angeles in the 1980s, the Philadelphia fiasco was repeated while in the 1990s police claims of success were made in the face of the most dramatic increase in gang homicides in modern history. The case for careful, independent program evaluation cannot be better made than by reference to the claims of such past programs.

The list of recommended articles below is for students particularly interested in developing ideas about assessing the impact of gang intervention efforts. The enforcement articles by L. Bloom, D. D. Saccente, and Marjorie Zatz set forth contrasting descriptions very effectively. The careful evaluations by Walter Miller and Malcolm Klein illustrate the value of social intervention assessment, while those of the Tarrant County Task Force, Charles Cooper, Marylyn Bibb, Pamela Robinson-Young, Hans Mattick and Gerald Caplan, and Ethel G. Ackley and Beverly R. Fliegel provide a cafeteria of available social intervention approaches. Finally, useful and highly readable policy approach statements are included by the Los Angeles District Attorney's Office, C. Ronald Huff, and J. B. Sibley. In a period of heavy debate over gang issues, nothing could please the editors of this volume more than to have its readers delve further into the complex issues of gang intervention and control policy. Current policymakers need all the help they can get and are truly crying out for it.

There is still one other way that we can consider our gang problems, and that is by comparing them with the situation in other countries. Given all that is being presented here about gangs in America, how unique are we? Is the gang a strictly American phenomenon, or are other nations facing the same problems? Various surveys have revealed gangs of one form or another, and one time or another, in over fifty nations. Europe, Africa, Russia, Southeast Asia, China and Japan, South and Central America—all have yielded descriptions of gangs, although few have yielded descriptions of gang intervention programs. A review of studies and reports elsewhere leads to several conclusions:

- Gangs do indeed exist in other nations, but are nowhere near as widespread.
- Most gangs elsewhere do not resemble typical American gangs. More unique forms can be found in Japan, the Philippines, England, Sweden, Germany, Brazil, and quite a few other locations.
- American-style street gangs can be found in Berlin, in several Russian cities of the Volga region, in Canada, Brussels, Port Moresby (Papua-New Guinea), and most recently have been reported in The Hague, Holland. These cases are exceptional, rather than the rule. Readers interested in these instances can refer to Malcolm Klein's *The American Street Gang*, Chapter 8, and other readings listed below. What is important here is to gain an understanding that our United States gangs, taken as a whole, do indeed mark our nation as a unique gang-involved nation. We have therefore to understand ourselves, as a nation, in order to understand our gangs.

Additional Readings

Intervention, Enforcement, and Policy

Ackley, Ethel G., & Fliegel, Beverly R., A social work approach to street-corner girls. *Social Work*, 1960, 5(4):27-36.

Amandes, Richard, Hire a gang leader: A delinquency prevention program that works. *Juvenile and Family Court Journal*, 1979, 30:27-40.

Bibb, Marylyn, Gang-related Services of Mobilization for Youth. In M.W. Klein (ed.), *Juvenile Gangs in Context: Theory, Research, and Action*. Englewood Cliffs, NJ: Prentice-Hall, 1967.

Bloom, L., Community policing nips gang problem in the bud. *Law and Order*, September 1992, 40(9):67-70.

Cooper, Charles N., The Chicago YMCA detached workers: Current status of an action program. In M.W. Klein (ed.), *Juvenile Gangs in Context: Theory, Research, and Action*. Englewood Cliffs, NJ: Prentice-Hall, 1967.

Huff, C. Ronald, Youth gangs and public policy. *Crime and Delinquency* 1989, 35:524-37.

Institute for Law and Justice (Alexandria, VA), Gang Prosecution Prosecutor Survey, June 1993.

Jackson, Patrick, & Rudman, Cary, Moral panic and the response to gangs in California. In Scott Cummings and Daniel J. Monti (eds.), *Gangs: The Origin and Impact of Contemporary Youth Gangs in the United States*. Albany: State University of New York Press, 1993.

Klein, M., Gang cohesiveness, delinquency, and a street-work program. *Journal of Research in Crime and Delinquency*, July 1969, pp. 135-66.

Mattick, Hans & Caplan, Gerald, The Chicago Youth Development Project, A Descriptive Account of Its Action Program and Research Designs. Ann Arbor: University of Michigan, February 1964.

Miller, Walter B., The impact of a 'total community' delinquency control project, *Social Problems*, Fall 1962, 10:168-91.

Molina, Alexander A., California's anti-gang Street Terrorism Enforcement and Prevention act: One step forward, two steps back? *Southwestern University Law Review*, 1993, 22(2):457.

Reiner, Ira, Gangs, Crimes and Violence in Los Angeles, Office of the District Attorney, County of Los Angeles, May 1992.

Robinson-Young, Pamela, Recreation's role in gang intervention. *Parks and Recreation*, 1992, 27(3):54-6.

Saccente, D. D., Gang intervention efforts: RAP to street gang activity. *Police Chief*, 1993, 60(2):28-31.

Sibley, J. B., Gang violence: Response of the criminal justice system to the growing threat. *Criminal Justice Journal.*, Spring 1989, 11(2):403-22.

Tarrant County (Dallas/Ft. Worth), Gangs in Tarrant County: Strategies for a Grass Roots Holistic Approach to Gang-Related Crime, October 1991.

Zatz, Marjorie S., Chicano youth gangs and crime: The creation of a moral panic. *Contemporary Classics II*, 1987, 2:129-58.

Gangs in Other Countries

Clinard, Marshall B., & Abbott, Daniel J., *Crime in Developing Countries: A Comparative Perspective*. New York, John Wiley and Sons, 1973.

Covey, Herbert C., Menard, Scott, & Franzese, Robert J., *Juvenile Gangs*. Chicago: Charles C. Thomas, 1992.

Rosen, Roger, & Petra McSharry (eds.), *Street Gangs: Gaining Turf, Losing Ground*. New York, Rosen Publishing Group, 1991.

Klein, Malcolm W., *The American Street Gang: Its Nature, Prevalence, and Control*. New York: Oxford University Press, 1995.

Spergel, Irving A., *Youth Gangs: Problems and Response*. New York: Oxford University Press, 1994. ✦

Social Intervention

29

The National Youth Gang Survey: A Research and Development Process[1]

Irving A. Spergel and G. David Curry

Given the increase in gangs across the United States, there is vast concern about the appropriate means of responding to gangs and gang members. Based on the National Youth Gang Survey, which was administered to agencies in cities with admitted gang problems, Spergel and Curry provide in this essay a thorough assessment of the types of intervention strategies implemented in gang cities in the United States.

The most significant finding to emerge from the National Youth Gang Survey is that agencies consistently fail to base their policy approaches on logically developed strategies grounded in an assessment of the causes of gang affiliation. Instead, actions tend to be measures taken with little thought given to the sources of gangs in their communities. Spergel and Curry's essay highlights the need for more careful evaluation in developing strategies for dealing with gangs. On a positive note, they report that community mobilization is a strategy consistently perceived as effective in dealing with the youth gang problem in the cities they investigated.

There is evidence of an increase of gangs, violent gang activity, and gang-member-related drug trafficking in a growing number of large and small cities, suburban areas, and even some small towns and rural areas. There are claims that the number and proportion of females in gangs and the severity of their crimes may be increasing. The literature on gangs has recently proliferated, mainly through the publication of many participant observation studies (Spergel, 1991). Quantitative analyses and surveys of the gang problem are also increasing, although at a slower pace to date. Federal and state agencies are funding an assortment of gang prevention, intervention, and suppression programs. However, there appears to be limited coordination or integration of various research studies, policies, and intervention programs bearing on the complex problem of youth gangs. One preliminary integrative research and development effort has been the National Youth Gang Suppression and Intervention Program, of which an important component was the National Youth Gang Survey.

Excerpted from *The Gang Intervention Handbook* (pp. 359-92), edited by A. P. Goldstein and C. R. Huff, 1993, Champaign, IL: Research Press.

Background

In 1987, the University of Chicago's School of Social Service Administration entered into a cooperative agreement with the United States Department of Justice's Office of Juvenile Justice and Delinquency Prevention (OJJDP) to establish the National Youth Gang Suppression and Intervention Program. The research and development program's primary goals, addressed in corresponding stages, were (a) to identify and assess promising approaches and strategies for dealing with the youth gang problem, (b) to develop prototypes or models from the information thereby gained, and (c) to produce technical assistance manuals for those who would implement the models.

During the first 2 years of the 4-year project, a survey gathered information on organized programs in the continental United States. Data were collected from 254 criminal justice and community-based agencies and grass-roots organizations in 45 cities and at six special program sites. The survey was intended to encompass every agency in the country that was currently or recently engaged in organized responses specifically intended to deal with gang crime problems. Categories of data collected concerned the nature and scope of the problem; its onset and development; the basis on which the problem was defined; the kind of goals, strategies, program structures, and activities developed; and the results of such interventions.

This chapter will deal primarily with the methodology and selected findings of the survey, which was an integral part of our program's assessment stage. It will conclude with a discussion of other aspects of the program, including an annotated bibliography of publications that resulted from program activities at various stages.[2] Specifically, these stages included the following: assessment (Stage 1); prototype development (Stage 2); and development of technical assistance manuals of the National Youth Gang Suppression and Intervention Program, with collaboration in the research and development process by policymakers, administrators, and practitioners, as well as current or former gang members (Stage 3).

In the present volume on intervention, our chapter has a dual role. On one hand, the National Youth Gang Survey is an intensive, nationwide study of the range of existing interventions. On the other, the survey and, even more, related and subsequent components of the larger research and development program exemplify research itself as intervention.

Study Sites and Agencies Surveyed

Survey sites were selected in a process that began with the screening of 101 cities. Selection criteria included (a) presence and recognition of a youth gang problem and (b) presence of a youth gang program as an organized response to the problem. In itself, the division of the cities according to 1987 data on gang problems and organized responses serves as a baseline for future national surveys of the distribution of such problems and responses. Table 1 lists all cities screened, showing those that were included and those excluded.

Table 1

Sites Screened for the National Youth Gang Survey

INCLUDED IN THE SURVEY		
Chronic gang problem cities (n = 21)		
Albuquerque, NM	Long Beach, CA	Phoenix, AZ
Chicago, IL	Los Angeles, CA	San Diego, CA
Chino, CA	Los Angeles County, CA	San Francisco, CA
Detroit, MI	New York, NY	San Jose, CA
East Los Angeles, CA	Oakland, CA	Santa Ana, CA
El Monte, CA	Pomona, CA	Stockton, CA
Inglewood, CA	Philadelphia, PA	Tucson, AZ
Emerging gang problem cities (n = 24)		
Atlanta, GA	Hialeah, FL	Reno, NV
Benton Harbor, MI	Indianapolis, IN	Rockford, IL
Cicero, IL	Jackson, MS	Sacramento, CA
Columbus, OH	Louisville, KY	Salt Lake City, UT
Evanston, IL	Madison, WI	Seattle, WA
Flint, MI	Miami, FL	Shreveport, LA
Fort Wayne, IN	Milwaukee, WI	Sterling, IL
Fort Worth, TX	Minneapolis, MN	Tallahassee, FL
EXCLUDED FROM THE SURVEY		
No declared organized youth gangs or gang activity (n = 24)		
Albany, NY	Des Moines, IA	New Orleans, LA
Baltimore, MD	Fresno, CA	Pasadena, CA
Buffalo, NY	Greenville, MS	Pittsburgh, PA
Cambridge, MA	Houston, TX	Portsmouth, ME
Charleston, SC	Jersey City, NJ	Racine, WI
Charlotte, NC	Kansas City, KS	San Antonio, TX
Chattanooga, TN	Lincoln, NE	Tulsa, OK
Denver, CO	Memphis, TN	Washington, DC
No organized response (n = 29)		
Anaheim, CA	Gary, IN	Omaha, NE
Berkeley, CA	Glendale, CA	Orlando, FL
Boston, MA	Hartford, CT	St. Petersburg, FL
Cincinnati, OH	Huntington Beach, CA	St. Louis, MO
Cleveland, OH	Jacksonville, FL	Spartanburg, SC
Compton, CA	Joliet, IL	San Bernardino, CA
East St. Louis, IL	Kansas City, MO	San Pedro, CA
El Paso, TX	Kenosha, WI	Springfield, MA
Fort Lauderdale, FL	Lakewood, CA	Wilmington, DE
Garden City, CA	Las Vegas, NV	
Excluded because outside U.S. mainland (n = 4)		
Honolulu, HI	Tonga	
San Juan, PR	Samoa	

In each city, a key agency, usually the police, was contacted initially by phone, and direct contact with an informed representative of the agency was established. The representative was asked two kinds of questions: The first was designed to ascertain the existence of a youth gang crime problem, and the second was intended to establish the existence of an organized agency or community response. A youth gang crime problem was simply one perceived or identified as such and eliciting a special agency and community reaction. An organized response was regarded as a program in existence for at least a year, having a current or recent set of articulated program goals, demonstrating a response to the problem that was more than simplistic and unitary (e.g., either police arrests alone or a youth gang recreation program alone), and possessing some means to describe the program's impact. Several cities were excluded from the analysis because information gathered indicated that, in 1987, the agency or city administration did not recognize the existence of a gang problem. Many of the excluded agencies and cities have since recognized the problem, or ceased to deny it. In fact, some of these cities have developed large-scale, sophisticated approaches to the problem. At this point in the survey, we had a population of 98 cities or localities. Of these, 74, or slightly more than three-quarters, reported the presence of organized youth gangs or gang activities. Of those cities or jurisdictions reporting a gang problem, 29, or 39.2%, had no organized response to the problem as just defined. This left 45 cities meeting the two selection criteria.

To explore all promising programs that we could possibly identify, we also considered a number of programs that were not part of a community-level response. Six of these single-program sites, listed in Table 2, were eventually included in the survey. The California Department of the Youth Authority is a state correctional agency that maintains contact with officials in several California cities or counties and offers a number of unique programs for gang-identified youths. The Sunrise House is a social service agency with a tradition of meeting the needs of gang youths. The Paramount public school system has a gang program that has received national recognition. The other three sites mentioned in Table 2 are correctional agencies with special programs designed for incarcerated gang youths.

Our survey analyses are based on the 45 cities (one a county area) and the six sites identified through the initial screening. Clearly, this is not a systematic sample from a known population of eligible cities or agencies. Rather, it is a fairly large group of cities and agencies generally recognized to have youth gang problems and organized programs to address them. Relatively complete individual agency and cross-agency and community group level data were carefully collected.

Our survey concerned the gang problem, and organized responses to it, in two types of cities: chronic gang problem cities, which often had a long history of serious gang problems, and emerging gang problem cities, often smaller cities that had recognized and begun to deal with a usually less serious but often acute gang problem since 1980. In chronic problem cities or contexts, gangs tended to be better organized and involved in more serious crime and drug trafficking activity. Of the 45 localities, 21 were classified as chronic and 24 as emerging youth gang problem cities (see Table 1). A somewhat greater proportion of the chronic problem cities had large or very large populations, but the category included a sizable number of small cities as well. Most of the cities in the emerging problem category were smaller, although some had populations of over 500,000. We also classified the correctional schools and special agency programs or sites under these two rubrics (see Table 2).

This distinction between chronic and emerging sites was a valuable component of the analyses reported here and has since been refined and elaborated. Although our classification is mainly a temporal one, referring to the onset of the problem, we have observed that in some cities the gang crime problem was serious or violent at emergence and that in some chronic problem cities the problem subsided and re-emerged later. Furthermore, the nature of the agency's or city's response to the gang crime problem helps determine whether it is in the emerging or chronic category.

Table 2

Sites Included in the National Youth Gang Survey

Chronic gang problem sites ($n = 2$)	Emerging gang problem sites ($n = 4$)
California Department of the Youth Authority	Ethan Allen School (WI)
Sunrise House (CA)	Glen Mills School (PA)
	McClaren School (OR)
	Paramount School (CA)

Study Procedures and Results

Once a city or jurisdiction was selected for inclusion in the survey, a snowball sampling technique was employed. The initial informed respondent was asked for a list of other key agencies involved in the community's organized gang response. An informed respondent at each of these agencies was then contacted and also asked for such a list; the interviewer for that city continued to contact respondents until all respondents' lists were exhausted. The response rate was 70.5%. Lack of response most commonly was associated with a respondent's determining, upon reflection, that his or her agency did not fall within the aims of our study.

We classified the 254 respondents into three major categories, with six criminal justice subcategories (see Table 3): law enforcement, mainly police (20.5%), prosecutors (10.2%); judges (5.5%); probation (12.6%): corrections (3.1%); parole (4.3%); school (13.3%), subdivided into academic and security personnel; community/service agencies (24.4%), subdivided into youth service, youth and family service/treatment, grass-roots groups, and comprehensive crisis intervention; community, county, or state planners (4.7%); and others (0.8%).

From these results, we know that the gang problem is addressed with some degree of complexity by a great variety of organizations located in small as well as large cities and jurisdictions in a number of states in the Union. We also know from federal agency reports (e.g., Drug Enforcement Administration, 1988; current research sponsored by the National Institute of Justice, 1991; and work of other federal and local agencies, including the Department of Health and Human Services) that the problem is widespread throughout almost all the states. Although the gang crime problem is national in scope, the development of organized community response programs probably lags behind the spreading problem.

Table 3

Respondent Categories

	CATEGORY		SUBCATEGORY	
	n	%[a]	n	%[a]
Law enforcement	52	20.5		
Prosecutors	26	10.2		
Judges	14	5.5		
Probation	32	12.6		
Corrections	8	3.1		
Parole	11	4.3		
School	35	13.8		
Academic			26	74.3
Security			9	25.7
Community/service	62	24.4		
Youth service agency			46	74.2
Youth and Family Service			8	12.9
Grass-roots			5	8.1
Comprehensive			3	4.8
Community planning	12	4.7		
Other	2	0.8		
	254	100.0		

a % = percent of all respondents.

Programmatic Strategies

Each agency or community organization responds to a problem such as gang crime in terms of its mission, goals, and objectives. Often abstract or highly generalized terms justify and sustain the programs and activities that these entities—public, private, nonprofit, and sectarian—carry out. Most respondents in our study represented organizations established to deal with issues and problems broader than gangs and gang crime and to conduct a corresponding range of activities. We, however, attempted to develop measures of the goals and objectives, key programs, or activities underlying the organizations' efforts to deal specifically with the gang problem. We have termed these measures strategies of intervention. Conceptually, they are situated between broad mission or goal statements and specific or discrete program activities.

Social problems wax and wane, but most organizations seek to sustain their missions and strategies as long as possible. Sooner or later, an organization must clarify the relationship between gang problem and strategy of intervention, for the sake of logic or common sense as well as public relations—and very often to justify requests for additional funding for gang problem initiatives. There is some evidence that a human service or social intervention strategy in respect to the youth gang problem, predominant in the 1950s and 1960s, gave way to a law enforcement or suppression strategy in the 1970s and 1980s. This occurred for a variety of reasons not yet fully researched (see Spergel, 1992).

To understand the current dynamics and structure of organizations' responses to gangs, we tried to describe and analyze their strategies and to discover how strategies were interrelated across types of organizations in a particular locality and how they might vary across localities. Our survey respondents answered five open-ended questionnaire items intended to elicit information on program activities, priority of strategies employed, and estimates of effectiveness of agency efforts. These items were as follows:

Item IV-1. What are your unit's or organization's goals and objectives in regard to the gang problem?

Item VI-2. What has your department (or unit) done that you feel has been particularly successful in dealing with gangs? Please provide statistics, if relevant and available.

Item VI-3. What has your department (or unit) done that you feel has been least effective in dealing with gangs?

Item VI-6. What do you think are the five best ways employed by your department or organization for dealing with the gang problem? (Rank in order of priority.)

Item IV-14. What activities do gang or special personnel perform in dealing with the problem? [Probe by telephone interviewers later to determine how these are tied to the problem as described and goals/objectives.]

We used the answers to these items to construct an empirically based and theoretically sensitive set of five underlying strategies. Our analysis relied most heavily on the responses to Item VI-6. The strategies to emerge were community organization or community mobilization, social intervention, opportunities provision, suppression, and organizational change and development (see Table 4). The strategies are defined and their indicators—that is, the statements or phrases of the respondents—are classified as follows.

Community Organization

Spergel's (1991) literature review . . . names community organization, or neighborhood mobilization, as one of four major strategies employed historically in efforts to deal with the gang problem: "Community organization is the term used to describe efforts to bring about adjustment, development, or change among groups and organizations in regard to community problems or social needs" (p. 3). Earlier, Spergel (1969) used the term interorganizing, a key dimension of community organization or community organizing, to refer to "efforts at enhancing, modification, or change in intergroup or interorganizational relationships to cope with a community problem" (p. 20). Issues of coordination as well as mobilization across neighborhood, organization, and governmental levels are addressed in this formulation.

Table 4

Distribution of Strategy Rankings: Number of Responses (% of Total Responses) for Each Priority Category

	Strategy Rank					
	1	2	3	4	5	Total
Community organization	22 (8.95%)	58 (23.4%)	35 (14.1%)	5 (2.0%)	1 (0.4%)	121 (21.2%)
Social intervention	78 (31.5%)	46 (18.5%)	19 (7.7%)	3 (1.2%)	0	146 (25.5%)
Opportunities provision	12 (4.8%)	38 (15.3%)	15 (6.0%)	4 (1.6%)	0	69 (12.0%)
Suppression	109 (44.0%)	35 (14.1%)	16 (6.5%)	4 (1.6%)	1 (0.4%)	165 (28.8%)
Organizational change and development	27 (10.9%)	21 (8.5%)	18 (7.3%)	5 (2.0%)	0	71 (12.4%)

Respondents used key words and phrases that at times clearly could be included in this community organization category and at other times could not. Decisions for inclusion of items in a category had to be based on some appropriate rationale. For example, the contemporary term networking was classified within the community organization strategy unless it referred to networking among law enforcement agencies, in which case it was classified under suppression. References to prevention, when they implied program or policy efforts across agencies, were coded as community organization. All references to meeting with community leaders and attending meetings of community organizations were regarded as reflecting a community organization strategy. After much consideration, we included advocacy for victims under the strategy of suppression rather than community organization because it can be viewed as part of a more basic strategy of crime control. Following are additional key words indicating goals or activities encompassed by the community organization strategy:

Cleaning up the community
Involving the schools
Mobilizing community
Building community trust
Involving parents (families)
Educating the community
Changing the community

Social Intervention

Spergel's literature review (1991) identifies youth agency outreach and street work as a second major gang program strategy. According to Spergel (1966), street work is

> the practice variously labeled detached work, street club, gang work, area work, extension youth work, corner work . . . the systematic effort of an agency worker, through social work or treatment techniques within the neighborhood context, to help a group of young people who are described as delinquent or partially delinquent to achieve a conventional adaptation. (p. 27)

This strategy involves the redirection or conversion of youth gangs to legitimate social gangs or conventional organizations. This requires the agent to work with or manipulate the people or other agency representatives who interact critically with members of the delinquent group.

The notion of traditional street work may be somewhat outdated and has now become part of a larger strategy of social intervention that focuses on individual behavioral rather than group value change or transformation (Klein, 1971). Therefore, we place street work under the more general category of social intervention, which also encompasses recreational and sports activities. Social intervention also includes counseling or direct attempts—informational or guidance oriented—to change youths' values in such a way as to make gang involvement less likely. Actions to improve general, specialized, remedial, or basic alternative educational programs are included under opportunities provision. Advocacy for individual gang members is classified as a social intervention goal. The following indicators fall in the social intervention category:

Crisis intervention
Service activities
Diversion
Outreach
Provision of role models
Leadership development
Intergang mediation
Group counseling
Temporary shelter
Tattoo removal
Referrals for services
Religious conversion
Counseling of gang members
Drug prevention/treatment
All psychological approaches
All social work approaches
Postsentence social services
Working with gang structure
Helping members leave gang

Opportunities Provision

Spergel (1991) names provision of opportunities in terms of employment, job training, and education as a third major gang strategy. Under this approach are included "large scale resource infusions and efforts to change institutional structures including schools, job opportunities, political participation, and the development of a new relationship between the federal government and local neighborhoods in the solution not only of delinquency but of poverty itself" (p. 7). This strategy encompasses efforts to stimulate the development of new and improved schools, special training and job programs, and business and industry involvement in the social and economic advancement of people, efforts directed toward gang youths in disadvantaged inner-city and rural areas. Following are key words or phrases included under opportunities provision:

Job preparation
Job training
Job placement
Job development
Assistance with school
Tutoring
Education of gang youths

Suppression

As the fourth major gang program strategy, Spergel (1991) identifies suppression—formal and informal social control, which includes arrest, incarceration, and other forms of criminal justice, along with youth agency or community group supervision. Under this approach gang members may be arrested, prosecuted, and removed from the community for short or long prison sentences. Tactical patrols by police gang units, vertical prosecution, intensive supervision and vertical case management by probation departments, legislation targeted at gang members, and interagency task forces involving criminal justice actors are placed in this category. Also included are information systems (i.e., gathering/collecting and maintaining information), as well as information sharing, or the distribution or publishing of information on gangs that facilitates law enforcement. Suppression, however, should be distinguished from law enforcement: Suppression is a broader concept, which therefore includes social agency monitoring or targeting of youths for special forms of supervision with the aim of controlling gang behaviors. The following other key words or phrases are included under suppression:

Enforcement
Neutralization
Investigation
Adjudication
Apprehension
Monitoring
Restraint
Arrest
Discipline
Intelligence
Identification
Legal consequences
Removal from community
Correctional placement
Law enforcement liaison
Supervision
Setting limits

Organizational Change and Development

A fifth category, which has a modified or limited agency structural or program developmental quality, has been added. It includes organizational adaptations and changes that facilitate the application of the other strategies. Especially characteristic is specialization that enables an organization to deal with the gang problem—for example, formation of a special gang unit within a police department. This strategy includes needs assessment and evaluation, along with the following other approaches:

Internal agency coordination
Improvement of organizational efficiency
Program development
Advocacy for legislation
Specialized training
Additional resources
Case management
Use of media

Classification of Strategies

Using written guidelines regarding the five strategies, the two senior members of the research team, working separately, classified the responses of the 254 respondents and interpreted the rankings of the strategies. We agreed independently on approximately 70% of the classifications of the hundreds of separate items. After hours of case-by-case discussion, we reached agreement on all item rankings. Not all respondents provided items for five separate strategies, and some items essentially repeated a particular strategy. If an item repeated a strategy already ranked, it was eliminated. Each item was ranked into one strategy only.

Distribution of Strategies

Table 4 shows the distribution of strategies by rank for all of the respondents. The most common first or primary strategy of agencies in our survey was suppression (44% of agencies), followed by social intervention (31.5%). Organizational change and development (10.9%) and community organization (8.9%) were comparably less common as first or primary strategies. Opportunities provision as a primary strategy was infrequent (4.8%). Over the total listing of strategies in the five categories—primary, secondary, and so on—suppression was still the most often chosen, and opportunities and organizational change and development were the least often chosen. Because the majority of respondents were from criminal justice agencies, this distribution is not surprising. In the aggregate analysis of all the categories of strategies, opportunities provision rose in the number of times mentioned, but it obviously was not a priority strategy.

Type of Strategy Across Communities

In this part of the analysis, we were interested in the community rather than the agency level. We concentrated on each agency's primary strategy. Our locality or site level measure reflects the proportion of agencies in each community using each of our five strategies as the primary strategy. As Table 5 shows, there were significant differences between chronic and emerging gang cities in the use of three of the five gang program strategies—community organization, social intervention, and opportunities provision—as primary.

A multivariate analysis of variance for the differences across community by gang problem type was significant at the 0.05 level. Discriminant analysis to generate a function that separated communities by gang problem type on the basis of these three primary strategies produced a function that could be used successfully to reclassify two-thirds (66.7%) of the communities by problem type. There is, therefore, at least tentative empirical support for the notion that primary strategy choices vary by community or city type.

Table 5

Mean Proportion of Respondents per Site Exhibiting Primary Strategy by City Type

	Chronic gang problem cities (n = 20)	Emerging gang problem cities (n = 22)
Community organization	.65	.160[a]
Social intervention	.283	.142[a]
Opportunities provision	.071	.017[a]
Suppression	.454	.573
Organizational change and development	.107	.085

[a] Student's t test significant at 0.05 level

Perceived Causes of the Gang Problem

Our first attempt to determine whether these strategies were effective in reducing or controlling the youth gang problem took place at the logical-conceptual level. We assumed that strategic intervention in a social problem should be related in some commonsense way to the cause of the problem. Effectiveness in addressing a problem ordinarily signified success in addressing its cause. On the one hand, we assumed that organizational strategies for a problem such as gangs were dependent on organizational mission, political-economic interests, specific disciplinary approaches, and contemporary ideology and fashion. On the other hand, we considered it likely that perceptions of cause of a problem might not be closely related to strategic interventions selected to ameliorate it. Furthermore, determination of the cause of a social problem might not be closely dependent on the organization's mission and political interest. To the extent that the strategy was not related to cause of the problem, it seemed logical to anticipate that the problem would not be addressed adequately and therefore not alleviated.

Thus, from a research and policy development perspective, we thought it important to elicit from the survey respondents some expression of causes of the gang problem and a ranking of such perceived causes. We asked the following question: "What do you think are the five most important causes of the gang problem in your city? (Rank in order of priority.)"

From our 254 respondents, we received 244 open-ended responses to this question. As with strategy determinations, the two senior members of the research team first classified all answers separately. The minimal conflicts in classification arising from these two separate content analyses were resolved through case-by-case discussion. This process yielded 23 categories of perceived cause, which we further grouped into 4 major categories (see Table 6).

The first set of perceived causes of the gang problem involved broad problems at the level of the social system, such as poverty, unemployment, criminal opportunities, increased prevalence and profitability of drug sales, patterns of migration and changes in population composition, and other conditions of urban life. The second set of causes related to the failure of basic institutions, the family and the schools in particular. The third set of causes focused on the individual and peer group, and included substance abuse, psychological explanations (most frequently lack of self-esteem or personal pathology), peer influence, and fear coupled with the desire for self-protection through gang affiliation. Finally, many of our respondents recognized the existence of the gang problem within the context of numerous attempts to resolve it. In other words, there was a perception that community agency responses themselves might be inappropriate or inadequate. Respondents expressed this perception by citing failure of the police, the courts, or other representatives of the legal system; liberalism; failure of community participation; lack of social services and recreational programs for youth; media influence; discrimination and race relations; the labeling phenomenon; lack of resources committed to dealing with the gang problem; politicians' use of the gang problem to fulfill their personal ambitions; denial that a gang problem exists; and exploitation of the legal system by adults using youths to perform criminal acts.

Analysis of the ranking of perceived causes showed that system level causes were deemed most important by 43.4% of our respondents. Another 30.3% blamed major institutions for not meeting the needs of youths. The remainder, a little more than one-fourth of the respondents, attributed their gang problems to individual or peer-group level cause (12.7%) or response effects (13.5%). Poverty and unemployment, drug trafficking, family breakdown, and school system failure were viewed as the key causes of the gang problem.

Table 6

Perceived Causes of the Gang Problem

	Respondents citing	% of respondents citing
Social system problems		
(Selecting)	222	91.0
(Ranking primary)	106	43.4
Poverty/unemployment	163	66.8
Criminal opportunity	33	13.5
Drug phenomena	101	41.4
Migration/demographics	20	8.2
Urban ecology	12	4.9
Institutional Failure		
(Selecting)	183	75.0
(Ranking primary)	74	30.3
Family breakdown/failure	135	53.1
School failure/dropout	114	46.7
Lack of role models	13	5.3
Individual and peer group level problems		
(Selecting)	125	49.2
(Ranking primary)	31	12.7
Drug/alcohol use	17	6.7
Psychological explanations	84	33.1
Peer/gang influence	55	22.5
Self-protection/fear	29	11.9
Response effects		
(Selecting)	152	62.3
(Ranking primary)	33	13.5
Legal system failure	25	10.2
Liberalism	3	1.2
Community failure	48	19.7
Lack of services/problems	73	28.7
Media	13	5.3
Discrimination/race relations	27	11.1
Labeling	1	0.4
Lack of committed resources	12	4.9
Politics	4	1.6
Denial	11	4.5
Adult exploitation of juvenile justice system	3	1.2
No response = 10		

Relationship Between Perceived Causes and Primary Strategies

Of particular interest for policy development is the degree of relationship between perceived causes and strategies selected to deal with the gang problem. Table 7 shows no observable relationship between perceived primary cause and primary response strategy. Chi-square tests of the distribution of each set of strategies by each perceived cause indicate that none of them is significantly different (at the 0.10 level) from the distribution of strategies for the entire population. Some researchers (Huff, 1989, Moore, 1988) have suggested that quick action, whether a police sweep or an expansion of a social intervention program, tends to follow upon a series of publicized crisis events. A systematic causal analysis did not often precede a course of agency action. There was little evidence of strategies based on logically related causes. Our analysis indicated, even on the basis of post hoc discussion with respondents, that coordination of cause and strategy was probably not occurring.

Measuring Program Effectiveness

In the absence of measures of direct program effectiveness, we examined three measures of perceived program effectiveness: perceived improvement in the gang problem since 1980, perceived agency effectiveness in 1987, and perceived community level effectiveness. Later, we will present and analyze independently gathered data that served as a validity check on perceptual data.

Table 7

Primary Strategy by Primary Perceived Cause: Number (Percent) of Responses per Perceived Cause

Primary Cause	Primary Strategy				
	Community organization	Social intervention	Opportunities provision	Suppression	Organizational change and development
Social system problems	10 (9.5%)	26 (24.8%)	7 (6.7%)	48 (45.7%)	14 (13.3%)
Institution failure	6 (8.3%)	24 (33.3%)	3 (4.2%)	31 (43.1%)	8 (11.1%)
Individual level problems	3 (9.7%)	11 (35.5%)	0 (0.0%)	14 (45.2%)	3 (9.7%)
Response effects	3 (9.1%)	16 (48.5%)	1 (3.0%)	11 (33.3%)	2 (6.1%)

We used the following items to generate the perceptual measures:

Item III-18. Has the gang situation changed since 1980?

Item III-19. If yes, how?

Item V-1. How effective do you think your unit was in 1987 in dealing with the gang problem?

very effective
moderately effective
hardly effective
not at all effective

Item IV-8. Are there any interagency task forces or community-wide organizations that attempted to coordinate efforts to deal with the gang problem in 1987?

Item IV-9. If yes, were these efforts:

very effective
somewhat effective
hardly effective
not at all effective?

Table 8

Normalized (PROBIT) Scores for Three Gang Program Effectiveness Measures

Improvement Since 1980		
	Yes = -1.63	No = 0.24
Evaluation of Program Effectiveness in 1987		
	Agency level	Community level
Very effective	-0.86	-1.02
Moderately effective	0.48	0.30
Hardly efffective	1.52	1.22
Not at all effective	2.37	1.88

We content analyzed the item concerning change since 1980 to produce a dichotomous variable of improvement versus nonimprovement. In transforming these three measures into a single evaluation measure, we chose not to give equal weight to each of these three variables, believing that the variables merited separate weights. We felt that these weights should be derived empirically from the structure of their covariation in this particular set of respondents. At the agency level, one of these variables was dichotomous, and the other two were sets of ordered categories. We chose to normalize these measures at the agency level using PC-PRELIS to generate normalized (PROBIT) scores for each of our categorical variables (see Table 8). A principal components analysis of the normalized (PROBIT) scores for the three measures resulted in the three eigenvalues, none of which approached zero. We used the first and largest of these eigenvalues (accounting for 45.5% of the variance) to generate the set of principal components coefficients to be used as weights for our three normalized measures (see Table 9).

The score generated for improvement since 1980, an agency rating of very effective, and a rating of very effective community level program is -2.18001. By adding 3.18001 to each score, one can easily transform this value so that it is equal to 1.0 and all subsequent values are positive. The result is a set of general effectiveness scores ranging from 1.0 to 5.87. It must be remembered in the analyses that follow that the lower the value of this measure of perceived general effectiveness, the greater the perceived effectiveness.

Table 9

Coefficients for First Principal Component

	Coefficient	% of variance explained
Improvement since 1980	0.411	31.5
Agency effectiveness	0.531	52.5
Community program effectiveness	0.531	52.4

Program Strategies and Perceived Effectiveness

By regressing our measure of perceived general effectiveness on the proportion of agencies within each locality exhibiting each strategy as primary, we were able to compare relationships between perceived effectiveness and primary strategy. (In moving toward a city level of analysis we included the statewide site, the California Department of the Youth Authority, along with the cities.)

Table 10 presents analysis of covariance results for each strategy by type of city (i.e., with chronic vs. emerging gang problem). A negative slope as indicated by the sign of the regression coefficient indicates a positive relationship between the proportion of agencies in each city exhibiting an expressed strategy and the strategy's perceived general effectiveness. Conversely, a positive regression coefficient indicates a negative relationship between the proportion of agencies in each city exhibiting a particular strategy and perceived general effectiveness.

Table 10

Analysis of Covariance Results: General Effectiveness Score by City Type With Primary Strategy as a Covariate

Primary Strategy	Regression Coefficient		Significance of Covariate
	Chronic	Emerging	
Community organization	-2.14	-3.01[a]	0.001
Social intervention	0.34	2.03	0.05
Opportunities	-3.62[b]	-2.70	
Suppression	0.48	0.67	
Organizational change and development	0.89	1.84	

[a] Significant at the 0.05 level
[b] Significant at the 0.01 level

Caution in interpreting these findings is justified by several conditions of the results. If the subsets of the cities were regarded as samples rather than populations, only two of the regression slopes—priority of community organization strategy in emerging problem settings and priority of opportunities provision strategy in chronic problem settings—would differ significantly from zero. Given the structural dependence that is built into the creation of the strategy measures and the assumptions of statistical techniques that decompose variance, the covariance scores inevitably will be negative, but this in fact indicates that a particular primary strategy is positively associated with the perception of general effectiveness.

In the context of these caveats, community organization as a primary strategy appears to be associated with greater perceived general effectiveness in emerging than in chronic problem settings. Social intervention as a primary strategy is differentially associated with lower perceived effectiveness in emerging and in chronic problem settings. Opportunities provision as a primary strategy is associated with greater perceived general effectiveness in chronic problem settings. (From Table 5, we know that opportunities provision is seldom exhibited as a primary strategy in emerging problem settings.)

The final step in our analysis at this point was construction of regression models of perceived general effectiveness. Though we considered a wide range of variables in our extended analyses of these data (Spergel & Curry, 1990), primary program strategy dominated any regression model of perceived general effectiveness regardless of type of problem setting. Table 11 shows the multiple regression models for predicting perceived general effectiveness from the proportion of agencies exhibiting a primary strategy. The findings suggest that different combinations of strategies were associated with a reduction in the youth gang problem in different kinds of cities.

In cities with chronic youth gang problems, agencies and community groups perceived a significant general effectiveness in reduction of the problem, mainly when the primary response strategy was the provision of social opportunities. Community organization or mobilization was also significantly related to perceived general effectiveness in reduction of the problem, but only when social opportunities were provided as well. When we look at the use of these two strategies together, we can explain almost 50% of the variance on the dependent variable. In the emerging youth gang problem cities, only community organization or community mobilization shows up as a significant independent variable, explaining 31% of the variance on the dependent variable, perceived general effectiveness.

Other Factors Contributing to Perceived Effectiveness

In an earlier paper (Curry & Spergel, 1988), we proposed that social disorganization, interacting with poverty variables, could account for much of the variance in the presence of gang problems in inner-city areas. It may be helpful to elaborate what we mean by social disorganization. The origin of what is called social disorganization theory is usually credited to Thomas and Znaniecki (1927) and their studies of the Chicago communities inhabited by Polish immigrants shortly after the turn of the century. The two social researchers whose work is most identified with ecological research, Shaw and McKay (1972), expanded the concept in explaining the distribution of delinquency and gang crime in the urban setting; eventually they came to substitute "differential social organization" for "social disorganization." Sutherland (1947) elaborates:

> The term "social disorganization" is not entirely satisfactory and it seems preferable to substitute for it the term "differential social organization." The postulate on which this theory is based, regardless of the name, is that crime is rooted in the social organization and is an expression of that social organization. A group may be organized for criminal behavior or organized against criminal behavior. Most communities are organized both for criminal and anticriminal behavior and in that sense the crime rate is an expression of the differential group organization. (p. 9)

As we use the concept, social disorganization remains linked to social, economic, and cultural transitions or disruptions such as population movements and changing labor market conditions. Social disorganization or "differential social organization" also signifies a lack of integration across key components of social life. Differences in goals, motivations, norms, values, and activities divide and sometimes create conflict between individual personalities, families, peer groupings, institutions, and segments of communities and the larger society. It should not be surprising that gang involvement is most likely to occur or begin in the interstitial period that is adolescence. Changes that weaken established ties to school, peers, and family can be critical. For example, there are seasonal rises in gang activity each fall as youths begin school, just before and after holiday periods, and during the late spring period of transition to summer vacation.

Table 11

Multiple Regression Models for Perceived General Effectiveness by Type of City or Jurisdiction

Problem setting type	Independent variable	b	Beta	R^2
Chronic gang problem cities	Proportion of agencies per community exhibiting opportunities provision as primary strategy	-4.18[a]	-0.634	0.497
	Proportion of agencies per community exhibiting community organization as primary strategy	-2.91[b]	-0.450	
Emerging gang problem cities	Proportion of agencies per community exhibiting community organization as primary strategy	-3.01[a]	-0.558	0.311

[a] Significant at the 0.01 level.
[b] Significant at the 0.05 level.

We feel that this approach does not make us vulnerable to criticisms of social disorganization such as those of Jankowski (1991), who argues that all social disorganization theories of gang formation assume "a lack of social control" (p. 22). We do not feel that our use of social disorganization requires us to reject Jankowski's hypothesis that

> low-income areas in American cities are, in fact, organized, but they are organized around an intense competition for, and conflict over, the scarce resources that exist in these areas. They comprise an alternative social order. In this Hobbesian world, the gang emerges as one organizational response—but not the only one—seeking to improve the competitive advantage of its members in obtaining an increase in material resources. (p. 22)

Social disorganization, as we define it, may or may not be related to racism, culture conflict (e.g., differences between an immigrant group's culture and that of the dominant community group), social isolation (e.g., environmental separation of a housing project from the neighborhood or the neighborhood from the city), or poverty. In fact, we believe that it is the interaction of at least two of these sets of variables, especially social disorganization and poverty, that creates high risks for different patterns of gang-related crime.

Our regression models, described earlier, showed that the one strategy associated with effectiveness in dealing with the youth gang problem, in both chronic and emerging problem areas, was community mobilization. We also expected other measures of community mobilization or of efforts toward community cohesion to be significantly associated with perceived general effectiveness, to the degree to which these responses reduced social disorganization. Although the possible combinations of variables are plentiful, several other variables in our national survey data that were designed to assess the level of community interorganizational relationship are worth examining for possible guidance in developing productive community responses to the gang problem.

Table 12

Mean General Effectiveness Scores by Categories of City and Primary Strategy Types and Presence of External Advisory Board

Category	n	Mean[a]	Standard Deviation	Significance of Difference[b]
Agencies by type of city				
Chronic	74	3.34	0.91	0.024
Emerging	56	2.94	1.07	
Primary strategy				
Community organization	11	2.54	1.33	0.001
Social intervention	45	3.54	0.90	
Opportunities provision	3	1.94	0.24	
Suppression	55	3.13	0.90	
Organizational change and development	17	2.87	0.77	
External advisory board				
Yes	79	3.02	0.95	0.034
No	53	3.40	1.01	

[a] The lower the mean score, the greater the perception of general effectiveness in dealing with the gang problem.
[b] t test or analysis of variance result.

One such variable is the presence of independent advisory boards or councils for individual organizations or agencies attempting to deal with the problem. Such boards usually comprise representatives of other agencies and community groups. We believe that the existence of such an external board indicates a connection of the agency's program with the community's system of concern and contributes to the integration of community efforts to address the problem. Table 12 shows the average general effectiveness scores for agencies in chronic and emerging gang problem cities. (Lower numeric scores indicate greater positive perception of general effectiveness in dealing with the gang problem.) There is a statistically significant difference between the effectiveness scores of agencies dealing with the gang problem in the two types of cities. Likewise. the significant differences across agencies choosing specific primary strategies that we saw in our regression analyses show up in the one-way analysis of variance results. The difference in average general effectiveness scores between agencies with and without external advisory boards is also statistically significant but does not seem so great.

It is only when we look at specific combinations of city type, primary strategy, and presence or absence of an external advisory board (see Table 13) that we see the most extreme differences in mean general effectiveness score. Presence of an external advisory board is associated with high levels of perceived effectiveness for respondents in chronic gang problem cities with opportunities provision as primary strategy and for respondents in emerging gang problem cities with community organization as primary strategy. In other words, the perceived effectiveness of select primary strategies can be enhanced significantly by the presence of external advisory boards that inevitably involve multiple interagency contacts and thereby extend community mobilization.

Table 13

Mean General Effectiveness Scores by Presence of External Advisory Board Across City Type and Primary Strategy: Comparing Two Types of Cities and Three Types of Primary Strategies

Presence of external advisory board	n	Mean[a]	Standard deviation	Significance of difference
Emerging gang problem city, social intervention as primary strategy, no external board.	4	3.86	0.83	0.0006[b]
Chronic gang problem city, community organization as primary strategy, no external board.	12	3.84	0.87	
Emerging gang problem city, community organization as primary strategy, external board.	6	1.88	1.01	
Chronic gang problem city, opportunities provision as primary strategy, external board.	2	1.80	0	

[a] The lower the mean score, the greater the perception of general effectiveness in dealing with the gang problem.
[b] Analysis of variance result.

Validity Check

To minimize potential criticism that our analysis was based only on perceptual data and to tie it to more concrete evidence of actual reduction in the gang problem, we recontacted law enforcement agencies in a random sample of 21 cities in our survey, 11 drawn from the 15 with the highest general effectiveness scores and 10 from the 15 with lowest general effectiveness scores. We obtained information on changes between 1980 and 1987 in five empirical indicators: numbers of gangs, gang members, gang-related homicides, gang-related assaults, and gang-related narcotic incidents. The data or numerical estimates were reasonably complete for most of the variables except number of gang-related narcotic incidents.

We found that the associations between perception of increased general effectiveness in reduction of the problem and actual or concrete data were perfectly correlated across the five empirical indicators—whether of improvement or deterioration in the gang situation—for 18 of the 21 cities or locations, a correspondence rate of 85.7%. A Fisher's Exact Test revealed that the hypothesis of no correspondence between perceptions and the set of empirical measures could be rejected at the 0.05 level of statistical significance. We thus have evidence that the perceptual data are grounded in the empirical world and that our causal models can now be accepted.

Use of Assessment Procedures to Select Program Strategies

The literature review conducted by the National Youth Gang Intervention and Suppression Program (Spergel, 1991) suggested that the predominant strategy for dealing with the gang problem during the 1950s and 1960s was social intervention, whereas the predominant strategy during the 1970s and 1980s was suppression. The analysis of data from the National Youth Gang Survey produced little evidence documenting the efficacy of either approach as a primary strategy for either chronic or emerging gang problem cities. On the other hand, strategies showing some promise of efficacy are community organization in emerging gang problem cities and opportunities provision in chronic gang problem cities. The survey results, the literature review, the field visit studies, and the various regional conferences of policymakers and practitioners engaged in testing the program's models and manuals all point to the importance of a collective awareness of appropriate and complementary strategies, especially when their implementation involves a division of labor across agencies.

Our analysis implies that both community disorganization and poverty are necessary but not sufficient causes of the gang problem. In other words, both must be present in some variable combination for the gang problem to emerge and develop (Curry & Spergel, 1988). A more direct conclusion of the analysis is that adequate resources and improved interagency or community cohesion are needed, again in some variable and appropriate combination, if the problem is to be reduced. This is especially true in cities where the gang problem has been chronic and is probably most severe. It is likely that a concerted, coordinated community attack on the problem, with federal support and accompanied by provision of educational, training, and job opportunities for gang or high-risk youths, would help alleviate the problem.

Caution is needed, however. Our analysis, while highlighting the promise in certain strategies, did not indicate that suppression of gang violence and gang-member-related drug trafficking is unimportant or that various forms of social intervention are unimportant. We found, rather, that these actions per se are less important and do not contribute to increased effectiveness in dealing with the problem. The strength of our community mobilization variable clearly indicates the need for various community organizations, including law enforcement and youth agencies, to play important interactive and collective roles in both emerging and chronic problem cities. But collective action alone—even assuming that it is genuine—may itself be insufficient, particularly in chronic problem cities, without the infusion of additional resources targeted appropriately to the problem.

A basic consideration may be that the proliferation of the gang problem signifies a progressive weakening of basic institutions of socialization, especially the family but also the schools and other community organizations. Secondary institutions in the community, particularly police, schools, and youth agencies, must assume additional support and control functions that perhaps formerly were fulfilled by families. At the least, these institutions must support families and one another in better carrying out those functions critical to the youth socialization process, especially in low-income areas. The process of community mobilization and resource development must aim not only to strengthen these secondary institutions but, in doing so, to nurture a coherent community in which problematic or at-risk youths can play a constructive and meaningful role. Such involvement can provide an alternative to the criminal youth gang as a source of social status and self-esteem.

Analysis of our survey data revealed no evidence that most agencies or community programs attempted to link selected primary strategies to perceived causes of the gang problem. Yet, the literature review (Spergel, 1991) and the analysis of socialization patterns (Curry & Spergel, 1992) mandate a concern for such linkage. The field visit reports (Spergel & Chance, 1990) further confirm the utility of tailoring organizational solutions to the unique social context in which gang problems emerge. For this reason, the guidelines offered in the technical assistance manuals of the National Youth Gang Suppression and Intervention Program treat assessment as crucial in constructing a locally successful response.

Testing of Intervention Models

One way to perpetuate the development of poorly coordinated, ill-focused gang response programs at the local level is to continue to start from scratch as each emerging gang problem is recognized. One way to avoid hastily contrived, crisis-spawned patchwork responses is to have a nationally coordinated, systematic paradigm for dealing with the gang problem. Although any effective national gang program must take into account the locally unique social, political, and economic factors that define a gang problem, such a program must also limit itself to a set of well-defined models or prototypes with proven potential for success.

Each experimental program that is initiated must be accompanied by technical support that emphasizes effective model implementation and information system construction. Only if these conditions are met can stringent program evaluations be developed. Methodical application and testing of models and prototypes is necessary if we are to move toward a systematic national gang program guided by rational policy decisions based on valid information about the evolving problem.

Notes

1. Prepared under Grant No. 90-JD-CX-K001 from the Office of Juvenile Justice and Delinquency Prevention, Office of Justice Programs, United States Department of Justice. Points of view or opinions in this document are those of the authors and do not necessarily represent the official position or policies of the U.S. Department of Justice.
2. [Editors' note: This bibliography has been omitted in this version of the paper.]

References

Curry, G. D. & Spergel, I. A. (1988). Gang homicide, delinquency and community. *Criminology*, 26, 381-405.

——(1992). Gang involvement and delinquency among Hispanic and African American males. *Journal of Research in Crime and Delinquency*, 29, 273-291.

Drug Enforcement Administration. (1988). *Crack cocaine availability and trafficking in the United States.* Washington, DC: U. S. Department of Justice. Drug Enforcement Administration. Cocaine Investigation Section.

Huff, C. R. (1989). Youth gangs and public policy. *Crime and Delinquency*, 35, 524-537.

Jankowski, M. S. (1991). *Islands in the street*. Berkeley: University of California Press.

Klein, M. W. (1971). *Street gangs and street workers*. Englewood Cliffs, NJ: Prentice Hall.

Moore, J. W. (1988). Introduction: Gangs and the underclass: A comparative perspective. In J. M. Hagedorn, *People and folks: Gangs, crime, and the underclass in a rustbelt city*. Chicago: Lake View.

National Institute of Justice. (1991, November 14). *NIJ FY 1991 gangs projects* (Research on Gangs). Washington, DC: U. S. Department of Justice.

Shaw, C. R., & McKay, H. D. (1972). *Juvenile delinquency in urban areas*. University of Chicago Press.

Spergel, I. A. (1966). *Street gang work: Theory and practice*. Reading, MA: Addison-Wesley.

——(1969). *Problem solving: The delinquency example*. University of Chicago Press.

——(1991). *Youth gangs: Problem and response*. Washington, DC: U. S. Department of Justice, Office of Juvenile Justice and Delinquency Prevention.

——(1992). Youth gangs: An essay review. *Social Service Review*, 66, 121-140.

Spergel, I. A., & Chance, R. L. (1990). *Community and institutional responses to the youth gang problem*. University of Chicago, School of Social Service Administration.

Spergel, I. A., & Curry, G. D. (1990). *Survey of youth gang problems and programs in 45 cities and 6 sites* (National Youth Gang Suppression and Intervention Program). Washington, DC: U. S. Department of Justice, Office of Juvenile Justice and Delinquency Prevention.

Sutherland, E. H. (1947). *Principles of criminology*. New York: Lippincott.

Thomas, W. I., & Znaniecki, F. (1927). *The Polish peasant in Europe and America*. New York: Knopf. ✦

30

Evaluation of the National Youth Gang Drug Prevention Program

Marcia I. Cohen, Katherine Williams, Alan M. Bekelman, and Scott Crosse

The following article provides an evaluation of prevention and reform projects developed to intervene on gang and drug activities among youths. The researchers' assessment of which types of services were most effective in meeting these goals is quite revealing. The projects they analyzed produced positive effects in the reduction of delinquent behavior, the use of illegal drugs and alcohol, and problematic behavior in school. On the other hand, the programs had little effect in keeping most youths from becoming involved in gangs, and had little influence on the gang involvement of youths who were gang members when the projects began. Instead, factors they report as distinguishing gang and nongang youths include such things as whether the youths have friends or family in gangs, have been in trouble in school, use alcohol or drugs, or have negative or positive attitudes about gangs.

Introduction and Program Background

In the late 1980s, a surge in youth gang activity, stimulated by growing drug use and sales and by urban violence, focused national attention on the need for strategies to help local communities respond to the problem of youth gangs. The Omnibus Anti-Drug Abuse Act (P.L. 100-690), passed in 1988, established the Drug Abuse Education and Prevention Program Relating to Youth Gangs (hereafter referred to as the Youth Gang Drug Prevention Program). This legislation specifically identifies the Administration on Children, Youth and Families (ACYF) of the Department of Health and Human Services' (HHS's) Administration for Children and Families as the administering agency, to emphasize the social service focus of the law. The program received its first appropriation of $15 million in FY 1989; during that year, ACYF funded 52 projects aimed at prevention of youth drug use and gangs.

Reprinted from *National Evaluation of The Youth Gang Drug Prevention Program*. Bethesda, MD: Development Services Group, Inc, June 1994. This study was conducted for The Adminstration on Children, Youth, and Families (ACYF), U.S. Department of Health and Human Services, Contract # 105-90-1704.

Scope of the National Evaluation

On May 29, 1990, ACYF issued a Request for Proposal calling for the evaluation of the 52 drug and gang prevention projects that were funded by ACYF's Family and Youth Services Bureau (FYSB) in FY 1989. Both process and outcome components were to be included in this study. The national evaluation was to assess:

- what the prevention projects tried to accomplish;
- how they went about meeting their goals;
- the problems they encountered and the solutions developed;
- what they achieved and what could not be accomplished;
- how they might improve their services; and
- the costs and funding sources of the overall program.

The national evaluation had four basic objectives:

(1) to describe the implementation of the prevention projects,
(2) to assess the influence of the policy environment on the projects,
(3) to describe the activities of the projects and the youths who participated in them, and
(4) to assess the projects' effectiveness.

The evaluation process included site visits to all 16 consortium projects, 5 of the 6 innovative support projects, and 15 of the 30 single-purpose demonstration projects. . . . Extensive interviews were conducted with project staff at each site as well as with representatives from schools, law enforcement, and other youth-serving agencies and with key members of each community. Data collection addressed the extent of the youth gang and drug problem in each community; needs assessment findings; project management, organization, staffing, and training; service delivery; recordkeeping and reporting systems; locally conducted evaluations; fiscal management; and overall project implementation and results. Collaborative efforts and interagency communication and coordination also were carefully examined, particularly at the consortium projects.

An outcome study comparing youth participants and nonparticipants was conducted at consortium sites that provided direct services. This study included in-person interviews with more than 250 participants and 250 nonparticipants to determine which types of services were most effective in preventing or reducing gang and drug activity.[1]

Consortia Projects

Community-based consortia projects were designed to increase community-level efforts to focus attention on current and emerging problems of youth gangs and to develop comprehensive, coordinated approaches to those problems. Broad-based partnerships drawing on the resources and experiences of many different groups were encouraged to prevent and divert youths from joining gangs. These consortia were intended to emphasize early intervention for junior high school youths, ages 11 to 14.

A community-based consortium was defined as a formal partnership of at least three city, county, town, neighborhood, or other local-level organizations and/or individuals with the capacity to generate sustained, collaborative, community-wide commitment to strategies addressing youth gang issues. A consortium could involve voluntary private agencies, law enforcement, local government, recreational agencies, youth organizations, businesses, churches, foundations, medical facilities, and colleges. Consortium projects were originally funded for 24 months; all received an additional 12 months of funding.

Methodology for Assessing Outcomes

The outcome component of the national evaluation of the Youth Gang Drug Prevention (YGDP) Program was designed to assess the effectiveness of the prevention projects in achieving certain key outcomes for youth participants. The outcome component addressed the following basic questions:

- Did some services or groups of services offered by the prevention projects appear to be more effective than others in preventing at-risk youth from participating in gangs that engaged in illicit drug-related activities?
- What participant and project characteristics were associated with positive outcomes for youths?
- Did the length of a youth's participation in project programming make a difference in the project's effectiveness?

Outcome Evaluation Methodology

This study used a quasi-experimental, retrospective pre-post design. The study was designed to enable comparisons of project outcomes for participants and nonparticipants in the 13 consortium projects; thus, data on both groups were collected and analyzed. The primary source of pre-post behavior was a self-report survey of participants and nonparticipants. The "pre" time period for project participants was prior to project participation; for nonparticipants, it was prior to one year before being interviewed. This is referred to as "time period 1." The "post" time period for project participants was since project participation; for nonparticipants, it was since one year before being interviewed. This is referred to as "time period 2." The self-reports are retrospective because youths were interviewed only once and asked to "think back" to the time before they entered the project or to one year ago.

"Participants" were defined as individuals who were 10 to 18 years old at the time of the study and who, within 3 months prior to the study, had actively engaged in project activities for at least 6 months or (for shorter, fixed-length projects) had completed at least 75 percent of a program. "Nonparticipants" were defined as individuals 10 to 18 years old at the time of the study who had never participated in the project, had participated for less than a month, or had completed less than 25 percent of a shorter, fixed-length program.

In-person interviews were conducted with eligible participants and nonparticipants selected from lists that the projects provided. Youths were asked to provide information on their current behavior (e.g., alcohol or other drug use) and on their behavior at a specified point in the past. Both descriptive and comparative analyses of these data were performed.

Sampling

With the assistance of project staff, the evaluation team first identified participants and nonparticipants who met the eligibility criteria and then constructed sampling frames of these youth. The team sought nonparticipants who had little or no exposure to the project, lived in the same geographic area as participants, and shared some of the same background (e.g., demographic) characteristics. Next, participants and nonparticipants were stratified by gender.

Random samples were drawn of participants and nonparticipants. Typically, equal numbers of participants and nonparticipants were selected for each project. As needed, additional samples were drawn for given projects. A sufficient number of participants and nonparticipants was sampled to provide adequate statistical power for comparisons even after allowing for nonresponses. (A statistical power analysis indicated that a sample size of at least 250 for each group of participants and nonparticipants would permit detection of even a fairly small difference between these groups [i.e., less than 25% of the standard error at $p<0.05$ and power = 0.80]).

Data Collection

Data were collected from September 1992 through February 1993. Prior to data collection, separate questionnaires for participants and nonparticipants were developed, and youths were recruited for the study. Many of the items in the two questionnaires were either identical or highly comparable. Each questionnaire consisted of the following five sections: (1) youth and family characteristics; (2) neighborhood characteristics; (3) exposure to and attitudes toward gangs; (4) program participation (for nonparticipants, this section focused on knowledge of the project and reasons for nonparticipation); and (5) past and current behavior related to the key outcomes. The vast majority of questionnaire items were closed-ended. Each draft questionnaire was pretested with fewer than nine respondents, and the drafts were revised based on the pre-tests. After pretesting, the evaluation team developed Spanish-language versions of each questionnaire. The evaluators considered developing questionnaires in languages other than English and Spanish (e.g., Vietnamese), but the small number of youths who would require interviews in other languages made this unnecessary.

Initially, selected youths' parents or guardians were contacted by mail. Letters to these individuals informed them about the study and requested their permission for their sons or daughters to participate in the study. Parents refusing permission were asked to notify the evaluation team of this decision.

Letters to selected youths informed them about the study, encouraged their participation, and indicated that project staff would be contacting them about the location and time of the interviews. Typically, project staff either mailed or hand-delivered the letters. Staff were given sample letters, which some projects revised and/or printed on their stationery (sometimes in several different languages).

Project staff typically scheduled youth for interviews. Interviewers conducted individual in-person interviews with each respondent. A diverse group of interviewers was hired and assigned to the projects to maximize the match of racial/ethnic backgrounds of interviewers and youth respondents.

In nearly all cases, the interviews took place at one of the facilities at which participants received program services. Some nonparticipants were interviewed in other locations, such as schools. Each interviewing location was chosen to offer privacy, security, and freedom from distractions. The interviews typically lasted about 1 hour each.

Successful interviews were conducted with 261 participants and 267 nonparticipants; hence, the sample size targets suggested by the power analysis were met. The overall response rates were 67 percent for participants and 58 percent for nonparticipants. ("Response rate" was defined as the number of completed interviews divided by the number of sampled, eligible potential respondents. Ineligible potential respondents included youths who failed to meet the selection criteria as well as those who had moved out of the geographical area or were otherwise not locatable.) Response rates varied by project, especially for nonparticipants. The major reason for nonresponse was failure to make the interview appointment. Only a few youths refused to be interviewed.

Methodological Strengths

The outcome evaluation used a valid baseline for assessing project effects: a comparison group composed of nonparticipants and new participants. This comparison group was similar to the participant group with respect to several key background characteristics. Comparability was achieved in part by including in the nonparticipant group youths who had recently begun participation; about a third of the nonparticipants (32.7%) were new participants, and these youths were likely to have many of the same characteristics as the participants (including motivation to participate).

The information collected directly from participants and nonparticipants covered a broad array of topics relevant to participation, project effects, and mediating factors. The study collected information on several outcome domains in addition to gang involvement (e.g., use of alcohol and other drugs) and on certain risk factors associated with these domains (e.g., exposure to persons who use alcohol and other drugs). Another strength of the outcome evaluation was the use of certain open-ended questions (e.g., about reasons for leaving gangs), which contributed to a deeper understanding of project effects.

Drawing on self-reports also helped evaluators learn about experiences and events that would have been missed in official records. Events that triggered record entries on delinquent behavior (usually, arrests) accounted for only a small percentage of the illegal activities in which youths engaged. Moreover, because organizations (e.g., schools and juvenile justice agencies) tend to maintain tight control of information on youths, such information would have been unavailable in many cases.

Limitations

The three chief limitations of the outcome study were the potential bias and error of youth self-reports, potential differences between the participant and nonparticipant groups in terms of the length of the followup or "time period 2," and the limited generalizability of results. First, information from youth self-reports, while sometimes highly useful, may have been intentionally distorted; for example, youths may have underreported their involvement in illicit activities or sought to satisfy (their perceptions of) interviewer and program staff expectations by responding in a way that exaggerated project effects. The evaluation team attempted to reduce these potential tendencies by conducting the interviews in person and matching interviewers with respondents' racial/ethnic characteristics so as to maximize rapport; in addition, interviewers stressed the confidentiality of interview data. (Youths often freely reported on their involvement in illicit activities.) Another potentially negative aspect of youth self-reports is that they were subject to recall error, especially for responses that required reporting on behaviors that had occurred in the past (e.g., a year before interviewing). Respondents were encouraged to "anchor" their reports to important events that had occurred at about the same time as the reported behavior or events (such as entrance into middle school).

A second limitation of the study is that the length of "time period 1" and "time period 2" differed for participants and nonparticipants. Although these periods were defined in terms of the beginning of participation in the program for participants, they were defined in terms of a year before data collection for nonparticipants. Hence, the length of the period during which youths were at risk of engaging in any given outcome behavior (e.g., alcohol or other drug use) could have varied by group. For example, a participant whose "time period 2" was only a month long would have been less likely than a nonparticipant to use alcohol or other drugs simply because the participant's "time period 2" was shorter. This is problematic to the extent that youths who were more likely to engage in outcome behaviors were also more likely to have shorter "time 2" (after) periods.

Three aspects of the study limit the degree to which study results can be generalized. First, only consortium projects were evaluated. These projects were the largest and most diverse of all the evaluated projects, and some of their features set them distinctly apart from the other types; hence, conclusions are best limited to the consortium projects and others that closely resemble them. A second issue concerns the timing of the study. Information was collected from youths during the fall and early winter of 1992-1993; during this time, some of the projects were closing their operations. To the extent that project activities and other aspects (e.g., staff attitudes) differed during these seasons or at this stage of the projects' operations, the study results may generalize poorly to other periods of operation.

Finally, respondents may not fully represent eligible participants and nonparticipants for two reasons. First, project staff decided whether specific youths met the selection criteria and contacted selected youths; although the evaluators were unaware of any error or bias in this selection process, the potential for problems (e.g., screening youth in or out of the sampling lists based on their attitude toward the program) did exist. Second, response rates (67% for participants and 58% for nonparticipants) were somewhat lower than expected. To the extent that nonrespondents differ from respondents (e.g., in motivation), the results may be biased. Although an analysis of this issue suggests that the respondents adequately represented the eligible participants and nonparticipants on demographic characteristics, the existence of other differences is unknown—as is their influence (if any) on study results.

It should be noted that although it is not possible to rule out any possible selection into the prevention program based on nondemographic factors, the controlled change analysis allows an examination of the possibility of "creaming," that is, recruiting individuals into a program who seem more amenable to help. Such "creaming" is truly avoidable only by random assignment from a pool of potential participants. It is possible, however, to check to some degree for "creaming" by comparing the incidence of prior anti-social behavior of participants and nonparticipants. If the "easier" young people were systematically involved in the program, then participants should show lower levels of anti-social behavior in "time period 1." The data on prior behavior indicate that assignment to participation in the program did not seem to represent such "creaming." If anything, the data give some limited evidence of "reverse creaming" (i.e., nonparticipants had better "time period 1" behavior). For example, in "time period 1," 51 percent of the participants compared to only 43 percent of the nonparticipants had done one or more of the items used in the specific delinquency scale. Conversely, 49 percent of the participants and 57 percent of the nonparticipants had done none of the items used in the delinquency scale.

Gang Involvement

This section reports on the effects of 13 Youth Gang Drug Prevention (YGDP) Program consortium projects on the gang involvement of youths who participated in these projects. First, the section describes these youths in terms of their exposure to gangs; for gang-involved participants, aspects of their involvement are examined. Second, the section presents the results of comparisons of project participants and nonparticipants with regard to gang involvement. The results of multivariate analyses on gang involvement are reported; these analyses consider several characteristics of participants and nonparticipants simultaneously. Many of these comparisons consider changes in youth behavior over time.

Table 1

Participant and Nonparticipant Exposure to Gangs

Interview Questions	Participants (%)	Non-participants (%)	Test Statistic[1]
Ever been picked on or hassled by a gang?	**(N = 258)**	**(N = 261)**	
Yes	23.3	24.9	$X^2 = 0.2$,
No	76.7	75.1	df = 1, NS
	100.0	100.0	
Ever been approached about joining a gang?	**(N = 259)**	**(N = 265)**	
Yes	29.3	30.2	$X^2 = <0.1$,
No	70.7	69.8	df = 1, NS
	100.0	100.0	
Have any friends been involved with a gang?	**(N =254)**	**(N = 257)**	
Yes	54.3	55.6	$X^2 = <0.1$,
No	44.7	44.7	df = 1, NS
	100.0	100.0	
If yes, how many friends?	**(N = 138)**	**(N = 143)**	
1-5	26.8	24.5	
6-10	18.8	25.9	$X^2 = 4.6$
11-20	16.7	21.7	df = 3, NS
21 or more	37.7	28.0	
	100.0	100.0	
If yes, are these your close friends?	**(N = 137)**	**(N = 138)**	
Yes	59.8	63.0	$X^2 = 0.3$
No	40.2	37.0	df = 1, NS
	100.0	100.0	
Have family members ever been involved with a gang?	**(N = 260)**	**(N = 263)**	
Yes	30.8	34.6	$X^2 = 0.9$
No	69.2	65.4	df = 1, NS
	100.0	100.0	

[1] For the X^2 test of statistical significance, NS = statistically nonsignificant.

Table 2
Participant and Nonparticipant Characteristics That May Be Associated With Gang Involvement

	Ever Gang Involved?					
	Participants			Nonparticipants		
Characteristic/Interview Question	**Yes (%)**	**No (%)**	**Test Statistic[1]**	**Yes (%)**	**No (%)**	**Test Statistic[1]**
Gender	(N = 59)	(N = 200)		(N = 60)	(N = 205)	
Male	74.6	61.0	$X^2 = 3.6$,	83.3	56.6	$X^2 = 14.2$
Female	25.4	39.0	df = 1, NS	16.7	43.4	df = 1,
	100.0	100.0		100.0	100.0	$p < 0.001$
Race/ethnicity	(N = 59)	(N = 199)		(N = 60)	(N = 205)	
African-American	27.1	39.7	$X^2 = 4.4$	26.7	26.3	$X^2 = < 0.1$,
Hispanic	45.8	32.2	df = 2, NS	55.0	54.2	df = 1, NS
Other	27.1	28.1		18.3	19.5	
	100.0	100.0		100.0	100.0	
Currently in school	(N = 59)	(N = 200)		(N = 60)	(N = 205)	
Yes	84.8	96.5	NA	76.7	93.2	$X^2 = 13.4$,
No	15.2	3.5		23.3	6.8	df = 1, NS
	100.0	100.0		100.0	100.0	
Length of time at current address	(N = 59)	(N =200)		(N = 59)	(N =205)	
Less than 6 months	22.0	8.0	$X^2 = 14.1$	17.0	12.2	$X^2 = 2.0$
6 - 11 months	13.6	6.5	df = 3,	6.8	4.4	df = 3, NS
12 - 24 months	18.6	18.5	$p < 0.01$	6.8	10.2	
Over 24 months	45.8	67.0		69.5	73.2	
	100.0	100.0		100.0	100.0	
Ever been approached about joining a gang?	(N = 58)	(N = 200)		(N = 60)	(N = 205)	
Yes	67.2	18.5	$X^2 = 51.4$	71.7	18.0	$X^2 = 63.3$
No	32.8	81.5	df = 1,	28.3	82.0	df = 1
	100.0	100.0	$p < 0.001$	100.0	100.0	$p<0.001$
Have any friends been involved with a gang?	(N = 59)	(N = 194)		(N = 60)	(N = 195)	
Yes	94.9	41.8	NA	95.0	44.1	NA
No	5.1	58.2		5.0	55.9	
	100.0	100.0		100.0	100.0	
Have any family members ever been involved with a gang?	(N = 59)	(N = 200)		(N = 60)	(N = 201)	
Yes	57.6	23.0	$X^2 = 25.6$,	61.7	26.9	$X^2 = 24.6$
No	42.4	77.0	df = 1,	38.3	73.1	df = 1,
	100.0	100.0	$p < 0.001$	100.0	100.0	$p < 0.001$

Exposure to Gangs

To the extent that direct or indirect contact with gangs can influence youths to become gang involved, the majority of participants and nonparticipants were at risk of joining gangs. About a quarter of the participants and nonparticipants had been picked on or hassled by a gang (see Table 1). A somewhat high percentage of participants (29.3%) and nonparticipants (30.2%) had actually been approached about joining a gang. Perhaps more telling is the finding that over half of the participants (54.3%) and nonparticipants (55.6%) had friends who had been gang members. In the majority of cases, these gang-involved individuals were close

***Table 2** (Continued)*
Participant and Nonparticipant Characteristics That May Be Associated With Gang Involvement

	Ever Gang Involved?					
	Participants			Nonparticipants		
Characteristic/Interview Question	**Yes (%)**	**No (%)**	**Test Statistic**[1]	**Yes (%)**	**No (%)**	**Test Statistic**[1]
Among the youths in your neighborhood, how important is it to be a member of a gang?	**(N = 58)**	**(N = 192)**		**(N = 60)**	**(N = 197)**	
Very important	22.4	9.4	$X^2 = 27.9$,	18.3	14.7	$X^2 = 11.8$
Somewhat important	37.9	17.2	df = 4,	33.3	16.8	df = 4,
Neither important nor unimportant	17.2	14.1	$p < 0.001$	15.0	13.2	$p < 0.05$
Somewhat unimportant	10.3	17.2		13.3	15.7	
Very unimportant	12.1	42.2		20.0	39.6	
	100.0	100.0		100.0	100.0	
How safe do you feel in your neighborhood?	**(N = 59)**	**(N = 200)**		**(N = 60)**	**(N = 205)**	
Very safe or fairly safe	83.0	73.5	$X^2 = 2.3$,	75.0	70.2	$X^2 = 4.2$,
Neither safe nor unsafe	8.5	12.0	df = 2, NS	6.7	16.6	df = 2, NS
Fairly unsafe or very unsafe	8.5	14.5		18.3	13.2	
	100.0	100.0		100.0	100.0	
Have you ever tried alcohol or any other drugs?	**(N = 59)**	**N = 200)**		**(N = 60)**	(N = 205)	
Yes	83.0	35.0	$X^2 = 42.4$	90.0	36.6	$X^2 = 53.0$
No	17.0	65.0	df = 1,	10.0	63.4	df = 1,
	100.0	100.0	$p < 0.001$	100.0	100.0	$p < 0.001$
Have the police ever accused you of committing a crime?	**(N = 59)**	(N = 200)		**(N = 60)**	**(N = 204)**	
Yes	74.6	25.5	$X^2 = 47.2$	66.7	15.2	$X^2 = 62.5$
No	25.4	74.5	df = 1,	33.3	84.8	df = 1,
	100.0	100.0	$p < 0.001$	100.0	100.0	$p < 0.001$
Have you ever been in trouble at school before participating in the program?[2]	**(N = 47)**	(N = 177)		**(N = 60)**	**(N = 205)**	
Yes	89.4	39.6	$X^2 = 36.9$	61.7	33.2	$X^2 = 15.8$
No	10.6	60.4	df = 1,	38.3	66.8	df = 1,
	100.0	100.0	$p < 0.001$	100.0	100.0	$p < 0.001$

[1] For the X^2 test of statistical significance, NS = statistically nonsignificant and NA = test inappropriate because cell sizes or marginal totals were too small.

[2] For nonparticipants, the time reference was before 1 year ago.

friends of the participants and nonparticipants. About one-third of the participants (30.8%) and nonparticipants (34.6%) had one or more family members who had been gang members. There were no differences between the participant and nonparticipant groups on any of these facets of exposure to gangs.

Factors Contributing to Participant Gang Involvement and Avoidance

In addition to exposure to gangs, several factors can contribute to the gang involvement or avoidance of a given youth. When asked directly about why they avoided gang involvement, participants most frequently reported that they had "no need to [join]" or "did not want to [join]" (34.9%) and "don't like [gangs]" (16.9%). These reasons indicate generally negative attitudes toward gangs; other reasons given by many participants suggest a belief that joining a gang can have negative consequences. For example, 26.2 percent of participants indicated that they avoided gang involvement because "it was threatening" or it "would get them into trouble."

To better understand the factors that contribute to gang involvement or avoidance, another approach is to compare the 22.8 percent of participants who had been involved with a gang with those who avoided gang involvement. A separate similar set of comparisons was made for nonparticipants. Among project participants, the only demographic characteristic that seems to be associated with gang involvement is length of time at the current address (see Table 2). Gang-involved participants tended to live at their current addresses for less time than participants who avoided gang involvement. For example, 35.6 percent of gang involved participants had lived at their current address for less than 12 months, as compared with only 14.5 percent of participants who avoided gang involvement. Among nonparticipants, gang involvement is associated with gender and current school enrollment. Gang-involved nonparticipants were more likely to be male than nonparticipants who avoided gang involvement. Gang-involved nonparticipants also were less likely to be enrolled in school; this finding is consistent with the finding for participants on gang involvement and school enrollment.

Table 3
Participant Age, Gender, and Race/Ethnicity (at Time of Initial Joining of a Gang)

Participant Characteristic	Age			Test Statistic[1]
	Less Than 14	14 and Over	Total	
Gender				
Male	73.9	26.1	100.0	X^2=0.3,
Female	68.0	32.0	100.0	df=1, NS
Race/ethnicity				
African-American	78.1	21.9	100.0	X^2=1.0,
Hispanic	72.4	27.6	100.0	df=2, NS
Other	66.7	33.3	100.0	
Overall	72.6	27.4	100.0	NA

Note: Percentages are row percents. The sample size is 117.
[1]For the X2 test of statistical significance, NS = statistically nonsignificant and NA = test inappropriate because cell sizes or marginal totals were too small.

Several social factors may have a greater potential influence on gang involvement or avoidance than demographic factors. Participants were more likely to have been gang involved if they had been approached about joining a gang, had gang-involved friends, or had family members who were gang involved. For example, about two-thirds of gang-involved participants (67.2%) had been approached, compared to only 18.5 percent of participants who avoided gang involvement. As expected, the perceived importance of gang membership also may affect whether youths become gang involved. This finding is consistent with the previously mentioned finding that participants who avoided gang involvement had generally negative attitudes toward gangs. Participant feelings of safety in their neighborhood appears unrelated to gang involvement. The findings for nonparticipants on social factors associated with gang involvement are very similar to those for participants.

A tendency toward social deviance and delinquent behavior is another factor that seems to be associated with gang involvement or avoidance. Participants who were gang involved were much more likely than other participants to have tried alcohol or other drugs (83% versus 35%), have been accused of committing a crime (74.6% versus 25.5%), or have been in trouble at school (89.4% versus 39.6%). The findings for nonparticipants on delinquent behavior associated with gang involvement are very similar to those for participants.

Table 4
Features of Gang Involvement for Participants Who Are or Were Gang Involved

Interview Question	Percentage of Total
Was drug-related activity part of your involvement?	**(N=59)**
No	44.1
Yes, using only	8.5
Yes, selling only	25.4
Yes, using and selling	22.0
	100.0
If still involved, for how many months?	**(N=30)**
4-12	13.3
13-24	33.3
25-36	20.0
Over 36	33.3
	100.0
If still involved, how many hours do you spend with gang members during a typical week?	**(N=30)**
No time	3.3
1-2	3.3
3-5	6.7
6-10	10.0
11-15	16.7
16-20	10.0
Over 20	50.0
	100.0
Would you like to get out?	**(N=31)**
Yes	32.3
No	67.7
	100.0
Are you able to get out?	**(N=10)**
Yes	70.0
No	30.0
	100.0

Features of Gang Involvement

Participants who were gang involved tended to begin their involvement at a young age—that is, an average age of 12.6 years old; nearly three-fourths of all gang-involved youths began their involvement before they were 14 years old (see Table 3). No relationship appeared to exist between age at the time of joining a gang and either gender or race/ethnicity.

For the majority of participants who were or had been gang involved, using or selling illicit drugs was part of that involvement (see Table 4). Some 8.5 percent of gang-involved participants used drugs, and

47.4 percent sold or used illicit drugs. It is perhaps surprising that the percentage of gang-involved participants without drug involvement (44.1%) is as high as it is.

Over half of the participants who had ever been gang involved (53.4%) were still involved. Some 86.6 percent of these participants had been involved for over a year. These individuals tended to spend large amounts of time with other gang members. During a typical week, over three-fourths (76.7%) spent more than 10 hours with gang youths; half of the participants who remained gang involved spent over 20 hours per week with gang youths.

Table 5
Participant and Nonparticipant Gang Involvement (by Time Period)

	Time Period 1[1]			Time Period 2[2]		
Gang Involved	Participants (%)	Nonparticipants (%)	Test Statistic[3]	Participants (%)	Nonparticipants (%)	Test Statistic[3]
	(N=259)	(N=265)	X^2=0.6, df=1, NS	(N=258)	(N=265)	X^2=<0.1, df=1, NS
Yes	20.8	18.1		12.0	11.7	
No	79.2	81.9		88.0	88.3	
	100.0	100.0		100.0	100.0	

[1]For participants, "time period 1" was prior to project participation; for nonparticipants, 1 year before being interviewed.
[2]For participants, "time period 2" was since project participation; for nonparticipants, since 1 year before being interviewed.
[3]For the X^2 test of statistical significance, NS = statistically nonsignificant.

Of the participants who remained gang involved, only about one-third (32.3%) wanted to leave their gangs. Seven of these 10 youths believed that they could leave their gangs if they chose to do so. This finding suggests that gang-involved participants remained involved for reasons other than feared retribution if they were to attempt to leave the gang.

Project Effects on Gang Involvement

Effects on Gang Avoidance

The projects seem to have had little or no influence on participants' gang involvement or avoidance. Participants and nonparticipants were very similar in terms of gang involvement: about 22.8 percent of participants and 22.6 percent of nonparticipants had been involved with a gang. With regard to the time period at which youths were gang involved, a similar pattern obtained. During "time period 1" of this evaluation (i.e., prior to project participation, for participants, and prior to one year before being interviewed, for nonparticipants), 20.8 percent of participants and 18.1 of nonparticipants were gang involved (see Table 5). During "time period 2" (i.e., since project participation, for participants, and since one year before being interviewed, for nonparticipants), 12.2 percent of participants and 11.7 percent of nonparticipants were gang involved. Thus, there were no differences between the groups in terms of gang involvement at either time.

There were also no apparent differences between the groups in terms of patterns of change in gang involvement at the individual level. Roughly 88 percent of both participants and nonparticipants remained uninvolved or experienced positive changes in gang involvement over time (i.e., remaining uninvolved during time periods 1 and 2 or changing from gang involved during "time period 1" to uninvolved in "time period 2") (see Table 6).

Table 6
Changes in Participant and Nonparticipant Gang Involvement (by Time Period)

Change in Gang Involvement	Participants (%)	Nonparticipants (%)
	(N=258)	(N=265)
Not involved before, not involved after	78.7	79.2
Not involved before, involved after	0.8	2.6
Involved before, not after	9.3	9.1
Involved before and after	11.2	9.1
	100.0	100.0

*Note:*For participants, the "before" period ("time period 1") was prior to project participation; for nonparticipants, prior to 1 year before being interviewed. For participants and nonparticipants, "after" ("time period 2") was at the time of being interviewed. A test of statistical significance was inappropriate because one or more cell sizes were too small.

Effects on Youths Already Gang Involved

The consortium projects also seem to have had little or no influence on the gang involvement of participants who were already involved. The projects encouraged gang-involved youth to leave gangs or, at a minimum, to reduce some of the negative behaviors often associated with involvement. No differences were found between gang-involved participants and nonparticipants in terms of the amount of time spent with gang members in "time period 2" (see Table 7). Also, no differences were found between the groups with respect to whether these youths wanted to leave their gangs. Of the gang-involved participants, only 9 youths (29%) believed that project participation had in some way affected their gang involvement.

The finding of no differences between participants and nonparticipants in terms of gang involvement is generally consistent with participant reports. For example, only 40.3 of the participants who avoided gang involvement indicated that the project had helped them avoid such involvement. Although the projects may have helped some participants avoid gang involvement, they appear not to have been the central factor in keeping most youths from becoming involved.

Multivariate Analyses of Project Effects on Gang Involvement

The first set of multivariate analyses compared participants and nonparticipants on gang involvement in "time period 2" after statistically adjusting for differences in terms of certain background characteristics (e.g., age, gender, race/ethnicity, and gang involvement in "time period 1") between participant and nonparticipant groups. The desired effect of the statistical adjustments was to reduce differences between the groups with regard to these background characteristics because they could interfere with understanding whether or not a project had influenced differences in the outcome variable (i.e., gang involvement in "time period 2"). To the extent that these analyses revealed that the participant group was less likely than the nonparticipant group to be gang involved in "time period 2"—even with the statistical adjustments—the evaluators would have support for the conclusion that the project, rather than differences in background characteristics, was primarily responsible for the group difference in terms of the outcome variable. If the first set of multivariate analyses indicated differences between the groups in terms of gang involvement in "time period 2," the evaluators planned to conduct a second set of analyses (with the participant group only) to identify youth and project characteristics that were associated with reduced gang involvement.

Table 7
Comparison of Participants and Nonparticipants Regarding Features of Gang Involvement for Youths Who Were or Are Gang Involved

Feature of Involvement	Participants (%)	Non-participants (%)	Test Statistic[1]
Change in amount of time spent with gang members[2,3]	**(N=31)**	**(N=30)**	
More time	9.7	33.3	
About the same	32.3	20.0	
Less time	58.1	46.7	
	100.0	100.0	
Amount of time spent with gang members weekly	**(N=30)**	**(N=31)**	
20 hours or less	50.0	45.2	X^2=0.1,
More than 20 hours	50.0	54.8	df=1,
	100.0	100.0	NS
Want to leave gang	**(N=31)**	**(N=31)**	
Yes	32.3	41.9	X^2=0.6,
No	67.7	58.1	df=1,
	100.0	100.0	NS

[1]For the X^2 test of significance, NS = statistically nonsignificant.
[2]Since program participation or, for nonparticipants, since 1 year before being interviewed.
[3]A test of statistical significance was inappropriate because one or more cell sizes were too small.

In both the first and second sets of multivariate analyses, the same outcome variable was to be used for gang involvement in "time period 2." Ideally, this variable would be sensitive to differences with respect to the severity or chronicity of youths' gang involvement. The evaluators considered two different approaches to defining this outcome variable. The first approach was to focus on changes, during "time period 2," in the amount of time that participants and nonparticipants spent with gang members. However, this approach was rejected because it would have reduced the sample sizes (i.e., it applied only to the relatively few participants and nonparticipants who were gang involved during both time periods 1 and 2); hence, multivariate analysis would have been inappropriate. The approach adopted was to define the outcome variable in terms of whether or not youths were gang involved in "time period 2." Because this variable is dichotomous, logistic regression rather than ordinary least squares regression was used in the analyses.

Analyses of Differences Between Groups on Gang Involvement

Several independent variables or covariates were selected for the first set of multivariate analyses on the difference between participants and nonparticipants regarding gang involvement in "time period 2." Because most of these covariates are theoretically linked to gang involvement, the evaluators sought to control statistically for differences between them for both groups. These covariates were chosen and categorized as follows:

- age: less than 14 years and 14 years or older;
- gender;
- race/ethnicity: African-American, Hispanic, and other;
- gang involvement in "time period 1": involvement and no involvement; and
- extent of gang problem in areas in which projects were located and youths resided: emerging and chronic gang problem (based on information from the process component of the national evaluation).

A sixth independent variable, the number of non-YGDP projects in which youths participated, was also considered. It would have aided an assessment of the influence of the FYSB program beyond the actual projects involved; however, it was not used because it failed to significantly differentiate the participants from nonparticipants in terms of gang involvement.

The first set of multivariate analyses found that participants were as likely as nonparticipants to be gang involved in "time period 2." These results are consistent with the results of the comparative analyses. However, because they are more rigorous, the multivariate analyses strengthen the argument for no effects of the projects on participant gang involvement.

When participants and nonparticipants were compared in the multivariate analyses, race/ethnicity and extent of gang problem were the only covariates on which the groups differed. Participants were more likely than nonparticipants to be African-American and in the "other" category (e.g., Asian-American/Pacific Islander and white) and less likely than nonparticipants to be Hispanic. When the effect of race/ethnicity was removed in the logistic regression, participants were still found to be as likely as nonparticipants to be gang involved in "time period 2." In other words, approximately the same percentage of participants and nonparticipants in each race/ethnicity category were gang involved in "time period 2."

Analyses that included the independent variable "extent of gang problem" produced results similar to those for race/ethnicity. Participants were more likely than nonparticipants to live in areas that had emerging gang problems. When the effect of "extent of gang problem" was removed in the logistic regression, participants were as likely as nonparticipants to be gang involved in "time period 2." In other words, approximately the same percentage of participants and nonparticipants in each "extent of gang problem" category were gang involved in "time period 2."

In summary, the first set of multivariate analyses indicated that the two groups differed in terms of certain background characteristics (e.g., race/ethnicity, extent of gang problem) that could account for the observed similarity in gang involvement in "time period 2." No differences were observed between the groups for other background characteristics (e.g., gender, age, gang involvement in "time period 1"). When the effects of differing background characteristics were removed, the participant group was still as likely as the nonparticipant group to be gang involved in "time period 2." This finding supports the hypothesis that the projects had no detectable influence on gang involvement among participants.

Analyses of Youth and Project Characteristics Associated With Reduced Gang Involvement

Because no differences in gang involvement were found between the participant and nonparticipant groups in "time period 2," no additional analyses were performed on factors associated with stronger effects of the projects on participants. These additional analyses would have been warranted only if the first set of analyses had indicated that the projects were associated with reduced gang involvement for participants.

Summary and Conclusions

Although the methodological limitations of the evaluation preclude definitive conclusions, the youth gang drug prevention consortium projects appear to have had little or no influence on participant gang involvement or avoidance. During time periods 1 and 2, the participant and nonparticipant groups were similar with respect to the percentages of youths who were gang involved and patterns of change in gang involvement at the individual level. The results also indicated no differences between gang-involved youths in these groups in terms of the amount of time spent with gang members and the desire to leave their gangs.

In addition, the evaluators found that the majority of participants and nonparticipants had at least a passing exposure to gangs. Several factors distinguished gang-involved participants from those who avoided gang involvement, including whether a participant:

- had ever been approached about joining a gang;
- had friends who were gang involved;
- had family members who were gang involved;
- perceived gang membership to be important among his or her peers;
- had used alcohol or other drugs;
- had been accused of committing a crime; and
- had been in trouble in school.

Many of the participants who avoided gang involvement seemed to have generally negative attitudes toward gangs and to be concerned about some of the potential negative consequences of gang invoment.

Notes

1. [Editors' note: The sections of the larger report excerpted for this volume cover only the evaluation of consortium projects and the findings concerning program effects on gang involvement.] ✦

31
G-Dog and the Homeboys

Celeste Fremon

Given the vast array of gang intervention approaches and the sometimes hopeless sense that nothing works, we conclude this section with the inspirational story of one individual's efforts to make a difference. In the following article, Fremon describes the one-man gang reform program found in Father Gregory Boyle of East Los Angeles. He offers schooling, job programs and counseling to the gang members in his community, as well as a caring, supportive relationship with these youth. While he touches the lives of so many of the gang members around him, it remains inevitable that the efforts of one person can do little to diminish the escalation of gang activity and violence.

At exactly 7 p.m. on an uncommonly warm night in early March, 1990, some 300 mourners, most of them members of the Latino gang the East L.A. Dukes, descend upon Dolores Mission Church at the corner of 3rd and Gless streets in Boyle Heights. They arrive by the carload and cram themselves into the scarred wooden pews that fill the sanctuary. As they file into the small stucco building, they cast edgy glances toward the street, as if expecting trouble. They are here for the funeral of Hector Vasquez, a.k.a. Flaco, 17, killed by a single shot to the head two nights before in a drive-by incident that took place at the nearby Aliso Village housing project.

The attire worn this night conforms to the unwritten gang code of dress. Girl gang members wear their hair long at the bottom and teased high at the crown, their lipstick blood-red. The boys sport perfectly pressed white Penney's T-shirts, dark Pendleton shirts and cotton work pants called Dickies, worn four sizes too big and belted, a contemporary interpretation of the old *pachuco* style. About 20 boys and girls wear sweat shirts emblazoned with iron-on Old English lettering that reads: "IN LOVING MEMORY OF OUR HOMIE FLACO R.I.P."

Outside the church, the police are very much in evidence. A couple of black-and-whites sit, just around the corner, motors running. Two beige unmarked cars, the kind favored by the LAPD's special gang unit, and one plain white Housing Police sedan continuously circle the block.

At first, the mood in the church is tense, expectant. But when taped synthesizer music throbs from loudspeakers, the sound seems to open an emotional spigot. The shoulders of the mourners start to shake with grief.

Behind the altar, a bearded man in glasses and priest's vestments sits quietly, watching the crying gangsters. When the music ends, Father Gregory Boyle rises and, taking a microphone, steps down to a point smack in front of the first row of mourners. From a distance, with his receding hair line and beard going to gray, he looks well past middle age. Up close, he is clearly much younger, not yet even 40.

Boyle takes a breath. "I knew Flaco for a long time," he says, his gaze traveling from face to face in the pews. "He used to work here at the church. I knew him as a very loving, great-hearted and kind man." Boyle pauses. "And now we shouldn't ask who killed Flaco, but rather *what* killed him. Flaco died of a disease that is killing La Raza, a disease called gang-banging." The crowd shifts nervously.

"So how do we honor Flaco's memory?" Boyle asks. "We will honor him best by doing what he would want us to do." Another pause. "He would want us to stop killing each other."

All at once, there is a commotion in the sixth row. A hard-eyed kid of 18 with the street name Magoo stands bolt upright and makes his way to the center aisle. Slowly, deliberately, he walks down the aisle, until he stands in front of Boyle, staring the priest straight in the eye. Then he turns and walks out a side door.

The air in the church is as brittle as glass when Boyle begins speaking again: "If we *knew* Flaco and *loved* Flaco, then we would stop killing each other."

Four more gangsters stand and walk out. Boyle's face reddens and then turns pale, as the mourners wait to see what he will do. Finally his jaw sets. "I loved Flaco," he says, his eyes starting to tear. "And I swear on Flaco's dead body that he would want us to stop killing each other."

The words explode in crisp, stunning bursts like so many rounds of live ammunition. Two more gang members get up and leave—but these boys walk with their heads down, their gaits rapid and scuttling. The rest of the mourners sit stock still, transfixed by the ferocity of Boyle's gaze. "We honor his memory," he says quietly, "if we can do this."

Father Gregory Boyle is the pastor of Dolores Mission Church, which serves a parish that is unique in several ways. First, it is the poorest in the Catholic Archdiocese of Los Angeles—it is dominated by a pair of housing projects: Pico Gardens and Aliso Village. Second, within the parish boundaries, which enclose about two square miles of Boyle Heights east of the

Reprinted with permission of the author from the *Los Angeles Times*, August 11, 1991.

Los Angeles River, seven Latino gangs and one African-American gang claim neighborhoods. This means that in an area smaller than the UCLA campus there are eight separate armies of adolescents, each equipped with small- and large-caliber weapons, each of which may be at war with one or more of the others at any given moment.

The Clarence Street Locos is the largest of the gangs, with close to 100 members; Rascals is the smallest, with 30 or so. The rest—Al Capone, the East L.A. Dukes, Cuatro Flats, The Mob Crew (TMC, for short), Primera Flats and the East Coast Crips (the single black gang in this predominantly Latino area)—hover in size from 50 to 80 teen-age boys and young men. However large the membership, the "'hood," or territory, that each gang claims is minuscule—no more than a block or two square. A member of one gang cannot safely walk the half-block from his mother's apartment to the corner store if that store is in enemy territory—much less walk the five or 10 blocks (across as many 'hoods) to reach his assigned junior high or high school.

According to statistics compiled by the Hollenbeck Division of the LAPD, gang-related crimes in East Los Angeles were up a sobering 20% from 1989 to 1990 and are rising again, up 11% over the same period last year. It is hardly surprising, therefore, that in his five years as parish priest Greg Boyle has buried 17 kids who were shot to death by rival gang members, and two who were shot to death by sheriff's deputies.[1] He himself has been in the line of fire seven times.

This is the tragic heart of the barrio, a bleak and scary part of Los Angeles that much of the rest of the city would like to block from its consciousness. Here junkies and baseheads pump gas for handouts at self-service filling stations, and bullet craters in the stucco walls of houses and stores serve as mnemonic devices, reminders of where this kid was killed, that one wounded. Yet surface impressions are not the whole of the matter in this parish: Beyond the most insistent images of gang violence, poverty and despair, a more redemptive vision comes into focus, a vision that comes clearest around Father Boyle.

Boyle lives simply. He wears the same burgundy zip-front sweat shirt every cold day, and the same rotating selection of five shirts when the days are sunny. His sleeping quarters are half a mile from the church, in a 1913-vintage two-story clapboard dwelling that he shares with six other Jesuits.

His days are long. They start at 7 a.m., often with a trip to Juvenile Court to testify in a gang member's behalf. They end close to midnight when Boyle takes one last bicycle ride around the projects to make sure that no trouble is brewing. In between, along with two assistants at Dolores Mission, he performs the conventional range of pastoral duties: saying Mass, hearing confessions, officiating at weddings and funerals or simply working in his monastic-cell of an office, dealing with parish business.

Whenever the door to Boyle's office opens, gang members swoop in like baby chicks for a feeding. They come to him to have their hair cut, to ask for a job through his Jobs for a Future program, to sign up to feed the homeless (to comply with court-ordered community service), to ask for admission to Dolores Mission Alternative, the school that he started as a sort of Last Chance U. for gang members. But mostly they come to hang out, to talk, to tease and be teased, to laugh. Around Boyle, the gangsters' defensive "screw you" expressions drop away. Twelve-year-old wanna-bes and 20-year-old tough-eyed *veteranos* jockey to be the favored child and sit next to Boyle in his car on his daily errands. They aren't afraid to cry in his presence. They find any excuse to touch him. The gangsters have even christened Boyle with his own *placa*, his street name: G-Dog. But most simply call him G.

"G. is always there when you need him," says one precariously reformed gangster. "I don't have a dad. So I think of him like my father. Even when I was in jail, he always had time to talk to me. Even when nobody else was there for me. And, you know, when I wanted to stop gang-banging, sometimes I would have so much anger that I wanted to do something, kill somebody. But I would talk to Father Greg and he would help me so I didn't explode inside. He's the one we can all look up to."

The term "dysfunctional family," one of the fashionable buzz phrases of the '90s, acquires a special meaning in the Dolores Mission parish. Not long ago, on a whim, Boyle sat down at his computer and made a list of all the gang kids who immediately came to mind. Next to each name he wrote a coded description of the youth's family situation: "AB" for father absent; "A" for alcoholic father; "AA" for alcoholic and abusive; "ABU" for just plain abusive, "S" for stepfather, "I" for intact original family.

"I didn't stack the deck or anything," he explains. "I just wrote down 67 names sort of stream-of-consciousness. I found that most fathers were absent. The second biggest categories were alcoholic and alcoholic/abusive." Out of 67 kids, only three had intact families with fathers who were not alcoholic or abusive.

Pick three, any three, of the gang members that hover around Boyle's door and delve into their family dynamics and the stories will disturb your sleep. There is Bandito[2], whose father died two years ago of a heroin overdose. There is Smiley[2], whose father is continually drunk and abusive. There is Gato[2], whose basehead mother sold his only warm jacket to buy another hit. Or Gustavo Martinez, Javier Villa and Guadelupe Lopez—Grumpy, Termite and Scoobie, respectively.

Grumpy's father was gone long before he was born. His mother beat him with the plug-end of the television cord, with the garden hose, a spiked belt—anything she could find. The beatings were so severe that she was jailed several times for child abuse. Some abusive parents are by turns affectionate and rejecting. Not this mother. In all the years of Grumpy's upbringing, he never received a birthday gift or a Christmas gift or even a card. "Imagine," says Boyle, "not one piece of concrete evidence of caring from a parent throughout a whole childhood."

In Termite's case, the blows were not to the body. His mother always professed great love for him. His father never hit him. What his father did was tell him he worthless, despicable and generally a bad seed. Even now, when Boyle drops Termite at home, a call will sometimes come minutes later. It will be Termite pleading to sleep in Boyle's office for the night. "My dad locked me out," he will say.

"I know he cares about me," says Termite, as if the words are a spell capable of making it so. But when pushed on the subject he averts his eyes. "I guess mostly he just acts like I'm not there."

Sometimes it is not the parents but life in the barrio that provides the abuse. Scoobie's last memory of his alcoholic father was when he was 3; his dad knocked his mother off her feet, cuffed Scoobie to the floor and snarled: "What're you lookin' at?" Scoobie's mother gathered her kids and fled. However, the hotel in which she found shelter was so crime-ridden that, before he was 5, Scoobie witnessed three lurid murders, virtually on his doorstep. Add to that the problems of a young single mother with no resources and no child care and the picture becomes still bleaker.

Scoobie's mother padlocked her preschool-age children in a darkened hotel room while she went to work for the day. "She was trying to keep us safe," says Scoobie. When he is asked if his childhood had any happy times, he thinks for a moment: "I remember this one day when my mom took us all to the park and let us run around. It was so great, you know. For once we weren't stuffed up in that little room. And we felt, I don't know, just—free!"

So what does a barrio kid do when family and society have failed him? When he turns 14 or 15, he joins a gang, a surrogate family, where he finds loyalty, self-definition, discipline, even love of a sort. "We all want to be attached to something," says Diego Vigil, an anthropology professor at USC who has studied gangs. "We want to connect and commit. If we can't find anywhere else to connect and commit, we'll connect and commit to the streets. The gang takes over the parenting, the schooling and the policing."

On a Sunday afternoon in January, 1991, Father Boyle takes Scoobie and Grumpy shopping for clothes. Both of them are large kids, bulky and muscular, each with a proclivity for fast, funny patter delivered half in English, half in Spanish. They are members of the Mob Crew and the Clarence Street Locos, respectively—traditionally friendly gangs whose neighborhoods are close to the church. Scoobie is 19 and Grumpy is 20, both *veteranos*, both too old to attend Dolores Mission Alternative. They are desperate to find employment. Their shopping destination is Sears. The idea is to get them non-gangster attire to wear to job interviews.

In the men's department, Boyle pulls out pants and shirts for them to try on. He is careful to choose light colors. Grumpy and Scoobie keep edging back in the direction of the gangster look: dark colors and a baggy fit.

"Hey G., these pants are too tight," wails Scoobie. In reality, the pants fit perfectly.

"They're fine," Boyle counters, and Scoobie relents.

"Look," Boyle says to Scoobie and Grumpy as he hands the cashier a Sears credit card, "I'm spending a lot of bank on this today, and the deal is you have to be dressed and in my office every morning at 9 a.m., ready to look for work." The two nod obediently and assure Boyle that they will indeed comply.

Both Scoobie and Grumpy are staying in Casa Miguel Pro, the temporary residence that Dolores Mission maintains for homeless women and children. "I'm trying an experiment in letting them stay there," Boyle explains. "A lot of folks aren't exactly thrilled that I'm doing this. But right now neither of them has anywhere else they can go."

After the shopping trip, Scoobie irons his new tan pants and shirt striped in shades of blue. Next he takes a bath. Finally he puts on the freshly pressed clothes and looks in a communal mirror.

"That ain't me. . ." he says softly to the mirror. He stands back a little and looks again. "I look like a regular person," he says, his expression so happy it borders on giddiness. "Not like the police say, not like another *gang member*."

When Greg Boyle first came to Dolores Mission in early July, 1986, at age 32 the youngest pastor in the L.A. Archdiocese, he hardly seemed likely to become "the gang priest." Raised in comfortable Windsor Square on the outskirts of Hancock Park, one of eight children of a third-generation dairyman, he attended Loyola High School, the Jesuit-run boys' school on Venice Boulevard, from 1968 to 1972. It was a wildly inspiring four years for an idealistic Catholic kid. His teachers led peace marches protesting the Vietnam War, and activist Jesuits were making news all over the country as liberation theology—which marries social justice to spiritual renewal—came to full flower.

Boyle spent the next 13 years in religious training, culminating in his 1984 ordination in Los Angeles. He was posted to Bolivia, the poorest country in the Western Hemisphere, where he became the parish priest in a small village. The experience radicalized the young, middle-class priest from Southern California. "Bolivia turned me absolutely inside out," says Boyle. "After Bolivia my life was forever changed." He realized he wanted to work with the poor. And few places were poorer than Dolores Mission.

Boyle's first year in the parish was tense and difficult. The priest before him had been a venerable *Mexicano*, and the community was slow to warm up to an Anglo, especially one so young. Since so few parishioners came to him, he decided to go to them. Every afternoon without fail, Boyle walked for hours through the neighborhood, particularly through the housing projects where most of his parishioners lived. He talked to people, listened to their complaints, played with their children. Over time he noticed that the majority of the complaints centered upon one issue: gangs.

Boyle made an effort to get to know the gangsters. He began by learning their names. At first, they brutally rejected the *gavacho* who spoke only passable Spanish. But he kept going back to them. "And you know," he says, "at some point it becomes sort of flattering that the priest knows who you are." Then he started going to Juvenile Hall to visit when kids got locked up, bringing messages from their homeboys. Or he'd rush to the hospital if they got shot.

He noticed that the kids who got into the most trouble were the kids who were not in school, and the reasons they were not in school were invariably gang-related. Either they had gotten kicked out of school because they had been fighting with enemy gang members, or the school itself was in enemy territory and deemed unsafe by the kids.

So in September, 1988, Father Boyle and one of his associates at Dolores Mission, Father Tom Smolich, opened a junior high and high school for gang members only. Dolores Mission Alternative was started on the third floor of Dolores Mission Elementary, the church's grammar school. Through home study and specially designed classes, the school aimed to get the kids back on an educational track, or at the least to help them pass the high-school equivalency exam.

Boyle also started hiring gang members to work around the church at $5 an hour. "And before I knew it there was no turning back," he laughs. "I felt like I sort of related to the gang members. They were fun and warm and eternally interesting. So gradually," he says, "it became a ministry within a ministry."

The rest of the parish, however, didn't find the gangsters quite so "warm" and "interesting." They saw only hair-netted homeboys doing heaven-knows-what in the same building with uniformed parochial-school children. Worse yet, these same "criminal types" were hanging out at the church as if it was their personal clubhouse. In the fall of 1989, Boyle's most virulent critics circulated a petition asking then-Archbishop Roger M. Mahony to remove him from the parish altogether.

Things came to a head one October night. Boyle had called a meeting to clear the air. The school basement was packed with Boyle supporters and *contras* when a swarm of gang members unexpectedly walked in, underlining the tension in the room. One by one, the homies got up and talked: "We're human beings, and we need help. And Father Greg is helping us."

Slowly the tension began to lift. Parish parents rose to speak: "Father Greg is right," they said. "These gang members are not the enemy. They are our children. And if we don't help them no one will."

That was the turning point. The parish stopped fighting Boyle's programs and began adopting them as their own. In short order, the Comité Pro Paz en el Barrio, the Committee for Peace in the Barrio, was formed to address the gang situation. Parish mothers who had never before attended so much as a PTA meeting suddenly became activists in the gangsters' behalf, organizing a peace march, holding a gang conference.

"What is going on at Pico-Aliso is very different than anything else I've seen elsewhere in the city," says Yolanda Chavez, for the last two years Mayor Tom Bradley's official liaison to the L.A. Latino community. "A lot of people are well-meaning, but they don't help people organize themselves. They do things for them. Father Greg's goal is always to help the people help themselves. He has become a focal point for their strength, empowering the community to provide the gang members with alternatives."

Scoobie has been job-hunting for three weeks straight, but now he is sitting in Boyle's office and he looks terrible. His lips and jaw are bruised and swollen. His hands are cut up, and an incisor on the lower left side of his jaw is broken. He has just returned from the dentist. Boyle will pay the dental bills, which may be close to a thousand dollars.

It happened two nights ago, says Scoobie, when he was stopped by two uniformed police officers. He was doing nothing in particular—just hanging out with the homies when the officers ordered him up against a car with his hands over his head. "Then they pushed me down on my knees," he says. Scoobie responded with a four-letter suggestion. At that point, according to Scoobie, one of the cops hit him in the mouth with a billy club. Then, he says, the cops made him lie down spread-eagled and stepped on his hands. Finally the police let him go without an arrest.

One of the activist parish mothers, Pam McDuffie, took Scoobie to the Hollenbeck Police Station to report the incident. The case is currently under investigation by Internal Affairs, but Boyle believes Scoobie's story implicitly. "This is one of many, many cases of the police beating the kids down," he says.

A few days after Scoobie's trip to the dentist, there is new trouble. Boyle arrives at his office in the morning to find a message on his answering machine. "Hey G.," says a young voice, "tell Grumpy I don't have the money for the gun but I'll have the money soon." Boyle stares at the machine boggle-eyed. It is nearly inconceivable that someone would leave such a message with him.

Boyle goes upstairs to Grumpy's room, and in a kind of false wall in the closet he finds a gun-cleaning kit and a metal strongbox. The box is heavy and the lid is stuck. Boyle carts it down to his office and shuts the door before prying the lid open. Inside, he finds $178 in cash, a neat list of investors and a box of 9-millimeter Beretta shells.

Boyle shuts the box, puts it in a desk drawer and waits for Grumpy's inevitable appearance. The confrontation goes as follows:

"Do you have a gun?"

"No, G."

"Are you collecting money for a gun?"

"No, G."

Boyle opens the drawer to reveal the strong box. "You've really let me down," he says quietly.

Grumpy's face turns to stone. "When do you want me to leave?" he asks. Then eyes averted and brimming, he turns and walks out.

Two hours later Grumpy is back. "G., I know I let you down! I let you down, *gacho*! I let you down big time!"

Boyle cannot bring himself to make Grumpy leave. "I know tough love is sometimes required," he philosophizes later. "I just don't know how tough the love should be."

A solution to the gang problem has been eluding Los Angeles Police Department for decades, and from law enforcement's point of view, the "love" should be very tough indeed. The ongoing police anti-gang program is dubbed Operation Hammer. "Hammer is a strategy in which we keep the pressure on," says Captain Nick Salicos, recently of the Hollenbeck Division. "On a Friday or a Saturday night, we go out with 30 or 40 officers to known gang locations and arrest gang members for anything we can. Drinking beer in public. Anything." If the crime can be shown to be gang related, and the arrestee is a known gang member, the sentence can be "enhanced"—made longer.

"The police try to make life as miserable as possible for gang members," Boyle says, "which is really redundant since gang members' lives are already miserable enough, thank you very much. And they hate me, I guess, because, No. 1, I refuse to snitch on gang members. No. 2, they can't understand how I could care about these kids. And I can't understand why they insist on criminalizing every kid in this community."

A visit to Hollenbeck Police Station reveals that Boyle is correct; the police don't like him much. Mention the priest's name to most Hollenbeck officers and there is invariably much rolling of eyes, followed by remarks that range from the suggestion that Boyle is "well-meaning but dangerously naive" to veiled charges that he is an accessory to gang crimes to intimations that he is under the influence of Communists.

A ride-along in a black-and-white provides an instructive perspective. The streets seem meaner from inside a patrol car. The stares the police gather are hostile, threatening. "Although our job is to try to prevent gang crime," explains Detective Jack Forsman of the LAPD's special gang unit, CRASH (Community Resources Against Street Hoodlums), "more often than not we can do little more than pick up the pieces once a crime has been committed."

"What I don't get," adds another officer who requested anonymity, "is why Father Boyle refuses to preach against using guns and being in gangs."

The remark infuriates Boyle. "Aside from the fact that it just isn't true," he bristles, "it has no respect for the complexity of the issue. It's Nancy Reagan writ large: 'Just Say No' to gangs. I would say getting kids out of gangs is the whole point of my work here. But what is ultimately persuasive is a job and self-esteem and education and having the kid feel that he or she can put together in his or her imagination a future that is viable. Now I can sit there and say, 'Get out of the gang!' but I don't know what value that would have. If any of this is going to be successful, you have to accept folks where they are. What they always get is: 'Where you are is a horrible place and you'd better change.' Well, look how successful that's been."

Boyle sighs wearily. "Part of the problem," he says, "is that when you're poor in the city of Los Angeles, you're hard-pressed to imagine a future for yourself. And if you can't imagine a future, then you're not going to care a lot about the present. And then anything can happen."

Although his approach is controversial, Boyle is by no means the only person working with gangs who decries the Just Say No approach as simplistic. "We have tried that," says Chavez from Mayor Bradley's office, "and it hasn't worked. Force hasn't worked. Police harassment hasn't worked. Jail and Juvenile Hall hasn't worked. Without options, gangs will thrive."

Mary Ridgeway and John Tuchek are the two officers in the L.A. County Probation Department's East L.A. Gang Unit who deal with arrested juveniles from Pico Gardens or Aliso Village. "There is the illusion," says Tuchek, "that we are rehabilitating these kids. And I'm here to tell you that the truth is we aren't even trying to rehabilitate them. We used to. But that doesn't happen down here any more. That's why what Father Greg is doing is so important. He's their only resource."

Ridgeway puts it another way. "At best, we can only deal with a fraction of the kids for a very short period of time, while *he's* there for all of them, all of the time. Father Greg and I are, in many ways, coming from a different point of view philosophically," she continues. "There are kids that I think should be locked up who he is reluctant to give up on—like a kid we both know who, fortunately, now is in Soledad. He was trouble every minute he was out on the streets.

"But, see," she smiles, "Father Greg loves everybody. In all my years in probation I've met maybe two people who have his courage. He's the kind of person we all wish we could be."

In the month after Boyle finds Grumpy's gun fund, the Pico-Aliso gangs begin to turn up the heat. By early March, Boyle is depressed. "Things have been awful around here," he says one Monday morning. It seems that Looney, an East Coast Crip, was killed on Thursday as a payback for Clown, a Primera Flats kid who was shot by a Crip in September, 1990. "That's how the game works," says Boyle grimly. The night after Looney was killed, two Latinos, one a transient and the other a basehead, were killed. No one is sure if these killings were gang-related or not. Moreover, the Crips and Al Capone, gangs that have traditionally gotten along, have had two fights in less than 48 hours.

The bad news didn't stop there. At about 8 p.m. on Saturday night, a kid from the Clarence Street Locos was headed down Gless Street to buy a beer when a Cuatro Flats kid approached him. Words were exchanged. Immediately each boy marched off to find his homies. In seconds, members of both gangs appeared from around corners, like magic rabbits, and began mad-dogging and dissing each other—glaring and shouting insults. A kid named Diablo from Cuatro hit Solo from Clarence, and someone yelled, "It's on!" War had been declared.

Suddenly, 80 gang members were blocking the intersection of 4th and Gless. Fists were flying, heads were bashed, ghetto blasters were swinging. All the while voices screamed, "It's on. It's on!"

It was then that Boyle showed up, almost by chance. He had just dropped a kid off at home when he saw traffic backed up, he pulled over and raced to investigate. Then the situation became surreal. Into a tangle of brawling gangsters ran Boyle, grabbing arms and shrieking every four-letter word he could think of. At his screamed orders, the Clarence group backed up. Cuatro stopped swinging and halted its advance. On the edge of the action, kids on bikes still circled, shotguns bulging underneath their Pendletons.

Finally, Boyle was able to herd the Clarence kids across 4th and down Gless; the Cuatro force moved off, dispersing into the neighborhood.

Afterward, Boyle was walking alongside Mando, who, with his identical twin, has a lot of juice with the Clarence Street Locos. "You *yelled* at us, G.," said Mando, shaking his head in genuine shock. "You used the *F word*!"

"In the moment," says Boyle later, "I'll do any damn thing that works."

It's raining. Four homies—Termite, Grumpy, Green and Critter—are hanging out in Boyle's office as he opens mail and does paper work.

Critter, a slim, handsome kid with long, fringed eyelashes and a heartbreaker's smile, rubs Boyle's ever-expanding forehead with the palm of his hand as Boyle unsuccessfully bats him away. "I'm rubbing your bumper for luck, G.!" says Critter, moving in for another rub.

"Hey, G.," interrupts Grumpy, "How come you're in such a good mood?" Turning to Green: "Have you ever noticed that whenever G. is in a good mood it rains?" Grumpy pauses, possessed of a new thought. "Hey, you think maybe G. is actually Mother Nature in disguise? That means the drought is his fault, right? You think the drought is your fault, G.?"

Boyle looks up at Grumpy. "Here's a letter here from a couple who want to adopt a child," he says, deadpan. "What do you think, Grumps? You think it's right for you?"

"Only if the *madre* is proper," sniffs Grumpy. Meanwhile, the imagined scene of an unsuspecting young couple being introduced to their new "child"—a 6-foot, 200-pound tattooed homie named Grumpy—throws the rest of the room into spasms of hilarity.

Grumpy is discouraged about his job prospects. He has been answering want ads for weeks to no avail, he says. "You go in there and you fill out an application. Then they say they'll call you but you can tell they're looking at your tattoos and they're not gonna, you know? It's like, when you leave, you see your application flying out the window made into a paper airplane."

Nonetheless, Grumpy has heard that applications are being taken at the post office on 1st Street. "C'mon, let's go," he says to Green.

"Nah," says Green, "they won't hire us."

"C'mon homes," Grumpy persists. "Let's just try it. Let's go." He attempts to drag Green. "C'mon homes." But Green remains immovable. Finally, Grumpy sits back down with a sigh. No one goes to the post office this day.

After the homies vacate his office, Boyle stares dolefully at his checkbook. "Right now, I have a hundred dollars in the bank. And I have to pay the kids working for me on Friday." He looks up. "But, you know, it's weird. Somehow the money always shows up. It usually happens on Thursday, my day off. There'll be no money in the bank on Wednesday and then I'll come in on Friday and there'll be a couple of checks on my desk. Checks coming from nowhere when they had to come—that's happened at least 50 times since I first came here." Boyle pauses. "It's not like I think it comes from God. My spirituality doesn't really take that form. But I do feel that if the work is meant to be done, somehow there'll be a way.

"Now all I have to do is find $150,000 to give kids jobs this summer," he continues. "Invariably, the violence in the neighborhood decreases in direct proportion to how many kids are working at any given time."

With the Jobs for a Future program, Boyle usually has three or four construction and maintenance crews working on church projects. In addition, he is on the phone daily to local businesses asking them to hire homies. "We will pay their salaries," he tells the potential employers. "All you have to do is give them a place to work." Boyle adds: "Of course, it would be great if the employers would pay the salaries. But unfortunately, that rarely happens.

"The myth about gang members and jobs," says Boyle, "is how're you gonna keep 'em down on the farm when they're making money hand over fist selling drugs—the implication being that they will never want to accept an honest job. Well, I have kids stop me on the street every single day of the week asking for jobs. And a lot of times these are kids I know are slanging, which is the street term for selling crack cocaine. I always say, 'If I get you a job, it means no more slanging.' And I've never once said that to a kid who didn't jump at the chance to do an honest day's work instead of selling drugs."

Four days later it is Saint Patrick's Day, a generally uneventful Sunday until Grumpy approaches Boyle, his clothes and hands covered in paint. "Oh, I've been doing some painting at Rascal's house," he says, in answer to Boyle's questioning look. Then he screws his face into a grimace. "You know, G.," he says. "I'm not going to look for a job anymore."

Boyle's expression darkens. "Why?" he asks.

"I'm just not going to," replies Grumpy. "No more job hunting."

Boyle looks truly distressed by this news. "What are you talking about . . . ?" Boyle begins.

"Nope. I'm not looking for a job any more," is all Grumpy will say.

Boyle throws up his hands. "What the hell am I supposed to do? Support you for the rest of your life?"

Finally, Grumpy's face breaks into a gigantic grin. "I'm not going to look for a job any more BECAUSE I FOUND A JOB, G.," he shouts. "I'm a painter! I'm painting stereo speakers!"

The rest of the day, Boyle cannot restrain himself. He tells Grumpy how proud he is, over and over. Grumpy tries to stay cool but his happiness is obvious and irrepressible.

Termite is one of the regulars in and around Boyle's office. He is 16, has the huge, dark eyes of a yearling deer and a smile that unfolds fast, wide and bright. His hair is cut Marine short, shaved by Boyle with the No. 4 attachment of the church's clippers. On his upper lip there sprouts a pale hint of brown velvet. When he is happy, Termite's face is transformed into that of a deliciously mischievous child. In repose, his expression suggests someone waiting patiently for a punishment. At all times, his shoulders slump more than is natural.

Termite is a Clarence Street Loco, jumped into the gang less than a year ago. So far, his gang-banging has been confined to compulsive tagging: Walk in any direction from Dolores Mission and you soon see the spray-painted message "CSL *soy* Termite." Termite is not a kid drawn to violence. "I don't mind if you want to go head up," he says. "But it would be better if nobody had guns."

Since last summer, Termite has been pestering Boyle for a job. Finally, the priest has talked a local self-storage company into hiring two homies, courtesy of Dolores Mission. Termite and Stranger, a kid from The Mob Crew, get the call.

The timing is fortuitous. Termite's father has just gone to visit family in Mexico, and with the weight of his dad's anger briefly lifted, Termite is a new person. Instead of partying with the homies till all hours, he asks Boyle to drive him home before dark every night. He has all but stopped tagging and has started showing up at the alternative school every day.

The day before Termite and Stranger are to start work, Boyle drives them to meet their new boss, the manager of the storage company, a matter-of-fact woman named Yolanda. The boys listen quietly while she explains their duties—gofering and general cleanup. Afterward Boyle takes the two kids to McDonald's to celebrate.

"We won't let you down, G." says Termite.

One week later, events have derailed Termite's promise. On the first Sunday in April, at about 5 p.m., Boyle is driving across 1st Street, from East L.A. Dukes territory in Aliso Village toward the church. He sees a group of five Clarence kids, Grumpy and Termite among them, running in Pecan Park near the baseball diamond. It is not a playful run. Termite has a long stick under his jacket, as if he's packing a shotgun. On instinct, Boyle turns to look behind him and sees a group of East L.A. Dukes near home plate, also running. The Dukes are sworn enemies of the Clarence Street Locos.

Boyle swerves his car to a halt on the wrong side of the street, rolls down his window and yells to the Clarence kids to get the blankety-blank out of there. Amazingly they do. As he raises his hand to open his door, there is a terrifying BOOM-BOOM-BOOM-BOOM-BOOM. Just behind Boyle's head, the car's rear window on the driver's side shatters. When the shooting stops, Boyle gets out to confront the Dukes. They disappear fast as lightning.

Later, he drives back into Dukes territory. This time he finds them. "Did you want to f—kin' kill me?" he yells, hoping to shock them into a new state of consciousness. "I prayed you would hit me so then maybe it would end. I'd be willing to die to end this." The Dukes stare at him, then at the missing car window and the bullet holes in his car, one in the door frame no more than an inch from where Boyle's head had been. They murmur frantic, ineffectual apologies.

Then one boy looks up just in time to see two gangsters on the hill above them—East Coast Crips. An instant later the noise comes again: BOOM-BOOM-BOOM-BOOM-BOOM-BOOM. Everyone dives behind Boyle's car as the sky rains bullets. Miraculously, no one is hit. Instead a bullet has punctured the car's right rear tire, just missing the gas tank, and come to rest inside the trunk.

The next day, Boyle wakes up with no obvious ill effects from the near misses except for a piercing headache. The pain is localized just behind his ear, where neck meets skull. In other words, about where the door-frame bullet would have hit if it had taken only a slightly different course.

As usual, violence spawns more violence. On Monday morning, when Boyle arrives at the church, he gets a call from Yolanda, the manager of the storage facility where Termite and Stranger are working. She is going to have to fire Termite, she says. It seems that on Friday he not only crashed the facility's motorized cart, but, when he was supposed to remove graffiti from a wall, he replaced it with new inscriptions: "CSL *soy* Termite."

It does not strike Boyle as entirely coincidental that Termite's father returned from Mexico a few hours before Termite began this orgy of acting out. Nor does it help matters that the mood of the Clarence homies in general is restless. Two Clarence Street homeboys have been killed by Dukes since January, 1990, and Clarence has not yet retaliated. After yesterday's shooting, they will probably begin to feel intolerably pressed. And most of the pressure will fall on the little heads, the younger gang members like Termite who have yet to prove themselves.

Boyle takes Termite to lunch to break the bad news about the job. First he gives him a stern lecture about responsibility and consequences. Then he turns Good Cop and assures Termite that losing the job is not the end of the world. "You know I'll never give up on you," Boyle says. "*Te quiero mucho*," he says finally. "*Como si fueras mi hijo*" ("I love you as if you were my son"). At this, Termite starts to cry. Once started he cries for a long while.

At the end of the day, Termite's actions are swinging farther out of control; he gets into a fight with one of his own homies. When Boyle sees him again, he is covered in blood. "It's nothin'," he mumbles.

Then at about 2 the next afternoon, Father Smolich sees Termite deep in Dukes territory with a can of spray paint; he is crossing out Dukes graffiti and replacing it with his own. It is a dangerously provocative act, considering the events of the last two days. Smolich demands that Termite hand over the spray can. Termite dances rebelliously away.

Two hours later, Termite is back in Clarence territory, on the pay phone at the corner of Third and Pecan streets talking with his girlfriend, Joanna. He sees Li'l Diablo[2], another "new bootie" from Clarence, walking north toward 1st Street and Pecan Park, and sensing that something is up, he follows. All at once, Termite sees what is up: Li'l Diablo has a gun, and there is a group of Dukes gathered in the park. Termite watches as Li'l Diablo raises the gun, a .22, and fires one shot into the air. The Dukes scatter, running for the projects across 1st Street. Li'l Diablo drops his weapon and runs in the other direction.

At first Termite follows him. But then, on an impulse he cannot later adequately explain, Termite turns back and picks up the gun. Then he points it in the direction of the by-now faraway Dukes and empties it. Most of the bullets fall harmlessly to the pavement. However, one bullet strays into an apartment on Via Las Vegas, where a 6-year-old girl named Jackie is watching television with her mother. Jackie kicks up her small foot just in time for it to meet the bullet. Blood spurts, and her mother begins to scream.

Holding the empty gun, Termite stands on the sidewalk still as a statue for a long moment. Finally he runs.

In short order, the neighborhood is alive with rumor, and word of what has happened quickly reaches Boyle. It is hours before he finds Termite, milling nervously with some other homies a block from the church. Wordlessly, Termite climbs into Boyle's car.

"I know what happened," Boyle tells him. "Did you do it?"

There is a silence. "Yeah," Termite says without meeting Boyle's gaze.

Boyle informs him that he has hit a little girl. Termite is horrified. "A lot of people say," Boyle tells him, "that in order to be a man you have to shoot a gun. But I'm telling you that isn't true. The truth is, in order to be a man you need to take responsibility for your actions. That means you need to turn yourself in."

Termite starts to protest. Then he is quiet for a long while. "Let's go, G." he says finally.

Inside Hollenbeck Police Station, two CRASH officers order Termite to spread his legs. As the officers briskly frisk him, he stands with his lips pursed, trying not to cry.

Everyone who meets Greg Boyle seems to go through the same two-step process. Step one is as follows: "Hey, this guy is really some kind of a saint!" And then step two: "There's got to be a dark side."

Yet when you get to know Boyle well, you find no ominous recesses of the psyche or murky hidden agendas. There are small things: a healthy-size ego, or the way he at times seems more quarrelsome with the police than might be necessary. But nothing you'd call dark. What you do find, however, is a man in the grip of a paradox.

The other priests at Dolores Mission, however fond they are of the gang members, admit that they keep an emotional distance between themselves and a situation that can be overwhelming and tragic on a daily basis. For Boyle, there seems to be no distance. He cares for the gang members as if they were literally his own children. Certainly it is Boyle's offer of unconditional love that is the source of his magic. Pure love heals. But what happens if you give your heart to 10 dozen kids, many of whom will die violently and young, the rest of whom are dying slow deaths of the spirit?

"Burn-out is the cost, I think," Boyle says. "Because I'm so invested in each kid, tragedies and potential tragedies kind of get into my gut in a way they probably don't get into other folks'." He laughs nervously. "A lot of it is the classic ministerial occupational hazard of co-dependency, where you get too invested. Only it's kind of writ larger here, I think. And it's also parental. It's like, 'Oh my God, my kid hasn't come home yet and it's midnight' times a hundred."

The analogy of Boyle as parent can lead to still riskier territory. If you ask most parents what they would die for, they reply, "My children." Boyle grows uncharacteristically quiet when the question is posed to him. "I would die for these kids," he says finally. "I don't know how that would play itself out. But I don't think there would be any question. It's not a choice, you know," he says. "It just *is*."

This is not the first time Boyle has considered the possibility. The day the Dukes' gunfire hit his car and came within an inch of killing him, he realized that a line had been crossed. It was not that they had tried to kill him; it was that they had known he was in the line of fire and they had shot anyway.

Two weeks later he had another close call. Late at night, Boyle was walking one of the younger kids home when the boy whispered, "Look out." Boyle turned to see gangsters, guns at the ready, creeping along the bushes that fringe the Santa Ana Freeway on the east edge of Aliso Village. They were headed toward a group of TMC homies. But this time, seeing Boyle, no one shot.

"It was very similar to the day that the Dukes shot," Boyle says. "But that time I arrived a split second too late and the action had already been put in motion. This time I think I arrived just early enough to stop it.

"As I walked home that night I felt so weird. I kept saying to myself, 'I really think this is where my life will end. I'm going to die in this barrio.' "

He pauses, his eyes searching some interior distance. "But you know, what should I do differently? Would I not have intervened that day between Clarence and East L.A.? Just kept driving instead? I don't think that would be possible.

"So what should I do differently?"

The question hangs in the air like smoke after a fire.

Even Dukes were impressed by the fact that Termite had turned himself in. "That's *firme*! That's *firme*!" they said. But Termite's father assessed his actions differently. We could have gotten you to Mexico, he told Termite, his voice scathing. "Can't you do anything right?"

At Termite's court hearing, his fortunes take an unexpected turn. His public defender—a fast-talking, upwardly mobile fellow named Brady Sullivan—not only undermines a witness's testimony but also gets

Termite's confession thrown out on a Miranda violation. Termite is set free.

As far as Boyle is concerned, this is good news and bad news. The good news is that a sensitive kid with no prior record will not get two to five in a California Youth Authority lockup. "Termite is a wonderful, wonderful kid," Boyle says. "And he shot a little girl. A lot of people can't hold those two thoughts together. But, the task of a true human being is do precisely that."

The bad news is that Termite will not go on a badly needed, if enforced, vacation. Instead, he will be back in the neighborhood and back in the gang life.

At first, Termite is euphoric at being free. But soon, reality sets in; the Dolores Mission neighborhood is no longer a safe place for him. His mother talks about sending him to live with an aunt in San Bernardino or his grandmother in Mexico, but Termite doesn't want to go. He says he wants to be near his girlfriend Joanna, a sunny-natured girl of 14. His mother relents on the condition that Termite stay away from the church and the projects.

For two weeks straight, Termite spends his days cooped up in a darkened house with his dad, who works at night. Predictably, it isn't long before the situation blows itself to smithereens. Termite is back hanging out, staying at friends' houses, tagging everything he can find, particularly in East L.A. Dukes territory.

Word is soon on the street that Termite is a marked man. His mother has answered the phone at home and heard the death threats. "It's hard to know what to do," Boyle worries out loud. "I don't want him to feel boxed in. When that happens a kid is likely to feel that the only thing to do is to go out in a blaze of glory, or take somebody else out in a blaze of glory."

When it is mentioned to Termite that he is all but asking to be killed, he cocks his head quizzically. "Sometimes I just don't care. Sometimes I feel like I want to die," he says, then looks away, "and I don't know why."

A week later, the inevitable has happened: Termite has been shot. He was hanging out with homies from both Clarence and TMC near the corner store at Gless and 4th. A truck whizzed by and dozens of bullets were fired. Only one connected. It grazed the left side of Termite's head above his ear and blew a crater an inch-and-a-half deep and six inches in diameter in the stucco wall behind him. There was lots of blood, but no serious damage.

No one knows for sure who the shooters were—or who the intended target was. But Termite believes he knows. "I didn't tell anybody," he says, "but I was thinking while I was lying there on the ground, 'This bullet was meant for me.'"

Like the volume of a boom box turned up notch by notch, the violence around Dolores Mission grows in frequency and intensity as the days move from spring to summer and on toward fall. Grumpy gets a bullet in the stomach. Two Jobs for a Future construction workers are shot on two different nights. Thumper, from Cuatro Flats, who was out walking with his girlfriend, has his hair parted down the middle by a bullet that skimmed neatly across the top of his skull. Sniper, from TMC, is shot twice in the shoulder and once below the heart. All his wounds are through-and-throughs—the .38-caliber bullets passed straight through his body and out again. An hour and a half after he is rushed to White Memorial Hospital emergency room, Sniper is back on the street, a jacket over his bandages. "He has no insurance so they wouldn't give him any pain killers," says Boyle, "not even some Tylenol."

And yet there are bright spots. Grumpy recovers and is still employed. Green finds a job making conga drums. Scoobie makes it onto one of Boyle's construction crews, and his foreman gives him rave reviews. The morning after Critter receives his diploma from Roosevelt High School (with some help from Mission Alternative) on the stage of the Shrine Auditorium, he starts a new job at a downtown law firm. "I think maybe after a while they're going to let me do some computer work," says Critter happily. "I told 'em I got an A-plus in my last computer class."

And then there is Termite. After he was shot, he asked if he could move into Casa Miguel Pro with Grumpy. "Casa Pro is supposed to be for mothers and children," explains Boyle. "If I let Termite in it would just open the flood gates. Grumpy genuinely has no where else he can go, but if I gave a room to every kid who has an intolerable family situation I could fill up Casa Pro plus the Hilton."

In the end Boyle found a compromise. He told Termite he could sleep on the floor of his office. For a time, things seemed to settle down.

Then, a few weeks later, the shooting starts again. Boyle is at Aliso Village talking to a group of TMC homies when unidentified gangsters open fire with automatics and "gauges"—shotguns. The shooting goes on for nearly two minutes. But, as is often the case, the gangsters are bad shots and no one is seriously hurt.

The next day, Termite is picked up by the police. He had been wandering in Dukes territory, carrying a loaded .38. He pleads guilty to a carrying a concealed weapon and is given a minimum sentence—approximately six months—in a county probation department youth camp.

It is 9:55 p.m. and Boyle has finished his bicycle rounds through the projects; things are quiet and he grows contemplative. "You know," he says, "people are always asking me what I consider to be my victories. But I can never think of things that way. With these kids, all you can do is take one a day at a time. A lot of days it's two steps forward and four steps back. On other days it's like the line in Tennessee Williams' play, 'A Streetcar Named Desire': 'Sometimes there's God so quickly.' Then it's joy upon joy, grace upon grace."

Grace or none, it is clear that Boyle loves this place and the job. "You go where the life is," he says. "And the life for me is here in this parish—especially with these kids. The happiness they bring me is beyond anything I can express in words. In the truest and most absolute sense, this work is a vocation." He laughs softly. "And for good or ill I can do no other."

There is an irony here. In July, 1992, Greg Boyle will in fact "do other." A Jesuit is normally assigned to a particular post for six years, no more. The goal is detachment—it should be the work, not the person, on which redemption depends.

Next summer marks the end of Boyle's assignment as pastor of Dolores Mission. He is then expected to spend the next 12 months in prayer, study and renewal before he takes his final vows. (Jesuits wait until a man hits his middle years before final vows are offered.) "After that," says Boyle, "I'll probably be able to come back here in some capacity, maybe as director of the school." But not even this is a sure thing.

When asked what effect his departure will have on the homeboys, Boyle is quick to be reassuring. "It'll be fine. The structures are in place now—the school, the Comité Pro Paz, the Jobs for a Future program. I am by no means irreplaceable at Dolores Mission."

Maybe, and maybe not. A look into the faces of the gang members who love Boyle as they love no one else in the world makes you wonder. One thing is sure: For good or ill, by this time next year, Father Gregory Boyle will be gone.[3]

Notes

1. [Editors' note: The article was written in 1991. By the end of 1994, Father Boyle had buried his 39th gang member in this parish.]
2. The name of this gang member—and others so marked—has been changed.
3. [Editors' note: And in 1994, Father Boyle returned to continue his work with his "homies," finding jobs and burial sites.] ✦

Law Enforcement

32

Policing Gangs: Case of Contrasting Styles

David Freed

This journalistic account presents two distinctive variations in police gang suppression. The two major Los Angeles departments define gangs similarly and yet organize their gang control operations quite differently. The relative effectiveness of the two approaches has never been adequately tested, but the readings in Section II on group process suggest that several of the operational activities described may produce unintended enhancement of gang cohesiveness.

Since this article was written, the LAPD CRASH units decentralized to the station level, but plans are currently underway for partial centralization. The gang homicide annual figures in both jurisdictions continued to increase steadily through 1992.

Friday night. A darkened street in Boyle Heights. Sgt. Faryl Fletcher, a Los Angeles police gang expert, cruises by in an unmarked car as 10 Latino gang members lean against a truck.

The faces of the gang members are frozen in Fletcher's spotlight, their eyes defiant. "Damn, I'd like to jam those guys," Fletcher says.

To "jam" is Los Angeles police jargon. It means to randomly stop, frisk and question. With so large a group, Fletcher needs backup, and he radios for assistance.

But other anti-gang officers are too busy to respond. "Damn," Fletcher sighs, "I wish we could jam 'em."

Friday night. A darkened street in Lynwood. Sgt. Curtis Jackson, a Los Angeles county sheriff's gang expert, cruises by in an unmarked car as a dozen black gang members shoot dice.

Hey homeys, wuz happenin'? Jackson asks the "home boys" (gang members) on the side walk, who wave and continue gambling. Their leader promises to finish the game "in a minute." Smiling, the sergeant takes him at his word but says he'll be back in two minutes.

"These people aren't dumb," he says, pulling away. "They're street soldiers. You gotta approach 'em like that. They got thinking minds just like policemen."

The two encounters speak volumes about the sharply contrasting philosophies, tactics and effectiveness of Los Angeles County's two largest law enforcement agencies in their struggles against the epidemic of street gang violence.

For the Los Angeles Police Department, the war on gangs is led by the 145 officers of CRASH—Community Resources Against Street Hoodlums.

Its counterpart in the Sheriff's Department is the 52-member Operation Safe Streets (OSS).

But except for common adversaries—gangs and gang violence—the two elite units share little else. In their missions, their manner, their training and turnover—and their apparent success in curbing gang violence—they are vastly different.

Gang crime statistics provided by both the police and sheriff's departments show that OSS—battling twice as many gang members with only a third as many officers—has done a more effective job in fighting gang violence than its more widely known counterpart, CRASH.

The CRASH mission is "total suppression" of Los Angeles' 160 street gangs and their 12,500 members.

In pairs and strike forces, CRASH officers, two-thirds of whom work in uniform, handle virtually every gang crime in the city. They also "jam," or harass, gang members wherever they find them, at the same time collecting intelligence on gang activities.

The OSS mission is "target suppression" of the 239 gangs and 25,000 gang members in the contract cities and unincorporated areas that are in the Sheriff's Department's jurisdiction.

OSS deputies, all of whom work in plainclothes, "jam" gangs as well, but only those they target as the most criminally active. Deputies say they do not ignore non-targeted gangs, but they usually do not make a point of arresting those gang members for minor transgressions, such as curfew violations.

"We just get on the case of the bad gangs until they knock off whatever they've been doing," OSS Sgt. Curtis Jackson said.

When gangs are targeted, OSS makes arrests for significant as well as minor crimes, including loitering and even swearing in public. The strategy, sheriff's officials believe, forces otherwise violent youths to police themselves.

Gangs remain targeted until they behave themselves and are no longer a major crime problem. Then, the deputies move on to other gangs but keep an eye on those already suppressed. There are currently 92 gangs on the OSS target list.

It's like eating a big block of ice," Jackson explained. "You can't eat the entire block at once, but you can chip off pieces of it and eat the whole thing eventually. That's what we're trying to do with gangs."

The strategy may be working. In 1979, OSS' first year of operation, the Sheriff's Department recorded 92 gang-related homicides. The Police Department had 115.

By 1985, the Sheriff's Department reported that its gang-related homicides had plummeted to 57—a drop of 38 percent—even though its jurisdiction had grown to include several additional contract cities where gangs are found. During the same period, the number of gang killings in the city of Los Angeles climbed slightly to 120.

A similar trend was seen in other categories of gang violence, particularly felony assaults. In 1979, there were 1,608 such assaults in the sheriff's jurisdiction, compared to 1,070 in the city. But by 1984, the sheriff's gang felony assaults had fallen 13 percent to 1,402; the Police Department's had climbed 44 percent to 1,548.

Both sheriff's and police officials acknowledge that the criteria used by each agency to define and report gang crime are virtually the same.

Overall gang violence has increased in both sheriff's and police jurisdictions over the last five years, but the comparative growth has been much slower under OSS.

In 1979, the Sheriff's Department logged 2,781 major, gang-related crimes, far exceeding the Police Department's 2,088, but in 1984 the OSS tally was 3,872 such crimes compared to CRASH's 3,985.

"That's not to say that their program doesn't work and ours does," observed Sheriff's Lt. Alan Chancellor, who heads OSS. "I just think that ours works a little better."

Police officials defend CRASH as having "held the line" against gang crime but conceded that major changes are being considered. Chief Daryl F. Gates is expected to take under review this month a long-range study on how to combat gangs.

"We've seen a 25 percent growth in the number of gang members and street gangs in the last five years, but we really haven't appreciably changed our deployment," said the Police Department's top anti-gang officer, Cmdr. Lorne C. (Larry) Kramer.

One proposal included in the study is to base CRASH officers at 12 station houses, rather than at three large bureaus in South, West and Central Los Angeles, as they are now, Kramer said.

The decentralization proposal would force regular patrol officers to become more involved in the fight against gangs, a responsibility that many street cops have "abdicated" since CRASH emerged in the late 1970s, Kramer said.

Further, Kramer acknowledged that last year CRASH adopted the OSS tactic of targeting particularly violent gangs. The Police Department, he said, also began sending patrol officers to an eight-hour gang awareness school at the Police Academy to remind them that policing gangs should not be left exclusively to CRASH.

"We don't have the resources for CRASH units to handle all gang crimes," Kramer said. ". . . Until we have the resolve of everybody, including the community, we're just going to continue to flounder."

Asked why the Sheriff's department has statistically outperformed the Police Department in slowing the rise of gang violence, Kramer replied:

"I don't know, but if there is an answer, it may be because the sheriff doesn't have the challenge of a highly concentrated, demographic urban area. The gang members we're talking about are confined to a much smaller space, which gives rise to more hostilities and more rivals between opposing gangs."

But police supervisors closer to the street and sheriff's deputies say that demographic differences between the two agencies' jurisdictions and the gangs themselves are not significant enough to explain so wide a statistical disparity.

'Same Kinds of Gangs'

"Basically, we're still talking the same kinds of street gangs . . . in the city and the county," said Lt. Robert P. Ruchhoft of the Police Department's 26-officer Gang Activities Section, which monitors CRASH and gangs throughout the city from police headquarters downtown.

"Maybe [OSS] is doing something we're not," he said.

Besides the contrasting gang-suppression tactics, OSS deputies say another difference may be OSS' emphasis on developing rapport with street sources—from gang members themselves to their mothers. Those sources, they say, frequently provide intelligence that can be used to help thwart violence before it occurs.

"A regular officer wearing his uniform and driving around in a black and white [patrol car] looks pretty formidable and is not really all that approachable," OSS' Sgt. Jackson said.

"We drive unmarked cars and wear [green-colored sheriff's] jackets. The 'gangbangers' know us, and we know them. They'll talk to us while they might not talk to a uniformed guy," he said.

During a recent ride-along in Lynwood, Jackson stopped regularly to talk and joke with gang members as well as other street sources. Some came out of their houses to lean into his car window and visit.

At one point, the deputy drove to the home of a teen-ager at the request of the youth's mother and spent 15 minutes counseling him about the dangers of gang involvement.

In contrast, on two nighttime patrols in Central and South Los Angeles, CRASH sergeants did not stop once to talk to gang members or others on the street, except at crime scenes, a *Times* reporter observed.

When CRASH officers did meet gang members, the atmosphere was confrontational, the dialogue hostile. Their contact with the gangs is rarely positive, officers say.

"We've found that being friendly with these guys just doesn't work," said Sgt. Thomas C. Jones, a three-year CRASH veteran who patrols in Watts.

Few gang members are deterred by anything but direct confrontation, he said and that requires "jamming" gangs to remind them that "they don't rule the streets."

While CRASH officers may not be hostile to each youth they stop, Los Angeles gang members say there is often a definite difference in the way they are treated by police and sheriff's specialists.

"The sheriff understands where you're coming from; he'll treat you like a man," said one gang leader from South Los Angeles. "They don't call you 'little punk' this and 'little punk' that, like the cops do. The sheriff'll kick your ass, but you gotta provoke him."

Gang leaders complain that they have seen CRASH patrol cars cruise through their neighborhoods flying ribbons or pennants in the colors of rival gangs to taunt them.

What's more, gang leaders say members have been picked up by CRASH officers and deposited dangerously deep inside rival gang territory.

"That's nonsense," CRASH Sgt. Jones said. "We're too busy to play games."

Others familiar with CRASH believe that officers often prejudge all gang members—or those they believe to be gang members. Consequently, many CRASH officers have alienated themselves from street sources whose information could help prevent violence, critics charge.

"The impression you're left with when you see [CRASH officers] out there is that they look at every kid as problematic," said Ruben R. Rodriguez, a Latino activist in the San Fernando Valley who has counseled gang members. "Under the police's system, it's impossible to build rapport between the two sides."

Still, CRASH supporters say that the unit is as effective as it can be given its resources.

"They're not a juvenile division; they're not out there to improve the quality of life," said Councilman Robert Farrell, whose district in South Los Angeles is considered a gang hot spot. "The workload is so high, unfortunately, that they have to spend all of their time knocking down crap."

Until the late 1970s, the Police Department had no formal gang unit, although a handful of officers had educated themselves on the gangs that have existed in Latino neighborhoods since the 1940s.

In 1977, with black gangs emerging as a formidable criminal element and Latino gangs continuing to pose problems, department administrators received a one-year federal grant for a special 44-man unit to concentrate on neighborhoods where gang crime was heaviest.

Based at the Hollenbeck Division in East Los Angeles, the unit was dubbed Total Resources Against Street Hoodlums (TRASH), but civic leaders thought the acronym disparaging. The word "community" was substituted. CRASH was judged a success and the city took over funding in 1979.

As gang violence escalated in Los Angeles—major crimes more than doubled from 2,088 in 1979 to 5,158 in 1981—CRASH evolved as the department's primary gang enforcement unit.

"The mutual purpose and intention of CRASH was to target specific hard-core gangs," Kramer noted. "I think that over a period of time, because of the mushrooming of gangs and gang members, CRASH was put in a position of having to deal with the much larger, overall problem."

Concept Emerges in 1976

The concept behind the sheriff's OSS unit emerged in 1976 when Sgt. Jackson, then assigned to the Firestone station in South-Central Los Angeles, proposed that deputies there focus all of their attention on one particularly violent gang. The result was impressive, according to sheriff's officials: gang-related crime statistics dropped 50 percent in six months in Firestone's patrol area.

After a one-year federal grant, OSS received county funding in 1979, and teams of deputies were assigned to sheriff's stations in East Los Angeles, Firestone, Lennox, Lynwood and Pico Rivera. OSS teams now are based at four additional stations—Carson, Industry, Lakewood and Norwalk—as well as the county's Central Jail.

"By conserving our resources and directing them to the most highly active, most violent gangs, we can have a direct impact," OSS' Chancellor said. "If we took our same resources and directed them at all 239 gangs, we would be largely ineffectual. Massive uniform suppression is not a panacea to the problem; it is only a stopgap solution."

Yet that, essentially, is what CRASH has been forced to do because of the growth of gang violence, Kramer said. As a result, the unit has been spread thin, he and others believe.

A year ago, after Gates named him the department's top anti-gang officer, Kramer wrote to the Chicago Police Department for suggestions on how to best handle gangs. Chicago, whose 345-officer gang unit is the largest in the country, utilizes both uniform and plainclothes "gang crime specialists" to gather intelligence on that city's 10,000 gang members. The unit also relies on uniformed "tactical officers" who patrol in marked cars and are assigned "directed missions"—covering specific areas of Chicago where gang members are known to congregate.

But despite its size and strategies, Chicago's gang unit could offer little help, according to Chicago's anti-gang commander, Edward C. Pleines, who responded to Kramer's letter.

In 1984, Chicago recorded 3,839 gang-related crimes, including 72 murders.

'Not Going Anywhere'

"We're not going anywhere," Pleines lamented in a recent telephone interview. ". . . There's no one button you can push that's going to eliminate [gang violence]."

In other cities, particularly New York and Philadelphia, gang membership and crime statistics have declined in recent years—but not by employing specialized police units to crush gang activity.

Instead, after studying the effectiveness of high-profile, CRASH-type enforcement, officials in those cities have put their emphasis on counseling programs.

"We spend a lot of time talking to the kids, and it has a big deterrent [effect] here," said Sgt. John Galea who heads the New York City Police Department's gang intelligence unit and has compared notes with Los Angeles police gang specialists.

"In L.A., I don't think there's a dialogue. The kids out there don't have anyone to talk to," he said.

When there is dialogue between CRASH officers and gang members, it is most likely after the gang members have been stopped and frisked. It is rarely a situation conducive to building rapport. Gang members are questioned about their gangs or others. Their answers are carefully noted, and their pictures are often taken.

'Don't Need Pictures'

The information gleaned in such field interviews finds its way into files so extensive that gang members can later be identified by their nicknames and their cars. Even photographs of their tattoos are filed, cross-referenced by body parts.

OSS also maintains thousands of mug shots of gang members taken not in the field, but in jail bookings. Deputies say they rely less on the photographs than on their street acumen.

"We don't need pictures to know who the gang members are," OSS Chancellor said.

Others would agree.

"The sheriff's people seemed better organized with a better grasp of the overall situation," said Deputy Dist. Atty. Fred Horn, who spent five years heading the district attorney's Hard Core Gang Division.

"[CRASH] did have some pretty good guys with a good understanding of the gang and where to find them," he said. "But unfortunately, they usually got promoted and transferred; then they'd bring in a new guy with no real gang experience."

GANG-RELATED CRIME
Los Angeles City and County, 1978-1984

	Homicides		Attempted Homicides		Felony Assaults		Armed Robberies		Total Gang-Related Major Crimes*	
	LAPD	Sheriff	**LAPD**	Sheriff	**LAPD**	Sheriff	**LAPD**	Sheriff	**LAPD**	Sheriff
1984	**119**	60	**236**	93	**1,548**	1,402	**1,836**	1,772	**3,985**	3,872
1983	**123**	57	**253**	72	**1,438**	1,431	**2,343**	1,858	**4,481**	3,988
1982	**103**	54	**326**	45	**1,697**	1,372	**2,655**	1,513	**5,175**	3,526
1981	**167**	64	**353**	63	**1,982**	1,607	**2,243**	1,408	**5,158**	3,894
1980	**192**	90	**420**	NA+	**1,825**	1,865	**1,145**	1,006	**3,952**	3,398
1979	**115**	92	**293**	NA+	**1,070**	1,608	**354**	676	**2,088**	2,781
1978	**92**	60	**281**	NA+	**849**	1,245	**255**	452	**1,682**	2,068

* includes homicides, attempted homicides, felony asssaults, battery on a police officer, rape, kidnap, robbery, arson and shooting at inhabited dwelling.

+ included under category—felony assaults—for years 1978, 1979, and 1980

While CRASH officers receive no formal gang training after being chosen for the unit, a new OSS deputy will spend 40 hours in class studying gangs. He later attends another 40-hour seminar on techniques of investigating juvenile crimes.

OSS has little turnover.

"Our people usually stay several years because they like it and because it takes that long to develop expertise," Jackson said. "We don't have very many vacancies."

In comparison, tours of duty in CRASH lasting less than two years are not uncommon. It is an assignment from which talented officers are often promoted and transferred swiftly.

Ruchhoft of the Police Department's Gang Activities Section said he believes that new officers bring to CRASH "fresh blood and fresh ideas." Familiarity with the streets, he said, is not sacrificed nor are street sources developed by CRASH officers who transfer from the unit.

"Any officer who can develop informants can pass them on to new guys," Ruchhoft said. Nonetheless, many residents who live in gang areas say they are hesitant to trust officers whom they've never seen before.

'Good Thing Going'

"We had a good thing going for a while with two CRASHers a couple of years ago," said Leon Watkins who runs an inner-city mission on South Vermont Avenue. "Those two officers got close with the gang members. Both sides knew each other. They got the gangs to paint buildings, and the officers came down on their off-duty time and helped. It showed what could be done with the proper people. . .

"Then they got transferred. I don't even know the officers out there now."

Ruchhoft said CRASH officers should be routinely transferred every three years because "there's a tendency after a while for a guy to sit back and rest on his expertise."

"You're gonna get all the [gang] expertise you need in six months anyway; anything else is gravy," Ruchhoft said.

OSS deputies scoff at that assertion.

"When it comes to gangs, knowing the players is everything," Jackson said. "You have to be out there talking to them, building your network of snitches. Six months isn't enough."

Police Agencies With Anti-Gang Units

	Officers in Anti-Gang Activities	Size of Police Department	No. of Gang Members in Department's Area	No. of Gangs in Respective Area
Chicago	345	12,000	10,000	110
LAPD	201	7,000	12,500	160
New York City	75	25,000	2,202	66
LA Sheriff	50	6,200	25,000	239
San Jose	11	1,000	125	5
San Diego	10	1,400	1,200	24
Phoenix	7	1,748	2,700	28
San Francisco	6	1,991	750	5

33

The Tri-Agency Resource Gang Enforcement Team: A Selective Approach To Reduce Gang Crime

Douglas R. Kent and Peggy Smith

Kent and Smith describe another Southern California city's approach to gang control—an all-out suppression program that emphasizes selective targeting of gang leaders and hardcore recidivists by focussing and coordinating police, probation, and prosecution resources. An evaluation after the second year of implementation found programmatic success in the arrest and conviction of a high proportion of the targeted gang members, and a reduction in serious gang-related crime. The possible displacement of gang activity into neighboring jurisdictions or changes in the type of criminal activity engaged in by gang members was not addressed by the evaluation, but the preliminary results suggest that focussed efforts of this type can produce positive effects in smaller gang cities.

Introduction

The City of Westminster's gang crime intervention program is an innovative multi-agency approach to fighting gang-related crime. It places the staff of the City Police Department, County Probation Department and the District Attorney's office together in the same location at the police facility, to focus on a very select group of gang leaders and recidivist criminals. This model is intended to maximize communication and coordination among the different agencies and to amplify their ability to suppress gang activity.

The program's design is particularly innovative because of its systemic approach to gang violence and the justice system's response to it. Rather than simply focusing on the policing issues involved, the City of Westminster is addressing enforcement, case preparation, witness support, prosecution, and sentencing disposition. This intervention consists of intensive investigation, vertical prosecution, or probation supervision efforts by experts in the field of gang crime using new legal tools available to them.

The program was implemented in January, 1992 after the Westminster Police Department, the Orange County Probation Department and the Orange County District Attorney's office entered into a Memorandum of Understanding establishing an interagency program. The goal of the Tri-Agency Resource Gang Enforcement Team (TARGET) program is to increase the flow of intelligence information between cooperating agencies, and to ensure a well-coordinated effort aimed at decreasing violent gang crimes.

The cooperative agreement between these discrete criminal justice agencies established a research committee for purposes of evaluating program effectiveness and providing feedback on program operations. All cooperating agencies are represented on the research committee which has met regularly to develop the research plan, review data collection strategies and assist in evaluating research information.

This chapter contains portions of a department report describing the organization and activities of the program and which documents evidence of its success. This chapter will: (1) describe the mission and goals of the program; (2) provide an overall description of how the program works; (3) describe the activities of its operational components; and (4) describe the impact observed on gang-related crime in the community.

TARGET Mission and Key Concepts

Mission and Goals

The TARGET program mission statement is to reduce gang-related criminal activity by: 1) Removing selected hardcore target subjects that impact the City of Westminster; (2) Gathering intelligence information on gangs as well as individual gang members for use in criminal investigations and trial preparation; (3) Developing innovative techniques toward controlling gangs; (4) Developing personnel expertise in detecting and analyzing gang crime; and (5) Documenting the effectiveness of program efforts.

The prevention of future criminal activity of selected hardcore target subjects is to be accomplished by keeping them in custody. The purpose of the TARGET team is to develop target subject selection criteria, share relevant information with other agencies and follow-up with intensified investigation, probation supervision, and prosecutorial efforts. Intelligence information is shared with other agencies, for investigative as well as training purposes. Networking and interfacing with other departmental bureaus, as well as refining information storage and retrieval systems improves the use of gang intelligence information. Innovative techniques toward gang control are explored, including utilization of Street Terrorism Enforcement and Prevention (STEP) Act laws, use of

Reprinted from the report of the Westminster (California) Police Department, 1994.

civil law in addition to criminal law to fight gang crime, as well as the increased awareness of criminal gang activity on the part of patrol officers. Finally, interest in identifying the effect of the program on crime in the City is of central importance to the program.

The research committee identified the following operational program goals: (1) Vigorous arrests of identified target subjects; (2) Effective prosecution and conviction of target subjects; (3) Vigilant supervision of target subject probationers; (4) Expanded intelligence and information-sharing between cooperating agencies; (5) Development and implementation of innovative crime-reduction tools; and (6) A reduction in gang-related crime from the baseline year, 1991 to first year of full operation, 1993. Each of these outcomes is addressed in later sections of this report.

Two Key Concepts

The TARGET model is based upon two key concepts: (1) Selective intervention: efficient deployment of resources directed at incarcerating gang leadership and the most chronic recidivists; and (2) Multiple-agency cooperation: the use of a focused, coordinated team representing three levels of the criminal justice system, whose members are able to maximize the efforts of all other members.

Selective Intervention. Given limited resources, law enforcement agencies are increasingly faced with the task of searching for ways to maximize impact on public safety. There is evidence that suggests that a small proportion of recidivist criminals account for a disproportionally large share of crime. Sociological studies of two birth cohorts have reported that a small percent of repeat offenders were responsible for a disproportionate share of crime (Wolfgang, Figlio & Sellin, 1972; Wolfgang, 1983). For example, Wolfgang et al. (1972) found that 18% of juveniles who had committed at least one crime were responsible for 52% of crime committed by that cohort.

Some studies have suggested that a selective intervention approach, focusing law enforcement efforts on individuals predicted to commit serious crimes frequently in the future, may be promising for reducing crime. The Repeat Offender Project, a specialized police unit in Washington, D.C. was organized to investigate and prosecute crimes committed by individuals believed to have been committing five or more felony offenses per week. An evaluation study yielded evidence of success, and concluded that selective apprehension units provide a promising strategy for major urban police departments (Martin & Sherman, 1986). However, the utilization of selective intervention approaches have been shown to be difficult. Such difficulties have been articulated well by Struckhoff (1987). Further, concerns that disadvantaged groups might be more likely to be designated as high rate offenders have been expressed (Decker & Salert, 1987).

The concept of selective intervention was employed in the design of the TARGET program. Criminal histories and law enforcement intelligence information were used to select hardcore recidivists and gang leaders. The program then directed its multiagency coordinated efforts toward this relatively small percentage of chronic offenders. These chronic offenders were individuals who were expected to account for a disproportionate share of gang crime in the community. Thus, placing these offenders in custody was expected to result in a reduction of gang crime in the community.

Multiple-Agency Cooperation. Program personnel, when operating as a team, fall under the general direction of the Detective Bureau Lieutenant and include: (1) a Police Department component (one sergeant and two police investigators); (2) a Probation Department component (one full time and one part time Deputy Probation Officers); (3) a prosecution component (one senior Deputy District Attorney and a District Attorney's Investigator); and (4) support staff (one Police Service Officer, one Special Service Clerk, and a part-time intern).

The prosecutor and probation officer are relocated from county facilities several miles away to the police department where they share an office with police investigators and support staff. Each team member interacts face-to-face with the others on a regular and ongoing basis. Because each is aware of the daily activities of other team members, coordinated action is greatly facilitated.

This approach essentially combines each of the justice system components into a single unit located at the front end of the criminal justice system. Team members select habitual offenders or gang leaders for vigorous surveillance and prosecution. When a crime is committed, however small, the defendant and the case undergo intensive investigation and prosecution for the most serious charges possible. The prosecutor and probation officer are able to direct their full attention to offenders affecting the City of Westminster. The prosecutor is able to give his maximum effort to each new offense, no matter how minor. The probation officer is able to give each new charge a heightened level of attention as well. When convicted, target subjects are either incarcerated or placed on probation under rigorous, gang-terms conditions. These conditions are then vigorously enforced by TARGET team probation officers.

Information-sharing with other agencies has proven to be tremendously useful in many criminal investigations. Internal information-sharing efforts include information bulletins and training for patrol officers. Team members have also become resource persons on the criminal activities of gangs, not only within the department, but also across agency and jurisdictional lines. Team members have presented gang suppression information at two conferences, the California Gang Investigators Conference and the Association of Criminal Justice Research. Furthermore, gang intelligence information furnished by the team has assisted other agencies in clearing gang-related crimes in many communities in the region.

The Target Model

The TARGET model uses intelligence-gathering and information-sharing to assist in the identification and appropriate selection of individuals and gangs for multi-agency intervention. Selection of specific hardcore gang members and intervention in their criminal activities should have an impact on future crime rates.

The first task of program implementation was to identify all gang members having contact with police officers in the City of Westminster. Prior to program implementation, there was no centralized database on known gang members. Because the program relies on selective identification of gang members, according to specified legal criteria, an early task of the implementation year was to establish central record-keeping on known gang members. All three agencies participated cooperatively in this process, and by December, 1993, had identified 2,158 known gang members having contact with Westminster Police Department over the past five years.

Of these gang members, information on individuals who are verifiable gang members is entered into the county-wide information database called the General Reporting Evaluation And Tracking (GREAT) System. Since 1990, 647 individuals have been verified by Westminster law enforcement officers as meeting GREAT gang membership verification criteria. A description of these 647 verified gang members and selection criteria are provided in the following section. From this group of 647 individuals, either individuals or the entire membership of a gang is targeted for program intervention. Figure 1 describes how the program intervention on selected gang members is expected to impact gang-related crime in the community.

Targeting Individual Gang Members

From this population of 647 verified gang members, individual target subjects are selected (77 by the end of 1993), then monitored for new criminal activity. . . . When a violation occurs, the incident is subject to intensified investigation by program detectives. When arrests are made, target subjects, as well as co-defendants, face vertical prosecution, enhanced penalties under a criminal law statutory scheme directed toward street gang activity and aggressive probation supervision. Thus, the prosecutor and probation officer join police on the front end of the criminal justice system—they are often integrally involved in developing case strategies before an arrest occurs.

Police detectives provide surveillance of identified gang members, investigate most gang-related crimes, maintain gang intelligence files, identify subjects to be targeted, and conduct probation searches with the deputy probation officer (DPO). The DPO provides intensive supervision of a caseload of hardcore gang members who have special "gang terms" (non-association with other gang members) of probation, authorizes probation searches, provides surveillance of known gang hangouts and provides needed information regarding probationer gang members.

Both police detectives and the DPO work with the Deputy District Attorney (DDA) and DA Investigator in gathering evidence for prosecution of probation violations and/or additional crimes committed. The intelligence information obtained on the gang membership serves an additional function as evidence in seeking enhanced sentencing under the STEP Act. The district attorney focuses efforts solely on the City of Westminster's target subject and other gang-related cases. He provides vertical prosecution (handling the case from filing to sentencing), enhances search warrant capabilities, and provides aggressive prosecution of probation violators. The DA investigator assists in trial preparation and witness management and protection.

Further, gang members may be legally served with a notice (although not required) informing individual gang members of the criminal nature of the member's gang and of the penal consequences for continued participation in the gang. The STEP Act involves a comprehensive series of laws and procedures dealing with criminal street gangs. It makes active participation in a criminal street gang a crime and adds additional sentence time to certain gang-related

Figure 1
Components Model of the Tri-Agency Resource Gang Enforcement Program

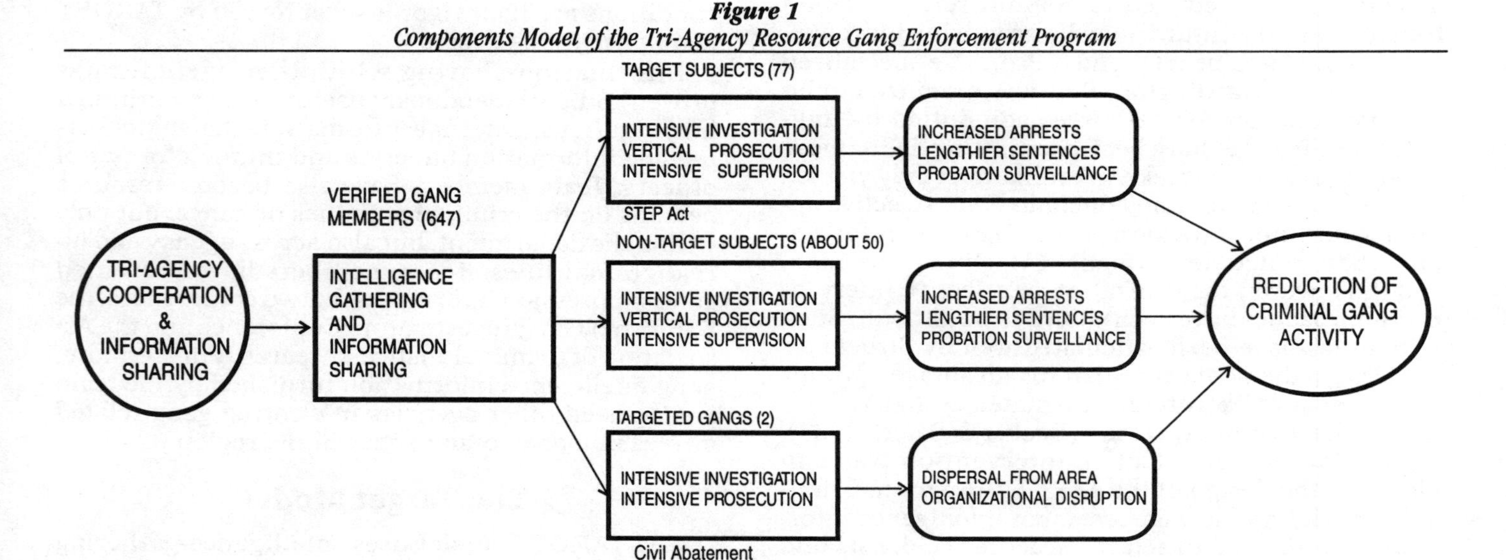

felonies. Meeting the various STEP Act gang membership verification criteria requires substantial documentation on gang membership and activity in a specific geographic area.

Non-Target Subjects

Individuals who associate with target subjects and participate in crimes committed by target subjects often become part of the case prosecuted by the TARGET DDA. When non-target subjects (about 50 by the end of 1993) are co-defendants or are believed to be involved in the criminal activities of a target subject, they too receive heightened attention by the TARGET team. On occasion, when the seriousness of a case warrants intensive service, other gang-related cases are investigated and prosecuted by the TARGET team.

Targeting The Entire Membership of a Gang

In addition to targeting specific individuals committing gang-related crimes, attention has also been focused on the entire membership of certain gangs. Target team detectives identify the group to be targeted and gather legal evidence of its impact on the community. This requires very specific and detailed information on each member in the gang and proof of gang affiliation. An innovative legal tool is now being used to suppress the activity of an entire gang. Under a process known as civil abatement, the entire membership of a gang is sued in civil court to abate an area of the city in which they engage in criminal activity.

The TARGET team DDA, in association with the City Attorney, sue the entire gang to abate a specified geographic area. Gang members are then served with a court order that prohibits members from associating with each other in a specified area of the community. This prohibition of association with other gang members disrupts the basic enabling mechanism of gang activity—group behavior. Violation of the court abatement order is punishable as criminal contempt of court. A major advantage of the civil abatement process is that any patrol officer (not just TARGET team detectives) can arrest an individual gang member for violating the court order.

An additional strategy used in intensive prosecution of criminal gang activity is the use of multiple-site search warrants. These warrants are becoming an important part of gang crime investigation because of the group context in which the crimes occur. Court orders are sought for multiple-sites because weapons, ammunition, and evidence are often shared among the group's membership. Multiple-site search warrants require much greater expertise in preparation than single-site warrants. When a serious gang-related crime is being investigated, multiple residential searches send a strong message to suspects that the crime committed is being vigorously pursued.

Program Outcomes

In the case of targeted individuals, arrests, lengthy sentences, and probation violations are expected. Each of these outcomes is expected to result in physical restrictions, either through incarceration and/or parole or probation restrictions. When the entire membership of a gang is targeted, dispersal from the area and organizational disruption is expected. By focusing enforcement efforts on a small number of selected target subjects and selected gangs, the program is expected to reduce a disproportionately large share of gang-related crime in the community.

Two years of program implementation and operation have produced significant progress in identifying and addressing the gang-related crime problem in the city of Westminster. To date, the program has accomplished the following:

- Identified and documented 2,158 gang members having contact with Police Officers in Westminster over the past five years.
- Identified and verified 647 individual gang members since 1990.
- Identified 95 gangs having two or more contacts with police in Westminster since 1992. Of these, members of 59 gangs were interviewed two or more times by police.
- Targeted 77 verified gang members for intensive investigation, probation supervision and prosecution. Of the 77 (12% of 647 verified gang members) subjects targeted for the high probability of their future involvement in crime, 53 (69%) are now in custody.
- Documented a 62% decrease in serious gang-related crime occurring in the same period that 53 (8% of 647 verified gang members) had been placed in custody.
- Found that 71% of victims of violent crimes committed by Westminster's hardcore gang members are innocent civilians.
- Initiated civil abatement procedures against two highly active gangs.
- Provided expertise in investigations, search warrants and prosecutions to criminal justice professionals in other agencies and jurisdictions.
- Supervised an average caseload of 52 probationers regarded as hardcore gang members.
- Prosecuted 145 cases involving 168 gang member defendants and achieved a 99% conviction rate since the program was implemented.
- Improved abilities to quantify unit operations and conducted statistical analyses of data on verified gang members.

The TARGET program has established procedures for documenting the criminal activities of gang members contacted by police, and developed computerized databases for storing essential subject characteristics and crime data. The ability to systematically identify and track gang-related criminal activity is a major advance over previous record-keeping procedures. The multi-agency team hasdemonstrated a significant impact on target subjects' ability to commit crime and the amount of gang-related crime in Westminster. Future indications of program effectiveness will focus on maintaining current low levels of gang-related crime. With only one year of full operation the TARGET program has demonstrated its ability to impact the criminal activity of street gangs in the City of Westminster.

References

Decker, S. H. & Salert, B. (1987). Selective incapacitation: A note on its impact on minorities. *Journal of Criminal Justice*, 15, pp. 287-299.

Martin, S. E. & Sherman, L. W. (1986). Selective apprehension: A police strategy for repeat offenders. *Criminology*, 24, pp. 155-173.

Struckhoff, D. R. (1987). Selective incapacitation: good theory, bad practice. *Corrections Today*, 49, p. 30.

Wolfgang, M.E. (1983). Delinquency in two birth cohorts. *American Behavioral Scientist*, 27, 75-86.

Wolfgang, M.E., Figlio, R.M., & Sellin, T. (1972). *Delinquency in a birth cohort*. Chicago: University of Chicago Press. ✦

Community Policing: An Approach to Youth Gangs in a Medium-Sized City

Jim Weston

This brief article describes an approach to gang policing that contrasts markedly with the first two pieces in this section. While sharing the element of selective targeting with the Westminster program, the community policing strategy adopted in Reno focuses upon engaging less committed gang members in intervention programs, community awareness about gangs, and community collaboration in law enforcement operation and policy. Working with the media to report more accurately and better inform the public about gang matters is another distinctive feature of this approach. This is one variation of the community mobilization strategy described by Spergel and Curry in the previous section.

Reno, Nevada, a tourist destination city of 135,000, serves a daily visitor population of 50,000 to 60,000. Its 315 sworn officers patrol 50 square miles, including several isolated geographical islands of the city. The 24-hour per day gaming and tourism industry draws a large number of transient, low-income service employees posing unique policing problems, such as a calls-for-service workload that frequently remains just as active on the late night shift as on the evening shift.

In 1986, after a series of violent crimes—including the gang rape of a 12-year-old girl—public outrage and demand for action prompted the Reno Police Department to form a gang unit, which was charged with developing a plan to gather gang intelligence information, adopt a zero-tolerance enforcement program targeted at gang members and educate the public concerning the dangers of youth gangs in the community.

Youths belonging to, or associated with, gangs were subject to constant scrutiny and arrest for a variety of violations. Drug sales activity being conducted by a black gang in a local park resulted in massive arrests and several violent confrontations between police and neighborhood youths. Although gang officers and detectives produced a high clearance rate for violent gang-motivated crime, gang membership continued to grow even as confrontations between police and neighborhood youths increased. Increased media attention to each gang incident fueled a public paranoia about the influence of gangs, although gang-motivated crime accounted for only a fraction of the violent crime in the city.

During this time, a survey revealed that 60 percent of Reno residents thought the police were not doing a good job and considered most officers to be "isolated and non-caring." The media portrayed the department as heavy-handed in its operations, and openly challenged the chief. The department had also suffered from 10 years of staff reductions coupled with increased workload, during which time two attempts to pass a ballot initiative to hire more officers were rejected by disgruntled voters.

Seeing a need for major change, then-Police Chief Robert Bradshaw embarked on a department-wide transformation to a community policing philosophy called "COP+." The "+" stood for a quality assurance bureau, which was charged with conducting continuing public surveys to assess the department's performance and obtain public feedback concerning its operations. Captains formed neighborhood advisory groups (NAGs) to provide them with feedback about the department. The department's command structure was flattened out, and operations were decentralized to allow supervisors and commanders the ability to deal with neighborhood problems more effectively.

The department leadership instituted radical changes in the way officers went about their business in every section of the department, from traffic services to animal control to employee training. One change resulted in the abandonment of the enforcement-oriented war against gangs philosophy in favor of a new Community Action Team (CAT) designed to work with the community to address a wide range of youth gang issues.

Community Action Team (CAT)

Community policing normally means that the community is included as a partner with police in dealing with community issues, allocation of resources and problem solving. The Reno Police Department carried this philosophy a step further, designing the new CAT team with guidance from members of the local minority neighborhoods, community service agencies and political leaders. A general order defining what comprised a gang and the manner in which police would collect intelligence was developed with considerable public input.

The result was a decision not to wage a war against gangs, but to create a highly specialized team of officers to target the top 5 percent of violent gang members with a repeat offender program. At the same time, the team would assume responsibility for coordinating efforts to address the 80 percent of local gang members who were not involved in criminal activity and not considered to be "hard core." The minority community and police agreed that any effort to totally eliminate gangs would experience the same failure as the war against drugs. It was acknowledged that youth gangs fill a need in the lives of disadvantaged or neglected youth and that outlawing gang membership would simply worsen the problem.

Ten officers and two detectives were initially assigned to CAT; the team was subsequently expanded to include a drug dog handler and a Hispanic liaison officer. CAT team activities encompassed the following areas.

Intelligence Gathering

To lessen the tension between gang members and the police during field contacts, CAT team officers received cultural sensitivity training and were provided with "gang kits" consisting of cameras, field interview cards and tape recorders. A passive gang member identification technique was developed that encouraged local gang members to allow their photographs to be taken and to provide gang affiliation, addresses and other personal data.

Additionally, an officer regularly visits the regional jail to interview incarcerated gang members. The goal is not to obtain information about the specific case for which these gang members were arrested, but to obtain current gang intelligence information. Automated gang moniker files were developed that allow field officers with laptop computers to enter partial information about suspects involved in gang-motivated crime and have this information matched with specific gangs. This data base has resulted in the quick resolution of many violent crimes.

While many agencies have developed similar intelligence systems, Reno has taken the additional step of requiring names to be purged from the files for such reasons as a period of inactivity, no contact with police or—under certain circumstances—a personal request. The minority community in Reno felt that this purge system was very important, since it helps to prevent gang members from being labeled for life and provides a more realistic tally of current gang membership.

To minimize the negative perception of police held by many minorities during traffic stops or field contacts, a brochure titled, "What To Do When Stopped by Police," was prepared and distributed throughout the community. Developed with the assistance of the county Legal Aid Society, the brochure provides information as to what procedures police follow on traffic stops, as well as advice concerning rights of citizens who are contacted by police.

Since the program began, thousands of field contacts with gang members have been made without generating one formal complaint of harassment or heavyhandedness.

Repeat Offender Targeting

A core group of CAT officers was assigned to target the most violent gang members, as well as those involved in weapons violations. As with most crimes, officers found that the vast majority of gang-motivated crime in Reno was committed by 10 to 15 percent of the city's gang members.

In 1992, the FBI and five local law enforcement agencies created a Violent Crime Task Force to target the top 1 percent of gang members responsible for the most serious crimes. Again, the minority community was consulted during the formation process, and periodic meetings have continued with the group to discuss its progress. The Repeat Offender Program was designed specifically to avoid the perception that gang membership was a primary criterion for enforcement.

In conjunction with the targeting efforts, efforts by the state legislature to criminalize membership in youth gangs and outlaw youth gangs engaged in criminal activity were opposed by both the police department and the community, who agreed that these measures would have created an unenforceable and unwinnable situation for the police. Such legislation also would have done little to deal with the real issues underlying youth gang violence.

Community Awareness

The CAT team was designed to allow its officers to be free of the regular calls-for-service work load, which in turn allowed them time to deal directly with the families of many younger gang members or "wannabes." For example, officers encountering a gang member painting graffiti or participating in minor crimes were able to take the child home and speak directly to the parents concerning the offense. Literature and counseling referral services were provided for families who normally only heard the child's side of stories involving the police.

Officers developed relationships with many families, who in turn became invaluable sources of intelligence information concerning the worst offenders in neighborhood gangs. As a result, when major gang crimes occurred, neighborhood residents would usually support the department's efforts to deal with the problem. For example, one father of a Hispanic gang member wanted for a stabbing during a neighborhood gang incident provided the CAT officers with his son's whereabouts and then provided a news interview supporting the efforts of the police.

Intervention Programs

CAT officers became directly involved in efforts to deter gang membership. A jobs program with local trades was developed, allowing CAT officers to refer gang members into apprenticeship work programs at construction companies, auto body shops and other businesses that provide better opportunities than the typical low-paying service job.

In conjunction with a local, private gang counseling organization, CAT officers operated a bicycle shop that paid gang members to refurbish and rebuild bicycles to be donated to disadvantaged children. The building housing the bike shop, as well as ongoing expenses, was funded by local businesses and grants. At its peak, the program was providing a neutral territory for more than 50 individuals associated with 12 different gangs. Counseling, education and referral services were made available for gang members who brought friends or family members to the bike shop.

The department also conducts a variety of other outreach programs, including:

- An annual COPS + Kids picnic attracting over 2,500 underprivileged youth gives police officers an opportunity to educate kids and their parents about the department and its operations. Thousands of dollars of prizes, food and services are given away.
- PAL wrestling, backpacking, water skiing and boxing programs are targeted to underprivileged and gang youth.
- Police funds are provided to support a number of minority youth programs operated by local ministers.

Northern Nevada Youth Gang Task Force

In 1988, more than a dozen local agencies formed a Northern Nevada Youth Gang Task Force consisting of officers involved in gang intelligence operations. The group shared automated intelligence files, and most agencies began participating in the automated GREAT (Gang Resistance Education and Training) gang intelligence system operated by the Los Angeles County Sheriff's Department.

Most members of the group adopted the press policy established by the Reno Police Department to limit sensationalization of gang activities. The chiefs and sheriffs of the major agencies collaborated on media statements concerning gang-related issues in the county.

NAGs Provide Feedback

In conjunction with the police department's COP+ program, the chief of police and area captains developed Neighborhood Advisory Groups (NAGs) in geographical areas throughout the city to solicit feedback from the community. An advisory group of local minority leaders involved in youth gang issues was also organized, as was a NAG of gang members. In developing the gang NAG, the department did not recognize specific gangs as representatives, but did allow persons belonging to a variety of different gangs to join the group, where they were given access to the chief of police to air their concerns.

NAGs became very useful when new enforcement programs were adopted because the groups were able to participate in the programs' development and offer suggestions. As mentioned earlier, the FBI Violent Crime Task Force targeting gang crime utilized the groups during the formation process and for continuing feedback concerning operations.

The minority NAG initially voiced much fear of "secretive" FBI enforcement tactics that would exclude the media and public from any knowledge of the operations. Consequently, after several meetings with the FBI special agent in charge and heads of the participating law enforcement agencies, a number of safeguards were written into the task force agreement to address these concerns. The result was that the task force enjoyed the public support of the NAGs, the NAACP and a local Hispanic group.

Similarly, the input and blessing of the NAGs are typically sought prior to the implementation of major gang/drug enforcement projects in the neighborhoods to avoid controversy later when the media began reporting the arrests and neighborhood gang activity.

Media

A media policy, developed in conjunction with the NAGs and other local agencies that provide youth gang services, recommends that while law enforcement agencies should avoid identifying individual gangs or gang members by name or address, they should provide complete and accurate information when gang-motivated crime occurs.

A pool of statistical information was maintained to de-escalate periodic attempts by the media to overplay the gang crime issue. A semi-annual report, "Status of Gangs in the City of Reno," was prepared for the general public providing information on the total gang population, numbers and types of gang crimes committed and, most importantly, the results of gang intervention programs.

Gang-motivated crimes were repeatedly compared with total Part I felony crimes, showing that only a fraction of a percent of the total reported felony crime in Reno was attributable to gang members. The monthly gang crime and membership statistics made available to the media had a tendency to curtail journalistic efforts to overstate the gang problem.

The first question normally asked by reporters covering a violent crime was, "Is it gang related?" If an answer was not provided by the department, reporters typically approached neighbors, witnesses or anyone else who would comment and ask the same question. Unfortunately, residents would often label a crime as gang related whether it was or not. Consequently, the department made it a priority to determine as quickly as possible whether or not gang involvement was present and relay this information to the media. In the majority of cases, gang motivation was not present. Additionally, the department created a network of other agencies and sources that agreed to the same media policy to prevent the media from pitting the police against other groups when discussing the gang situation in Reno. One of these groups was the Gang Alternatives Partnership (GAP).

GAP

Formed in 1991 to coordinate the resources from public and private agencies involved in dealing with youth gangs, GAP included representatives from law enforcement, the district attorney's office, juvenile probation, the school district, several private agencies, businesses and private individuals. The group recognized early that any one group would have a limited impact on the youth gang issue. Thus, the partnership became invaluable in balancing the member agencies' enforcement, intervention and education efforts, as well as in providing a single source of information for the community on youth gang issues. Too often, the police had been targeted as the "experts" on youth gangs, resulting in a tendency for the media and community to focus on violence and enforcement programs.

Through community donations, a full-time executive director is being hired to administer grant programs, contribution drives and other resources. Public statements concerning the status of youth gangs, the effectiveness of intervention programs and the best approach to certain issues were jointly agreed upon and presented by the group.

Summary

In 1988, the citizens of Reno passed a ballot initiative that increased the number of police officers in Reno by 40 percent. Over the years since the first semi-annual community survey was conducted in 1987, the department's standing has improved to the point that nine out of every 10 residents report that they believe the police are doing a good job. A deputy chief responsible for the CAT team received the local NAACP chapter's Freedom Citation in recognition of the department's efforts, specifically with gang-related issues.

Youth gang violence in Reno has been minimal in comparison with total felony crime and, although gang membership continues to increase at a moderate rate, fear is no longer simply linked to an increase in gang membership. The minority community supports tough enforcement efforts against repeat violent offenders in gangs, and officers have been very effective in solving gang-related crime. Although it is difficult to prove definitively, it would appear that limited violence and limited growth in gang membership is related to the many success stories resulting from intervention efforts.

A lesson learned early in Reno was that there was no aspect of policing that could not benefit from a collaboration with the community. The traditional law enforcement mentality that the police are the expert "technicians" who know best how to deal with crime problems is simply a myth. There is no rule book that dictates how the police can best deal with crime or community issues, and there are certainly few proven methods for dealing with youth gang issues. One fact does remain, however. A community that participates in the process also willingly supports the efforts of the police. ✦

35

An Evaluation of Operation Hardcore: A Prosecutorial Response to Violent Gang Criminality

Judith Dahmann

Operation Hardcore, initiated by the Los Angeles District Attorney's Office, was the first prosecution program to target serious, violent gang-related offenses. Its special features include reduced caseloads, vertical prosecution (that is, one attorney handles the case from start to finish), additional investigative support, and resources for assisting victims. This article summarizes an independent evaluation of the program, performed two years after its initiation in 1979.

The research found that Operation Hardcore had been implemented consistent with its design and resulted in more convictions, for more serious charges and higher incarceration rates, than either a comparison group of cases not receiving the specialized handling and cases prosecuted prior to Hardcore's implementation. While flaws in this research design (for example, the lack of random assignment to the program) leave the comparability of the comparison groups open to question, Operation Hardcore continues to be highly regarded. It has been replicated throughout the nation.

Executive Summary

Operation Hardcore is a specialized prosecution program operated by the Los Angeles District Attorney's Office designed to improve the prosecution of violent gang offenses. The program was instituted in response to rising levels of gang violence in Los Angeles. It began in 1979 and it is in operation today.

The concept underlying the Operation Hardcore program is based on a series of assumptions linking gang criminality and effective criminal prosecution:

1.Gang criminality is characterized by certain features which distinguished it from other types of crime.

2.These distinctive features pose particular problems for criminal prosecution of gang-related cases.

3.These prosecutorial problems can be addressed through specific actions on the part of the criminal prosecutor.

4.These special prosecutorial actions will lead to improved prosecution of gang-related cases and thus increased criminal sanctions to defendants in these cases.

Reprinted with the permission of the author, report dated October 1982.

The research described here considers these assumptions and presents empirical evidence which supports the expectations of improved prosecution of gang cases through the use of specialized prosecutorial practices.

In terms of distinguishing features of gang criminality and the problems posed by these features for criminal prosecution, there are three areas of particular importance.

The *first* is the collective nature of most gang criminality including the involvement of both multiple suspects and defendants in gang incidents and the juvenile/adult mix common among gang defendants. The criminal justice system is designed primarily to deal with individuals not groups. The collective nature of gang crime poses problems for prosecution in several ways:

1. *Prosecutorial Strategy*. The Criminal Justice System is oriented toward identifying the one individual responsible for the commission of an offense. It can be argued that given the collective nature of gang crimes, this is an inappropriate response in gang cases.

2. *Legal Limitations*. The law does not lend itself to the prosecution of a group of offenders for a single incident. Evidence required to support allegations of conspiracy or aiding and abetting is often difficult to obtain without special investigatory resources.

3. *Logistical Problems*. Given the assembly line methods of case handling found in most large prosecutors' offices and the bifurcation of juvenile and adult adjudication, prosecution of multiple defendant cases involving both juveniles and adults faces particular problems.

Second are the witness problems commonly associated with prosecution of gang violence, including the reluctance of witnesses to participate and witness intimidation. These witness problems are the result of certain characteristics of gang cases:

1.Witnesses are often gang members themselves who for obvious reasons are not often willing witnesses.

2.Non gang members are also reticent to participate in a gang prosecution. Their homes, families and jobs are often located in areas controlled by gangs and thus are vulnerable to retaliatory action on the part of other gang members.

Third, prosecution of gang cases faces a major problem of the credibility of gang motives to juries. Gang subculture, gang values and the gang way of life are alien to most members of juries. In order to effectively present a gang case the prosecutor faces the task of credibility introducing the jury to a subculture, in some cases without prejudicing them against prosecution witnesses who may be gang members themselves.

In short, gang cases are a far cry from the ideal case for prosecution in which you have a single, clearly identified suspect perpetrating an offense against an innocent victim, in the presence of innocent cooperative witnesses. Gang cases typically involve a collective act of violence against an individual or gang who often look more like the gang suspects than the jurors. Further, the witnesses typically either resemble the suspects or at least share their disdain for the criminal justice system or, out of fear of retribution, are unwilling to cooperate with the prosecution.

In order to address these problems in Los Angeles, a specialized, self-contained unit devoted to the prosecution of incidents of gang violence was created. This unit, Operation Hardcore, sought to address the problems described above through the addition of resources, in the form of:

- A highly motivated and qualified attorney staff,
- Special investigative support attached directly to the Unit, and
- Low caseloads for both attorneys and Unit investigators;

through changes in case management:

- Early involvement in case preparation and investigation including preparation of search warrants,
- Continuous or vertical prosecution with one deputy handling the full range of prosecutorial functions for his cases from filing to disposition and sentencing,
- Special attention to witness problems including using available witness relocation funds, providing witness protection, taking taped or sworn witness statements, prosecuting instances of witness intimidation, and
- Prosecution of both juvenile and adult suspects by the same deputy;

and through policy actions:

- Working closely with law enforcement agencies,
- Preparing written motions and points of authority early in cases,
- Settling early or going to trial, and
- Prosecuting both juveniles and adults and accessories as well as the "shooters."

Operation Hardcore Unit uses these resources and activities to address the problems prosecution faces with violent gang cases described above, namely:

- Evidentiary and logistical problems due to the collective nature of gang criminal incidents;
- Problems due to witness reluctance to participate and to witness intimidation by the gangs; and
- Problems due to the alien nature of the gang lifestyle which threatens the credibility of gang evidence and motives to juries.

Of the three areas, Operation Hardcore addresses problems involving witnesses most directly. Witness problems are the most often cited difficulty with gang cases. Witnesses hesitate to become involved in gang-related prosecutions for a number of reasons. Hardcore attorneys have the time to devote to their cases to assess the situations and motivations of witnesses and to deal with each individual as appropriate. Those who have been threatened or who are fearful can be relocated or protected. Those who are reluctant can be pinned down early and efforts can be made to hold them to their original statements. Taped interviews can be conducted and sworn statements can be taken, which can then be used throughout a case prosecution to aid in maintaining consistency in witness testimony. The collective nature of gang criminality and the age composition of gang members poses logistical problems for prosecution. Multiple defendant cases are subject to severance and time delays simply due to the management problems associated with handling the case. These problems are further exacerbated when both juveniles and adults are involved in an incident and separate filings are made in different courts. The vertical approach to case handling of Hardcore cases coupled with the ability of Hardcore attorneys to prosecute juveniles as well as adults, directly addresses these problems. With his low caseload, a Hardcore attorney can comprehensively oversee the entire processing of the case.

Evidentiary and legal problems are also associated with multiple defendant cases. In cases involving multiple suspects, a tendency among prosecutors is to file charges on only the central individual, given difficulties with legally holding the accompanying individuals accountable for their involvement. Charges of conspiracy or aiding and abetting require the prosecution to demonstrate associations among the group members as well as to show a commonly held motive. The evidence needed to substantiate charges such as these requires special police attention. Operation Hardcore has been able to work closely with local law enforcement agencies, and in particular law enforcement gang specialists, early in the investigation of gang cases to develop needed evidence. By specifying in search warrants material related to gang involvement, evidence needed to pursue the prosecution of the whole group of suspects can be sought.

Along the same lines, because they work with gangs all the time, the Hardcore attorneys have developed a base of expertise in gang operations, motives, etc., which aids them in developing their cases and in convincing juries of the credibility of their arguments.

The results of an analysis of defendants and cases handled by the Operation Hardcore program, as compared to similar defendants and cases handled by non-program attorneys both before and during program operations, indicate that this program is having the expected effects on criminal justice performance. There have been more convictions, fewer dismissals, and more convictions to the most serious charge among cases handled by Operation Hardcore. Where there exists sentencing discretion in the commitment of convicted young adults to the California Youth Authority (a form of sentence bargaining), the program shows a higher rate of state prison commitments.

These results suggest that selective prosecution has been an effective strategy in Los Angeles and that the Operation Hardcore program has obtained demonstrable improvements in the criminal justice handling of gang defendants and their cases. ✦

36

Attempting Gang Control by Suppression: The Misuse of Deterrence Principles

Malcolm W. Klein

The selections in this section reflect the national pre-eminence of suppressive approaches in law enforcement programming. In this final article, Klein outlines the theoretical underpinnings of such approaches and describes the pitfalls in the application of deterrence principles to gang settings. In their current form, suppression programs fail to recognize core properties of gang dynamics, but Klein argues that this need not be the case. He suggests that the careful articulation of deterrence principles in program development could yield salutary preventive effects on at-risk youth.

Abstract

American crime policy has been encapsulated in successive decades by prominent theoretical positions. Moving by stage through the medical prevention model, to opportunity theory, then to labeling theory, and currently in a 180 degree reversal to deterrence theory, each stage has provided the opportunity for the testing of these criminological models. Deterrence theory has seemed more impervious to test, however, perhaps because of its ideological overload.

In the U.S., the growing proliferation of street gangs has yielded greater focus on deterrence through the development of special gang suppression programs. With gang-like structures receiving more attention in other nations, the U.S. experience with deterrence and suppression is timely. This paper therefore describes the context for the development of suppression programs, reviews the basic tenets of deterrence theory and tests of its viability, describes suppression programs that emerge from a deterrence philosophy, and discusses their shortcomings in the context of the properties of street gangs.

Introduction

A famous American athlete once offered this advice: Don't look back, someone may be gaining on you. The street gang is still largely an American product—and a rapidly proliferating one within the U.S. borders—but its counterparts in other nations are becoming more visible. Gang-like structures are reported in Stockholm, Berlin, Frankfurt, London, Manchester, Zurich, Madrid, and half a dozen cities in Russia among other western cities. Melbourne, Papua-New Guinea, Beijing, Tokyo, and Hong Kong are among Eastern cities from which gang reports are emerging. South America and Canada provide additional nominations.

It behooves us then, not to dismiss street gangs as "just an American problem," but to learn from the American experience and the failures there to control gang crime and promote pro-social life styles for potential gang members. In particular, the current U.S. reliance on gang suppression programs calls for special attention, especially as an exercise in deterrence principles at work. Over the past decade, the U.S. has all but given up on gang prevention programs.

The Context of Anti-Gang Enforcement Efforts

Defining as ambiguous a phenomenon as street gangs is a somewhat arbitrary process, but for purposes of this discussion the following depiction may suffice:

A street gang is a collectivity of youth (adolescent and adult), primarily male, who see themselves as a distinct entity (usually with a group name) with an anti-social orientation. It is generally perceived in its neighborhood as both distinct and anti-social, and has been involved in enough criminal activity to call forth a consistent negative response from community residents and enforcement officials. The street gang is generally but not always territorial and generally but not always composed of ethnic or racial minorities. Its crime pattern is versatile.

Drug distribution gangs often appear to be a variant of street gangs, developing independently or as offshoots of established street gangs. They are far more focussed on drug sales and associated criminal activities than are traditional street gangs, and less likely to be territorially oriented.

Excluded from this depiction are terrorist groups, motorcycle gangs, car clubs, "stoner" groups, normal peer networks, and organized adult criminal groups.

An assessment of current law enforcement approaches to gang activity makes most sense when placed in the context of enforcement efforts over the past several decades. The current emphasis on gang suppression has emerged from at least four developments which can be seen as both shaping and justifying its status. The four developments are:

© Excerpted and reprinted from *Studies on Crime and Crime Prevention*, 1993, pp. 88-111. Scandinavian University Press, Stockholm, Sweden.

1. A growing acknowledgement that treatment/rehabilitation approaches have been unsuccessful;
2. The growth in gang intelligence sophistication and technologies;
3. Pressures from the emergence of various gang forms in several hundred American cities, and their expansion in size and violence in such gang hubs as Los Angeles and Chicago;
4. Pressures generated by real and purported involvements of urban gangs in drug distribution, most notably in crack distribution.

Deterrence

In this section, I cover four background issues: The components of deterrence theory, pertinent portions of the deterrence literature, deterrence and drugs, and then deterrence and gangs.[1] As we discuss the elements of deterrence theory and their limitations, the reader may be aided by having in mind some of the gang suppression programs to which the deterrence principles will be applied. Included, and described more fully in a later section, are the following:

- *Street sweeps*, in which hundreds of police officers—usually with public forewarning—crack down on high-intensity gang and drug distribution neighborhoods, round up hundreds of suspects, and subject them to an accelerated booking and disposition process.
- *Special gang probation and parole caseloads*, in which officers deal with gang members only, employ high surveillance techniques and revoke probation and parole status for any violation noted, returning the suspects to detention.
- *Prosecution programs* that target gang leaders and serious gang offenders for intensive vertical prosecution and special court handling to increase successful prosecution rates to 95% or more.
- *Various civil procedures*—use of civil abatement laws, using gang membership to define arrest for conspiracy or unlawful association—in order to emphasize the special nature of gang membership and the special enforcement activities to which gang members may be subjected.
- *School programs*, including overt surveillance and covert buy-bust operations.

These are examples of suppression programs that exemplify various deterrence principles. Obviously, it is not the case that enforcement officials or city councils have undertaken careful analyses of deterrence theory and then designed intervention programs based upon the theory. But in explaining the rationale and value of such programs, officials *do* explicitly make reference to propositions that are immediately recognizable as articulating deterrence theory. Public statements—even promises—have been made about "obliterating" gangs. Programs are described as "sending a message" to drug dealers in gangs. Speed of enforcement (celerity) and certainty of punishment are stressed; severity of sanctions is promised, and laws promulgated to increase it; targeting for sanctions is both broadened by increasing gang intelligence and pinpointed by the concentration of enforcement efforts and development of special control units in the various agencies. Gang leaders are selected for special attention to spread the effect, while known gang symbols such as graffiti and "colors" are singled out for special attention. Yet, what is missing in all this is any considered attention to the gap between message delivered and message received. This gap, in a broad sense, should be the eventual target of suppression program evaluations.

Theoretical Components

Deterrence theory comes not so much in many forms as in many emphases. The watershed in illuminating the theory came in the mid-1970s with the publication of Zimring and Hawkins' *Deterrence: The Legal Threat in Crime Control* (1973) and Gibbs' *Crime, Punishment, and Deterrence* (1975).

Suppression approaches are loosely based on a deterrence perspective, especially among justice officials (Zimring and Hawkins). Gibbs and others make it clear that deterrence is a component of "preventive consequences of punishment." This is especially true with respect to general deterrence. Thus one can turn to deterrence theory to sharpen the operations encompassed under the suppression rubric, thereby increasing the chances for useful prevention.

Two of the properties of deterrence are celerity and severity of applied punishment. The use of aperiodic massive police sweeps in high drug and gang neighborhoods is said to serve as a general deterrent for actual and potential gang members and crack sellers. Sweeps, it is claimed, send an unmistakable message about the punitive consequences of drug distribution by gang members.

But what takes place in such a sweep? On a typical weekend in Los Angeles, it may yield four-hundred arrests, half gang, many mere traffic violations, other warrants already outstanding; quick booking and release; prior warning (sometimes first night, always subsequent nights). The general impression is one of a police gnat attack—we know it's coming, its targets are diffuse, it leads for some persons to minor sanctions quickly abated by quick release. Sherman's (1990) review of police crackdowns, including those aimed at drug sales, defines them as increases in *either* certainty or severity of sanctions. But, *celerity* is achieved at the expense of *certainty* and *severity*—two of the three major properties of deterrence theory. This contradictory implication involving different deterrence properties is foreshadowed by Nagel's (1982) suggestions about the interaction between certainty and severity and is in accord as well with data reported by Tittle (1980).

The police say they are sending a message (presumably of certainty and celerity). But, especially given the group processes in the gang world, one might guess that the messages *received*—interpreted, reinterpreted, cognitively altered to serve the purposes of the gang audience—may well be: "the police are incompetent", "I can beat the rap", "They're just getting minor offenders", "Only fools get caught, or guys who want some excitement." The *objective* (Gibbs' "presumptive") properties here are questionable. The subjective or *perceived* properties may actually work *against* the desired deterrent effect; their preventive value may be essentially nil. Gang group process can turn a street sweep into a source of gang bravado and cohesiveness.

Each of various suppression operations described in this paper involves the potential application of deterrence propositions, but also carries the potential for a boomerang effect. The failure to achieve prevention via suppression operations can be due to poorly operationalized deterrence properties, or to the failure to consider the perceptual or broader cognitive counterpart to the objective or presumptive property.

To set the stage for this enterprise, I need to offer a brief review of the state of deterrence theory and its principal propositions. Among many writers, there has been a good deal of pessimism about constructing a comprehensive theory of deterrence. As Zimring and Hawkins put it in 1973, ". . . the net effect of increasing attention and study is something less than a knowledge explosion" (1973:3). But this kind of pessimism is sometimes hard to discern among public officials or the general public who, to quote Zimring and Hawkins again, ". . . seem to think in a straight line about the deterrent effect of sanctions; if penalties have a deterrent effect in one situation, they will have a deterrent effect in all; if some people are deterred by threats, then all will be deterred; if doubling a penalty produces an extra measure of deterrence, then trebling the penalty will do still better. . . . This style of thinking imagines a world in which armed robbery is in the same category as illegal parking, burglars think like district attorneys . . ." (1973:19).

Part of the problem in this "straight line" thinking is one of distinguishing between *specific deterrence* and *general deterrence*. Another is a blurring of *severity*, *certainty*, and *celerity* of sanctions. Yet another is the distinction between *objective* (or "presumptive") and *perceived* properties of deterrence. Then there is the place of deterrence among *other processes* related to crime levels, and the relation of deterrence to the broader notion of prevention. These issues were succinctly covered in Gibbs (1975), and little improved upon since, so we rely rather heavily on that volume to lay out for the reader some basic components of deterrence theory.

Specific deterrence has to do "with the impact of legal punishment on those who have suffered it."[2]

General deterrence pertains "to the impact of legal punishment on the public at large."

It is worth noting at this point that specific deterrence is loosely based on behavioristic learning theories for individuals while general deterrence applies these mechanistic principles to non-involved populations with little attention to intervening processes. This is mirrored in gang suppression programs.

Severity is generally described as an observable, measurable characteristic of sanctions in terms of the punitive consequences of the sanctions on the offender. Greater severity should lead to greater deterrence. Zimring and Hawkins cite an earlier practice in Beijing of displaying, next to the 15 mph speed signs, the severed heads of those caught exceeding the limit. In 1982, we found that practice supplanted by the use of photographs of the executed. No comparative impact statement is available.

Certainty represents the probability that a sanction will be applied to an offender as a consequence of a particular offense or pattern of offenses out of many. Higher certainty should lead to greater deterrence.

Celerity refers to the speed with which a sanction is applied, i.e., how close in time to the offense; the closer in time, the greater the deterrence.

These are objective properties of sanctions, but are not related to their effect in a simple linear fashion. For instance, low levels of severity may be relatively indistinguishable in effect, while above a reasonably high level, any additional quantum of severity may be superfluous. Or consider the problem with certainty, given the fact that juvenile offenses in general and many minor offenses may have a commission-to-detection ratio of 20 to 1. Increasing such a low level to ratios of 20 to 2 or 20 to 5 may well be inconsequential, even unnoticeable. As to celerity, any student of American enforcement and judicial processes can recite the delays which normally occur between the commission of a criminal act and subsequent official detection, apprehension, and court sanction.

Applicability was offered by Zimring and Hawkins as the degree to which a sanction is believed to apply personally to the offender. Higher applicability yields greater deterrence—specific deterrence in particular.

Credibility, also added by Zimring and Hawkins, refers to the belief that the sanctioning agency can indeed deliver on its threat. Higher credibility leads to greater deterrence, in part, we assume, through higher levels of certainty.

The reader may discern in these latter two propositions a shift away from the objective level to the perceived level. While economists and other rational choice theorists prefer to eschew the perceptual level, much deterrence theory and research pertains directly to the objective/perceptual distinction and the capacity of measures of the *perceived* properties to predict deterrent efforts at higher levels of impact.

Perceived severity, certainty, and celerity (and other properties such as applicability and credibility) are the processual translations between general deterrence and specific deterrence, such that higher perceived levels should produce greater deterrence. However, from our point of view in translating deterrence into prevention among the non-sanctioned, these *perceived properties* become paramount as well. It helps in the translation to turn again to Gibbs who notes several levels of importance to us:

- Some people never *contemplate* committing the acts in question. They are beyond the concern of deterrence, and beyond our concern in this paper.
- "Absolute deterrence" refers to those who never commit criminal acts because of a general risk assessment. This is clearly in the arena of primary prevention, and of interest to us.
- "Restrictive deterrence" is defined in terms of the perceived odds for a given individual to be

punished. This seems to combine the notions of applicability and credibility above, and also relates directly to our interests.

Thus *absolute and restrictive deterrence* are also relevant properties, with higher levels of each yielding greater deterrent impact. This proposition, along with that on perceived properties, leads us on the path of equating deterrent and preventive effects. Lest the reader underestimate the complexity of the propositional status of deterrence theory, consider that Logan (1982) developed a set of 26 interrelated hypotheses. This path from deterrence to prevention is far from simple.

Deterrence, Gangs, and Group Process

Our own research consistently has revealed gangs as qualitatively different from other delinquent or criminal collectivities (Klein, 1971; Maxson, Gordon, and Klein, 1985; also see Short and Strodtbeck, 1965). Gangs are not merely located toward the end of some criminal continuum; internal group processes and the mutual interactions between such groups and their communities—schools, playgrounds, police, store owners, etc.—set the gangs apart qualitatively. Street gangs, by self and other definition, become set apart so as to be distinctive from other peer groups in which some criminal involvement is evidenced. Gang suppression takes on a different character (as will be seen from our description of gang suppression programs) but also must be studied in some special ways because of the influence of group process on the way program components are received and interpreted.

Deterrence in the gang setting is difficult. Consider, for example, the non-gang findings of Erickson and Gibbs (1978) that the positive correlation between perceived certainty and crime rate disappears when one controls on the social condemnation of crime; Alcorn's (1978) finding that while deterrent properties had no effect, delinquent peers and values did, and Meier, Burkett, and Hickman's (1984) confirmation that sanction threats had no effect but peer influences did.

The Gang/Drug connection over the years has been more assumed than demonstrated. What the literature suggests about the gangs and drugs connection would seem to be confusing. Many people *assume* the connection, but to judge from the literature, the potential for the gang/drug connection has not to date been fulfilled.

Chein's (1964) report on 18 New York City gangs found very low drug usage and absolutely no organized sale procedures. Short and Strodtbeck (1965) found marijuana use and sales to rank 48th in a list of 69 gang activities, while narcotics use and sales ranked 59th (in contrast to alcohol at the 22nd position). Retreatist gangs were almost non-existent in this Chicago research. Carney, Mattick, and Calloway (1969), also in Chicago, found hard drug use very uncommon in gangs: "The drug user was held in contempt." In Philadelphia, Robin (1967) found gang member drug offenses too few to register in his offense categories. Neither the incisive account by Cohen (1955) nor by Suttles (1968) mentions the problem. The report of the New York City Youth Board (1960) acknowledges drugs among its gangs only briefly as part of the "full gamut of juvenile offenses." Los Angeles gangs described by Klein (1971) had drug *and* alcohol offenses comprising from three to eleven percent of recorded offenses prior to intervention efforts. In later reports from Chicago, Cartwright, Tompson, and Schwartz (1975) suggest the place of drug involvement in gangs by reference to the gang leader who "belt-whipped a member of his gang suspected of using drugs." Short (1968), while describing minor use to be common in groups, found that hard drugs were unusual except in one gang, and that "addiction was virtually unknown." Blum's (1972) extensive study in the Bay Area yielded 350 pages on dealers with not one mention of street gangs.

In sum, with almost unbroken consistency the earlier literature yielded the counter-intuitive conclusion that gang involvement in the drug world had been relatively minor, and had emphasized "soft" rather than "hard" drugs. Moore's (1978) research with ex-convict, older gang members in East Los Angeles offers the only principal exception.

The situation of drug distribution is no better: experience with and observation of drug sales systems has not been well captured in the empirical literature. For instance, major reviews such as those by Ray (1983), Gottschalk, McGuire, Heiser, Dinovo, and Birch (1979), Gandossy, Williams, Cohen, and Harwood (1980), and O'Donnell, Voss, Clayton, Slatin, and Room (1976) cover drug use and users extensively, but not distributors (beyond their role as users). Chin and Fagan's 1990 analysis of violence among users and user/sellers of crack shows little increment over prior violence levels, and *no* consideration of gang involvement.

Typically, older studies of drug distribution have described systems principally involving white, middle-class actors (Adler and Adler, 1983; Blum, 1972; Atkyns and Hanneman, 1974; Langer, 1977; Mouledoux, 1972; Lieb and Olsen, 1976). Descriptions by Hughes, Crawford, Barker, Schumann, and Jaffe (1971), Preble and Casey (1969), Blum (1972), and Goldstein (1981) deal with various distribution roles among heroin users. Cocaine distribution is almost untouched in this literature.

One exception to some of the above is Ianni's (1974) article on black and Hispanic intrusion into Mafia-controlled rackets, including drug trafficking. Another is the Goldstein, Brownstein, Ryan, and Bellucci (1989) graphic and disheartening descriptions of violence and death related to what he calls the "systemic" aspect of drugs, referring to the interaction between use and distribution systems.

However, research during the past few years has suggested a trend toward stronger and more direct connections between gangs and both drug use and drug sales. Our own gang/crack research in Los Angeles (Maxson and Klein, 1990) revealed gang members involved in up to 25% of all crack sales arrests, most of these being at the street level. Hagedorn (1988) reports similar levels of general drug sales and high levels of use as well. Skolnick, Correl, Navarro, and Rabb (1988) have reported even closer relations at the middle levels of crack distribution. Taylor (1989) describes an almost complete involvement of gangs and drugs in the deteriorating heart of Detroit. Hayeslip concludes that "In many cities, gangs control street sales" (1989:3).

But the picture is mixed. In Los Angeles, the police department and the Sheriff's department differ considerably in imputing gang involvement to drug sales and violence. A. Goldstein (1990) cites a recent New York Task Force report as concluding that gang involvement in the drug business is very low. In Washington, D.C., now famous for its high levels of crack, little evidence exists of gang involvement. Washington has in fact never been among the major gang cities.

Fagan (1989) probably has drawn the most accurate picture: gangs, drugs, and violence are often found together, and yet there are many instances of gangs without much drug involvement, drugs sales groups that are not gangs, and both gangs and drug systems with and without violence. The connections are probably both spurious and causal, and the former can become the latter. Thus, Spergel concludes that "effective but exclusive suppression of gang activity may also be associated with conversion of the gang to more criminal gain-oriented activity such as drug trafficking" (1990:3), and Clayton (1986:13) cites the conclusion of the Select Committee on Narcotics Abuse and Control that the federal Office of Juvenile Justice and Delinquency Prevention "... should consider the problem of gangs and gang violence in relation to drug abuse both in its research and programmatic endeavors."

Gang suppression efforts have received scant attention in the research literature. Hayeslip (1989), writing for the National Institute of Justice, makes the gang/drug equation and then gives brief attention to street enforcement techniques, including police sweeps, and to civil abatement procedures. But Stapleton and Needle noted in one of the very first descriptions of gang enforcement procedures that:

> Contemporary gang prevention and control practices are in an early developmental stage, not primitive, but certainly not approaching maturity. The state-of-the-art barely approaches that found in newer police program areas, such as community crime prevention or riot control, let alone the more fundamental areas such as patrol and investigations. Basic collective technology—proven practices, standard training curriculum, job specifications, evaluations, evaluation methodologies, and even a body of literature—has not yet emerged in this area of police concern (1982:xiii).

In a following section of this paper I will provide brief sketches of the various suppression programs to be found specifically in selected American cities such as Los Angeles, but following the description by Stapleton and Needle above, only one significant effort has been undertaken to describe *generic* suppression approaches to gang activity (with or without connections to drug use and sales). This is the national assessment recently completed at the University of Chicago under the direction of Irving Spergel. Spergel and his co-authors state about police suppression programs, "A principal assumption is that gangs and gang members should not be tolerated or even helped" (1989:171). This police strategy, they say

> . . . is clear and simple. It is to arrest, prosecute, and sentence gang members, especially hard-core or leaders, quickly, effectively and to keep them in jail as long as possible. The strategy is achieved through such tactics as surveillance, stake-out, aggressive patrol and enforcement, follow-up investigation, the development of extensive intelligence, and infiltration of gangs in contexts in which gangs are found, e.g. schools. Gangs are to be broken up and harassed. Saturation patrol and sweeps are periodically employed. The aim often is to acquire improved fire power to deal with "drug gangs". . . .

Spergel also describes suppressive approaches to probation and parole gang caseloads, based in large part on the Los Angeles approach. The "primary emphasis is strict supervision, search of the homes of youths, with police protection." The trend has been away from younger members "to target more 'hard-core youth' similar to those served by the Los Angeles Police and Sheriff's gang units." There is also a Gang Drug Pushers and Sellers Program using heavier sanctions and electronic surveillance of gang drug sellers, and daily assignment of probation officers to a school Crime Suppression Program to deal with gang activities on school campuses.

Other school based components have been described by the National School Safety Center, including dress codes, graffiti removal, crisis management, and so on. The Center, we might add, has adopted and widely disseminated an image of youth gangs that perpetuates a violence orientation far beyond reality; the image may well justify extreme suppression and surveillance, but it is a false image.

Finally, although in less detail, the Spergel group has described gang suppression programs run by prosecutor's offices. With an emphasis on obtaining high conviction rates and maximum sentences, these programs try to avoid plea bargaining, and put some of their best efforts into gathering intelligence through special warrant and search training for investigators, concentration on gang leaders and the most serious gang offenders, and the use of vertical prosecution. Whether this translates into any form of deterrence other than that of specific offender incapacitation is the kind of question requiring our attention.

Let me be clear about the foregoing: the message is not so much that suppression does or does not "work:" evidence one way or the other is sorely lacking. *There are logical, as well as experiential, reasons to believe that suppression programs can have deterrent effects and thus, by our reasoning, can contribute substantially to gang and drug activity prevention.* But there is also evidence to the contrary from the continued rise in gang violence in Chicago and Los Angeles, cities with suppression emphases. The issue for us is finding ways that such programs may be effectively sharpened so that they do not shoot themselves in the foot, as experience and our understanding of group process suggest they do.

The Gang Suppression Programs

Gibbs reminds us "that individuals cannot be deterred from an act unless they regard it as criminal and therefore subject to some kind of punishment" (1975:227). There needs to be, he notes, a "cognitive consensus" in the relevant populations. Zimring and Hawkins move us further: "It follows that communication can be of decisive importance in the process. For the effective operation of deterrence as a means of social control must depend, among other things, on the effective communication of threats of punishment and their concrete exemplifications to the public." And again, "The deterrence threat may perhaps be best viewed as a form of advertising" (1973:141). And yet again: "If the first task of a threatening agency is the communication of information, its second task is persuasion" (1973:149).

Communication and persuasion are social psychological processes. They take place most effectively with group support (see any standard text). They also are blocked or reinterpreted most effectively by group processes. The group—in our case, the street and drug gangs—becomes, therefore, a strong actor in turning suppression programs into justifications of gang offending, *or* into the prevention of the same. How well, then, do the various gang and drug suppression programs seem formulated to do the one or the other? Here I will illustrate the question by reference to the cafeteria of gang suppression programs in my own city of Los Angeles:

CRASH and OSS

CRASH (Community Resources Against Street Hoodlums) is the Los Angeles Police Department's special gang control operation, with 235 officers in gang patrol units in each of the department's geographic bureaus. OSS is the Sheriff's Department counterpart of about 110 officers, with units located in each of the individual stations with gang problems. There is also a central OSS command group which coordinates and collects gang intelligence, whereas in the Los Angeles Police Department the centralized gang intelligence unit is divorced from CRASH.

CRASH is a high profile gang control operation, carried out by uniformed patrol officers, stressing high visibility, street surveillance, pro-active suppression activities, and investigative follow-through on arrests. As is typical of Los Angeles Police Department operations, officer transfer and turnover is relatively rapid as new officers replace CRASH operatives after, typically, a two-year period. In deterrence terms, the emphasis is on specific deterrence through implied certainty and severity of sanctions. Applicability and credibility may be weak.

OSS is a less high profile operation. It concentrates on targeted gangs (an approach recently favored more by Los Angeles Police Department as well), and places more emphasis on the intelligence function in proportion to control. OSS officers often stay with their assignment over many years, becoming experts on the local community and surprisingly close to traditional gangs in that community. The central OSS unit maintains an updated gang roster not only for its jurisdiction but for the county as a whole (including Los Angeles Police Department gangs). Because of the roster system and the greater emphasis on gang intelligence, LASD has emerged with a wider image for its gang expertise, while Los Angeles Police Department has emerged with more of a street control and suppression image. Compared to CRASH, the OSS operation lays less stress on severity and, by reputation at least, has higher credibility.

Operation Hammer

This is the aperiodic street sweep program operated by Los Angeles Police Department, primarily in South Bureau, which encompasses the largest portions of Los Angeles Police Department's gang areas. Over a two-day period, typically, Operation Hammer sends a coordinated force of between 200 and a thousand officers into a predesignated area to react to every legal violation and suspicious setting possible. Armed as well with prior warrants, the officers crack down on the area with high visibility, often announced beforehand and with heavy media coverage. A typical sweep will net several hundred arrests, primarily for misdemeanors including traffic violations, about half of which are gang-related in some way.

Because of the massive arrests, Hammer also consists of an expedited booking and release system in a mobile command post, thus maximizing officers' time in the sweep rather than its resulting paperwork.

The stated purposes of Operation Hammer are to crack down on gang and street dealing (specific deterrence) and to "send a message" to the local community (general deterrence). After several years of operations, it has been noted that gang violence has declined in South Bureau, with the implication that the message has been received. Skeptics, on the other hand, point to other activities in the community and question the direct ties between the times and locations of Operation Hammer and those of the reported decline. Even Hammer officials belatedly are acknowledging the need for community involvement.

More pertinent to our purposes are the questions raised about the suppressive or deterrent character of the operation. For example:

a. The medium proportion of *gang* arrests may weaken the gang-specificity of the message;

b. The high proportion of arrests for minor incidents and hence low sanction severity may weaken the image of the suppression of serious gang and drug offenses;

c. The timing and media coverage may decrease the deterrent effects—Hammer comes as little surprise to the community;

d. The quick booking and release may mitigate the perceived severity of sanctions, as well as allow gang members to return to their group claiming victory over a low-credibility police operation.

Other jurisdictions have eschewed following the Los Angeles Police Department example for some of the reasons noted above.

Operation Cul de Sac

Particular blocks and neighborhoods that have become open drug markets are targeted for traffic barricades to stop all vehicular traffic, concurrently with intensive police surveillance and crackdown and the encouraging of resident mobilization against street dealers. Program audiences are primarily the local dealers and secondarily local residents. Issues of displacement (of dealing) or expansion (of community-level control) have not been confronted.

Operation Hardcore

This is the vertical prosecution program in the District Attorney's office. Originally aimed at gang leaders and serious gang offenders it now must concentrate on gang-related homicide cases because of their increasing prevalence (771 gang-related homicides in the county in 1991). Working closely with police agencies on gang intelligence, warrant procedures, and witness protection, Hardcore deputy District Attorneys seek high conviction rates and full sentences (incapacitation), with the further general deterrence *intention* of having these gang convictions provide examples of the consequences of serious gang involvement. So far as we can determine, however, no serious attempt is made to follow through on this message; its successful dissemination is assumed.

Specialized Gang Supervision Program

This is a project in the Los Angeles County Probation Department. Carefully selected probation officers are given greatly reduced caseloads consisting of gang members only, juvenile and adult. The emphasis is on those convicted of violent offenses; there is close liaison with enforcement agencies; operations stress close surveillance of gang probationers and, in the case of detected probation violations, returning cases to court for recommitment to secure institutions. Program objectives are stated in specific deterrence terms only with no attention to the broader implications of the program. Certainty of sanctions is emphasized in a specific deterrence context. This stands in stark contrast to the handling of drug offenders, now so overloading the system that many convicted offenders receive no or minimal jail time, while many of their companions are simply released without being charged. The deterrence *context* is weak.

Parole Gang Program

This is the parole counterpart to the above, run by the California Youth Authority for its wards following their release from secure placement.

Street Terrorism Enforcement Program (STEP)

This is a new approach enabled by the state legislature. STEP operates on the legal finding that gang membership is based on knowledge of the criminal involvement of the group. But in order to be on safe constitutional grounds, the legislation provides that gang members be given formal notice of their suspected affiliation. Then charges of complicity and conspiracy can be lodged against them in connection with offenses charged against the group. Deputy city or district attorneys or police officers typically move into a targeted gang area with their gang rosters to deliver notices to individual members. Thereafter, arrest can lead to convictions with more severe sentencing. The STEP approach translates general deterrence messages into individual specific messages and comes close to a direct primary prevention mechanism by emphasizing certainty and applicability properties. But it is in conflict with the realities of an overloaded system that sends back a message of minimum sanctions.

Civil Abatement

Especially in connection with drug distribution, the city attorney's office has turned to a number of statutes which can be used to harass and discourage those who facilitate gang and drug activities operating out of homes, apartments, or business settings. These statutes include plumbing and electrical inspections; zoning rule adherence; unlawful gatherings; graffiti removal; and occupancy and use limitations. Because drug trafficking tends to become concentrated in areas of tolerance, especially if accompanied by intimidation related to gang presence, these civil abatement procedures are designed less to prevent illicit operations as much as to keep them disorganized, on the move, and ineffective as market systems. We see low credibility and applicability as limiting the value of this program as currently constituted.

School Programs

These come in a number of forms, including closed campuses, increased use of armed and uniformed security personnel, undercover drug buys followed by mass arrests at the end of each semester (Los Angeles Police Department and Los Angeles city schools), and placement of police and probation units on campus. One may reasonably expect these approaches, and variations on the theme, to proliferate in the context of the increasing gang and drug problems in Los Angeles. They tend to be school-specific and thus need to be monitored at the individual school level. Relationship to DARE and SANE drug and gang prevention/education programs should also be carefully noted—prevention from opposite ends of the continuum. However, in the concentrated peer group atmosphere of the school campus, one can speculate that the DARE and SANE programs may have more long-term effect because they deliberately *employ* aspects of group process while the suppression programs may well be *subverted* by group process.

Group Process and Prevention Directions

I have made the point, and need not dwell on it long, that the straightforward intentions of gang suppression programs may backfire. Their implicit deterrent properties and messages may be altered by the receiving gang members. This is less likely to be the case with nongang audiences, although drug dealing cliques may evidence the same character as traditional street gangs. We must, in due time, survey the effects of suppression programs on both grouped and non-grouped audiences but for the moment I am concerned specifically with the group setting. In interstitial and inner city areas where formal social controls are weak, group processes more easily emerge to direct youthful behaviors.

This gang setting, it should be added, has derived increasing importance in recent years because of the impact of more sophisticated theoretical *and* methodological advances in understanding developmental phases for delinquency and drug use. Longitudinal research outcomes reveal, with great consistency, peer relations as becoming the most important, proximal contributor to drug and delinquency involvement (e.g., Elliott, Huizinga, and Menard, 1989; Thornberry, 1990; Farrington et al., 1990).

Moore and Vigil suggest quite properly that "gangs maintain an oppositional, rather than a deviant subculture," and thus represent "an institutionalized rejection of the values of adult authority—especially as exhibited in the Anglo-dominated schools and the police department" (1989:31). In a context in which a major law enforcement official declares that his department will "obliterate" gangs and that "casual drug users should be shot," the oppositional value system makes sense. War mentalities distort the communications between the antagonists.

The gang literature—that portion of it that derives directly from researchers' field time spent with gang members—is replete with descriptions of the oppositional, reinterpreting pattern of gang members (Short and Strodtbeck, 1965; Klein, 1971; Horowitz, 1983; Hagedorn, 1988). It is effectively restated in deterrence terms by Zimring and Hawkins:

- "It seems possible that threats of punishment, so far from being disincentives to crime, may in these [gang] circumstances even function as incentives to it" (1973:216).
- "The operation of deterrence is greatly complicated when group pressures may not only inhibit the expression of the fear of sanctions but also in some instances convert stigmata into status symbols" (1973:317).

The gang setting discourages the acceptance or assignment of legitimacy to police, prosecution, and court accounts of acceptable behaviors. It denies the wrongfulness of many offense incidents (though not of all offenses *per se*). It encourages the bravado that accompanies anti-social deeds and utterances. It legitimates violence in the setting of gang rivalry and protection of drug dealing; it accepts the gang's moral superiority in unequal battles and its predicates against both the weak and those in authority. In the drug arena in particular, where personal indulgence and profits are immediate and personalized, the credibility of anti-drug messages is seriously endangered. And in the context of a neighborhood that tolerates trafficking, straightforward deterrence messages fall on deaf ears. The differences in effect between such programs as Operation Hammer and STEP may provide considerable illumination on how to use suppressive deterrence programming for prevention purposes.

These are very practical issues in prevention. There are two principal ways in which *successful specific deterrence* can be preventive. First, in the tertiary prevention sense, it will reduce the sanctioned activity—e.g., drug use or dealing, gang recruiting, and various related criminal offenses. Secondly, one can fairly assume that such success can have primary or secondary preventive success with those at-risk youth (gang sibs, elementary and junior high school students) in the inner city who model, imitate or otherwise are influenced by their directly sanctioned peers and elders. Here, group process both by itself and as affected by deliberate interventions can be used for preventive ends. Thus a *successful* Operation Hammer or STEP or Probation Gang Caseload, guided by well-articulated deterrence principles and deliberate follow-up interventions with at-risk youth, could greatly expand their targeted populations.

Similarly, *successful general deterrence*, using messages with appropriate content for appropriate audiences, can have a direct primary prevention effect on at-risk youth. Here one would most certainly want to enlist the collaboration of the schools, the media, and a number of community youth-serving organizations to pass on and train in the program messages. Where prevention/education programs are already in place, the collaboration could be particularly effective.

But—in order to facilitate these preventive procedures and help shape their form and substance, we must learn more about the processes taking place via the available suppression programs. For illustration, let us take just a few examples out of the many possible.

- Suppose the Operation Hammer message is interpreted to be that sanctioning is over rapidly and is mild. One might advise the police to give up the mobile booking operation as part of Hammer, thus forcing the swept-up arrestees into the normal, longer, less clearly manageable arrest and arraignment procedures. Both severity and credibility are increased.
- Suppose that STEP properly notifies known gang members of their liability for arrest and conviction, but would-be gang members are untouched (properly) by this legal process. There are other avenues—the media, the schools—by which they could be made clearly aware of the legal risks associated with membership. Certainty and applicability are increased.
- Suppose that Operation Hardcore, being limited to the most serious gang offenders, successfully incapacitates most of its "clients," but because these are strictly individual convictions they remain relatively unknown to others. One can imagine various procedures whereby drug dealers and others willing to commit violence to protect their trade can be alerted to Hardcore results—not only the severity of the sanctions, but the truly high rate of conviction, i.e., certainty. An experiment using posters with name and picture of convicted violent offenders is currently underway.

- Suppose that drug offenders subjected to electronic surveillance and intensive supervision are so successfully deterred that, from the point of view of their peers or former criminal colleagues, they all but disappear from the scene: out of sight, out of mind. Their plight will not affect other offenders on the street. It seems clear that probation, school, and other officials could easily heighten the awareness of these restricted lives among the at-risk populations. We then get at least some increment in certainty and credibility.

Of course, we cannot know in the absence of careful research whether such examples are realistic but they do illustrate the kinds of connections that can be made between successful or improvable suppression programs and the targets for rationally planned prevention intervention. What I think we *do* know about street gangs is that, once formed, they have a life of their own that feeds off their surroundings. The urban setting of their development serves to maintain them. Gang rivalries serve to strengthen them. And little that we have devised by way of intervention seems to weaken them. My informed hunch is that suppression programs, left to their own devices, may deter a few members but also increase the internal cohesiveness of the group.

By focussing on the gang *per se*, calling special attention to it, calling out its leaders, derogating its members, these programs will provide the very status and identity that youths join gangs to receive in the first place. The logic of deterrence fails in suppression programs because the programs assume, erroneously, a rational gang world. The gang world is not a rational choice model, but a social psychological one. Deterrence principles will act through group-determined perceptual processes. The critical task then is to understand these processes so that deterrence principles do not boomerang, thus creating more of the monster they are designed to modify.

Notes

1. [Editors' note: extended reviews of the scholarly literature on deterrence theory are included in the original article, but excluded here for the sake of brevity.]
2. Gibbs' preference for limiting deterrence to legal punishment is not necessary, and not followed in most literature or this paper.

References

Adler, P.A. & Adler, P. (1983). Shifts and oscillations in deviant careers: The case of Upper-level drug dealers and smugglers. *Social Problems* 31:195-207.

Alcorn, D.S. (1978). *A social psychological perspective of deterrence: Development and test of a causal model.* Ann Arbor: University Microfilms.

Atkyns, R.L. & Hanneman, G.J. (1974). Illicit drug distribution and dealer communication behavior. *Journal of Health and Social Behavior* 15:36-43.

Blum, R.H. (1972). *The dream sellers*. San Francisco: Jossey-Bass.

Carney, F.J., Mattick, H.W., and Callaway, J.D. (1969). Action in the streets: A handbook for inner city youth work. New York: Association Press.

Cartwright, D.S., Tomson, B., & Schwartz, H., eds., (1975). *Gang delinquency*. Monterey, CA: Brooks/Cole.

Chein, I. (1964). Narcotics use among juveniles. In Cavan, R., ed., *Readings in Juvenile Delinquency*. New York: J.P. Lippincott.

Chin, K. & Fagan, J. (1990). The impact of crack on drug and crime involvement. Paper read at the meeting of the American Society of Criminology.

Clayton, R.R. (1986). Drug use among children and adolescents. Paper prepared for the OJJDP Workshop, Annapolis, MD. Lexington, KY: University of Kentucky.Cohen, A.K. (1955). *Delinquent boys: The culture of the gang*. New York: Free Press.

Cohen, A.K. (1955). *Delinquent boys: The culture of the gang*. New York: Free Press.

Elliott, D.S., Huizinga, D. & Menard, S. (1989). *Multiple problem youth: Delinquency, substance use, and mental health problems*. New York: Springer-Verlag.

Erickson, M.L. & Gibbs, J.P. (1978). Objective and perceptual properties of legal punishment and the deterrence doctrine. *Social Problems*. 25:253-64.

Fagan, J. (1989). The social organization of drug use and drug dealing among urban gangs. *Criminology*, 27(4):633-669.

Farrington, D.P., Loeber, R., Elliott, D.S., Hawkins, J.D., Kandel, D.B., Klein, M.W., McCord, J., Rowe, D.C., & Tremblay, R.E. (1990). Advancing knowledge about the onset of delinquency and crime. In Lahey, B.J., & Kazdin, A.D., eds., *Advances in Clinical Child Psychology*. New York: Plenum.

Gandossy, R.P., Williams, J.R., Cohen, J., & Harwood, H.J. (1980). *Drugs and crime: A survey and analysis of the literature*. Washington, D.C.: National Institute of Justice.

Gibbs, J.P. (1975). *Crime, punishment, and deterrence*. New York: Elsevier.

Goldstein, A. (1990). *Delinquent gangs: A psychological perspective*. A pre-publication manuscript. Syracuse University.

Goldstein, P.J. (1981). Getting over economic alternatives to predatory crime among street users. In Inciardi, J.A., ed., *The Drugs-Crime Connection*. Beverly Hills, CA: Sage Publications.

Goldstein, P.G., Brownstein, H.H., Ryan, P.J., & Bellucci, P.A. (1989). Crack and homicide in New York City, 1988. *Contemporary drug problems*, 16(4):651-87.

Gottschalk, L.A., McGuire, F.L., Heiser, J.F., Dinovo, E.C., & Birch, H. (1979). *Drug Abuse deaths in nine cities: A survey report*. Washington, D.C.: National Institute of Drug Abuse.

Hagedorn, J.M. (1988). *People and folks: Gangs, crime and the underclass in a Rustbelt city*. Chicago: Lake View Press.

Hayeslip, D.W.,Jr. (1989). Local-level drug enforcement: New strategies. *Research in Action* #213. Washington, D.C.: National Institute of Justice.

Horowitz, R. (1983). *Honor and the American dream*. New Brunswick: Rutgers University Press.

Hughes, P.H., Crawford, G.A., Barker, N.W., Schumann, S., & Jaffe, J.H. (1971). The social structure of a heroin copping community. *American Journal of Psychiatry* 128:551-8.

Ianni, F.A. (1974). New mafia: black, Hispanic, and Italian styles. *Society* 2.

Klein, M.W., ed., (1971). *Street gangs and street workers*. Englewood Cliffs: Prentice-Hall.

Klein, M.W., Maxson, C.L. (1989). Street gang violence. In: Weiner, N. & Wolfgang, M. E., eds. *Violent crimes, violent criminals*. Newbury Park: Sage Publications.

Langer, J. (1977). Drug entrepreneurs and dealing culture. *Social Problems* 24:377-86.

Lieb, J. & Olsen, S. (1976). Prestige, paranoia, and profit: On becoming a dealer of illicit drugs in a university community. *Journal of Drug Issues* 6:356-67.

Logan, C.H. (1982). Propositions for deterrence theory at [the] aggregate level. Presentation to the Panel on Deterrence, meetings of the American Society of Criminology.

Maxson, C.L., Gordon, M.A. & Klein, M.W. (1985). Differences between gang and nongang homicides. *Criminology* 23:209-22.

Maxson, C.L. & Klein, M.W. (1990). Street gang violence: Twice as great or half as great? In Huff, R., ed., *Gangs in America: Diffusion, diversity, and public policy.* Newbury Park: Sage Publications.

Meier, R.F., Burkett, S.R. & Hickman, C.A. (1984). Sanctions, peers, and deviance: preliminary models of a social control process. *Sociological Quarterly* 25:67-82.

Moore, J.W. (1978). *Homeboys: Gangs, drugs, and prison in the barrios of Los Angeles*. Philadelphia: Temple University Press.

Moore, J.W. & Vigil, D. (1989). Chicano gangs: Group norms and individual factors related to adult criminality. *Aztlan* 18:27-44.

Mouledoux, J. (1972). Ideological aspects of drug dealership. In Westhues, K., ed., *Society's Shadow: Studies in the Sociology of Countercultures*. Toronto: McGraw-Hill.

Nagel, S.S. (1982). Tradeoffs in crime reduction among certainty, severity, and crime benefits. *Rutgers Law Review* 35:100-32.

New York City Youth Board. (1960). *Reaching the fighting gangs*. New York: New York City Youth Board.

O'Donnell, J.A., Voss, H.L., Clayton, R.R., Slatin, G.T., Room, R.G.W. (1976). *Young men and drugs—A nationwide survey*. Rockville, MD: National Institute of Drug Awareness.

Preble, E.A. & Casey, J.J., Jr. (1969). Taking care of business—the heroin user's life on the street. *International Journal of the Addictions* 4:1-24.

Ray, O. (1983). *Drugs, Society and Human Behavior*. St. Louis: C.V. Mosby.

Robin, G.D. (1967). Gang member delinquency in Philadelphia. In Klein, M.W., ed., *Juvenile Gangs in Context: Theory, Research, and Action*. Englewood Cliffs: Prentice-Hall.

Sherman, L.W. (1990). Police crackdowns. *NIJ Reports*, 219 (March/April):2-6.

Short, J.F., Jr., ed., (1968). *Gang delinquency and delinquent subcultures*. New York: Harper and Row.

Short, J.F., Jr. & Strodtbeck, F.L. (1965). *Group process and gang delinquency*. Chicago: University of Chicago Press.

Skolnick, J.H., Correl, T., Navarro, E., and Rabb, R. (1988). The social structure of street drug dealing. Sacramento: Office of the Attorney General of the State of California.

Spergel, I.A. (1990). Youth gangs: Continuity and change. In Tonry, M. & Norris, N., eds., *Crime and Justice, Vol. 12*. Chicago: University of Chicago Press.

Spergel, I.A., Curry, G.D., Kane, C., Chance, R., Ross, R., Alexander, A., Rodriquez, P., Seed, D., and Simmons, E. (1989a). Youth Gangs: Problem and Response. A Review of the Literature. A draft report of the National Gang Suppression and Intervention Project. Chicago: University of Chicago, School of Social Service Administration.

Stapleton, W.V., and Needle, J.A. (1982). Police handling of youth gangs. Sacramento: American Justice Institute.

Suttles, G.D. (1968). *The social order of the slum: Ethnicity and territory in the inner city*. Chicago: University of Chicago Press.

Taylor, C.S. (1989). *Dangerous society*. East Lansing: Michigan State University Press.

Thornberry, T.P. (1990). Empirical support for interactional theory: A review of the literature. Working paper #5, Rochester Youth Development Study. Albany: The University at Albany.

Tittle, C.R. (1980). *Sanctions and social deviance: The question of deterrence*. New York: Praeger.

Zimring, F.E. (1978). Policy experiments in general deterrence: 1970-1975. In Blumstein, A., Cohen, J, & Nagin, D., eds., *Deterrence and Incapacitation: Estimating the Effects of Criminal Sanctions on Crime Rates*. Washington D.C.: National Academy of Sciences.

Zimring, F.E. & Hawkins G.J. (1973). *Deterrence: The legal threat in crime control*. Chicago: University of Chicago Press. ✦

Policy Issues

37

Gangs, Neighborhoods, and Public Policy

John M. Hagedorn

Urban underclass conditions have spread across the United States in ways that parallel the growth of gangs. Recognizing this pattern and the connection between the lack of effective social institutions, poverty, and gangs, Hagedorn presents a public policy strategy that emphasizes investing in the communities from which gangs emerge. His work is in contrast to much of the popular policy of the contemporary era, which merely emphasizes suppression and overlooks the need to combat the conditions that lead to gangs.

Abstract

This article uses research from three recent Milwaukee studies to show that deindustrialization has altered some characteristics of youth gangs. Gang members tend to stay involved with the gang as adults, and many have turned to the illegal drug economy for survival. Poor African-Americans in neighborhoods where gangs persist have both similarities and differences to Wilson's underclass concept. What characterizes these neighborhoods is not the absence of working people but the absence of effective social institutions. Public policy ought to stress jobs and investment in underclass neighborhoods, evaluation of programs, family preservation, and community control of social institutions.

Are today's youth part of an "underclass"? What policies should communities adopt to control their gang problem? Based on recent gang research and experience in reforming Milwaukee's human service bureaucracy, we can address these questions and suggest practical local policies that go beyond the usual nostrums of "more cops" and "more jobs."

In the last few years a number of researchers have suggested that today's gangs have changed in some fundamental ways and may be part of an urban minority "underclass" (Moore 1985, Short 1990b, Taylor 1990, Vigil 1988). The nature of the "underclass," however, has been the subject of controversy (Aponte 1988, Gans 1990, Jencks 1989, Ricketts, Mincy, and Sawhill 1988, Wilson 1991). This paper uses data gathered from three different Milwaukee studies over the past five years to examine the changing nature of Milwaukee's gangs, the characteristics of Milwaukee's poorest African-American neighborhoods, and the relationship between gangs and neighborhoods.

For the first study, completed in 1986, 47 of the founding members of Milwaukee's 19 major gangs, including 11 of the 19 recognized leaders, were interviewed (Hagedorn 1988). That study described the origins of Milwaukee gangs, their structure and activities, and documented how gangs came to be seen as a social problem. It also tracked the education, employment, drug use, incarceration experience, and the level of gang participation of the 260 young people who founded the 19 gangs, including the 175 founders of 12 African-American male gangs.

A brief follow-up study in spring of 1990 looked at the patterns of drug abuse and the structure of gang drug dealing in three African-American gangs. This pilot study tracked the employment, incarceration, and drug use status of the 37 founding members of the three gangs since the original study. It began a process of exploring the relationship between Milwaukee gangs and drug dealing businesses or "drug posses."

Finally, as part of a human services reform plan, Milwaukee County commissioned a needs assessment in two neighborhoods where several of Milwaukee's gangs persist (Moore and Edari 1990b). Residents were hired to survey heads of households drawn from a probability sample of 300 households in ten census tracts in two neighborhoods. These neighborhoods had a high percentage of residents living in poverty and a clustering of social problems associated with the "underclass."

This article first looks at how Milwaukee gangs have changed due to deindustrialization. Second, the paper explores some volatile social dynamics occurring within poor but still heterogeneous African-American neighborhoods. Finally, based on the analysis of gangs and their neighborhoods, other underclass research, and on the author's own experience in reforming the delivery of social services, the article suggests several local policies to strengthen and assist community institutions with gang troubles.

Macro-Economic Trends and Gangs in Milwaukee

The underclass has been conceptualized as a product of economic restructuring that has mismatched African-Americans and other minority workers with radically changed employment climates (Bluestone and Harrison 1982, Kasarda 1985, Sullivan 1989). Milwaukee epitomizes this mismatch: between 1979 and 1986 over 50,000 jobs were lost or 23 percent of

Milwaukee's manufacturing employment (White et al. 1988:2-6). African-American workers were hit especially hard. In 1980 prior to the downturn, 40 percent of all African-American workers were concentrated in manufacturing (compared to 31 percent of all city workers). By 1989 research in five all-black Milwaukee census tracts found that only about one quarter of all black workers were still employed in manufacturing (Moore and Edari 1990b). African-American unemployment rates in Milwaukee have reached as high as 27 percent over the past few years.

Another way to view economic changes in the African-American community is to look at social welfare over the last thirty years. Like European immigrants before them, African-Americans came to Milwaukee with the hopes of landing good factory jobs (Trotter 1985) and large numbers succeeded. But as industrial employment declined and good jobs were less available, reliance on welfare increased (Piven and Cloward 1987:83). In 1963, when black migration to Milwaukee was still rising, fewer than one in six of Milwaukee's African-Americans were supported by AFDC. However by 1987, nearly half of all Milwaukee African-Americans and two thirds of their children received AFDC benefits. Seven out of every ten Milwaukee African-Americans in 1987 were supported by transfer payments of some kind accounting for half of all 1987 black income in Milwaukee County (Hagedorn 1989a).

Coinciding with reduced economic prospects for African-Americans, Hispanics, and other working people, gangs reemerged in Milwaukee and other small and medium-sized cities across the Midwest. While the popular notion at the time was that these gangs had diffused from Chicago, gangs in Milwaukee and the Midwest developed from corner groups and break-dancing groups in processes nearly identical to those described by Thrasher fifty years before (Hagedorn 1988, Huff 1989). The economy may have been changing, but the way gangs formed had not.

In 1986 we interviewed 47 of the 260 Milwaukee gang founders or members of the initial groups of young people who started the 19 major gangs in the early 1980s. At the time of our interviews, the founders were all in their early twenties and at an age when young people typically "mature out" of gang life. We asked the 47 founders to report on the current status of all the members who were part of the gang when it started. To our surprise, more than 80 percent of all male gang founders were reported as still involved with the gang as twenty to twenty-five year old adults.

We concluded at the time that the *economic basis* for "maturing out" of a gang—those good paying factory jobs that take little education, few skills, and only hard work—was just not there any more. As Short wrote in a recent review of gang literature, "There is no reason to believe that boys hang together in friendship groups for reasons that are very different now than in the past. . . . What has changed are the structural economic conditions . . ." (Short 1990a).

Moore (1991) has also documented economic effects of deindustrialization on the "maturing out" process of Chicano gangs. She finds that members of recent gang cliques in East Los Angeles are less likely to have found good jobs than members of older gang cliques. She concludes, "It is not that the men from recent cliques were more likely to have dropped out of the labor market, nor were they more likely to be imprisoned. It may be that they could not get full-time stable jobs."

Table 1
Employment and Adult Gang Involvement

	% Black Male	% Hisp. Male	% Wh. Male	% Female
Full Time	9.7	10	10	8.6
Part Time	14.0	0	40	11.4
Unemployed	70.3	82.5	40	63.0
Involved with the Gang as an Adult	81.1	70	100	8.6
Totals	N=175	N=40	N=10	N=35

The difficulty in finding a good job today is offset by the abundance of part-time jobs in the illegal drug economy. In preparation for a proposal to the National Institute on Drug Abuse to examine the impact of drug abuse and drug dealing on Milwaukee's gangs, we updated our rosters on the current status of the 37 founding members of three African-American gangs. By 1990, less than one in five (19 percent) of the founders, now in their mid to late twenties, were engaged in full-time work. However, three times as many of the founders (59 percent) graduated from the gang into drug "posses" or high-risk small businesses selling drugs. "High risk" is perhaps an understatement. Almost all of the 37 (86 percent) had spent significant time in prison since 1986, most for drug offenses. Three quarters (76 percent) had used cocaine regularly within the last three years and three had been murdered. While five of the 37 were said to be working as entrepreneurs (called "hittin' 'em hard"), the others involved with drug distribution worked part time ("makin' it") or sporadically ("day one") and continued to live on the margins.

Table 2
1990 Status of 37 Founding Members of Three African-American Gangs

Involved in Regular Sales of Cocaine	Used Cocaine Routinely Since 1987	Spent Time in Prison	Presently Working Full Time	Murdered
59%	76%	86%	19%	8%
N=22	N=28	N=32	N=7	N=3

As Don, a leader of the 1-9 Deacons told us in 1985: "I can make it for two or three more years. But then what's gonna happen?" The answer to Don's question is now clear. The lack of access to good jobs has had a direct effect of making illegal drug sales, no matter how risky, more attractive to Milwaukee's gang founders as an occupation for their young adult years.

Frederick Thrasher pointed out sixty years ago: "As gang boys grow up, a selective process takes place; many of them become reincorporated into family and community life, but there remains a certain criminal residue upon whom gang training has for one reason or another taken hold" (Thrasher 1963:287). The loss of entry level manufacturing jobs appears to have turned Thrasher's "selective process" on its head. Today most of the young adult gang founders rely on the illegal economy for guarantees of survival. It is only the "residue" who, at this time in Milwaukee, are being "reincorporated into family and community life."

There are also some indirect effects of economic changes. In Milwaukee most of the founders still identify somewhat with their old gang and often hang out in the same neighborhoods where they grew up, coexisting with a new generation of gang youth. This mixing of older members of drug "posses" with younger siblings and other young gang members has produced disturbing intergenerational effects. Older gang members with a street reputation employed in the fast life of drug dealing are modeling dangerous career paths for neighborhood youth. These intergenerational effects also appear in Anderson's latest work (1990). He finds that "old heads," older residents who upheld and disseminated traditional values, are being replaced by new "old heads" who "may be the product of a street gang" and who promote values of "hustling," drugs, and sexual promiscuity (103). This "street socialization" may contribute to reproducing an underclass rather than socializing young people into conventional lifestyles (Short 1990b, Vigil 1988).[1]

In summary, contemporary gangs have changed from the "delinquent boys" of fifties literature: There is a growing relationship between the youth gang, illegal drug-based distribution, and survival of young adult gang members in a post-industrial segmented economy. Clearly, powerful economic forces are affecting contemporary gangs as Wilson and other underclass theorists would predict. But when we take a closer look at the impact of economic, demographic, and institutional changes on processes within Milwaukee's poorest African-American neighborhoods, the situation becomes more complicated.

Gangs and Neighborhood Segmentation

Gangs have always been associated with neighborhoods and African-American gangs have been no exception. Thrasher found "Negroes" had "more than their share" of gangs (Thrasher 1963:132) as far back as the 1920s. In the neighborhood that Suttles studied, gangs were functional "markers" or signs by which neighborhood youth could know who may be harmful and who is not and thus were an important part of a neighborhood's search for order. Suttles' black gangs were not in any significant way distinct from white ethnic gangs (Suttles 1968:157). Similarly, the black Chicago gang members that Short and Strodtbeck (1965:108) studied were quite similar to nongang black youth though they were more lower class than white gang members. Until the 1960s, the sociological literature largely viewed black gangs as functional parts of black neighborhoods.

But things have been changing. Perkins, summarizing the history of black Chicago gangs, wrote that gangs first became disruptive to their communities in the late 1960s due to the influence of drugs, corrupting prison experiences, and the failure of community-based programs (Perkins 1987:40-42). Cloward and Ohlin theorized that housing projects and other big city "slums" tended to be disorganized and "produce powerful pressures for violent behavior among the young in these areas" (Cloward and Ohlin 1960:172). They correctly predicted that "delinquency will become increasingly violent in the future as a result of the disintegration of slum organization" (203).

Increasing violence in central cities has prompted angry responses from residents. Cooperation by broad elements of the black community with police sweeps of gang members in Los Angeles and elsewhere and the founding of "mothers against gangs" and similar organizations throughout the country are examples of community hostility to gangs. Gangs today are seen by both law enforcement and many community residents as basically dysfunctional. Today's gangs are a far cry from the "Negro" street gangs of Suttles' Addams area which contained the "best-known and most popular boys in the neighborhood" (Suttles 1968:172).

Based on our Milwaukee interviews, we concluded that gang members reciprocated the hostility of "respectables." While the gang founders were hostile toward police and schools as expected, they also severely criticized African-American community agencies which they felt were mainly "phoney." The black founders agreed their gangs were dysfunctional for their neighborhoods: two thirds of those we interviewed insisted that their gang was "not at all" about trying to help the black community. Some were shocked at even the suggestion that their gang would be concerned about anything but "green power" (i.e., money). The role model of choice for many of the founders we interviewed was not Dr. Martin Luther King, Jesse Jackson, or any African-American leader, but Al Capone.

One explanation for this intracommunity alienation in Milwaukee is the peculiar way black gangs formed. Gang formation in Milwaukee coincided with desegregation of the schools: a one-way desegregation plan that mandatorially bused only black children. While gangs originally formed from neighborhood groups of youth in conflict with youth from other neighborhoods, busing complicated the situation. School buses picking up African-American students often stopped in many different neighborhoods, mixing youth from rival gangs and transforming the buses into battlegrounds. Gang recruitment took place on the buses and in the schools as well as from the neighborhood. The black founders told us in 1985-86 that a majority of the members of their gangs no longer came from the original neighborhood where the gang formed.

Consequently, when the gang hung out on neighborhood corners, they were not seen by residents as just the "neighbors' kids" messing up. "I'll tell your Mama" did not work when no one knew who "mama" was or where she lived. Informal social controls were ineffective, so calling the police became the basic method to handle rowdiness and misbehavior as well as more serious delinquency. Hostility between the gangs and the neighborhood increased with each squad car arriving on the block.

A second explanation for intra-community hostility is provided by 1989 research in five of Milwaukee's poorest and all-black census tracts (Moore and Edari 1990b) where several of the gangs I had studied were founded. These neighborhoods exhibit many of the criteria of an "underclass" area, but they also differ in many respects from very poor ghetto neighborhoods described by Wilson and others.

Household income of the tracts was very low—1980 census data (before the eighties downturn) show more than 30 percent of the families in the five tracts living below poverty. The five tracts experienced a 42 percent population loss between 1960 and 1985. In 1989, when the interviews were completed, most (53.8 percent) respondents received AFDC and nearly twenty percent (19 percent) did not have a phone. A majority of residents in the five tracts presently live below the poverty line. The tracts certainly qualify as "underclass" areas by standard definitions (Ricketts and Mincy 1988).

But these neighborhoods are not uniformly poor. One quarter of the residents (28.6 percent) owned their own home—fifteen percent less than the city-wide average, but still a stable base within a very poor neighborhood. Half of the household heads lived at their current residence for five or more years. While stable employment had drastically declined in these tracts since 1980, still nearly one third of working respondents had held their current job for 10 or more years. Unlike the "densely settled ghetto areas" Sampson describes (1987:357) where residents have "difficulty recognizing their neighbors," 80 percent of the Milwaukee respondents said the best thing about their neighborhood *was* their "neighbors." Nearly three in five (59.2 percent) visited with neighbors at least once a week.

More striking were strong kinship ties, supporting earlier work by Stack (1974) and others. Nearly half of all respondents visited their parents every day and over ninety percent visited their parents monthly. An even higher percentage visited siblings at least once a month. Finally, more than three quarters belonged to families that held family reunions—and 77 percent of those respondents regularly attended those reunions. Even child protective clients, who are among the most transient residents, had extensive kinship networks (Moore and Edari 1990a).[2]

But the neighborhoods are not regarded positively by most residents. Less than one fifth (19.7 percent) said the neighborhood was a "good place to live," and 52 percent said they would move if they could. While the respondents liked their neighbors as the best thing about their community, the top three worst things were said to be drugs (64 percent), violence (52 percent), and gangs (20 percent). About half said things had gotten worse the past two years, and a majority (54.5 percent) believed things will continue to get worse. And the problems were not "around the corner" or in an adjacent neighborhood, but right on the blocks where the interviews took place. The interviewers were often told by respondents to not go to a certain house or to avoid a certain side of the street because of dangerous drug or gang problems.

The area also has few basic social institutions. Zip code 53206 is a 20 by 20 square block area with 40,000 residents in the heart of Milwaukee, containing the census tracts where the interviews took place. This area has no large chain grocery stores. There are no banks or check-cashing stores in the entire zip code area. Bars and drug houses are in plentiful supply and the area has the highest number of Milwaukee drug arrests. Still, in 1989, this zip code area did not have a single alcohol/drug treatment facility. Even community agencies are located overwhelmingly on the periphery of 53206, circling the neighborhoods they serve, but not a part of them.[3] Community programs, churches, and social workers were seldom mentioned by survey respondents as a resource to call in times of neighborhood trouble.[4]

In summary, while these poor African-American neighborhoods have characteristics of Wilson's notion of the underclass, they also exhibit important differences. On the one hand, central city Milwaukee neighborhoods have been getting poorer due to deindustrialization and have experienced substantial population loss. They are home to the poorest and most troubled of all Milwaukee's residents. The area's lack of basic institutions is reminiscent of descriptions by Thrasher (1927) and Shaw and McKay (1969) and supports aspects of Wilson's underclass thesis.

On the other hand, large numbers of working class African-American families still reside in these neighborhoods. Some want to leave but cannot because of residential segregation (Massey and Eggers 1990) or lack of affordable housing. But many stay because they want to. Rather than neighborhoods populated overwhelmingly by a residue left behind by a fleeing middle and working class, as Wilson described, Milwaukee's "underclass" neighborhoods are a checkerboard of struggling working class and poor families, coexisting, even on the same block, with drug houses, gangs, and routine violence.

This ecological coexistence explains much of the intra-community tension between poor and working families and underclass gangs. Clearly when drug deals gone bad turn into midnight shoot-outs, residents of a neighborhood will be scared and angry. Contrary to Wilson's claim, events in one part of the block or neighborhood are often of vital concern to those residing in other parts (Wilson 1987:38). With a lack of effective community institutions, residents can either ignore the gunshots in the night, arm themselves for self-protection, call "911"—or give in to the fear and despair by moving out.[5]

While Milwaukee neighborhoods are not the socially disorganized underclass area reported by Wilson, neither are they the highly organized neighborhoods described by Whyte (1943) or Suttles (1968). Milwaukee's poor neighborhoods have segmented and an uneasy peace reigns between nervous factions. Suttles (1968) saw the 1960s Addams area as representing "ordered segmentation," where firm boundaries between ethnic neighborhoods helped make "a decent world within which people can live" (234). Instead, Milwaukee's neighborhood segments have become a prime source of instability.

This picture of neighborhood segmentation is consistent with Anderson's portrait of "Northton," a poor African-American community in a large eastern city (Anderson 1990). "Old heads" in Northton are not so much missing, as they have become demoralized and their advice shunned (78-80). Respectable residents are confronted by a growing street culture that increases community distrust of young people, victimizes neighborhood residents, and lures children into dangerous activities (92). Police simplistically divide the neighborhood between the "good people" and those linked to drug trafficking (202-3). Conflict between neighborhood segments inevitably increases, and "solidarity" is sacrificed to the imposed order of police patrols, vigilante justice, and prisons.

These heterogeneous but segmented neighborhoods in "Northton" and Milwaukee may be characteristic of many "underclass" communities across the United States (Jencks 1990). How to stabilize such neighborhoods is one of the major policy debates of the nineties.

Gangs, Neighborhoods, and Public Policy

In light of these findings, what do we make of this contradictory picture of gangs and their neighborhoods? What policies ought to be followed? The data suggest the drug economy nourishes in large part because of the absence of good jobs. It is hard to argue with the response from a 1986 interview:

> Q: OK. we're at the end here. The Governor comes in. He says, Darryl, I'm gonna give you a million dollars to work with gangs. Do what you want with it.
>
> A: Give 'em all jobs.

But while jobs are certainly needed, there is no reason to believe hundreds of thousands of good paying entry-level jobs will appear anytime soon from either the private or public sector. In the absence of sufficient jobs, pressure will continue to mount for more police and more prisons as the policy option of choice to curtail violence. This militarization of our neighborhoods is inevitable unless community residents and public officials can be persuaded that alternative policies are plausible and can be effective. But what alternative policies should be advocated?

One popular option is to work with city hall and call for more federal resources to come to cities. While we clearly need more resources, a more critical issue is how money is spent. As Spergel says in summarizing his recommendations in the National Youth Gang Survey "the implication of our findings is that more resources alone for police or even human service programs would not contribute much to dealing effectively with the youth gang problem" (Spergel and Curry 1990:309). In the absence of institutional reform and guarantees that resources will get to those that need it, more resources alone will not necessarily contribute to solving gang problems.[6]

The development of effective policy will require a struggle within cities over where new and existing programs are physically located, who will be served, and how the massive public bureaucracies (which gobble most resources intended for the poor) should be structured. Rather than proposing specific new model gang programs or narrowly calling for a federal office of gang control (Miller 1990), our data suggests a focus on strengthening neighborhood social institutions. Our experience in reforming Milwaukee's human service system suggests that we should adopt four policies to strengthen neighborhood-level social control.

1. Public spending and private investment must be concentrated in the most impoverished areas. This does not mean spend more human service dollars "for" the underclass by funding well-intentioned programs run by middle-class white providers located on the periphery of the poorest neighborhoods. Rather, I suggest we should insist that money be spent mainly on programs physically located *in* underclass neighborhoods, run by people with ties to the neighborhoods they intend to serve. This policy has the effect of targeting programs for the underclass while also strengthening minority agencies or creating new agencies within very poor neighborhoods. These agencies provide not only services but also can provide jobs for neighborhood residents. As employment opportunities increase and better funded local agencies become centers for social action, pressures for working- and middle-class residents to flee should decrease.

For example, in Milwaukee, close examination of where human service dollars were spent by zip code exposed that less than 1 percent of $100 million of Department of Health and Human Service contract dollars in 1988 was spent on programs located in two of Milwaukee's poorest zip code areas (53206 and 53204). These two areas contain only eight percent of Milwaukee County's population but are home to 25 percent of Milwaukee's human service clients. These figures were used by our reform administration to direct several million dollars in purchase contracts to agencies physically located in the two zip code areas, helping build an institutional infrastructure. Boarded up buildings are being rehabilitated to house the new agencies, employing neighborhood youth in the rehabbing effort.

Redirecting existing money is not an easy task. When we sent more than "crumbs" to neighborhood organizations, the mainly white traditional agencies—which are located downtown or in integrated, more stable neighborhoods—howled "reverse discrimination" and lobbied against us. Funding new programs is a zero sum game: if agencies located in poor neighborhoods are to get funded, agencies located elsewhere stand to lose. Those providers will almost certainly have more political power and connections than poor neighborhood organizations.

But as our research shows, while very poor neighborhoods have been devastated by economic and demographic changes, they also have important strengths to build on. The residents who live in poor neighborhoods need stable, well-funded agencies and institutions in which to participate. This recommendation is a call for sustained local political struggle over *where* money is spent to better stabilize impoverished neighborhoods.

2. Programs should be fully evaluated to see if they are having a positive impact on gangs or those most in need. It is not only important where the money is spent, but it is also critical whether anyone besides the agency or bureaucracy benefits. The inability of traditional agencies to serve the "hard to reach" has a long history: the Chicago Area Project (Schlossman, Zellman, and Schavelson 1984) was initiated to fill just such a gap. Geis cites the 1960s New York City Youth Board as an example of the need for innovative programming to replace the traditional agencies which were unable "to respond readily to new ideas and approaches" (Geis 1965:43). And some programs do "work." Lizbeth Schorr lists numerous contemporary programs that have been effective and could be replicated (Schorr 1988).

Large public bureaucracies are seldom concerned with formal results of programs. Once programs are funded, their continuation is often all that is offered as proof of effectiveness. In Milwaukee, research on agencies which received more than $20 million dollars worth of contracts to work with delinquents discovered the Department of Social Services kept no records at all of client outcomes of these programs. Funding decisions were based almost solely on routine approval of the re-funding of those agencies funded the year before (Hagedorn 1989b).

Programs thus continue with no regard for their effectiveness for clients. Lindblom points out the apparent absurdity that "In an important sense, therefore, it is not irrational for an administrator to defend a policy as good without being able to specify what it is good for" (Lindblom 1959:84). James Q. Wilson, in a forum on "Can Government Agencies be Managed?" recommended the novel idea that managers be judged on program results, a prospect he doubted would happen because "It is in no one's interest in Washington, D.C.," to do it (Wilson 1990:33). Many organizational theorists have pointed out that program evaluation serves only ceremonial functions for public bureaucracies (Meyer and Rowan 1981, Weick 1976). If sociologists are not among those insisting that social programs be evaluated and show results for the clients they are intended to serve, who will?

3. Fund family preservation programs. One of the most encouraging developments in the past decade in social work has been family preservation programs (Nelson, Landsman, and Duetelman 1990). These short-term intensive empowerment model programs which focus not on an individual client but rather the needs of the entire family have been remarkably successful.[7] In dozens of states and cities these programs, many of them modeled after the successful "homebuilders" projects funded by the Edna McConnell Clark Foundation, have reduced out of home placements and helped families learn how to stay together during a crisis.

Families where an older sibling is involved with gangs may be ideal candidates for these types of intensive, coordinated efforts. Our data show that many child protective clients have extensive family networks whose strengths could be utilized by intensive interventions. Milwaukee received a $1 million dollar grant from the Philip Morris Companies to fund a "homebuilders" model program. An agency located in one of the poorest areas of the city was awarded the contract to implement the program and collaborate with the public school system. As noted above, there was considerable resistance to the program from elements within the social welfare bureaucracy where family-based, results-oriented programming was viewed as a threat to business as usual (Nelson 1988). Yet, strategies were developed to confront the opposition, and the program was implemented.

4. Finally, large public bureaucracies should become more neighborhood based and more open to input from clients and the neighborhoods they serve. Reminiscent of the 1960s community control movement (Altschuler 1970), current research suggests that social control is least effective when imposed by outside forces. Community controls are strengthened most when informal community level networks are voluntarily tied to external bureaucracies and other resources (Figueira-McDonough 1991).[8] Public dollars for social programs today are largely used to support "street level bureaucrats" whose structure of work often makes it difficult to deliver services that improve the quality of life of their clients (Lipsky 1980). Diverse reform trends in policing, education, and social services all stress more community involvement in public bureaucracies (Chubb and Moe 1990, Comer 1972, Goldstein 1977, Kamerman and Kahn 1989). These reforms, insofar as they increase client and neighborhood control and break down existing bureaucratic barriers, merit support.

While Lipsky and others comment that it will be difficult to reform public bureaucracies in the absence of social movement (Lipsky 1980:210, Wineman 1984:240), unfavorable conditions should not be an excuse for inaction. The Milwaukee experience of creating multi-disciplinary teams of human service workers, moving them into the neighborhoods, and creating neighborhood councils to increase accountability is one example of such a reform.

Conclusion

Deindustrialization has altered the nature of gangs, creating a new association between the youth gang, illegal drug-based distribution, and survival of young adult gang members in a post-industrial segmented economy. While it would be a mistake to see all gangs as drug-dealing organizations, the lack of opportunity for unskilled delinquents creates powerful strains on gang members to become involved in the illegal economy. Without a major jobs program, illegal traffic in drugs and related violence seem likely to continue at unacceptable levels (Goldstein 1985, Johnson et al. 1989).

Although neighborhood changes are clearly relevant to gang activities, Wilson's characterization of the underclass as living in neighborhoods from which middle and working class African-Americans have fled and abandoned social institutions (Wilson 1987:56) does not fully apply in cities like Milwaukee. Instead, there are deteriorating neighborhoods with declining resources and fractured internal cohesion. In cities like Milwaukee, it is not the absence of working people that define underclass neighborhoods but more the absence of effective social institutions. Without community controlled institutions, conventional values will have diminished appeal, neighborhoods will segment, solidarity will weaken, and working residents will continue to flee. The research on Milwaukee is consistent with the basic tenet of social theory, that the lack of effective institutions is related to crime and delinquency. The data support Spergel and other who call for "community mobilization and more resources for and reform of the educational system and job market" (Spergel and Curry 1990:309) as the most effective approach to gang control.

This article does support Wilson and others who call for massive new federal job programs. While lobbying for new state and federal job programs, social scientists should also focus on ways to encourage private and public investment in poor neighborhoods and advocate for more community control of social institutions. This means a stepped up involvement by academics in the workings of the large public bureaucracies which control resources needed to rebuild these communities.[9]

In the words of C. Wright Mills, bureaucracies "often carry out series of apparently rational actions without any ideas of the ends they serve" (Mills 1959:168). All too often the ends public bureaucracies serve are not helpful for poor communities. This article can be read as a call for social scientists to step up the struggle to make public bureaucracies more rational for the truly disadvantaged.[10]

Notes

1. Moore (1991) also finds a mixing of gang cliques in Los Angeles gangs. Short's (1990) 1960 Nobles were mainly employed in the early 1970s when they were restudied, in contrast to Vicelords, virtually all of whom had more prison experience, many of whom still identified with the Vicelords and were involved in illegal operations more than a decade after they were first studied.
2. Child protective clients, however, more than other residents, turned to police for help with problems than asking help from their relatives or neighbors.
3. In contrast, zip code 53204, a predominantly Hispanic area home to several Hispanic gangs, is dotted with community agencies, banks, merchants, and grocery stores. While this area is a neighborhood of first settlement for Mexican immigrants, it does not have the characteristics of social disorganization of the predominantly African-American 53206 neighborhoods. Those who use "percent Hispanic" as a proxy for social disorganization should take note of these findings (cf. Curry and Spergel 1988:387).
4. There are other institutions in the area with a high profile, particularly law enforcement. But the strong police presence plays to a mixed review. While most residents (38.3 percent) called the police for any serious problems in the neighborhood before they called relatives or friends, one in eight (12.1 percent) listed police as one of the three top "bad things" about the neighborhood. Police are still viewed with suspicion and fear in African-American communities.
5. It must be remembered, however, that the illegal drug economy, while disruptive, is also sustained by a local demand. Workers in drug houses assert that most Milwaukee cocaine sales are to people within the neighborhood, not to outsiders (in contrast to Kornblum and Williams [1985:11]). But when illegal activities bring trouble to the neighborhood, particularly violence, police are often welcomed in ousting drug dealers and combatting gang problems (Sullivan 1989:128).
6. City hall may be as capable today of using academics against Washington for its own purposes as Washington in the sixties was adept at using academics to attack city hall (Gouldner 1968, Piven and Cloward 1971).
7. Recent control group evaluations have questioned these programs' effectiveness in reducing out of home placements. The main conclusion from the evaluations is the incapacity of social service bureaucracies to refer the appropriate clients to the programs. The evaluations found family preservation programs are so effective that social workers try to place families in the programs even though they do not fit project guidelines (cf. Feldman 1990, Schuerman et al. 1990, Yuan 1990). These evaluations also point out the important role social scientists can play in insisting programs be properly implemented.
8. This was also Suttles' conclusion: as community ties to external forces increased, so did its internal social control—it became more "provincial" (1968:223-224). Social disorganization and social control, Sullivan also points out, is not linear, but varies widely between poor neighborhoods (Sullivan 1989:237).
9. This recommendation is not a call for revisiting the Chicago Area Project which relied on private financing and performed a "mediating role" with local institutions (Schlossman and Sedlak 1983, Sorrentino 1959), nor is it a call for a new war on poverty with built in antagonism between city hall and short lived federally funded agencies (Marris and Rein 1967, Moynihan 1969). Rather, it is a call for academics to directly engage in local struggles over how and where large public bureaucracies distribute existing resources.
10. This article is based on several previous papers. The first was presented on April 24, 1990, to the U.S. Conference of Mayors in Washington, D.C. Two others were presented at the 85th Annual ASA Meetings, also in Washington D.C., August, 1990. Joan Moore, Carl Taylor, Howard Fuller, and Clinton Holloway made helpful comments on various earlier drafts. *Social Problems*' anonymous reviewers also added valuable insights. Correspondence to Hagedorn, University of Wisconsin—Milwaukee, Urban Research Center, P.O. Box 413, Milwaukee, WI 53201.

References

Altshuler, Alan A. 1970. *Community Control, The Black Demand for Participation in Large American Cities*. New York: Pegasus.

Anderson, Elijah. 1990. *Streetwise: Race, Class, and Change in an Urban Community*. Chicago: University of Chicago Press.

Aponte, Robert. 1988 "Conceptualizing the underclass: An alternative perspective." Paper presented at Annual Meetings of the American Sociological Association. August. Atlanta, Georgia.

Bluestone, Barry, and Bennett Harrison. 1982. *The Deindustrialization of America: Plant Closings, Community Abandonment, and the Dismantling of Basic Industry*. New York: Basic Books.

Chubb, John E., and Terry M. Moe. 1990. *Politics, Markets, and America's Schools*. Washington, D.C.: The Brookings Institute.

Cloward, Richard, and Lloyd Ohlin. 1960. *Delinquency and Opportunity*. Glencoe, Ill: Free Press.

Comer, James P. 1972. *Beyond Black and White*. New York: Quadrangle Books.

Curry, G. David, and Irving A. Spergel. 1988 "Gang homicide, delinquency, and community." *Criminology* 26:381-405.

Feldman, Leonard. 1990. "Evaluating the impact of family preservation services in New Jersey." Trenton, N.J.: New Jersey Division of Youth and Family Services.

Figueira-McDonough, Josefina. 1991. "Community structure and delinquency: A typology." *Social Service Review* 65:68-91.

Gans, Herbert J. 1990. "The dangers of the underclass: Its harmfulness as a planning concept." New York: Russell Sage Foundation, Working Paper #4.

Geis, Gilbert. 1965. "Juvenile gangs." Washington, D.C.: President's Committee on Juvenile Delinquency and Youth Crime.

Goldstein, Herman. 1977. *Policing a Free Society*. Cambridge, Mass.: Ballinger Publishing.

Goldstein, Paul J. 1985. "The drugs-violence nexus: A tripartite conceptual framework." *Journal of Drug Issues* 15:493-506.

Gouldner, Alvin. 1968. "The sociologist as partisan: Sociology and the welfare state." *The American Sociologist* May: 103-116.

Hagedorn, John M. 1988. *People and Folks: Gangs, Crime, and the Underclass in a Rustbelt City*. Chicago: Lakeview.

——. 1989a. "Roots of Milwaukee's underclass." Milwaukee, Wis.: Milwaukee County Department of Health and Human Services.

——. 1989b. "Study of youth released from residential treatment, day treatment, and group homes in 1989." Milwaukee, Wi.: Milwaukee County Department of Health and Human Services.

Huff, C. Ronald. 1989. "Youth gangs and public policy." *Crime and Delinquency* 35:524-537.

Jencks, Christopher. 1989. "Who is the underclass—and is it growing."*Focus* 12:14-31.

Johnson, Bruce, Terry Williams, Kojo Dei, and Harry Sanabria. 1989. "Drug abuse in the inner city." In *Drugs and the Criminal Justice System*, ed. Michael Tonry and James Q. Wilson, Chicago: University of Chicago.

Kamerman, Sheila B., and Alfred J. Kahn. 1989. "Social services for children, youth, and families in the United States." Greenwich, Conn.: The Annie E. Casey Foundation.

Kasarda, John D. 1985. "Urban change and minority opportunities." In *The New Urban Reality*, ed. Paul E. Peterson, 33-65. Washington, D.C.: The Brookings Institute.

Kornblum, William, and Terry Williams. 1985. *Growing Up Poor*. Lexington, Mass: Lexington Books.

Lindblom, Charles E. 1959. "The Science of 'Muddling Through.' " *Public Administrative Review* 19: 79-88.

Lipsky, Michael. 1980. *Street-Level Bureaucracies: Dilemmas of the Individual in Public Services*. New York: Russell Sage.

Marris, Peter, and Martin Rein. 1967. *Dilemmas of Social Reform, Poverty, and Community Action in the United States*. Chicago: University of Chicago.

Massey, Douglas S., and Mitchell L. Eggers. 1990. "The ecology of inequality: Minorities and the concentration of poverty, 1970-1980." *American Journal of Sociology* 95:1153-1188.

Meyer, John M., and Brian Rowan. 1981. "Institutionalized organizations: Formalized structure as myth and ceremony." In *Complex Organizations: Critical Perspectives*, ed. Mary Zey-Ferrell and Michael Aiken, 303-321. Glenview, Ill.: Scott, Foresman, and Company.

Miller, Walter. 1990. "Why the United States has failed to solve its youth gang problem." In *Gangs in America*, ed. C. Ronald Huff, 263-287. Beverly Hills, Calif.: Sage.

Mills, C. Wright. 1959. *The Sociological Imagination*. London: Oxford University Press.

Moore, Joan W. 1985. "Isolation and stigmatization in the development of an underclass: The case of Chicano gangs in East Los Angeles." *Social Problems* 33:1-10.

——. 1991. *Going Down to the Barrio*. Philadelphia: Temple University Press.

Moore, Joan W., and Ronald Edari. 1990a. "Survey of Chips clients: Final report." Milwaukee, Wis.: University of Wisconsin—Milwaukee Urban Research Research Center.

——. 1990b. "Youth initiative needs assessment survey: Final report." Milwaukee, Wis.: University of Wisconsin—Milwaukee.

Moynihan, Daniel P. 1969. *Maximum Feasible Misunderstanding: Community Action in the War on Poverty*. New York: The Free Press.

Nelson, Douglas. 1988. "Recognizing and realizing the potential of 'family preservation.' " Washington, D.C.:Center for the Study of Social Policy.

Nelson, Kristine, Miriam J. Landsman, and Wendy Deutelman. 1990. "Three Models of Family-Centered Placement Protection Services." *Child Welfare* 69:3-21.

Perkins, Useni Eugene. 1987. *Explosion of Chicago's Street Gangs*. Chicago: Third World Press.

Piven, Frances Fox, and Richard A. Cloward. 1971. *Regulating the Poor: The Functions of Public Welfare*. New York: Pantheon.

——. 1987. "The contemporary relief debate." In *The Mean Season: The Attack On the Welfare State*, ed. Fred Block, Richard A. Cloward, Barbara Ehrenreich, and Frances Fox Piven, 45-108. New York: Pantheon.

Ricketts, Erol, and Ronald Mincy. 1988. "Growth of the underclass: 1970-1980." Washington, D.C.: Changing Domestic Priorities Project, The Urban Institute.

Ricketts, Erol, Ronald Mincy, and Isabel V. Sawhill. 1988. "Defining and measuring the underclass." *Journal of Policy Analysis and Management* 7:316-325.

Sampson, Robert J. 1987. "Urban black violence: The effect of male joblessness and family disruption." *American Journal of Sociology* 93:348-382.

Schlossman, Steven, and Michael Sedlak. 1983. "The Chicago Area Project revisited." Santa Monica, Calif.: Rand Corporation.

Schlossman, Steven L., Gail Zellman, and Richard Schavelson. 1984. *Delinquency Prevention in South Chicago*. Santa Monica, Calif.: Rand Corporation.

Schorr, Lisbeth. 1988. *Within our Reach*. New York: Doubleday.

Schuerman, John R., Tina L. Pzepnicki, Julia H. Littell, and Stephen Budde. 1990. "Some intruding realities." Chicago: University of Chicago, Chapin Hall Center for Children.

Shaw, Clifford R., and Henry D. McKay. 1969. *Juvenile Delinquency and Urban Areas*. Chicago: University of Chicago.

Short, James F. 1990a. "Gangs, neighborhoods, and youth crime." Houston, Tex.: Sam Houston State University Criminal Justice Center.

——. 1990b. "New wine in old bottles? Change and continuity in American gangs." In *Gangs in America*, ed. C. Ronald Huff, 223-239. Beverly Hills, Calif: Sage.

Short, James F., and Fred L. Strodtbeck. 1965. *Group Process and Gang Delinquency*. Chicago: University of Chicago.

Sorrentino, Anthony. 1959. "The Chicago Area Project after 25 years." *Federal Probation* 23:40-45.

Spergel, Irving A., and G. David Curry. 1990. "Strategies and perceived agency effectiveness in dealing with the youth gang problem." In *Gangs in America*, ed. C. Ronald Huff, 288-309, Beverly Hills, Calif.: Sage.

Stack, Carol B. 1974. *All Our Kin*. New York: Harper Torchback.

Sullivan, Mercer L. 1989. *Getting Paid: Youth Crime and Work in the Inner City*. Ithaca, N.Y: Cornell University Press.

Suttles, Gerald D. 1968. *The Social Order of the Slum*. Chicago: University of Chicago.

Taylor, Carl. 1990. *Dangerous Society*. East Lansing, Mich: Michigan State University Press.

Thrasher, Frederick. [1927] 1963. *The Gang*. Chicago: University of Chicago.

Trotter, Joe William. 1985. *Black Milwaukee: The Making of an Industrial Proletariat 1915-1945*. Chicago: University of Illinois.

Vigil, Diego. 1988. *Barrio Gangs*. Austin, Tex: University of Texas Press.

Weick, Karl E. 1976. "Educational organizations as loosely coupled systems." *Administrative Science Quarterly* 21:1-19.

White, Sammis, John F. Zipp, Peter Reynolds, and James R. Paetsch. 1988. "The Changing Milwaukee Industrial Structure." Milwaukee, Wis.: University of Wisconsin-Milwaukee, Urban Research Center.

Whyte, William Foote. 1943. *Street Corner Society*. Chicago: University of Chicago.

Wilson, James Q. 1990. "Can government agencies be managed?" *The Bureaucrat*. 9:29-33.

Wilson, William Julius. 1985. "Cycles of deprivation and the underclass debate." *Social Service Review* 59:541-559.

——. 1987. *The Truly Disadvantaged*. Chicago: University of Chicago.

——. 1991. "Studying inner-City social dislocations: The challenge of public agenda research." *American Sociological Review* 56:1-14.

Wineman, Steven. 1984. *The Politics of Human Services*. Boston: South End Press.

Yuan, Ying-Ying T. 1990. "Evaluation of AB 1562 in-home care demonstration projects." Sacramento, Calif.: Walter R. McDonald and Associates. ✦

Civil Gang Abatement: A Community Based Policing Tool of the Office of the Los Angeles City Attorney

L.A. City Attorney Gang Prosecution Section

The current thrust in gang policy is toward gang suppression and deterrence at the expense of prevention, rehabilitation, and efforts to change the social conditions that make gangs viable options for more and more youths today. Civil Gang Abatement provides an example of this approach, one which raises serious issues about the civil rights of gang members, as the use of civil abatement laws provides the police with the right to arrest individuals in gangs for acts that would otherwise be non-criminal. In addition to the fact that these measures are undertaken without also providing alternatives for gang youth, it is likely, given our reading on group process in Section II, that these efforts will increase gang cohesiveness rather than diminish it.

The L.A. City Attorney "Civil Gang Abatement" is a coordinated effort by police, prosecutors, and local residents to significantly reduce illegal gang, drug and other criminal activity while simultaneously identifying and providing resources to measurably improve the guality of life for residents of a targeted neighborhood. While the legal proceeding which is entitled "Civil Gang Abatement" is, by itself, a legal proceeding aimed at obtaining an injunction against a criminal element such as a street gang to prohibit them from engaging in conduct which facilitates criminal activity, the *ultimate* goal of the Civil Gang Abatement is to act as a *vehicle* for the coordination of various community-based policing efforts such as Neighborhood Watch, graffiti abatement, building abatements, at-risk youth identification, and employment recruitment as well as the more traditional law enforcement efforts to suppress narcotics trafficking and gang activity through undercover narcotics operations and the vertical (specialized) prosecution of hard-core gang members. When the Civil Gang Abatement is coordinated with other government and community-based efforts, as described in the "Broken Windows"[1] theory, crime is not only reduced but the neighborhood's *quality of life* is visibly improved and a mechanism remains to insure its continued improvement. Because the Civil Gang Abatement, by definition, begins through the mobilization of the community through meetings of local residents, police and prosecutors to identify problems which exist in the neighborhood in support of the prosecutor's request for an injunction, the Civil Gang Abatement also becomes a means to identify those resources which are necessary to improve the quality of life in a particular neighborhood. Such community meetings invariably identify needed community resources beyond law enforcement deployment, such as child care, parenting classes, street maintenance, graffiti removal, and increased employment opportunities. The Civil Gang Abatement is successful because it includes the coordination of resources to address these problems while simultaneously reducing criminal activity through the injunction and other law enforcement efforts. As such, the Civil Gang Abatement is a complete program which begins as a means to identify specific criminal elements and to provide an innovative legal solution to abate such criminal activity while simultaneously identifying other community needs and providing those resources which will bring about a measurable improvement in the quality of life for residents of the targeted area. The following is an illustration of how the Civil Gang Abatement can simultaneously mobilize a community through community based policing, identify and suppress drug dealing by a local street gang and also begin the revitalization of the community as a result of the community empowerment brought about by the Civil Gang Abatement process.

Gang Related Drug Dealing *Without* a 'Civil Gang Abatement'

Without a "Civil Gang Abatement," *uniformed* police vainly attempt to enforce drug laws against street dealers. All day long, gang members stand at intersections known for drug sales, wear pagers, dress in gang attire, flash handsigns, and wave at and approach passing vehicles and pedestrians for what are certainly offers to buy drugs. Yet, because all of these activities (i.e. wearing pagers, flashing handsigns, waving at and approaching vehicles, etc.) are lawful conduct, the gang members are immune from arrest unless an actual exchange of money for drugs is observed. Since the uniformed officer typically observes only the lawful activity preceding the actual sale, he

Prepared by the Gang Unit, Los Angeles City Attorney's Office, Los Angeles, California, Martin Vranicar, Supervisor. Edited by Jule Bishop, Deputy City Attorney. Reprinted by permission.

is forced to drive past in frustration while law abiding citizens look on in disgust.

Although it is true that an *undercover* officer may be able to successfully arrest and convict a limited number of gang members for drug sales and hopefully obtain lengthy prison terms (which is almost impossible in Los Angeles due to jail overcrowding), undercover enforcement fails to have any measurable impact on the *ability of the gang to profit*. This is because the "removal" of even a substantial number of drug dealing gang members by undercover officers, for no matter how long, merely creates a "vacancy" in the ranks of the gang's organization, with an endless supply of young recruits ready to assume that enviable position on the street corner dealing the gang's narcotics. Even under the best of circumstances, the gang will successfully consummate hundreds, if not thousands, of drug transactions while suffering only a handful of unsuccessful sales due to undercover enforcement. Add to this the fact that undercover narcotics officers are few in number and that all police departments rely, for the most part, upon uniformed personnel to achieve crime suppression and reduction, it is not surprising that while some gang members may serve long prison sentences, conspicuous drug dealing by the gang continues unabated.

Gang Related Drug Dealing *With* a 'Civil Gang Abatement'

With a "Civil Gang Abatement," *uniformed* officers are given the tools to effectively impact a gang's ability to profit from drug dealing, while simultaneously providing the means for the community to improve the quality of life for all its residents. The legal procedure known as a "Civil Gang Abatement" is similar to a situs or building abatement.[2] However, unlike a building abatement which may result in a court ordered injunction against a *property owner*, the "Civil Gang Abatement" seeks a series of court orders against *members of a street gang*. For those unfamiliar with building abatements, the legal procedure known as a "Civil Gang Abatement" is easily understood when likened to an ordinary labor strike.

Consider, for a moment, an emotional labor strike wherein picketers grow in number and eventually become unruly, interfering with the ability of the employer and working employees to enter the work place. Once it becomes evident that routine police action will not be able to insure the protection of those choosing to cross the picket lines and violence appears certain, the employer and/or police provide evidence to a judge that the strikers are creating a dangerous nuisance. The court helps "abate" or reduce the nuisance by issuing orders which prohibit or "enjoin" the strikers from doing certain things, such as picketing too close to the entrance of the work place, limiting the number of picketers and other restrictions which will help to curb anticipated violence. These orders are in the form of an injunction which applies to every striker who chooses to picket and possibly interfere with the employer's ability to conduct business during the strike. If, after the strikers are formally notified of the injunction, they choose to ignore the orders of the court (e.g. picketing closer to the work entrance than the court injunction permits), the strikers are subject to arrest for Penal Code Section 166.4.[3]

Thus, aggressive enforcement of an injunction enables law enforcement to effectively *prevent* imminent criminal activity by arresting persons for *prohibited patterns of conduct which are known to precede and facilitate these crimes*. In the case of the strikers, this pattern of conduct includes strikers congregating in dangerously large groups, standing too close to a work place entrance and carrying signs which could be used as weapons. Since, in the case of gang activity, law enforcement can also identify many patterns of lawful activity by gang members which contribute to and normally precede the commission of certain crimes, such as drug dealing, the goal of the Civil Gang Abatement, as in the labor strike analogy, is to identify otherwise lawful conduct by gang members which precedes and furthers criminal activity and then seek to enjoin or prohibit it.[4]

Many gang members wear pagers, "dress down" in gang attire, flash "handsigns," approach and solicit business from pedestrians and passing vehicles, and congregate at known drug sales locations, all for the express purpose of selling illegal narcotics. If, however, this conduct is enjoined (prohibited) by a court, uniformed police are, for the first time, able to make arrests *before* drug deals are consummated, thus impairing the gang's ability to *profit* from drug dealing (which ultimately *prevents* gang-related drug dealing). Simply put, instead of consummating hundreds of illegal drug transactions and earning large profits before suffering an arrest for sale of narcotics, gang members are now subject to arrest for simply doing the things that are *necessary* for them to do *before* they can begin to sell the drugs and earn the profits. Since even standing on a particular corner or wearing a beeper can subject a gang member to arrest, the previously helpless *uniformed* officer is now able to *interfere* with and *reduce* the gang's ability to profit from drug sales by arresting the gang members *before* they are able to consummate a drug transaction. This effort, combined with undercover strategies, can effectively interfere with the gang's ability to profit while incarcerating an increasing number of drug dealing gang members.[5] Since the gang's potential for profits is diminished, the chronic and daily drug dealing on neighborhood street corners ceases and other forces are able to work together to significantly improve the overall quality of life for the residents of the community.

Civil Gang Abatement: How It Works

The L.A. City Attorney "Civil Gang Abatement" brings together specially assigned police, prosecutors and residents of the targeted neighborhood to gather the evidence which will prove to a judge that identified patterns of conduct such as the wearing of pagers, approaching pedestrians and passing vehicles and congregating at known drug locations furthers the illegal drug activity of the local gang and deserves to be enjoined by the court. Through the use of police, resident and community leader declarations, photographs and videos, crime and arrest statistics, and anything else that helps describe the gang's effect on the community, the Civil Gang Abatement persuades the judge to issue an injunction prohibiting the gang members, as a group, from engaging in the patterns of conduct identified by the community and police. Before the injunction is issued, a "Notice" by the City or District Attorney is distributed throughout the community warning the gang that if it does not stop (abate) its illegal criminal activities, the City or District Attorney's Office will seek an injunction against the gang.[6] If statistics and other evidence indicate that the gang is not complying with the Notice to Abate, then the prosecutor files a complaint requesting issuance of an injunction which includes court orders designed to help abate the criminal activity of the defendant street gang. Once the injunction is issued, the police can serve copies of the injunction on all gang members and immediately enforce the orders of the court through arrests for disobedience of a court order.[7] Ideally, those gang members arrested for violating the court injunction should be prosecuted by the City or District Attorney assigned to the Civil Gang Abatement. This special prosecutor not only will seek significant jail terms but more importantly, pursue probation conditions (such as "search and seizure" conditions, "do not associate with other gang members," and even "exclusion" from the neighborhood) which were not included in the terms of the civil injunction. Thus, even if a gang member violates the injunction and suffers only a small jail sentence with probation, a subsequent violation of probation can result in significant jail sentences and the virtual removal of that gang member from the neighborhood.[8]

Coordination of Other Efforts: 'The Community Impact Team'

While the effort to obtain an injunction against a drug dealing street gang can be, by itself, effective in interfering with a gang's ability to profit from drug dealing and thus reduce the gang's other criminal activities, the "Civil Gang Abatement" can and should be combined with other law enforcement strategies to address the many other problems that are certain to occur in the targeted neighborhood, as described in the "Broken Windows Theory." The creation of "Community Impact Teams" composed of specially assigned police and prosecutors facilitates the coordination of these efforts, as well as the gathering of the evidence necessary to obtain an injunction against the street gang.[9] For example, the Community Impact Teams (or whatever name one assigns to such a group) schedules a number of community meetings attended by local residents, landlords, merchants, regular patrol and narcotics officers and probation officers. At these meetings, the "Community Impact Team" explains the concept of the "Civil Gang Abatement" and its reliance upon the participation of the community. Residents, merchants and property owners attending these meetings are asked to document how the local gang and its criminal activities have negatively impacted their quality of life. Citizens maintain diaries or "logs" of life in the area controlled or frequented by the gang. Not only is gang activity recorded but, importantly, the *consequences* of gang activity are also documented. As such, the logs not only include descriptions of gunshots going off each night and routine intimidation by gang members but also describe how municipal sanitation trucks avoid the neighborhood for fear of gang violence and streets remain in disrepair because maintenance workers are afraid to enter the area. These logs not only serve to mobilize the community against a local street gang but become the primary evidence in court to justify the issuance of an injunction.[10]

'Broken Windows Theory' and Community-Based Policing:[11] A Non-Traditional Approach to Law Enforcement

Because the consequences of gang activity include the deterioration of the normal municipal services such as street maintenance, garbage collection and other services critical to the quality of life of any community (see Broken Window, above), the logs also become an important resource for use by the "Community Impact Team" in determining what other remedies are required to restore the quality of life in the neighborhood. For example, if residents describe trash and debris in alleys, the Team may discover that sanitation trucks do not regularly pick up trash in alleys for fear of violence or simply out of disgust because the gang quickly replaces the trash within hours of its pickup. The "Community Impact Team" thus, through its coordination with other governmental entities including the Department of Sanitation, takes necessary action to insure that future trash pickups include alleys in the targeted neighborhood. The "Civil Gang Abatement" is, accordingly, not only an effective and logical law enforcement tool for the permanent abatement of drug dealing street gangs, but a vehicle to assist a "Community Impact Team" in improving the *quality of life* in a neighborhood. Because the law enforcement activity is scheduled to occur *at the same time* that municipal services are restored by a "Community Impact Team," the lessons learned from the "Broken Window Theory" are realized and the community enjoys a renewed sense of calm as crime is reduced and the neighborhood actually begins to *look* and *feel* safer, all at the same time.

Some may question the wisdom of employing police and prosecutors, at significant taxpayer expense, to spearhead an effort to improve the quality of life for a neighborhood besieged by gangs and drugs. Why not use staff from offices of elected officials, especially since the "Broken Windows Theory" involves the coordination of municipal services normally not under the control or supervision of law enforcement? The reason, however, is simple. Since the coordination of all the efforts, both law enforcement strategies and municipal services, must be carefully timed in relation to when successes are achieved by police and prosecutors, only prosecutors and police are able to know *when* the restoration of municipal services is best implemented.

If, for instance, sanitation resumes trash collection in targeted areas before law enforcement has taken appropriate action to keep gang members from continually undermining sanitation efforts, trash collectors will quickly realize the futility in resuming trash collection and, once again, abandon the area. In addition, it is through the gathering of declarations from residents describing how the gang has negatively affected the community that one knows precisely what municipal services are required to improve the quality of life in the targeted neighborhood.

Moreover, it is the application of esoteric and little used laws (i.e. building abatement and nuisance laws, local codes and ordinances, special sentencing procedures) that require a special prosecutor who can use these laws to force compliance by landlords, residents and gang members. All too often, governmental entities responsible for insuring compliance with local laws (such as Building & Safety or Health & Safety Codes) are unsure of little used but effective legal strategies known to a prosecutor which can effectuate compliance and help contribute to the improved quality of life for the community. Thus, a building and safety inspector frustrated in his attempts to enforce Building and Safety Code violations against a property owner who allows gang and drug activity may be more successful if his efforts are linked with the strategies of the prosecutor and police of the Civil Gang Abatement.

In addition, the building inspector may not realize that in the course of inspecting a drug and gang infested building for code violations, the *timing and coordination* of his efforts with law enforcement could not only result in building code compliance but a marked reduction in gang activity. This, of course, is based on a fundamental concept that criminal activity can be dramatically reduced if the environment supporting the criminal activity is changed. Simply put, to the extent that the building inspector can use his legal weapons to force a property owner to improve a building's quality and appearance *at the same time* that other law enforcement efforts are in progress to abate gang and drug activity, he is able to create an environment in that building that will discourage criminal activity and likewise encourage occupancy by law abiding tenants. A building inspector who works closely with the Civil Gang Abatement prosecutor and local police can play a major role in bringing about a marked and permanent reduction in gang related crime in a neighborhood. On the other hand, a building inspector who fails to coordinate his efforts with an experienced prosecutor and local police will do little more than bring about temporary compliance with local codes and miss an opportunity to contribute to a community's enhanced quality of life.

Sadly, even when governmental agencies are knowledgeable about unusual or little used strategies, many prosecutors are not familiar with such strategies and thus fail to aggressively enforce such efforts in court. A specially assigned prosecutor, on the other hand, will not only aid in the discovery of effective albeit little used legal strategies, but insure their enforcement and support in court. Lastly, only a specially trained prosecutor working closely with police can insure that the Civil Gang Abatement is brought to a successful conclusion notwithstanding its uniqueness in our criminal justice system. Certainly, elected officials and other governmental representatives should be involved in the coordination effort. But, because this is clearly a law enforcement strategy in combination with other municipal efforts, law enforcement should and must take a leading role.

City of Los Angeles vs. the Playboy Gangster Crips

In the first application of the "Civil Gang Abatement" (against a West Los Angeles street gang, the Playboy Gangster Crips),[12] conspicuous street dealing was out of control while a number of apartment buildings were effectively controlled by the local street gang as a result of poor management by property owners. In coordination with the gathering of evidence for the civil injunction against the local street gang, the local prosecutor used California building abatement laws to force property owners to take corrective action to discourage gang and drug activity at their property locations. The prosecutor ordered the owners to remove graffiti daily, erect security gates, install lighting, remove abandoned vehicles, initiate evictions of known drug dealers and even trim shrubbery so as to effectively discourage gang and drug activity. Sample leases, property management advice, advice regarding enforcement of state trespass laws and other special police patrols were simultaneously offered to help the property owners effectively discourage and remove unwanted gang activity. In addition, the prosecutor applied pressure to other governmental entities to pave streets, restore street lighting, and improve garbage collection. Instead of merely seeking easily obtained court orders against the landlords, the prosecutor applied the concepts embodied in "community-based policing," and *proactively assisted* property owners in taking corrective steps *before* their property deteriorated to the point where prosecution was indicated.

Although prior efforts by police failed to reduce the gang's control over the neighborhood, the "Civil Gang Abatement" reduced criminal activity significantly and, in effect, forced the gang out of the community. More importantly, the "Civil Gang Abatement" not only *statistically* reduced crime but brought about a significant and visibly measurable improvement in the *quality of life*. in the area. Residents, once again, were observed walking their dogs, watering their lawns and painting their homes. "For Sale" signs came down and property values went up. Potholes were repaired, street lights replaced and garbage was collected on a daily basis. The project was so effective that it provided the impetus for the Mayor to create a permanently established program to coordinate such community efforts, appropriately called the "Model Neighborhood Program." Lastly, because the "Civil Gang Abatement" not only reduces criminal activity but also mobilizes the community as an effective voice in government, a mechanism was in place to insure that long after the police and prosecutor have moved on to other neighborhoods, crime in the area would remain low while the quality of life would continue to improve.

In conclusion, while the "Civil Gang Abatement" can be effective as a single law enforcement tool, it is clearly most effective when used as a *vehicle* for the coordinated application of 1) aggressive law enforcement strategies (including traditional narcotics enforcement such as "buy-busts," specialized criminal prosecutions and building abatements); 2) efforts to mobilize the community; *and* 3) the restoration of critical municipal services which are essential for improving the quality of life for residents of the neighborhood. Moreover, while it is conceivable that police departments may be able to begin the abatement process on their own, the early formation of "Community Impact Teams" involving specially assigned police-prosecutor teams is critical to insure that the efforts of the police and other agencies are aggressively supported in court. Furthermore, this special police-prosecutor team is essential to *coordinate* the application of law enforcement strategies with the restoration of critical municipal services so as to bring about a noticeable improvement in quality of life. If police departments and prosecuting agencies are willing to assign the relatively few resources necessary to implement a Civil Gang Abatement, the rewards can be astonishing—a community that experiences significantly reduced gang activity, drug dealing and truancy while enjoying a noticeable and long lasting improvement in the quality of life for all its residents.

[Editors' note: We present below the original abatement notice used by the City Attorney's Office. Later notices have undergone some revisions.]

NOTICE TO ABATE PUBLIC NUISANCE AND OF INTENT TO SEEK A PRELIMINARY AND PERMANENT INJUNCTION IN LIEU OF VOLUNTARY ABATEMENT

TO: *WATTS VARIO GRAPE STREET aka WVG, aka GRAPE STREET WATTS, aka GSW, aka GRAPE STREET, aka GS, aka WATTS BABY LOCO CRIPS, aka WBLC, aka BABY LOCO CRIPS, aka BLC, aka BABY LOCS, aka LOCO CRIPS, aka LOCS, aka TINY LOCO CRIPS, aka TLC, aka TINY LOCS, aka TL, aka EAST SIDE KIDS, aka ESK, aka PLAYBOY HOO RIDE CRIPS, aka PHRC, aka HOO RIDE CRIPS, aka HRC, aka SOUTH SIDE GRAPE STREET, aka SSG ST, aka YOUNG PANTHERS*, an UNINCORPORATED ASSOCIATION AND STREET GANG AS DEFINED IN CODE SECTION 186.22 OF THE CALIFORNIA PENAL CODE, AND ALL OF ITS MEMBERS, ASSOCIATES, AGENTS AND ALL OTHER PERSONS ACTING UNDER, IN CONCERN WITH, FOR THE BENEFIT OF, AT THE DIRECTION OF, OR IN ASSOCIATION WITH THEM:

THE PEOPLE OF THE STATE OF CALIFORNIA, BY AND THROUGH JAMES K. HAHN, CITY ATTORNEY FOR THE CITY OF LOS ANGELES, HEREBY PUT YOU ON NOTICE THAT:

You are creating, maintaining and encouraging, and permitting others to create and maintain, a public nuisance in that you are engaging in and encouraging, and permitting others to engage in, continuing, repeated and ongoing acts of:

a. murder;
b. open and conspicuous narcotics trafficking;
c. open and conspicuous narcotics possession and use;
d. assaults and other acts of violence;
e. use and possession of dangerous weapons and ammunition;
f. vandalism to public and private property including, but not limited to, graffiti;
g. congregating at locations including, but not limited to, the 2000 to 2100 blocks between 101st and 102nd Streets, the 2000 to 2200 blocks on the north side of 103rd Street, in the City of Los Angeles, so as to attract persons who seek to purchase narcotics and other contraband, and attract members of rival street gangs who intend to commit acts of violence and other violations of law;
h. congregating at or near Jordan Down Public Housing Project, in sufficiently large numbers and in such a rude and threatening manner, so as to interfere with lawful law enforcement investigations and activities and threaten the safety and well-being of law abiding citizens;
i. blocking the free flow of vehicular traffic and emergency vehicles by approaching passing vehicles and engaging passengers in conversation;
j. blocking and obstructing sidewalks and pedestrian thoroughfares so as to annoy, threaten and intimidate law abiding citizens;
k. wearing and possessing certain identifiable hats, shirts, belts, jackets, sweat shirts, shoe laces, handkerchiefs, and other articles of clothing which identify the wearer as a member or associate of the criminal street gang known as Watts Vario Grape Street, so as to intimidate law abiding citizens, facilitate recruitment of younger law abiding citizens to join said criminal street gang and commit illegal acts, and encourage and induce members of rival street gangs to acts of violence;
l. yelling of words and phrases and making certain identifiable hand and body movements in public which are intended to warn other gang members, narcotics traffickers, and potential customers of narcotics, that police officers and representatives of the Housing Authority of the City of Los Angeles are present;

m. soliciting, inducing and encouraging others, either verbally, in writing, or by hand and body movements, to commit acts of violence to law abiding citizens, police officers, and other gang members;

n. possessing paging devices (beepers) and portable and cellular telephones at or near narcotic locations described in paragraph g. (above) so as to facilitate the trafficking of narcotics by respondent street gang.

THE ABOVE DESCRIBED ACTIVITIES ARE A PUBLIC NUISANCE, ARE OFFENSIVE TO THE SENSES, ARE INJURIOUS TO HEALTH, AND ARE INDECENT, SO AS TO INTERFERE WITH THE COMFORTABLE ENJOYMENT OF LIFE AND PROPERTY BY AN ENTIRE NEIGHBORHOOD AND A CONSIDERABLE NUMBER OF PERSONS IN THE COMMUNITY.

THEREFORE,

You are hereby commanded to halt, discontinue and abate the creation and maintenance of the public nuisance described above.

In the event that you should fail to abate said public nuisance, notice is hereby given that the People of the State of California, by and through James K. Hahn, City Attorney of the City of Los Angeles, will seek a preliminary and permanent injunction prohibiting the continuance of said nuisance.

THE VIOLATION OF AN INJUNCTION CAN BE PUNISHED BY CRIMINAL PROSECUTION AND CIVIL CONTEMPT RESULTING IN JAIL, FINES, OR BOTH!

JAMES K. HAHN
City Attorney

Notes

1. The "Broken Windows Theory" explains the deterioration of a community by comparing a building suffering a single broken window to the deterioration of a neighborhood riddled with crime. The theory states that when a single window is broken in an otherwise fit building but is not *immediately* repaired, soon afterwards many other windows will be vandalized in succession. It is a common phenomenon which many have observed in society. It follows that if a building *already* suffers from numerous broken windows, the only way to effectively restore the building to a fit condition is to repair *all* windows at the same time. Anything less than full *coordination* of the repairs will result in an endless attempt to keep fixing some windows while more are vandalized in the interim.

   By the same token, if government fails to *coordinate* its efforts to improve a neighborhood so that law enforcement strategies are timed with the restoration and improvement of municipal and social services, the entire effort will fail. If, for example, police make a major drive to reduce gang crime in winter, while municipal government doesn't take steps to repair streets, lighting and garbage collection until the summer, by the time government *begins* to restore municipal services, the successes achieved by the police during the winter months will have already been reversed and gone to nought. On the other hand, if municipal and social services are improved *at the same time* that police reduce gang crime, then the environment which supported the criminal activity will have been altered so as to sustain the successes achieved by the police.
2. Situs (building) abatement laws in California generally state that a property owner can suffer fines, jail and/or the loss of one's real property if he causes, maintains or permits a property to become a public nuisance. In real terms, this means that if a landlord fails to take reasonable steps to prevent illegal drug or gang activity at a location, the landlord can face stiff penalties including the seizure of the property. In most cases, the property owner is held strictly liable and is *not* excused because the police were unable to control the problem. Not surprisingly, this is one of the most powerful and successful law enforcement tools in California.
3. California Penal Code §166.4 states, in pertinent part, that: "Every person guilty of any contempt of court . . . of the following kinds, is guilty of a misdemeanor: . . . Willful disobedience of any process or order lawfully issued by any court."
4. The "Civil Gang Abatement" can be based on any type of nuisance activity engaged in by a street gang. The most likely nuisance upon which to base a Civil Gang Abatement, however, is ongoing narcotic activity. This is simply because street sales of narcotics typically involve easily identifiable patterns of conduct (e.g. possession of pagers and approaching vehicles from known narcotics locations) which facilitate the gang's successful narcotics sales. Accordingly, an injunction prohibiting such conduct could be expected to be successful at abating such narcotic sales. However, this certainly does not preclude the use of a "Civil Gang Abatement" approach to other organized criminal activity where law enforcement can identify patterns of lawful conduct which, if enjoined by a court, would reduce or eliminate the illegal activity.
5. While undercover efforts, by themselves, are often ineffective in abating gang-motivated drug dealing, they should still be included as part of any drug abatement effort. To be sure, undercover officers are best able to identify and target gang *leaders* for felony arrests leading to significant jail and prison sentences, thus inhibiting continued recruitment and coordination of the gang's illegal activities.
6. The open distribution of the warning revitalizes community support and mobilizes the residents to further support the efforts of law enforcement, including their willingness to complete logs for the "Civil Gang Abatement." But even more striking, the distribution of this warning notice can be most effective in lawfully "intimidating" the targeted gang into abating its criminal activity. In Los Angeles, such a warning notice has been distributed three times in anticipation of a request for an injunction against three different local street gangs. In two instances (one against the notorious Grape Street Gang in Jordan Downs Housing Project, the other against the Harbor City Crips in the Harbor area of Los Angeles), the distribution of the warning notices themselves, without further court action, brought about a remarkable 50% reduction in gang related crime. Even more surprising, that reduction in crime was sustained for several months. This phenomenon has been observed with the distribution of other legal warnings to gangs (e.g. S.T.E.P. notices) with similar, although not quite as remarkable, reductions in crime. We leave it to sociologists and others to speculate on the reasons why the neighborhood distribution of such documents to gang members has such a dramatic and sometimes long lasting effect on their previously unabatable criminal activity.

7. A phenomenon was observed during the serving of the court orders on individual gang members that cannot go unnoticed. While it was *enforcement* of the terms of the injunction in combination with other efforts described in this paper that was largely responsible for the successes achieved during the first "Civil Gang Abatement," police noticed that gang members actually feared and went to great lengths to avoid being personally served with the court orders. Even though there was no attempt to intimidate gang members during service of the orders, something that was actually impossible due to wide scale media coverage of the event, gang members ran and hid when they observed a police officer holding the large manila envelope containing the court's injunction and proof of service. Gang members who once boldly sold drugs within a few steps of a uniformed officer now remained indoors to avoid receiving that most feared document, the civil injunction. Naturally, however, after most gang members had eventually been served, they resumed their open sales of narcotics. That is, of course, until the police and assigned prosecutors aggressively enforced the terms of the injunction.
8. Previous experience has shown, however, that abatement *deters* future violations of the injunction following the first few aggressive prosecutions for a violation of the injunction. In the first use of the Civil Gang Abatement in Los Angeles, several gang members "tested" the injunction by immediately violating the orders. One gang leader, for instance, threw the court order in the street minutes after being handed it by a police officer. He was immediately arrested for violating the injunction since one of the orders was not to litter. While clearly surprised to learn that he was going to eventually serve three days in jail for an apparently minor violation of law, he was even more shocked to learn that the prosecutor obtained (and his public defender recommended that he agree to) a condition of probation banishing him from the targeted neighborhood for two years! News of that sentence spread rapidly throughout the targeted gang and had the desired effect of virtually insuring future compliance of the injunction by all other members of the gang. Moreover, the littering gang leader obeyed his "banishment" condition and was never again seen in the targeted neighborhood, nor was he observed to participate in future gang activity.
9. While the creation of "Community Impact Teams" is not a necessary requirement for implementation of a Civil Gang Abatement, such teams can dramatically increase the effectiveness of the process by insuring coordination of the various efforts as called for in the "Broken Windows Theory" of community decline and restoration, as described herein.
10. Residents are, however, given assurances that their logs will only be included in the Civil Gang Abatement with their consent. Moreover, the prosecutor should request and will normally receive a court order "sealing" or "sanitizing" the logs to prevent gang members from obtaining sufficient information to retaliate against residents. If such an order is not obtained, then the logs can be removed from the court file and other evidence can be relied upon to justify the injunction, *including* the fact that residents were afraid to submit declarations for fear of retaliation.
11. A law enforcement philosophy which encourages police to work closely with residents, property owners and merchants to encourage compliance with the law. Instead of relying chiefly upon arrests and convictions, community-based policing is premised upon the fact that the quality of life of a neighborhood cannot improve unless citizens actively participate with police and elected officials in the restoration of the neighborhood. It also calls for police to attempt to secure compliance from cooperative citizens rather than relying exclusively upon confrontation and court proceedings.
12. The American Civil Liberties Union unsuccessfully challenged the L.A. City Attorney's request for an injunction against the local street gang, the Playboy Gangster Crips. Although the court did not enjoin all activity requested by the prosecutor, the court did find that the street gang was subject to a civil injunction and subsequently issued a number of useful injunctive orders. In the following year, twenty-six gang members were arrested for violation of the injunction. Twenty-two pled guilty while the remaining cases were dismissed for insufficient evidence. Many of the defendants who pled guilty complied with a probation order to stay out of the neighborhood for two years. ✦

39

County Takes First Step to Prohibiting Gangs From Parks

Amy Pyle

Among the legal efforts to suppress gangs in Los Angeles County is the use of ordinances to ban gangs from public facilities such as parks. In this article, Pyle describes the process by which these ordinances are being enacted, the arguments in favor of doing so, and the legal challenges waged against them by the American Civil Liberties Union. It should be noted that while these ordinances ban gang youths from public parks, they do not include efforts to deal with where the gang members will congregate as a result.

The Los Angeles County Board of Supervisors on Tuesday stepped into the legal battle over banning gang members from public parks, asking park officials and the Sheriff's Department to identify gang-plagued county parks where such a ban should be imposed.

Supervisor Mike Antonovich asked that a list of parks "overcome with gang activity" be provided to the board in a month to be considered for a ban similar to the ordinance adopted by the city of San Fernando in September.

That ordinance, thought to be the first of its kind in the nation, is being challenged in a Los Angeles Superior Court lawsuit brought by the American Civil Liberties Union of Southern California on the grounds that gang members have a constitutionally protected right to free assembly.

But the approach has been gaining support from elected officials and their constituents. In December, the city of Pomona banned gang members from two of its parks and officials in several other cities, including Los Angeles, are discussing similar crackdowns.

Supervisors voted unanimously to look into the need for such a ban at county parks and to join San Fernando in fighting the ACLU lawsuit by offering legal help.

ACLU Executive Director Ramona Ripston said she hoped the county would wait for the lawsuit to be resolved before acting.

"We understand the problem," Ripston said. "I want to be safe too. But we don't have to sacrifice the Constitution in order to have safety."

Two county supervisors and several members of the public expressed concerns Tuesday about the legal grounds for a ban. But many also applauded the success so far in San Fernando, where Las Palmas Park—used almost exclusively by gangs last year—again attracts families.

"I support San Fernando's remedy and . . . it may work in other areas when these problems arise," said Supervisor Gloria Molina. "But I'm concerned about implementation, about if anybody who looks like a gang member is going to be harassed. There's a lot of people who believe that every minority belongs to a gang."

The San Fernando City Council approved the ban after a mother and her three children were wounded in the cross-fire of a gang turf war in the park. Under the ordinance, members of groups identified by local law enforcement officers—under the guidelines contained in a state law—as criminal street gangs are warned to stay away from the park. A first violation of the law brings a warning and the second offense carries a $250 fine.

Supervisor Ed Edelman said he fears that forcing gangs out of parks merely pushes them into the surrounding neighborhoods, where they continue to pose a threat. A report produced by the ACLU indicated that two fatal gang shootings in October occurred within 100 yards of Las Palmas Park.

Only a few of the county's more than 100 parks are likely to meet the gang prohibition criteria, said Rodney E. Cooper, county director of parks and recreation. In general, he said, gang problems are already being controlled by county park police and by a community safety program in the parks.

Both the San Fernando and Pomona ordinances were crafted by the Los Angeles County district attorney's office, which has offered its services to other governmental bodies.

Dist. Atty. Ira Reiner, who spoke at length during Tuesday's meeting, said he believes the ordinances will withstand legal challenges. ✦

Reprinted with permission from the *Los Angeles Times*, January 15, 1992.

40

Safe Streets Don't Require Lifting Rights

Paul Hoffman and Mark Silverstein

In their essay, Hoffman and Silverstein argue that many of the recent attempts at legal intervention into the lives of gang members, particularly those which criminalize their non-criminal activities, are a violation of their constitutional rights. The authors highlight the dangers found in such sweeping measures, in particular the harassment of many law-abiding youths who may fit police stereotypes of gang members, and the negative effects this will have on community-police relations.

No one can disagree that gang violence is a plague in our community. But the absence of real solutions and the tendency to attack the symptom and not the disease creates pressure to get the job done at the expense of civil liberties.

City Attorney James K. Hahn has once again succumbed to these pressures. He filed a lawsuit asking the court to declare a constitutional "free-fire" zone in a large section of the San Fernando Valley bounded by Sepulveda Boulevard, Valerio Street, Van Nuys Boulevard and Chase Street.

Hahn seeks an order that would forbid each of 500 unnamed but alleged members of the Blythe Street gang from engaging in a wide variety of ordinarily lawful everyday activities that are protected by the Constitution. A hearing is now scheduled for March 25.

Unlike Hahn, we do not believe that suspending constitutional rights is necessary to deal with the gang's criminal activities. Murder, mayhem, drug dealing, assault, intimidation, robbery and burglary all are prohibited by law. The Constitution does not protect criminal activity. Criminals should be arrested, prosecuted and sentenced. There is no need to choose between safe streets and the Constitution.

The order Hahn seeks tramples unjustifiably on fundamental constitutional rights of association, privacy and expression. It forbids lifelong friends, even brothers in the same family, from associating with one another. It bans certain clothes and certain jewelry. It bars 500 yet-to-be-named individuals from discussing or referring to the Blythe Street gang in any way, and forbids talk about any subject at all while riding in cars.

The proposed order forbids each of the 500 people from waiting for a bus or otherwise staying in any public place longer than five minutes. Under the order, parents could not take their children to stores, restaurants, hospitals or churches after 8 p.m. Some individuals would be banished from the neighborhood entirely, forbidden even to stay overnight with relatives.

The proposed order would forbid 500 alleged gang members from engaging in the most ordinary lawful conduct on their own property and in their own homes. Children could not climb trees or fences. Parents could not patch the family's roof. Fixing bicycles on the front steps would be banned. Shaving with razor blades would be prohibited. Baseball bats, flashlights, even screwdrivers would become contraband.

Under the proposed order, 500 unnamed individuals would be required to carry special papers to prove that their everyday activities are lawful. They would need written permission to visit a neighbor's house, written authorization to change a tire and valid proof of purchase for every auto part they possess. After 8 p.m., teens under 18 would be confined to their homes without special written documentation, and adults without proof of residence would be banned entirely from the neighborhood.

Because Hahn's lawsuit does not identify the 500 alleged gang members, police will inevitably attempt to apply the court's order to any Latino youths they believe to be members of the gang. There is no surer recipe for the harassment of many law-abiding Latino youths. After its independent investigation of the Los Angeles Police Department, the Christopher Commission's report was filled with examples of the destructive effects of such harassment on police-community relations.

Hahn's suit is like a rerun of an unsuccessful film. He filed and lost essentially the same suit against the Playboy Gangster Crips in 1987. The judge at that time agreed with the American Civil Liberties Union's arguments, finding that Hahn's lawsuit was "far, far overreaching."

Once again, Hahn is overreaching the boundaries of the law. If he is attempting to wage war against crime at the expense of civil liberties, then the result must be the same. The United States is not a police state. The judge must deny Hahn the power to prosecute suspected gang members for ordinary, everyday noncriminal activities that are protected by the Constitution. City officials can maintain safe streets and safe neighborhoods without asking for a wholesale suspension of civil liberties. ✦

Los Angeles Times, Op-ed, March 11, 1993. Reprinted with permission of the authors.